Convergence of Human Resources Technologies and Industry 5.0

Pawan Kumar
Lovely Professional University, India

Sunil Kumar
Shoolini University, India

Rajesh Verma
Lovely Professional University, India

Sumesh Dadwal
London South Bank University, UK

IGI Global
PUBLISHER of TIMELY KNOWLEDGE

A volume in the Advances in Human Resources Management and Organizational Development (AHRMOD) Book Series

Published in the United States of America by
IGI Global
Business Science Reference (an imprint of IGI Global)
701 E. Chocolate Avenue
Hershey PA, USA 17033
Tel: 717-533-8845
Fax: 717-533-8661
E-mail: cust@igi-global.com
Web site: http://www.igi-global.com

Library of Congress Cataloging-in-Publication Data

CIP PENDING

Convergence of Human Resources Technologies and Industry 5.0
Pawan Kumar, Sunil Kumar, RAJESH VERMA, Sumesh Singh Dadwal
2024 Business Science Reference

ISBN: 979-8-3693-1343-5
eISBN: 979-8-3693-1344-2

This book is published in the IGI Global book series Advances in Human Resources Management and Organizational Development (AHRMOD) (ISSN: 2327-3372; eISSN: 2327-3380)

British Cataloguing in Publication Data
A Cataloguing in Publication record for this book is available from the British Library.

For electronic access to this publication, please contact: eresources@igi-global.com.

Advances in Human Resources Management and Organizational Development (AHRMOD) Book Series

Patricia Ordóñez de Pablos
Universidad de Oviedo, Spain

ISSN:2327-3372
EISSN:2327-3380

Mission

A solid foundation is essential to the development and success of any organization and can be accomplished through the effective and careful management of an organization's human capital. Research in human resources management and organizational development is necessary in providing business leaders with the tools and methodologies which will assist in the development and maintenance of their organizational structure.

The **Advances in Human Resources Management and Organizational Development (AHRMOD) Book Series** aims to publish the latest research on all aspects of human resources as well as the latest methodologies, tools, and theories regarding organizational development and sustainability. The **AHRMOD Book Series** intends to provide business professionals, managers, researchers, and students with the necessary resources to effectively develop and implement organizational strategies.

Coverage

- Executive Education
- Human Relations Movement
- Worker Behavior and Engagement
- Coaching and Mentoring
- Performance Improvement
- Workplace Discrimination
- Talent Identification and Managcment
- Succession Planning
- Personnel Policies
- Corporate Governance

IGI Global is currently accepting manuscripts for publication within this series. To submit a proposal for a volume in this series, please contact our Acquisition Editors at Acquisitions@igi-global.com or visit: http://www.igi-global.com/publish/.

The Advances in Human Resources Management and Organizational Development (AHRMOD) Book Series (ISSN 2327-3372) is published by IGI Global, 701 E. Chocolate Avenue, Hershey, PA 17033-1240, USA, www.igi-global.com. This series is composed of titles available for purchase individually; each title is edited to be contextually exclusive from any other title within the series. For pricing and ordering information please visit http://www.igi-global.com/book-series/advances-human-resources-management-organizational/73670. Postmaster: Send all address changes to above address.

Titles in this Series

For a list of additional titles in this series, please visit: http://www.igi-global.com/book-series/advances-human-resources-management-organizational/73670

Building Sustainable Human Resources Management Practices for Businesses
Cristina Raluca Gh. Popescu (University of Bucharest, Romania & The Bucharest University of Economic Studies, Romania) Javier Martínez-Falcó (University of Alicante, Spain & University of Stellenbosch, South Africa) Bartolomé Marco-Lajara (University of Alicante, Spain) Eduardo Sánchez-García (University of Alicante, Spain) and Luis A. Millán-Tudela (University of Alicante, Spain)
Business Science Reference • copyright 2024 • 364pp • H/C (ISBN: 9798369319949) • US $275.00 (our price)

Demystifying the Dark Side of AI in Business
Sumesh Dadwal (Northumbria University, UK) Shikha Goyal (Lovely Professional University, India) Pawan Kumar (Lovely Professional University, India) and Rajesh Verma (Lovely Professional University, India)
Business Science Reference • copyright 2024 • 268pp • H/C (ISBN: 9798369307243) • US $275.00 (our price)

Organizational Management Sustainability in VUCA Contexts
Rafael Perez-Uribe (Universidad de la Salle, Colombia) David Ocampo-Guzman (Santo Tomas University, Colombia & EAN University, Colombia) Carlos Salcedo-Perez (Politecnico Grancolombiano, Colombia) and Andrés Carvajal-Contreras (EAN University, Colombia)
Business Science Reference • copyright 2024 • 435pp • H/C (ISBN: 9798369307205) • US $275.00 (our price)

Fostering Organizational Sustainability With Positive Psychology
Elif Baykal (Istanbul Medipol University, Turkey)
Business Science Reference • copyright 2024 • 338pp • H/C (ISBN: 9798369315248) • US $275.00 (our price)

Overcoming Cognitive Biases in Strategic Management and Decision Making
Enis Siniksaran (Istanbul University, Turkey)
Business Science Reference • copyright 2024 • 295pp • H/C (ISBN: 9798369317662) • US $285.00 (our price)

Human Relations Management in Tourism
Marco Valeri (Niccolò Cusano University, Italy) and Bruno Sousa (Polytechnic Institute of Cavado and Ave, Portugal)
Business Science Reference • copyright 2024 • 316pp • H/C (ISBN: 9798369313220) • US $275.00 (our price)

Innovative Human Resource Management for SMEs
Shuja Iqbal (School of Management, Jiangsu University, China) Komal Khalid (King Abdulaziz University, Saudi Arabia) and Andi Cudai Nur (Universitas Negeri Makassar, Indonesia)
Business Science Reference • copyright 2024 • 449pp • H/C (ISBN: 9798369309728) • US $250.00 (our price)

IGI Global
PUBLISHER of TIMELY KNOWLEDGE

701 East Chocolate Avenue, Hershey, PA 17033, USA
Tel: 717-533-8845 x100 • Fax: 717-533-8661
E-Mail: cust@igi-global.com • www.igi-global.com

Editorial Advisory Board

Table of Contents

Detailed Table of Contents

The chapter discusses the transformation of human resources (HR) in the era of Industry 5.0, highlighting the importance of digital HR implementation in driving business growth. It discusses the strategic integration of digital tools, analytics, and automation within HR functions to improve workforce agility, productivity, and engagement. This chapter discusses the benefits of digital HR solutions, including talent acquisition optimization, performance management enhancement, learning facilitation, and employee experience enrichment. It emphasizes the importance of organizational agility, change management, and continuous innovation for successful adoption. By aligning HR strategies with Industry 5.0 needs, businesses can drive sustainable growth, foster innovation, and maintain a competitive edge in the global marketplace.

The integration of digital technologies has significantly transformed the way organizations operate, especially in the field of human resources (HR). This chapter explores the importance of creating effective HR strategies that are tailored to the modern workplace, focusing on navigating the digital frontier. By utilizing digital tools, HR professionals can streamline processes, improve employee engagement, and optimize talent management practices. The chapter also discusses the challenges and opportunities of digital transformation in HR, including recruitment, on-boarding, performance management, and employee development. It provides actionable guidance for HR leaders to harness digital technologies to create agile, resilient, and future-ready workplaces.

This chapter delves into the role of digital HR in developing economies, focusing on the intersection of technology, human resources, and economic development. It highlights the opportunities and challenges of digitalization, such as HR leveraging digital tools to enhance workforce efficiency and foster innovation. The chapter also discusses the implications of Industry 5.0, emphasizing the integration of AI, automation, and IoT in reshaping HR practices. The potential benefits of digital HR include improved talent management and increased productivity, but also address challenges like infrastructure constraints and skill gaps. The chapter forecasts trends in Digital HR specific to developing economies, aligning with Industry 5.0 principles. The chapter explores the effects of digitalization on workforce dynamics, organizational structures, and the economy, addressing challenges like digital literacy, data privacy, and socio-economic disparities. It highlights the potential of digital HR in bridging skill gaps, promoting inclusive growth, and stimulating innovation.

The incorporation of digital human resources (HR) technologies has emerged as a key force behind organizational change in today's quickly changing global environment. This chapter takes a close look at the potential and problems that come up when deploying digital HR technologies in the special environment of developing nations. The first point made in the chapter emphasizes how transformative digital HR solutions can be, from easier hiring processes and more employee engagement to data-driven decision-making. The chapter then turns its attention to emerging nations, where issues including socioeconomic inequality, poor infrastructure, and varied cultural values create particular obstacles to the adoption of technology. An in-depth examination of roadblocks such as a lack of digital infrastructure, a lack of technical awareness, and reluctance to change within established organizational structures reveals the central topic of obstacles. These elements not only prevent the seamless integration of digital HR systems but also force the creation of context-specific implementation strategies. The chapter also highlights a range of promising opportunities among these difficulties. Developing nations may transform HR procedures and promote more inclusivity and accessibility by embracing digital HR solutions. The opportunity to enhance personnel management and spur productivity and creativity lies in improved data analytics

Blue wind energy combines offshore wind energy with cutting-edge technology, addressing sustainability in urbanization. This chapter investigates its application, focusing on integrating blue wind energy, AI, and IoT for smart energy management. Urgently needed due to urban energy demand and environmental concerns, conventional methods fall short. Blue wind energy, with AI and IoT, offers a sustainable alternative, but integration challenges exist. The amalgamation of blue wind energy, AI, and IoT presents a groundbreaking solution to urban energy needs. Urbanization necessitates sustainable energy solutions, with blue wind energy utilizing offshore wind resources effectively. Offshore wind farms near cities offer better energy production but require complex energy management systems for full potential realization.

Any organization's growth and stability depend on its recruitment and selection process, which attracts top talent. HR metrics quantify and rate human resource processes. This study aims to integrate human resource metrics into the recruitment and selection process throughout. In this exploratory study, human resource managers discuss metrics and their use in evaluating recruitment and selection procedures. Manufacturing HR managers are being surveyed about the KPIs in question. Most HR managers (out of 15, at least 10 HR managers) have reported nine metrics as actively used in their firm, while a minority (out of 15, less than 10 HR managers) have reported 10 metrics as rarely used and six calculated metrics. This chapter will interest researchers and practitioners who identify, design, and deploy metrics to measure an organization's recruitment and selection process. The chapter identifies metrics to demonstrate how metrics encourage HR practitioners to adopt and measure skilled workforce in recruitment and selection. This contributes to the HR metrics debate.

Foreword

For Industry 5.0 humans are more than resources, and this is why for many years already we point out the need to treat humans as treasures instead. Industry 5.0 recovers the missing link between nature and human-made ecosystems. This is why it is recognizing and preventing five types of waste:

- Physical waste
- Social waste
- Urban waste
- Process waste
- Wasting of time

The prevention of social waste is an important part of Industry 5.0 ecosystems and this is why using the tools introduced, helps in the elimination of the social waste before it occurs. It is not just the HR, but the setup of social-economical system, that is creating the social waste already in the setup, because it divides the human life (and not only human) into three sections:

1. Pre-Productive
2. Productive
3. Post-Productive

Number one and three are understood by society as social waste because the image of society is based on economic ground-stones and not on natural and logical approach applied in nature. The companies adopted the ill socio-economical modules, and its main aim is to exploit the resources in shortest time possible and terminate after exchanging it with the "new resource."

Industry 5.0 is the first industrial evolution ever led by man (human). The term human is not a buzzword, but the key Living in the times of digitalization and virtualization it seems like the only one that needs to be digitalized is human itself. But if this would be realized the home of human will be dark, because data do not need any light. Industry 5.0 prevents this to happen by changing the role of human in the system. Instead of being a "component" it will become the "soul, brain, and heart." Nature never exploits its own resources leaving no space for recovery, the same Industry 5.0. It brings back meaningfulness of work resulting in meaningfulness of life. In 1959, in a video interview, Carl Gustav Jung says "the man cannot live meaningless life" One of the world´s most famous psychologists were right, saying that just 14 years after the end of the biggest war in human history. There is a Czech proverb which we have to keep in mind:

Fire is a great servant, but a very bad master.

The same is with technology, AI, machines, robots. The life in which robots utilize the addiction of humans on machines, was well described in the screenplay and novel in which the term "robot" was used for the first time in a human history. It is called "R.U.R", author Karel Čapek, and it was published in 1921.

Michael Rada
IBCSD LAB s.r.o., Czech Republic

Preface

In an era marked by rapid technological advancements and the pervasive influence of the digital age, the realm of Human Resources (HR) has undergone a profound evolution. The convergence of digital HR technologies and the emergence of Industry 5.0 signify a paradigm shift, presenting both unprecedented opportunities and formidable challenges, particularly for developing economies. It is within this dynamic landscape that our exploration unfolds.

In *Convergence of Human Resources Technologies and Industry 5.0*, authored by Pawan Kumar, Sunil Kumar, Rajesh Verma, and Sumesh Dadwal, we embark on a journey to delve into the effects, implementation, and implications of digital HR technologies within the context of Industry 5.0, with a specific focus on developing economies.

This collaborative effort embraces a comprehensive approach, drawing upon theoretical frameworks, empirical research, and practical insights from academia and industry alike. Through a blend of case studies, real-world examples, and quantitative analyses, we aim to provide readers with a nuanced understanding of the subject matter. Our objective is clear: to equip HR professionals, executives, managers, researchers, policymakers, and students with actionable insights and strategies to navigate the complexities of digital HR technologies adeptly.

The thematic scope of this book encompasses a multitude of pertinent topics, including the conceptualization of Industry 5.0 within developing economies, an exploration of digital HR technologies and their transformative potential, and an examination of the challenges and opportunities inherent in their adoption. Furthermore, we delve into the implications of digital HR technologies on critical facets such as workforce management, talent acquisition, and performance evaluation, while also addressing the ethical and legal considerations that accompany their utilization.

Chapter 1: It embarks on a journey to explore the transformation of Human Resources (HR) in the era of Industry 5.0. By emphasizing the strategic integration of digital tools, analytics, and automation within HR functions, we elucidate the key role of digital HR implementation in driving business growth. The chapter delves into the benefits of digital HR solutions, ranging from talent acquisition optimization to performance management enhancement and employee experience enrichment. Moreover, it underscores the importance of organizational agility, change management, and continuous innovation for successful adoption. By aligning HR strategies with the evolving needs of Industry 5.0, organizations can pave the way for sustainable growth, foster innovation, and maintain a competitive edge in the global marketplace.

Chapter 2: Explores the significant impact of digital technologies on modern HR strategies, focusing on navigating the digital frontier to create effective HR practices tailored to the contemporary workplace. Through a discussion on utilizing digital tools to streamline processes, improve employee engagement, and optimize talent management practices, the chapter offers actionable guidance for HR leaders. Additionally, it addresses the challenges and opportunities of digital transformation in HR, providing insights for creating agile, resilient, and future-ready workplaces.

Chapter 3: Delving into the realm of developing economies, this chapter examines the intersection of technology, human resources, and economic development. It highlights the opportunities and challenges of digitalization in HR, showcasing how digital tools can enhance workforce efficiency and foster innovation. The implications of Industry 5.0 are discussed, with an emphasis on integrating AI, automation, and IoT to reshape HR practices. Furthermore, the chapter forecasts trends specific to digital HR in developing economies, addressing challenges such as infrastructure constraints and skill gaps while exploring the potential for inclusive growth and innovation.

Chapter 4: Focused on the unique environment of developing nations, this chapter scrutinizes the potential and challenges of deploying digital HR technologies. It emphasizes the transformative nature of digital HR solutions while addressing obstacles such as socioeconomic inequality and poor infrastructure. By examining specific challenges such as a lack of digital literacy and resistance to change, the chapter offers insights into crafting context-specific implementation strategies to overcome barriers to integration.

Chapter 5: The concept of the circular economy in the manufacturing sector is explored in this chapter, emphasizing the role of digital technologies and data analytics in promoting sustainable practices. Through the lens of IoT, AI, and blockchain, the chapter highlights how these technologies enhance visibility, traceability, and collaboration in manufacturing supply chains. Challenges of implementing circular economy principles are discussed alongside potential economic benefits, with case studies providing practical examples of successful implementation.

Chapter 6: Investigating employee retention in the Indian automobile industry within the framework of Industry 5.0, this chapter explores various factors influencing retention, including organizational culture, reward recognition, and training. Through quantitative analysis, the chapter identifies training and development as a significant factor affecting employee retention. Furthermore, it offers insights into Industry 5.0 interventions for enhancing employee retention in the automobile industry.

Chapter 7: Providing an overview of Industry 5.0, this chapter outlines the integration of human insight with machine productivity to increase production efficiency and customize goods. It explores potential applications such as smart education, manufacturing, healthcare, and supply chain management, highlighting the transformative potential of Industry 5.0 technologies.

Chapter 8: Delving into the integration of AI into digital services, this chapter explores the influence of AI on user experience, security, and scalability. It addresses both the challenges and prospects presented by AI-driven strategies, stressing the importance of a comprehensive approach that considers technical, ethical, and regulatory dimensions.

Chapter 9: Focused on transitioning to inclusive and sustainable economies, this chapter discusses India's commitments to global development agendas such as the 2030 agenda and the Paris Agreement. It highlights the need for sustainable growth strategies that advance social justice, environmental protection, and equality.

Chapter 10: Investigating the recruitment and selection process, this chapter examines the integration of HR metrics into HR practices. Through interviews with HR managers, it identifies key metrics used in recruitment and selection processes, offering insights for researchers and practitioners aiming to optimize their workforce recruitment strategies.

Chapter 11: This chapter explores the relationship between employee training and job performance in Punjab's retail sector, emphasizing the importance of effective training in meeting customer demands and ensuring consistent satisfaction. It introduces a conceptual framework and moderation analysis to understand how training initiatives influence performance outcomes.

Chapter 12: Focusing on the Strategic HR Value Chain Model, this chapter aligns HR practices with organizational goals to drive sustainable growth. It emphasizes the importance of strategic alignment, technological integration, and a people-centric approach in optimizing talent management and fostering a positive workplace culture.

Chapter 13: Addressing the role of Industry 5.0 in bancassurance, this chapter explores the implications of digital banking and emerging trends in the banking sector. It offers insights into the association between Industry 5.0 and bancassurance, aiming to provide a comprehensive view for bankers, policymakers, and researchers.

Chapter 14: This chapter investigates the cultural factors influencing the adoption of digital HR strategies in entrepreneurial ventures. It highlights the importance of cultural sensitivity and cross-cultural communication in promoting sustainable entrepreneurship practices through digital HR tools.

Chapter 15: Exploring the integration of AI, IoT, and agricultural sensors in agriculture, this chapter discusses the potential of self-sustaining agro-technological ecosystems. It addresses challenges in implementing these technologies and provides insights into their future trajectory, offering guidance for sustainable and efficient agricultural practices.

Chapter 16: Focused on the convergence of HR practices with Industry 5.0 technologies, this chapter explores various HR technologies and their applications. It provides an overview of the evolution of HR technologies and their importance in enhancing HR processes and decision-making, offering insights for researchers, practitioners, and students alike.

As editors, we have endeavored to compile a compendium that not only sheds light on existing practices but also anticipates future trends and advancements in the field. Our hope is that this book serves as a catalyst for dialogue, innovation, and informed decision-making in the realm of HR, ultimately contributing to the sustainable growth and development of organizations within developing economies.

We extend our sincere gratitude to the contributors who have generously shared their expertise and insights, as well as to the readers who embark on this intellectual journey with us. May the exploration that lies ahead inspire curiosity, foster collaboration, and empower positive change in the ever-evolving landscape of HR.

Pawan Kumar
Lovely Professional University, India

Sunil Kumar
Shoolini University, India

Rajesh Verma
Lovely Professional University, India

Sumesh Dadwal
London South Bank University, UK

Acknowledgment

With great pleasure, we want to thank everyone, who has directly or indirectly supported us on this book project.

Prayers to almighty God, for granting us thoughts and wisdom to mediate this project as editors.

First of all, we are grateful to Michael Rada, known as the father of Industry 5.0 for his remarkable foreword section which is an eye opener for readers on demystifying the meaning of Industry5.0

This book required contributions from several authors. We are very grateful to each author as they have given their valuable time to share their knowledge with our readers by writing and revising and thus produced good quality pieces of work.

Deepest gratitude to the reviewers as well as our Editorial board team members, for their insights, critiques, and constructive feedback thus resulting in the successful publication of this book.

We would be grateful to the previous researchers and writers whose sources have been used and cited in this book.

We are grateful to our colleagues and people in our network for their constructive feedback and motivation.

We are very lucky and so thankful to our family members for letting us snatch time from them and use it on this project. Thank you so much!

Last but not least, we want to convey my thanks to IGI publishing and their team for their continued support and for shaping this project into a final work.

Thanks to the readers as the main motivation for this book.

Chapter 1
Digital HR Implementation for Business Growth in Industrial 5.0

Sampath Boopathi
https://orcid.org/0000-0002-2065-6539
Department of Mechanical Engineering, Muthayammal Engineering College, India

ABSTRACT

The chapter discusses the transformation of human resources (HR) in the era of Industry 5.0, highlighting the importance of digital HR implementation in driving business growth. It discusses the strategic integration of digital tools, analytics, and automation within HR functions to improve workforce agility, productivity, and engagement. This chapter discusses the benefits of digital HR solutions, including talent acquisition optimization, performance management enhancement, learning facilitation, and employee experience enrichment. It emphasizes the importance of organizational agility, change management, and continuous innovation for successful adoption. By aligning HR strategies with Industry 5.0 needs, businesses can drive sustainable growth, foster innovation, and maintain a competitive edge in the global marketplace.

INTRODUCTION

Industry 5.0 is a new industrial era that integrates advanced technologies with human-centric processes, transforming how businesses operate and interact with their environments. HR, traditionally associated with personnel management, is at the heart of this transformation, navigating the complexities of a digital landscape. This introduction explores the convergence of digital HR implementation and business growth within the context of Industry 5.0(Erro-Garcés & Aramendia-Muneta, 2023a). Industry 5.0 represents a departure from the mechanistic and automated approach of its predecessors, emphasizing the symbiotic relationship between humans and machines. The role of HR in this era is pivotal in orchestrating this harmonious coexistence and leveraging technology to augment human capabilities. The evolution of industrial paradigms, from mechanization in Industry 1.0 to automation and mass production in Indus-

DOI: 10.4018/979-8-3693-1343-5.ch001

try 2.0, and the digitalization and connectivity of processes in Industry 3.0 and 4.0, has brought about profound changes in work and organizational structures(Sulistyaningsih, 2023a).

In Industry 5.0, HR is shifting from administrative tasks like recruitment and payroll management to a strategic role at the intersection of technology, talent, and organizational objectives. HR professionals are expected to drive workforce agility, foster innovation, and promote employee engagement. They must also navigate the ethical and societal implications of emerging technologies like artificial intelligence, automation, and augmented reality in the workplace(Parameswaran, 2021a). The digital HR landscape in Industry 5.0 is characterized by a variety of technologies, including cloud-based HRIS, AI-powered recruitment platforms, and predictive analytics tools, which enhance HR processes and decision-making. These solutions help organizations streamline operations, gain insights into workforce dynamics, and personalize employee experiences. They also facilitate remote and distributed work models, particularly in response to global events like the COVID-19 pandemic(Cillo et al., 2022a).

Digital HR is crucial for business growth in Industry 5.0, where innovation and agility are significant. It optimizes talent acquisition, nurtures high-potential employees, and aligns individual goals with organizational objectives. Digital HR also enables data-driven decision-making, identifying trends, anticipating future skill requirements, and mitigating workforce risks. This catalyst drives productivity, innovation, and competitive advantage in a rapidly evolving business environment(Orlova, 2021). This explores the role of digital HR implementation in Industry 5.0 business growth. It highlights the opportunities and challenges of integrating technology and human capital. By adopting digital HR solutions and fostering a culture of continuous learning, businesses can position themselves for sustained success in the digital age. It provides strategic imperatives, best practices, and case studies for organizations to thrive in this era(Kraus et al., 2023).

Evolution of Industry Paradigms

The evolution of industry paradigms is a complex process characterized by technological innovation and societal transformation. New technologies have significantly impacted production, business organization, and economic function. This understanding is crucial for comprehending Industry 5.0 and the role of digital HR in driving business growth within this framework(Erro-Garcés & Aramendia-Muneta, 2023b; Sulistyaningsih, 2023a, 2023b).

Industry 1.0: The "First Industrial Revolution," or Industry 1.0, began in the late 18th century with the mechanization of production processes, including steam power, weaving looms, and the steam engine invented by James Watt. This led to mass production, factories, and mechanization of manual tasks, focusing on harnessing mechanical power for increased efficiency and output, laying the groundwork for modern industrialization.

Industry 2.0: The Second Industrial Revolution, spanning from the late 19th to early 20th century, saw a rapid acceleration in technological innovation and industrialization. Electricity and assembly line production revolutionized manufacturing processes, making them more flexible, efficient, and scalable. Henry Ford's assembly line technique in automobile manufacturing exemplified mass production and standardization. Industry 2.0 saw the rise of large-scale corporations and industry consolidation, driving economic growth and urbanization.

Industry 3.0: Industry 3.0, also known as the "Third Industrial Revolution," began in the mid-20th century with the widespread adoption of computers, automation, and digital technologies. Key innovations like PLCs, CAD, and robotics revolutionized manufacturing, leading to "smart" factories. Industry

3.0 emphasized efficiency, precision, and connectivity, laying the groundwork for the interconnected global economy we live in today.

Industry 4.0: Industry 4.0, also known as the "Fourth Industrial Revolution," is the convergence of physical and digital technologies, blurring the boundaries between the physical, digital, and biological worlds. It involves the digitization of entire value chains, the rise of cyber-physical systems, and new business models centered on data-driven decision-making and customization. This paradigm shift has profound implications for businesses, societies, and economies worldwide, as it transforms how goods are produced, services are delivered, and value is created.

The evolution of industry paradigms, from mechanization in Industry 1.0 to digitalization in Industry 4.0, has led to transformative changes in our lives, work, and interactions. As we approach Industry 5.0, which combines advanced technologies with human-centric processes, it's crucial to reflect on past revolutions and embrace the opportunities presented by the digital age, recognizing the lessons learned from past revolutions.

Scope and Objectives

The chapter explores the strategic implementation of digital HR practices in Industry 5.0, focusing on the evolving role of HR in the digital age and the landscape of digital HR solutions. It also explores the integration of digital technologies, data analytics, and automation into HR functions to drive business growth and foster innovation(Erro-Garcés & Aramendia-Muneta, 2023b; Parameswaran, 2021b; Sulistyaningsih, 2023b).

- **To analyze the Evolution of Industry Paradigms:** The chapter will begin by tracing the historical evolution of industry paradigms from the First Industrial Revolution to the current era of Industry 5.0. By understanding the progression of industrialization and technological innovation, readers will gain insight into the contextual backdrop against which digital HR practices are evolving.
- **To elucidate the Strategic Importance of Digital HR:** A main objective is to highlight the strategic significance of digital HR for organizational growth and competitiveness in Industry 5.0. Through case studies, best practices, and industry insights, the chapter will demonstrate how digital HR initiatives can optimize talent acquisition, performance management, and employee engagement, thereby driving business success.
- **To provide Practical Guidance for Digital HR Implementation:** Another objective is to offer practical guidance and actionable recommendations for organizations seeking to implement digital HR solutions effectively. This includes discussions on change management, technology selection, and organizational readiness, as well as insights into overcoming common challenges and pitfalls associated with digital HR adoption.
- **To Explore Future Directions of Digital HR:** Lastly, the chapter aims to explore emerging trends and future directions in the field of digital HR, anticipating how advancements in technology and changing workforce dynamics will shape HR practices in the years to come. By providing a forward-looking perspective, the chapter seeks to equip readers with the knowledge and foresight needed to stay ahead in the rapidly evolving landscape of Industry 5.0.

The chapter provides a thorough and comprehensive analysis of digital HR implementation for business growth in the era of Industry 5.0.

ROLE OF HUMAN RESOURCES IN INDUSTRY 5.0

Industry 5.0, a shift towards advanced technologies and human-centric processes, has significantly transformed the role of Human Resources (HR). HR plays a strategic role in facilitating business success by coordinating the harmonious coexistence of technology and talent. HR professionals are using digital technologies, data analytics, and automation to improve workforce agility, productivity, and engagement. A human-centric approach, fostering innovation, learning, and well-being amidst technological disruption, unlocks the full potential of human capital and positions organizations for success in the digital age(Zizic et al., 2022).

Figure 1 illustrates the role of Human Resources in Industry 5.0, emphasizing its strategic importance in facilitating business success, integrating technology and talent, utilizing digital tools and analytics, and promoting a human-centric approach to unlock the full potential of human capital.

Evolution of HR Function in Response to Technological Advancements

The HR function has evolved significantly due to technological advancements, adapting to changing organizational needs and priorities in response to changing business landscapes. Traditionally focused

Figure 1. The role of human resources in Industry 5.0

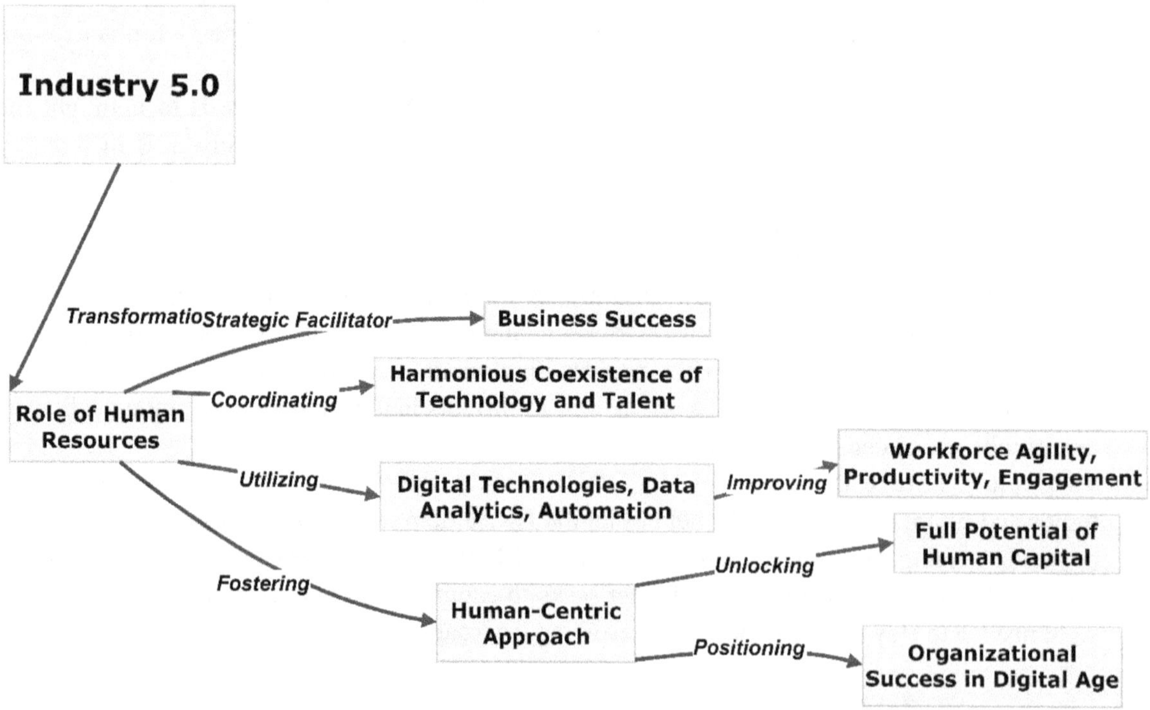

on administrative tasks such as payroll processing and personnel management, HR has evolved into a strategic partner that leverages technology to drive organizational success. With the advent of digital technologies, HR has embraced automation, data analytics, and artificial intelligence to streamline processes, enhance decision-making, and improve the employee experience. For example, cloud-based HRIS (Human Resource Information Systems) have revolutionized data management, enabling HR professionals to access real-time insights and make data-driven decisions(Cillo et al., 2022b). Recruitment processes have been augmented by AI-powered tools that analyze resumes, screen candidates, and predict job fit with greater accuracy. Moreover, the rise of remote work has necessitated the adoption of digital collaboration platforms and virtual onboarding solutions, transforming how HR interacts with employees across geographies. In essence, the evolution of the HR function in response to technological advancements underscores its pivotal role in driving organizational agility, efficiency, and innovation in the digital age(Gift et al., 2024).

Importance of Human-Centric Approach in the Digital Era

In the digital era, a human-centric approach is crucial for businesses, as automation and artificial intelligence dominate the world. Organizations must not overlook the human element that drives innovation, creativity, and collaboration. A human-centric approach to HR emphasizes empathy, inclusivity, and personalized experiences, recognizing that employees are more than just cogs in a machine. It entails fostering a supportive work environment that prioritizes employee well-being, professional development, and work-life balance. Moreover, in the face of digital disruption and rapid technological change, a human-centric approach enables organizations to navigate uncertainty with resilience and adaptability(Adel, 2022). By investing in employee engagement initiatives, promoting a culture of trust and transparency, and empowering employees to contribute their unique perspectives and talents, organizations can unlock the full potential of their workforce and achieve sustainable success in the digital era.

DIGITAL HR LANDSCAPE IN INDUSTRY 5.0

Industry 5.0 involves the integration of advanced technologies into HR functions to improve efficiency, agility, and employee experiences. Digital HR solutions leverage tools such as artificial intelligence, data analytics, cloud computing, and automation to streamline processes, enable data-driven decision-making, and personalize employee interactions. From recruitment and onboarding to performance management and learning and development, digital HR solutions encompass a wide range of applications designed to optimize HR operations and drive business growth in the digital era(Ghobakhloo et al., 2022).

Figure 2 illustrates Industry 5.0's Digital HR Landscape, integrating advanced technologies like artificial intelligence, data analytics, and automation. It demonstrates how these solutions streamline processes, enable data-driven decision-making, and personalize employee interactions across recruitment, onboarding, performance management, and learning and development, driving business growth in the digital era.

Figure 2. Industry 5.0's digital HR landscape, integrating advanced technologies

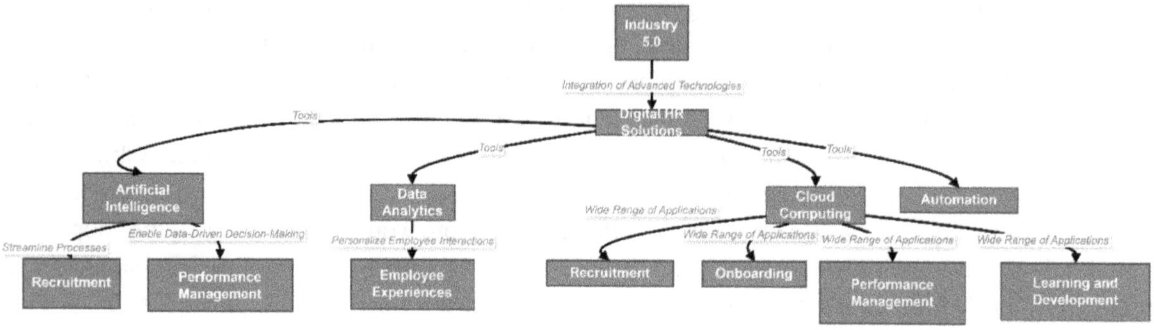

Trends Shaping Digital HR Strategies

The digital HR landscape in Industry 5.0 is rapidly evolving due to transformative technologies and changing workforce dynamics. Understanding important trends is crucial for organizations to leverage HR as a strategic enabler for business growth and innovation, with five prominent trends shaping the landscape(Erro-Garcés & Aramendia-Muneta, 2023b; Kraus et al., 2023).

- **Data-Driven Decision-Making:** Data analytics is revolutionizing HR practices, enabling organizations to derive actionable insights from vast volumes of workforce data. By leveraging advanced analytics tools, HR professionals can identify trends, predict future talent needs, and optimize HR processes for greater efficiency and effectiveness. From workforce planning and talent acquisition to performance management and employee engagement, data-driven decision-making is becoming a cornerstone of digital HR strategies in Industry 5.0.
- **Personalization and Employee Experience:** In the digital era, employees expect personalized experiences tailored to their unique preferences and needs. Digital HR strategies are increasingly focused on enhancing the employee experience through personalized communication, learning and development opportunities, and recognition programs. By adopting technologies such as AI-powered chatbots and personalized learning platforms, organizations can create a more engaging and supportive work environment that fosters employee satisfaction and retention.
- **Remote Work and Digital Collaboration:** The shift towards remote work accelerated by global events has necessitated a rethinking of traditional HR practices. Digital HR strategies now emphasize remote-friendly policies, virtual collaboration tools, and flexible work arrangements to support remote and distributed teams. Cloud-based HRIS, virtual onboarding platforms, and digital communication tools are essential components of modern HR infrastructure, enabling seamless collaboration and communication across geographies(Boopathi, 2023).
- **Skills Development and Continuous Learning:** With the rapid pace of technological change, skills development and continuous learning have become imperative for maintaining workforce agility and competitiveness. Digital HR strategies focus on providing employees with access to on-demand learning resources, personalized training programs, and upskilling opportunities to adapt to evolving job roles and industry trends. By investing in employee

development, organizations can future-proof their workforce and drive innovation in Industry 5.0(Prabhuswamy et al., 2024).

- **AI and Automation in HR Operations:** AI and automation technologies are revolutionizing HR operations, automating repetitive tasks, and optimizing workflows for greater efficiency. Chatbots and virtual assistants are being deployed to streamline employee queries and HR service delivery, while AI-powered recruitment tools are enhancing candidate sourcing and selection processes. By embracing AI and automation, HR departments can free up time for strategic activities, reduce human error, and deliver a more seamless employee experience(Boopathi, 2024).

The digital HR landscape in Industry 5.0 combines technologies and trends to improve workforce agility, productivity, and engagement. By embracing data-driven decision-making, prioritizing employee experience, facilitating remote work, investing in skills development, and leveraging AI and automation, organizations can develop sustainable growth strategies.

Technologies Driving Digital HR Transformation

Industry 5.0's digital HR landscape integrates advanced technologies to improve HR functions, optimize workforce management, and drive organizational success. Businesses are utilizing digital solutions to transform traditional HR processes and adapt to the digital age's changing demands. The digital HR landscape in Industry 5.0 is influenced by various technologies that are revolutionizing traditional HR processes, improving workforce management, and driving organizational performance. By embracing these technologies, organizations can position themselves for success in the digital age(Erro-Garcés & Aramendia-Muneta, 2023b, 2023a). Figure 3 illustrates the integration of advanced technologies in driving digital HR transformation in Industry 5.0 through visual representation.

Artificial Intelligence (AI) and Machine Learning: AI and machine learning algorithms are revolutionizing HR processes by enabling predictive analytics, automation, and personalized experiences. AI-powered recruitment platforms can analyze resumes, assess candidate fit, and predict job performance with greater accuracy, streamlining the talent acquisition process and reducing bias. Similarly, AI-driven chatbots and virtual assistants are enhancing employee self-service capabilities, providing instant support for HR inquiries, onboarding processes, and training initiatives(Paramita, 2020; Pillai & Sivathanu, 2020).

- **Data Analytics and Predictive Modeling:** Data analytics tools are empowering HR professionals to make data-driven decisions and optimize workforce management strategies. By analyzing workforce data, such as employee performance metrics, engagement levels, and turnover rates, organizations can identify trends, anticipate future skill requirements, and mitigate workforce-related risks. Predictive modeling techniques enable HR to forecast talent needs, succession planning, and workforce trends, thereby enabling proactive talent management strategies(Prabhuswamy et al., 2024).
- **Cloud-Based Human Resource Information Systems (HRIS):** Cloud-based HRIS platforms provide a centralized repository for managing employee data, streamlining HR processes, and facilitating collaboration across departments. These systems offer scalability, flexibility, and accessibility, allowing HR professionals to access real-time information, automate routine tasks, and track employee records with ease. Additionally, cloud-based HRIS platforms sup-

Figure 3. Integration of advanced technologies in driving digital HR transformation

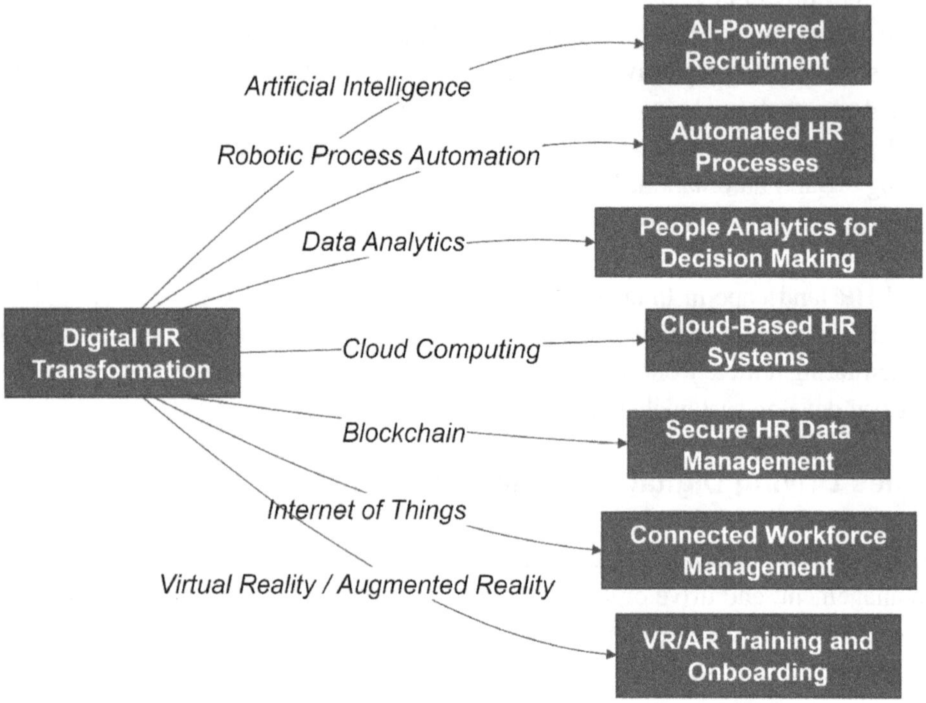

port remote work arrangements and enable seamless integration with other business applications, enhancing organizational agility and efficiency(Nanda et al., 2024; Rahamathunnisa et al., 2023).

- **Employee Self-Service Portals:** Employee self-service portals empower employees to manage their HR-related tasks independently, reducing administrative burden and enhancing user experience. Through self-service portals, employees can update personal information, view pay stubs, request time off, and access training resources from any device with internet connectivity. By empowering employees to take control of their HR processes, organizations can improve efficiency, engagement, and satisfaction levels across the workforce.
- **Virtual Reality (VR) and Augmented Reality (AR):** VR and AR technologies are revolutionizing HR training and development initiatives by providing immersive learning experiences and simulating real-world scenarios. VR-based simulations allow employees to practice skills in a risk-free environment, such as customer interactions or emergency response scenarios. AR applications enhance on-the-job training by overlaying digital information onto physical environments, providing real-time guidance and support. By leveraging VR and AR technologies, organizations can enhance employee learning outcomes, improve retention rates, and foster a culture of continuous learning and development(Revathi et al., 2024).

STRATEGIC IMPORTANCE OF DIGITAL HR FOR BUSINESS GROWTH

Enhancing Talent Acquisition Processes Through Digital Solutions

In Industry 5.0, talent acquisition is crucial for organizational success, and digital HR solutions enhance processes to attract, engage, and retain top talent more effectively. Digital HR solutions are crucial for organizations to drive business growth and maintain a competitive edge in Industry 5.0. They can widen the talent pool, streamline recruitment, improve candidate experience, enable data-driven decision-making, and promote diversity and inclusion, attracting and retaining top talent, and achieving sustainable success in the digital era(Pillai & Sivathanu, 2020).

- **Widening Talent Pool:** Digital HR platforms expand the reach of talent acquisition efforts beyond traditional boundaries. Online job boards, social media recruiting, and AI-powered candidate sourcing tools enable organizations to tap into a diverse pool of candidates from across the globe. By leveraging digital channels, organizations can access talent with specialized skills and niche expertise, enhancing their competitive advantage in the market.
- **Streamlining Recruitment Processes:** Digital HR solutions streamline the recruitment process, reducing administrative burdens and improving efficiency. Applicant tracking systems (ATS) automate routine tasks such as resume screening, candidate communication, and interview scheduling, freeing up HR professionals to focus on strategic activities. Moreover, video interviewing platforms enable remote assessments, accelerating the hiring timeline and reducing time-to-fill vacancies.
- **Enhancing Candidate Experience:** Digital HR technologies enhance the candidate experience, from initial engagement to onboarding. Mobile-responsive career portals, personalized communication channels, and interactive application processes create a seamless and engaging experience for candidates. By providing transparency, feedback, and support throughout the recruitment journey, organizations enhance their employer brand and reputation, attracting top talent and fostering long-term relationships.
- **Data-Driven Decision-Making:** Digital HR analytics provide valuable insights into recruitment performance, candidate demographics, and hiring trends. By analyzing data such as time-to-hire, cost-per-hire, and applicant demographics, organizations can identify areas for improvement, optimize recruitment strategies, and allocate resources more effectively. Predictive analytics tools enable organizations to forecast future talent needs, anticipate skill shortages, and develop proactive recruitment strategies to stay ahead of the competition.
- **Promoting Diversity and Inclusion:** Digital HR solutions support diversity and inclusion initiatives by removing biases from the recruitment process and promoting equitable hiring practices. AI-driven recruitment platforms can anonymize candidate data, mitigate unconscious biases, and ensure fair and objective candidate evaluation. Moreover, digital tools enable organizations to track diversity metrics, set diversity goals, and measure progress towards creating more inclusive workplaces.

Optimizing Performance Management With Data Analytics

Performance management is crucial for organizational success, and in Industry 5.0, digital HR is strategically integrating data analytics to optimize performance management processes. This approach enhances employee performance, fosters continuous improvement, and drives sustainable business growth by harnessing data-driven insights (Eliza, 2023).

a) **Enhanced Decision-Making:** Digital HR enables organizations to collect, analyze, and interpret vast amounts of performance-related data in real-time. By leveraging data analytics tools and dashboards, HR professionals can gain deeper insights into employee performance trends, identify areas for improvement, and make informed decisions to optimize workforce productivity and effectiveness.
b) **Personalized Performance Assessments:** Traditional performance management systems often rely on standardized metrics and subjective evaluations, which may not accurately capture individual contributions or developmental needs. Digital HR solutions leverage data analytics to personalize performance assessments based on objective performance metrics, skill proficiency, and job-specific criteria. This enables HR to provide targeted feedback, coaching, and development opportunities tailored to each employee's unique strengths and areas for growth.
c) **Continuous Feedback Loops:** Digital HR platforms facilitate continuous feedback loops between managers and employees, fostering ongoing dialogue and collaboration to improve performance outcomes. Through features such as real-time performance tracking, goal setting, and feedback mechanisms, organizations can create a culture of transparency, accountability, and continuous improvement. By providing timely feedback and recognition, digital HR promotes employee engagement, motivation, and retention, ultimately driving business success.
d) **Predictive Analytics for Talent Management:** In addition to monitoring current performance metrics, digital HR leverages predictive analytics to forecast future talent needs and identify high-potential employees. By analyzing historical performance data, employee demographics, and market trends, HR can anticipate skill gaps, succession planning requirements, and workforce trends, enabling proactive talent management strategies. This strategic approach to performance management ensures that organizations have the right talent in place to support their growth objectives and remain competitive in the marketplace.
e) **Alignment with Organizational Goals:** Digital HR aligns performance management initiatives with organizational goals and objectives, ensuring that individual efforts are directed towards achieving strategic priorities. By cascading organizational goals down to individual performance objectives, HR can create a clear line of sight between employee contributions and business outcomes. This alignment fosters a sense of purpose, accountability, and ownership among employees, driving performance excellence and contributing to overall business growth.

Organizations must optimize performance management with data analytics to leverage digital HR capabilities for business growth in Industry 5.0. This holistic approach enhances decision-making, personalizes performance assessments, fosters continuous feedback loops, uses predictive analytics for talent management, and aligns performance initiatives with organizational goals. This holistic approach unlocks workforce potential and achieves sustainable success in the digital age.

Facilitating Learning and Development Initiatives Using Digital Platforms

In Industry 5.0, continuous learning and development are crucial for a skilled workforce. Digital HR facilitates these initiatives by integrating digital platforms. Organizations can deliver personalized, engaging learning experiences, empowering employees to acquire new skills, adapt to change, and drive business growth by leveraging technology-enabled solutions(Shaddiq et al., 2023).

Figure 4 illustrates the iterative learning and development process in Industry 5.0, where employees continuously use digital platforms to enhance skills, adapt to business changes, and drive collective growth. Digital platforms are crucial for organizations to foster a culture of continuous learning and drive business growth in Industry 5.0. By utilizing technology-enabled solutions, they can provide personalized, engaging, and effective learning experiences, empowering employees to acquire new skills,

Figure 4. Iterative learning and development process in Industry 5.0

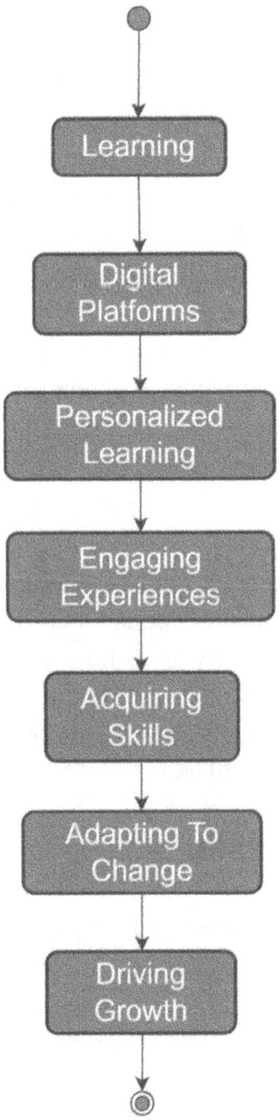

adapt to change, and contribute to organizational success (Pillai & Sivathanu, 2020; Shaddiq et al., 2023; Zehir et al., 2020).

i. **Accessibility and Flexibility:** Digital learning platforms provide employees with anytime, anywhere access to a diverse range of learning resources, including online courses, videos, webinars, and interactive modules. This accessibility and flexibility allow employees to engage in learning activities at their own pace and convenience, overcoming barriers such as geographical constraints and scheduling conflicts. Whether in the office, at home, or on the go, employees can access relevant learning content tailored to their individual needs and preferences.
ii. **Personalized Learning Paths:** Digital learning platforms leverage data analytics and machine learning algorithms to create personalized learning paths for employees based on their skills, knowledge gaps, and career aspirations. By analyzing employee performance data, training history, and competency assessments, HR can recommend targeted learning resources and development opportunities aligned with each employee's unique learning objectives. This personalized approach enhances learning effectiveness, engagement, and retention, ultimately driving employee growth and performance.
iii. **Interactive and Engaging Content:** Digital learning platforms employ interactive and multimedia-rich content formats to engage learners and enhance knowledge retention. Features such as gamification, simulations, quizzes, and virtual reality (VR) experiences make learning more immersive, interactive, and enjoyable. By incorporating elements of interactivity and gamification into learning activities, organizations can increase learner motivation, participation, and satisfaction, leading to more effective skill acquisition and application in the workplace.
iv. **Collaboration and Knowledge Sharing:** Digital learning platforms facilitate collaboration and knowledge sharing among employees through social learning features, discussion forums, and peer-to-peer networking opportunities. Employees can connect with colleagues, subject matter experts, and mentors to exchange ideas, seek advice, and share best practices. This collaborative learning environment fosters a culture of continuous improvement, innovation, and knowledge sharing, enriching the learning experience and driving organizational performance.
v. **Data-Driven Insights and Analytics:** Digital learning platforms provide HR with valuable insights and analytics on learning engagement, completion rates, skill acquisition, and learning effectiveness. By tracking significant performance indicators (KPIs) and learning metrics, HR can assess the impact of learning initiatives, identify areas for improvement, and tailor future learning interventions to meet evolving organizational needs. Data-driven insights enable HR to make informed decisions, allocate resources effectively, and demonstrate the return on investment (ROI) of learning and development initiatives to stakeholders.

Successful Digital HR Implementations

To successfully implement digital HR solutions, organizations must follow important steps and best practices. These steps enhance efficiency, effectiveness, and employee satisfaction, driving business growth and success in the digital age. Stakeholder engagement and strategic approach are also crucial for successful implementation (Strohmeier, 2020; Wargo et al., 2021; Zehir et al., 2020).

- **Define Clear Objectives:** Start by defining clear objectives and desired outcomes for the digital HR implementation. Identify specific pain points or areas for improvement within HR processes that digital solutions can address. Whether it's streamlining recruitment, enhancing performance management, or improving employee engagement, clarity on objectives will guide the selection and implementation of appropriate digital HR tools.
- **Engage Stakeholders:** Involve significant stakeholders, including HR professionals, departmental leaders, IT personnel, and end-users, in the planning and decision-making process. Solicit feedback, address concerns, and ensure alignment of objectives and expectations across all stakeholders. Collaboration and buy-in from stakeholders are critical for successful implementation and adoption of digital HR solutions.
- **Conduct Thorough Needs Assessment:** Conduct a thorough needs assessment to identify the specific requirements and functionalities needed from digital HR solutions. Evaluate existing HR processes, systems, and workflows to pinpoint areas of inefficiency or gaps that digital solutions can address. Consider factors such as scalability, integration capabilities, user-friendliness, and compliance requirements when selecting digital HR tools.
- **Select the Right Technology:** Choose digital HR technologies that align with your organization's goals, budget, and technological infrastructure. Evaluate various options, including HRIS platforms, recruitment software, performance management systems, learning management systems (LMS), and employee engagement tools. Prioritize solutions that offer scalability, customization options, and robust support services to meet your organization's evolving needs.
- **Plan for Change Management:** Implementing digital HR solutions involves significant changes to workflows, processes, and organizational culture. Develop a comprehensive change management plan to prepare employees for the transition, mitigate resistance, and foster acceptance of new technologies. Provide training, resources, and support to help employees adapt to the changes and maximize the benefits of digital HR implementations.
- **Ensure Data Security and Compliance:** Prioritize data security and compliance throughout the implementation process. Choose reputable vendors with robust security measures and data protection protocols in place. Ensure that digital HR solutions comply with relevant regulatory requirements, such as GDPR, HIPAA, or industry-specific regulations. Implement safeguards to protect sensitive employee data and mitigate risks of data breaches or privacy violations.
- **Monitor and Measure Performance:** Continuously monitor the performance and effectiveness of digital HR implementations through significant performance indicators (KPIs) and metrics. Track adoption rates, user satisfaction, process efficiency, and business outcomes to assess the impact of digital HR solutions on organizational performance. Use feedback and insights gathered to refine processes, optimize workflows, and drive continuous improvement.

Real-World Examples of Digital HR for Effective Implementation

Organizations are utilizing digital HR solutions like AI-powered recruitment tools, digital learning platforms, performance management redesigns, VR training programs, and productivity analytics to attract, develop, and retain talent in the digital age, resulting in tangible business outcomes (Eliza, 2023; Gilch & Sieweke, 2021; Paramita, 2020; Zavyalova et al., 2022).

- **IBM's Watson Recruitment Tool:** IBM's Watson Recruitment tool utilizes artificial intelligence (AI) to streamline the recruitment process and identify top talent. By analyzing resumes, social media profiles, and other data sources, Watson Recruitment identifies candidates who best match job requirements and cultural fit. This tool significantly reduces time-to-hire and improves the quality of hires by leveraging data-driven insights to make informed recruitment decisions (Domakonda et al., 2022; Samikannu et al., 2022; Venkateswaran et al., 2023).
- **Unilever's Digital Learning Platform:** Unilever's digital learning platform, known as the "ULearn" platform, provides employees with access to a wide range of online courses, resources, and interactive learning modules. The platform utilizes personalized learning paths and gamification elements to engage employees and enhance knowledge retention. By empowering employees to take ownership of their learning and development, ULearn has contributed to improved employee skills, performance, and career progression within the organization.
- **Deloitte's Performance Management Redesign:** Deloitte revamped its performance management system by transitioning from annual performance reviews to a continuous feedback and coaching model. Leveraging digital tools and platforms, Deloitte implemented a real-time feedback system that allows managers and employees to provide and receive feedback on an ongoing basis. This shift has improved communication, transparency, and accountability within the organization, leading to higher employee engagement and performance levels.
- **Accenture's Virtual Reality (VR) Training Program:** Accenture developed a virtual reality (VR) training program to enhance employee learning and development initiatives. The VR program simulates real-world scenarios, such as client interactions or technical skills training, in a virtual environment. By immersing employees in realistic training simulations, Accenture has improved learning outcomes, accelerated skill acquisition, and reduced training costs compared to traditional classroom-based training methods (Das et al., 2024; Durairaj et al., 2023; Sharma et al., 2024).
- **Microsoft's MyAnalytics Tool:** Microsoft's MyAnalytics tool utilizes data analytics and machine learning algorithms to provide employees with insights into their work habits, productivity trends, and collaboration patterns. By analyzing email communication, meeting attendance, and task completion rates, MyAnalytics helps employees identify opportunities for time management, prioritization, and work-life balance. This tool has empowered employees to optimize their productivity and well-being, leading to improved job satisfaction and performance outcomes.

CONSIDERATIONS FOR IMPLEMENTING DIGITAL HR

Adapting HR Strategies to Rapidly Changing Business Environments

Organizational agility is crucial in today's fast-paced business environment, and digital HR implementations must adapt strategies to rapidly changing business environments. Prioritizing agility helps organizations navigate complexities, position themselves for sustained growth, and enhance competitiveness in the digital age (Arslan et al., 2022; Tessema et al., 2022).

Figure 5 highlights the importance of organizational agility in adapting HR strategies to rapid business environment changes, ensuring competitiveness and sustained growth.

Figure 5. Importance of organizational agility in adapting HR strategies

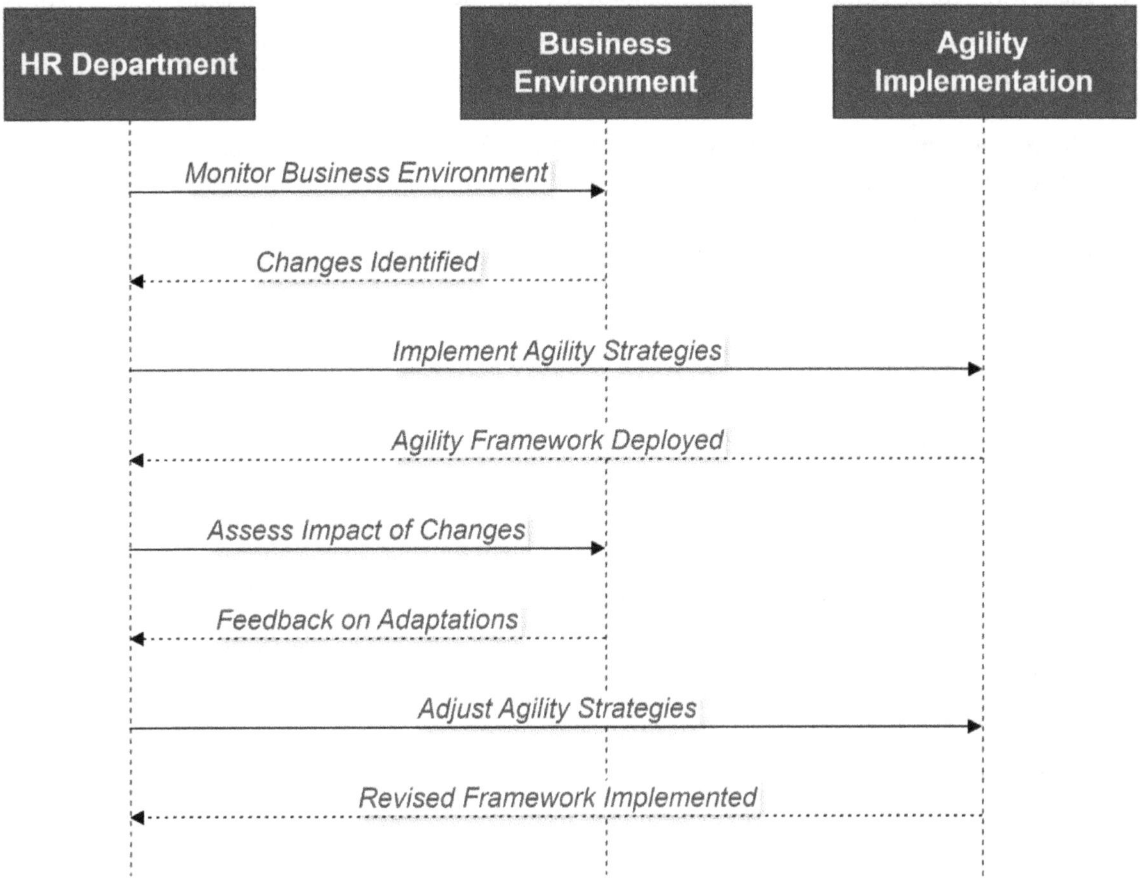

- **Flexibility in HR Processes:** Implement flexible HR processes that can quickly adapt to changing business needs and market conditions. Digital HR solutions should be configurable and customizable to accommodate evolving requirements, workflows, and regulatory changes without significant disruptions to operations.
- **Scalability of Digital HR Systems:** Choose digital HR systems that are scalable and capable of supporting organizational growth and expansion. Scalable solutions can accommodate fluctuations in workforce size, geographic locations, and business units, ensuring seamless scalability without compromising performance or user experience.
- **Agile Talent Management Practices:** Adopt agile talent management practices that enable organizations to identify, develop, and deploy talent rapidly in response to changing business priorities. Implement talent mobility programs, cross-functional training initiatives, and talent pools to build a flexible and adaptable workforce capable of meeting evolving business demands.
- **Real-Time Data Analytics:** Leverage real-time data analytics and predictive insights to inform HR decision-making and strategy formulation. Digital HR systems should provide HR professionals with access to timely, accurate, and actionable data on workforce trends, performance metrics, and talent analytics, enabling proactive responses to emerging opportunities and challenges.

- **Continuous Learning and Development:** Foster a culture of continuous learning and development within the organization to equip employees with the skills and competencies needed to thrive in a rapidly changing environment. Offer digital learning resources, upskilling programs, and on-the-job training opportunities to empower employees to adapt and grow alongside evolving business needs(Kumar et al., 2023).
- **Cross-Functional Collaboration:** Encourage cross-functional collaboration and communication between HR, IT, finance, and other departments to ensure alignment of digital HR initiatives with broader organizational objectives. Collaboration enables holistic decision-making, resource allocation, and implementation of digital HR solutions that support organizational agility and drive business success.

Change Management: Overcoming Resistance and Fostering Adoption

- **Communication and Transparency:** Effective communication is essential for overcoming resistance to change and fostering adoption of digital HR initiatives. Keep employees informed about the rationale behind the changes, the benefits they will bring, and how they will impact day-to-day work. Transparency builds trust and reduces uncertainty.
- **Stakeholder Involvement:** Involve important stakeholders, including HR professionals, departmental leaders, and end-users, in the change management process. Solicit their input, address concerns, and involve them in decision-making to ensure buy-in and ownership of the digital HR initiatives.
- **Training and Support:** Provide comprehensive training and support to employees to build their skills and confidence in using digital HR tools and platforms. Offer workshops, tutorials, and resources to familiarize employees with new technologies and processes. Additionally, establish a support system to address any questions or challenges that may arise during implementation.
- **Feedback and Adaptation:** Continuously gather feedback from employees throughout the implementation process and be prepared to adapt and refine digital HR initiatives based on their input. Encourage open dialogue, listen to concerns, and address issues promptly to demonstrate responsiveness and commitment to employee satisfaction.

Continuous Innovation: Embracing Emerging Technologies to Stay Ahead

- **Stay Abreast of Trends:** Keep abreast of emerging technologies and trends in digital HR to stay ahead of the curve and remain competitive in the marketplace. Regularly evaluate new tools, platforms, and innovations that have the potential to enhance HR processes and improve organizational performance.
- **Pilot Projects:** Experiment with pilot projects or proof-of-concept initiatives to test the feasibility and effectiveness of emerging technologies in a controlled environment. Pilot projects allow organizations to assess the impact of new technologies on HR processes, identify challenges, and refine implementation strategies before scaling up.
- **Partnerships and Collaborations:** Foster partnerships and collaborations with technology vendors, startups, and industry experts to leverage their expertise and access to cutting-edge solutions. Collaborative initiatives enable organizations to co-create innovative digital HR solutions tailored to their specific needs and objectives.

- **Cultural Readiness:** Cultivate a culture of innovation, experimentation, and continuous learning within the organization to embrace emerging technologies and drive digital HR transformation. Encourage employees to explore new ideas, take calculated risks, and challenge conventional ways of thinking to foster a culture of innovation that permeates throughout the organization.

Implementing digital HR strategies based on these factors can help organizations overcome resistance, promote adoption, and embrace emerging technologies in the ever-evolving HR management landscape.

FUTURE DIRECTIONS OF DIGITAL HR IN INDUSTRY 5.0

The future of digital HR in Industry 5.0 is marked by emerging trends and technologies that will transform HR processes, workforce dynamics, and business operations. Organizations can capitalize on these trends to achieve sustainable success in the digital age(Cooke et al., 2021; Zavyalova et al., 2022; Zehir et al., 2020).

- **AI and Machine Learning:** AI and machine learning technologies will continue to play a central role in shaping the future of HR by enabling predictive analytics, automation, and personalized experiences. AI-powered chatbots, virtual assistants, and predictive analytics tools will streamline HR processes, enhance decision-making, and improve employee engagement.
- **Blockchain Technology:** Blockchain technology has the potential to revolutionize HR processes such as credential verification, payroll management, and employee records management. By providing a secure, tamper-proof platform for storing and sharing sensitive HR data, blockchain technology can enhance data security, reduce fraud, and improve trust in HR transactions.
- **Augmented Reality (AR) and Virtual Reality (VR):** AR and VR technologies will transform employee training and development initiatives by providing immersive, interactive learning experiences. VR simulations, AR overlays, and virtual training environments will enable employees to acquire new skills, practice complex tasks, and engage in realistic scenarios without the need for physical equipment or resources.
- **People Analytics:** People analytics, also known as workforce analytics or HR analytics, will continue to gain prominence as organizations seek to leverage data-driven insights to optimize workforce management strategies. Advanced analytics tools and algorithms will enable HR professionals to analyze workforce trends, predict future skill requirements, and identify opportunities for performance improvement and talent development.

Anticipated Impacts of Digital HR Evolution on Business Operations and Workforce Dynamics

- **Increased Efficiency and Productivity:** The evolution of digital HR will lead to increased efficiency and productivity across HR processes, resulting in cost savings, improved resource allocation, and faster decision-making. Automation of routine tasks, streamlined workflows, and data-driven insights will enable HR to focus on strategic initiatives and value-added activities.
- **Enhanced Employee Experience:** Digital HR initiatives will enhance the employee experience by providing personalized, seamless interactions and access to self-service tools and resources. Employee-centric platforms, mobile apps, and virtual support services will empower employees

to manage their HR-related tasks, access learning opportunities, and engage with HR professionals anytime, anywhere.

- **Agile Workforce Management:** Digital HR evolution will enable organizations to adopt agile workforce management practices, such as flexible work arrangements, contingent staffing models, and remote work options. Digital platforms and collaboration tools will facilitate communication, collaboration, and coordination among distributed teams, enabling organizations to adapt to changing business needs and market dynamics more effectively.
- **Shift Towards Data-Driven Decision-Making:** The evolution of digital HR will facilitate a shift towards data-driven decision-making in HR management, enabling organizations to make informed, evidence-based decisions about talent acquisition, performance management, and employee development. By leveraging advanced analytics and predictive modeling techniques, HR professionals can anticipate future workforce trends, identify emerging skill gaps, and align HR strategies with organizational goals and objectives.

CONCLUSION

Digital HR is crucial in Industry 5.0 for driving sustainable business growth. It optimizes workforce management, enhances employee experience, and keeps organizations ahead of competition. Digital HR solutions, including recruitment, talent management, learning, and development, offer opportunities to streamline processes, improve efficiency, and foster innovation. AI-powered recruitment tools help organizations attract top talent, while digital learning platforms enable employees to acquire new skills. Performance management systems use data analytics to enhance employee productivity and engagement, while virtual reality training programs revolutionize learning experiences and skill development. By embracing digital HR solutions, organizations can unlock their workforce's full potential and position themselves for success in the digital era.

Digital HR is not just about technology; it's about people. Organizations can leverage digital HR for sustainable business growth by adopting a human-centric approach. By providing employees with self-service tools, personalized learning resources, and virtual support services, they can enhance their experience and satisfaction, leading to retention and loyalty. A strategic mindset, commitment to innovation, and focus on the human element are essential. Aligning digital HR initiatives with organizational goals, fostering a culture of continuous learning, and embracing emerging technologies can build agile, resilient, and future-ready workforces. As Industry 5.0 unfolds, organizations prioritizing digital HR will emerge as industry leaders.

Abbreviations

AI: Artificial Intelligence
AR: Augmented Reality
ATS: Applicant Tracking System
CAD: Computer-Aided Design
COVID: Coronavirus Disease (2019)
GDPR: General Data Protection Regulation
HIPAA: Health Insurance Portability and Accountability Act

HR: Human Resources
HRIS: Human Resource Information System
IBM: International Business Machines Corporation
IT: Information Technology
KPI: Key Performance Indicator
LMS: Learning Management System
PLC: Programmable Logic Controller
ROI: Return on Investment
UL: Underwriters Laboratories (may refer to other entities as well)
VR: Virtual Reality

REFERENCES

Adel, A. (2022). Future of industry 5.0 in society: Human-centric solutions, challenges and prospective research areas. *Journal of Cloud Computing (Heidelberg, Germany)*, *11*(1), 40. doi:10.1186/s13677-022-00314-5 PMID:36101900

Arslan, A., Cooper, C., Khan, Z., Golgeci, I., & Ali, I. (2022). Artificial intelligence and human workers interaction at team level: A conceptual assessment of the challenges and potential HRM strategies. *International Journal of Manpower*, *43*(1), 75–88. doi:10.1108/IJM-01-2021-0052

Boopathi, S. (2023). Internet of Things-Integrated Remote Patient Monitoring System: Healthcare Application. In *Dynamics of Swarm Intelligence Health Analysis for the Next Generation* (pp. 137–161). IGI Global. doi:10.4018/978-1-6684-6894-4.ch008

Boopathi, S. (2024). Implementation of Green Manufacturing Practices in Automobile Fields: A Review. *Sustainable Machining and Green Manufacturing*, 221–248.

Cillo, V., Gregori, G. L., Daniele, L. M., Caputo, F., & Bitbol-Saba, N. (2022a). Rethinking companies' culture through knowledge management lens during Industry 5.0 transition. *Journal of Knowledge Management*, *26*(10), 2485–2498. doi:10.1108/JKM-09-2021-0718

Cillo, V., Gregori, G. L., Daniele, L. M., Caputo, F., & Bitbol-Saba, N. (2022b). Rethinking companies' culture through knowledge management lens during Industry 5.0 transition. *Journal of Knowledge Management*, *26*(10), 2485–2498. doi:10.1108/JKM-09-2021-0718

Cooke, F. L., Xiao, M., & Chen, Y. (2021). Still in search of strategic human resource management? A review and suggestions for future research with China as an example. *Human Resource Management*, *60*(1), 89–118. doi:10.1002/hrm.22029

Das, S., Lekhya, G., Shreya, K., Shekinah, K. L., Babu, K. K., & Boopathi, S. (2024). Fostering Sustainability Education Through Cross-Disciplinary Collaborations and Research Partnerships: Interdisciplinary Synergy. In Facilitating Global Collaboration and Knowledge Sharing in Higher Education With Generative AI (pp. 60–88). IGI Global.

Domakonda, V. K., Farooq, S., Chinthamreddy, S., Puviarasi, R., Sudhakar, M., & Boopathi, S. (2022). Sustainable Developments of Hybrid Floating Solar Power Plants: Photovoltaic System. In Human Agro-Energy Optimization for Business and Industry (pp. 148–167). IGI Global.

Durairaj, M., Jayakumar, S., Karpagavalli, V., Maheswari, B. U., Boopathi, S., & ... (2023). Utilization of Digital Tools in the Indian Higher Education System During Health Crises. In *Multidisciplinary Approaches to Organizational Governance During Health Crises* (pp. 1–21). IGI Global. doi:10.4018/978-1-7998-9213-7.ch001

Eliza, E. (2023). Human Resource Management Strategies to Improve Performance in the Digital Era. *Implikasi: Jurnal Manajemen Sumber Daya Manusia*, *1*(2), 132–139.

Erro-Garcés, A., & Aramendia-Muneta, M. E. (2023). The role of human resource management practices on the results of digitalisation. From Industry 4.0 to Industry 5.0. *Journal of Organizational Change Management*, *36*(4), 585–602. doi:10.1108/JOCM-11-2021-0354

Ghobakhloo, M., Iranmanesh, M., Mubarak, M. F., Mubarik, M., Rejeb, A., & Nilashi, M. (2022). Identifying industry 5.0 contributions to sustainable development: A strategy roadmap for delivering sustainability values. *Sustainable Production and Consumption*, *33*, 716–737. doi:10.1016/j.spc.2022.08.003

Gift, M. D. M., Senthil, T. S., Hasan, D. S., Alagarraja, K., Jayaseelan, P., & Boopathi, S. (2024). Additive Manufacturing and 3D Printing Innovations: Revolutionizing Industry 5.0. In Technological Advancements in Data Processing for Next Generation Intelligent Systems (pp. 255–287). IGI Global. doi:10.4018/979-8-3693-0968-1.ch010

Gilch, P. M., & Sieweke, J. (2021). Recruiting digital talent: The strategic role of recruitment in organisations' digital transformation. *German Journal of Human Resource Management*, *35*(1), 53–82. doi:10.1177/2397002220952734

Kraus, N., Kraus, K., Manzhura, O., Ishchenko, I., & Radzikhovska, Y. (2023). Digital Transformation of Business Processes of Enterprises on the Way to Becoming Industry 5.0 in the Gig Economy. *WSEAS Transactions on Business and Economics*, *93*(20), 1008–1029. doi:10.37394/23207.2023.20.93

Kumar, P. R., Meenakshi, S., Shalini, S., Devi, S. R., & Boopathi, S. (2023). Soil Quality Prediction in Context Learning Approaches Using Deep Learning and Blockchain for Smart Agriculture. In Effective AI, Blockchain, and E-Governance Applications for Knowledge Discovery and Management (pp. 1–26). IGI Global. doi:10.4018/978-1-6684-9151-5.ch001

Nanda, A. K., Sharma, A., Augustine, P. J., Cyril, B. R., Kiran, V., & Sampath, B. (2024). Securing Cloud Infrastructure in IaaS and PaaS Environments. In Improving Security, Privacy, and Trust in Cloud Computing (pp. 1–33). IGI Global. doi:10.4018/979-8-3693-1431-9.ch001

Orlova, E. V. (2021). Design of personal trajectories for employees' professional development in the knowledge society under Industry 5.0. *Social Sciences (Basel, Switzerland)*, *10*(11), 427. doi:10.3390/socsci10110427

Parameswaran, H. (2021). Industry 5.0: Can it be a change management gizmo in Human resource development? *Parameswaran, Hima,(2021), Industry, 5.*

Paramita, D. (2020). *Digitalization in talent acquisition: A case study of AI in recruitment*. Academic Press.

Pillai, R., & Sivathanu, B. (2020). Adoption of artificial intelligence (AI) for talent acquisition in IT/ITeS organizations. *Benchmarking*, *27*(9), 2599–2629. doi:10.1108/BIJ-04-2020-0186

Prabhuswamy, M., Tripathi, R., Vijayakumar, M., Thulasimani, T., Sundharesalingam, P., & Sampath, B. (2024). A Study on the Complex Nature of Higher Education Leadership: An Innovative Approach. In *Challenges of Globalization and Inclusivity in Academic Research* (pp. 202–223). IGI Global. doi:10.4018/979-8-3693-1371-8.ch013

Rahamathunnisa, U., Sudhakar, K., Murugan, T. K., Thivaharan, S., Rajkumar, M., & Boopathi, S. (2023). Cloud Computing Principles for Optimizing Robot Task Offloading Processes. In *AI-Enabled Social Robotics in Human Care Services* (pp. 188–211). IGI Global. doi:10.4018/978-1-6684-8171-4.ch007

Revathi, S., Babu, M., Rajkumar, N., Meti, V. K. V., Kandavalli, S. R., & Boopathi, S. (2024). Unleashing the Future Potential of 4D Printing: Exploring Applications in Wearable Technology, Robotics, Energy, Transportation, and Fashion. In Human-Centered Approaches in Industry 5.0: Human-Machine Interaction, Virtual Reality Training, and Customer Sentiment Analysis (pp. 131–153). IGI Global.

Samikannu, R., Koshariya, A. K., Poornima, E., Ramesh, S., Kumar, A., & Boopathi, S. (2022). Sustainable Development in Modern Aquaponics Cultivation Systems Using IoT Technologies. In *Human Agro-Energy Optimization for Business and Industry* (pp. 105–127). IGI Global.

Shaddiq, S., Irpan, M., & ... (2023). Governance of Human Resources Management in the Digital Era. *Journal of Business and Management Studies*, *5*(3), 80–96. doi:10.32996/jbms.2023.5.3.8

Sharma, D. M., Ramana, K. V., Jothilakshmi, R., Verma, R., Maheswari, B. U., & Boopathi, S. (2024). Integrating Generative AI Into K-12 Curriculums and Pedagogies in India: Opportunities and Challenges. *Facilitating Global Collaboration and Knowledge Sharing in Higher Education With Generative AI*, 133–161.

Strohmeier, S. (2020). Digital human resource management: A conceptual clarification. *German Journal of Human Resource Management*, *34*(3), 345–365. doi:10.1177/2397002220921131

Sulistyaningsih, E. (2023). Improving Human Resources Technology Innovation as a Business Growth Driver in the Society 5.0 Era. *ADI Journal on Recent Innovation*, *4*(2), 149–159.

Tessema, M. T., Tesfom, G., Faircloth, M. A., Tesfagiorgis, M., & Teckle, P. (2022). The "great resignation": Causes, consequences, and creative HR management strategies. *Journal of Human Resource and Sustainability Studies*, *10*(1), 161–178. doi:10.4236/jhrss.2022.101011

Venkateswaran, N., Vidhya, R., Naik, D. A., Raj, T. M., Munjal, N., & Boopathi, S. (2023). Study on Sentence and Question Formation Using Deep Learning Techniques. In *Digital Natives as a Disruptive Force in Asian Businesses and Societies* (pp. 252–273). IGI Global. doi:10.4018/978-1-6684-6782-4.ch015

Wargo, E., Carr Chellman, D., Budge, K., & Canfield Davis, K. (2021). On the digital frontier: Stakeholders in rural areas take on educational technology and schooling. *Journal of Research on Technology in Education*, *53*(2), 140–158. doi:10.1080/15391523.2020.1760753

Zavyalova, E., Sokolov, D., Kucherov, D., & Lisovskaya, A. (2022). The digitalization of human resource management: Present and future. *Foresight and STI Governance*, *16*(2), 42–51. doi:10.17323/2500-2597.2022.2.42.51

Zehir, C., Karaboğa, T., & Başar, D. (2020). The transformation of human resource management and its impact on overall business performance: Big data analytics and AI technologies in strategic HRM. *Digital Business Strategies in Blockchain Ecosystems: Transformational Design and Future of Global Business*, 265–279.

Zizic, M. C., Mladineo, M., Gjeldum, N., & Celent, L. (2022). From industry 4.0 towards industry 5.0: A review and analysis of paradigm shift for the people, organization and technology. *Energies*, *15*(14), 5221. doi:10.3390/en15145221

Chapter 2
Crafting Effective HR Strategies for the Modern Workplace:
Navigating the Digital Frontier

Boopathi S
Muthayammal Engineering College, India

S. Gopi
Department of Electronics and Communication Engineering, Muthayammal Engineering College, India

ABSTRACT

The integration of digital technologies has significantly transformed the way organizations operate, especially in the field of human resources (HR). This chapter explores the importance of creating effective HR strategies that are tailored to the modern workplace, focusing on navigating the digital frontier. By utilizing digital tools, HR professionals can streamline processes, improve employee engagement, and optimize talent management practices. The chapter also discusses the challenges and opportunities of digital transformation in HR, including recruitment, on-boarding, performance management, and employee development. It provides actionable guidance for HR leaders to harness digital technologies to create agile, resilient, and future-ready workplaces.

INTRODUCTION

The role of Human Resources (HR) has significantly changed due to the influence of digital technologies. Traditional HR functions have evolved to include strategic initiatives for organizational success in the digital age. This transformation necessitates a reevaluation of HR strategies to navigate the complexities of the modern workplace. As organizations rely on technology for efficiency and productivity, HR departments must leverage digital tools to attract, retain, and develop talent in a competitive environment. This includes recruitment, onboarding, performance management, and employee engagement, redefining every aspect of HR practice (Billett, 2020).

DOI: 10.4018/979-8-3693-1343-5.ch002

Effective HR strategies require a deep understanding of the digital landscape and its implications for workforce management. This involves adopting innovative technologies and a mindset shift towards agility, adaptability, and continuous improvement. Utilizing data analytics, artificial intelligence, and automation, HR professionals can identify workforce trends, talent gaps, and tailor interventions to meet organizational needs. Talent management, covering the entire employee lifecycle, is central to the modern HR paradigm. In an era of rapid technological advancements and evolving skill requirements, talent acquisition and retention are strategic imperatives. Digital platforms provide opportunities for talent sourcing, enabling HR professionals to access global talent pools and enhance candidate experiences (Tessema et al., 2022).

The digitalization of HR processes has significantly impacted employee onboarding and performance management. Virtual onboarding techniques, interactive training modules, and digital collaboration platforms have become essential tools for a seamless onboarding experience, improving employee satisfaction, accelerating productivity, and reducing turnover rates. Performance management is now facilitated by digital tools, allowing employees to take ownership of their development journey and fostering a culture of accountability. This data-driven approach helps identify high-potential employees, address performance gaps, and drive overall organizational performance (De Klerk et al., 2021).

Effective HR strategies, especially in remote and hybrid work arrangements, rely on employee engagement. Digital platforms provide opportunities for connection, collaboration, and community among teams. HR professionals can use technology to cultivate a sense of belonging and purpose, enhancing morale, productivity, and retention. A proactive approach to digital transformation and technology optimization is crucial for creating agile, resilient, and future-ready organizations. This chapter explores key components of digital HR strategies and offers actionable guidance for HR leaders to navigate the complexities of the modern workplace(Manjula & others, 2021).

The role of Human Resources (HR) has evolved significantly due to digital technologies and changing workplace dynamics. Previously, HR was primarily administrative, managing personnel, but now plays a strategic role in talent acquisition, development, and retention. Digitalization has transformed recruitment practices, enabling HR departments to use applicant tracking systems, AI algorithms, and online job platforms to identify and attract top talent. Digital tools allow HR professionals to access diverse talent pools and engage with candidates globally. Data analytics capabilities help organizations track recruitment strategies, optimize job postings, and identify areas for improvement in the hiring process (Piwowar-Sulej, 2021).

The modern workplace has transformed the onboarding process, incorporating virtual techniques, interactive training modules, and digital collaboration platforms. This not only accelerates time-to-productivity but also enhances the employee experience by providing access to resources, training materials, and support networks. HR professionals can use digital tools to make new hires feel connected, engaged, and empowered to contribute to the organization's success (Azizi et al., 2021).

Digital technologies have revolutionized performance management, enabling agile and continuous feedback mechanisms. Real-time performance tracking software, goal-setting platforms, and peer-to-peer recognition systems enable employees to receive timely feedback, set actionable goals, and track progress towards key objectives. This fosters accountability, transparency, and helps organizations identify high-potential employees, address performance gaps, and align individual goals with strategic objectives. Employee engagement is a critical focus for HR in the digital age, especially with remote and hybrid work arrangements. Digital platforms offer opportunities for connection, collaboration, and community among dispersed teams, creating a sense of belonging and purpose. Digital communication tools facilitate open dialogue, feedback loops, and transparent channels, fostering trust and empowerment within the organization (Azizi et al., 2021).

The digital age has transformed HR, enabling strategic workforce planning and development. Utilizing data analytics, predictive modeling, and machine learning algorithms, HR professionals can understand workforce trends, anticipate future skill needs, and address talent gaps. This allows organizations to make informed decisions about recruitment, training, and succession, ensuring the right talent is in place for success in a competitive environment (Aust et al., 2020). The digital age has transformed HR practices from transactional to strategic, enabling HR professionals to optimize recruitment, enhance employee experience, improve performance management, and foster innovation. This digitalization has enabled organizations to attract, develop, and retain top talent, driving growth and success in the modern workplace.

Effective HR strategies are crucial for organizations to thrive in today's competitive business environment. They help attract, develop, and retain top talent, driving organizational success. These strategies align with organizational goals and address challenges and opportunities in the digital age. They enable organizations to adapt to changing market conditions, technological advancements, and workforce demographics. By proactively addressing talent management issues like recruitment, onboarding, performance management, and employee engagement, organizations can maintain a competitive edge and position themselves for long-term growth and sustainability (Cooke et al., 2021).

Effective HR strategies enhance employee experience by promoting engagement, collaboration, and innovation within an organization. By investing in employee development and well-being, organizations can create a motivated workforce committed to achieving shared goals and driving organizational success. Crafting effective HR strategies is crucial for attracting, retaining, and developing talent for the digital age (Arslan et al., 2022).

Gap Analysis

The study investigates the use of AI and machine learning algorithms in recruitment, the effectiveness of social media platforms and niche job boards in reaching diverse talent pools, and strategies for optimizing candidate experience through personalized communication and virtual hiring events. It also evaluates the use of VR simulations for immersive onboarding experiences and gamification's role in enhancing engagement and knowledge retention. The study investigates performance management using data analytics, predictive modeling, and digital platforms for agile management. It also examines the role of mobile applications for real-time tracking and goal alignment. The research evaluates the effectiveness of personalized learning platforms, AI-driven career pathing tools, and strategies for fostering a continuous learning culture. It also assesses employee engagement, social recognition platforms, and strategies for improving communication and virtual team-building in remote work environments.

Scope of the Chapter

This chapter explores the relationship between human resources (HR) and digital technologies in the modern workplace, focusing on recruitment, onboarding, performance management, employee development, and engagement. It also discusses the challenges and opportunities associated with digital HR and offers insights into overcoming implementation barriers. The chapter emphasizes the importance of leveraging digital tools and strategies for optimizing HR practices.

Objectives

- Digital technologies have significantly transformed HR practices, transforming aspects like recruitment, onboarding, performance management, employee development, and engagement within organizations.
- The text provides guidance and strategies for HR leaders to effectively navigate the complexities of digital transformation and overcome common obstacles in adopting digital HR strategies.
- This study explores the impact of digital HR initiatives on organizational culture, employee engagement, and overall employee experience, highlighting emerging trends and technologies in HR management.

DIGITAL FRONTIER

The digital revolution is transforming HR practices by optimizing recruitment, enhancing employee experiences, and driving organizational success. However, it also presents challenges like data privacy, cybersecurity risks, and the need for digital literacy and skills development. Addressing these can position organizations for long-term growth and competitiveness. The digital frontier is transforming the way organizations operate and interact with employees, driven by important trends that fundamentally alter workplace dynamics and present both challenges and opportunities for human resources (HR) practices in today's rapidly evolving business landscape (Hadi et al., 2024).

Figure 1 illustrates how the digital frontier is transforming HR practices, focusing on recruitment optimization, employee experience enhancement, and organizational success, while acknowledging challenges like data privacy and cybersecurity risks.

Trends Shaping the Modern Workplace

a) **Remote Work and Telecommuting:** The widespread adoption of digital communication tools and cloud-based technologies has facilitated the rise of remote work and telecommuting arrangements. This trend has been accelerated by the COVID-19 pandemic, forcing organizations to rethink tra-

Figure 1. Digital frontier transforming HR practices

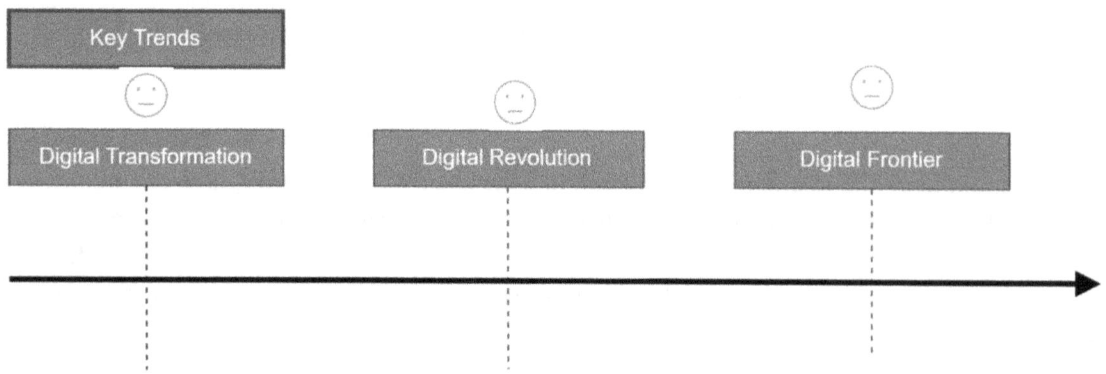

ditional office-based work models and embrace flexible remote work policies to adapt to changing circumstances.

b) **Gig Economy and Flexible Workforce:** The emergence of digital platforms and online marketplaces has facilitated the growth of the gig economy, where individuals engage in short-term, freelance, or contract work arrangements. This trend has led to the proliferation of flexible workforce models, allowing organizations to access specialized talent on-demand and adapt quickly to fluctuating market demands.

c) **Artificial Intelligence and Automation:** Advances in artificial intelligence (AI) and automation technologies are reshaping the nature of work across industries. From predictive analytics and machine learning algorithms to robotic process automation (RPA) and chatbots, AI-powered tools are augmenting human capabilities, streamlining repetitive tasks, and enabling more efficient decision-making processes.

d) **Data Analytics and Predictive Modeling:** The abundance of data generated by digital platforms and systems has unlocked new opportunities for HR professionals to gain insights into workforce trends, predict future talent needs, and optimize HR practices. Data analytics tools and predictive modeling techniques enable organizations to make informed decisions about recruitment, performance management, and employee engagement, driving strategic workforce planning initiatives.

e) **Employee Experience and Well-being:** As organizations compete for top talent in a competitive market, employee experience and well-being have emerged as critical priorities. Digital HR solutions, such as employee self-service portals, wellness apps, and virtual communication platforms, enable organizations to create personalized and engaging experiences for employees, fostering a culture of inclusivity, collaboration, and support.

Impact of Digital Transformation on HR Practices

The digital transformation in HR practices is transforming the entire employee lifecycle, from recruitment to talent development, by optimizing processes, enhancing efficiency, and enhancing employee experience (Wargo et al., 2021).

- **Recruitment and Talent Acquisition:** Digital platforms and AI-powered tools enable HR professionals to reach a broader pool of candidates, automate candidate screening processes, and identify top talent more effectively. Recruitment analytics provide insights into the effectiveness of recruitment strategies, allowing organizations to refine their approach and attract the right candidates for the job.
- **Onboarding and Employee Integration:** Virtual onboarding techniques, online training modules, and digital collaboration platforms facilitate seamless onboarding experiences for new hires, regardless of their location. Digital onboarding ensures that employees feel connected, informed, and equipped to succeed from day one, accelerating their time-to-productivity and integration into the organization.
- **Performance Management and Feedback:** Digital performance management systems enable real-time feedback, goal setting, and performance tracking, fostering a culture of continuous improvement and accountability. These systems facilitate ongoing dialogue between managers and employees, providing actionable insights for coaching, development, and performance evaluation.

- **Employee Development and Learning:** E-learning platforms, microlearning modules, and personalized development plans empower employees to acquire new skills and knowledge at their own pace. Digital learning solutions enable organizations to deliver targeted training programs, address skill gaps, and support career advancement opportunities for employees.
- **Employee Engagement and Communication:** Digital communication tools, such as instant messaging apps, social intranets, and virtual meeting platforms, facilitate open communication, collaboration, and knowledge sharing among employees. These tools foster a sense of community and belonging within the organization, promoting employee engagement, morale, and retention.

DIGITAL TOOLS AND TECHNOLOGIES IN HR

This section explores the role of digital tools and technologies in modern human resources (HR) to optimize processes, improve employee experiences, and drive organizational success. It examines the variety of digital solutions available and their integration strategies (Strohmeier, 2020).

Figure 2 illustrates the use of digital tools and technologies in HR to optimize processes, improve employee experiences, and drive organizational success through various integration strategies.

Digital Solutions

- **Applicant Tracking Systems (ATS):** ATS streamlines the recruitment process by automating job postings, candidate screening, and applicant tracking. These systems enable HR professionals to manage candidate pipelines efficiently, identify top talent, and ensure compliance with hiring regulations.

Figure 2. Use of digital tools and technologies in HR

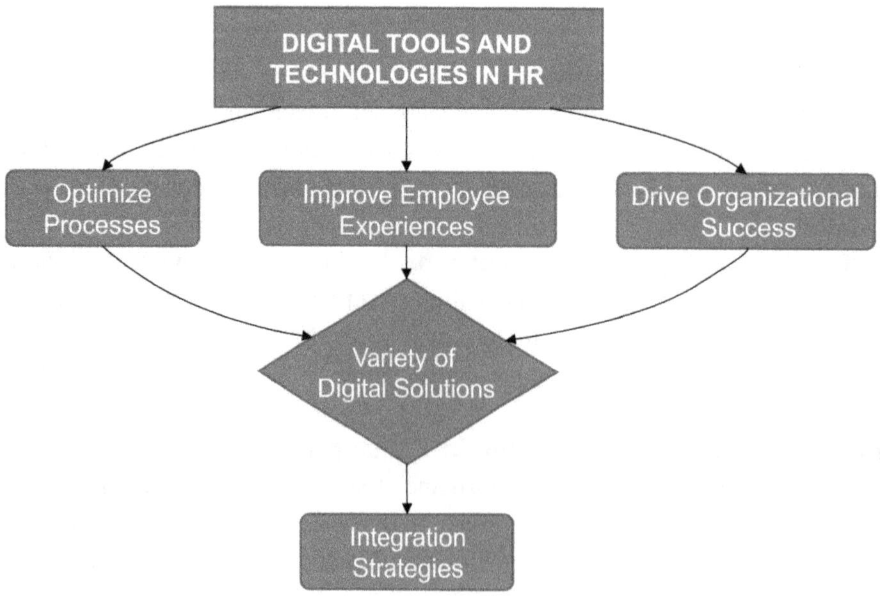

- **HR Management Systems (HRMS):** HRMS centralizes HR data and processes, providing a unified platform for managing employee information, payroll, benefits administration, and performance management. These systems improve data accuracy, streamline administrative tasks, and enable data-driven decision-making.
- **Learning Management Systems (LMS):** LMS facilitates employee training and development through online learning modules, course management, and skills tracking. These systems support personalized learning paths, enable self-paced learning, and provide analytics to measure training effectiveness.
- **Performance Management Software:** Performance management software automates performance evaluations, goal setting, and feedback processes. These tools facilitate ongoing performance discussions, foster employee engagement, and provide insights for coaching and development.
- **Employee Engagement Platforms:** Employee engagement platforms enhance communication, collaboration, and recognition within the organization. These platforms include features such as pulse surveys, social recognition, and virtual team-building activities to foster a positive workplace culture and improve employee morale.
- **Digital Onboarding Solutions:** Digital onboarding solutions streamline the onboarding process for new hires through online documentation, training modules, and virtual orientation sessions. These solutions ensure a smooth transition for new employees, accelerate time-to-productivity, and improve retention rates.
- **Workforce Analytics Tools:** Workforce analytics tools leverage data to gain insights into workforce trends, identify performance patterns, and forecast talent needs. These tools enable HR professionals to make data-driven decisions about recruitment, succession planning, and workforce optimization.

Integration Strategies for HR Systems

HR professionals can improve organizational performance by utilizing digital tools and effective integration strategies. These tools enable HR departments to adapt to changing business needs, utilize data-driven insights, and deliver value to the organization and workforce (Zehir et al., 2020).

- **API Integration:** Application Programming Interface (API) integration allows different HR systems to communicate and share data seamlessly. By integrating APIs, organizations can synchronize employee data across multiple platforms, eliminate data silos, and improve data accuracy.
- **Single Sign-On (SSO):** Single Sign-On enables employees to access multiple HR systems using a single set of credentials. SSO enhances user experience, improves security, and reduces the administrative burden associated with managing multiple login credentials.
- **Middleware Platforms:** Middleware platforms serve as intermediaries between disparate HR systems, facilitating data exchange and synchronization. These platforms enable organizations to integrate legacy systems with cloud-based solutions, automate workflows, and improve system interoperability.
- **Custom Integration Solutions:** Custom integration solutions involve developing tailored connectors or scripts to integrate specific HR systems. While more resource-intensive, custom integrations offer flexibility and scalability to meet unique business requirements and system architecture.

- **Data Mapping and Transformation:** Data mapping and transformation involve mapping data fields between different HR systems and transforming data formats to ensure compatibility. This process enables organizations to standardize data across systems, reconcile discrepancies, and maintain data integrity.

Applications of VR and AR in HR Practices

VR and AR technologies provide immersive recruitment experiences, offering virtual VR and AR technologies enhance employee engagement and learning by providing immersive experiences and engaging learning opportunities. These technologies stimulate curiosity and motivation, leading to higher knowledge retention and skill acquisition. The experiential nature of VR and AR also fosters active learning and skill development, resulting in better performance and job satisfaction compared to traditional methods (Agrawal et al., 2023; Durairaj et al., 2023).

- workplace tours and job simulations to assess skills and cultural fit. They also facilitate interactive training modules for new hires to familiarize themselves with company policies and procedures.
- VR and AR enable experiential learning by simulating real-world scenarios, providing hands-on training in a safe environment, enhancing employees' skills and confidence by allowing them to practice complex tasks.
- VR and AR can enhance performance management by providing interactive feedback and personalized coaching experiences, enabling employees to receive real-time feedback and engage in virtual role-playing exercises for communication and leadership improvement.

RECRUITMENT AND TALENT ACQUISITION

The digital age has transformed recruitment and talent acquisition by utilizing digital platforms, analytics, and automation tools. HR professionals can use these tools for talent sourcing, applicant tracking, and recruitment analytics, enhancing the recruitment process, attracting top talent, and driving organizational success in the competitive labor market (Strohmeier, 2020).

Figure 3 illustrates how digital platforms, analytics, and automation tools have transformed recruitment and talent acquisition, enhancing the process of talent sourcing, applicant tracking, and recruitment analytics, ultimately attracting top talent and driving organizational success in the competitive labor market.

Leveraging Digital Platforms for Talent Sourcing

Digital platforms have significantly impacted the recruitment process, allowing organizations to attract and engage with potential candidates. Job boards, professional networking sites, social media, and online talent marketplaces provide vast talent pools, enabling HR professionals to reach passive candidates and target specific demographics or skill sets. Social media platforms like LinkedIn, Facebook, and Twitter are powerful tools for talent sourcing and employer branding, allowing recruiters to showcase company culture, share job postings, and engage with candidates directly. AI-driven sourcing tools and talent marketplaces further enhance this process (Paramita, 2020).

Figure 3. Recruitment and talent acquisition process

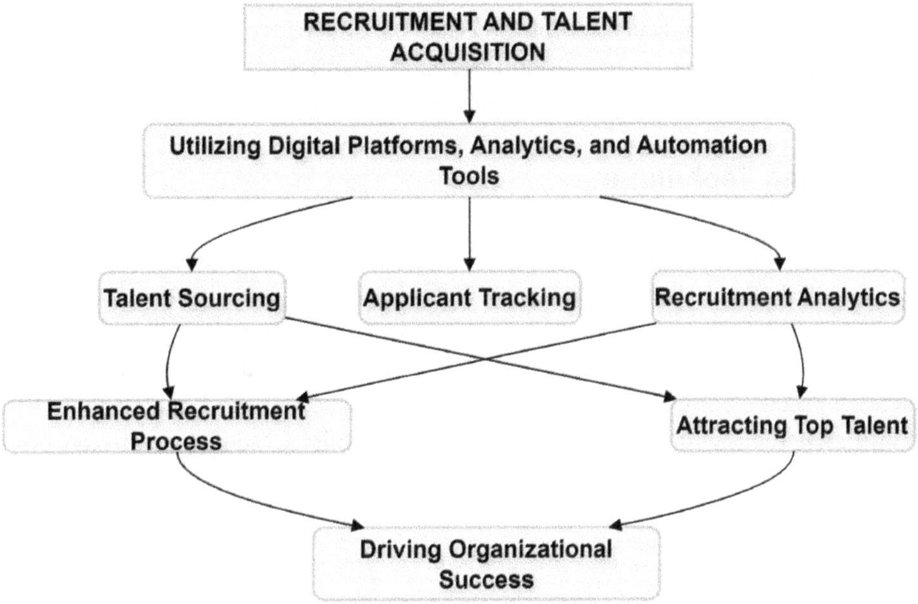

Niche job boards and industry-specific websites help organizations target candidates with specific skill sets or domain expertise. These platforms provide access to highly qualified candidates who may not actively seek employment but are open to new opportunities. By leveraging digital platforms, HR professionals can reduce time-to-fill and improve hire quality.

Applicant Tracking Systems and Recruitment Analytics

Applicant Tracking Systems (ATS) automate the recruitment process by managing job postings, candidate applications, and communication with applicants. They streamline administrative tasks like resume screening and interview scheduling, allowing recruiters to focus on higher-value activities like candidate engagement. Recruitment analytics help optimize the process by analyzing data like time-to-fill, cost-per-hire, and source-of-hire. HR professionals can identify trends, assess channel performance, and make data-driven decisions to improve recruitment outcomes, enabling organizations to allocate resources more efficiently and optimize the candidate experience (Gilch & Sieweke, 2021).

Predictive analytics tools use historical recruitment data to predict future talent needs, anticipate hiring trends, and identify potential talent gaps, enabling organizations to address workforce planning challenges, develop targeted recruitment strategies, and build a qualified candidate pipeline.

ONBOARDING AND EMPLOYEE INTEGRATION

This section discusses the importance of digital onboarding in employee lifecycle, highlighting how virtual platforms can enhance the experience, accelerate productivity, and demonstrate an organization's commitment to digital transformation. It also discusses strategies for creating a seamless digital onboarding experience for new hires (Pillai & Sivathanu, 2020).

Figure 4 illustrates the digital onboarding process, starting with pre-onboarding preparation, progressing through virtual welcome sessions, online training modules, virtual tours, mentor programs, and regular check-ins, ultimately leading to the completion of the onboarding process.

Virtual Onboarding Techniques

Virtual onboarding is a digital process that enables remote orientation, training, and integration of new hires, ensuring a consistent and standardized experience across distributed teams (Zavyalova et al., 2022).

- **Pre-Onboarding Preparation:** Before the first day, new hires can be provided with access to digital resources, such as employee handbooks, training materials, and onboarding checklists. This helps familiarize them with the organization's culture, policies, and expectations before they start.

Figure 4. Strategies for creating a seamless digital onboarding experience

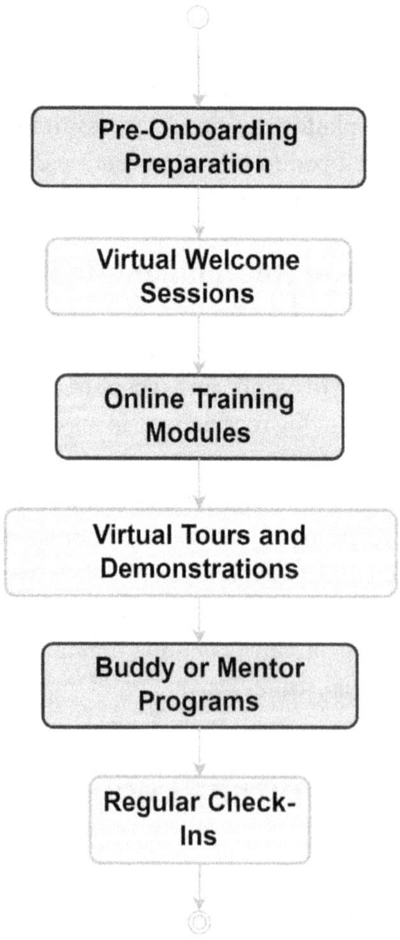

- **Virtual Welcome Sessions:** Hosting virtual welcome sessions via video conferencing platforms allows new hires to meet important stakeholders, including their manager, team members, and HR representatives. These sessions provide an opportunity to introduce the company, its values, and the team dynamics.
- **Online Training Modules:** Digital learning management systems (LMS) can be used to deliver online training modules covering topics such as compliance, job-specific skills, and company processes. These modules can be completed at the new hire's own pace, enabling self-directed learning.
- **Virtual Tours and Demonstrations:** Virtual tours of the office facilities, introductions to internal tools and systems, and demonstrations of software applications can be conducted remotely to familiarize new hires with their work environment and tools they will use.
- **Buddy or Mentor Programs:** Pairing new hires with experienced employees as buddies or mentors provides them with a support system and a resource for asking questions, seeking guidance, and acclimating to the organization's culture and practices.
- **Regular Check-Ins:** Regular check-ins with the new hire's manager or mentor via video conferencing or instant messaging platforms help track their progress, address any concerns, and provide feedback and support.

Building a Digital Onboarding Experience

A successful digital onboarding experience necessitates strategic planning, thoughtful design, and the use of suitable digital tools and platforms (Pillai & Sivathanu, 2020).

- **Personalization:** Tailoring the onboarding experience to the individual needs and preferences of each new hire helps create a personalized and engaging experience. This can involve customizing training modules, assigning relevant tasks, and providing opportunities for interaction and feedback.
- **Integration with HR Systems:** Integrating digital onboarding platforms with HR systems, such as the HRMS and ATS, enables seamless data transfer, automates administrative tasks, and ensures a consistent and efficient onboarding process.
- **Interactive Content:** Incorporating interactive elements, such as videos, quizzes, simulations, and gamified activities, enhances engagement and retention of onboarding content. Interactive content makes the onboarding experience more dynamic, immersive, and memorable for new hires.
- **Mobile Accessibility:** Ensuring that digital onboarding platforms are accessible via mobile devices allows new hires to complete onboarding tasks and access resources on-the-go, making the process more convenient and flexible.
- **Feedback Mechanisms:** Soliciting feedback from new hires about their onboarding experience helps identify areas for improvement and ensures continuous refinement of the digital onboarding process. Feedback can be collected through surveys, focus groups, or one-on-one discussions.

PERFORMANCE MANAGEMENT IN THE DIGITAL ERA

Performance management is undergoing a significant transformation in the digital era due to the need for continuous feedback, data-driven insights, and agility in response to changing business environments. Organizations are leveraging continuous feedback mechanisms and performance evaluation software and tools to enhance their practices, improve employee engagement and productivity, and drive organizational success in a competitive and dynamic business environment. Digital performance management allows organizations to adapt to evolving workforce trends, leverage data-driven insights, and foster a culture of continuous improvement and excellence (Eliza, 2023).

Figure 5 shows how performance management is transforming in the digital era, using continuous feedback and performance evaluation software to improve practices, employee engagement, and productivity. This allows organizations to adapt to workforce trends, use data-driven insights, and foster a culture of continuous improvement and excellence.

Continuous Feedback Mechanisms

Traditional performance management systems often rely on annual or semi-annual performance reviews, which can be time-consuming, subjective, and disconnected from day-to-day work. Continuous feedback mechanisms facilitate real-time communication between managers and employees, promoting transparency, collaboration, and continuous improvement, and include various methods (Shaddiq et al., 2023).

Figure 5. Performance management in the digital era

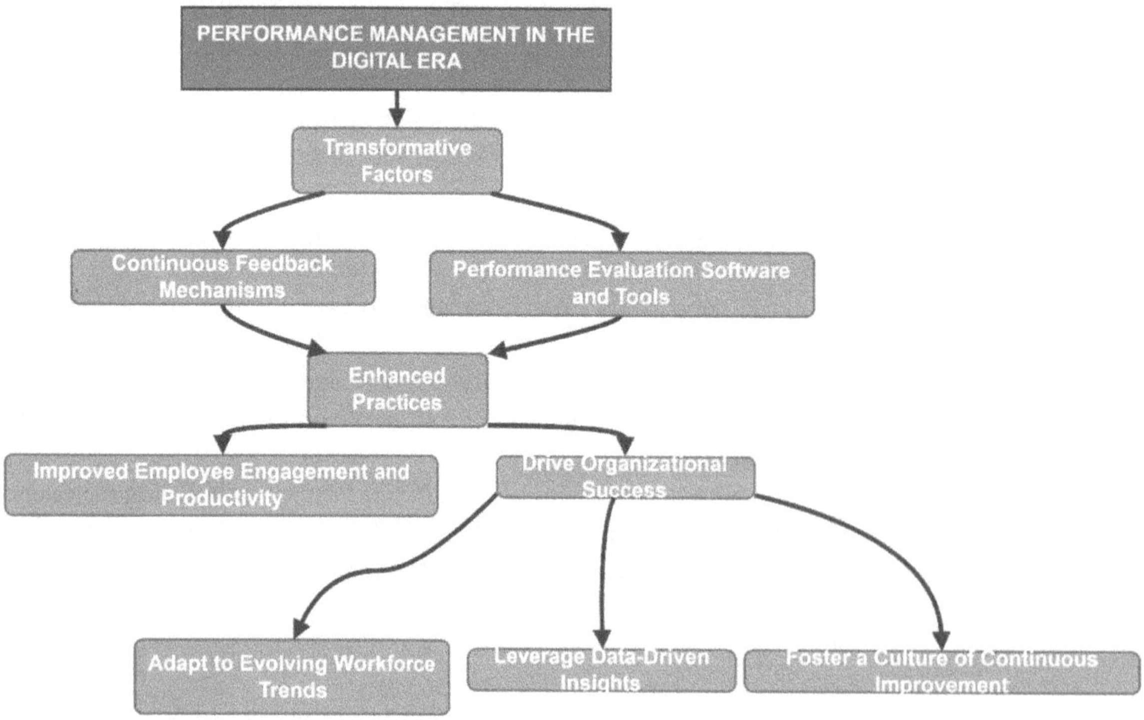

- **Regular Check-Ins:** Regular one-on-one meetings between managers and employees provide an opportunity to discuss goals, progress, challenges, and development opportunities in a timely manner. These check-ins promote open communication, address issues proactively, and build stronger relationships between managers and employees.
- **360-Degree Feedback:** 360-degree feedback involves soliciting feedback from multiple sources, including managers, peers, subordinates, and external stakeholders, to provide a comprehensive view of an employee's performance. Digital tools and platforms streamline the collection and analysis of 360-degree feedback, enabling organizations to identify strengths, development areas, and areas for improvement.
- **Continuous Performance Feedback Tools:** Digital performance management platforms and apps facilitate ongoing feedback exchange between managers and employees, allowing them to provide feedback in real-time on specific tasks, projects, or behaviors. These tools enable immediate recognition of achievements, timely course corrections, and personalized coaching opportunities (Das et al., 2024; Durairaj et al., 2023).
- **Pulse Surveys:** Pulse surveys are short, frequent surveys administered to employees to gauge their satisfaction, engagement, and performance perceptions. Digital survey platforms allow organizations to collect feedback quickly, analyze trends over time, and identify areas for improvement in performance management processes.
- **Social Recognition Platforms:** Social recognition platforms enable employees to publicly acknowledge and appreciate their peers' contributions and achievements. These platforms foster a culture of recognition and appreciation, reinforcing desired behaviors and values and enhancing employee morale and engagement.

Performance Evaluation Software and Tools

Performance evaluation software streamlines the process, providing managers with data and insights to make informed decisions about employee performance (Eliza, 2023).

- Performance review software digitizes the performance evaluation process, allowing managers to set goals, track progress, and conduct performance reviews online. These platforms standardize evaluation criteria, ensure consistency, and provide a centralized repository for performance-related data.
- Goal management systems enable organizations to set SMART (Specific, Measurable, Achievable, Relevant, Time-bound) goals, cascade them across teams, and track progress in real-time. These systems align individual goals with organizational objectives, foster accountability, and drive performance improvement.
- Data analytics and reporting tools provide insights into performance trends, identify high-performing employees, and pinpoint areas for improvement. These tools enable organizations to make data-driven decisions about talent development, succession planning, and performance improvement initiatives.
- Performance calibration tools facilitate objective and fair evaluations by standardizing rating scales, eliminating bias, and ensuring consistency across evaluators. These tools enable organizations to calibrate performance ratings, identify outliers, and mitigate rater bias effectively.

- Feedback and coaching apps provide managers with prompts, templates, and best practices for delivering constructive feedback, setting development goals, and coaching employees to improve performance. These apps promote continuous learning and development, empower managers to support their teams effectively, and drive performance improvement.

EMPLOYEE DEVELOPMENT AND LEARNING

Digital resources like e-learning platforms and microlearning modules are being used by organizations to provide personalized development plans for employees. This approach helps employees acquire new skills, stay relevant in a changing workplace, and contribute effectively to business objectives. It empowers employees to take ownership of their learning, drive performance improvement, and foster a culture of continuous learning. Digital learning initiatives help organizations adapt to changing business needs and invest in their workforce's future success (Das et al., 2024; Prabhuswamy et al., 2024).

E-Learning Platforms and Microlearning Modules

E-learning platforms have revolutionized employee development by offering flexible, convenient access to various learning resources, including online courses, webinars, videos, and interactive modules. Microlearning modules, particularly their bite-sized format, are popular for their easy-to-digest content (Durairaj et al., 2023).

- **Accessibility and Convenience:** E-learning platforms eliminate barriers to learning by providing access to training materials from any location with an internet connection. Employees can complete courses during downtime, on-the-go, or outside of traditional working hours, enabling them to balance learning with their other responsibilities.
- **Personalized Learning Paths:** E-learning platforms use data analytics and machine learning algorithms to recommend personalized learning paths based on employees' interests, skill gaps, and career aspirations. These platforms track employees' progress, suggest relevant courses, and adapt content to match their learning preferences and objectives.
- **Interactive and Engaging Content:** E-learning platforms leverage multimedia elements, such as videos, quizzes, simulations, and gamified activities, to create engaging learning experiences. Interactive content promotes active participation, enhances retention, and caters to different learning styles and preferences.
- **Self-Paced Learning:** E-learning platforms empower employees to take control of their learning journey by offering self-paced courses that accommodate individual learning styles and schedules. Employees can progress through courses at their own speed, revisit concepts as needed, and focus on areas where they need improvement.
- **Scalability and Cost-Effectiveness:** E-learning platforms enable organizations to scale training initiatives rapidly and cost-effectively, without the need for physical classrooms or travel expenses. By leveraging digital resources, organizations can train employees across geographically dispersed locations and accommodate diverse learning needs.

Personalized Development Plans Using Digital Resources

Personalized development plans enable organizations to tailor learning experiences to the unique needs, goals, and preferences of individual employees. Digital resources play a crucial role in creating and delivering personalized development plans, offering flexibility, accessibility, and customization options (Agrawal et al., 2023).

- **Skills Assessment and Gap Analysis:** Digital tools and assessments help identify employees' current skills, competencies, and areas for improvement. By conducting skills assessments and gap analyses, organizations can pinpoint skill gaps, prioritize development opportunities, and tailor learning interventions accordingly.
- **Learning Recommendations and Resources:** Digital platforms use algorithms to recommend relevant learning resources, such as courses, articles, videos, and podcasts, based on employees' development goals and interests. These recommendations help employees discover new opportunities for learning and growth and stay aligned with their career aspirations.
- **Goal Setting and Progress Tracking:** Digital tools enable employees to set SMART (Specific, Measurable, Achievable, Relevant, Time-bound) development goals and track their progress over time. Goal setting and progress tracking features provide visibility into employees' achievements, milestones, and areas for further improvement, fostering accountability and motivation.
- **Feedback and Coaching:** Digital platforms facilitate ongoing feedback and coaching from managers, mentors, and peers, providing employees with actionable insights and guidance to support their development efforts. Feedback and coaching features enable continuous learning and improvement, driving performance and career growth.
- **Integration with Performance Management Systems:** Integrating personalized development plans with performance management systems allows organizations to align employees' learning and development goals with organizational objectives and performance metrics. By linking development activities to performance outcomes, organizations can ensure that learning initiatives contribute to business success and employee advancement.

ENHANCING EMPLOYEE ENGAGEMENT

Employee engagement is crucial for organizational success, productivity, and retention. In the digital era, organizations are using gamification strategies and social collaboration tools to foster a culture of collaboration and connection. These strategies help create a dynamic work environment where employees feel connected, motivated, and empowered. They also enable organizations to adapt to remote and hybrid work environments, overcome communication barriers, and build resilient teams. Overall, digital engagement initiatives are essential for fostering a positive organizational culture and fostering a positive work environment (Naveeenkumar et al., 2024; Ravisankar et al., 2024).

Figure 6 highlights the importance of employee engagement for organizational success, productivity, and retention. Organizations are using gamification strategies and social collaboration tools to create a dynamic work environment, fostering a sense of connection, motivation, and empowerment. These strategies help adapt to remote and hybrid work environments, overcome communication barriers, and build resilient teams, ultimately fostering a positive organizational culture.

Figure 6. Activities for enhancing employee engagement

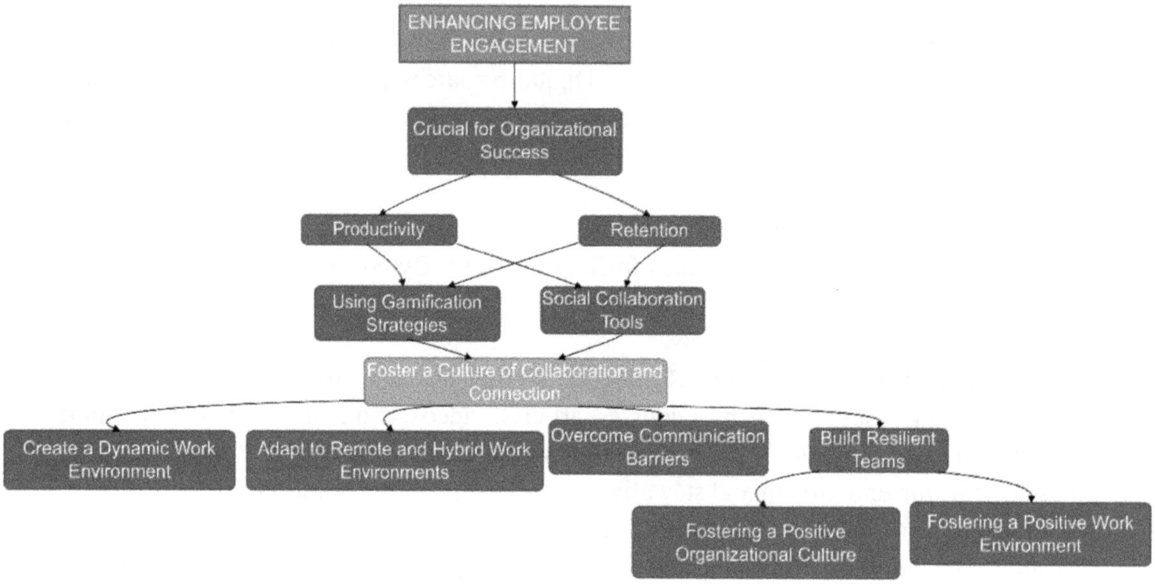

Gamification Strategies for Engagement

Gamification involves incorporating game-like elements, such as challenges, rewards, and competitions, into non-game contexts to motivate and engage employees. By gamifying work processes and activities, organizations can enhance employee engagement, drive performance, and promote a sense of achievement and recognition (Hanumanthakari et al., 2023).

- **Goal-Based Challenges:** Setting clear, achievable goals and milestones and rewarding employees for reaching them encourages progress and achievement. Gamified goal-setting platforms allow employees to track their progress, earn badges or points, and compete with colleagues or teams, fostering healthy competition and motivation.
- **Recognition and Rewards:** Recognizing and rewarding employees for their contributions, achievements, and milestones reinforces positive behaviors and encourages continued engagement. Gamified reward systems, such as virtual badges, leaderboard rankings, and digital currency, provide tangible incentives and recognition for employees' efforts.
- **Skills Development and Learning Games:** Gamified learning platforms and simulations make training and development more engaging and interactive. Incorporating game-like elements, such as quizzes, challenges, and scenario-based exercises, into learning programs enhances retention, encourages participation, and reinforces learning outcomes.
- **Team-Based Collaboration:** Encouraging teamwork and collaboration through gamified challenges and projects promotes camaraderie, communication, and mutual support among team members. Gamified collaboration platforms facilitate task assignments, progress tracking, and team-based competitions, fostering a sense of belonging and collective achievement.

- **Wellness and Health Challenges:** Promoting employee well-being and health through gamified wellness programs encourages healthy behaviors and lifestyle choices. Gamified wellness apps and platforms offer challenges, rewards, and social support networks to motivate employees to stay active, manage stress, and prioritize self-care.

Social Collaboration Tools and Internal Communication Platforms

Social collaboration tools and internal communication platforms enable communication, knowledge sharing, and collaboration among employees, regardless of location or role. They foster open dialogue, transparency, and community, fostering a connected and engaged workforce (Das et al., 2024).

- **Enterprise Social Networks (ESNs):** ESNs provide a digital space for employees to connect, share ideas, and collaborate in real-time. These platforms offer features such as newsfeeds, group discussions, file sharing, and instant messaging, enabling employees to communicate and collaborate across departments, locations, and time zones.
- **Team Collaboration Apps:** Team collaboration apps, such as Slack, Microsoft Teams, and Google Workspace, facilitate communication and collaboration within teams through channels, chat, video conferencing, and document collaboration features. These apps streamline communication, reduce email overload, and promote agile teamwork and decision-making.
- **Knowledge Sharing Platforms:** Knowledge sharing platforms centralize organizational knowledge and expertise, making it accessible to employees across the organization. These platforms enable employees to share best practices, lessons learned, and resources, fostering a culture of continuous learning and innovation (Das et al., 2024; Sharma et al., 2024).
- **Employee Feedback and Idea Sharing Tools:** Employee feedback and idea sharing tools provide a platform for employees to share feedback, suggestions, and innovative ideas with management and colleagues. These tools promote employee voice, engagement, and involvement in decision-making processes, driving organizational improvement and innovation.
- **Virtual Town Halls and All-Hands Meetings:** Virtual town halls and all-hands meetings bring together employees from across the organization to hear updates from leadership, ask questions, and participate in discussions. Digital platforms enable organizations to host engaging and interactive virtual events, fostering a sense of community and alignment around shared goals and values.

OVERCOMING CHALLENGES IN DIGITAL HR

Digital HR initiatives offer numerous benefits but also present challenges. Addressing data privacy and security issues, managing change, and building digital literacy are crucial for successful implementation. Prioritizing data protection measures, adopting change management strategies, and investing in training and support resources can help organizations unlock the full potential of digital HR. A strategic, holistic approach, guided by clear objectives, strong leadership, and a commitment to continuous learning and improvement, is essential for successful digital HR transformation (Azizi et al., 2021; Manjula & others, 2021).

Addressing Data Privacy and Security Concerns

- **Compliance with Regulations:** Ensure compliance with data protection regulations such as GDPR (General Data Protection Regulation) and CCPA (California Consumer Privacy Act) by implementing robust data privacy policies, obtaining explicit consent for data processing, and maintaining transparent communication with employees regarding data usage.
- **Data Encryption and Access Controls:** Implement encryption mechanisms to secure sensitive HR data both in transit and at rest. Utilize access controls and role-based permissions to restrict access to confidential information only to authorized personnel, mitigating the risk of data breaches and unauthorized access.
- **Regular Security Audits and Training:** Conduct regular security audits and risk assessments to identify vulnerabilities and areas for improvement. Provide comprehensive training and awareness programs for HR staff and employees on cybersecurity best practices, phishing awareness, and data protection protocols to minimize the likelihood of security incidents.
- **Vendor Due Diligence:** Perform thorough due diligence when selecting third-party vendors for digital HR solutions, ensuring they adhere to industry standards for data security and privacy. Establish clear contractual agreements outlining data protection responsibilities and rights, including data breach notification procedures and indemnification clauses.

Managing Change and Building Digital Literacy

- **Change Management Strategies:** Develop a comprehensive change management strategy that emphasizes clear communication, stakeholder engagement, and organizational readiness assessments. Identify potential resistance to change and proactively address concerns through targeted communication, training, and support mechanisms.
- **Executive Sponsorship and Leadership Alignment:** Secure executive sponsorship and leadership alignment for digital HR initiatives to demonstrate commitment from senior management and facilitate buy-in from across the organization. Engage leaders as champions of change, encouraging their active participation and advocacy for digital transformation efforts (Prabhuswamy et al., 2024).
- **Training and Upskilling Programs:** Offer training and upskilling programs to equip HR staff and employees with the digital literacy and skills necessary to navigate new digital HR systems and tools effectively. Provide hands-on training sessions, online tutorials, and self-paced learning resources tailored to different learning styles and proficiency levels.
- **User-Friendly Design and Support Resources:** Design digital HR systems with user-friendly interfaces and intuitive navigation to enhance usability and adoption. Provide comprehensive support resources, including FAQs, user guides, and helpdesk support, to assist users with troubleshooting issues and maximizing the benefits of digital HR solutions.
- **Feedback Mechanisms and Continuous Improvement:** Establish feedback mechanisms to gather input from HR staff and employees on their experiences with digital HR systems and processes. Use feedback to identify pain points, areas for improvement, and opportunities for enhancement, driving continuous iteration and refinement of digital HR initiatives.

ETHICAL AND LEGAL IMPLICATIONS IN DIGITAL HR

Organizations must consider ethical and legal implications of data privacy, compliance, and fairness in AI-driven processes as they adopt digital HR strategies.

- **Data Privacy and Compliance:** Organizations must comply with strict data privacy regulations like GDPR in the EU and CCPA in the US, ensuring transparent data collection, explicit employee consent for processing, and robust security measures to protect sensitive information (Agrawal et al., 2023).
- **Fairness in AI-driven Processes:** AI algorithms in recruitment, performance management, and HR functions should be ethically designed and implemented to prevent biases and discrimination. Regular audits and validations are necessary to identify and mitigate biases that may disproportionately affect certain groups (Naveeenkumar et al., 2024).
- **Employee Training and Upskilling:** Organizations should prioritize employee training and upskilling initiatives for successful adoption of digital HR tools and technologies. This includes comprehensive training on data privacy protocols, ethical AI practices, and responsible use of digital HR platforms. Empowering employees with necessary skills can mitigate risks and foster ethical decision-making.
- **Transparency and Accountability:** Organizations should ensure transparency in the use of digital HR technologies, including data collection, processing, and utilization. Employees should have clear visibility into decision-making algorithms and criteria, and accountability mechanisms like ethical review boards or compliance committees can help ensure adherence to ethical standards and regulatory requirements.
- **Continuous Monitoring and Adaptation:** Digital HR strategies should be continuously monitored and adjusted to address ethical and legal challenges. This involves staying updated on regulatory frameworks, conducting regular audits, and seeking employee feedback. Fostering an ethical culture and upholding fairness, transparency, and compliance can help organizations navigate the complexities of digital HR.

REAL-WORLD EXAMPLES

- **Google's People Analytics:** Google employs advanced data analytics to enhance HR functions like recruitment, performance management, and employee engagement, identifying patterns and trends in employee feedback to facilitate proactive interventions for improved workplace satisfaction and productivity.
- **IBM's Digital Onboarding Platform:** IBM has developed a digital onboarding platform that utilizes AI to offer personalized experiences for new hires, including virtual tours, interactive training modules, and chatbots to facilitate a smooth transition into the company culture.
- **Salesforce's Learning Experience Platform:** Salesforce has launched Trailhead, a learning experience platform that provides personalized paths, interactive tutorials, and badges to encourage skill development and career growth among employees, aligning with the company's business objectives.

- **Microsoft's Viva Insights:** Microsoft's Viva Insights uses workplace analytics to analyze employee well-being, productivity, and collaboration patterns, offering personalized recommendations and resources like mindfulness exercises and work-life balance tips.
- **HubSpot's Employee Engagement Initiatives:** HubSpot uses digital platforms and communication channels to boost employee engagement, especially in remote work, through virtual team-building activities, peer recognition programs, and online communities, fostering collaboration and creativity.

FUTURE DEVELOPMENTS

As organizations continue to adapt to the evolving landscape of work and technology, the future of HR strategies in the modern workplace will be shaped by several significant developments. Anticipating and leveraging these trends will be essential for crafting effective HR strategies that drive organizational success (Cooke et al., 2021).

AI and Automation Integration: The integration of artificial intelligence (AI) and automation technologies into HR processes will become more prevalent, enabling organizations to streamline administrative tasks, personalize employee experiences, and make data-driven decisions. AI-powered chatbots, predictive analytics, and robotic process automation (RPA) will revolutionize recruitment, onboarding, performance management, and employee development processes (Rahamathunnisa et al., 2023; Sengeni et al., 2023).

Enhanced Employee Experience: Employee experience will emerge as a top priority for organizations seeking to attract and retain top talent in a competitive market. HR strategies will focus on creating personalized, seamless, and meaningful experiences for employees throughout their lifecycle, from recruitment to retirement. Digital HR platforms, wellness programs, flexible work arrangements, and career development opportunities will be central to enhancing employee engagement, satisfaction, and retention.

Remote Work and Hybrid Models: The shift towards remote and hybrid work models is expected to persist due to digital advancements, evolving employee preferences, and business agility. HR strategies must accommodate diverse work arrangements, promote virtual collaboration, and ensure equitable access to resources. Significant enablers include flexible policies, virtual team-building initiatives, and technology-enabled workspace solutions (Domakonda et al., 2022).

Data-Driven Decision Making: Data analytics will play an increasingly important role in HR decision-making, enabling organizations to gain insights into workforce trends, predict future talent needs, and optimize HR processes. HR strategies will leverage advanced analytics tools and predictive modeling techniques to inform recruitment, performance management, talent development, and succession planning initiatives. Data-driven HR practices will drive efficiency, effectiveness, and agility in responding to changing business needs.

Emphasis on Diversity, Equity, and Inclusion (DEI): Organizations will prioritize diversity, equity, and inclusion (DEI) initiatives to create a more inclusive and equitable workplace culture. HR strategies will focus on recruiting and retaining diverse talent, promoting inclusive leadership behaviors, and fostering a sense of belonging among employees from different backgrounds. DEI metrics, training programs, and accountability mechanisms will be integrated into HR processes to drive meaningful change and create a more diverse and inclusive workforce.

Agile HR Practices: Agile methodologies will be applied to HR practices, enabling organizations to adapt quickly to changing business conditions, customer demands, and workforce preferences. Agile HR strategies will emphasize cross-functional collaboration, iterative experimentation, and continuous feedback loops to drive innovation, responsiveness, and resilience in HR processes. Agile HR teams will embrace flexibility, collaboration, and learning as core principles to drive organizational agility and performance.

HR strategies for the modern workplace must adapt to technological advancements, work dynamics, and employee expectations. By embracing AI, automation, enhancing employee experience, accommodating remote work, leveraging data-driven insights, prioritizing diversity, and adopting agile practices, organizations can attract, engage, and empower their workforce for innovation and competitive advantage.

CONCLUSION

In conclusion, crafting effective HR strategies for the modern workplace requires a forward-thinking approach that embraces innovation, flexibility, and a deep understanding of evolving workforce dynamics. Throughout this chapter, we have explored the evolution of HR in the digital age, the importance of leveraging digital tools and technologies, and strategies for enhancing important HR functions such as recruitment, onboarding, performance management, employee development, engagement, and overcoming challenges in digital HR.

As organizations navigate the digital frontier, they must anticipate and adapt to future developments such as AI and automation integration, remote work and hybrid models, data-driven decision-making, emphasis on diversity, equity, and inclusion, and agile HR practices. By embracing these trends and leveraging digital solutions, organizations can create a more agile, resilient, and employee-centric workplace that drives innovation, productivity, and business success. The future of HR lies in leveraging technology to enhance employee experiences, enable data-driven decision-making, foster collaboration and inclusion, and drive organizational agility. By crafting effective HR strategies that prioritize digital transformation, organizations can position themselves for success in a rapidly changing business environment, attract and retain top talent, and create a culture of continuous learning, growth, and innovation.

In essence, the journey towards crafting effective HR strategies for the modern workplace is ongoing and dynamic, requiring organizations to adapt and evolve in response to emerging trends, technological advancements, and evolving employee expectations. By embracing digitalization and fostering a culture of innovation and agility, organizations can stay ahead of the curve and build a workforce that is equipped to thrive in the digital age.

ABBREVIATIONS

AI: Artificial Intelligence
API: Application Programming Interface
ATS: Applicant Tracking System
CCPA: California Consumer Privacy Act
COVID: Coronavirus Disease
DEI: Diversity, Equity, and Inclusion

ESN: Enterprise Social Network
FAQ: Frequently Asked Questions
GDPR: General Data Protection Regulation
HR: Human Resources
HRMS: Human Resources Management System
LMS: Learning Management System
RPA: Robotic Process Automation
SSO: Single Sign-On

REFERENCES

Agrawal, A. V., Pitchai, R., Senthamaraikannan, C., Balaji, N. A., Sajithra, S., & Boopathi, S. (2023). Digital Education System During the COVID-19 Pandemic. In Using Assistive Technology for Inclusive Learning in K-12 Classrooms (pp. 104–126). IGI Global. doi:10.4018/978-1-6684-6424-3.ch005

Arslan, A., Cooper, C., Khan, Z., Golgeci, I., & Ali, I. (2022). Artificial intelligence and human workers interaction at team level: A conceptual assessment of the challenges and potential HRM strategies. *International Journal of Manpower*, *43*(1), 75–88. doi:10.1108/IJM-01-2021-0052

Aust, I., Matthews, B., & Muller-Camen, M. (2020). Common good HRM: A paradigm shift in sustainable HRM? *Human Resource Management Review*, *30*(3), 100705. doi:10.1016/j.hrmr.2019.100705

Azizi, M. R., Atlasi, R., Ziapour, A., Abbas, J., & Naemi, R. (2021). Innovative human resource management strategies during the COVID-19 pandemic: A systematic narrative review approach. *Heliyon*, *7*(6), e07233. doi:10.1016/j.heliyon.2021.e07233 PMID:34124399

Billett, S. (2020). *Learning in the workplace: Strategies for effective practice*. Routledge. doi:10.4324/9781003116318

Cooke, F. L., Xiao, M., & Chen, Y. (2021). Still in search of strategic human resource management? A review and suggestions for future research with China as an example. *Human Resource Management*, *60*(1), 89–118. doi:10.1002/hrm.22029

Das, S., Lekhya, G., Shreya, K., Shekinah, K. L., Babu, K. K., & Boopathi, S. (2024). Fostering Sustainability Education Through Cross-Disciplinary Collaborations and Research Partnerships: Interdisciplinary Synergy. In Facilitating Global Collaboration and Knowledge Sharing in Higher Education With Generative AI (pp. 60–88). IGI Global.

De Klerk, J. J., Joubert, M., & Mosca, H. F. (2021). Is working from home the new workplace panacea? Lessons from the COVID-19 pandemic for the future world of work. *SA Journal of Industrial Psychology*, *47*(1), 1–14. doi:10.4102/sajip.v47i0.1883

Domakonda, V. K., Farooq, S., Chinthamreddy, S., Puviarasi, R., Sudhakar, M., & Boopathi, S. (2022). Sustainable Developments of Hybrid Floating Solar Power Plants: Photovoltaic System. In Human Agro-Energy Optimization for Business and Industry (pp. 148–167). IGI Global.

Durairaj, M., Jayakumar, S., Karpagavalli, V., Maheswari, B. U., Boopathi, S., & ... (2023). Utilization of Digital Tools in the Indian Higher Education System During Health Crises. In *Multidisciplinary Approaches to Organizational Governance During Health Crises* (pp. 1–21). IGI Global. doi:10.4018/978-1-7998-9213-7.ch001

Eliza, E. (2023). Human Resource Management Strategies to Improve Performance in the Digital Era. *Implikasi: Jurnal Manajemen Sumber Daya Manusia*, *1*(2), 132–139.

Gilch, P. M., & Sieweke, J. (2021). Recruiting digital talent: The strategic role of recruitment in organisations' digital transformation. *German Journal of Human Resource Management*, *35*(1), 53–82. doi:10.1177/2397002220952734

Hadi, R., Melumad, S., & Park, E. S. (2024). The Metaverse: A new digital frontier for consumer behavior. *Journal of Consumer Psychology*, *34*(1), 142–166. doi:10.1002/jcpy.1356

Hanumanthakari, S., Gift, M. M., Kanimozhi, K., Bhavani, M. D., Bamane, K. D., & Boopathi, S. (2023). Biomining Method to Extract Metal Components Using Computer-Printed Circuit Board E-Waste. In *Handbook of Research on Safe Disposal Methods of Municipal Solid Wastes for a Sustainable Environment* (pp. 123–141). IGI Global. doi:10.4018/978-1-6684-8117-2.ch010

Manjula, P., & ... (2021). Human Resource Coping Strategies in „New Normal" and their Impact on Work Places: Systematic Review. *Journal of Contemporary Issues in Business and Government*, *27*(1), 1746–1759.

Naveeenkumar, N., Rallapalli, S., Sasikala, K., Priya, P. V., Husain, J., & Boopathi, S. (2024). Enhancing Consumer Behavior and Experience Through AI-Driven Insights Optimization. In *AI Impacts in Digital Consumer Behavior* (pp. 1–35). IGI Global. doi:10.4018/979-8-3693-1918-5.ch001

Paramita, D. (2020). *Digitalization in talent acquisition: A case study of AI in recruitment.*

Pillai, R., & Sivathanu, B. (2020). Adoption of artificial intelligence (AI) for talent acquisition in IT/ITeS organizations. *Benchmarking*, *27*(9), 2599–2629. doi:10.1108/BIJ-04-2020-0186

Piwowar-Sulej, K. (2021). Human resources development as an element of sustainable HRM–with the focus on production engineers. *Journal of Cleaner Production*, *278*, 124008. doi:10.1016/j.jclepro.2020.124008 PMID:32901179

Prabhuswamy, M., Tripathi, R., Vijayakumar, M., Thulasimani, T., Sundharesalingam, P., & Sampath, B. (2024). A Study on the Complex Nature of Higher Education Leadership: An Innovative Approach. In *Challenges of Globalization and Inclusivity in Academic Research* (pp. 202–223). IGI Global. doi:10.4018/979-8-3693-1371-8.ch013

Rahamathunnisa, U., Subhashini, P., Aancy, H. M., Meenakshi, S., Boopathi, S., & ... (2023). Solutions for Software Requirement Risks Using Artificial Intelligence Techniques. In *Handbook of Research on Data Science and Cybersecurity Innovations in Industry 4.0 Technologies* (pp. 45–64). IGI Global.

Ravisankar, A., Shanthi, A., Lavanya, S., Ramaratnam, M., Krishnamoorthy, V., & Boopathi, S. (2024). Harnessing 6G for Consumer-Centric Business Strategies Across Electronic Industries. In AI Impacts in Digital Consumer Behavior (pp. 241–270). IGI Global.

Sengeni, D., Padmapriya, G., Imambi, S. S., Suganthi, D., Suri, A., & Boopathi, S. (2023). Biomedical waste handling method using artificial intelligence techniques. In *Handbook of Research on Safe Disposal Methods of Municipal Solid Wastes for a Sustainable Environment* (pp. 306–323). IGI Global. doi:10.4018/978-1-6684-8117-2.ch022

Shaddiq, S., Irpan, M., & ... (2023). Governance of Human Resources Management in the Digital Era. *Journal of Business and Management Studies, 5*(3), 80–96. doi:10.32996/jbms.2023.5.3.8

Sharma, D. M., Ramana, K. V., Jothilakshmi, R., Verma, R., Maheswari, B. U., & Boopathi, S. (2024). Integrating Generative AI Into K-12 Curriculums and Pedagogies in India: Opportunities and Challenges. *Facilitating Global Collaboration and Knowledge Sharing in Higher Education With Generative AI*, 133–161.

Strohmeier, S. (2020). Digital human resource management: A conceptual clarification. *German Journal of Human Resource Management, 34*(3), 345–365. doi:10.1177/2397002220921131

Tessema, M. T., Tesfom, G., Faircloth, M. A., Tesfagiorgis, M., & Teckle, P. (2022). The "great resignation": Causes, consequences, and creative HR management strategies. *Journal of Human Resource and Sustainability Studies, 10*(1), 161–178. doi:10.4236/jhrss.2022.101011

Wargo, E., Carr Chellman, D., Budge, K., & Canfield Davis, K. (2021). On the digital frontier: Stakeholders in rural areas take on educational technology and schooling. *Journal of Research on Technology in Education, 53*(2), 140–158. doi:10.1080/15391523.2020.1760753

Zavyalova, E., Sokolov, D., Kucherov, D., & Lisovskaya, A. (2022). The digitalization of human resource management: Present and future. *Foresight and STI Governance, 16*(2), 42–51. doi:10.17323/2500-2597.2022.2.42.51

Zehir, C., Karaboğa, T., & Başar, D. (2020). The transformation of human resource management and its impact on overall business performance: Big data analytics and AI technologies in strategic HRM. *Digital Business Strategies in Blockchain Ecosystems: Transformational Design and Future of Global Business*, 265–279.

Chapter 3
Digital Transformation in Developing Economies:
Forecasting Trends, Impact, and Challenges in Industry 5.0

Rekha Pasumarthy
https://orcid.org/0000-0003-3904-2964
Department of Humanities and Mathematics, G. Narayanamma Institute of Technology and Science, India

Shariq Mohammed
Department of Department of Accounting, College of Commerce and Business Administration, India

Vishnu Laxman
https://orcid.org/0009-0007-1233-1703
Department of Economics, GITAM University, India

V. Krishnamoorthy
Department of Management Studies, Kongu Engineering College, India

S. Durga
Department of Management Studies, Vignan Foundation for Science Technology and Research, India

Sampath Boopathi
https://orcid.org/0000-0002-2065-6539
Department of Mechanical Engineering, Muthayammal Engineering College, India

ABSTRACT

This chapter delves into the role of digital HR in developing economies, focusing on the intersection of technology, human resources, and economic development. It highlights the opportunities and challenges of digitalization, such as HR leveraging digital tools to enhance workforce efficiency and foster innovation. The chapter also discusses the implications of Industry 5.0, emphasizing the integration of AI, automation, and IoT in reshaping HR practices. The potential benefits of digital HR include improved talent management and increased productivity, but also address challenges like infrastructure constraints and skill gaps. The chapter forecasts trends in Digital HR specific to developing economies, aligning with Industry 5.0 principles. The chapter explores the effects of digitalization on workforce dynamics, organizational structures, and the economy, addressing challenges like digital literacy, data privacy, and socio-economic disparities. It highlights the potential of digital HR in bridging skill gaps, promoting inclusive growth, and stimulating innovation.

DOI: 10.4018/979-8-3693-1343-5.ch003

INTRODUCTION

In the contemporary global landscape, the rapid pace of technological advancement has ushered in an era of unprecedented change, often referred to as Industry 5.0. As developed economies seamlessly integrate digital technologies into their industrial processes, the focus now shifts towards understanding the implications and opportunities for developing economies in the context of digital transformation. This introduction provides a foundational overview of the burgeoning paradigm of Industry 5.0, emphasizing its potential impact on developing economies. It sets the stage for an in-depth exploration of the forecasting trends, nuanced impacts, and inherent challenges associated with digital transformation in these dynamic contexts (Sánchez-Bayón & Aznar, 2020).

The term Industry 5.0 encapsulates the fusion of cyber-physical systems, the Internet of Things (IoT), and artificial intelligence (AI) in industrial processes. Building upon the foundations of Industry 4.0, this new phase seeks to harmonize human-centric approaches with advanced technologies, creating a symbiotic relationship between humans and machines. In the developed world, this transformation has led to increased efficiency, innovation, and economic growth. However, as we embark on this journey, it becomes imperative to examine how developing economies, often characterized by diverse socio-economic landscapes and unique challenges, can harness the power of digital transformation for sustainable development (Strohmeier, 2020a).

Developing economies, despite facing initial barriers, are positioned to leverage digital transformation to leapfrog traditional developmental stages. The integration of digital technologies holds the promise of addressing longstanding challenges in areas such as healthcare, education, and infrastructure. Yet, it is crucial to acknowledge the multifaceted nature of this transition. The impact of Industry 5.0 extends beyond the industrial sector, permeating various facets of society, from governance and education to healthcare and beyond. Thus, understanding the trends, impacts, and challenges within the specific context of developing economies becomes paramount for policymakers, businesses, and the global community at large (Costan et al., 2021).

Digital technologies can significantly drive inclusive growth by providing access to information, services, and markets, creating a more equitable environment. However, challenges like digital literacy, infrastructural limitations, and socio-economic disparities need to be addressed to ensure seamless integration. Addressing these obstacles can unlock the full potential of Industry 5.0 and guide developing economies towards sustainable development, thereby promoting a more equitable playing field (Thite, 2022a).

This study explores the complex nature of digital transformation in developing economies, forecasting trends, examining impacts on sectors, and addressing challenges to fully utilize Industry 5.0's potential. It aims to illuminate the future, inspire dialogue, and foster a future where digital transformation is a powerful force for positive change in these economies (Rane, 2023). Digital Human Resources (HR) is a crucial aspect of Industry 5.0, integrating technology, workforce management, and organizational efficiency. It plays a significant role in sustainable growth in developing economies, where diverse labor markets and unique socio-economic challenges exist. Digitalization in HR practices can foster inclusive and equitable development, highlighting the importance of HR in addressing these challenges and promoting sustainable development.

Digital HR is a crucial tool for developing economies, enabling scalable solutions for talent acquisition, management, and development. By leveraging digital platforms, these economies can tap into a global talent pool, fostering a more diverse and skilled workforce. This aligns with Industry 5.0 principles, which emphasize the integration of technology for efficiency and creating a globally connected workforce (Karmaker et al., 2023). Industry 5.0 is a shift in work, requiring digital HR to equip the workforce with necessary skills. Digital HR platforms facilitate training and development programs, bridging skills gaps and empowering employees to navigate Industry 5.0's complexities. In developing economies, digital HR promotes lifelong learning, upskilling, and adaptability, especially in areas where educational disparities hinder workforce readiness due to educational disparities.

Digital HR enhances organizational structures by transforming traditional hierarchies into flexible, collaborative frameworks, allowing for quicker decision-making and adaptability to market changes. This approach is particularly beneficial in developing economies where bureaucratic processes may hinder operations, streamlining operations and improving overall efficiency (Mourtzis et al., 2022). Digital HR is gaining momentum in developing economies due to its potential to foster sustainable development, enhance workforce capabilities, and contribute to Industry 5.0 principles. However, challenges such as digital literacy, access to technology, and data privacy need to be addressed. Governments, businesses, and educational institutions must work together to overcome these obstacles. Digital HR is seen as a beacon, guiding the way towards a future where technology drives efficiency, empowers individuals, and promotes inclusive growth (Adel, 2022).

Objectives

- Explore how these trends align with the principles and requirements of Industry 5.0, understanding the evolution of HR in the digital age.
- Examine how Digital HR practices contribute to creating a more dynamic, adaptable, and collaborative workforce aligned with the needs of Industry 5.0.
- Explore the extent to which Industry 5.0 principles influence organizational structures, fostering agility and responsiveness.
- Understand how the integration of digital HR strategies can spur innovation, enhance productivity, and contribute to overall economic growth in alignment with Industry 5.0 principles.
- Explore the opportunities presented by the adoption of Digital HR in developing economies, such as improved efficiency, talent acquisition, and skill development.

DIGITAL HR LANDSCAPE IN DEVELOPING ECONOMIES

The current state of Digital HR practices within developing economies reflects a dynamic landscape marked by both challenges and opportunities. While some regions have made significant strides in adopting digital HR technologies, others are still navigating the initial phases of this transformation. The exploration of the Digital HR landscape in developing economies unveils key characteristics and trends that shape the approach towards human resource management in the era of Industry 5.0 (Costan et al., 2021; Kshetri, 2021).

- **Adoption Levels and Varied Maturity:** Developing economies showcase a diverse range of adoption levels and maturity in Digital HR practices. Some countries and industries have embraced digital HR technologies to streamline processes, enhance employee experiences, and drive efficiency. However, there are instances where the adoption remains at an early stage, influenced by factors such as economic constraints, cultural considerations, and technological infrastructure limitations.

- **Talent Acquisition and Management:** Digital HR in developing economies has a significant impact on talent acquisition and management. Advanced technologies, such as AI-driven recruitment tools and data analytics, are increasingly being utilized to identify and attract skilled professionals. This shift marks a departure from traditional recruitment methods, offering more streamlined and data-driven approaches to talent acquisition.
- **Cloud-Based HR Solutions:** Cloud-based HR solutions are gaining traction in developing economies due to their scalability and cost-effectiveness. These solutions offer flexibility in managing HR processes, enabling businesses to adapt to changing demands without significant upfront investments. The cloud facilitates the accessibility of HR services, particularly in regions where physical infrastructure may be a constraint.
- **Focus on Employee Experience:** Digital HR practices in developing economies are placing a growing emphasis on enhancing the overall employee experience. Mobile applications, self-service portals, and online training modules contribute to a more user-friendly and engaging HR environment. This focus aligns with the broader trend in Industry 5.0, emphasizing the importance of a human-centric approach to technology.

The Digital HR landscape in developing economies faces challenges such as digital literacy, workforce disparities, and concerns about data privacy and security. This transition is complex, with some regions implementing advanced practices while others navigate a difficult one. Factors such as adoption levels, talent management focus, cloud-based solution utilization, employee experience emphasis, and existing challenges shape the trajectory of Digital HR practices within Industry 5.0.

Analysis of the Adoption Levels and Emerging Trends

The adoption levels of Digital HR technologies in developing economies display a spectrum ranging from early-stage exploration to advanced implementation. While certain sectors and countries showcase a proactive embrace of digital HR practices, others are still at the nascent stages of adoption. Economic factors, technological infrastructure, and organizational culture play pivotal roles in determining the adoption landscape. Industries with higher digital maturity tend to integrate a broader array of digital HR tools, while others may focus on incremental advancements (Adel, 2022; Kshetri, 2021; Strohmeier, 2020a).

Technologies in Digital HR

- **AI and Machine Learning:** Adoption of AI and machine learning in developing economies is gaining momentum, particularly in talent acquisition and employee engagement. These technologies power predictive analytics for identifying suitable candidates, forecasting workforce trends, and personalizing employee experiences (Boopathi, 2024a).
- **Cloud-Based Solutions:** Cloud-based HR solutions are pivotal in providing scalable and accessible HR services. The flexibility and cost-effectiveness of cloud platforms make them particularly attractive in resource-constrained environments. Developing economies are increasingly leveraging cloud technology for managing HR processes efficiently (Hema et al., 2023).

- **Mobile Applications:** Mobile applications are integral to enhancing the accessibility of HR services. With a significant portion of the population accessing the internet through mobile devices, HR applications facilitate real-time communication, self-service functionalities, and on-the-go access to critical HR information.
- **Employee Self-Service Portals:** Employee self-service portals are becoming prevalent, empowering individuals to manage their HR-related tasks independently. This includes accessing pay stubs, updating personal information, and enrolling in training programs. Such portals contribute to a more streamlined and efficient HR workflow.
- **People Analytics:** Developing economies are increasingly recognizing the value of people analytics in making informed HR decisions. By leveraging data analytics, organizations can gain insights into employee performance, identify areas for improvement, and align HR strategies with broader business goals.

Emerging Trends in Digital HR

The analysis reveals that developing economies are strategically adopting key technologies and emerging trends to improve their Digital HR capabilities. Factors such as economic conditions, industry requirements, and workforce digital readiness influence this trajectory. As these technologies evolve, these economies are poised to leverage Digital HR for sustainable growth and increased competitiveness in Industry 5.0. The figure 1 depicts the latest trends in digital HR.

- **Focus on Employee Well-being:** There is a growing trend in developing economies towards prioritizing employee well-being through digital HR initiatives. This includes mental health support,

Figure 1. Emerging trends in digital HR

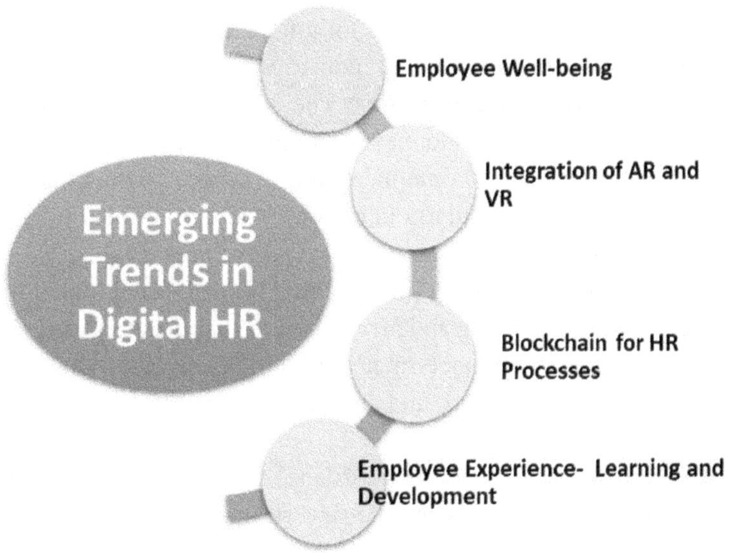

wellness programs, and flexible work arrangements, reflecting a broader Industry 5.0 emphasis on the holistic development of the workforce (Strohmeier, 2020a; Thite, 2022a).

- **Integration of Virtual Reality (VR) and Augmented Reality (AR):** While still in the early stages, some industries within developing economies are exploring the integration of VR and AR technologies in HR practices. This includes virtual onboarding processes, simulated training environments, and enhanced collaboration through AR-enhanced communication tools (Revathi et al., 2024).
- **Blockchain for HR Processes:** Blockchain technology is gradually gaining attention in HR processes, particularly in developing economies aiming to enhance data security and streamline verification processes. Blockchain can be utilized for secure storage of employee records, credential verification, and ensuring data integrity.
- **Enhanced Employee Experience Platforms:** Developing economies are witnessing a trend towards comprehensive employee experience platforms. These platforms integrate various HR functions, such as performance management, learning and development, and employee feedback, to create a cohesive and engaging experience for employees.
- **Personalized Learning and Development:** With the rise of digital HR, there is a shift towards personalized learning and development initiatives. AI-driven platforms analyze individual skill gaps and preferences, offering tailored training programs to enhance employee skills, aligning with the principles of Industry 5.0.

FORECASTING TRENDS IN DIGITAL HR

This study provides a comprehensive analysis of the anticipated trends in Digital HR pertaining to developing economies (Abdeldayem & Aldulaimi, 2020a, 2020b).

- **Increased Adoption of AI for Talent Acquisition:** Developing economies are expected to witness a surge in the use of Artificial Intelligence (AI) for talent acquisition. AI-driven tools will play a crucial role in automating the recruitment process, from resume screening to candidate matching. This trend is driven by the need for efficiency and effectiveness in identifying and attracting qualified candidates, especially in industries facing skill shortages.
- **Expansion of Cloud-Based HR Solutions:** The adoption of cloud-based HR solutions is forecasted to expand in developing economies. As organizations seek scalable and cost-effective HR solutions, cloud platforms will become increasingly popular. This trend aligns with the need for flexibility and accessibility, particularly in regions where traditional infrastructure may be a constraint (Boopathi, 2024b; Venkateswaran, Vidhya, Ayyannan, et al., 2023).
- **Emphasis on Employee Well-being and Mental Health:** Anticipated trends include a heightened focus on employee well-being and mental health support. As Digital HR evolves, developing economies recognize the importance of holistic employee care. Digital platforms will be employed to provide resources, support, and programs that address the mental health and well-being of the workforce.
- **Mobile-First HR Strategies:** With the prevalence of mobile devices, Digital HR in developing economies will see a shift towards mobile-first strategies. HR applications and platforms will prioritize mobile accessibility, allowing employees to access HR services seamlessly on their

smartphones. This trend caters to the widespread use of mobile technology and ensures inclusivity in HR services.

- **Continued Integration of People Analytics:** Developing economies are expected to continue integrating people analytics into HR processes. The use of data analytics to make informed decisions about workforce management, employee engagement, and performance optimization will become more sophisticated. This trend reflects a commitment to evidence-based HR strategies and aligns with Industry 5.0 principles.
- **Enhanced Focus on Learning and Development:** The forecast includes an enhanced focus on personalized learning and development initiatives. Digital HR platforms will leverage AI to analyze individual skills, preferences, and performance data, providing tailored training programs. This trend addresses the need for upskilling and reskilling in the evolving job landscape (Das et al., 2024; Durairaj et al., 2023).
- **Expansion of Virtual Collaboration Tools:** The anticipation is an expansion of virtual collaboration tools within Digital HR, especially in developing economies where remote work and virtual collaboration have become more prevalent. Virtual reality (VR) and augmented reality (AR) technologies may find increased application in HR processes, such as virtual onboarding and immersive training experiences.
- **Blockchain Integration for Data Security:** Forecasted trends include the exploration of blockchain technology to enhance data security in HR processes. Developing economies may leverage blockchain for secure storage of employee records, credential verification, and ensuring the integrity of sensitive HR data. This trend addresses concerns related to data privacy and security (Mohanty et al., 2023; Sundaramoorthy et al., 2024).
- **Agile HR Practices:** Anticipated trends involve the adoption of agile HR practices, allowing organizations in developing economies to respond swiftly to changing market dynamics. This includes agile performance management, flexible organizational structures, and adaptive talent management strategies to align with the principles of Industry 5.0.
- **Continued Embrace of Employee Experience Platforms:** Digital HR in developing economies is expected to witness a continued embrace of comprehensive employee experience platforms. These platforms integrate various HR functions to create a seamless and engaging experience for employees. The trend focuses on improving overall employee satisfaction and aligns with the human-centric approach of Industry 5.0.

The forecasting trends in Digital HR for developing economies suggest a shift towards technology-driven efficiency, employee-centric approaches, and innovative solutions to tackle unique challenges, positioning Digital HR as a crucial driver of sustainable development and competitiveness in Industry 5.0.

Trajectory of Industry 5.0

The forecasted trends in Digital HR for developing economies align seamlessly with the trajectory of Industry 5.0, a paradigm that emphasizes the harmonious collaboration between humans and advanced technologies. The integration of Artificial Intelligence (AI) for talent acquisition aligns with Industry 5.0's human-centric approach by automating routine tasks, enabling HR professionals to focus on strategic and empathetic aspects of recruitment. This shift reflects a move towards a symbiotic relationship between human intuition and AI-driven efficiency, fostering a balanced and effective talent acquisition process in line with Industry 5.0 principles (Mourtzis et al., 2022; Rane, 2023).

The expansion of cloud-based HR solutions resonates with the core tenets of Industry 5.0, emphasizing flexibility and accessibility. Cloud platforms enable developing economies to overcome traditional infrastructure limitations, promoting a decentralized and interconnected approach to HR processes. This aligns with the broader Industry 5.0 vision of creating interconnected, agile systems that enhance efficiency and adaptability. The mobile-first HR strategies also contribute to this trajectory, recognizing the need for ubiquitous accessibility and ensuring that HR services are available to a diverse and dispersed workforce, aligning with the principles of Industry 5.0.

The forecasted emphasis on employee well-being and mental health in Digital HR trends is in line with the human-centric ethos of Industry 5.0. The industry acknowledges the importance of holistic employee care, emphasizing not only productivity but also the well-being of individuals. As Industry 5.0 seeks to create environments that prioritize human experiences, the integration of digital HR platforms to address mental health concerns demonstrates a commitment to fostering a supportive and inclusive workplace.

The continued integration of people analytics reflects the Industry 5.0 principle of informed decision-making through data-driven insights. Developing economies leveraging people analytics in Digital HR are aligning with the broader trend of using advanced technologies to enhance strategic decision-making, optimize workforce performance, and align HR strategies with organizational goals. This trend ensures that the human element is not overshadowed but rather augmented by data, fostering a more informed and responsive HR approach.

Furthermore, the adoption of agile HR practices and the exploration of blockchain for data security represent the adaptive and innovative nature encouraged by Industry 5.0. Agile HR practices allow organizations to respond swiftly to changing dynamics, mirroring the agile and responsive systems advocated by Industry 5.0. The integration of blockchain ensures data integrity and security, aligning with the emphasis on trust and transparency within Industry 5.0. These trends collectively underscore the role of Digital HR in shaping workplaces that resonate with the principles of Industry 5.0, fostering collaboration, innovation, and a human-centric approach within developing economies.

IMPACT OF DIGITAL HR ON WORKFORCE DYNAMICS

Evaluation of the Transformative Effects of Digitalization

The impact of Digital Human Resources (HR) on workforce dynamics is transformative, reshaping the structure, skills, and composition of the workforce in profound ways. Digital HR technologies have ushered in a new era where the traditional boundaries of work and the nature of employment are evolving, responding to the demands of an increasingly digitized and interconnected world (Tiwari & Mondal, 2022).

Structural Changes: Digital HR brings about structural changes in the workforce by facilitating remote work and flexible arrangements. Virtual collaboration tools, enabled by digitalization, allow employees to connect and collaborate from different locations, leading to the deconstruction of traditional organizational hierarchies. This transformation supports Industry 5.0 principles by fostering agile and dynamic organizational structures that adapt to changing market needs. The workforce becomes more decentralized, breaking down geographical barriers and enabling a more diverse and globally connected working environment (Boopathi, 2024c; Boopathi et al., 2022).

Skills Evolution: The impact of Digital HR on workforce skills is revolutionary, demanding a shift towards digital literacy and the acquisition of new competencies. Automation, AI, and data analytics are integrated into various HR functions, necessitating employees to possess not only technical skills but also critical thinking, adaptability, and problem-solving abilities. Digital HR platforms often provide personalized learning and development opportunities, promoting continuous upskilling and reskilling. This skills evolution aligns with the principles of Industry 5.0, emphasizing the fusion of human capabilities with advanced technologies to drive innovation and productivity (Boopathi et al., 2023; Kumar et al., 2023).

Enhanced Employee Experience: Digital HR contributes to an enhanced employee experience by providing self-service portals, mobile applications, and other user-friendly tools. These platforms empower employees to manage their HR-related tasks independently, creating a more streamlined and engaging experience. This focus on enhancing the employee experience aligns with Industry 5.0, which emphasizes human well-being and satisfaction as essential components of a productive and innovative workforce. Digital HR platforms cater to individual needs, fostering a workplace environment that prioritizes employee satisfaction and engagement.

Talent Acquisition and Retention: Digital HR technologies revolutionize talent acquisition and retention strategies. AI-driven recruitment tools streamline the hiring process, enabling HR professionals to identify and attract suitable candidates more efficiently. The use of data analytics in workforce planning enhances strategic decision-making, ensuring that organizations can anticipate skill needs and recruit talent proactively. This impact on talent acquisition and retention aligns with the industry 5.0 goal of creating a collaborative and skilled workforce that can drive innovation and sustainable growth.

Diversity and Inclusion: Digital HR platforms play a crucial role in promoting diversity and inclusion within the workforce. By leveraging data analytics, organizations can identify and address biases in recruitment processes, ensuring fair and equitable opportunities. Virtual collaboration tools facilitate communication and collaboration among diverse teams, breaking down traditional barriers. This impact on diversity and inclusion aligns with the societal goals of Industry 5.0, emphasizing the importance of social responsibility and inclusivity in the workplace.

Digital HR has a significant impact on workforce dynamics, involving structural changes, skill evolution, enhanced employee experiences, and talent acquisition and retention. This aligns with Industry 5.0 principles, promoting a collaborative, adaptive, and human-centric work environment in developing economies. Organizations adopting digitalization in HR practices create a technologically adept, resilient, diverse, and prepared workforce for the digital age.

Digital HR Practices for Employee Engagement, Productivity, and Satisfaction

Digital HR practices exert a significant influence on employee engagement, productivity, and satisfaction, shaping a work environment that fosters both professional growth and personal well-being (Burnett & Lisk, 2021; Tiwari & Mondal, 2022). The figure 2 depicts digital HR practices that enhance employee engagement, productivity, and satisfaction.

- **Improved Employee Engagement:** Digital HR platforms contribute to enhanced employee engagement by providing interactive and accessible tools for communication, collaboration, and feedback. Employee self-service portals and mobile applications enable individuals to easily ac-

Figure 2. Digital HR practices for employee engagement, productivity, and satisfaction

cess relevant information, participate in surveys, and contribute to decision-making processes. Virtual collaboration tools foster real-time communication and collaboration, bridging geographical gaps and promoting a sense of connectedness. This heightened engagement is crucial for cultivating a positive workplace culture, aligning with Industry 5.0's emphasis on human-centric approaches to technology.

- **Enhanced Productivity through Automation:** The integration of automation and AI in HR processes streamlines routine tasks, freeing up time for employees to focus on more strategic and value-added activities. Automation in recruitment, onboarding, and administrative tasks reduces manual workloads, allowing HR professionals and employees to allocate their time more efficiently. This improved productivity not only aligns with Industry 5.0's goal of optimizing operational efficiency but also contributes to a more fulfilling work experience, as employees can invest their efforts in tasks that require creativity and critical thinking (Boopathi, 2023; Gnanaprakasam et al., 2023).
- **Personalized Learning and Development Opportunities:** Digital HR platforms support personalized learning and development initiatives, tailoring training programs to individual employee needs. AI-driven analytics identify skill gaps and recommend targeted learning modules, enabling employees to enhance their competencies and stay relevant in their roles. This personalized approach fosters a sense of individual growth and investment in employees' professional development, directly impacting their satisfaction and engagement.
- **Real-Time Performance Feedback:** Digital HR facilitates real-time performance feedback, moving away from traditional annual reviews to continuous performance management. Through

digital platforms, managers can provide timely and constructive feedback, helping employees understand their strengths and areas for improvement. This approach not only enhances performance but also contributes to a culture of transparency and open communication, reinforcing employee satisfaction and engagement.

- **Employee Well-being and Satisfaction:** Digital HR practices contribute to employee well-being and satisfaction by addressing work-life balance and mental health concerns. Remote work arrangements, enabled by digital tools, provide flexibility that allows employees to better manage their personal and professional lives. Well-being programs, accessible through digital platforms, offer resources and support for physical and mental health. These initiatives align with the industry 5.0 emphasis on creating workplaces that prioritize the holistic well-being of employees (Boopathi, 2024a; Maheswari et al., 2023).

Digital HR practices significantly impact employee engagement, productivity, and satisfaction by enhancing communication, streamlining processes, and supporting personal and professional development. These practices align with Industry 5.0 principles, emphasizing the importance of putting humans at the center of technological advancements. They contribute to operational efficiency, overall workforce satisfaction, and well-being, ensuring a positive and empowering workplace environment.

ORGANIZATIONAL STRUCTURES IN THE ERA OF DIGITAL HR

The impact of Digital Human Resources (HR) on traditional organizational structures is profound, leading to a paradigm shift towards more agile and flexible models. Digital HR technologies are catalysts for change, influencing how organizations are structured, operate, and adapt to the evolving demands of the digital era (Strohmeier, 2020b).

- **Flattening of Hierarchies:** Digital HR contributes to the flattening of traditional organizational hierarchies. With the automation of routine administrative tasks and the decentralization of HR functions through digital platforms, there is a reduced need for multiple hierarchical layers. These streamlining fosters quicker decision-making processes, facilitates direct communication channels, and promotes a more collaborative work environment. The result is a move away from rigid, top-down structures toward more agile and responsive organizational frameworks.
- **Decentralization and Remote Work:** The integration of digital HR practices facilitates decentralization, allowing organizations to operate beyond traditional centralized offices. Remote work becomes more feasible as digital platforms enable seamless communication, collaboration, and HR management irrespective of geographical locations. This shift towards decentralized work models challenges the conventional idea of a centralized physical office and encourages a more distributed, flexible workforce that aligns with the principles of Industry 5.0 (Boopathi & Myilsamy, 2021; Subha et al., 2023).
- **Agile Organizational Structures:** Digital HR accelerates the adoption of agile organizational structures. These structures prioritize adaptability, collaboration, and responsiveness to change. Agile methodologies, commonly used in software development, are now being applied to HR processes, allowing for iterative development, continuous improvement, and quick responses to

evolving business needs. This agility is essential for organizations to thrive in the fast-paced, dynamic landscape shaped by technological advancements.

- **Cross-Functional Teams:** Digital HR practices foster the creation of cross-functional teams that operate collaboratively across different departments and functions. By breaking down silos and leveraging digital platforms for communication and project management, organizations can create teams that bring diverse skills and perspectives together. This approach encourages innovation, problem-solving, and efficient decision-making, reinforcing the shift towards more flexible and collaborative organizational structures.
- **Focus on Employee Networks:** Digital HR encourages the development of employee networks, emphasizing connections and collaboration beyond formal reporting structures. Social collaboration platforms and digital communication tools enable employees to connect, share knowledge, and work together on projects irrespective of hierarchical positions. This networked approach promotes a culture of inclusivity and collective problem-solving, aligning with the collaborative principles of Industry 5.0.
- **Data-Driven Decision-Making:** Digital HR facilitates data-driven decision-making, empowering organizations to base strategic decisions on real-time analytics. This shift from intuition-based decision-making to data-driven insights enhances organizational effectiveness and agility. By leveraging digital technologies for workforce analytics, organizations can adapt their structures based on actual performance data, ensuring a more responsive and efficient organizational design.

Digital HR has significantly impacted traditional organizational structures, promoting flexibility, decentralization, and agility. This shift is driven by the transformative power of digital technologies, allowing organizations to navigate the digital era with resilience. As organizations adopt digital HR practices, they move towards structures that optimize efficiency, foster innovation, and align with Industry 5.0 principles (AlHamad et al., 2022).

ECONOMIC DEVELOPMENT AND DIGITAL HR

The role of Digital Human Resources (HR) in fostering economic development within developing economies is significant, representing a transformative force that contributes to innovation, productivity, and overall growth. Digital HR strategies serve as catalysts for positive changes, influencing how businesses operate, manage talent, and contribute to the broader economic ecosystem (AlHamad et al., 2022; Thite, 2022b). The figure 3 depicts the significant impact of digital HR on economic development.

- **Talent Acquisition and Retention:** Digital HR strategies streamline talent acquisition processes, enabling organizations in developing economies to attract and retain skilled individuals more efficiently. By leveraging technology for recruitment, onboarding, and talent management, companies can build high-performing teams. This strategic approach to human capital directly impacts productivity and innovation, fostering an environment conducive to economic development (Ravisankar et al., 2023).
- **Skill Development and Workforce Readiness:** Digital HR platforms play a crucial role in skill development and workforce readiness. By offering personalized learning and development programs, organizations can address skill gaps and enhance the capabilities of their workforce. A

Figure 3. Role of digital HR on economic development

digitally skilled workforce is better equipped to contribute to innovation, adapt to technological advancements, and drive economic growth in sectors that demand cutting-edge expertise.

- **Agile Organizational Structures:** Digital HR contributes to the adoption of agile organizational structures, allowing businesses to respond swiftly to market dynamics and changes in consumer demands. This agility enhances overall organizational efficiency and flexibility, creating an environment where innovation can flourish. The ability to adapt quickly to evolving business landscapes is a key factor in fostering economic development, and digital HR strategies play a pivotal role in enabling this adaptability.
- **Enhanced Productivity and Efficiency:** Automation and digitalization in HR processes lead to increased productivity and efficiency. Digital HR platforms automate administrative tasks, allowing HR professionals and employees to focus on more strategic and value-added activities. This efficiency translates into optimized workflows, reduced operational costs, and improved resource allocation – all essential factors for sustainable economic development.
- **Data-Driven Decision-Making:** Digital HR strategies enable data-driven decision-making, providing organizations with valuable insights into workforce trends, performance metrics, and employee engagement. Informed decision-making based on real-time analytics enhances organizational effectiveness. This data-driven approach contributes to the development of strategies that align with business objectives, fostering innovation and supporting economic growth.

- **Innovation in HR Practices:** The adoption of digital HR strategies encourages innovation in HR practices, fostering a culture of continuous improvement. From performance management to employee engagement initiatives, digitalization allows organizations to experiment with new approaches and refine strategies based on data and feedback. This innovative mindset permeates the entire organization, contributing to a culture where creativity and forward-thinking are valued – essential elements for sustained economic development (Boopathi, 2024b; Rahamathunnisa et al., 2023).
- **Access to Global Talent and Markets:** Digital HR facilitates access to global talent pools and markets. Through online recruitment platforms and digital collaboration tools, organizations in developing economies can tap into a diverse talent base and expand their reach beyond local borders. This global connectivity enhances competitiveness, stimulates innovation, and contributes to economic development by fostering international collaborations and partnerships.

Digital HR plays a crucial role in economic development in developing economies by addressing talent acquisition, skill development, organizational agility, productivity, and innovation. These strategies contribute significantly to overall economic growth and development, aligning with Industry 5.0 principles and the digital transformation era, making them integral components of organizational practices.

OPPORTUNITIES IN DIGITAL HR ADOPTION

The integration of digital HR practices presents numerous opportunities for organizations, creating a landscape where efficiency, talent acquisition, and decision-making are significantly enhanced. The adoption of digital HR technologies opens doors to transformative possibilities that can positively impact various aspects of human resource management and organizational dynamics (Burnett & Lisk, 2021; Thite, 2022b). The figure 4 illustrates the potential for the integration of digital HR practices.

- **Increased Efficiency and Streamlined Processes:** One of the primary opportunities in adopting digital HR practices is the potential for increased efficiency and streamlined processes. Automation of routine tasks, such as payroll processing, leave management, and performance evaluations, reduces manual workload and minimizes the likelihood of errors. This efficiency allows HR professionals to focus on more strategic initiatives, fostering a workplace where time and resources are utilized effectively.
- **Global Talent Acquisition:** Digital HR platforms provide opportunities for global talent acquisition, allowing organizations to access a diverse pool of candidates beyond geographical boundaries. Online recruitment platforms, AI-driven candidate matching, and video interviewing tools facilitate a more streamlined and inclusive talent acquisition process. This global reach enhances the potential for finding the right skills and expertise, contributing to a more competitive and diverse workforce.
- **Personalized Learning and Development:** Digital HR creates opportunities for personalized learning and development initiatives. AI-driven analytics can identify individual skill gaps and recommend tailored training programs. This personalized approach enhances employee engagement, supports continuous learning, and ensures that training efforts align with the unique

Figure 4. Opportunities for integration of digital HR practices

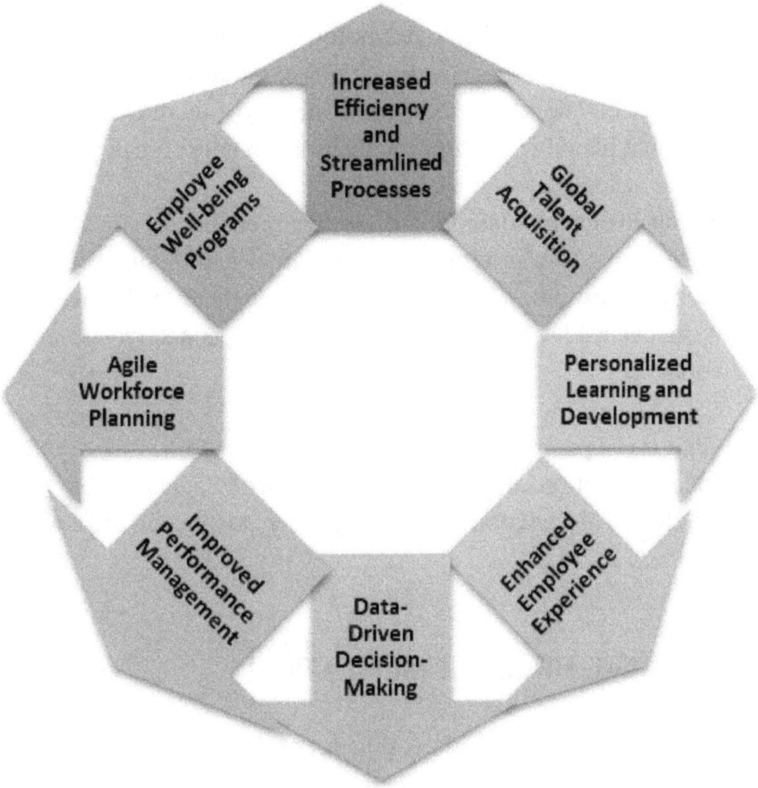

needs of each employee. The result is a more skilled and adaptable workforce, contributing to organizational growth (Agrawal et al., 2023; Durairaj et al., 2023; Venkateswaran, Vidhya, Naik, et al., 2023).

- **Enhanced Employee Experience:** The integration of digital HR practices offers opportunities to enhance the overall employee experience. Employee self-service portals, mobile applications, and virtual collaboration tools create a user-friendly environment where individuals can access HR services and information seamlessly. This improved employee experience contributes to higher satisfaction levels, increased engagement, and a positive workplace culture.
- **Data-Driven Decision-Making:** Digital HR platforms provide opportunities for data-driven decision-making. The collection and analysis of HR-related data enable organizations to gain insights into workforce trends, performance metrics, and employee engagement levels. Informed decision-making based on real-time analytics ensures that HR strategies align with broader business objectives, fostering a culture of evidence-based management.
- **Improved Performance Management:** Digital HR practices offer opportunities for enhanced performance management. Continuous feedback mechanisms, goal-setting tools, and data analytics enable organizations to assess employee performance more effectively. This facilitates a proac-

tive approach to talent development, aligning individual goals with organizational objectives and promoting a culture of continuous improvement (Janardhana et al., 2023).

- **Agile Workforce Planning:** Digital HR technologies create opportunities for agile workforce planning. By leveraging data analytics, organizations can forecast future skill requirements, identify potential talent gaps, and develop strategies for proactive recruitment and talent development. This agility in workforce planning allows organizations to adapt quickly to changing market conditions and stay ahead of industry trends.
- **Employee Well-being Programs:** Digital HR platforms enable organizations to implement comprehensive employee well-being programs. From mental health support to wellness initiatives, digital tools can provide resources and support that contribute to the overall well-being of employees. This, in turn, can lead to increased job satisfaction, reduced turnover, and a more resilient and productive workforce.

The integration of digital HR practices offers numerous opportunities for organizations to optimize their human resource management processes, including efficiency gains, global talent acquisition, and data-driven decision-making. This creates a technologically advanced, employee-centric workplace aligned with broader business goals.

CHALLENGES IN DIGITAL HR IMPLEMENTATION

Implementing digital HR strategies comes with its share of challenges, ranging from technical obstacles to human-centric concerns. Addressing these challenges is crucial for organizations seeking to navigate the digital transformation of their HR practices successfully (Costan et al., 2021; Kshetri, 2021; Mourtzis et al., 2022).

Digital Literacy and Training: A significant challenge in digital HR implementation is the varying levels of digital literacy among employees. Resistance to change and a lack of familiarity with digital tools may hinder the adoption of new HR technologies. To overcome this, organizations need to invest in comprehensive training programs to ensure that employees at all levels have the necessary skills to effectively use digital HR platforms.

Data Privacy and Security Concerns: The collection, storage, and processing of sensitive employee data in digital HR systems raise significant concerns about data privacy and security. Organizations must implement robust data protection measures, comply with relevant regulations, and establish transparent policies to build trust among employees. Addressing these concerns is crucial for maintaining the integrity and confidentiality of HR-related information.

Integration with Existing Systems: Many organizations already have established HR systems and processes in place. Integrating new digital HR technologies seamlessly with existing systems can be a complex challenge. Compatibility issues, data migration, and the need for interoperability may arise, requiring careful planning and technical expertise to ensure a smooth transition without disrupting ongoing HR operations.

Change Management and Cultural Shift: The shift to digital HR often involves a cultural transformation within the organization. Resistance to change, fear of job displacement, and a reluctance to adopt new practices can impede successful implementation. Change management strategies, effective communication, and fostering a culture of continuous learning are essential to navigate this challenge and ensure that employees embrace the digitalization of HR processes.

Cost and Resource Constraints: Implementing digital HR strategies may require significant financial investments in technology infrastructure, software, and training programs. Small and medium-sized enterprises (SMEs) or organizations with limited resources may face challenges in allocating budgets for these initiatives. Striking a balance between cost-effectiveness and the adoption of efficient digital HR solutions is crucial for organizations with resource constraints.

Accessibility and Inclusivity: Ensuring that digital HR platforms are accessible to all employees, regardless of their location or abilities, is a challenge. Socio-economic disparities, varying levels of technology access, and differences in internet connectivity can create barriers to adoption. Organizations must prioritize inclusivity, considering the diverse needs of their workforce and implementing measures to ensure equitable access to digital HR resources.

Overreliance on Technology: While digital HR brings efficiency, there is a risk of overreliance on technology at the expense of human interactions. Maintaining a balance between automated processes and the human touch in HR practices is essential. The challenge lies in finding the right equilibrium to ensure that the digitalization of HR enhances rather than diminishes the overall employee experience.

Evolving Regulatory Landscape: The regulatory landscape around data privacy and HR practices is constantly evolving. Keeping up with changes in regulations, such as GDPR or other regional data protection laws, poses a challenge for organizations. Failure to stay compliant with these regulations can lead to legal and reputational risks, emphasizing the need for ongoing monitoring and adaptation of digital HR strategies.

To successfully implement digital HR strategies, organizations must adopt a holistic approach that integrates technological solutions with human-centered considerations. This includes fostering digital literacy, ensuring data privacy, and managing cultural shifts, ultimately contributing to the overall success of the digital transformation journey.

SOCIO-ECONOMIC IMPACT OF DIGITAL HR

The adoption of Digital Human Resources (HR) practices extends beyond organizational benefits, influencing society and the economy at large. The socio-economic impact of digital HR is multifaceted, contributing to skill development, inclusive growth, and fostering innovation (Rahardja et al., 2021; Samoilovych et al., 2022).

- **Narrowing the Skill Gap:** Digital HR plays a crucial role in narrowing the skill gap by providing opportunities for continuous learning and development. Personalized training programs, often facilitated by AI-driven analytics, enable employees to acquire the skills necessary for the evolving job market. This not only enhances employability but also contributes to a workforce that is more adaptable and resilient in the face of technological advancements.
- **Inclusive Growth and Accessibility:** Digital HR practices contribute to inclusive growth by making HR services and opportunities more accessible. Remote work facilitated by digital platforms allows individuals in diverse geographical locations to participate in the workforce. Online learning and development initiatives ensure that skill-building opportunities are accessible to a broader demographic, reducing barriers to entry and fostering inclusivity in the workforce.

- **Flexible Work Arrangements:** Digital HR enables flexible work arrangements, providing employees with the opportunity to balance work and personal life more effectively. This flexibility is especially impactful for segments of the population facing socio-economic challenges, such as caregivers, individuals with disabilities, or those living in remote areas. The ability to work remotely can contribute to economic participation and empowerment for a more diverse workforce (Malathi et al., 2024).
- **Democratization of Opportunities:** The digitalization of HR processes democratizes opportunities by removing traditional barriers to entry. Online recruitment platforms and AI-driven candidate matching ensure that individuals are evaluated based on their skills and competencies rather than traditional factors. This fosters a more meritocratic approach, promoting diversity and equal opportunities for individuals from various socio-economic backgrounds.
- **Innovation and Entrepreneurship:** Digital HR contributes to fostering innovation and entrepreneurship. By optimizing talent acquisition, providing opportunities for skill development, and creating a culture of continuous learning, organizations become more innovative. Moreover, the rise of remote work allows for the formation of diverse and global teams, fostering a collaborative environment that stimulates creativity and the generation of new ideas.
- **Economic Productivity and Competitiveness:** The adoption of digital HR practices enhances economic productivity by optimizing HR processes, reducing administrative burdens, and promoting efficient talent management. A skilled and engaged workforce, facilitated by digital HR, contributes to organizational competitiveness. This, in turn, has broader economic implications as companies become more agile, adaptive, and capable of contributing to overall economic growth (Babu et al., 2022; Mohanty et al., 2023; Ravisankar et al., 2023).
- **Job Resilience and Adaptability:** Digital HR platforms support job resilience and adaptability. As the workforce acquires digital skills and experiences continuous learning, individuals become more resilient in the face of economic disruptions. The ability to adapt to changing job requirements and industry demands positions workers for greater job security and sustainability, contributing to a more resilient and future-ready workforce.
- **Data-Driven Policy Formulation:** The data generated by digital HR practices can inform policymakers and industry leaders about workforce trends, skills gaps, and areas of opportunity. This data-driven approach enables more informed policy formulation at the macroeconomic level. Understanding the evolving needs of the workforce allows for targeted interventions to address skill shortages and promote sustainable economic development.

Digital HR significantly impacts societal and economic dynamics by bridging skill gaps, promoting inclusivity, and contributing to economic productivity. It shapes a future workforce that is technologically adept, adaptable, and inclusive.

CONCLUSION

The chapter explores the transformation of Digital Human Resources in developing economies, focusing on Industry 5.0. It highlights the benefits of digital HR practices like increased productivity, talent acquisition, and better decision-making. It emphasizes the need for a holistic approach that balances technology with human-centric considerations, overcoming digital literacy, data privacy concerns, and system integration.

The socio-economic impact of digital HR is explored in-depth, emphasizing its role in narrowing the skill gap, fostering inclusive growth, and promoting innovation. It also discusses the democratization of opportunities, flexibility introduced by remote work arrangements, and the potential for economic resilience and adaptability. Digital HR practices extend beyond organizational boundaries to shape a workforce that is technologically adept, socially inclusive, and economically competitive. The chapter advocates for strategic considerations in the implementation of digital HR, acknowledging the evolving nature of digital technologies, regulatory landscape, and dynamic workforce. It emphasizes the importance of data-driven decision-making and the human-centric approach in leveraging digital HR for long-term success.

In summary, the chapter serves as a comprehensive guide to understanding the nuances of Digital HR adoption in developing economies, positioning digital HR as a transformative force that can reshape organizations and contribute to economic development and inclusive growth.

ABBREVIATIONS

HR - Human Resources
AI - Artificial Intelligence
VR - Virtual Reality
AR - Augmented Reality
SMEs - Small and Medium sized Enterprises

REFERENCES

Abdeldayem, M. M., & Aldulaimi, S. H. (2020). Trends and opportunities of artificial intelligence in human resource management: Aspirations for public sector in Bahrain. *International Journal of Scientific and Technology Research*, *9*(1), 3867–3871.

Adel, A. (2022). Future of industry 5.0 in society: Human-centric solutions, challenges and prospective research areas. *Journal of Cloud Computing (Heidelberg, Germany)*, *11*(1), 1–15. doi:10.1186/s13677-022-00314-5 PMID:36101900

Agrawal, A. V., Pitchai, R., Senthamaraikannan, C., Balaji, N. A., Sajithra, S., & Boopathi, S. (2023). Digital Education System During the COVID-19 Pandemic. In Using Assistive Technology for Inclusive Learning in K-12 Classrooms (pp. 104–126). IGI Global. doi:10.4018/978-1-6684-6424-3.ch005

AlHamad, A., Alshurideh, M., Alomari, K., Kurdi, B., Alzoubi, H., Hamouche, S., & Al-Hawary, S. (2022). The effect of electronic human resources management on organizational health of telecommuni-cations companies in Jordan. *International Journal of Data and Network Science*, *6*(2), 429–438. doi:10.5267/j.ijdns.2021.12.011

Babu, B. S., Kamalakannan, J., Meenatchi, N., Karthik, S., & Boopathi, S. (2022). Economic impacts and reliability evaluation of battery by adopting Electric Vehicle. *IEEE Explore*, 1–6.

Boopathi, S. (2023). Deep Learning Techniques Applied for Automatic Sentence Generation. In Promoting Diversity, Equity, and Inclusion in Language Learning Environments (pp. 255–273). IGI Global. doi:10.4018/978-1-6684-3632-5.ch016

Boopathi, S. (2024a). Advancements in Machine Learning and AI for Intelligent Systems in Drone Applications for Smart City Developments. In *Futuristic e-Governance Security With Deep Learning Applications* (pp. 15–45). IGI Global. doi:10.4018/978-1-6684-9596-4.ch002

Boopathi, S. (2024b). Balancing Innovation and Security in the Cloud: Navigating the Risks and Rewards of the Digital Age. In Improving Security, Privacy, and Trust in Cloud Computing (pp. 164–193). IGI Global.

Boopathi, S. (2024c). Energy Cascade Conversion System and Energy-Efficient Infrastructure. In Sustainable Development in AI, Blockchain, and E-Governance Applications (pp. 47–71). IGI Global. doi:10.4018/979-8-3693-1722-8.ch004

Boopathi, S., Kumar, P. K. S., Meena, R. S., Sudhakar, M., & Associates. (2023). Sustainable Developments of Modern Soil-Less Agro-Cultivation Systems: Aquaponic Culture. In Human Agro-Energy Optimization for Business and Industry (pp. 69–87). IGI Global.

Boopathi, S., & Myilsamy, S. (2021). Material removal rate and surface roughness study on Near-dry wire electrical discharge Machining process. *Materials Today: Proceedings*, *45*(9), 8149–8156. doi:10.1016/j.matpr.2021.02.267

Boopathi, S., Thillaivanan, A., Mohammed, A. A., Shanmugam, P., & VR, P. (2022). Experimental investigation on Abrasive Water Jet Machining of Neem Wood Plastic Composite. *IOP: Functional Composites and Structures, 4*, 025001.

Burnett, J. R., & Lisk, T. C. (2021). The future of employee engagement: Real-time monitoring and digital tools for engaging a workforce. In *International Perspectives on Employee Engagement* (pp. 117–128). Routledge. doi:10.4324/9781003142492-9

Costan, E., Gonzales, G., Gonzales, R., Enriquez, L., Costan, F., Suladay, D., Atibing, N. M., Aro, J. L., Evangelista, S. S., Maturan, F., Selerio, E. Jr, & Ocampo, L. (2021). Education 4.0 in developing economies: A systematic literature review of implementation barriers and future research agenda. *Sustainability (Basel)*, *13*(22), 12763. doi:10.3390/su132212763

Das, S., Lekhya, G., Shreya, K., Shekinah, K. L., Babu, K. K., & Boopathi, S. (2024). Fostering Sustainability Education Through Cross-Disciplinary Collaborations and Research Partnerships: Interdisciplinary Synergy. In Facilitating Global Collaboration and Knowledge Sharing in Higher Education With Generative AI (pp. 60–88). IGI Global.

Durairaj, M., Jayakumar, S., Karpagavalli, V., Maheswari, B. U., Boopathi, S., & ... (2023). Utilization of Digital Tools in the Indian Higher Education System During Health Crises. In *Multidisciplinary Approaches to Organizational Governance During Health Crises* (pp. 1–21). IGI Global. doi:10.4018/978-1-7998-9213-7.ch001

Gnanaprakasam, C., Vankara, J., Sastry, A. S., Prajval, V., Gireesh, N., & Boopathi, S. (2023). Long-Range and Low-Power Automated Soil Irrigation System Using Internet of Things: An Experimental Study. In Contemporary Developments in Agricultural Cyber-Physical Systems (pp. 87–104). IGI Global.

Hema, N., Krishnamoorthy, N., Chavan, S. M., Kumar, N., Sabarimuthu, M., & Boopathi, S. (2023). A Study on an Internet of Things (IoT)-Enabled Smart Solar Grid System. In *Handbook of Research on Deep Learning Techniques for Cloud-Based Industrial IoT* (pp. 290–308). IGI Global. doi:10.4018/978-1-6684-8098-4.ch017

Janardhana, K., Singh, V., Singh, S. N., Babu, T. R., Bano, S., & Boopathi, S. (2023). Utilization Process for Electronic Waste in Eco-Friendly Concrete: Experimental Study. In Sustainable Approaches and Strategies for E-Waste Management and Utilization (pp. 204–223). IGI Global.

Karmaker, C. L., Bari, A. M., Anam, M. Z., Ahmed, T., Ali, S. M., de Jesus Pacheco, D. A., & Moktadir, M. A. (2023). Industry 5.0 challenges for post-pandemic supply chain sustainability in an emerging economy. *International Journal of Production Economics*, *258*, 108806. doi:10.1016/j.ijpe.2023.108806

Kshetri, N. (2021). Evolving uses of artificial intelligence in human resource management in emerging economies in the global South: Some preliminary evidence. *Management Research Review*, *44*(7), 970–990. doi:10.1108/MRR-03-2020-0168

Kumar, M., Kumar, K., Sasikala, P., Sampath, B., Gopi, B., & Sundaram, S. (2023). Sustainable Green Energy Generation From Waste Water: IoT and ML Integration. In Sustainable Science and Intelligent Technologies for Societal Development (pp. 440–463). IGI Global.

Maheswari, B. U., Imambi, S. S., Hasan, D., Meenakshi, S., Pratheep, V., & Boopathi, S. (2023). Internet of things and machine learning-integrated smart robotics. In Global Perspectives on Robotics and Autonomous Systems: Development and Applications (pp. 240–258). IGI Global. doi:10.4018/978-1-6684-7791-5.ch010

Malathi, J., Kusha, K., Isaac, S., Ramesh, A., Rajendiran, M., & Boopathi, S. (2024). IoT-Enabled Remote Patient Monitoring for Chronic Disease Management and Cost Savings: Transforming Healthcare. In Advances in Explainable AI Applications for Smart Cities (pp. 371–388). IGI Global.

Mohanty, A., Venkateswaran, N., Ranjit, P., Tripathi, M. A., & Boopathi, S. (2023). Innovative Strategy for Profitable Automobile Industries: Working Capital Management. In Handbook of Research on Designing Sustainable Supply Chains to Achieve a Circular Economy (pp. 412–428). IGI Global.

Mourtzis, D., Angelopoulos, J., & Panopoulos, N. (2022). A Literature Review of the Challenges and Opportunities of the Transition from Industry 4.0 to Society 5.0. *Energies*, *15*(17), 6276. doi:10.3390/en15176276

Rahamathunnisa, U., Subhashini, P., Aancy, H. M., Meenakshi, S., Boopathi, S., & ... (2023). Solutions for Software Requirement Risks Using Artificial Intelligence Techniques. In *Handbook of Research on Data Science and Cybersecurity Innovations in Industry 4.0 Technologies* (pp. 45–64). IGI Global.

Rahardja, U., Aini, Q., Budiarty, F., Yusup, M., & Alwiyah, A. (2021). Socio-economic impact of Blockchain utilization on Digital certificates. *Aptisi Transactions on Management*, *5*(2), 106–111. doi:10.33050/atm.v5i2.1508

Rane, N. (2023). *Transformers in Industry 4.0, Industry 5.0, and Society 5.0: Roles and Challenges.* Academic Press.

Ravisankar, A., Sampath, B., & Asif, M. M. (2023). Economic Studies on Automobile Management: Working Capital and Investment Analysis. In Multidisciplinary Approaches to Organizational Governance During Health Crises (pp. 169–198). IGI Global.

Revathi, S., Babu, M., Rajkumar, N., Meti, V. K. V., Kandavalli, S. R., & Boopathi, S. (2024). Unleashing the Future Potential of 4D Printing: Exploring Applications in Wearable Technology, Robotics, Energy, Transportation, and Fashion. In Human-Centered Approaches in Industry 5.0: Human-Machine Interaction, Virtual Reality Training, and Customer Sentiment Analysis (pp. 131–153). IGI Global.

Samoilovych, A., Popelo, O., Kychko, I., Samoilovych, O., & Olyfirenko, I. (2022). Management of Human Capital Development in The Era of the Digital Economy. *J. Intell. Manag. Decis, 1*(1), 56–66. doi:10.56578/jimd010107

Sánchez-Bayón, A., & Aznar, E. T. (2020). Business and labour culture changes in digital paradigm: Rise and fall of human resources and the emergence of talent development. *Cogito: Multidisciplinary Res. J., 12*, 225.

Strohmeier, S. (2020). Digital human resource management: A conceptual clarification. *German Journal of Human Resource Management, 34*(3), 345–365. doi:10.1177/2397002220921131

Subha, S., Inbamalar, T., Komala, C., Suresh, L. R., Boopathi, S., & Alaskar, K. (2023). A Remote Health Care Monitoring system using internet of medical things (IoMT). *IEEE Explore*, 1–6.

Sundaramoorthy, K., Singh, A., Sumathy, G., Maheshwari, A., Arunarani, A., & Boopathi, S. (2024). A Study on AI and Blockchain-Powered Smart Parking Models for Urban Mobility. In *Handbook of Research on AI and ML for Intelligent Machines and Systems* (pp. 223–250). IGI Global.

Thite, M. (2022). Digital human resource development: Where are we? Where should we go and how do we go there? *Human Resource Development International, 25*(1), 87–103. doi:10.1080/13678868.2020.1842982

Tiwari, M., & Mondal, S. R. (2022). Technological dynamism of workforce management for effective education service delivery during and after Covid-19. *HR Analytics and Digital HR Practices: Digitalization Post COVID, 19*, 199–215. doi:10.1007/978-981-16-7099-2_8

Venkateswaran, N., Vidhya, K., Ayyannan, M., Chavan, S. M., Sekar, K., & Boopathi, S. (2023). A Study on Smart Energy Management Framework Using Cloud Computing. In 5G, Artificial Intelligence, and Next Generation Internet of Things: Digital Innovation for Green and Sustainable Economies (pp. 189–212). IGI Global. doi:10.4018/978-1-6684-8634-4.ch009

Venkateswaran, N., Vidhya, R., Naik, D. A., Raj, T. M., Munjal, N., & Boopathi, S. (2023). Study on Sentence and Question Formation Using Deep Learning Techniques. In *Digital Natives as a Disruptive Force in Asian Businesses and Societies* (pp. 252–273). IGI Global. doi:10.4018/978-1-6684-6782-4.ch015

Chapter 4
Digitalizing HR in Emerging Markets:
A Comprehensive Study of Implementation Challenges and Opportunities

Jaskiran Kaur
https://orcid.org/0000-0002-4452-1807
Lovely Professional University, India

Amit Dutt
Lovely Professional University, India

Geetika Madaan
https://orcid.org/0000-0001-8141-9935
Chandigarh University, India

ABSTRACT

The incorporation of digital human resources (HR) technologies has emerged as a key force behind organizational change in today's quickly changing global environment. This chapter takes a close look at the potential and problems that come up when deploying digital HR technologies in the special environment of developing nations. The first point made in the chapter emphasizes how transformative digital HR solutions can be, from easier hiring processes and more employee engagement to data-driven decision-making. The chapter then turns its attention to emerging nations, where issues including socioeconomic inequality, poor infrastructure, and varied cultural values create particular obstacles to the adoption of technology. An in-depth examination of roadblocks such as a lack of digital infrastructure, a lack of technical awareness, and reluctance to change within established organizational structures reveals the central topic of obstacles. These elements not only prevent the seamless integration of digital HR systems but also force the creation of context-specific implementation strategies. The chapter also highlights a range of promising opportunities among these difficulties. Developing nations may transform HR procedures and promote more inclusivity and accessibility by embracing digital HR solutions. The opportunity to enhance personnel management and spur productivity and creativity lies in improved data analytics

DOI: 10.4018/979-8-3693-1343-5.ch004

and automation. The chapter also emphasizes the importance of digital platforms in democratizing HR services and enabling both businesses and employees to succeed in a changing labor market. This chapter offers a thorough framework for comprehending the complex dynamics of implementing digital HR technology by drawing on a variety of case studies and scholarly ideas. In order to fully realize the revolutionary potential of digital HR technologies in the distinctive setting of developing countries, it needs a sophisticated approach that strikes a balance between technology improvements and local contextualization. This chapter is an excellent resource for scholars, practitioners, and policymakers navigating the uncharted territory of digital HR adoption in various socio-economic contexts as firms try to remain competitive and relevant.

INTRODUCTION

Contemporary organizations are strongly affected by digital "(r)evolution" in many different ways and on multiple levels. The effects of digitalization directly impact all the processes in an organization internally and in relation to external stakeholders (Bajer, 2017; Horváth et al., 2019). In that sense, digitalization is a process of utmost importance for economies and societies which started a long time ago, receiving forceful acceleration by development and adoption of newest technologies such as data mining, Internet of Things, Artificial intelligence, Blockchain technology, Big Data Analytics, etc. (Kagermann, 2015; Schwanholz et al., 2018; Rachinger et al., 2019).

According to previous research, digitalization has been studied mainly in the light of its influence and consequences of its adoption on customer preferences, buying behaviour, marketing, and business performance, while research on how it affects an organization's internal processes and behavior especially in terms of implication to human resources management was fairly seldom (Burchardt et al., 2019; Branca et al., 2020).

Rapid development and adoption of technologies such as Cloud Computing, Edge Computing, Mobile Apps, Social, Big Data Analytics and IoT help organizations to exploit characteristics of such transformative technologies in terms of improving business agility, accelerating innovation and transforming business processes, and introducing new business models (Bajer, 2017; Schwanholz et al., 2018; Rachinger et al., 2019; Zehir et al., 2020).

The adoption of new technologies and digitalization of organizational processes have forced the rapid evolution of HRM practices, requiring the development and adoption of new HR competencies, new forms of employment, and agile HR processes (Kagermann, 2015; Horváth et al., 2019). In that respect and to enable and accommodate rapid technological change and development, organizations are expected to develop procedures and establish practices for a continuous reappraisal of employee competencies, and also to introduce new forms of work organization (Sakellaridis et al., 2011; Götz et al., 2020).

Most of today's HR practices are developed stable and long-lasting employment forms and it can be challenging for an organization to apply those practices to new forms of employment such as permanently changing conditions of contracts based on project principles (Demartini et al., 2018; Cichosz et al., 2020). Thereby, as a result of the adoption of accelerated technological changes, those increasing new flexible employment forms affect also competence and career development practices representing the changeable work environment (Rachinger et al., 2019).

Digitalization implies a complete transformation of business, revision and upgrading or development of new business models, and continuous revision of business strategy and fundamental innovation of business processes (Kagermann, 2015; Schwanholz et al., 2018; Parida et al., 2019). To achieve and maintain business performance, digitalization requires organizations to change organizational culture, and introduce a new type of leadership such as open leadership and self-leadership (Burchardt et al., 2019; Cortellazzo et al., 2019).

To better understand this technological transformation and its impact on organizational functioning, the difference and context between digitization and digitalization (Parviainen et al., 2017; Branca et al., 2020). Digitization means "the action or process of digitizing; the conversion of analog data into digital form" (Berman et al., 2014), while the term digitalization denotes the transformation of business functions and business models into the digital form (Legner et al., 2017; Burchardt et al., 2019; Ritter et al., 2020). Digitalization is also used to denote the integration of digital technologies into various areas of a business.

Digital Transformation

The digital transformation is the crucial facet of the current radical changes in the functioning of modern economies. The emergence and rapid development of digital technologies such as Big Data, Machine Learning (ML), Artificial Intelligence (AI), Internet-of-Things (IoT), Internet-of-Services, Mechatronics, and Advanced Robotics, Cloud Computing, Cybersecurity, Additive Manufacturing, Digital Twin, and Machine to Machine (M2M) communication enable organizations to develop new business models and new employee skills and competencies resulting in achieving efficient product optimization and improving overall organizational performance and competitiveness (Sakellaridis et al., 2011; Bajer, 2017; Demartini et al., 2018; Branca et al., 2020; Zehir et al., 2020).

The concept of digital transformation is widely used to depict various processes of digitization or digitalization of processes and practices within organizations, but there is no consensus regarding a unified definition of it (Li, 2018; Burchardt et al., 2019; Gong et al., 2021). It is defined and described as a strategy (Legner et al., 2017; Schwanholz et al., 2018; Rachinger et al., 2019), a process (Kagermann, 2015; Gong et al., 2021), or a business model (Sakellaridis et al., 2011; Parida et al., 2019; Horváth et al., 2019; Ritter et al., 2020). In general, digital transformation is described as "the use of new digital technologies (..) to enable major business improvements" (Fitzgerald et al., 2014).

It is important to point out that digital transformation is not defined as unique technology, but rather it is viewed as a set of significant change interventions based on a "combination of information, computing, communication, and connectivity technologies"(Bharadwaj et al., 2013). Another definition describes the concept of digital transformation as "a fusion of advanced technologies" that are integrating physical and digital systems (Li, 2018; Burchardt et al., 2019; Cichosz et al., 2020).

The key effect of digital transformation is value creation in terms of operational effectiveness, successful business model, organizational performance, and competitive advantage (Legner et al., 2017; Branca et al., 2020; Gong et al., 2021). It includes also superior customer experience, better relationships with stakeholders, significant cost reduction, and enhanced strategic differentiation (Götz et al., 2020). Digital transformation also implies new concepts and rules of business at both, internal and external levels (Nivlouei, 2014; Demartini et al., 2018; Rachinger et al., 2019).

The digital transformation is considered as a set of ongoing processes affected in great measure with organizational readiness and digital maturity (Rachinger et al., 2019), where under the term digital maturity is understood (a) digital capabilities, which indicate the intensity of digital initiatives (Nivlouei, 2014; Horváth et al., 2019; Mirković et al., 2019) and (b) transformation management capabilities in terms of leadership, culture, change management, governance (Cichosz, 2018; Parida et al., 2019; Gong et al., 2021).

As research results indicate, the implementation of digital transformation processes is a very complex and demanding activity that can be slowed down or stopped by various obstacles that can affect its success. Therefore, the identification of obstacles and understanding their nature and assessment of the probability of their occurrence is an important element of successful adoption of the concept of digital transformation (Horváth et al., 2019; Cichosz et al., 2020). Among numerous possible obstacles, various studies identified employees as the biggest challenge and key factor of success for digital transformation emphasizing employee's competency traps, difficulties with changing employee's mindsets and beliefs and employee's IT knowledge, skills, and capabilities (Bajer, 2017; Legner et al., 2017; Cortellazzo et al., 2019).

Establishing an organizational digital transformation strategy creates a framework for an organization to leverage all the possibilities and features of available new technologies.

The implementation of digital technologies enables organizations to deploy various new processes along the whole value chain. In that respect, digital transformation can be considered as a holistic approach that encompasses all functions, areas, and processes enabling it to utilize organizational digital potentials (Nivlouei, 2014; Rachinger et al., 2019; Mirković et al., 2019). In that sense, digital transformation is not just a transfer of data and documents from analog to digital form, but business processes networking, the development of effective interfaces, and integrated data exchange and management (Legner et al., 2017; Ritter et al., 2020; Kurek, 2021).

Successfully implemented digital transformation supports organizations in:

- Ensuring continuous responsiveness in the context of changing future demand and securing the market position; (Demartini et al., 2018);
- Maintaining competitiveness by applying efficient processes with cost and resources saving;
- Achieving higher product quality (Li, 2018);
- Maximizing organizational performance (Sakellaridis et al., 2011);
- Planning a flexible production (Cichosz et al., 2020)

These can be achieved by the development of features such as real-time capability, interoperability, and the horizontal and vertical integration of production systems (Sakellaridis et al., 2011; Horváth et al., 2019). Besides, it allows organizations to deploy flexible work, through self-organization and multitasking skills, according to education and lifelong learning initiatives.

HRM Challenges Caused By Digital Transformation

"Given the impact of digital transformation on organizational processes and therefore the ability of organizations to adopt more flexible working arrangements for renewal and further development of organizational culture will be a top priority for human resource management (Nivlouei, 2014; Demartini et al., 2018; Gong et al., 2021). Cultural transformation as a consequence of digital transformation is an uncharacteristic challenge for modern HRM practice and requires the integration of HRM strategy with organizational strategy and goals, as well as the development of procedures and standards that support employees operating in changing working conditions and customer requirements (Selmer et al., 2004; Marler et al., 2016; Branca et al., 2020).

The existing organizational culture must find answers related to the shift towards a hybrid work model that takes advantage of remote and office work (Ancarani et al., 2018; Am et al., 2020). Different working conditions such as reduced face-to-face interaction and increasing dispersion of the workforce will lead to a change in social dynamics among employees (Bajer, 2017; Götz et al., 2020).

The introduction of remote working has dramatically changed the way we work, and some employees might undergo the need for additional learning to achieve the same level of efficiency.

Furthermore, due to the effects of digital transformation, the HRM function can introduce a performance management system based on the results achieved, where employee performance is measured exclusively based on their performance and not on time spent at work (Ulrich et al., 2013; Demartini et al., 2018; Horváth et al., 2019). In that sense, digital transformation allows organizations to introduce performance monitoring technology to track employee work performance and results achieved (Nivlouei, 2014; Li, 2018).

Adoption of new technologies enables HRM function in the organization to develop sound succession planning strategies by identifying and rethinking critical roles and establishing contingency plans using scenario-based planning instead of traditional HR planning (Selmer et al., 2004; Sakellaridis et al., 2011; Bajer, 2017). The key success element of this process is effective communication to ensure employee readiness.

In performing its strategic role, learning and development are an integral part of contemporary HRM practice. It especially refers to the improvement of the knowledge and skills of its employees with transferable and specialized skills, thus providing them with a competitive advantage and making them more resistant to change (Ulrich et al., 2013; Ancarani et al., 2018; Kurek, 2021).

An important element of organizational HR strategy is workforce analysis. The implemented digital technologies allow HRM function to measure employee experience, engagement, and satisfaction (Selmer et al., 2004; Fenech et al., 2019). The use of analytics enables organizations to better assess workforce requirements, monitor employees' performance and productivity, optimize revenue, and reduce costs of operation (Nivlouei, 2014; Marler et al., 2016; Li, 2018). It also helps to establish a strategy for talent acquisition, and redefine recruitment processes creating a cost-effective and effective operating model (Horváth et al., 2019; Sima et al., 2020).

The increasing use and growth of remote working have enabled the emergence of alternative employment strategies such as the application of a virtual environment in the process of planning, searching, evaluating, selecting, and hiring of talents (Marler et al., 2016; Rashid, 2017; Cortellazzo et al., 2019). Digital transformation of HRM function is driven by the implementation of technologies such as Artificial Intelligence (AI), Virtual Reality (VR), Augmented Reality (AR), and Blockchain complemented with data science, at the same time enabling the establishment of a decision-making system at the level of the entire organization free from bias (Ancarani et al., 2018; Sima et al., 2020; Zehir et al., 2020; Kurek, 2021).

These technologies may be used to improve all HR functions. Using data science and AI applications, organizations can reduce costs and time by using automated CV screening processes in hiring cycles (Rashid, 2017; Demartini et al., 2018; Götz et al., 2020). Big data and data analytics may be used to improve the recruitment process by helping to identify top talent and assess workforce performance and capacity requirements (Sakellaridis et al., 2011; Manuti et al., 2018; Am et al., 2020). AR and VR technology may be used to improve the orientation process through virtual office tours, without requiring new employees to be physically present. Using virtual and digital learning platforms will enable organizations to accelerate and make re-skilling and up-skilling processes more efficient without investing in the infrastructure and logistics required for hands-on training (Ancarani et al., 2018; Bajer, 2017; Zehir et al., 2020; Sankar et al., 2021).

Some studies have reported also some critical aspects of the implementation of digital technologies. Digital transformation does not only bring positive effects, having particularly negative impacts on low-skilled works and repetitive tasks (Manuti et al., 2018; Fenech et al., 2019; Gong et al., 2021). Despite all the positive perspectives of digital transformation, human experience cannot be replaced. However, to realize all the opportunities provided by the digital transformation, the organization needs to ensure the development of knowledge, skills, and abilities of the workforce to maintain the required level of competitiveness and organizational performance (Demartini et al., 2018; Am et al., 2020). The processes of upgrading knowledge and skills will enable the creation of a workforce adaptable to the rapidly changing new conditions and requirements brought by the application of digital technologies (Ulrich et al., 2013; Marler et al., 2016; Sankar et al., 2021).

Redesigning business processes and integrating them with new digital technologies and aligning jobs and employees will certainly help improve the overall success of the organization (Ancarani et al., 2018; Kurek, 2021). Furthermore, in the context of digital transformation, the opportunity opens up for HRM to influence changes in organizational culture, contribute to improving the relationship between employees and the organization and create an environment that has a positive effect on employee engagement and well-being (Rimon, 2017; Cortellazzo et al., 2019; Sima et al., 2020).

Numerous studies have shown that changes in employee behavior, attitudes, and expectations induced by the implementation of digital transformation processes are the main challenges modern HRM functions are facing within an effort to meet the requirements of operational and strategic adjustment and prepare organizational processes for a changing profile of modern workforce (Ulrich et al., 2013; Manuti et al., 2018; Sankar et al., 2021). In that sense, that way defined so-called digital employees represent significant challenges and areas of intervention for the HR profession (Marler et al., 2016; Fenech et al., 2019).

As confirmed by researches conducted at the level of organizations, the fundamental challenges that HRM will need to address in the context of the application of digital technologies are, among other;

- The impact of digital trends such as cyber, data, cloud, social media and networking, and mobile devices (Kurek, 2021).
- A multi-generation workforce (Sima et al., 2020).
- Hyperconnected employees with integrated work and lifetimes
- Emergence of digitally qualified employees, ie digital citizens (Götz et al., 2020)
- The emergence of business models that have to deal with the challenges of digital disruption (Demartini et al., 2018)
- An employee becomes a consumer of an employer's brand

According to Rimon (2017), six main elements will characterize the perspectives of digital transformation of HRM;

- The consumerization of HR systems - employees will use HR processes as consumers, not just as employees. Establishing a digital employee-manager dialogue (Mirković et al., 2019).
- The transformation of learning (Fenech et al., 2019). • Influence on goal setting (Selmer et al., 2004).

- Efficiency of feedback due to the application of digital transformations using analytical solutions (Demartini et al., 2018).
- Analytics - in-depth analysis, presenting immediate insights into actions for managers and HR professionals (Rimon, 2017).

For the digital transformation to be successful in the domain of responsibility of the HRM function, the participation of employees, managers, and other stakeholders and acceptance of the changes brought by the application of new technologies is crucial. In doing so, HRM processes must be harmonized with the overall organizational strategy and goals in the field of digital transformation (Manuti et al., 2018; Cichosz et al., 2020; Kurek, 2021).

Recently, the principles of digital transformation are applied to both organizations and their employees. Organizations are in search of talents to make recruitment and selection processes as simple as possible, and therefore initiate fact-gathering processes on how digital technologies and tools affect employees (Rashid, 2017; Fenech et al., 2019; Am et al., 2020).

Digital transformation enables mobility and remote work. In that respect, cloud computing offers off-premises applications, and therefore mobility and remote working are becoming standard for many organizations (Ulrich et al., 2013; Ancarani et al., 2018; Am et al., 2020; Kurek, 2021). Various digital tools for work and reporting are available to employees, while managers are given the freedom to seek and recruit employees with adequate qualifications and skills regardless of their place of residence (Schwanholz et al., 2018; Cortellazzo et al., 2019; Sankar et al., 2021). Successful and fluid communication in these working conditions is enabled by various digital tools - social networks, intranets, e-mail and instant messaging applications, forums, VoIP, etc. (Fenech et al., 2019; Gong et al., 2021).

Digital transformation also provides superior features of employee analysis and reporting but also enables performance measurement and prediction of employee activities that were previously difficult to record, greatly improving interaction and collaboration with HR professionals and organization management (Selmer et al., 2004; Marler et al., 2016; Demartini et al., 2018). The use of digital tools has a positive effect on the optimization of work processes and enables the faster and more efficient achievement of organizational goals.

In a digitalized era of businesses, and business processes the traditional management is no longer sufficient. Complicated business processes are manageable only by technology. Increased development throughout the business has diversified and manipulated management and involvement of human capital. Information management has become more systematically manageable through digitalization. Human Resources Management (HRM) has become Digital Human Resources Management (Digital HRM) due to this transformation (Kirilmaz, 2020). While digitalization brings many benefits to the organization and its stakeholders without a doubt, it holds disadvantages related to the application and implementation of these functions. Digitalization of human resource functions in many organizations lacks a clear long-term strategy to apply the transformation, which impact employee's security and loyalty. In addition, a lack of specific budgets to enable the implementation of these short- and long-term goals. In some organization, the process implementation may vary according to the agility level of the organization and resistance towards change. Lack of democracy and agility may lead to longer period when applying upgrades to the digital systems. Furthermore, resistance may come from top level management to adopt or invest in digitalization. This struggle may arise from lack of awareness or lack of expertise in utilizing digital transformation to enhance operation.

Ethical Considerations

Human resource management (HRM) systems are undergoing a digital revolution, which presents a number of ethical issues and difficulties, especially with regard to digital privacy (Zhang & Chen, 2023). Organisations must negotiate a challenging terrain of moral conundrums and privacy issues when they use technology to improve employee experiences and expedite HR procedures.

The collecting and use of employee data is a major ethical concern in the digitization of HRM systems (Divyashree & Mithun, 2023). Organisations get access to a multitude of personal data as they implement technologies for sentiment analysis, performance tracking, and predictive analytics (Bag et al., 2023). It's difficult to strike the correct balance between protecting employees' right to privacy and using this data for organisational gain. In order to guarantee transparent data practises, it is imperative to set ethical rules that explicitly inform employees about the intended use of their data and give them the chance to provide their consent.

In HRM, the problem of informed consent is closely related to digital privacy. Workers might not be completely aware of how much information on them is being gathered and examined (Malik et al., 2020). Organisations must place a high priority on open and understandable communication on data usage to make sure that workers understand the privacy implications of digital HRM technologies (Lumi, 2020). Employees are empowered to make knowledgeable decisions about the use of their personal information because of this transparency, which also builds confidence.

The monitoring of employees presents another ethical conundrum. Real-time tracking of work activities is made possible by digital tools, but there is a thin line separating appropriate monitoring for productivity goals from overbearing surveillance (Renkema, 2021). Establishing moral guidelines that specify appropriate monitoring procedures while upholding the dignity and liberty of workers is vital for organisations. Tighter rules and regulations can aid in preventing abuse and overuse of monitoring powers

One of the most important ethical concerns with the digitalization of HRM technologies is data protection. It is essential to protect confidential employee data from cyber threats, illegal access, and data breaches in order to preserve ethical standards and foster public trust (Singh et al., 2023). To safeguard the confidentiality and integrity of employee data, organisations need to make significant investments in strong cybersecurity measures, carry out frequent audits, and keep up with the latest security risks.

Additionally, the application of machine learning (ML) and artificial intelligence (AI) algorithms in HRM technology carries the danger of algorithmic bias. These algorithms have the potential to reinforce and magnify preexisting biases in hiring, performance reviews, and decision-making procedures if they were trained on biased datasets (Bresciani et al., 2021). Organisations must aggressively address and reduce algorithmic bias in order to promote justice and equity in HR procedures, as required by ethical considerations.

Legal problems and ethical challenges are intimately related in the digitization of HRM systems. To maintain compliance and safeguard individual rights, organisations must abide by data protection rules, such as the General Data Protection Regulation (GDPR), and other pertinent regulations. In addition to putting one at risk legally, breaking these rules compromises the moral underpinnings of digital HR procedures.

Psychological Impact of Digitalisation on Employees

HR is undergoing a digital revolution, and this has a significant psychological impact on workers' experiences, attitudes, and well-being at work. While digitization increases productivity and convenience, it also presents new difficulties that may have a negative psychological effect on workers.

The shift in communication styles and work dynamics is one important factor. Traditional forms of engagement are frequently altered by digital tools, which place a greater emphasis on virtual communication channels (Zahariev et al., 2022). For people who get their energy from in-person relationships, in particular, this change may cause feelings of alienation and detachment. Lack of face-to-face interaction can exacerbate feelings of alienation, which could harm morale among staff members and the cohesiveness of the team.

Furthermore, the lines between work and personal life may become more hazy due to the continuous contact that digital HR technologies enable. Burnout and elevated stress can result from the expectation of being accessible 24/7 and replying to emails and messages outside of typical business hours (Zahariev et al., 2023). Employees who are under constant pressure to be reachable may experience psychological distress as a result of their inability to strike a balance between their personal and professional lives.

The implementation of digital HR systems for performance tracking and data-driven evaluations may have psychological effects on staff members. An environment that is high-pressure and encourages anxiety and apprehension may be created by the continuous evaluation and monitoring of individual performance (Mosca, 2020). Workers' self-esteem and job satisfaction may be negatively impacted by the feeling that they are under continual review. Organisations must make sure that employees feel supported rather than monitored and must communicate openly about the objective of performance measures.

Positively, HR digital transformation can increase worker engagement and empowerment. A sense of autonomy and progress can be facilitated by having access to learning opportunities, individualised development plans, and real-time feedback (Sharma et al., 2022). When used carefully, digital tools can raise morale by giving staff members the tools and data they require for both professional and personal growth.

In summary, the psychological effects of HR digital transformation on staff members are a complicated mix of advantageous and difficult factors. Employers need to be aware of the emotional and mental health of their staff members and address issues with performance reviews, work-life balance, and communication. Fostering a healthy and psychologically supportive work environment requires striking a balance between the benefits of digital HR tools and a thoughtful consideration of the human element of work.

Global Variations in Adoption of Digitalisation of HRM

Globally, there are wide variations in the adoption of digital human resource management (HRM), which can be attributed to a variety of factors including organisational readiness, cultural norms, regulatory contexts, and technology infrastructure. While the implementation of digital HRM may be slowed down in other areas of the world due to infrastructural and cultural preference issues, it tends to be more prevalent and smooth in technologically advanced nations.

Businesses are more likely to adopt digital HRM solutions in developed economies like the US, Western Europe, and some regions of Asia (Malik et al., 2020). These areas frequently have strong technological infrastructures, workers who are proficient in digital technologies, and legislative environments that promote the use of digital solutions for HR tasks. The need for efficiency, data-driven decision-making, and the competitive edge that modern HR solutions provide are what are driving adoption.

However, there can be obstacles in the way of the broad implementation of digital HRM in emerging economies (Tapiwa et al., 2022). Advanced HR system deployment may be hindered by lower digital literacy rates, restricted access to technology, and financial limitations. In certain areas, businesses might give more weight to entry-level HR features than complex digital solutions, concentrating on core functions like payroll and attendance monitoring.

The adoption of digital HRM is significantly influenced by cultural variables as well. Certain cultures might be more accepting of technology in the workplace because they see it as a means of advancement and productivity (Mosca, 2020). Others, on the other hand, could be more traditionalist and value face-to-face interactions in HR procedures. Digital HRM adoption frequently depends on ensuring that technology solutions complement current work practises rather than upend them and that they are in line with cultural norms.

Global differences are also evident in regulatory environments. Strict data protection laws, like the General Data Protection Regulation (GDPR) in Europe, can affect how businesses go about putting digital HRM systems into place. Adherence to local rules and regulations assumes paramount importance in ascertaining the viability and extent of digital HRM implementation (Bag et al., 2023)

In summary, there are significant regional differences in the uptake of digital HRM, which can be attributed to a variety of technological, cultural, economic, and legal variables. To guarantee successful implementation and alignment with local practises, organisations must carefully negotiate these dynamics and customise their approach to the unique environment of each region.

Purpose and Methods

The global economic situation forced for better preparedness for competitive challenges on digitalization of all the process. As the consequences of rapid technological development, organizations are faced with an implementation of digitization in all the processes. Digitalizing the HRM is the hot topic these days in all the corporate world. The purpose of this paper is to understand the opportunities and challenges of digitalizing the human resource management by evaluating the previous literature in a broader spectrum of digitalized HRM functions, that would illustrate a more balanced perspective of Digital HRM. According to Creswell & Creswell (2017), search methods determine how the researcher will collect, analyze, and understand the data of a specific study. This study was based on a secondary data analysis on the opportunities and challenges of digitalizing the HRM functions. Secondary analysis is a systematic process with procedural and evaluative steps to develop the research objective, then the identification of the dataset, and thorough evaluation the dataset (Johnston, 2017).

Opportunities of Digitalizing Human Resource Management

Digital transformation budgets according to Deloitte e-survey were going to increase by 25 percent in 2020 with the beginning of digitalized function and automated resources such as artificial intelligence (AI), blockchain, automated performance management and machine learning. This transformation will vary depending on Human resources management team and their perception, capabilities, and flexibility. In today's worlds that are numerous organizations that still rely on Excel sheets to gather and analyze data to make decisions. Digitalizing some of these data collection and analysis function will impact the

HR role, competency, and processes. The digital transformation and automated processes will allow time reduction, and remove repetitive tasks and actions, maximize employee's engagement, and enhanced time management to benefit the organization. In addition, digitalization will improve the time span of introducing digital solutions to improve the organization. Employees will get more freedom from repetitive tasks like filing and organizing and allow additional time to focus on introducing creative tasks. Digitalization will provide more simplicity and easy solutions when it comes to addressing employees needs and departments requirements. Anonymity is also an extra advantage especially during employee feedback, KPI evaluation and or whistleblowing actions. Moreover, there are countless of advantages and benefits to implement digitalization across the organization. The fast-paced characteristics of digitalization have a more significant wide-reaching impact than perhaps is expected, in the sense that it is changing human behavior and thus will lead to a profound domino effect on organizations. Therefore, it is of relevance for every human resource manager to relate to this digitalization (Al Haziazi et al, 2021). For the organization to implement digitalization it must start at the human resource management level. The organization should define the goal to implement digital transformation. Then identify the implementation process within the human resources team with the time frame of the implementation.

Afterwards, prepare the organization for the digitalization change and the intervention process at whichemployees will be involved in. Change within the organization or among the stakeholder will always face resistance, either towards the technology or the execution of the technology. Therefore, it's important for the organization to maintain a level of consistency in the transformation so it does not affect the benefit that would be derived out.

CONCLUSION

Mobility and remote working as significant consequences of the introduction of the digital transformation process have proven to be very successful, so organizations will build hybrid work models based on the intensive application of digital tools that support remote working and thus achieve increased productivity and efficiency. The role of the HRM function in this context will relate to the transformation of jobs and organizational structures and their adaptation to new standards and the need to increase operational efficiency. Digital transformation will enable the creation of a very flexible organizational structure and, accordingly, open space for the effective transfer of workers. The discussed processes will lead to the creation of organizational forms whose basic characteristics will be flexibility, scalability, and adaptability to new uncertain business conditions. HRM will play a very important role in these processes with a focus on retraining and upgrading the knowledge and skills of existing employees, which will require the use of effective digital tools (big data analytics) and extensive reporting due to the need to map employee competencies. The consequence of such trends will be that jobs will increasingly be designed for employees who possess transferable skills and can use them in a broader context. Digitization will enable organizations to design flexible work arrangements whose basic characteristics are flexible working hours and place of work. From the conducted research, it became obvious that the digital transformation has made significant changes in the organization and the way employees work in the organization. The change is also reflected in the change in the role that HRM has played in measuring employee performance. the application of digital technologies enables the establishment of a performance management system that is oriented towards the evaluation of the achieved results of employees and not about the time spent at work. It also implies the redesign of the employee appraisal system and its harmonization with new circumstances and needs arising from the implementation of the digital transformation process in the organization and especially within the HRM function. Using big data analytics and AI for digitization of working places caused changes in the organization of work and working environment and adoption of modern working methods. The transformation of HRM driven by the use of modern digital technologies has also strongly impacted an organization's overall business performance. Digital transformation processes in organizations have contributed to reducing the need for physical and repetitive work operations and created an increased need for a highly-skilled workforce. As a result of the application of digital technologies, the ways of hiring and selecting employees have changed. The digital transformation has conditioned radical changes in the organization of work, but also the functioning of the organization at all levels. It should be noted that in the context of digital transformation, not all organizations see the need to introduce modern digital solutions. The reason for this can be found in the specifics of organizational culture as well as employee resistance to change. There is evidence in the available literature that the application of digital tools based on artificial intelligence is not always the cause of staff reductions, but maybe a reason for better utilization and advanced management of employee knowledge and skills Although digital transformation introduces many positive perspectives, uncritically insisting on change can cause negative effects and jeopardize the achievement of optimal results. It is very important to detect possible risks related to information security, data access, and confidentiality and to find strategies to reduce or eliminate security threats by improving infrastructure and security processes.

REFERENCES

Al Haziazi, M., Muthuraman, S., Al Yahyaei, N., & Al Balusi, A. (2021, March). Influence of HR Digital Transformation in the Cognitive Technology Era of the Sultanate of Oman. In *2021 7th International Conference on Information Management (ICIM)* (pp. 123-127). IEEE. 10.1109/ICIM52229.2021.9417155

Am, E. N., Affandi, A., Udobong, A., Sarwani, S., & Hernawan, H. (2020). „Implementation of human resource management in the adaptation period for new habits. *International Journal of Educational Administration, Management, and Leadership*, *1*(1), 19–26. doi:10.51629/ijeamal.v1i1.4

Ancarani, A., & Di Mauro, C. (2018). Successful digital transformations need a focus on the individual. In F. Schupp & H. Wöhner (Eds.), *Digitalisierung im Einkauf* (pp. 11–26). Springer Gabler. doi:10.1007/978-3-658-16909-1_2

Bag, S., Srivastava, G., Cherrafi, A., Ali, A., & Singh, R. K. (2023). Data-driven insights for circular and sustainable food supply chains: An empirical exploration of big data and predictive analytics in enhancing social sustainability performance. *Business Strategy and the Environment*.

Bajer, J. (2017). „Digital transformation needs the human touch. *Strategic HR Review*, *16*(2), 91–92. doi:10.1108/SHR-02-2017-0011

Berman, S., & Marshall, A. (2014). The next digital transformation: From an individual centered to an everyone-to-everyone economy. *Strategy and Leadership*, *42*(5), 9–17. doi:10.1108/SL-07-2014-0048

Bharadwaj, A., El Sawy, O., Pavlou, P., & Venkatraman, N. (2013). Digital business strategy: Toward the next generation of insights. *Management Information Systems Quarterly*, *37*(2), 471–482. doi:10.25300/MISQ/2013/37:2.3

Branca, T. A., Fornai, B., Colla, V., Murri, M. M., Streppa, E., & Schröder, A. J. (2020). „The challenge of digitalization in the steel sector. *Metals*, *10*(2), 288–311. doi:10.3390/met10020288

Bresciani, S., Ferraris, A., Romano, M., & Santoro, G. (2021). Human resource management and digitalisation. In *Digital transformation management for agile organizations: A compass to sail the digital world* (pp. 117–138). Emerald Publishing Limited. doi:10.1108/978-1-80043-171-320211007

Burchardt, C., & Maisch, B. (2019). „Digitalization needs a cultural change–examples of applying Agility and Open Innovation to drive the digital transformation. *Procedia CIRP*, *84*, 112–117. doi:10.1016/j.procir.2019.05.009

Cichosz, M. (2018). Digitalization and competitiveness in the logistics service industry. *Ementor*, *77*(5), 73–82. doi:10.15219/em77.1392

Cichosz, M., Wallenburg, C. M., & Knemeyer, A. M. (2020). „Digital transformation at logistics service providers: Barriers, success factors and leading practices. *International Journal of Logistics Management*, *31*(2), 209–238. doi:10.1108/IJLM-08-2019-0229

Cortellazzo, L., Bruni, E., & Zampieri, R. (2019). The role of leadership in a digitalized world: A review. *Frontiers in Psychology*, *10*, 1–21. doi:10.3389/fpsyg.2019.01938 PMID:31507494

Creswell, J. W., & Creswell, J. D. (2017). *Research design: Qualitative, quantitative, and mixed methods approaches*. Sage Publications.

Demartini, M., Pinna, C., Tonelli, F., Terzi, S., Sansone, C., & Testa, C. (2018). Food industry digitalization: From challenges and trends to opportunities and solutions. *IFAC-PapersOnLine*, *51*(11), 1371–1378. doi:10.1016/j.ifacol.2018.08.337

Divyashree, K. M., & Mithun, R. (2023). A study on digitalization in HRM practices. *Commerce and Management*, *II*, 95.

Fenech, R., Baguant, P., & Ivanov, D. (2019). „The changing role of human resource management in an era of digital transformation. *Journal of Management Information and Decision Sciences*, *22*(2), 1–10.

Fitzgerald, M., Kruschwitz, N., Bonnet, D., & Welch, M. (2014). Embracing digital technology: A new strategic imperative. *MIT Sloan Management Review*, *55*(2), 1–16.

Gong, C., & Ribiere, V. (2021). Developing a unified definition of digital transformation. *Technovation*, *102*, 102217. doi:10.1016/j.technovation.2020.102217

Götz, M., & Jankowska, B. (2020). Adoption of Industry 4.0 Technologies and Company Competitiveness: Case Studies from a Post-Transition Economy. *National Research University Higher School of Economics*, *14*(4), 61–78. doi:10.17323/2500-2597.2020.4.61.78

Horváth, D., & Szabó, R. Z. (2019). Driving forces and barriers of Industry 4.0: Do multinational and small and medium-sized companies have equal opportunities? *Technological Forecasting and Social Change*, *146*, 119–132. doi:10.1016/j.techfore.2019.05.021

Johnston, M. P. (2017). Secondary data analysis: A method of which the time has come. *Qualitative and Quantitative Methods in Libraries, 3*(3), 619-626.

Kagermann, H. (2015). Change through digitization - Value creation in the age of Industry 4.0. In *Management of permanent change* (pp. 23–45). Springer Gabler. doi:10.1007/978-3-658-05014-6_2

Kirilmaz, S. (2020). Digital Transformation and Human Resources Management: Digital HRApplication Examples of Businesses. *Pressacademia, 11*(1), 224–225. doi:10.17261/Pressacademia.2020.1199

Kurek, D. (2021). Use of Modern IT Solutions in the HRM Activities: Process Automation and Digital Employer Branding. *European Research Studies, 24*(1), 152–170. doi:10.35808/ersj/2035

Legner, C., Eymann, T., Hess, T., Matt, C., Böhmann, T., Drews, P., Mädche, A., Urbach, N., & Ahlemann, F. (2017). Digitalization: Opportunity and challenge for the business and information systems engineering community. *Business & Information Systems Engineering, 59*(4), 301–308. doi:10.1007/s12599-017-0484-2

Li, F. (2018). The digital transformation of business models in the creative industries: A holistic framework and emerging trends. *Technovation.*

Lumi, A. (2020). The impact of digitalisation on human resources development. *Prizren Social Science Journal, 4*(3), 39–46. doi:10.32936/pssj.v4i3.178

Malik, A., Srikanth, N. R., & Budhwar, P. (2020). Digitisation, artificial intelligence (AI) and HRM. *Human resource management: Strategic and international perspectives, 88.*

Manuti, A., & de Palma, P. D. (2018). How to Develop Digital HRM Practices in the Cognitive Technology Era: Evidences from a Case Study. In *Digital HR* (pp. 67–79). Palgrave Macmillan. doi:10.1007/978-3-319-60210-3_5

Marler, J. H., & Parry, E. (2016). Human resource management, strategic involvement and e-HRM technology. *International Journal of Human Resource Management*, *27*(19), 2233–2253. doi:10.1080/09585192.2015.1091980

Mirković, V., Lukić, J., Lazarević, S., & Vojinović, Ž. (2019). Key characteristics of organizational structure that supports digital transformation. *International Scientific Conference Strategic Management and Decision Support Systems in Strategic Management.* 10.46541/978-86-7233-380-0_46

Mosca, M. (2020). *Digitalization of HRM: A study of success factors and consequences in the last decade* (Master's thesis, University of Twente).

Nivlouei, F. B. (2014). Electronic Human Resource Management System: The Main Element in Capacitating Globalization Paradigm. *International Journal of Business and Social Science*, *5*(2), 147–159.

Parida, V., Sjödin, D., & Reim, W. (2019). Reviewing literature on digitalization, business model innovation, and sustainable industry: Past achievements and future promises. *Sustainability (Basel)*, *11*(2), 391–410. doi:10.3390/su11020391

Parviainen, P., Tihinen, M., Kääriäinen, J., & Teppola, S. (2017). Tackling the digitalization challenge: how to benefit from digitalization in practice. *International Journal of Information Systems and Project Management, 5*(1), 63-77.

Rachinger, M., Rauter, R., Müller, C., Vorraber, W., & Schirgi, E. (2019). Digitalization and its influence on business model innovation. *Journal of Manufacturing Technology Management*, *30*(8), 1143–1160. doi:10.1108/JMTM-01-2018-0020

Rashid, B. (2017). Digital Transformation And Innovation In Today's Business World. Available at https://www.forbes.com/sites/brianrashid/2017/06/13/digital-transformationandinnovation-in-todays-business-world

Renkema, M. (2021). AI, Digitalisation, and HRM: Foundations, Extensions, and New Directions on AI, Digitalisation, and HRM. In New Directions in the Future of Work (pp. 77-96). Emerald Publishing Limited.

Rimon, G. (2017). Six surprising truths about how digital transformation will change HR. *Strategic HR Review*, *16*(2), 102–104. doi:10.1108/SHR-02-2017-0010

Ritter, T., & Pedersen, C. L. (2020). Digitization capability and the digitalization of business models in business-to-business firms: Past, present, and future. *Industrial Marketing Management*, *86*, 180–190. doi:10.1016/j.indmarman.2019.11.019

Sakellaridis, K., & Stiakakis, E. (2011). Business model change due to ICT integration: An application to the entertainment industry. *International Journal of Computer Information Systems and Industrial Management Applications*, *3*, 539–551.

Sankar, J. P., & Yogan, G. (2021). Human Resource Digital Transformation of IT Sector in India. *Webology*, *18*(1), 219–232. doi:10.14704/WEB/V18I1/WEB18085

Schwanholz, J., & Graham, T. (2018). Digital Transformation: New Opportunities and Challenges for Democracy? In J. Schwanholz, T. Graham, & P. T. Stoll (Eds.), *Managing Democracy in the Digital Age* (pp. 1–7). Springer. doi:10.1007/978-3-319-61708-4_1

Selmer, J., & Chiu, R. (2004). Required human resources competencies in the future: A framework for developing HR executives in Hong Kong. *Journal of World Business*, *39*(4), 324–336. doi:10.1016/j.jwb.2004.08.001

Sharma, A., Tyagi, R., Verma, A., & Paul, A. (2022). Review on Digitalisation and Artificial Intelligence in human Resource function of Energy sector. *Water and Energy International*, *65*(2), 38–46.

Sima, V., Gheorghe, I. G., Subić, J., & Nancu, D. (2020). Influences of the industry 4.0 revolution on the human capital development and consumer behavior: A systematic review. *Sustainability (Basel)*, *12*(10), 1–28. doi:10.3390/su12104035

Singh, G., Tiwari, P., & Garg, V. (2023). HRM Digitalisation: Exploring Success and Outcomes. In The Adoption and Effect of Artificial Intelligence on Human Resources Management, Part B (pp. 199-219). Emerald Publishing Limited.

Tapiwa, G. G., Pedzisai, P., Bernard, N., & Mervis, C. (2022). Digitalisation of Human Resources Systems and Process Necessary for Public Sector Transformation in Zimbabwe. In *Transformational Human Resources Management in Zimbabwe: Solutions for the Public Sector in the 21st Century* (pp. 61–74). Springer Nature Singapore. doi:10.1007/978-981-19-4629-5_5

Technologies, A. I. Strategic HRM. In U. Hacioglu (Ed.), *Digital Business Strategies in Blockchain Ecosystems, Contributions to Management Science*. Springer.

Ulrich, D., Younger, J., Brockbank, W., & Ulrich, M. D. (2013). The state of the HR profession. *Human Resource Management, 52*(3), 463–464. doi:10.1002/hrm.21536

Zahariev, A., Ivanova, P., Zaharieva, G., Slaveva, K., Mihaylova, M., & Todorova, T. (2023). Interplay between CSR and the Digitalisation of Bulgarian Financial Enterprises: HRM Approach and Pandemic Evidence. *Journal of Risk and Financial Management, 16*(9), 385. doi:10.3390/jrfm16090385

Zahariev, A., Zaharieva, G., Mihaylova, M., & Ivanova, K. (2022). Digitalisation in human resource management: Evidence from the Bulgarian banking and insurance sectors. *Economic and Social Development: Book of Proceedings*, 261-269.

Zehir, C., Karaboğa, T., & Başar, D. (2020). The transformation of human resource management and its impact on overall business performance: big data analytics and AI technologies in strategic HRM. *Digital Business Strategies in Blockchain Ecosystems: Transformational Design and Future of Global Business*, 265-279.

Zhang, J., & Chen, Z. (2023). Exploring Human Resource Management Digital Transformation in the Digital Age. *Journal of the Knowledge Economy*, 1–17. doi:10.1007/s13132-023-01214-y

Chapter 5
Embracing Circular Economy Principles for Sustainable Green Supply Chain Management in Manufacturing Industries

K. Sankara Moorthy
https://orcid.org/0000-0002-6853-6878
Faculty of Management, SRM Institute of Science and Technology, India

L. Raja
Department of Electronics and Communication Engineering, Sri Eshwar College of Engineering, India

G. Balakrishnan
Department of Commerce, Faculty of Science and Humanities, SRM Institute of Science and Technology, India

A. Vijayalakshmi
Department of Chemistry, R.M.K. Engineering College, Thiruvallur, India

S. Satheesh Kumar
Department of Business Administration, Panimalar Engineering College, Chennai, India

ABSTRACT

The circular economy is a sustainable approach in the manufacturing sector that focuses on long-lasting product design, remanufacturing, recycling, and waste reduction. This approach optimizes resource utilization, reduces reliance on finite resources, and minimizes waste generation, contributing to environmental conservation and mitigating climate change's effects. Digital technologies and data analytics play a crucial role in promoting a circular economy in manufacturing supply chains, with IoT, AI, and blockchain enhancing visibility, traceability, and collaboration. The challenges of implementing circular economy principles are discussed, along with the potential economic benefits of sustainable production and consumption patterns. Case studies from successful manufacturing companies are also examined.

DOI: 10.4018/979-8-3693-1343-5.ch005

INTRODUCTION

The concept of a circular economy has gained significant traction in recent years as a sustainable alternative to the traditional linear economy model. In a linear economy, resources are extracted, processed into products, consumed, and then discarded as waste, leading to resource depletion and environmental degradation. In contrast, a circular economy aims to decouple economic growth from resource consumption by promoting the reuse, recycling, and regeneration of materials and products. This paradigm shift towards circularity holds immense promise for addressing pressing environmental challenges and fostering sustainable development across various industries, including manufacturing (Kazancoglu et al., 2021).

The manufacturing sector is crucial for the global economy, but traditional practices often prioritize efficiency over environmental considerations, leading to resource depletion, pollution, and waste generation. The linear production and consumption model exacerbates these issues. The adoption of circular economy principles offers a chance for manufacturing industries to transition towards sustainable and resource-efficient business models. By embracing circularity, manufacturers can rethink product design, production processes, and supply chain management, reducing their environmental footprint and enhancing long-term resilience (Kazakova & Lee, 2022).

The circular economy emphasizes the importance of designing products with longevity and durability, reducing resource consumption and waste generation. This approach involves focusing on durability, reparability, and upgradability, allowing manufacturers to extend product lifespans and minimize frequent replacements. Disassembly and recycling also promote resource circulation. Remanufacturing and refurbishment are key components of the circular economy, extending product life and minimizing waste. Remanufacturing involves restoring used products to like-new condition, often incorporating upgrades to enhance performance and functionality. This approach captures value from existing resources and reduces demand for virgin materials (M. Hussain & Malik, 2020).

Recycling is a key aspect of the circular economy, enabling manufacturers to recover valuable resources and reduce the need for virgin raw materials. Advanced recycling technologies can recover high-quality materials from complex products like electronics and automotive components, enhancing resource efficiency and waste reduction. The circular economy aims for waste reduction and optimization of resource utilization, with manufacturers adopting lean production principles and minimizing waste generation at every stage. This leads to cost savings and reduced environmental impact (Karmaker et al., 2023).

The integration of circular economy principles into manufacturing operations requires a comprehensive approach that includes product design, production processes, supply chain management, and end-of-life strategies. Collaboration among stakeholders, including manufacturers, suppliers, consumers, and policymakers, is crucial for systemic change and overcoming barriers to adoption. The transition towards a circular economy can transform the manufacturing industry, create value from waste, minimize resource consumption, and contribute to natural ecosystem preservation. Collaboration, innovation, and bold leadership are key drivers for success (Edwin Cheng et al., 2022).

The need for sustainable practices in manufacturing industries is growing due to global concerns over environmental degradation, resource scarcity, and climate change. The need for a shift towards sustainable green supply chain management (GSCM) is urgent. This introduction explores the challenges and opportunities of integrating sustainability principles into manufacturing supply chains, focusing on environmental stewardship, social responsibility, and economic viability. Traditional manufacturing practices, such as a linear flow of materials from extraction to disposal, pose significant environmental and social risks, including resource depletion, pollution, labor exploitation, and social inequality (Edwin Cheng et al., 2022).

Sustainable green supply chain management (GSCM) is a strategic approach that combines economic development, environmental preservation, and social equity. It covers the entire supply chain, from raw material sourcing to end-of-life disposal. By integrating sustainability considerations, manufacturers can reduce their environmental footprint, enhance operational efficiency, and create shared value for stakeholders. The principle of environmental stewardship is central to GSCM, focusing on minimizing resource consumption, reducing waste generation, and mitigating environmental impacts throughout the product lifecycle. This approach offers numerous opportunities for manufacturers to implement sustainable practices and improve environmental performance (Ciliberto et al., 2021).

Sustainable GSCM involves social responsibility, fair labor practices, human rights protection, and community engagement. It enhances manufacturers' reputation, mitigates risks, and builds resilience in a global marketplace. Economic viability is crucial, as sustainable practices can lead to cost savings, operational efficiencies, and enhanced brand value. Lean manufacturing, supply chain optimization, product innovation, and market differentiation are all opportunities for driving business growth and creating shared value for all stakeholders. Despite potential additional costs, sustainable GSCM offers numerous opportunities for business growth and shared value (Lu et al., 2024).

The transition to sustainable green supply chain management necessitates visionary leadership, strategic collaboration, and innovative solutions. This approach mitigates environmental risks, ensures regulatory compliance, and opens new growth opportunities. Principles of environmental stewardship, social responsibility, and economic viability guide the industry towards a prosperous future (Jaeger & Upadhyay, 2020).

Objectives of the Chapter

- The chapter provides a thorough understanding of sustainable green supply chain management (GSCM) in the manufacturing industry, outlining key principles, challenges, and opportunities, laying the groundwork for further exploration and analysis.
- The chapter explores the integration of sustainability principles into manufacturing supply chains, focusing on product design, production processes, procurement, logistics, and end-of-life management. It uses case studies, best practices, and empirical evidence to illustrate the practical implications of sustainable GSCM in real-world settings.
- The chapter evaluates the environmental, social, and economic impacts of sustainable GSCM practices in manufacturing industries, focusing on the benefits and challenges of these initiatives, providing insights into the triple bottom line implications of adopting sustainable GSCM strategies.
- The chapter explores the obstacles and enablers to implementing sustainable GSCM practices in manufacturing supply chains, focusing on factors like organizational culture, regulatory frameworks, technological capabilities, and stakeholder collaboration, to help overcome obstacles and maximize success.
- The chapter offers actionable recommendations for advancing sustainable GSCM practices in manufacturing industries, based on research, industry best practices, and expert perspectives. It covers policy interventions, technological innovations, capacity-building initiatives, and stakeholder engagement strategies to drive positive change and foster sustainability.

THEORETICAL FRAMEWORK

The circular economy is a shift from traditional production and consumption models, focusing on regenerative materials through reuse, repair, remanufacturing, and recycling. It aims to decouple economic growth from resource depletion and environmental degradation, promoting sustainable development and long-term prosperity (Kazancoglu et al., 2021; Maranesi & De Giovanni, 2020).

Important Principles of the Circular Economy

- ***Design for Durability and Longevity:*** Emphasizing product design that prioritizes durability, reparability, and longevity can extend the lifespan of products and reduce the need for frequent replacements. Designing products for disassembly and modularization facilitates easier repair, refurbishment, and recycling, thereby promoting resource efficiency and waste reduction (Vignesh et al., 2018).
- ***Closed-Loop Material Flows:*** Central to the circular economy is the concept of closing the loop of material flows by maximizing the recovery and reuse of materials and components. Through practices such as remanufacturing, refurbishment, and recycling, manufacturers can extract maximum value from end-of-life products and minimize the extraction of virgin resources, thereby reducing environmental impacts and conserving natural resources (Dhanya et al., 2023a).
- ***Resource Optimization and Waste Reduction:*** By optimizing resource use and minimizing waste generation throughout the product lifecycle, the circular economy seeks to maximize resource efficiency and minimize environmental footprint. Lean manufacturing principles, resource-efficient production processes, and waste reduction strategies play a crucial role in achieving these objectives, leading to cost savings, operational efficiencies, and environmental benefits (Reddy et al., 2023).
- ***Collaborative Networks and Circular Business Models:*** Collaboration among stakeholders across the value chain is essential for implementing circular economy principles effectively. Circular business models, such as product-as-a-service, sharing platforms, and closed-loop supply chains, foster collaboration and incentivize resource conservation and reuse. By shifting from a transactional to a relational approach, businesses can create shared value for stakeholders while advancing sustainability goals (Z. Hussain et al., 2023a; Ingle et al., 2023a).

Relationship Between Circular Economy and Green Supply Chain Management

Green supply chain management (GSCM) and the circular economy are closely related, as they both aim to promote sustainability and minimize environmental impacts throughout the supply chain. Both concepts complement and enhance each other, ensuring a more sustainable and efficient supply chain. Both concepts are mutually reinforcing in their goals (Maranesi & De Giovanni, 2020; Zhang et al., 2023). The circular economy and GSCM are interconnected concepts aimed at promoting sustainability and minimizing environmental impacts in manufacturing supply chains. Integrating circular economy principles into GSCM practices can improve resource efficiency, reduce waste, and create value for stakeholders.

- ***Resource Efficiency and Waste Reduction:*** Both the circular economy and GSCM aim to optimize resource use and minimize waste generation throughout the supply chain. By adopting circular economy principles such as remanufacturing, recycling, and waste reduction strategies, manufacturers can reduce their environmental footprint and enhance resource efficiency, thereby advancing the goals of GSCM.
- ***Sustainable Procurement and Supply Chain Collaboration:*** GSCM emphasizes sustainable procurement practices, including the selection of suppliers based on environmental criteria, ethical sourcing, and supply chain transparency. The circular economy encourages collaboration among stakeholders across the supply chain to promote resource conservation, reuse, and recycling. By integrating circular economy principles into procurement processes and fostering collaboration with suppliers, organizations can enhance the sustainability of their supply chains and reduce environmental risks (Mohanty et al., 2023a; Verma et al., 2024a).
- ***Product Lifecycle Management and End-of-Life Strategies:*** Both the circular economy and GSCM recognize the importance of managing products throughout their lifecycle and implementing effective end-of-life strategies to minimize waste and maximize resource recovery. By designing products for disassembly, repair, and recycling, manufacturers can facilitate the transition to a circular economy and reduce the environmental impact of products throughout their lifecycle. GSCM provides a framework for integrating these principles into supply chain management practices, ensuring that environmental considerations are addressed from product conception to disposal.

STRATEGIES FOR IMPLEMENTING CIRCULAR ECONOMY PRINCIPLES IN MANUFACTURING

Product Design for Longevity and Durability

Product design plays a crucial role in promoting sustainability and circularity in manufacturing processes and supply chains by prioritizing durability, reparability, and longevity, thereby extending product lifespan, reducing resource consumption, and minimizing waste. Product design for longevity and durability is crucial for advancing circular economy principles in the manufacturing industry (Agrawal, Magulur, et al., 2023; Gift et al., 2024). By prioritizing durability, reparability, and resource efficiency,

Figure 1. Strategies for implementing circular economy principles in manufacturing

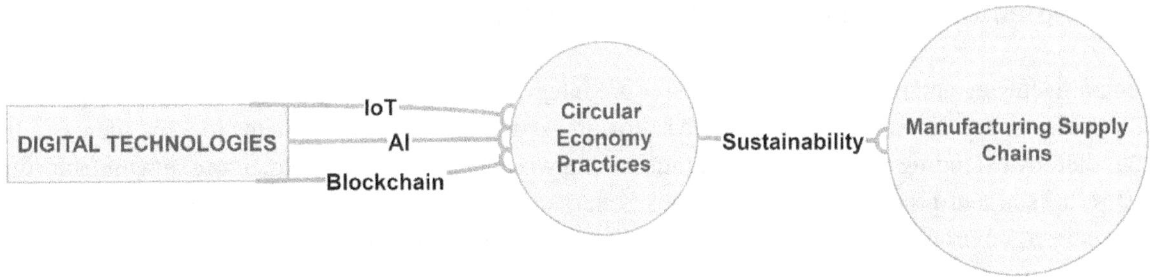

manufacturers can create sustainable products that meet consumer and stakeholder needs, driving positive change and shaping a sustainable future for generations to come (Edwin Cheng et al., 2022; M. Hussain & Malik, 2020). The figure 1 illustrates various strategies for implementing circular economy principles in manufacturing.

- ***Durability Assessments:*** Conducting thorough durability assessments during the product design phase to identify potential weaknesses, failure points, and areas for improvement. By designing products to withstand prolonged use and environmental stressors, manufacturers can enhance product lifespan and reduce the frequency of replacements.
- ***Material Selection:*** Choosing high-quality, durable materials with minimal environmental impact is essential for designing long-lasting products. Selecting materials that are recyclable, biodegradable, or derived from renewable sources promotes resource conservation and facilitates end-of-life recovery and recycling (Murali et al., 2023).
- ***Modular Design:*** Adopting a modular design approach enables products to be easily disassembled, repaired, and upgraded, prolonging their lifespan and reducing the need for replacement. Modular design allows for the replacement of individual components or modules, rather than the entire product, reducing costs and minimizing waste.
- ***Standardization and Compatibility:*** Standardizing product components and interfaces enhances compatibility and interoperability, enabling interchangeability and facilitating repairs, upgrades, and replacements. Designing products with standardized parts and interfaces promotes resource efficiency and simplifies end-of-life management.
- ***Design for Repairability:*** Incorporating features that facilitate repair and maintenance, such as accessible fasteners, removable panels, and diagnostic capabilities, empowers consumers and service providers to extend the lifespan of products through timely repairs and maintenance. Designing products for ease of repair reduces the likelihood of premature disposal and contributes to resource conservation.
- ***Extended Producer Responsibility (EPR):*** Embracing the principles of extended producer responsibility involves assuming responsibility for products throughout their lifecycle, including end-of-life management. Implementing take-back programs, product stewardship initiatives, and recycling schemes enables manufacturers to recover valuable materials and components from end-of-life products, closing the loop and promoting circularity.
- ***User-Centric Design:*** Engaging end-users in the design process and soliciting feedback on product preferences, usability, and durability can inform design decisions and ensure that products meet the needs and expectations of consumers. User-centric design fosters customer satisfaction, loyalty, and brand reputation, while also promoting sustainable consumption patterns.

Remanufacturing and Refurbishment Processes

Remanufacturing and refurbishment processes are integral components of a circular economy approach in manufacturing. These processes involve restoring used products or components to a like-new condition, thereby extending their lifespan and minimizing waste generation. Implementing remanufacturing and refurbishment practices offers numerous benefits, including resource conservation, cost savings, and reduced environmental impact. The strategies and considerations for integrating remanufacturing and refurbishment processes into manufacturing operations are explained (Ferreira & Gonçalves, 2021; Zacharaki et al., 2021).

- ***Product Assessment and Disassembly:*** The remanufacturing process begins with the assessment of used products or components to determine their condition and suitability for remanufacturing. Products are disassembled into individual components, which are inspected for wear, damage, or defects. Components that meet quality standards are selected for refurbishment, while those that are beyond repair are responsibly recycled (Ali et al., 2024; Myilsamy Sureshkumar, 2018; Vennila et al., 2022).
- ***Cleaning and Repair:*** Once disassembled, components undergo thorough cleaning and repair to remove contaminants, restore functionality, and address any defects or damage. Cleaning processes may involve degreasing, sandblasting, or chemical treatments to remove surface contaminants and corrosion. Repair activities may include welding, machining, or replacing worn or damaged parts to restore components to their original specifications.
- ***Replacement of Wear Parts:*** In some cases, worn or damaged parts may need to be replaced with new or refurbished components to ensure product performance and reliability. Replacement parts may be sourced from original equipment manufacturers (OEMs), aftermarket suppliers, or internal inventory. Selecting high-quality replacement parts is essential to maintaining product quality and prolonging the lifespan of remanufactured products.
- ***Reassembly and Testing:*** After cleaning, repair, and replacement activities are completed, remanufactured components are reassembled into finished products using standardized procedures and quality control measures. Products undergo rigorous testing to verify performance, functionality, and compliance with quality standards. Testing may include functional tests, performance tests, and quality inspections to ensure that remanufactured products meet or exceed customer expectations.
- ***Packaging and Distribution:*** Once remanufactured products have been tested and approved for sale, they are packaged and prepared for distribution to customers or retailers. Packaging materials should be designed for minimal environmental impact, such as using recycled or biodegradable materials and minimizing packaging waste. Efficient logistics and distribution processes help minimize transportation-related emissions and reduce the environmental footprint of remanufactured products.
- ***Customer Support and Warranty:*** Providing robust customer support and warranty services is essential to building trust and confidence in remanufactured products. Offering warranties on remanufactured products demonstrates the manufacturer's commitment to quality and reliability, while also providing peace of mind to customers. Customer support services, such as technical assistance and product troubleshooting, help ensure a positive customer experience and encourage repeat business (Revathi et al., 2024).
- ***Continuous Improvement:*** Implementing remanufacturing and refurbishment processes requires ongoing monitoring, evaluation, and continuous improvement to optimize performance and efficiency. Collecting feedback from customers, suppliers, and internal stakeholders can identify areas for improvement and inform future process enhancements. By embracing a culture of continuous improvement, manufacturers can refine remanufacturing processes, reduce costs, and enhance the sustainability of their operations (Yupapin et al., 2023).

Remanufacturing and refurbishment processes are crucial in promoting a circular economy in manufacturing by extending product lifespan, conserving resources, and minimizing waste. Effective implementation unlocks economic value, reduces environmental impact, and meets evolving customer and stakeholder needs in a sustainable and responsible manner.

Recycling and Material Recovery Techniques

Recycling and material recovery techniques are crucial for sustainable manufacturing practices, promoting resource conservation, waste reduction, and environmental stewardship. They involve recovering valuable materials from end-of-life products or waste streams, reintroducing them into the production cycle. Effective implementation requires careful planning, infrastructure investment, and stakeholder collaboration (Xiao et al., 2022). The figure 2 depicts recycling and material recovery techniques for sustainable manufacturing practices.

- ***Waste Characterization and Sorting:*** The first step in recycling and material recovery is to characterize and sort waste streams to identify recyclable materials and separate them from non-recyclable waste. Automated sorting technologies, such as optical scanners, magnetic separators, and eddy current systems, can help efficiently separate different types of materials based on their properties, such as size, shape, density, and composition.

Figure 2. Recycling and material recovery techniques for sustainable manufacturing practices

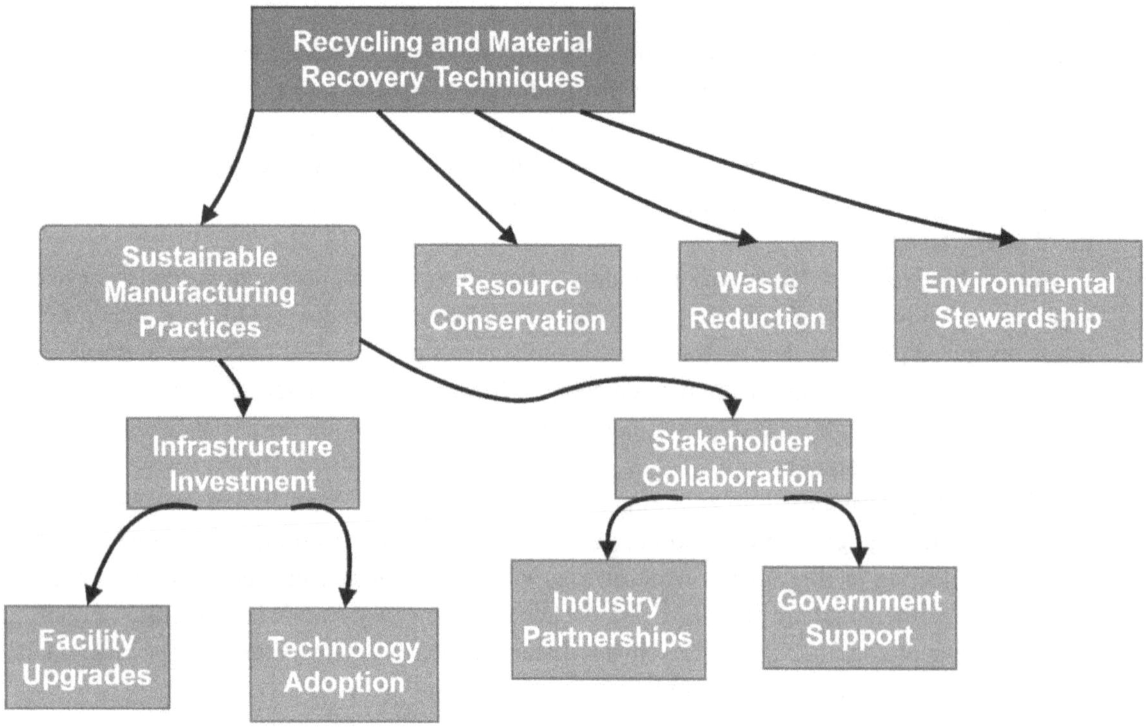

- ***Collection and Aggregation:*** Once recyclable materials have been sorted, they are collected and aggregated for processing. Collection systems may vary depending on the type of material and the scale of operations, ranging from curbside collection programs for household recyclables to centralized collection centers or material recovery facilities (MRFs) for industrial and commercial waste streams.
- ***Mechanical and Biological Treatment:*** Recyclable materials undergo mechanical or biological treatment processes to prepare them for recycling. Mechanical treatment involves shredding, grinding, or crushing materials to reduce their size and facilitate further processing. Biological treatment, such as composting or anaerobic digestion, may be employed for organic waste materials to produce compost or biogas for energy recovery (Saravanan et al., 2022).
- ***Material Separation and Recovery:*** After treatment, recyclable materials are further separated and recovered through various techniques, including screening, air classification, gravity separation, and magnetic separation. These techniques help isolate different types of materials, such as metals, plastics, glass, paper, and organic matter, for subsequent processing and recycling.
- ***Recycling and Reclamation:*** Recovered materials are processed and recycled into new products or raw materials through recycling and reclamation processes. Recycling involves converting materials, such as plastics, metals, glass, and paper, into new products or materials through melting, extrusion, molding, or other manufacturing processes. Reclamation involves recovering valuable components or resources from waste streams, such as extracting precious metals from electronic waste or recovering energy from organic waste through anaerobic digestion or incineration.
- ***Quality Control and Assurance:*** Quality control measures are essential to ensure the purity and integrity of recycled materials and products. Quality control processes may include material testing, inspection, and certification to verify compliance with quality standards and specifications. By maintaining high-quality standards, manufacturers can enhance the marketability and value of recycled products and materials (Boopathi, 2021a; Venkatasubramanian et al., 2024).
- ***Market Development and End-Market Partnerships:*** Developing robust markets for recycled products and materials is critical to creating demand and driving investment in recycling infrastructure. Manufacturers can collaborate with end-market partners, such as product manufacturers, retailers, and consumers, to promote the use of recycled materials in new products and applications. By creating incentives and market demand for recycled products, manufacturers can close the loop and foster a more circular economy (Ravisankar et al., 2024).
- ***Continuous Improvement and Innovation:*** Recycling and material recovery techniques are continually evolving, driven by technological advancements, regulatory requirements, and market trends. Manufacturers should invest in research and development to explore innovative recycling technologies, improve process efficiency, and overcome technical challenges. By embracing a culture of continuous improvement and innovation, manufacturers can stay ahead of the curve and position themselves as leaders in sustainable manufacturing practices.

Recycling and material recovery techniques are vital for promoting resource conservation, waste reduction, and environmental sustainability in manufacturing operations. Effective implementation minimizes environmental footprint, reduces reliance on virgin resources, and contributes to a circular economy. Collaboration among stakeholders and infrastructure investment are essential.

Waste Reduction and Resource Optimization Measures

Waste reduction and resource optimization are crucial strategies for promoting sustainability and circularity in manufacturing operations. These measures aim to minimize waste generation, maximize resource efficiency, and optimize production processes to reduce environmental impact and improve operational performance (Khalid et al., 2022; Xiao et al., 2022). The figure 3 depicts waste reduction and resource optimization.

- ***Lean Manufacturing Principles:*** Lean manufacturing principles, such as just-in-time production, value stream mapping, and continuous improvement, are foundational to waste reduction and resource optimization. By eliminating waste, streamlining processes, and improving efficiency, manufacturers can minimize resource consumption, reduce production costs, and enhance overall productivity (Boopathi, 2024; Ingle et al., 2023a).
- ***Material Efficiency and Minimization:*** Material efficiency measures aim to minimize the consumption of raw materials and inputs throughout the production process. This can include redesigning products to use less material, optimizing cutting patterns to minimize waste during fabri-

Figure 3. Waste reduction and resource optimization

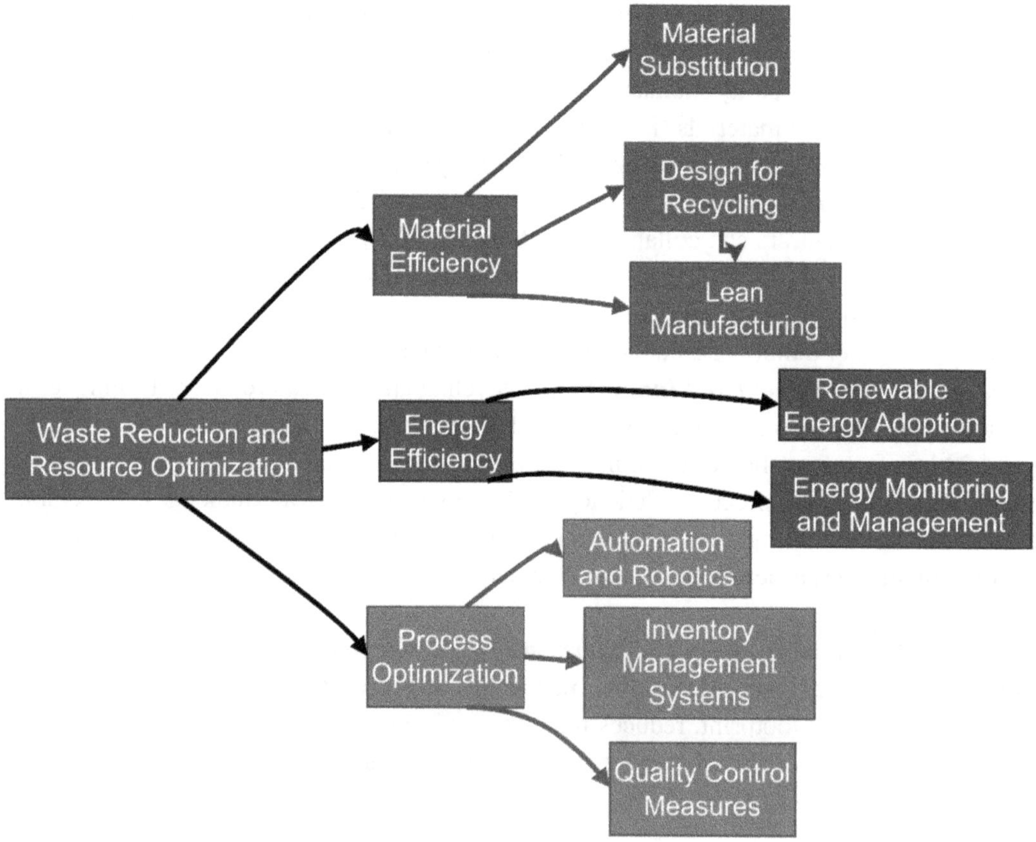

cation, and implementing inventory management systems to reduce excess inventory and material waste (Hanumanthakari et al., 2023; Harikaran et al., 2023; Janardhana et al., 2023).

- ***Energy Efficiency and Conservation:*** Energy efficiency initiatives focus on reducing energy consumption and improving energy performance across manufacturing operations. This can involve upgrading equipment and machinery to more energy-efficient models, implementing energy management systems to monitor and control energy usage, and adopting renewable energy sources, such as solar or wind power, to reduce reliance on fossil fuels (Agrawal, Shashibhushan, et al., 2023; Nishanth et al., 2023).
- ***Water Management and Conservation:*** Water management strategies aim to minimize water usage, reduce water waste, and optimize water treatment and recycling processes. This can include implementing water-saving technologies, such as low-flow fixtures and water-efficient equipment, optimizing water reuse and recycling systems, and conducting regular maintenance and audits to identify and address leaks and inefficiencies (Jeya et al., 2023; Rahamathunnisa et al., 2024).
- ***Process Optimization and Automation:*** Process optimization involves analyzing and improving manufacturing processes to enhance efficiency, productivity, and resource utilization. This can include optimizing production scheduling to minimize downtime and idle time, automating repetitive tasks to reduce labor and resource inputs, and implementing advanced manufacturing technologies, such as robotics and artificial intelligence, to optimize production processes and reduce waste (Boopathi, 2022; Saravanan et al., 2022).
- ***Closed-Loop Supply Chains:*** Closed-loop supply chain strategies involve designing supply chains that minimize waste and maximize resource recovery and reuse. This can include establishing reverse logistics systems to collect and recover end-of-life products and materials, partnering with suppliers to optimize packaging and transportation efficiency, and collaborating with customers to facilitate product returns and remanufacturing.
- ***Product Lifecycle Management:*** Product lifecycle management (PLM) encompasses the management of products from conception through disposal, with a focus on optimizing resource use and minimizing environmental impact at each stage of the lifecycle. This can include designing products for disassembly and recyclability, implementing take-back programs to recover and recycle end-of-life products, and conducting lifecycle assessments to evaluate and improve product sustainability.
- ***Employee Engagement and Training:*** Engaging employees and providing training and education on waste reduction and resource optimization practices is essential to driving sustainable behavior change and fostering a culture of continuous improvement. This can include providing training on waste reduction techniques, implementing employee suggestions and feedback for process improvement, and recognizing and rewarding employees for their contributions to sustainability initiatives.

Sustainable manufacturing practices involve waste reduction and resource optimization to minimize environmental impact, reduce costs, and improve operational efficiency. These strategies enhance competitiveness, meet customer expectations, and contribute to a circular economy. Collaboration among stakeholders, investment in technology and innovation, and continuous improvement are crucial for meaningful progress (P. Das et al., 2024; Rahamathunnisa et al., 2024; Vijayakumar et al., 2024).

Figure 4. Role of digital technologies in advancing circular economy practices

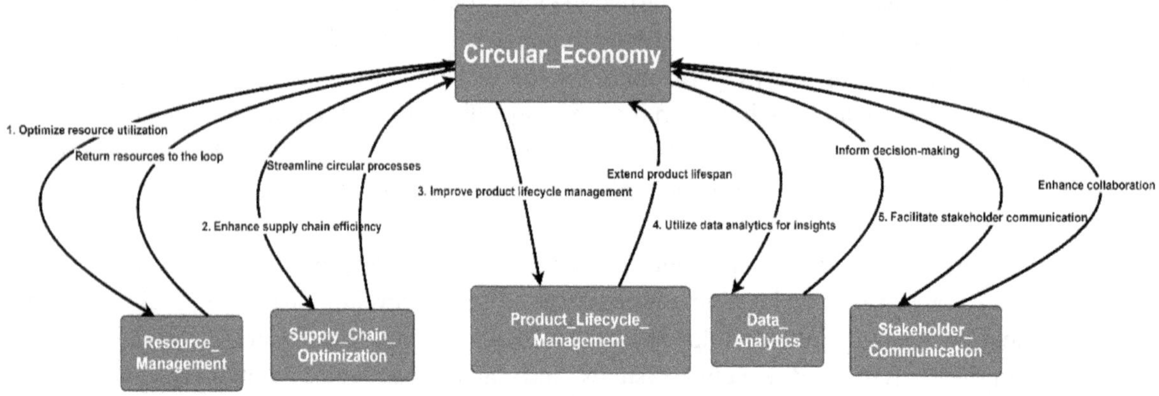

ROLE OF DIGITAL TECHNOLOGIES IN ADVANCING CIRCULAR ECONOMY PRACTICES

The Internet of Things (IoT) is playing a crucial role in enhancing circular economy practices, especially in supply chain management. IoT devices, embedded with sensors and software, collect and exchange data, enhancing visibility, traceability, efficiency, and sustainability throughout the product lifecycle. These applications contribute to a more sustainable and efficient supply chain management system (Ferreira & Gonçalves, 2021; Xiao et al., 2022). The role of digital technologies in promoting circular economy practices is highlighted in Figure 4.

- ***Enhanced Visibility and Transparency:*** IoT-enabled sensors and devices provide real-time visibility into various aspects of the supply chain, including inventory levels, product location, and environmental conditions. This enhanced visibility enables stakeholders to track the movement of products and materials, identify inefficiencies, and optimize resource utilization. By improving transparency, IoT helps ensure accountability and compliance with sustainability standards and regulations (Hema et al., 2023; Samikannu et al., 2022; Syamala et al., 2023).
- ***Optimized Inventory Management:*** IoT applications enable automated inventory tracking and management, reducing the risk of overstocking or stockouts and minimizing excess inventory and waste. By monitoring inventory levels, demand patterns, and consumption trends in real-time, organizations can optimize production planning, reduce storage costs, and minimize waste throughout the supply chain.
- ***Condition Monitoring and Predictive Maintenance:*** IoT sensors can monitor the condition and performance of equipment, machinery, and assets in real-time, enabling proactive maintenance and minimizing downtime. Predictive maintenance algorithms analyze sensor data to detect potential issues and predict maintenance needs before they escalate into costly failures. By optimizing equipment performance and extending asset lifespan, IoT helps reduce resource consumption and minimize waste in manufacturing operations (Vignesh et al., 2018).
- ***Track and Trace for Product Lifecycle Management:*** IoT-enabled track-and-trace systems provide end-to-end visibility into the entire product lifecycle, from raw material sourcing to end-

of-life disposal. By tracking products and materials throughout their journey, organizations can ensure compliance with environmental regulations, verify sustainable sourcing practices, and facilitate responsible disposal and recycling at the end of the product lifecycle. This transparency fosters trust among consumers and stakeholders and supports circular economy initiatives.

- ***Supply Chain Optimization and Collaboration:*** IoT facilitates collaboration and information sharing among supply chain partners, enabling seamless coordination and optimization of operations. By exchanging real-time data on inventory levels, production schedules, and transportation routes, organizations can optimize logistics, reduce lead times, and minimize waste in the supply chain. Collaboration enabled by IoT fosters innovation and agility, allowing organizations to adapt quickly to changing market conditions and consumer preferences.
- ***Waste Monitoring and Recycling Management:*** IoT sensors can monitor waste generation, composition, and disposal practices in manufacturing operations, providing insights into opportunities for waste reduction and recycling. By tracking waste streams and analyzing data on material flows, organizations can identify inefficiencies, optimize recycling processes, and divert waste from landfills. IoT-enabled recycling management systems help organizations achieve their sustainability goals by maximizing resource recovery and minimizing environmental impact (Koshariya et al., 2023; Reddy et al., 2023).

The Internet of Things (IoT), Artificial Intelligence (AI), and Blockchain are revolutionizing supply chain management by improving visibility, optimizing resources, and fostering collaboration. These technologies drive innovation and facilitate the transition towards a circular economy, enabling manufacturers to optimize resource utilization, operational efficiency, and promote transparency and collaboration across supply chain networks. This is contributing to a more circular and resilient economy.

Internet of Things (IoT) Applications in Supply Chain Management

The Internet of Things (IoT) is a network of interconnected devices that collect, exchange, and analyze real-time data. It is used in supply chain management to provide manufacturers with unprecedented visibility and control over their operations. By integrating IoT sensors into manufacturing equipment, products, and logistics processes, manufacturers can track key metrics like resource usage, energy consumption, and product lifecycle status. This data enables proactive decision-making, predictive maintenance, and optimization of resource allocation, leading to improved efficiency and sustainability in supply chain operations (Hugos, 2024).

Artificial Intelligence (AI) for Enhanced Resource Management

Artificial Intelligence (AI) technologies, including machine learning algorithms and predictive analytics, can significantly improve manufacturing resource management and operational efficiency. By analyzing vast data, AI can identify patterns, trends, and insights, enabling data-driven decisions and resource allocation (Koshariya et al., 2023; Venkateswaran et al., 2023). AI-driven predictive maintenance systems can anticipate equipment failures, reduce downtime, and extend asset lifespan. AI-powered demand forecasting and production planning systems can anticipate customer demand, optimize production schedules, and minimize excess inventory. This enables cost savings, improved efficiency, and reduced environmental impact throughout the product lifecycle (Sonia et al., 2024).

Blockchain Technology for Supply Chain Transparency

Blockchain technology provides a decentralized, transparent platform for recording and verifying transactions in supply chain networks, enhancing transparency, traceability, and accountability. It enables manufacturers to track material flow from sourcing to disposal, fostering trust and confidence among consumers and partners (Kumar et al., 2023; Sundaramoorthy et al., 2024). Blockchain-based smart contracts facilitate automated transactions, such as product returns and recycling incentives, streamlining processes and reducing administrative overhead. By leveraging blockchain technology for supply chain transparency, manufacturers can promote sustainability, mitigate risks, and create value throughout the entire value chain (Sundaramoorthy et al., 2024).

Digital technologies like IoT, AI, and blockchain are revolutionizing circular economy practices by optimizing resource utilization, enhancing operational efficiency, and promoting transparency. These technologies can accelerate the transition towards a sustainable, circular economy, achieving environmental, social, and economic benefits. However, collaboration among industry partners, investment in technology, and data-driven decision-making are crucial for maximizing the full potential of digital technologies in advancing circular economy practices.

CHALLENGES AND OPPORTUNITIES

The transition to a circular economy offers numerous benefits like resource efficiency, waste reduction, and cost savings, but also presents challenges and opportunities for manufacturers. Important challenges include overcoming obstacles and overcoming obstacles to achieve these benefits (Sharma et al., 2024; Venkatasubramanian et al., 2024).

Challenges

- One of the primary challenges in implementing circular economy practices is ensuring economic viability and profitability. Many circular economy initiatives require upfront investment in technology, infrastructure, and process redesign, which can be financially challenging for manufacturers, particularly small and medium-sized enterprises (SMEs). Balancing the short-term costs of implementation with the long-term benefits of resource efficiency and cost savings is a significant challenge for manufacturers.
- Another challenge is the lack of awareness and understanding of circular economy principles among manufacturers, suppliers, and other stakeholders. Many businesses may be unfamiliar with the concept of circular economy or may perceive it as complex or impractical. Educating stakeholders about the benefits and opportunities of circular economy practices is essential for overcoming resistance to change and fostering buy-in at all levels of the organization.
- Regulatory and policy constraints, such as waste management regulations, environmental standards, and product labeling requirements, can pose barriers to the implementation of circular economy practices. Inconsistent or ambiguous regulations may hinder innovation and investment in circular economy initiatives, creating uncertainty for manufacturers. Aligning regulatory frameworks with circular economy objectives and providing incentives for sustainable practices can help overcome these barriers.

- Implementing circular economy practices often requires advanced technologies, infrastructure, and expertise, which may not be readily available or accessible to all manufacturers. Limited access to recycling facilities, remanufacturing capabilities, and resource recovery technologies can hinder the scalability and effectiveness of circular economy initiatives. Investing in research and development, technology transfer, and capacity-building initiatives can help overcome technological and infrastructure limitations.
- The complexity and fragmentation of global supply chains pose challenges for implementing circular economy practices, particularly in industries with complex value chains and multinational operations. Coordinating and collaborating with multiple suppliers, partners, and stakeholders to implement circular economy initiatives requires robust communication, collaboration, and trust. Developing partnerships, networks, and collaborative platforms can help streamline supply chain operations and overcome barriers to implementation.

Opportunities

- The circular economy offers opportunities for innovation and collaboration across industries, sectors, and value chains. By fostering partnerships, networks, and ecosystems, manufacturers can leverage collective expertise to develop innovative solutions and overcome shared challenges. Collaborative initiatives like industry consortia, innovation hubs, and research partnerships can accelerate circular economy practices (Dhanya et al., 2023a; Ingle et al., 2023a).
- Circular economy practices offer manufacturers a competitive advantage by addressing the growing demand for environmentally friendly and socially responsible products and services. By adopting sustainable business models, products, and processes, manufacturers can attract environmentally conscious consumers and strengthen their brand reputation.
- Circular economy practices enable manufacturers to enhance resource efficiency, reduce waste, and achieve cost savings throughout the product lifecycle. By optimizing material usage, reducing energy consumption, and minimizing waste generation, manufacturers can lower production costs, increase profitability, and enhance operational resilience, resulting in substantial financial returns over time.
- Circular economy practices can help manufacturers achieve regulatory compliance and mitigate risks like environmental regulations, supply chain disruptions, and reputational damage by aligning with sustainability standards, certifications, and best practices, demonstrating their commitment to responsible business practices and reducing regulatory fines and legal liabilities.

Overcoming Barriers to Implementation of Circular Economy

- Economic Viability: Explore opportunities to incentivize circular economy practices through government subsidies, tax incentives, and grants. Encourage collaboration with financial institutions to develop innovative financing mechanisms for circular economy projects. Conduct cost-benefit analyses to demonstrate the long-term economic benefits of circular practices (Dhanya et al., 2023b; Z. Hussain et al., 2023b).

- Lack of Awareness and Education: Develop educational programs and awareness campaigns targeting manufacturers, policymakers, and consumers to increase understanding of circular economy principles and benefits. Foster knowledge-sharing networks and partnerships with industry associations, academic institutions, and non-profit organizations to disseminate information and best practices (S. Das et al., 2024; Prabhuswamy et al., 2024; Sharma et al., 2024; Venkatasubramanian et al., 2024).
- Regulatory and Policy Constraints: Advocate for supportive policies and regulatory frameworks that incentivize circular economy practices, such as extended producer responsibility (EPR) laws, eco-labeling schemes, and procurement policies favoring sustainable products. Engage policymakers in dialogue and consultation to address regulatory barriers and promote alignment with circular economy objectives.
- Technological and Infrastructure Limitations: Invest in research and development to develop and commercialize innovative technologies and solutions for resource recovery, waste valorization, and product lifecycle management. Foster collaboration with technology providers, startups, and research institutions to leverage expertise and resources in developing scalable and cost-effective circular solutions.
- Supply Chain Complexity: Strengthen collaboration and communication within supply chains through partnerships, supplier engagement programs, and supply chain transparency initiatives. Implement supply chain mapping and risk assessment tools to identify opportunities for circularity and address barriers related to sourcing, logistics, and end-of-life management.

Identifying Opportunities for Collaboration and Innovation

The transition to a circular economy requires a multifaceted approach that addresses economic, regulatory, technological, and social challenges, fostering collaboration and innovation across sectors for sustainable growth (Rahamathunnisa et al., 2023; Srinivas et al., 2023).

- Industry Consortia and Networks: Form industry consortia and collaborative networks to facilitate knowledge exchange, joint research, and pre-competitive collaboration on circular economy initiatives. Share best practices, lessons learned, and success stories to inspire innovation and drive systemic change across sectors.
- Cross-Sector Partnerships: Foster partnerships with stakeholders from diverse sectors, including government agencies, non-profit organizations, academia, and civil society, to address complex challenges and leverage complementary expertise and resources. Collaborate on pilot projects, demonstration initiatives, and innovation challenges to test and scale circular solutions.
- Open Innovation Platforms: Establish open innovation platforms and crowdsourcing initiatives to harness the collective creativity and expertise of stakeholders in developing circular economy solutions. Invite external stakeholders, including startups, entrepreneurs, and independent innovators, to contribute ideas, prototypes, and technologies to address specific challenges and opportunities.
- Circular Business Models: Explore opportunities to transition from linear to circular business models, such as product-as-a-service, sharing platforms, and circular supply chains. Collaborate with partners along the value chain to design and implement innovative business models that pri-

oritize resource efficiency, waste reduction, and value creation through product lifecycle extension (Dhanya et al., 2023a).
- Community Engagement and Stakeholder Dialogue: Engage local communities, customers, and employees in dialogue and co-creation processes to identify opportunities for circularity and address local sustainability challenges. Establish community-based initiatives, such as repair cafes, recycling hubs, and community gardens, to promote circular practices and empower grassroots innovation.

BEST PRACTICES ON INTEGRATION OF CIRCULAR ECONOMY PRINCIPLES IN MANUFACTURING

Manufacturers can effectively incorporate circular economy principles into their operations, promoting sustainability, innovation, and resilience in the transition towards a more circular economy (Dhanya et al., 2023b; Mohanty et al., 2023b; Ravisankar et al., 2023).

- Design for Circular Economy: Eco-design principles, including durability, reparability, and recyclability, should be integrated into product development processes, while modular design and standardization facilitate product disassembly and remanufacturing, and life cycle assessments are used for environmental impact evaluation.
- Resource Optimization: Implement lean manufacturing principles to reduce waste and optimize resource use, implement closed-loop material flows for resource recovery, and optimize material sourcing, procurement, and inventory management to reduce excess inventory and waste.
- Waste Reduction and Recycling: To minimize waste generation, implement waste reduction strategies like source reduction, reuse, and recycling. Establish robust recycling and material recovery systems for end-of-life products and waste streams. Collaborate with suppliers, partners, and customers to promote circularity.
- Remanufacturing and Refurbishment: The project aims to enhance the remanufacturing and refurbishment of used products, implement reverse logistics systems for product collection and reintroduction, and provide remanufactured products as a sustainable, quality, and reliable alternative to new products.
- Digitalization and Innovation: The text emphasizes the importance of utilizing digital technologies like IoT, AI, and blockchain to optimize resource utilization, enhance operational efficiency, and promote transparency in manufacturing operations. It also advocates for fostering innovation and collaborating with startups, research institutions, and technology providers to pilot and scale innovative circular economy solutions.
- Collaboration and Partnerships: The text emphasizes the importance of forming partnerships and networks with stakeholders across the value chain, engaging in pre-competitive collaboration to address challenges and opportunities related to circular economy implementation, and participating in industry consortia and standards development organizations.
- Stakeholder Engagement and Education: The initiative aims to educate stakeholders about the benefits and principles of circular economy practices, engage with local communities and civil society organizations, and offer training and capacity-building programs to equip employees with the necessary skills for effective implementation.

- Measurement and Reporting: The circular economy strategy involves setting KPIs and metrics to track progress, conducting regular audits to assess the effectiveness of initiatives, and reporting transparently on the performance and impact to stakeholders like customers, investors, and regulators.

FUTURE TRENDS

Figure 5 presents emerging trends to overcome implementation challenges. Emerging trends offer innovative solutions for implementing circular economy principles in sustainable green supply chain management, enabling manufacturers to drive transformative change, enhance operational efficiency, and promote sustainability in their industries (Boopathi, 2021b; Ingle et al., 2023b; Rebecca et al., 2024).

i. Circular Business Models: The adoption of circular business models, such as product-as-a-service, sharing platforms, and circular supply chains, is expected to accelerate. These models prioritize resource efficiency, waste reduction, and value creation through product lifecycle extension, offering new opportunities for sustainable growth and innovation.
ii. Digitalization and Industry 4.0: The integration of digital technologies, such as IoT, AI, blockchain, and big data analytics, will continue to play a pivotal role in advancing circular economy and green supply chain management practices. These technologies enable real-time monitoring, optimization, and transparency across supply chains, driving efficiency, resilience, and sustainability (Boopathi & Kumar, 2024).
iii. Circular Design and Materials Innovation: Innovations in eco-design, biomimicry, and sustainable materials will enable the development of products and packaging that are more durable, recyclable, and biodegradable. Advances in materials science, such as bio-based materials, nanotechnology, and 3D printing, will offer new opportunities for resource-efficient manufacturing and waste reduction (Boopathi et al., 2023; Palaniappan et al., 2023; Senthil et al., 2023).
iv. Collaborative Partnerships and Ecosystems: Collaboration among stakeholders across industries, sectors, and value chains will become increasingly important for driving systemic change and scaling circular economy initiatives. Industry consortia, public-private partnerships, and multi-stakeholder platforms will foster collaboration, knowledge-sharing, and collective action towards common sustainability goals.
v. Regulatory and Policy Support: Governments and regulatory bodies are expected to play a more active role in promoting circular economy and sustainability through policy frameworks, incentives, and regulations. Extended producer responsibility (EPR) laws, eco-design standards, and circular procurement policies will incentivize businesses to adopt circular practices and drive market transformation.
vi. Circular Economy Metrics and Reporting: The development of standardized metrics, frameworks, and reporting guidelines for circular economy performance will enable better measurement, benchmarking, and transparency. Companies will increasingly integrate circular economy metrics into their sustainability reporting and disclosure practices to demonstrate their commitment to environmental stewardship and accountability.

Figure 5. Emerging trends to overcome the challenges for implementation

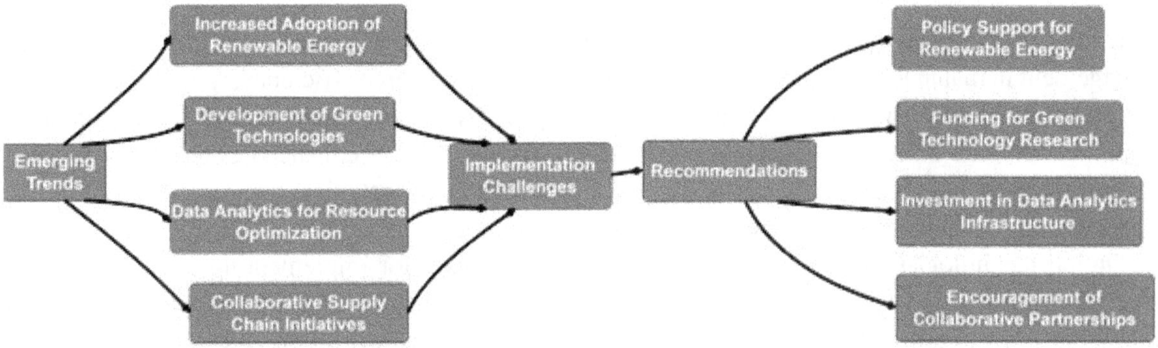

Research and Industry Action

- Longitudinal Studies: Conduct longitudinal studies to assess the long-term environmental, social, and economic impacts of circular economy practices on businesses, supply chains, and society. Track key performance indicators (KPIs) over time to understand trends, identify best practices, and inform decision-making.
- Lifecycle Assessments: Conduct comprehensive lifecycle assessments (LCAs) to evaluate the environmental footprint and sustainability performance of products, processes, and supply chains. Use LCAs to identify hotspots, prioritize interventions, and quantify the benefits of circular economy initiatives (Ingle et al., 2023b).
- Cross-Sector Collaboration: Foster cross-sector collaboration and knowledge exchange to leverage insights, expertise, and resources from diverse industries and disciplines. Collaborate with academia, research institutions, and non-profit organizations to address complex sustainability challenges and drive innovation.
- Pilot Projects and Demonstrations: Implement pilot projects and demonstration initiatives to test and validate circular economy solutions in real-world settings. Collaborate with industry partners, suppliers, and customers to co-create and co-implement circular economy initiatives and assess their feasibility and scalability.
- Capacity Building and Training: Invest in capacity building and training programs to develop the skills, knowledge, and capabilities needed to implement circular economy practices effectively. Provide training on circular design, materials innovation, supply chain management, and sustainability reporting to empower employees and stakeholders.
- Policy Advocacy and Engagement: Engage in policy advocacy and dialogue with policymakers, regulators, and industry associations to shape supportive policy frameworks and regulations for circular economy and sustainability. Advocate for incentives, funding mechanisms, and market-based instruments that encourage investment in circular economy initiatives and drive market transformation (Mohanty et al., 2023b; Verma et al., 2024b).

CONCLUSION

The chapter emphasizes the importance of circular economy principles in sustainable green supply chain management in manufacturing industries. This shift focuses on resource efficiency, waste reduction, and environmental stewardship throughout the product lifecycle. By integrating circular economy principles, manufacturers can achieve cost savings, regulatory compliance, and enhanced brand reputation. By adopting eco-design, resource optimization, and waste reduction strategies, businesses can minimize their environmental footprint and create value for stakeholders.

Digital technologies like IoT, AI, and blockchain are crucial for implementing circular economy practices by providing real-time monitoring, optimization, and transparency across supply chains. These enable manufacturers to make data-driven decisions, optimize resource utilization, and foster collaboration. Despite challenges like economic viability, regulatory constraints, and technological limitations, there are opportunities for innovation, collaboration, and policy advocacy. Manufacturers can overcome these barriers by forming partnerships, advocating for policies, and investing in research and development.

Manufacturing industries must continue advancing circular economy practices, embracing emerging trends, and driving systemic change towards sustainability and resilience. By embracing circular economy principles, manufacturers can reduce environmental impact, create value, drive innovation, and contribute to a sustainable future for generations to come.

ABBREVIATIONS

AI - Artificial Intelligence
GSCM - Green Supply Chain Management
EPR - Extended Producer Responsibility
OEM - Original Equipment Manufacturer
MRF - Material Recovery Facility
PLM - Product Lifecycle Management
SME - Small and Medium-sized Enterprises
KPI - Key Performance Indicator
LCA - Life Cycle Assessment

REFERENCES

Agrawal, A. V., Magulur, L. P., Priya, S. G., Kaur, A., Singh, G., & Boopathi, S. (2023). Smart Precision Agriculture Using IoT and WSN. In *Handbook of Research on Data Science and Cybersecurity Innovations in Industry 4.0 Technologies* (pp. 524–541). IGI Global. doi:10.4018/978-1-6684-8145-5.ch026

Agrawal, A. V., Shashibhushan, G., Pradeep, S., Padhi, S., Sugumar, D., & Boopathi, S. (2023). Synergizing Artificial Intelligence, 5G, and Cloud Computing for Efficient Energy Conversion Using Agricultural Waste. In Sustainable Science and Intelligent Technologies for Societal Development (pp. 475–497). IGI Global.

Ali, M. N., Senthil, T., Ilakkiya, T., Hasan, D. S., Ganapathy, N. B. S., & Boopathi, S. (2024). IoT's Role in Smart Manufacturing Transformation for Enhanced Household Product Quality. In *Advanced Applications in Osmotic Computing* (pp. 252–289). IGI Global. doi:10.4018/979-8-3693-1694-8.ch014

Boopathi, S. (2021). Improving of Green Sand-Mould Quality using Taguchi Technique. *Journal of Engineering Research.*

Boopathi, S. (2022). Experimental investigation and multi-objective optimization of cryogenic Friction-stir-welding of AA2014 and AZ31B alloys using MOORA technique. *Materials Today. Communications, 33*, 104937. doi:10.1016/j.mtcomm.2022.104937

Boopathi, S. (2024). Minimization of Manufacturing Industry Wastes Through the Green Lean Sigma Principle. *Sustainable Machining and Green Manufacturing*, 249–270.

Boopathi, S., Khare, R., KG, J. C., Muni, T. V., & Khare, S. (2023). Additive Manufacturing Developments in the Medical Engineering Field. In Development, Properties, and Industrial Applications of 3D Printed Polymer Composites (pp. 86–106). IGI Global.

Boopathi, S., & Kumar, P. (2024). Advanced bioprinting processes using additive manufacturing technologies: Revolutionizing tissue engineering. *3D Printing Technologies: Digital Manufacturing, Artificial Intelligence, Industry 4.0*, 95.

Ciliberto, C., Szopik-Depczyńska, K., Tarczyńska-Łuniewska, M., Ruggieri, A., & Ioppolo, G. (2021). Enabling the Circular Economy transition: A sustainable lean manufacturing recipe for Industry 4.0. *Business Strategy and the Environment, 30*(7), 3255–3272. doi:10.1002/bse.2801

Das, P., Ramapraba, P., Seethalakshmi, K., Mary, M. A., Karthick, S., & Sampath, B. (2024). Sustainable Advanced Techniques for Enhancing the Image Process. In *Fostering Cross-Industry Sustainability With Intelligent Technologies* (pp. 350–374). IGI Global. doi:10.4018/979-8-3693-1638-2.ch022

Das, S., Lekhya, G., Shreya, K., Shekinah, K. L., Babu, K. K., & Boopathi, S. (2024). Fostering Sustainability Education Through Cross-Disciplinary Collaborations and Research Partnerships: Interdisciplinary Synergy. In Facilitating Global Collaboration and Knowledge Sharing in Higher Education With Generative AI (pp. 60–88). IGI Global.

Dhanya, D., Kumar, S. S., Thilagavathy, A., Prasad, D., & Boopathi, S. (2023). Data Analytics and Artificial Intelligence in the Circular Economy: Case Studies. In Intelligent Engineering Applications and Applied Sciences for Sustainability (pp. 40–58). IGI Global.

Edwin Cheng, T., Kamble, S. S., Belhadi, A., Ndubisi, N. O., Lai, K., & Kharat, M. G. (2022). Linkages between big data analytics, circular economy, sustainable supply chain flexibility, and sustainable performance in manufacturing firms. *International Journal of Production Research, 60*(22), 6908–6922. doi:10.1080/00207543.2021.1906971

Ferreira, C., & Gonçalves, G. (2021). A systematic review on life extension strategies in industry: The case of remanufacturing and refurbishment. *Electronics (Basel), 10*(21), 2669. doi:10.3390/electronics10212669

Gift, M. D. M., Senthil, T. S., Hasan, D. S., Alagarraja, K., Jayaseelan, P., & Boopathi, S. (2024). Additive Manufacturing and 3D Printing Innovations: Revolutionizing Industry 5.0. In Technological Advancements in Data Processing for Next Generation Intelligent Systems (pp. 255–287). IGI Global. doi:10.4018/979-8-3693-0968-1.ch010

Hanumanthakari, S., Gift, M. M., Kanimozhi, K., Bhavani, M. D., Bamane, K. D., & Boopathi, S. (2023). Biomining Method to Extract Metal Components Using Computer-Printed Circuit Board E-Waste. In *Handbook of Research on Safe Disposal Methods of Municipal Solid Wastes for a Sustainable Environment* (pp. 123–141). IGI Global. doi:10.4018/978-1-6684-8117-2.ch010

Harikaran, M., Boopathi, S., Gokulakannan, S., & Poonguzhali, M. (2023). Study on the Source of E-Waste Management and Disposal Methods. In *Sustainable Approaches and Strategies for E-Waste Management and Utilization* (pp. 39–60). IGI Global. doi:10.4018/978-1-6684-7573-7.ch003

Hema, N., Krishnamoorthy, N., Chavan, S. M., Kumar, N., Sabarimuthu, M., & Boopathi, S. (2023). A Study on an Internet of Things (IoT)-Enabled Smart Solar Grid System. In *Handbook of Research on Deep Learning Techniques for Cloud-Based Industrial IoT* (pp. 290–308). IGI Global. doi:10.4018/978-1-6684-8098-4.ch017

Hugos, M. H. (2024). *Essentials of supply chain management.* John Wiley & Sons.

Hussain, M., & Malik, M. (2020). Organizational enablers for circular economy in the context of sustainable supply chain management. *Journal of Cleaner Production*, *256*, 120375. doi:10.1016/j.jclepro.2020.120375

Hussain, Z., Babe, M., Saravanan, S., Srimathy, G., Roopa, H., & Boopathi, S. (2023). Optimizing Biomass-to-Biofuel Conversion: IoT and AI Integration for Enhanced Efficiency and Sustainability. In Circular Economy Implementation for Sustainability in the Built Environment (pp. 191–214). IGI Global.

Ingle, R. B., Swathi, S., Mahendran, G., Senthil, T., Muralidharan, N., & Boopathi, S. (2023). Sustainability and Optimization of Green and Lean Manufacturing Processes Using Machine Learning Techniques. In *Circular Economy Implementation for Sustainability in the Built Environment* (pp. 261–285). IGI Global. doi:10.4018/978-1-6684-8238-4.ch012

Jaeger, B., & Upadhyay, A. (2020). Understanding barriers to circular economy: Cases from the manufacturing industry. *Journal of Enterprise Information Management*, *33*(4), 729–745. doi:10.1108/JEIM-02-2019-0047

Janardhana, K., Singh, V., Singh, S. N., Babu, T. R., Bano, S., & Boopathi, S. (2023). Utilization Process for Electronic Waste in Eco-Friendly Concrete: Experimental Study. In Sustainable Approaches and Strategies for E-Waste Management and Utilization (pp. 204–223). IGI Global.

Jeya, R., Venkatakrishnan, G. R., Rengaraj, R., Rajalakshmi, M., Pradeep Mohan Kumar, K., & Boopathi, S. (2023). Water Resource Managements in Soil and Soilless Irrigation Systems Using AI Techniques. In Advances in Environmental Engineering and Green Technologies (pp. 245–266). IGI Global. doi:10.4018/979-8-3693-0338-2.ch014

Karmaker, C. L., Al Aziz, R., Ahmed, T., Misbauddin, S., & Moktadir, M. A. (2023). Impact of industry 4.0 technologies on sustainable supply chain performance: The mediating role of green supply chain management practices and circular economy. *Journal of Cleaner Production, 419*, 138249. doi:10.1016/j.jclepro.2023.138249

Kazakova, E., & Lee, J. (2022). Sustainable manufacturing for a circular economy. *Sustainability (Basel), 14*(24), 17010. doi:10.3390/su142417010

Kazancoglu, I., Sagnak, M., Kumar Mangla, S., & Kazancoglu, Y. (2021). Circular economy and the policy: A framework for improving the corporate environmental management in supply chains. *Business Strategy and the Environment, 30*(1), 590–608. doi:10.1002/bse.2641

Khalid, M. Y., Arif, Z. U., Ahmed, W., & Arshad, H. (2022). Recent trends in recycling and reusing techniques of different plastic polymers and their composite materials. *Sustainable Materials and Technologies, 31*, e00382. doi:10.1016/j.susmat.2021.e00382

Koshariya, A. K., Khatoon, S., Marathe, A. M., Suba, G. M., Baral, D., & Boopathi, S. (2023). Agricultural Waste Management Systems Using Artificial Intelligence Techniques. In *AI-Enabled Social Robotics in Human Care Services* (pp. 236–258). IGI Global. doi:10.4018/978-1-6684-8171-4.ch009

Kumar, P. R., Meenakshi, S., Shalini, S., Devi, S. R., & Boopathi, S. (2023). Soil Quality Prediction in Context Learning Approaches Using Deep Learning and Blockchain for Smart Agriculture. In Effective AI, Blockchain, and E-Governance Applications for Knowledge Discovery and Management (pp. 1–26). IGI Global. doi:10.4018/978-1-6684-9151-5.ch001

Lu, H., Zhao, G., & Liu, S. (2024). Integrating circular economy and Industry 4.0 for sustainable supply chain management: A dynamic capability view. *Production Planning and Control, 35*(2), 170–186. doi:10.1080/09537287.2022.2063198

Maranesi, C., & De Giovanni, P. (2020). Modern circular economy: Corporate strategy, supply chain, and industrial symbiosis. *Sustainability (Basel), 12*(22), 9383. doi:10.3390/su12229383

Mohanty, A., Venkateswaran, N., Ranjit, P., Tripathi, M. A., & Boopathi, S. (2023). Innovative Strategy for Profitable Automobile Industries: Working Capital Management. In Handbook of Research on Designing Sustainable Supply Chains to Achieve a Circular Economy (pp. 412–428). IGI Global.

Murali, B., Padhi, S., Patil, C. K., Kumar, P. S., Santhanakrishnan, M., & Boopathi, S. (2023). Investigation on hardness and tensile strength of friction stir processing of Al6061/TiN surface composite. *Materials Today: Proceedings.*

Myilsamy Sureshkumar, Boopathi, & Sabareesh. (2018). The improving Wear Resistance Properties of Molybdenum Alloy Under Cryogenic Treatment. *International Journal of Mechanical and Production Engineering Research and Development, 8*(7), 724–728.

Nishanth, J., Deshmukh, M. A., Kushwah, R., Kushwaha, K. K., Balaji, S., & Sampath, B. (2023). Particle Swarm Optimization of Hybrid Renewable Energy Systems. In *Intelligent Engineering Applications and Applied Sciences for Sustainability* (pp. 291–308). IGI Global. doi:10.4018/979-8-3693-0044-2.ch016

Palaniappan, M., Tirlangi, S., Mohamed, M. J. S., Moorthy, R. S., Valeti, S. V., & Boopathi, S. (2023). Fused Deposition Modelling of Polylactic Acid (PLA)-Based Polymer Composites: A Case Study. In Development, Properties, and Industrial Applications of 3D Printed Polymer Composites (pp. 66–85). IGI Global.

Prabhuswamy, M., Tripathi, R., Vijayakumar, M., Thulasimani, T., Sundharesalingam, P., & Sampath, B. (2024). A Study on the Complex Nature of Higher Education Leadership: An Innovative Approach. In *Challenges of Globalization and Inclusivity in Academic Research* (pp. 202–223). IGI Global. doi:10.4018/979-8-3693-1371-8.ch013

Rahamathunnisa, U., Subhashini, P., Aancy, H. M., Meenakshi, S., Boopathi, S., & ... (2023). Solutions for Software Requirement Risks Using Artificial Intelligence Techniques. In *Handbook of Research on Data Science and Cybersecurity Innovations in Industry 4.0 Technologies* (pp. 45–64). IGI Global.

Rahamathunnisa, U., Sudhakar, K., Padhi, S., Bhattacharya, S., Shashibhushan, G., & Boopathi, S. (2024). Sustainable Energy Generation From Waste Water: IoT Integrated Technologies. In Adoption and Use of Technology Tools and Services by Economically Disadvantaged Communities: Implications for Growth and Sustainability (pp. 225–256). IGI Global.

Ravisankar, A., Sampath, B., & Asif, M. M. (2023). Economic Studies on Automobile Management: Working Capital and Investment Analysis. In Multidisciplinary Approaches to Organizational Governance During Health Crises (pp. 169–198). IGI Global.

Ravisankar, A., Shanthi, A., Lavanya, S., Ramaratnam, M., Krishnamoorthy, V., & Boopathi, S. (2024). Harnessing 6G for Consumer-Centric Business Strategies Across Electronic Industries. In AI Impacts in Digital Consumer Behavior (pp. 241–270). IGI Global.

Rebecca, B., Kumar, K. P. M., Padmini, S., Srivastava, B. K., Halder, S., & Boopathi, S. (2024). Convergence of Data Science-AI-Green Chemistry-Affordable Medicine: Transforming Drug Discovery. In *Handbook of Research on AI and ML for Intelligent Machines and Systems* (pp. 348–373). IGI Global.

Reddy, M. A., Gaurav, A., Ushasukhanya, S., Rao, V. C. S., Bhattacharya, S., & Boopathi, S. (2023). Bio-Medical Wastes Handling Strategies During the COVID-19 Pandemic. In Multidisciplinary Approaches to Organizational Governance During Health Crises (pp. 90–111). IGI Global. doi:10.4018/978-1-7998-9213-7.ch006

Revathi, S., Babu, M., Rajkumar, N., Meti, V. K. V., Kandavalli, S. R., & Boopathi, S. (2024). Unleashing the Future Potential of 4D Printing: Exploring Applications in Wearable Technology, Robotics, Energy, Transportation, and Fashion. In Human-Centered Approaches in Industry 5.0: Human-Machine Interaction, Virtual Reality Training, and Customer Sentiment Analysis (pp. 131–153). IGI Global.

Samikannu, R., Koshariya, A. K., Poornima, E., Ramesh, S., Kumar, A., & Boopathi, S. (2022). Sustainable Development in Modern Aquaponics Cultivation Systems Using IoT Technologies. In *Human Agro-Energy Optimization for Business and Industry* (pp. 105–127). IGI Global.

Saravanan, M., Vasanth, M., Boopathi, S., Sureshkumar, M., & Haribalaji, V. (2022). Optimization of Quench Polish Quench (QPQ) Coating Process Using Taguchi Method. *Key Engineering Materials*, *935*, 83–91. doi:10.4028/p-z569vy

Senthil, T., Puviyarasan, M., Babu, S. R., Surakasi, R., Sampath, B., & Associates. (2023). Industrial Robot-Integrated Fused Deposition Modelling for the 3D Printing Process. In Development, Properties, and Industrial Applications of 3D Printed Polymer Composites (pp. 188–210). IGI Global.

Sharma, D. M., Ramana, K. V., Jothilakshmi, R., Verma, R., Maheswari, B. U., & Boopathi, S. (2024). Integrating Generative AI Into K-12 Curriculums and Pedagogies in India: Opportunities and Challenges. *Facilitating Global Collaboration and Knowledge Sharing in Higher Education With Generative AI*, 133–161.

Sonia, R., Gupta, N., Manikandan, K., Hemalatha, R., Kumar, M. J., & Boopathi, S. (2024). Strengthening Security, Privacy, and Trust in Artificial Intelligence Drones for Smart Cities. In *Analyzing and Mitigating Security Risks in Cloud Computing* (pp. 214–242). IGI Global. doi:10.4018/979-8-3693-3249-8.ch011

Srinivas, B., Maguluri, L. P., Naidu, K. V., Reddy, L. C. S., Deivakani, M., & Boopathi, S. (2023). Architecture and Framework for Interfacing Cloud-Enabled Robots. In *Handbook of Research on Data Science and Cybersecurity Innovations in Industry 4.0 Technologies* (pp. 542–560). IGI Global. doi:10.4018/978-1-6684-8145-5.ch027

Sundaramoorthy, K., Singh, A., Sumathy, G., Maheshwari, A., Arunarani, A., & Boopathi, S. (2024). A Study on AI and Blockchain-Powered Smart Parking Models for Urban Mobility. In *Handbook of Research on AI and ML for Intelligent Machines and Systems* (pp. 223–250). IGI Global.

Syamala, M., Komala, C., Pramila, P., Dash, S., Meenakshi, S., & Boopathi, S. (2023). Machine Learning-Integrated IoT-Based Smart Home Energy Management System. In *Handbook of Research on Deep Learning Techniques for Cloud-Based Industrial IoT* (pp. 219–235). IGI Global. doi:10.4018/978-1-6684-8098-4.ch013

Venkatasubramanian, V., Chitra, M., Sudha, R., Singh, V. P., Jefferson, K., & Boopathi, S. (2024). Examining the Impacts of Course Outcome Analysis in Indian Higher Education: Enhancing Educational Quality. In Challenges of Globalization and Inclusivity in Academic Research (pp. 124–145). IGI Global.

Venkateswaran, N., Vidhya, K., Ayyannan, M., Chavan, S. M., Sekar, K., & Boopathi, S. (2023). A Study on Smart Energy Management Framework Using Cloud Computing. In 5G, Artificial Intelligence, and Next Generation Internet of Things: Digital Innovation for Green and Sustainable Economies (pp. 189–212). IGI Global. doi:10.4018/978-1-6684-8634-4.ch009

Vennila, T., Karuna, M., Srivastava, B. K., Venugopal, J., Surakasi, R., & Sampath, B. (2022). New Strategies in Treatment and Enzymatic Processes: Ethanol Production From Sugarcane Bagasse. In Human Agro-Energy Optimization for Business and Industry (pp. 219–240). IGI Global.

Verma, R., Christiana, M. B. V., Maheswari, M., Srinivasan, V., Patro, P., Dari, S. S., & Boopathi, S. (2024). Intelligent Physarum Solver for Profit Maximization in Oligopolistic Supply Chain Networks. In *AI and Machine Learning Impacts in Intelligent Supply Chain* (pp. 156–179). IGI Global. doi:10.4018/979-8-3693-1347-3.ch011

Vignesh, S., Arulshri, K., SyedSajith, S., Kathiresan, S., Boopathi, S., & Dinesh Babu, P. (2018). Design and development of ornithopter and experimental analysis of flapping rate under various operating conditions. *Materials Today: Proceedings*, *5*(11), 25185–25194. doi:10.1016/j.matpr.2018.10.320

Vijayakumar, G. N. S., Domakonda, V. K., Farooq, S., Kumar, B. S., Pradeep, N., & Boopathi, S. (2024). Sustainable Developments in Nano-Fluid Synthesis for Various Industrial Applications. In Adoption and Use of Technology Tools and Services by Economically Disadvantaged Communities: Implications for Growth and Sustainability (pp. 48–81). IGI Global.

Xiao, Z., Pramanik, A., Basak, A. K., Prakash, C., & Shankar, S. (2022). Material recovery and recycling of waste tyres-A review. *Cleaner Materials, 5*, 100115. doi:10.1016/j.clema.2022.100115

Yupapin, P., Trabelsi, Y., Nattappan, A., & Boopathi, S. (2023). Performance improvement of wire-cut electrical discharge machining process using cryogenically treated super-conductive state of Monel-K500 alloy. *Iranian Journal of Science and Technology. Transaction of Mechanical Engineering, 47*(1), 267–283. doi:10.1007/s40997-022-00513-0

Zacharaki, A., Vafeiadis, T., Kolokas, N., Vaxevani, A., Xu, Y., Peschl, M., Ioannidis, D., & Tzovaras, D. (2021). RECLAIM: Toward a new era of refurbishment and remanufacturing of industrial equipment. *Frontiers in Artificial Intelligence, 3*, 570562. doi:10.3389/frai.2020.570562 PMID:33733214

Zhang, A., Venkatesh, V., Wang, J. X., Mani, V., Wan, M., & Qu, T. (2023). Drivers of industry 4.0-enabled smart waste management in supply chain operations: A circular economy perspective in china. *Production Planning and Control, 34*(10), 870–886. doi:10.1080/09537287.2021.1980909

Chapter 6
Exploring Employee Retention in the Era of Industry 5.0:
An Empirical Investigation of Indian Automobile Industry

Amit Kumar
https://orcid.org/0000-0002-1686-3279
Eternal University, India

Anupriya Kaur
Jaypee University of Information Technology, India

Tanisha Thakur
Eternal University, India

Shaweta Sandhu
L.R. Institute of Management, India

Yashpal Azad
https://orcid.org/0000-0003-2957-8917
Eternal University, India

ABSTRACT

This study investigated the factors affecting employee retention in the Indian automobile industry in the era of Industry 5.0, including the factors such as organizational culture and climate, reward recognition and pay, leadership style and quality, job security, work-life balance, training and development, autonomy, promotions, and career growth. The convenience sampling technique was used to collect data from 141 employees of selected automobile companies using a self-administered questionnaire. The data were analyzed by employing multiple regression and multivariate analysis of variance (MANOVA). The findings of the study revealed that all the selected factors significantly affect employee retention. Training and development is the most influencing factor affecting employee retention in the Indian automobile industry. Additionally, the demographic variables taken in this study have demonstrated differential effects in context of the factors affecting employee retention. This study has also offered insights to automobile industry on Industry 5.0 interventions for employee retention.

DOI: 10.4018/979-8-3693-1343-5.ch006

1. INTRODUCTION

Amidst globalization and fierce competition, managing the workforce is a primary challenge that organizations are facing (Mukherjee et al. 2020). Employees are the most vital assets for any organization as every organization needs employees to survive in today's competitive scenario (Mukherjee et al., 2020; Muo, 2013, Rakhra, 2018; Kumar & Kaur, 2022). Having the right person at the right place at the right time is the triumph mantra to be followed by every organization (Narayanan et al., 2019). For an organization nothing could make a better impression than having a productive and satisfied workforce as it ensures customer satisfaction, increased productivity and healthy interpersonal relationships (Charity, 2016; Aruna & Anitha, 2015). Attracting, developing, and retaining a company's quality employees is the core role of personnel management (Mohammed, 2015; Iqbal and Hashmi, 2015).

Furthermore, in today's worldwide economy and in the era of industry 5.0, employee retention has become a difficult problem for organizations (Haider et al., 2015). Employee retention is the process of encouraging employees to stick around the company for as long as possible or until the project is finished (McDonnell et al., 2012; Chatterjee et al., 2014; Presbitero et al., 2016). Employers should make a concerted effort to develop an atmosphere that motivates current employees to stay with the company by putting policies and procedures in place that cater to their various demands (Mukherjee et al., 2020; McDonnell et al., 2012; Tanwar & Prasad, 2016). A lack of an effective retention plan can result in job disruption, a reduction in output and productivity, lower performance, and significant financial loss (Ballinger et al., 2011; Bryant & Allen, 2013; Khalid and Nawab, 2018). Employee retention is crucial since it prevents organizational problems such as investment on training, productivity loss and recruitment expenditure (Kundu & Lata, 2017). Due to industry 5.0 changes organizations are undergoing constant change, and the employees that work there are also being impacted by this shifting environment.

Human resources must be utilized effectively for resource utilization and to maximize organizational efficiency (Fletcher et al., 2018). Management of human resources is crucial in this context (Teclaw et al., 2014). Nowadays, all organizations face the critical challenge of employee retention. Numerous factors influence whether employees choose to stay with the company or quit it (Sinnott et al. 2002). It could be caused by internal reasons, external reasons, or a combination of the two (detailed in literature review section). It is imperative that human resource managers determine the needs of the employee before developing retention measures (Latha, 2013). One policy does not work for everyone because everyone has different priorities. Past research has shown that employee retention can boost an organization's performance overall, but because employee retention depending on the factors such as type of business or organization, the position of the employee within the organization, employee demographic attributes etc. consequently, it is difficult to develop a universal retention strategy for different industry (Fahim, 2018; Bibi et al. 2016). Therefore, a key and likely area of research would be to examine employee retention specifically in the industry (which has not been or has been less researched in the past in this context, such as the automobile industry). With growth of the automobile industry in the Indian economy, a sufficient number of opportunities existing in the market has increased competition. Consequently, each company needs to have a competitive edge (in terms of quality and stable employees) for a longer period of time.

In the world of advanced manufacturing, particularly in the automobile sector embracing Industry 5.0, holding onto skilled and experienced employees has become absolutely crucial (Cillo et al. 2022). The automobile industry is characterized by constant and rapid technological progress, making it vital to preserve the wealth of knowledge within the workforce. Experienced employees are the driving force behind innovation, a key element of Industry 5.0 that seamlessly incorporates cutting-edge technologies like AI, robotics, and IoT (Demir et al. 2019). Success in implementing these technologies depends heavily on a stable workforce, well-versed in both traditional manufacturing methods and the latest advancements. Employee retention is not just important to keeping operations smooth but it also acts as a strategic financial move. The costs involved in employee turnover, recruitment, and training can be substantial. Additionally, maintaining a stable team contributes significantly to upholding quality and safety standards is the critical factor in the automobile industry. Furthermore, in an era focused on customer satisfaction, keeping skilled and experienced employees ensures consistency and helps build lasting relationships with customers (Laskowska & Laskowski, 2022). As the automobile industry is transitioning to Industry 5.0, its success hinges on retaining a skilled and experienced workforce capable of navigating the evolving landscape while staying true to the industry's core principles. This study is the first of its kind to explore the factors affecting employee retention and to propose some insights to automobile industry in the transition of industry 5.0. Employees constantly learn new and innovative ideas to transform their organization. It is the employees who make things happen in all organizations. When an organization succeeds in managing their employees and creating them loyal and stable, they find it easy to manage the performance of the company. The Indian automobile industry is highlighted in the following section.

1.1. Industry/Organisation in Study

The automobile industry is the most important driver of the economic growth of India. The automobile industry includes an extensive range of companies and organizations involved in design, development, manufacturing and selling of automobiles (IBEF, 2022). The core products in automobile industries include motorcycles, scooters, cars, trucks, pickups, vans, and sport utility vehicles. As of 2020, India is the fifth largest automobile marketplace in the world, with the 3.49 million units sold in the passengers and commercial vehicles groups (IBEF, 2022). India is also a projecting auto exporter and has solid export growth opportunities for the near upcoming future (IBEF, 2022). In addition, numerous initiatives by the Indian government and automobile players in the Indian marketplace are expected to create India a leader in the automobile marketplace in the world within 2030 (IBEF, 2022). The growth of the automobile industry has created ample opportunities in the market; resulting in increased competition which made it important to hold efficient employees for longer time for the growth of organization (Kumar & Kaur, 2024). Employee retention is a matter of great concern especially nowadays when the plethora of opportunities are available for talented employees (Explained in introduction). The automobile industry offers services to a huge part of the population in India. Therefore, the role of the automobile industry cannot be ignored in the Indian manufacturing industry. The major companies in the Indian automobile industry are Maruti Suzuki, Hindustan Motors, Fiat India Pvt. Limited, Ford India Limited, Hyundai Motors India Limited, General Motors India Pvt. Ltd., Honda Siel Cars India Limited, Skoda India Pvt. Ltd., TVS, Ashok Leyland, Toyota Kirloskar Motors Ltd., Mahindra and Mahindra, Eicher Motors etc. (IBEF, 2022).

The purpose of this research is -1) to explore the factors that significantly influences the employee retention in Indian automobile industry; 2) to examine the differential effects of demographic factors in context of the factors of employee retention considered in this study; 3) to offer some insights on the industry 5.0 interventions for employee retention in automobile industry. In the sections that follow firstly, literature review and hypothesis development are presented. Next, the research material & methods and results are presented. The concluding section discusses the summery of findings and the conclusion.

2. LITERATURE REVIEW AND HYPOTHESIS DEVELOPMENT

Employee retention is the ability of a company to keep its personnel for a predetermined amount of time (Chatterjee et al., 2014; Mukherjee et al., 2020). As it can directly affect an organization's productivity, profitability, and competitiveness, it is a crucial component of human resource management (McDonnell, 2011). Researchers and academics have confirmed that employee retention can boost an organization's performance, while its absence might impair productivity (Park & Shaw, 2013; Hancock et al., 2013; Samuel & Chipunza, 2009). One of the most common theories related to employee retention is the social exchange theory. This theory proposes that employees stay with an organization when they perceive that they are receiving a fair exchange for their work. This can include tangible rewards such as compensation and benefits, as well as intangible rewards such as recognition, job satisfaction, and a positive work environment. As discussed in introduction section that there are numerous factors that influence employee retention. In the next section the literature on the factors that influence employee retention is discussed.

2.1 Factors Influencing Employee Retention

Previous studies found that a variety of factors, rather than just one, influence employee commitment and retention. First, job satisfaction is a crucial element in employee retention. Job satisfaction and employee retention have been linked favorably in a number of studies. For example, in a study by Tett & Meyer (1993), they found that employees who were satisfied with their job were more likely to stay with the organization. Similarly, in a study by Saks (1995), author found that employees who experienced high levels of job satisfaction were less likely to quit their jobs. Organizational culture is also an important factor in employee retention. A positive organizational culture can lead to higher levels of employee engagement, job satisfaction, and ultimately, retention. In a study by Denison & Mishra (1995), they found that companies with strong cultures were more likely to have lower turnover rates. Similarly, a study by Cameron & Sine (1999), concluded that organizations with a strong culture of innovation were more likely to have higher levels of employee retention. Programmes for training and development may also have an effect on staff retention. Employee retention is higher when there are opportunities for them to grow professionally and rise within the company. According to research by Holtom et al. (2008), businesses with training and development initiatives had reduced employee turnover rates. Walangitan et al. (2014) assert that training, empowerment, and involvement all significantly improve employee retention. Training and development will make organizations more competitive because they will be able to retain stability, deliver high-quality performance, and accomplish their objectives (Wareth & Amirah, 2020). Compensation and benefits also impact employee retention. While employees may not stay with an organization solely for monetary reasons, competitive compensation and benefits play an important role in retention. According to Heneman et al. (2002) remuneration is a key element of employee retention. Other research (Samuel & Chipunza, 2009) that took into account a variety of retention characteristics came to the conclusion that training, workplace autonomy, and job security are important predictors of employee retention. On the other hand, (Latha, 2013) said that compensation, peer relationships & support, performance reviews, and career advancement are the key predictors of employee retention. According to Hill & Tande (2006); Hassan et al. (2013), staff retention patterns and practices have altered and go beyond traditional practices like standard salary and financial benefits. According to Sandhya & Kumar (2011), encouraging the staff through a range of means, such as open communication, staff recognition programmes, career advancement programmes, performance-oriented bonuses, amenities for recreation, and gifts on important occasions, can boost employee retention. Organizations will be able to identify employees' perspectives on the position and organization if they invite their input into decision-making and the creation of retention strategies (Kaur & Dilawari, 2015). According to Naz et al. (2020), there is a substantial positive link between the endogenous variable of employee retention and the exogenous variable of a supportive work environment. The factors that affect employees socially, psychologically, and economically include their expectations from the job, an unfavorable work environment, a job that is not a good fit for them, irregular hours, stress, a lack of work-life balance, and inadequate compensation (Mangal et al., 2021). The analysis of the literature on employee retention shows that it is a complicated and multifaceted issue that calls for an integrated and strategic approach. The exploration of literature also demonstrates that there is no one-size-fits-all approach to employee retention because various factors may have varying effects on certain individuals depending on the situation. So, in order to personalize their retention strategy, businesses need to be aware of the wants and needs of their workforce. Next, the factors influencing employee retention and considered for current study are discussed in Table 1.

2.2 Differential Effect of Demographic Factors on Selected Factors of Employee Retention

Demographic factors have drawn a lot of attention among the many variables that affect employee retention because of their potential impact on job satisfaction and employee retention. According to Agyeman & Ponnaih (2014) a stable association between retention and turnover intentions was discovered in the literature analysis of demographic factors (age, gender, experience, education, and income levels). Almalki et al. (2012) discovered strong correlations between demographic factors such gender, age, and marital status and employee retention in a different study. In case of age older employees tend to exhibit higher retention rates due to factors such as increased job tenure, reduced job mobility, and higher levels of organizational commitment (Yusoff et al. 2013; Teclaw et al. 2014). However, younger employees may prioritize career growth and opportunities for development, which can impact their decision to stay with an organization (Rani & Samuel, 2016; Govindaraju, 2018). The relationship between gender and employee retention is complex and context-dependent. While some studies indicate that gender has no significant effect on retention, others highlight that women may face unique challenges in the workplace, such as work-life balance issues and limited career advancement opportunities, which impact their retention rates (George, 2015). Educational level has been found to have mixed effects on employee retention. While higher levels of education are generally associated with higher job satisfaction and increased opportunities, some studies suggest that highly educated employees may be more likely to pursue new opportunities and change jobs more frequently (Kumar & Babu, 2017).

$H_{2:}$ *Selected factors of employee retention (*OCC, RRP, LSQ, JS, WLB, TD, AUT and PCG*) are significantly varying in context of demographic factors (gender, age, occupation, work experience and education).*

Table 1. Factors influencing employee retention

Factor	Definition/Meaning
Organizational culture and climate (OCC)	Organizational culture represents the underlying values, beliefs, and practices that define an organization's identity, while organizational climate refers to the current perceptions and experiences of employees within that organization. Both culture and climate play crucial roles in shaping employee behavior, attitudes, and performance, and organizations that foster positive cultures and climates tend to have higher levels of employee satisfaction, engagement, and productivity.
Reward recognition and pay (RRP)	Reward recognition and pay are all essential components of an organization's compensation and motivation system. Rewards serve as positive incentives, recognition expresses appreciation for employees' efforts, and pay provides financial compensation for their work. By effectively implementing these elements, organizations can foster a motivating and rewarding work environment that contributes to employee satisfaction, engagement, and productivity.
Leadership style and quality (LSQ)	Leadership style refers to the approach a leader takes in guiding and influencing others, while leadership quality encompasses the characteristics and skills that make a leader effective. Effective leaders exhibit a leadership style that aligns with the needs of their team or organization and possess key leadership qualities that inspire, motivate, and guide their followers towards achieving common goals.
Job security (JS)	Job security refers to the assurance or confidence that an individual has in the continuity and stability of their employment within an organization. It represents the level of confidence an employee has that their job will remain secure, without the imminent risk of being terminated or laid off. Job security can be influenced by various factors, including economic conditions, organizational stability, industry trends, and individual performance.
Work life balance (WLB)	Work-life balance refers to the equilibrium and harmony between an individual's work life and personal life. It refers to the ability to effectively manage and allocate time and energy to various aspects of life, including work, family, relationships, leisure activities, and personal well-being. Achieving work-life balance is important as it allows individuals to maintain a healthy and fulfilling lifestyle, where they can fulfil their professional responsibilities while also enjoying personal pursuits and maintaining their overall well-being.
Training and development (TD)	Training and development refer to activities and initiatives designed to enhance employees' knowledge, skills, abilities, and competencies in order to improve their job performance and support their professional growth and career advancement. It involves planned and systematic efforts to provide learning opportunities that are aligned with organizational goals and individual needs.
Autonomy (AUT)	Autonomy refers to the extent to which employees have the freedom and discretion to make decisions related to their job tasks, work methods, and problem-solving approaches. Autonomy in the workplace allows employees to have a sense of ownership and control over their work, enabling them to exercise their judgment, creativity, and expertise.
Promotion and career growth (PCG)	Promotion and career growth are related concepts that involve advancement and progression in an individual's professional journey within an organization or a chosen field. While they are interconnected, promotion refers specifically to the upward movement to a higher position or rank within the organizational hierarchy, while career growth encompasses the overall development and advancement of an individual's career path over time. Organizations play a role by providing clear career paths, offering training and development opportunities, and establishing fair and transparent promotion processes.

$H_{1:}$ There is a statistically significant positive effect of all the selected factors (OCC, RRP, LSQ, JS, WLB, TD, AUT and PCG) on employee retention in automobile industry.

3. RESEARCH METHOD

3.1 Sample and Data Collection

This quantitative study is organised according to survey design. Information was gathered from the staff of seven automobile companies in north India. Since there are many outlets of automobile companies in the chosen location, convenience sampling was utilised to identify the survey pool.

3.2 Material and Design

A survey instrument (consisting of two parts) was developed for data collection. The first part consisted of the demographic information of the respondents. The second part consisted of statements related to variables such as OCC, RRP, LSQ, JS, WLB, TD, AUT and PCG to examine employee retention. A 24 items scale was considered to measure the construct. The measurement of variables was based on established scales. A brief description of the measures adopted is as follows: OCC (3 items) from Mukherjee et al. (2020) and Kumar & Santosh (2014), RRP (3 items) from Verma & Chaurasia (2016), LSQ (3 items) from Mukherjee et al. (2020), JS (3 items) from Mukherjee et al. (2020), WLB (3 items) from Kumar & Santosh (2014), TD (3 items) from Mukherjee et al. (2020), AUT (3 items), PCG (3 items) taken from Mukherjee et al. (2020) and Kumar & Santosh (2014). Every item on the scale was on a five-point Likert scale, with 1 denoting strongly disagree and 5 denoting strongly agree. The use of personal interviews was made to elicit responses from the survey pool, 141 fully completed questionnaires were taken into account for the study out of a total of 200 that were distributed.

3.3 Reliability Measure

The consistency of the scale was assessed through Cronbach's alpha (α). According to Hair et al. (2009) the Cronbach's alpha value above 0.6 is considered acceptable. Cronbach's alpha value for all the variables were found above the threshold value of 0.6 and hence inferred that the scale used in the study was reliable (Refer Table 3).

3.4 Demographic Profile of the Respondents

The demographic profile of the respondents includes information related to gender, age, occupation, work experience and qualification of respondents. Table 2 presents the respondent's profile. The majority of the respondents were male (66%) in the age group of 25-30 years (65%) working at operational level (49%) with experience of 0-5 years (60%). The majority of the respondents have qualified on graduation level (70%). Detail of the respondent's demographic information is given in Table 2.

3.5 Data Analysis

The statistical analysis of the data was accomplished through IBM SPSS version 25. Initially descriptive analysis was computed which follows the calculation of multiple regression to describe the rapport amongst a dependent (employee retention) and multiple independent factors (OCC, RRP, LSQ, JS, WLB, TD, AUT and PCG) in this study. Further, multivariate analysis of variance (MANOVA) has been performed to explore the differential effects of demographic factors such as gender, age, occupation, experience and education on the selected factors of employee retention in this study.

Table 2. Socio-demographic profile of respondents (N=141)

Particulars	No. of Respondents	Percentage (%)
Gender		
Male	93	66
Female	48	34
Age		
Below 25 years	24	17
25-30 years	91	65
31-40 years	26	18
Occupation/Designation		
Employee at managerial level	33	23
Employee at operational level	69	49
Supervisors	17	12
Worker	22	16
Work experience		
0-5 years	85	60
6-10 years	45	32
11-15 years	11	8
Education		
Intermediate	14	10
Graduate	99	70
Post graduate &above	28	20

Source: Field Survey, 2022

4. RESULTS OF DATA ANALYSIS

4.1 Descriptive Statistics

The descriptive statistics of the variables are presented in Table 3. The mean and standard deviation values of the variables demonstrate the level and variation in the respondent's score. In the study, the respondents show higher rating for LSQ (4.34), JS (4.30), RRP (4.27), WLB (4.24), OCC (4.22), PCG (4.13), TD (4.04) and AUT (3.96).

4.2 Multiple Regression Analysis

In order to check the impact of selected factors on employee retention multiple regressions was used. A multiple regression model is usually used to examine the influence of the set of independent factors on a single dependent factor. Selected factors affecting employee retention are independent factors and employee retention is dependent factor in this study. Table 4 shows the summary of multiple regression model.

Table 3. Descriptive statistics

Variable and Item		Mean	S.D.	Cronbach's Alpha (α) value
OCC		**4.22**	**0.572**	
OCC 1	Suggestions & grievances considered and disposed then off	4.06	0.827	
OCC 2	Employees treated fairly with due respect	4.28	0.555	**0.835**
OCC 3	Work life culture & climate meet my expectancy by comparison to other players in the sector	4.28	0.584	
RRP		**4.27**	**0.499**	
RRP 1	Good work is recognized	4.28	0.584	**0.751**
RRP 2	Usually rewarded for successful job accomplishment	4.26	0.660	
RRP 3	Salary and other benefits are more than those working under other players in the sector	4.28	0.584	
LSQ		**4.34**	**0.467**	
LSQ 1	Organization's leader's approachability is extremely acceptable	4.30	0.590	
LSQ2	Superior is helpful, impartial and protective & use tactful decision	4.33	0.572	**0.694**
LSQ 3	Commitments toward the company increase because of the quality & style of my leader/ Supervisor	4.40	0.616	
JS		**4.30**	**0.493**	
JS 1	Feel secured in my job as chance of getting jobless is less	4.28	0.586	**0.762**
JS 2	Job security improve my sense of reliability toward the organization	4.33	0.628	
JS 3	Increased job safety give lift to my moral	4.28	0.548	
WLB		**4.24**	**0.377**	
WLB 1	Job is neither stressful nor boring	4.36	0.581	**0.715**
WLB 2	Work programming and timing meet my expectation	4.15	0.546	
WLB 3	I enjoy an accurate balance among work and personal-life	4.21	0.523	
TD		**4.04**	**0.819**	
TD 1	Specific training programme identified and given to me	4.10	0.877	
TD 2	Instruction training given to me which reflected the real scenario of the work and company	4.05	0.891	**0.891**
TD 3	Training given to me is at parity with the change dynamics as compared to other players in sector	3.98	0.911	
AUT		**3.96**	**0.714**	
AUT 1	Usually get extreme degree of independency to execute a job	4.05	0.790	**0.832**
AUT 2	Involved in main conclusions relating to my job	3.85	0.971	
AUT 3	Supervisor advantages in decision-making and consider my suggestions and opinions	4.00	0.713	
PCG		**4.13**	**0.553**	
PCG 1	Job has good promotion opportunity	4.20	0.576	**0.776**
PCG 2	Promotion procedure is good and don't need change	4.03	0.735	
PCG 3	Career growth objectives are fulfilled to my expectation	4.18	0.676	

Table 4. Model summary of multiple regression model

Model		Adjusted	*F* Ratio	*P* Value
I	0.604	0.583	30.04	0.002

Significance at 5% Level

The results revealed that R-square value which determine the proportion of variance in dependent variable is 0.604 or 60.4 per cent. Which means that 60.4 per cent of the variance is explained by the combination of independent variables on the dependent variable. The F-ratio measures whether the model as a whole has statistical significance or not. The *F*–ratio (30.04) and ($P = 0.002$) indicate that model is statistically significant and having a good predictive power. Therefore, it can be inferred that the selected factors have a considerable impact on employee retention and the multiple regression model is statistically significant and having a good predictive power. Therefore, it can be inferred that the selected factors in this study have considerable influence on employee retention. Next, the standardized Beta value is assessed to examine which independent factor accounts for the strongest contribution to explaining the dependent variable i.e., employee retention. The Beta value of each variable has been considered for individual variable analysis. From the results in Table 5, it was found that all the factors taken in this study i.e., OCC (0.586), RRP (0.412), LSQ (0.446), JS (0.418), WLB (0.582), TD (0.594), AUT (0.448) and PCG (0.488) have positive and significant impact on employee retention (Refer Table 5) and hence H_1 was accepted.

4.3 Multivariate Analysis of Variance (MANOVA)

Next, to determine different effects in selected factors of employee retention in terms of demographical variables (gender, age, occupation, income, experience and education) MANOVA was used. Results of MANOVA analysis are summarized in Table 6. In case of gender, results of MANOVA analysis revealed that male and female investors display differential effect *(Wilks' $\lambda = 0.818$; $F = 1.287$; $P = 0.001$; $\eta 2 = 0.182$).* Partial eta squared (0.182) evidenced that gender explain 18.2 per cent of variance in context of factors of employee retention. Furthermore, from the mean analysis, it was found that male consumers reported a comparatively higher degree for (OCC, RRP, WLB, TD, AUT, PCG) whereas female employees shown higher degree for (LSQ, JS,). With regard to age, results of MANOVA analysis revealed that age displays a differential effect *(Wilks' $\lambda = 0.830$; $F = 0.598$; $P < 0 .000$; $\eta 2 = 0.089$).* Partial eta squared (0.089) indicating that age explains 8.9 per cent of variance in employee retention factors. Furthermore,

Table 5. Coefficients in multiple regression.

Independent Variables	Dependent Variable- Employee Retention			
	Beta	Coefficient Std. Error	t-Value	Sig.
OCC	0.586	0.134	5.461	0.000
RRP	0.412	0.171	3.439	0.007
LSQ	0.446	0.180	3.800	0.004
JS	0.418	0.173	3.508	0.001
WLB	0.582	0.202	5.447	0.000
TD	0.594	0.092	5.620	0.002
AUT	0.448	0.086	3.453	0.009
PCG	0.488	0.148	4.257	0.004

from the mean analysis of factors of employee retention, it was found that employees under 25-30 age group reported a comparatively higher degree for (OCC, RRP, LSQ, AUT,) whereas employees under 31-40 age group shown higher degree for (WLB, TD, PCG). Considering occupation, results of MANOVA analysis revealed that occupation displays a differential effect *(Wilks' $\lambda = 0.496$; $F = 1.594$; $P < 0.002$; $\eta 2 = 0.209$)*. Partial eta squared (0.209) indicated that occupation explains 20.9 per cent of variance in employee retention factors. Mean analysis of factors of employee retention revealed that employee at managerial level reported a comparatively higher degree for (OCC, RRP, JS, WLB, AUT, PCG) whereas employee working at operational shown higher degree for (LSQ) and worker shown higher degree (TD). With regard to work experience, results of MANOVA analysis for employee retention revealed differential effects *(Wilks' $\lambda = 0.787$; $F = 0.778$; $P < 0.000$; $\eta 2 = 0.113$)*. Partial eta squared (0.113) indicated that occupation explains 11.3 per cent of variance in employee retention factors. Mean analysis of factors of employee retention, it was found that employees having work experience of 11-15 years reported a comparatively higher degree for (OCC, RRP, LSQ, JS, WLB, TD, AUT, and PCG). Considering education, results of MANOVA analysis also displays differential effects *(Wilks' $\lambda = 0.548$; $F = 2.153$; $P < 0.004$; $\eta 2 = 0.260$)*. Partial eta squared (0.260) evidenced reasonably good effect size, indicating that occupation explains 26 per cent of variance in employee retention factors. Furthermore, from the mean analysis of factors of employee retention, it was found that employees that were qualified at intermediate level reported a comparatively higher degree for (OCC, TD) whereas employees qualified at post graduate & above level reported higher degree for (RRP, JS, WLB, AUT, PCG). Hence based on the results of MANOVA, H_2 was accepted.

4.4 Summary of Finding

The following discussion summarizes the findings. The findings reveal that all factors demonstrate adequate reliability and validity and can benefit future researchers in this field of study. This research identified OCC, RRP, LSQ, JS, WLB, TD, AUT and PCG as the significant influencing factors of employee retention and 60.4 per cent variation is caused by these factors towards employee retention. The variable TD have the highest coefficient value, indicating that it strongly influences employee retention. A one-point rise in TD causes a 0.594 points positive change in employee retention. Another variable that has a strong influence on employee retention was OCC. Organization with positive work culture and climate can hold employees for longer time period with them. The employee retention was positively affected by 0.586 points for every single point increase in the OCC. WLB was also emerged as a strong factor that affect employee retention. A one-point rise in WLB results in a 0.582 points improvement in employee retention. PCG opportunities also an appealing factor for employees in the organization. One point rise in PCG results in a 0.488 points improvement in employee retention. Remaining set of factors such as AUT, LSQ also indicated a positive influence on employee retention. A one-point rise in these factors results in a 0.488 and 0.446 points improvement in employee retention respectively. Out of the selected factors in this study surprisingly the least influencing factors identified were JS and RRP, in which one point increase can improve the employee retention 0.418 and 0.416 respectively. The results also gain support from the previous studies (Bibi et al., 2016; Ambrosius, 2018). The results of current study contradict the findings of (Oladapo, 2014), who examined the relationship between employee retention and job security, compensation, and career advancement chances and came to the conclusion that these factors do not influence retention. Another study by Reiche (2008) in the same line showed that training and career advancement have no bearing on employee retention, while job security has the least

Table 6. Results of multivariate analysis

Value label	OCC	RRP	LSQ	JS	WLB	TD	AUT	PCG
	Mean Values							
Gender								
Male	4.31	4.34	4.30	4.37	4.27	4.10	4.3	4.20
Female	3.97	4.14	4.41	4.41	4.12	3.87	3.75	3.89
Wilks' $\lambda = 0.818$; $F = 1.287$; $P = 1.387$; $\eta2 = 0.182$								
Age								
Below 25	4.02	4.28	4.35	4.33	4.20	3.87	3.89	3.94
25 – 30	4.28	4.31	4.36	4.33	4.23	4.07	3.97	4.13
31 – 40	4.20	4.20	4.12	4.33	4.29	4.16	3.95	4.35
Wilks' $\lambda = 0.830$; $F = 0.598$; $P = 0.089$; $\eta2 = 0.089$								
Occupation								
Employee at managerial level	4.30	4.26	4.30	4.26	4.31	4.06	4.07	4.04
Employee at operational level	4.16	4.31	4.40	4.33	4.17	3.97	3.85	4.10
Supervisor	4.73	4.60	4.33	4.73	4.33	4.20	4.53	4.80
Worker	3.58	3.90	4.00	3.91	4.16	4.25	3.33	3.83
Wilks' $\lambda = 0.496$; $F = 1.594$; $P = 0.209$; $\eta2 = 0.209$								
Work experience								
0-5 years	4.10	4.22	4.31	4.26	4.18	3.87	3.83	4.08
6-10 years	4.31	4.29	4.33	4.26	4.31	4.26	4.03	4.07
11-15 years	4.66	4.73	4.46	4.73	4.33	4.40	4.46	4.60
Wilks' $\lambda = 0.787$; $F = 0.778$; $P = 0.113$; $\eta2 = 0.113$								
Education								
Intermediate	4.46	3.86	4.00	3.86	4.06	4.13	3.53	4.13
Graduate	4.13	4.26	4.36	4.30	4.25	4.07	3.95	4.07
Post Graduate& above	4.41	4.55	4.36	4.55	4.25	3.88	4.13	4.27

Wilks' $\lambda = 0.548$; $F = 2.153$; $P = 0.260$; $\eta2 = 0.260$

Source: As per the author's computation

impact. Additionally, the results of current study showed the differential effect of demographic factors on the factors that influence employee retention. The literature (Gaines et al., 2018; Yeves et al., 2019) also supports these findings. Thus, it is suggested that rather than having a common retention strategy, it is more viable to consider differential retention strategies based on demographics of employee.

4.5 Industry 5.0 Interventions for Employee Retention in Automobile Industry

Industry 5.0 represents the next phase of industrial evolution, focusing on human-technology collaboration. Employee retention remains a critical concern in this era, and several interventions can be implemented to address this challenge. Some insights for the automobile industry considering the industry 5.0 interventions for employee retention are discussed next.

Personalized Training

Instead of generic training, companies can offer personalized programs based on each employee's skills and career goals. Advanced tech like AI can help tailor these programs to individual strengths and weaknesses.

Interactive Training with Augmented Reality (AR)

Organizations can try to make training programs more engaging with using augmented reality. The training programs like this will be simulate real work environment and results in more confident and skilled employees.

Smart Scheduling System

Employees can be allowed for flexible work hours by using smart scheduling systems. It will create an environment accommodating different lifestyles.

Blockchain Technology for Employee Appraisal

Blockchain technology will a good option to create a transparent appraisal system in the organization. Organization can utilize smart contracts to automate fair acknowledgment of employee achievements.

Predictive Analytics to Access employee Well-Being

Predictive analytics can be used to proactively identify the signs of employee burnout or dissatisfaction. By using predictive analytics organizations can offer timely support and make necessary adjustments.

Collaborative Robotics

To encourage collaborative work environment between human workers and robots at workplace, organizations can use collaborative robotics for repetitive kind of tasks and human workers can be engaged in others intellectual assignments.

Virtual Reality for Team Building

To inculcate team spirit among remotely dispersed teams, organizations can use virtual reality technology for performing team building exercises. It will be helpful to create a sense of belonging among employees.

Real Time Feedback With IoT

Organizations can establish a real time feedback mechanism using IOT. This kind of feedback system will be instrumental in providing immediate insights to employees on their performance. It will also setup a culture of continuous improvement and growth with regular feedback from peers and supervisors (Kumar & Kaur, 2023).

Artificial Intelligence Tools for Mental Health Support

Organizations can prioritize mental health of employees by offering resources and counselling services. It could be best done by artificial intelligence tools to detect signs of stress or mental health issues among employees.

By putting these strategies into action, companies can create a work environment that is not only technologically advanced but also supportive, collaborative, and focused on the well-being and growth of its employees. This, in turn, enhances retention and ensures long-term employee satisfaction.

5. CONCLUSION

In this study, the impact of various factors on employee retention in the automobile industry was examined. The study's findings will aid management and employers in keeping hold of their top talent for a longer period of time. The factors affecting employee retention such as organisational culture and climate, reward recognition and pay, leadership style and quality, job security, work-life balance, training and development, autonomy and promotion, career advancement were considered in this study. The study's findings demonstrate that employee retention in the automobile industry is primarily influenced by training and development. The demographic factors also had a substantial impact on the retention factors that were chosen. Based on the findings, it can be said that the management should implement measures to make organization a better place to work. The notable insights from the current research suggests that the: Training & development is one of the most essential factors in the automobile industry. Different styles and methods should be adopted by the company which can improve employees' productivity. It enables the reskilling and upskilling of the workforce, which boosts their long-term employability and earning potential. Particularly companies can: a) conduct a skill audit to identify skill gaps; b) to set specific and measurable goals; c) surveying and collecting feedback from employees to plan learning methods. Keeping a healthy work culture can act as a major aspect for employee retention. A negative or deadly culture can lead to unfortunate or unengaged staff members, inferior work, and high turnover. Organizations should try to clearly articulate their values, beliefs, and behavior that makes the organizational environment. Clear communication of the company's culture and its reflectivity makes it easier for employees to realize and embrace the values. A flexible schedule and state humanities could be an effective measure. Work from home can be act as an effective measure but unfortunately due to the nature of work in the automobile industry cannot be implemented fully. To provide a level of job autonomy to employees at the workplace could be another effective employee retention measure. The organization should provide employees the freedom to work in a way that suits them. Job autonomy will help employees to put creativity in the workplace and provide self-advocacy among employees. Additionally, in the era of industry 5.0 organizations are suggested to utilize interactive training with augmented reality, flexible work hours, blockchain technology for employee reward and recognition, predictive analytics to assess employee well being and other issues, team building exercises with virtual reality, real time feedback system etc. as interventions to strengthen employee retention in automobile industry. As far as employee retention is concerned in the automobile industry certain or selected automobile companies are providing several benefits to their employees consequently, the satisfaction level of the employees with these organization is greater which is a good symbol of harmonious relation among organization and the employees. Since employees are the foundation of any business, the HR department should place a high priority on employee retention. The management needs to recognise the crucial elements that influence employee retention and take the required actions to enhance them. The management should also take the necessary steps to determine the causes of employees' voluntary leaves. We may therefore draw the conclusion that the organisation should focus on addressing employees' requirements with regard to their employment, careers, families, etc. so that the organization's positive approach would boost employee retention.

REFERENCES

Agyeman, C. M., & Ponniah, V. M. (2014). Employee demographic characteristics and their effects on turnover and retention in MSMEs. *International Journal of Recent Advances in Organizational Behaviour and Decision Sciences*, *1*(1), 12–29.

Almalki, M. J., FitzGerald, G., & Clark, M. (2012). The relationship between quality of work life and turnover intention of primary health care nurses in Saudi Arabia. *BMC Health Services Research*, *12*(1), 1–11. doi:10.1186/1472-6963-12-314 PMID:22970764

Ambrosius, J. (2018). Strategic talent management in emerging markets and its impact on employee retention: Evidence from Brazilian MNCs. *Thunderbird International Business Review*, *60*(1), 53–68. doi:10.1002/tie.21799

Aruna, M., & Anitha, J. (2015). Employee retention enablers: Generation Y employees. *SCMS Journal of Indian Management*, *12*(3), 94.

Ballinger, G., Craig, E., Cross, R., & Gray, P. (2011). A stitch in time saves nine: Leveraging networks to reduce the costs of turnover. *California Management Review*, *53*(4), 111–133. doi:10.1525/cmr.2011.53.4.111

Bibi, P., Ahmad, A., & Majid, A. H. (2016). The moderating role of work environment on the relationship between compensation, job security, and employee's retention. *Journal of Economic & Management Perspectives*, *10*(4), 726–738.

Bryant, P. C., & Allen, D. (2013). Compensation, benefits and employee turnover: HR strategies for retaining top talent. *Compensation and Benefits Review*, *45*(3), 171–175. doi:10.1177/0886368713494342

Cameron, K., & Sine, W. (1999). A framework for organizational quality culture. *The Quality Management Journal*, *6*(4), 7–25. doi:10.1080/10686967.1999.11919208

Charity, E. (2016). Human resource management practices and retention of core employees in the oil and gas industry in Nigeria. *Human Resource Management*, *6*(7).

Chatterjee, S., Nankervis, A., & Connell, J. (2014). Framing the emerging talent crisis in India and China: A human capital perspective. *SA Journal of Human Resource Management*, *1*(1), 25–43.

Cillo, V., Gregori, G. L., Daniele, L. M., Caputo, F., & Bitbol-Saba, N. (2022). Rethinking companies' culture through knowledge management lens during Industry 5.0 transition. *Journal of Knowledge Management*, *26*(10), 2485–2498. doi:10.1108/JKM-09-2021-0718

Demir, K. A., Döven, G., & Sezen, B. (2019). Industry 5.0 and human-robot co-working. *Procedia Computer Science*, *158*, 688–695. doi:10.1016/j.procs.2019.09.104

Denison, D. R., & Mishra, A. K. (1995). Toward a theory of organizational culture and effectiveness. *Organization Science*, *6*(2), 204–223. doi:10.1287/orsc.6.2.204

Fahim, M. G. A. (2018). Strategic human resource management and public employee retention. *Review of Economics and Political Science*, *3*(2), 20–39. doi:10.1108/REPS-07-2018-002

Fletcher, L., Alfes, K., & Robinson, D. (2018). The relationship between perceived training and development and employee retention: The mediating role of work attitudes. *International Journal of Human Resource Management*, *29*(18), 2701–2728. doi:10.1080/09585192.2016.1262888

Gaines, B., Dugan, A., & Cherniack, M. (2018). The relationship between retirement expectations and job insecurity among the aging us workforce. *Innovation in Aging*, *2*(Suppl 1).

George, C. (2015). Retaining professional workers: What makes them stay? *Employee Relations*, *37*(1), 102–121. doi:10.1108/ER-10-2013-0151

Govindaraju, N. (2018). Demographic factors influence on employee retention. *International Journal of Engineering Studied and Technical Approach*, *7*, 10–20.

Haider, M., Rasli, A., Akhtar, C. S., Yusoff, R. B. M., Malik, O. M., Aamir, A., & Tariq, F. (2015). The impact of human resource practices on employee retention in the telecom sector. *International Journal of Economics and Financial Issues*, *5*(1), 63–69.

Hair, J. F. Jr, Black, W. C., Babin, B. J., & Anderson, R. E. (2009). *Multivariate Data Analysis: A Global Perspective*. Pearson Education.

Hancock, J. I., Allen, D. G., Bosco, F. A., McDaniel, K. R., & Pierce, C. A. (2013). Meta-analytic review of employee turnover as a predictor of firm performance. *Journal of Management*, *39*(3), 573–603. doi:10.1177/0149206311424943

Hassan, W., Razi, A., Qamar, R., Jaffer, R., & Suhail, S. (2013). The effect of training on employee Retention. *Global Journal of Management and Business Research Administration and Management*, *13*(6), 16–20.

Heneman, R. L., Greenberger, D. B., & Fox, J. A. (2002). Pay increase satisfaction: A reconceptualization of pay raise satisfaction based on changes in work and pay practices. *Human Resource Management Review*, *12*(1), 63–74. doi:10.1016/S1053-4822(01)00041-9

Hill, B., & Tande, C. (2006). *Total Rewards: The Employee Value Proposition*. Workspan.

Holtom, B. C., Mitchell, T. R., Lee, T. W., & Eberly, M. B. (2008). 5 turnover and retention research: A glance at the past, a closer review of the present, and a venture into the future. *The Academy of Management Annals*, *2*(1), 231–274. doi:10.5465/19416520802211552

India Brand Equity Foundation (IBEF). (2022). Automobile industry in India. https://www.ibef.org/industry/india-automobiles

Iqbal, S., & Hashmi, M. S. (2015). Impact of perceived organizational support on employee retention with mediating role of psychological empowerment. *Pakistan Journal of Commerce and Social Sciences*, *9*(1), 18–34.

Kaur, A., & Dilawari, K. (2015). A study to identify the factors affecting employee retention. *International Journal of Scientific Research*, *6*(5), 1827–1831.

Khalid, K., & Nawab, S. (2018). Employee participation and employee retention in view of compensation. *SAGE Open*, *8*(4). doi:10.1177/2158244018810067

Kumar, A., & Kaur, A. (2022, November). A Multivariate Analysis on Employee Competencies. *2022 5th International Conference on Multimedia, Signal Processing and Communication Technologies (IMPACT)*, 1-5. 10.1109/IMPACT55510.2022.10029153

Kumar, A., & Kaur, A. (2023). Predicting complaint voicing or exit amidst Indian consumers: A CHAID analysis. *Journal of Advances in Management Research*, *20*(1), 55–78. doi:10.1108/JAMR-03-2022-0054

Kumar, A., & Kaur, A. (2024). Indian consumers' tendency to exit amidst a complaint: A SEM approach. *International Journal of Management Practice*, *17*(1), 19–50. doi:10.1504/IJMP.2024.135189

Kumar, G. G., & Santhosh, C. (2014). Exploring the dimensions of employee retention in BPO industry in Kerala. *Asia Pacific Journal of Research*, *1*, 61–78.

Kumar, V. M., & Babu, P. (2017). A review of the factors affecting employee retention in the workplace. *International Journal of Current Research*, *9*(11), 61791–61794.

Kundu, S. C., & Lata, K. (2017). Effects of supportive work environment on employee retention: Mediating role of organizational engagement. *The International Journal of Organizational Analysis*, *25*(4), 703–722. doi:10.1108/IJOA-12-2016-1100

Laskowska, A., & Laskowski, J. F. (2022). "Silver" Generation at Work—Implications for Sustainable Human Capital Management in the Industry 5.0 Era. *Sustainability (Basel)*, *15*(1), 194. doi:10.3390/su15010194

Latha, K. L. (2013). A study on employee attrition and retention in manufacturing industries. *BVIMSR's. Journal of Management Research*, *5*(1), 1–23.

Mangal,, E., Lalwani, S., Dadhich, M., & Chauhan, D. (2021). A study of factors delivering competitive edge in employee retention. *Turkish Journal of Computer and Mathematics*, *12*(7), 2555–2571.

McDonnell, A., Collings, D. G., & Burgess, J. (2012). Guest editors' note: Talent management in the Asia Pacific. *Asia Pacific Journal of Human Resources*, *50*(4), 391–398. doi:10.1111/j.1744-7941.2012.00035.x

Mohammed, A. (2015). The impact of talent management on employee engagement, retention and value addition in achieving organizational performance. *International Journal of Core Engineering & Management*, *1*(12), 142–152.

Mukherjee, B., Chandra, B., & Singh, S. (2020). Talent retention in Indian public sector units (PSUs): An empirical investigation. *Kybernetes*, *49*(6), 1783–1810. doi:10.1108/K-03-2019-0165

Muo, I. K. (2013). Identifying and minimizing risks in the change management process: The case of Nigerian banking industry. *Issues in Business Management and Economics*, *1*(6), 148–162.

Narayanan, A., Rajithakumar, S., & Menon, M. (2019). Talent management and employee retention: An integrative research framework. *Human Resource Development Review*, *18*(2), 228–247. doi:10.1177/1534484318812159

Naz, S., Nisar, A., Khan, M., Ahmad, N., & Anwar, T. (2020). A study in the relationship between supportive work environment and employee retention: Role of organizational commitment and person-organization fit as mediator. *SAGE Open*, *4*(2), 1–20. doi:10.1177/2158244020924694

Oladapo, V. (2014). The impact of talent management on retention. *Journal of Business Studies Quarterly*, *5*(3).

Park, T. Y., & Shaw, J. D. (2013). Turnover rates and organizational performance: A meta-analysis. *The Journal of Applied Psychology*, *98*(2), 268–309. doi:10.1037/a0030723 PMID:23244224

Presbitero, A., Roxas, B., & Chadee, D. (2016). Looking beyond HRM practices in enhancing employee retention in BPOs: Focus on employee–organisation value fit. *International Journal of Human Resource Management*, *27*(6), 635–652. doi:10.1080/09585192.2015.1035306

Rakhra, H. K. (2018). Study on factors influencing employee retention in companies. *International Journal of Public Sector Performance Management, 4*(1), 57-79.

Rani, N., & Samuel, A. (2016). A study on generational differences in work values and person-organization fit and its effect on turnover intention of Generation Y in India. *Management Research Review*, *39*(12), 1695–1719. doi:10.1108/MRR-10-2015-0249

Reiche, B. S. (2008). The configuration of employee retention practices in multinational corporations' foreign subsidiaries. *International Business Review*, *17*(6), 676–687. doi:10.1016/j.ibusrev.2008.09.004

Saks, A. M. (1995). Longitudinal field investigation of the moderating and mediating effects of self-efficacy on the relationship between training and newcomer adjustment. *The Journal of Applied Psychology*, *80*(2), 211–225. doi:10.1037/0021-9010.80.2.211 PMID:7737934

Samuel, M. O., & Chipunza, C. (2009). Employee retention and turnover: Using motivational variables as a panacea. *African Journal of Business Management*, *3*(9).

Sandhya, K., & Kumar, D. P. (2011). Employee retention by motivation. *Indian Journal of Science and Technology*, *4*(12), 1778–1782. doi:10.17485/ijst/2011/v4i12.34

Sinnott, G. C., Madison, G. H., & Pataki, G. E. (2002). *Employee Retention*. McGraw-Hill.

Tanwar, K., & Prasad, A. (2016). Exploring the relationship between employer branding and employee retention. *Global Business Review*, *17*(3), 186S–206S. doi:10.1177/0972150916631214

Teclaw, R., Osatuke, K., Fishman, J., Moore, S. C., & Dyrenforth, S. (2014). Employee age and tenure within organizations: Relationship to workplace satisfaction and workplace climate perceptions. *The Health Care Manager*, *33*(1), 4–19. doi:10.1097/01.HCM.0000440616.31891.2d PMID:24463586

Tett, R. P., & Meyer, J. P. (1993). Job satisfaction, organizational commitment, turnover intention, and turnover: Path analyses based on meta-analytic findings. *Personnel Psychology*, *46*(2), 259–293. doi:10.1111/j.1744-6570.1993.tb00874.x

Verma, D. S., & Chaurasia, R. (2016). A study to identify the factors affecting employee turnover in small scale industries. *International Journal of Engineering Sciences & Research Technology*, *5*(7), 638–652.

Walangitan, N., Pangemanan, S., & Tumewu, F. (2014). The analysis of factors affecting employee retention at pt. hasjrat abadi manado. *Journal EMBA*, *2*(1), 490–498.

Wareth, H., & Amirah, N. (2020). A review of training and development towards employee retention in the banking sector. *The Journal of Management Theory and Practices*, *1*(2), 16–21.

Yeves, J., Bargsted, M., Cortes, L., Merino, C., & Cavada, G. (2019). Age and perceived employability as moderators of job insecurity and job satisfaction: A moderated moderation model. *Frontiers in Psychology*, *10*, 10. doi:10.3389/fpsyg.2019.00799 PMID:31031675

Yusoff, R. M., Khan, F., Mubeen, A. & Azam, K. (2013). A study about factors influencing the university performance. *Sains Humanika, 64*(2).

Chapter 7
Future of Industry 5.0:
Added Features, Enabling Technologies, and Human-Centric Solutions

Geetika Madaan
https://orcid.org/0000-0001-8141-9935
Chandigarh University, India

Jaskiran Kaur
https://orcid.org/0000-0002-4452-1807
Lovely Professional University, India

Sanjeet Singh
Chandigarh University, India

Satish Kumar Asthana
Chandigarh University, India

ABSTRACT

Industry 5.0, the next step in industrial development, seeks to combine the knowledge and insight of humans with the productivity, intelligence, and accuracy of machines to produce goods that are more cost-effective and more popular with end users than those produced by Industry 4.0. The goal of Industry 5.0 is to increase production and streamline the delivery of customized goods through the use of a suite of cutting-edge technology and apps. This chapter aims to give a foundational overview of Industry 5.0 by outlining some of the possible uses and enabling technologies of this emerging sector. First, the study defines Industry 5.0 and explains numerous new ideas from the point of view of several experts in the field. The study then details some of the possible applications or uses of Industry 5.0, including smart education, smart manufacturing, intelligent healthcare, supply chain management, supply chain management, and cyber-physical systems.

INTRODUCTION

Over the course of many centuries, humans, with or without the assistance of animals, have created a wide variety of vehicles, clothes, housing, and weapons (Nahavandi, 2019). When Industry 1.0 first appeared in 1974, it triggered a dramatic shift in the manufacturing sector (Grabowska, Saniuk, & Gajdzik, 2022). In Fig. 1 we see a timeline that spans the development of Industrial X.0. Approximately 100 years passed between each of the first three revolutions, and only 40 years separated the third and fourth. Industry 1.0 emerged in the 1780 with the advent of mechanised production facilities for steam and water-driven

DOI: 10.4018/979-8-3693-1343-5.ch007

machinery (Humayun, 2021). The economy has benefited greatly from the rise in production capacity, which has led to a dramatic improvement in the economy. In 1870, the introduction of electric power and assembly line manufacturing paved the way for what is now known as "Industry 2.0." Companies in the industrial sector were able to boost their output thanks to Industry 2.0's emphasis on mass production and the distribution of workloads. The ideas of electronic, semi-automatic, and information technology gave birth to what is now known as Industry 3.0 in 1970. Industry 4.0, or "smart manufacturing for the next generation," is a notion that emerged in 2011. The prime goal is to optimise output and enter mass manufacturing with the help of cutting-edge technologies. Industry 5.0 (started in 2020) is an impending transformation that will combine the ingenuity of human experts with the efficacy, intelligence, and accuracy of machines.

Industry 5.0

Industry 5.0 is a concept that represents the next phase in the evolution of industrial manufacturing, building upon the principles of Industry 4.0 while emphasizing the centrality of human workers in tandem with advanced technologies. Unlike previous industrial revolutions that focused primarily on automation and digitalization (Industry 4.0), Industry 5.0 seeks to integrate human skills, creativity, and decision-making into the manufacturing process alongside robotic and AI technologies. This approach aims to strike a balance between automation and human involvement, harnessing the strengths of both to create more efficient, adaptable, and sustainable industrial systems.

Key characteristics of Industry 5.0 include:

1. **Human-Centricity**: Industry 5.0 places humans at the forefront of manufacturing processes, recognizing their unique capabilities in problem-solving, creativity, and quality assurance. Rather than replacing human workers with machines, Industry 5.0 aims to augment human skills and empower workers to collaborate effectively with advanced technologies.
2. **Collaborative Robotics (Cobots)**: The adoption of collaborative robots (cobots) is a hallmark of Industry 5.0. Cobots are designed to work alongside humans, assisting with repetitive or physically demanding tasks while ensuring safety and productivity. This collaborative approach enhances operational efficiency and optimizes resource utilization.
3. **AI-Augmented Decision Making**: Industry 5.0 leverages artificial intelligence (AI) to support human decision-making. AI-driven analytics and predictive algorithms provide real-time insights, enabling workers to make informed decisions and optimize manufacturing processes based on data-driven recommendations.
4. **Skill Development and Training**: Industry 5.0 emphasizes continuous skill development and training for the workforce. As manufacturing technologies evolve, upskilling and reskilling programs ensure that workers remain adaptable and proficient in utilizing advanced tools and systems.
5. **Flexible and Adaptive Manufacturing**: Industry 5.0 promotes flexible and adaptive manufacturing systems that can quickly reconfigure production lines based on changing market demands and customer preferences. This agility enables manufacturers to respond swiftly to dynamic market conditions.
6. **Quality Assurance and Ethical Considerations**: Human oversight remains essential in Industry 5.0 for maintaining quality standards, identifying defects, and ensuring ethical and sustainable practices throughout the manufacturing process.

Overall, Industry 5.0 represents a shift towards a more holistic and inclusive approach to industrial manufacturing, where the synergy between human intelligence and technological innovation drives continuous improvement and innovation. By embracing human-centric principles alongside advanced technologies, Industry 5.0 aims to create smarter, more resilient, and socially responsible industrial environments that benefit both businesses and society as a whole.

"The breakdown of the article's remaining content is as follows. In Section 2, the existing study summarise the literature on the development of Industry 5.0 and define its distinguishing characteristics in light of preceding industrial revolutions. In Chapter 3, the study explores Industry 5.0's added features. The applications of Industry 5.0 are discussed in Section 4, and that include smart manufacturing, smart education, supply chain management, smart healthcare, and cyber physical systems. In Section 5, the study focusses on the Opportunities via Industry 5.0 Discussion as well as the Challenges and Open Issues in Industry 5.0 Development. Section 6 concludes this study and presents final findings.

Review of Literature

- **Rationale behind the Evolution of Industry 5.0**

"Artificial intelligence (AI), the Internet of Things (IoT), cloud computing, cyber physical systems (CPS), and cognitive computing" are just a few of the technologies that the industry 4.0 standard has brought together to change the industrial sector(Özdemir & Hekim, 2018). The goal of Industry 4.0 is to create a "smart" manufacturing sector by introducing a network of interconnected machines and other devices capable of controlling one another at all stages of the production cycle(Paschek, Mocan, & Draghici, 2019). The goal of Industry 4.0 is to reduce the amount of time and effort workers need to spend on individual tasks. The goal of Industry 4.0 is to increase overall efficiency and output by connecting and sharing machine-learned intelligence among various electronic equipment and software programmes. The

Figure 1. Industry revolution 5.0 adapted from Humayun (2021)

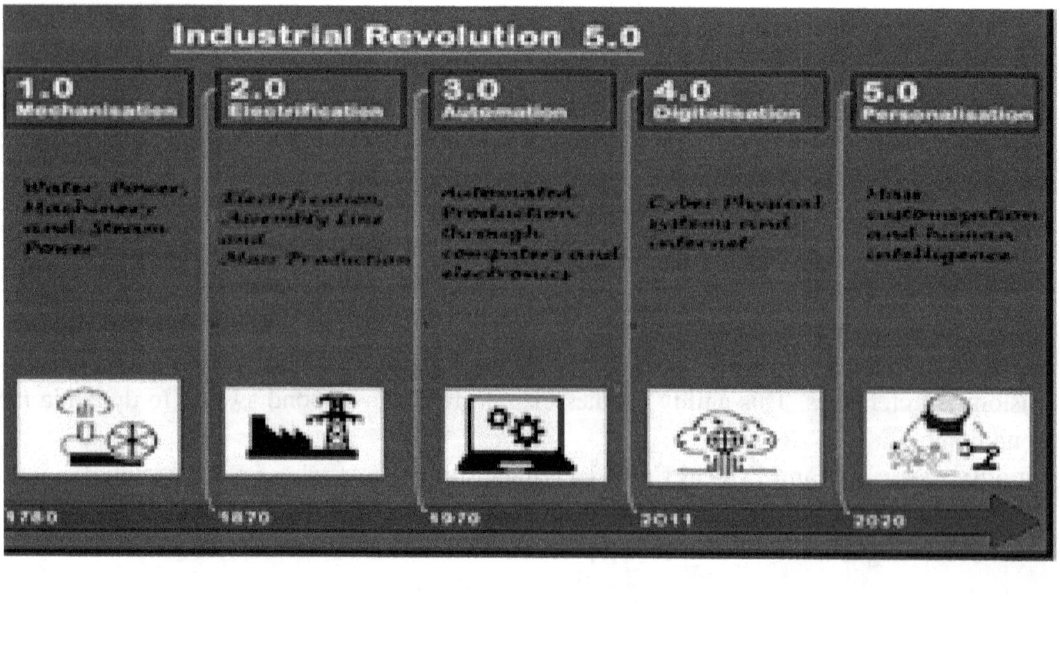

present vision of Industry 5.0 centres on the synergy between human experts' one-of-a-kind creativity and robust, intelligent, and precise machines(Javaid & Haleem, 2020). Industry 5.0, in the eyes of many technically minded futurists, will restore the human element to manufacturing. Industry 5.0 is supposed to bring together super-fast, super-accurate machines with human-level critical thinking. Industry 5.0 has also contributed greatly to mass personalization, which allows consumers to select products that are tailored specifically to their preferences and requirements. As a result of Industry 5.0, industrial productivity will grow dramatically, and humans and robots will be able to work together in new and more flexible ways, with shared control and ongoing oversight. The teamwork of humans and machines is meant to speed up manufacturing. Industry 5.0 has the potential to improve output quality by dividing labour between humans and machines, with the latter taking on more intellectually demanding duties (Javaid & Haleem, 2020; Lee, Bagheri, & Kao, 2015; Maddikunta et al., 2022).

Since intellectual professionals now work alongside robots, Industry 5.0 encourages the creation of additional highly trained positions. There will be a large emphasis on individualization under Industry 5.0, and humans will ultimately direct robots in this setting (Skobelev & Borovik, 2017). Large-scale production is well underway with robots in Industry 4.0, while the focus of Industry 5.0 is on improving the experience of the end user. Connected production systems (CPS) are the primary emphasis of Industry 4.0, while applications of Industry 4.0 and the utilisation of collaborative robots are the focus of Industry 5.0. Another perk of Industry 5.0 is that it offers environmentally friendly alternatives to the previous iterations of industrial transformation, which have not paid much attention to conservation efforts. Models built with the use of predictive analytics and operating intelligence in Industry 5.0 are intended to produce more reliable and consistent results than their predecessors. Most of the manufacturing process will be automated in Industry 5.0 due to the use of real-time data collected by machines and analysed by highly trained professionals (Kumar, Gupta, Singh, & Jain, 2021).

Though Industry 5.0 seems to be everywhere these days, we have yet to come across a comprehensive review piece on the topic. As a result of this realisation, we set out to write the first comprehensive assessment article of Industry 5.0.

- **Future Industrial Environments Focusing on Humans**

Embracing the harmonious integration of sophisticated technologies with the unique talents of human workers, Industry 5.0 represents a dramatic change towards a human-centric industrial environment in the future. Industry 5.0 acknowledges the critical importance of human intervention in production, in contrast to its forerunners, which mostly prioritized digitization and automation, such as Industry 4.0. Instead of trying to replace humans, this paradigm is based on the idea that technology can only improve our skills and capacities. Industry 5.0 aims to improve industrial systems through making them more efficient, flexible, and sustainable while also focusing on the well-being of workers and fostering innovation (Demir & Cicibaş, 2019).

Collaboration robots, or cobots, are one of the cornerstones of the fifth industrial revolution. Collaborating with humans, these robots can do risky, repetitious, or otherwise difficult jobs. Cobots improve efficiency and production while protecting employees from harm. In addition to improving production processes, this team effort fosters a more welcoming and inclusive workplace in which humans and machines can play to each other's strengths (Olaizola, Quartulli, Garcia, & Barandiaran, 2022).

In addition, AI-driven decision support systems are a key component of Industry 5.0, allowing human workers to make well-informed choices. Artificial intelligence (AI) does not intend to supplant human decision-makers but rather to supplement them with real-time data insights and predictive analytics. Employees are able to streamline operations, resolve issues, and promote continuous development through the use of data-driven recommendations, all thanks to this integration, which boosts overall quality and efficiency (Zizic, Mladineo, Gjeldum, & Celent, 2022).

Industry 5.0 is not just about integrating technology, but also about developing and educating human workers' skills. Workers' adaptability and competence in utilizing new technologies are ensured through constant upskilling and reskilling programs, which are essential in today's increasingly complex and networked production processes. In addition to preparing workers for the future, investing in their human capital encourages a spirit of creativity and continuous learning in manufacturing (Grabowska et al., 2022).

The development of more adaptable production methods is another important part of Industry 5.0. These systems are able to quickly modify production configurations in response to human input, real-time data, and shifting market demands. Industrial environments can improve their competitiveness and sustainability by making them more responsive to consumer needs through fast adaptation and agility (Humayun, 2021).

Industry 5.0 also places a strong emphasis on fostering adaptive and flexible production methods. Using real-time data, human interaction, and shifting market demands, these systems can quickly change production setups. Improved competitiveness and sustainability are outcomes of industrial settings that allow for quick adaptation and agility in response to consumer demands (Skobelev & Borovik, 2017).

The shift to Industry 5.0 is, however, not a picnic. It necessitates a significant change in organizational mindset towards embracing human-machine collaboration, as well as major investments in technological infrastructure. There are already enough of challenges with greater connection and automation without adding the added complexity of protecting personal information, keeping it secure, and taking ethical concerns into account (Breque, Lars De Nul, & Petridis, 2021).

To sum up, Industry 5.0 is the beginning of a new age in which industrial settings are designed with people in mind, using cutting-edge technology to enhance and empower workers. Industry 5.0 improves manufacturing processes in terms of adaptability, efficiency, and sustainability by encouraging human and machine collaboration. This change in thinking promotes innovation and productivity while also laying the groundwork for a more equitable and successful industrialization in the future by placing a premium on worker welfare, skill development, and ethical standards (Lee et al., 2015).

RESULT

Features of Industry 5.0

The fifth industrial revolution, or Industry 5.0, builds on the successes of the industry 4.0. In this part, we'll go over the features that come with Industry 5.0.

- **Hyper Personalization**

To this end, Industry 4.0 has sought to establish networks of interconnected machines, develop smart supply chains, encourage the manufacturing of intelligent products, and separate humans from the manufacture of automated goods. However, hyper customisation is used by Industry 5.0 to deal with the increasing demand for customization, which Industry 4.0 has been unable to handle (Fukuda, 2020). Hyper-personalization, or hyper-customization, is a form of individualised marketing strategy that makes use of cutting-edge technologies like "artificial intelligence (AI), machine learning (ML), cognitive systems (CS), and computer vision (CV)" in conjunction with real-time data to tailor offerings to each individual consumer. The ability to mass-customize items is greatly aided by the fusion of human and robotic intelligence. This is accomplished through disseminating multiple versions of the product's functional material to other staff members, all with the end goal of providing customers with more options to better suit their needs (Demir, Döven, & Sezen, 2019). While the goal of Industry 4.0 was mass manufacturing with little waste and maximum efficiency, the goal of Industry 5.0 is mass customisation with minimal expense and maximum precision. The coordination of production processes to accommodate for customer and market changes is made possible by the combination of human labour and robotics, aided by cognitive systems. One of the first steps towards hyper personalization is adopting a more flexible production method and supply chain. Furthermore, this requires the participation of humans, a production crew, and the tastes of the target audience. The created items' affordability is also crucial to the practicality of hyper customization (Akundi et al., 2022).

- **Cyber Physical Cognitive Systems**

Smart wearable gadgets, the Internet of Things, cloud computing, and big data analytics have all contributed to CPS's recent rise in popularity. The transition from fully manual to computerised production

Figure 2. Hyper personalization (Akundi et al., 2022)

systems (CPS) is a result of the Fourth Industrial Revolution. Industry 4.0's foundation rests on the data exchanged by CPSs with the aid of the Internet of Things. Cloud computing allows for the safe and efficient transfer and storage of massive amounts of data(Adel, 2022). Multiple applications use cognitive approaches to improve system performance, including "surveillance, industrial automation, smart grid, vehicular networks, and environmental monitoring" and hence known as cyber physical cognitive system (CPCS). The CPCS nodes represent a set of cognitive talents, such as the ability to monitor and analyse one's surroundings and act accordingly. The pillars of CPCS judgement are learning and knowledge. The CPCS is intended for use in human-robot collaboration (HRC) production settings. In the manufacturing division, the HRC works with a robot and a human to carry out the assembly of components. For this kind of collaborative work to occur in real time, we model and implement the fusion of machine and human cognition(Demir & Cicibaş, 2019). In the fifth industrial revolution, the benefits of the previous one has been capped, and human labour is once again essential to the production process. Industry 5.0 is a new industrial revolution that brings together robotics and skilled labour to create individualised goods and services.

- **Smart Additive Manufacturing**

Current manufacturing industries increasingly favour the use of sustainable manufacturing practices because of their low cost since it helps manufacturers carry out development objectives while decreasing pollution and optimising resource usage all through the product's life cycle. Industrial production has adopted a sustainable method called additive manufacturing, which involves building the product part layer by layer instead of in a single solid block, resulting in parts that are both lighter and stronger. It builds up 3D models layer by layer with material (Demir & Cicibaş, 2019). With the help of artificial intelligence (AI) algorithms and computer vision, smart additive manufacturing improves upon traditional 3D printing in terms of precision and visual representation of product design. Now, newer forms of additive manufacturing, such as 5D printing, are used to create superior materials. Smart manufactur-

Figure 3. Cyber physical cognitive systems (Olaizola et al., 2022)

ing goods have recently become the focus of research and development efforts by both businesses and academic institutions (Montazeri, 2019). Smart empowering technologies are gaining popularity and have significantly bolstered the growth of smart manufacturing in recent years thanks to the proliferation of cutting-edge technologies like "artificial intelligence (AI), internet of things (IoT), cloud computing (Cloud), big data (Big Data), communication protocol standards (CPS), fifth generation (5G), distributed technology (DT), and electronic components." Advantages of smart manufacturing include increased profitability, efficiency, and sustainability. "Smart additive manufacturing (SAM)" has emerged as a promising field of research in the past decade. The utilisation of Smart additive manufacturing, or 3D printing, to create environmentally friendly production methods is one of the most eye-catching features of Industry 5.0. Industry 4.0's application of additive manufacturing prioritised happy customers by integrating useful features in a variety of goods and services. Additionally, it allows for openness, compatibility, automation, and real-world understanding(Breque et al., 2021). SAM outlines the procedures that take place as new materials are added to an already existing design to create the final manufactured component. SAM has the potential to conserve energy, aids in decreasing material and resource usage, and ultimately results in the production of an environment free of pollution. When SAM is used in tandem with integrated automation capacity, the supply chain can be managed more efficiently, and products may be delivered sooner, thus maximising the promise of Industry 5.0 (Javaid & Haleem, 2020; Lee et al., 2015; Maddikunta et al., 2022).

Figure 4. Smart additive manufacturing (authors' elaboration)

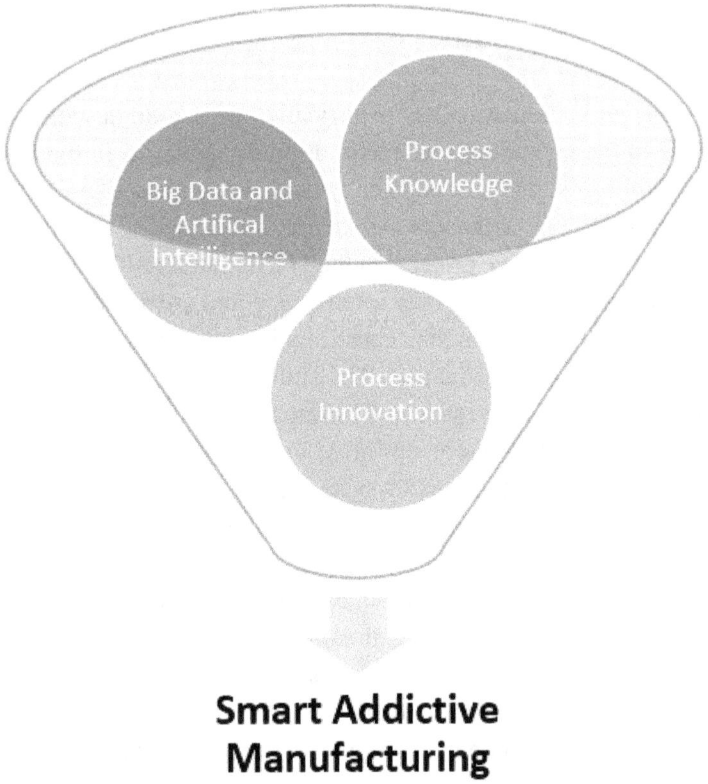

Predictive Maintenance

As the international economy continues its march towards globalisation, many businesses are confronted with formidable new difficulties. Because of this, factories have no choice but to implement future changes like predictive maintenance. Manufacturers have recently adopted new technologies, such as CPS methods and cutting-edge analytical techniques, to increase output and efficiency. In order to predict production capacity and supply, businesses need the ability to detect and evaluate risks, which is what transparency provides. In general, production plans count on constant access to machinery. However, this situation never actually occurs in the working world's industries (Breque et al., 2021; Montazeri, 2019). Accordingly, factories need to adopt predictive maintenance to improve their visibility. Application of cutting-edge prediction tools is required for this change, as the data must be transformed into information in a systematic manner, with the uncertainties defined, so that the workforce may make informed decisions. With the help of IoT, smart equipment and sensor networks can do predictive maintenance. The primary objective of predictive maintenance is to impart self-aware capabilities upon systems and devices. A crucial component of predictive maintenance technology is the use of a smart computational agent, which may take the form of specially designed smart software with built-in predictive modelling capabilities. Instead of waiting for problems to emerge before performing maintenance, Industry 5.0 uses PdM to execute maintenance in order to prevent them (Grabowska et al., 2022; Humayun, 2021).

Applications in Industry 5.0

The potential uses of Industry 5.0 are discussed below with the help of a visual representation (Fig. 2).

Smart Manufacturing/Production

The introduction of robots and automation has historically been credited with ushering in a period of profound transformation in the manufacturing sector around the world. In the past, robots in factories have been used for dangerous, repetitive, or physically demanding tasks like welding and painting automobiles and lifting and carrying big shipments. As smarter, more connected devices are introduced into the workplace, The goal of collaborative projects in the "Fifth Industrial Revolution," or "Industry 5.0," is to integrate cognitive computers with human intelligence and creativity. Since this is the case, it is possible that the fifth industrial revolution may cause significant paradigm shifts and lead to new ways of thinking about manufacturing and production. The authors of one of the study offered several takeaways from the fifth iteration's realisation state and its impact on productivity and the economy(Paschek et al., 2019). "Networked sensor data interoperability, multiscale simulation and dynamic modelling, production tracking, virtual training, autonomous systems, and machine cognition" are only some of the technologies included in this research as foundational to Industry 5.0. Fifth iteration cobot tasks were also proposed, with analysis of human intent preceding analysis of the task itself. Due to this, the cobots would be able to know when their human partner in collaboration needs help (Javaid & Haleem, 2020). Since many business industrialists continue to adhere to the outdated ideas of Industry 4.0, the study concludes that we are still far from implementing Industry 5.0. Given that many business industrialists continue to adhere to the outdated ideas of Industry 4.0, the study shows that we are far from ready to fully adopt Industry 5.0. Human-machine interaction, however, was determined to be an area where the fifth generation may make a positive contribution to employment. Significant indicators for Industry

Figure 5. Predictive maintenance (Humayun, 2021)

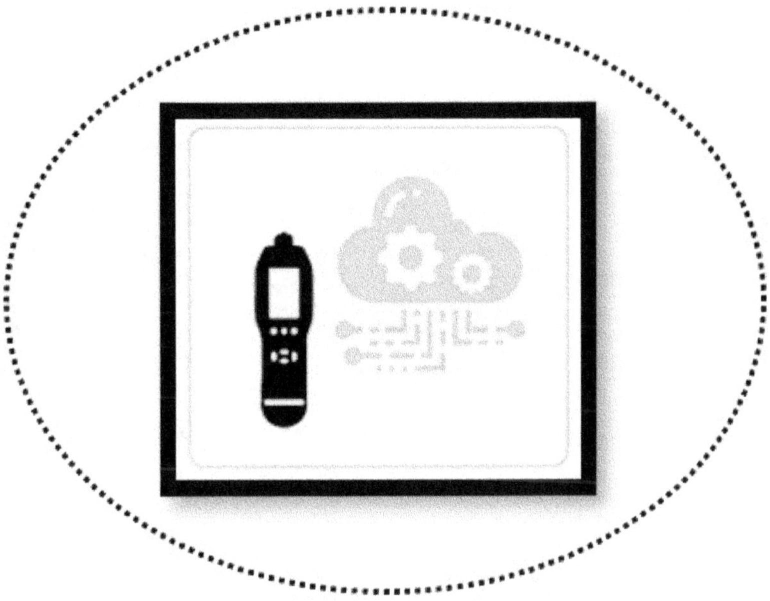

5.0 for the implementation of manufacturing highlighted by Humayun, Mamoona, (2021) (Humayun, 2021). This study examines the practical difficulties encountered by manufacturers when implementing 17 key features of the Fifth Industrial Revolution. Using Industry 5.0 in production, the authors concluded, would increase the value of the company and the satisfaction of its customers. Industry 5.0 was first proposed for use in the textile industry by Cary Sherburne. In the near future, the textile sector will be able to implement the characteristics of Industry 5.0 thanks to the foundation provided by their qualitative study (Maddikunta et al., 2022).

Supply Chain Management

Aligning the intelligence and creativity of humans with the disruptive technologies that enable Industry 5.0 can aid businesses in keeping up with demand for increasingly individualised goods while also increasing the speed with which they can supply them. The incorporation of "mass customization", a central notion in fifth industrial revolution, into supply chain management processes is facilitated by new revolution. Warehouses, stock levels, assets, and logistics may all be recreated in digital form using DT, just like the rest of the supply chain. The DT includes production facilities, raw material suppliers, subcontractors, transportation routes, distribution hubs, and retail outlets. From the initial design phase through building, commissioning, and operations, DT is there to provide a hand at every stage of the SCM's life-cycle. By mimicking real-time SCM systems, DT is able to collect data from the real world via IoT sensors. This information can be used by ML, big data, etc. to foresee challenges in later SCM stages. Consequently, businesses may preventatively address errors and losses throughout the SCM process and can aid in the speedy delivery of individualised merchandise to consumers. Businesses can use DT to weigh the pros and cons of various "capacity, service, inventory, and total landed cost configurations." Additionally, DT can assist businesses in improving their profit margins and cutting costs in the workplace across many

Figure 6. Applications in Industry 5.0 (Adapted from Skobelev & Borovik, 2017)

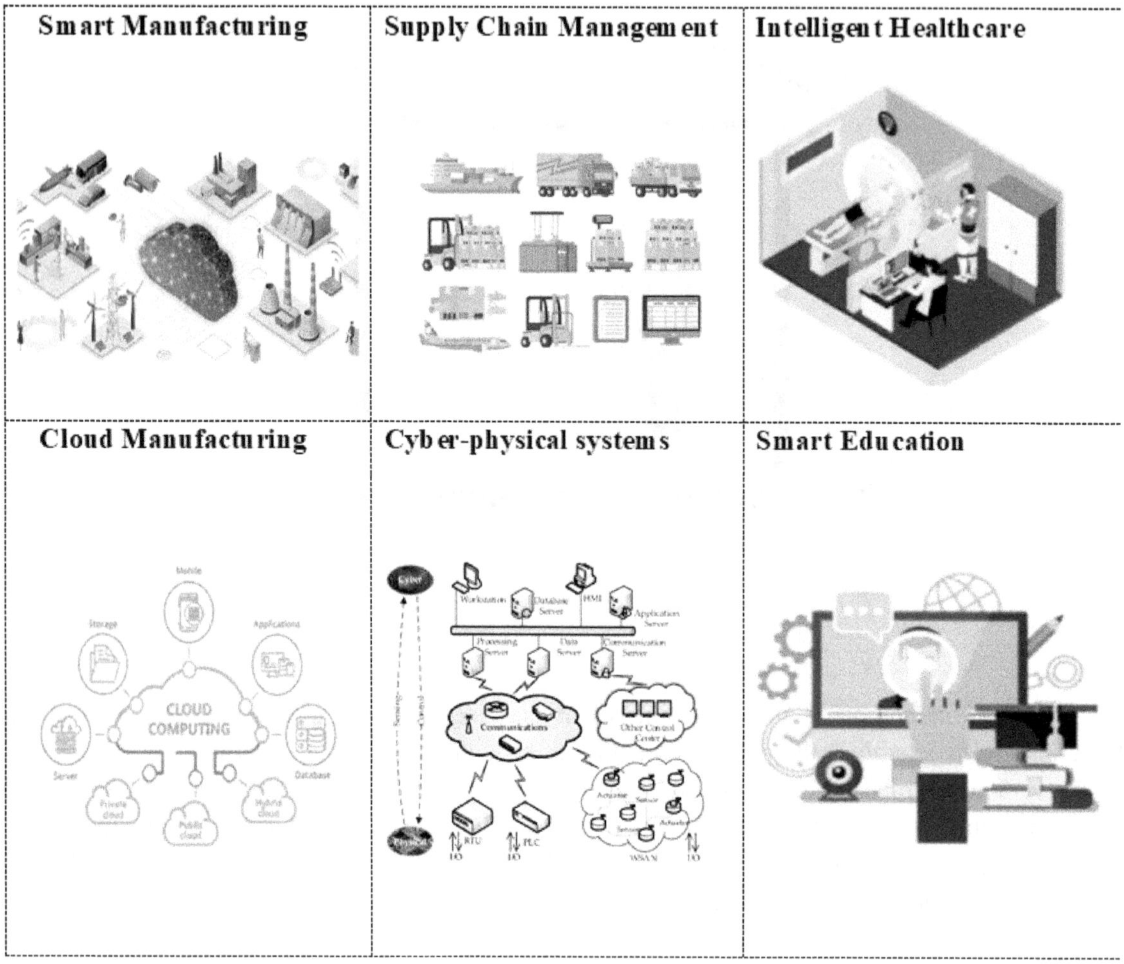

SCM processes. Several recent papers that propose DT as a method to address SCM are reviewed here. "Defraeye" suggested a DT-based method that models the temperature changes that occur in mangoes during cold-chain shipping. They have also invented a novel sensing device that acts as a fruit simulator in order to verify a temperature model for fruit pulp (Skobelev & Borovik, 2017). The authors showed that DT could shed light on the "thermo-behaviour" of fruits throughout the distribution process. The supply chain management (SCM) sector will benefit from these findings because it will be able to pinpoint the locations at which temperature-sensitive fruits are lost in transit and implement preventative actions to reduce this problem. The use of DT in the logistics and refrigeration industry can help cut down on waste and make a green supply chain a reality. The advantages of DT in cutting down on SCM costs in the building sector were discussed in this article (Kumar et al., 2021). To strengthen the pharmaceutical company's SCM process, Marmolejo recommended a DT (Fukuda, 2020). Using "solvers, simulators, and analytical tools", the author has created this technology. Different "inventory, supply, production, and distribution scenarios" for a pharmaceutical company have been modelled and examined by the author. As a result of DT's efforts, the pharmaceutical industry is better prepared for supply chain disruptions and changes thanks to predictive analytics and enhanced lines of communication.

The use of cobots in supply chain management (SCM) can be crucial. Work that is both common and potentially harmful, such as packing, quality control inspections, lifting big objects, etc., that things humans avoid doing can be carried out by robots, freeing up human expertise to be applied to more intricate tasks in the SCM life cycle. Cobots have a wide range of possible uses in the supply chain management (SCM) ecosystem, such as "material handling, assembly of the materials, packing, performing quality checks, transportation, delivery of the products to the customers and picking the return of the products from the customers." The SCM industries can lower their cost of ownership with the help of cobots. Consequently, cobots facilitate all SCM activities, including organised stock management, stock tracking, order fulfilment, and product returns (Zizic et al., 2022).

Intelligent Healthcare

These days, ML models are used to assist doctors in making diagnoses about their patients' health. This aids in increasing the precision with which diseases are diagnosed, which ultimately saves patients a great deal of time and money. But in the present circumstances, that is not enough. With the help of their doctors, patients need a system that can monitor their vitals, such as blood pressure and glucose levels, and provide them with medication tailored specifically to them. This is now feasible thanks to Industry 5.0. Smart watches, smart sensors, and other intelligent wearable devices can continuously capture the patient's healthcare data in real-time and save it in the cloud. Then we can utilise ML algorithms to determine the patients' medical conditions (Demir et al., 2019). These high-tech gadgets are able to share information with one another, so if medical treatment is needed, the doctors will be notified and may treat the patient based on the most up-to-date information. Cobots allow surgeons to collaborate with robots that are capable of two-way communication during procedures. Just a few ways that healthcare can be transformed by Industry 5.0 are listed above. The production of one-of-a-kind medical gadgets, implants, etc., has been greatly aided by this. Industry 5.0 promises to automate many mundane tasks, including checkups currently handled by doctors. This allows medical professionals to focus on more advanced tasks. Surgical corobots, guided by human input, can conduct even the most complex procedures with pinpoint accuracy. Medical professionals can provide more individualised care for their patients with the use of DT technologies like medicine prescribing. The following section explores the current literature on the potential medical uses of Industry 5.0 (Akundi et al., 2022).

According to Haleen et al. (Wickramasurendra, Jagoda, & Rathnayake, 2021), a fundamental need in orthopaedics is the production of patient-specific implants. Industry 5.0 holds great promise in this regard (Wickramasurendra et al., 2021). Furthermore, they provide examples of how Industry 5.0 might aid in facilitating more precise surgical procedures. Potential uses of Industry 5.0 in the field of medical education are being discussed. Key enabling technologies in Industry 5.0 have been investigated by Javaid and Haleem (2020) that can aid in patient treatment during the Covid-19 pandemic. They proposed ways in which corobots and other important Industry 5.0 enabling technologies can facilitate non-contact medical care for patients. They also proposed ways in which clinicians and intelligent robots may work together to scan and treat Covid-19 patients, thereby lowering the likelihood that patients would be exposed in emergency settings. Priadytmama et al. (Demir & Cicibaş, 2019) have advocated that assistive technology (AT), traditionally utilised for impaired or handicapped persons, be made available to everyone in order to increase functional independence (Demir & Cicibaş, 2019). Industry 5.0 disruptors like 3D printing were cited as a way to bring about widespread adoption of assistive technology. Using the aforementioned technologies, a user's orthoses, limb prostheses, or exoskeleton can be tailored to their specific anatomical needs.

Cloud Manufacturing

By leveraging cutting-edge innovations like cloud computing, the Internet of Things, virtualization, and service-oriented computing, cloud manufacturing is transforming the age-old production model into a cutting-edge production process. Global players in the manufacturing industry will work together in the cloud to run a lean, cheap operation. Cloud manufacturing is distinguished by its dependability, excellent quality, low cost, and capacity to produce on demand. In addition, it has a favourable effect on the environment because raw materials for production don't need to be transported over great distances using cloud manufacturing. Cloud manufacturing is also ahead of other innovative manufacturing methods like additive manufacturing and the manufacturing grid. The study depicts the international teamwork inherent in a typical cloud manufacturing ecosystem. By putting their design files for manufactured things in the cloud with strict permissions, designers may safeguard their intellectual property. This allows them to make use of manufacturing resources located in a variety of different parts of the world. This allows designers the flexibility to locate factories near inexpensive sources of raw materials and labour. In this setup, the cloud is responsible for managing the factory's machinery and carrying out the various tasks involved in the production life cycle, including service composition and scheduling. The Internet of Things allows for the collection and analysis of sensor data from the manufacturing process in the cloud. Li and Tao introduced the cloud manufacturing model as a service-oriented strategy for producing goods. Pay-as-you-go is just one of the several models Xu et al. (Zizic et al., 2022) suggested for monetizing cloud production. Next-generation cloud manufacturing systems are being developed as part of Industry 5.0 to meet the varied and intricate needs of these industries in engineering, production, and logistics. Future cloud manufacturing systems have the potential to vastly increase their capabilities as a result of developments in "artificial intelligence (AI) and machine learning (ML) technology, electronic commerce (EC) features, and 5G-based telecommunication networks."

Cyber-Physical Systems

CPSs refer to the fourth generation of these systems, which aimed to serve as a bridge between the real world and the virtual one in real time by means of cloud computing and the Internet of Things. The Fourth Industrial Revolution was triggered by a German government strategic project that aimed to merge the best features of the physical and digital worlds to transform the production sector. One of the biggest problems with Industry 4.0 is that it optimises and improves productivity without properly accounting for the human cost. Experts believe this issue will worsen as Industry 4.0 develops, and that governments and labour unions will likely put-up stiff opposition to it. To address this problem head-on and ensure that cutting-edge technologies are still being put to good use in the name of efficiency, Industry 5.0 has been proposed as the fifth iteration. Chen et al. (Akundi et al., 2022) centred the fifth stage of industrial evolution on "human-cyber-physical systems." Next-generation wind turbines could benefit from human-cyber-physical systems, as the authors have proposed (Kumar et al., 2021). The study only offered the model conceptually, but it lists the essential enabling technologies, such as "structural health monitoring, information translators, and damage prediction models", that can be attained over the amalgamation of "IoT, and AI based methodologies." The new challenges in human-cyber-physical systems were brought to light by Longo et al. (Demir & Cicibaş, 2019). The study, which was based on a survey of businesses, concluded that concerns about ethical technology and values in the workplace do not require immediate action. They also suggested using the value sensitive design technique to create a framework for the factory of the future that takes into account human values and prospective design phases.

Smart Education

Education is widely regarded as both a fundamental human right and the bedrock of any successful political transformation. Adapting to changes in society and industry, learning systems produce the skilled workers and innovative ideas that will drive economic growth in the years to come. However, while the goal of training in Industry 4.0 was to make robots more efficient than humans, the goal of training in Industry 5.0 is to make autonomous machines and humans work together more effectively. Combining high-powered machinery with highly-trained experts will result in a production that is efficient, environmentally friendly, and risk-free. As part of the shift to Industry 5.0, a new position will emerge: Chief Robotics Officer (Montazeri, 2019). This expert has worked in domains including robots and AI, and specialises in improving the communication between humans and machines. Education 5.0 skills, or the integration of technological, communicative, and leadership abilities, are essential for him to perform in his role at the company and make judgments involving these factors.

Discussion on Opportunities Through Industry 5.0

Using "artificial intelligence (AI), big data (Big Data), and the internet of things (IoT)", a study of Industry 5.0 was presented in. They advocate for the development of safer and more complex networks with an extremely high number of connections that has the potential to become a game-changer in a variety of industries, for instance, electronic medication that check up on patients to make sure they're taking their medicines. With the help of AI, IoT, and Industry 5.0, big data may be accumulated in a variety of digital settings (Breque et al., 2021). Industry 5.0 tools ("holography, 4D scans, humanoid robots, telemedicine, and smart inhalers") have been deployed to combat the spread of the COVID pandemic. Using the capabilities of Industry 5.0, a number of solutions were presented to the issues brought on by the COVID pandemic, including tracking of patients, therapy based on automation tailoring, optimization of supply chain, "digital medicine", manufacturing of medicines, campaigns related to awareness, and monitoring of crowd. Payments based on contactless, tracing kidnappers, scutinizing and treating patients, and other similar tasks are all possible in the "post-COVID" era due to the development of cobot. Some suggestions for a value-aware layout of smart factories are presented in. The potential of human-machine interaction, an integral part of Industry 5.0, is explored. Furthermore, the value-based design was used to show how problems with implementing the mutualistic Industry 5.0 might be avoided. Managers need a firm grasp of innovation ecosystems, business strategies, and design thinking in order to meet the demands of the industry 5.0 and Internet of Things. However, the study does not discuss the framework's actual implementation or the security precautions implemented while integrating it with business activities (Olaizola et al., 2022).

The benefits of Industry 5.0 compared to its forerunner were the subject of a study conducted in. Industry 5.0, according to the report, allows for smart manufacturing by means of "intelligent data usage", amid the integration of various industrial information and cutting-edge technology, resulting in the production of more customisable products. By freeing robots from mundane repetitive duties and freeing up human brainpower for creative problem solving, the newly established methods and technology speed up the process (Adel, 2022; Akundi et al., 2022; Demir & Cicibaş, 2019; Demir et al., 2019; Zizic et al., 2022). Industry 5.0 in algal biorefinery has been discussed in a recent survey, which highlights the potential for this sector to personalise production, enable real-time monitoring of algae growth, and decrease operational costs. Algae cultivation employing Industry 5.0's individualised "bioenergy" ("solid, liquid, and gas biofuels") manufacture and apparatuses, methods and restrictions. Industry 5.0's use of "human intelligence, machine smarts, 5G networks, and other technologies" that can bring about extraordinary improvement in the transportation sector as improved solutions for traffic management difficulties still exist. With the help of Industry 5.0's networked and collaborative smart technologies, we can create a more sophisticated autonomous vehicle. The textile sector as a whole stand to gain as well, with greater opportunities to offer bespoke garments to consumers. Fibre computing allows for more product customization in Industry 5.0, which in turn promotes more eco-friendly textile production. So, Industry 5.0 can be used in practically any sector to provide a more customised experience for consumers (Javaid & Haleem, 2020; Lee et al., 2015; Özdemir & Hekim, 2018; Paschek et al., 2019).

Future Implementation Challenges

Cognitively empowered manufacturing is at the heart of Industry 5.0, allowing for highly individualised client service. Few of the probable execution issues highlighted in this segment need to be resolved in order to provide seamless services (Breque et al., 2021). The issue of security is one of the possible obstacles. Security flaws in the processing of heterogeneous data and the usage of cloud services for a wide variety of user and industrial data management must be examined repeatedly as we progress toward more digitised computation. While providing consumers with increasingly customised and predictive offerings, it is important to keep in mind concerns related to privacy, including data privacy during transactions, data privacy throughout data accumulation, and ethical concerns. The return of human labour to the factory floor may be beneficial, but proper training is necessary to address the logistical challenges and ensure compliance associated with integrating human intellect with that of machines. Customized customer service through collaborative human-robot work must take into account issues related to expanding the number of users and the number of manufacturing processes (Lee et al., 2015). Moreover, the ethical concerns surrounding the widespread use of AI need to be taken into account in order to forestall unintended consequences.

CONCLUSION

We provided a comprehensive overview of the technologies that enable Industry 5.0 and their possible uses in this paper. To kick off this project, we defined some key principles of Industry 5.0 from the perspectives of both industry and academia. Possible applications of Industry 5.0 were then examined, including "intelligent healthcare, cloud manufacturing, supply chain management, manufacturing production", and so on; this was followed by a discussion of the technologies important to the expansion of "Industry 5.0". In nutshell, "Industry 5.0" is an idea that seeks to consistently improve both human and machine productivity in the workplace. Improved industrial output and customer happiness are two of the goals of the forthcoming Industry 5.0, which will be empowered through a wide range of new software and enabling technologies. In addition, we highlighted a number of difficulties and unresolved issues, including those related to safety, privacy, human-robot collaboration in the workplace, scalability, and the availability of appropriately trained workers that need to be addressed if Industry 5.0 is to become a reality any time soon.

REFERENCES

Adel, A. (2022). Future of industry 5.0 in society: Human-centric solutions, challenges and prospective research areas. *Journal of Cloud Computing (Heidelberg, Germany)*, *11*(1), 40. Advance online publication. doi:10.1186/s13677-022-00314-5 PMID:36101900

Akundi, A., Euresti, D., Luna, S., Ankobiah, W., Lopes, A., & Edinbarough, I. (2022). State of Industry 5.0—Analysis and Identification of Current Research Trends. *Applied System Innovation*, *5*(1), 1–14. doi:10.3390/asi5010027

Breque, M., De Nul, L., & Petridis, A. (2021). *Industry 5.0: Towards a sustainable, human-centric and resilient European industry*. Directorate-General for Research and Innovation. doi:10.2777/308407

Demir, K. A., & Cicibaş, H. (2019). The next industrial revolution: Industry 5.0 and discussions on industry 4.0. *Industry 4.0 from the MIS Perspective*, (February), 247–260.

Demir, K. A., Döven, G., & Sezen, B. (2019). Industry 5.0 and Human-Robot Co-working. *Procedia Computer Science*, *158*, 688–695. doi:10.1016/j.procs.2019.09.104

Fukuda, K. (2020). Science, technology and innovation ecosystem transformation toward society 5.0. *International Journal of Production Economics*, *220*(July), 107460. doi:10.1016/j.ijpe.2019.07.033

Grabowska, S., Saniuk, S., & Gajdzik, B. (2022). Industry 5.0: Improving humanization and sustainability of Industry 4.0. *Scientometrics*, *127*(6), 3117–3144. doi:10.1007/s11192-022-04370-1 PMID:35502439

Humayun, M. (2021). Industrial Revolution 5.0 and the Role of Cutting Edge Technologies. *International Journal of Advanced Computer Science and Applications*, *12*(12), 605–615. doi:10.14569/IJACSA.2021.0121276

Javaid, M., & Haleem, A. (2020). Critical components of industry 5.0 towards a successful adoption in the field of manufacturing. *Journal of Industrial Integration and Management*, *5*(3), 327–348. doi:10.1142/S2424862220500141

Kumar, R., Gupta, P., Singh, S., & Jain, D. (2021). Human Empowerment by Industry 5.0 in Digital Era: Analysis of Enablers. *Lecture Notes in Mechanical Engineering*, (February), 401–410. doi:10.1007/978-981-33-4320-7_36

Lee, J., Bagheri, B., & Kao, H. A. (2015). A Cyber-Physical Systems architecture for Industry 4.0-based manufacturing systems. *Manufacturing Letters*, *3*(December), 18–23. doi:10.1016/j.mfglet.2014.12.001

Maddikunta, P. K. R., Pham, Q. V., B, P., Deepa, N., Dev, K., Gadekallu, T. R., Ruby, R., & Liyanage, M. (2022). Industry 5.0: A survey on enabling technologies and potential applications. *Journal of Industrial Information Integration*, *26*(July), 100257. Advance online publication. doi:10.1016/j.jii.2021.100257

Montazeri, M. (2019). *Smart Additive Manufacturing: in-Process Sensing and Smart Additive Manufacturing: in-Process Sensing and Data Analytics for Online Defect Detection in Metal Data Analytics for Online Defect Detection in Metal Additive Manufacturing Processes Additive Man.* University of Nebraska - Lincoln. Retrieved from https://digitalcommons.unl.edu/mechengdisshttps://digitalcommons.unl.edu/mechengdiss/148

Nahavandi, S. (2019). Industry 5. 0—A Human-Centric Solution. *Sustainability, 11*(4371), 43–71.

Olaizola, I. G., Quartulli, M., Garcia, A., & Barandiaran, I. (2022). Artificial Intelligence from Industry 5.0 perspective: Is the Technology Ready to Meet the Challenge? *CEUR Workshop Proceedings*, 3214.

Özdemir, V., & Hekim, N. (2018). Birth of Industry 5.0: Making Sense of Big Data with Artificial Intelligence, "the Internet of Things" and Next-Generation Technology Policy. *OMICS: A Journal of Integrative Biology, 22*(1), 65–76. doi:10.1089/omi.2017.0194 PMID:29293405

Paschek, D., Mocan, A., & Draghici, A. (2019). Industry 5. 0 – The Expected Impact of Next Industrial Revolution. *Managment Knowledge Learning International Conference*, 125–132. Retrieved from http://www.toknowpress.net/ISBN/978-961-6914-25-3/papers/ML19-017.pdf

Skobelev, P., & Borovik, Y. (2017). On the Way From Industry 4. 0 To Industry 5.0. *International Scientific Journal "Industry 4.0," 2*(6), 307–311. Retrieved from https://stumejournals.com/journals/i4/2017/6/307/pdf

Wickramasurendra, J. M., Jagoda, D. J., & Rathnayake, R. M. L. (2021). Factors Influencing Social Media Addiction among G.C.E. Advanced Level Students in Sri Lanka: A Case Study in Colombo District, Sri Lanka. *Sri Lanka Journal of Social Sciences and Humanities, 1*(2), 1–11. doi:10.4038/sljssh.v1i2.33

Zizic, M. C., Mladineo, M., Gjeldum, N., & Celent, L. (2022). of Paradigm Shift for the People, Organization and Technology. *Energies, 15*(14), 5221. doi:10.3390/en15145221

Chapter 8
Future Trends in ICT and E-Services Through Advanced Assessment Metrics:
Harnessing the Power of AI

R. Pitchai
https://orcid.org/0000-0002-3759-6915
Department of Computer Science and Engineering, B V Raju Institute of Technology, India

R. Krishna Kumari
https://orcid.org/0000-0002-1802-628X
Career Development Centre, SRM Institute of Science and Technology, India

S. Satheesh Kumar
Department of Business Administration, Panimalar Engineering College, Chennai, India

L. Raja
Department of Electronics and Communication Engineering, Sri Eshwar College of Engineering, India

R. Sujatha
https://orcid.org/0000-0002-4071-0096
Department of Computer Science, Subbalakshmi Lakshmipathy College of Science, Madurai, India

M. Sudhakar
Department of Mechanical Engineering, Sri Sai Ram Engineering College, India

ABSTRACT

In the ever-evolving digital landscape, the integration of artificial intelligence (AI) into information and communication technology (ICT) and e-services is paramount. This chapter delves into the profound influence of AI on user experience, security, and scalability within digital services. It sheds light on both the hurdles and prospects presented by AI-driven strategies, underscoring the importance of adopting a holistic approach that encompasses technical, ethical, and regulatory dimensions. By offering valuable insights, this chapter guides organizations seeking to harness AI's capabilities in digital services, stressing the significance of a thorough and inclusive strategy.

DOI: 10.4018/979-8-3693-1343-5.ch008

INTRODUCTION

Artificial Intelligence (AI) is revolutionizing ICT and e-Services by enabling automation, data analysis, and decision-making. It simulates human intelligence processes, transforming the way digital services are delivered. This chapter examines AI's impact on ICT and e-Services, its evolution, applications, and future trends, examining its evolution, applications, and implications. AI is crucial in ICT and e-Services, enabling organizations to optimize operations, streamline processes, and provide personalized experiences. It is used for tasks like network optimization, resource allocation, predictive maintenance, and anomaly detection. Telecom companies can improve network efficiency, minimize downtime, and enhance service quality, ensuring a seamless user experience. AI is revolutionizing e-Services by providing tailored recommendations, personalized assistance, and predictive insights (Stegaru et al., 2015).

E-commerce platforms use AI-powered engines to analyze user behavior and preferences, enhancing the shopping experience. AI chatbots are also being deployed to provide instant customer support, enhancing satisfaction and retention. This chapter provides an in-depth analysis of AI's impact on ICT and e-Services, examining its evolution, applications, challenges, and opportunities. It also delves into advanced assessment metrics for evaluating AI-driven services, focusing on user experience, security, and scalability, and highlights the importance of security in implementing AI-driven solutions. This analysis will showcase how organizations are using AI to improve digital services, drive innovation, and gain market competitiveness. It will also discuss future trends and innovations in AI in ICT and e-Services, offering insights and recommendations for organizations to effectively utilize AI's potential (Seri et al., 2014).

This chapter provides a comprehensive understanding of AI's transformative impact on ICT and e-Services, offering insights for practitioners, researchers, and policymakers. It examines AI's evolution, applications, and future trends in digital services, facilitating informed decision-making and strategic planning in the evolving digital landscape. Artificial Intelligence (AI) is a significant advancement in computing, enabling machines to mimic human cognitive functions like learning, reasoning, problem-solving, and decision-making (Reggi et al., 2014). It focuses on developing algorithms and systems that interpret data, recognize patterns, and adapt autonomously to achieve specific objectives. AI subfields include machine learning, natural language processing, computer vision, robotics, and expert systems. Machine Learning is a subset of AI that uses algorithms to learn from data iteratively and improve performance over time. Common approaches include supervised learning, unsupervised learning, and reinforcement learning for tasks like classification and decision-making. Natural Language Processing (NLP) enables computers to understand and generate human language, facilitating communication between humans and machines. NLP algorithms process and analyze text and speech data for tasks like sentiment analysis and voice recognition (Agarwal & Thakur, 2019).

Computer Vision is a technology that enables computers to interpret and analyze visual information, similar to human vision. It uses techniques like image recognition, object detection, and segmentation to identify objects, recognize faces, and understand spatial relationships. Robotics, on the other hand, combines AI technologies with mechanical systems to create intelligent machines capable of autonomous tasks, enabling applications in manufacturing, healthcare, agriculture, and more. Expert Systems use knowledge representation and reasoning techniques to model human expertise in specific domains, enabling computers to make decisions and solve problems (Afacan & Arifoğlu, 2015). They are essential in fields like healthcare diagnosis, financial analysis, and engineering design. AI is a transformative force driving innovation, automation, and efficiency in various industries. As AI technologies advance, their integration into diverse applications and services could revolutionize work, communication, and interaction with technology, paving the way for a future powered by intelligent systems (Ronchi, 2019).

Artificial Intelligence (AI) is revolutionizing the delivery, management, and experience of digital services in Information and Communication Technology (ICT) and e-Services. AI automates repetitive tasks, optimizes processes, and automates system maintenance, network configurations, and customer service interactions. This improves operational efficiency and resource allocation, enabling organizations to better utilize their resources and enhance their digital services. AI enhances e-Services by analyzing user data to create personalized content, recommendations, and interactions (Mahmood et al., 2021). In e-commerce, AI-powered recommendation systems use past purchases, browsing behavior, and demographics to suggest relevant products, improving shopping experiences and sales conversion rates. AI algorithms can also analyze large datasets to identify patterns, trends, and insights, enabling decision-making and strategy development in ICT and e-Services. Predictive analytics can forecast customer demand, network failures, and cybersecurity threats (Montagnier & Ek, 2021).

AI-powered chatbots and virtual assistants are increasingly used in e-Services to provide round-the-clock customer support, answer questions, troubleshoot technical issues, and guide users through complex processes. These systems improve customer satisfaction and reduce human support agents' workload. AI also enhances cybersecurity measures in ICT and e-Services by analyzing network traffic patterns, detecting potential threats, identifying malware or phishing attacks, and responding to incidents in real-time (Reggi et al., 2014). NLP technologies enable advanced user interactions in e-Services by generating human language, enabling voice assistants, translation services, sentiment analysis tools, and chatbots. AI-driven data management tools help organizations extract actionable insights from large data volumes, enabling data driven decisions and optimizing services. AI is reshaping the ICT and e-Services landscape, driving innovation, efficiency, and personalization. By leveraging AI technologies, organizations can enhance digital offerings, improve customer experiences, and stay competitive in an increasingly digital world (Stegaru et al., 2015).

Scope and Objectives of the Chapter

This chapter provides a comprehensive understanding of AI's role in ICT and e-Services, offering insights for practitioners, researchers, policymakers, and stakeholders interested in utilizing AI for digital transformation and superior services, with the primary objectives being (Das et al., 2024; Sharma et al., 2024):

- It provides an in-depth understanding of how AI is transforming ICT and e-Services, examining its historical evolution and current trends like AI-driven automation, personalization, and predictive analytics, while also discussing its applications, benefits, and challenges.
- It explores the applications of AI in ICT and e-Services, highlighting its use in sectors like telecommunications, e-commerce, customer service, cybersecurity, and data management. It also evaluates the impact of AI on digital services, highlighting its benefits in efficiency, scalability, personalization, and user experience enhancement.
- It discusses the challenges and opportunities of implementing AI in ICT and e-Services, including technical barriers, ethical considerations, regulatory compliance, and talent acquisition, and introduces advanced assessment metrics for evaluating AI-driven services.
- It provides a comprehensive analysis of future trends in AI integration within ICT and e-Services, highlighting emerging technologies and strategic implications. It also offers insights and best

practices for organizations to effectively utilize AI to enhance digital services, drive innovation, and gain a competitive advantage.

EVOLUTION OF DIGITAL SERVICES: TRENDS AND CHALLENGES

The evolution of digital services has been marked by significant milestones and transformative shifts, from the internet to mobile technologies and cloud computing. Each era presents new opportunities and challenges for organizations to leverage technology to deliver innovative services to their customers (Agrawal, Pitchai, et al., 2023; Boopathi, 2024a; Venkateswaran, Vidhya, Naik, et al., 2023).

Figure 1 illustrates the evolution of digital services, starting with the internet and progressing to mobile technologies, cloud computing, IoT, AI, blockchain, 5G networks, and quantum computing. Each milestone shapes the landscape, offering new opportunities and challenges for organizations. The journey of ICT and e-Services began with the development of early computer networks in the mid-20th century, which laid the foundation for the digital revolution that would follow. The emergence of the internet in the late 20th century revolutionized communication and commerce, enabling the rapid exchange of information and the creation of new digital marketplaces. E-Services, ranging from online banking and e-commerce to digital media and social networking, emerged as key drivers of this digital transformation, reshaping industries and consumer behavior (Revathi et al., 2024; Venkateswaran, Kumar, et al., 2023).

The evolution of digital technologies has led to the rise of e-Services, allowing users to access digital services anytime, anywhere. Mobile apps and responsive web design have become essential components of e-Service delivery, catering to the growing demand for seamless, personalized experiences on smartphones and tablets. The rise of cloud computing has significantly transformed ICT and e-Services, democratizing access to computing resources and enabling organizations to harness scalable, on-demand infrastructure. It has facilitated the development and deployment of innovative e-Services, such as Software-as-a-Service (SaaS) applications and cloud-based storage and collaboration tools, driving efficiency and agility in the digital economy (Boopathi, 2023; Venkateswaran, Vidhya, Naik, et al., 2023).

Digital transformation presents numerous opportunities, but organizations face challenges in navigating the rapidly evolving ICT and e-Services landscape. One major challenge is keeping up with technological advancements and consumer expectations. Rapid innovation has shorten product lifecycles and intensified competition, forcing organizations to continually innovate and adapt to remain relevant in the digital marketplace. Organizations face cybersecurity threats and data privacy concerns in an interconnected world. The proliferation of digital services and vast amounts of data make cybercriminals targets. Ensuring customer data security and privacy is a top priority, necessitating robust cybersecurity measures and compliance with regulatory requirements like GDPR and CCPA (Boopathi & Kumar, 2024; Durairaj et al., 2023).

Organizations face challenges in embracing new technologies and delivering modern e-Services due to the complexities of legacy systems and infrastructure. These systems often lack flexibility and scalability, requiring costly migration efforts. The evolution of digital services in ICT and e-Services has brought transformative trends and challenges. To succeed in the digital economy, organizations must navigate the complexities of the digital landscape, address evolving consumer expectations, cybersecurity threats, and legacy infrastructure (Sharma et al., 2024).

Figure 1. Evolution of digital services: Trends and challenges

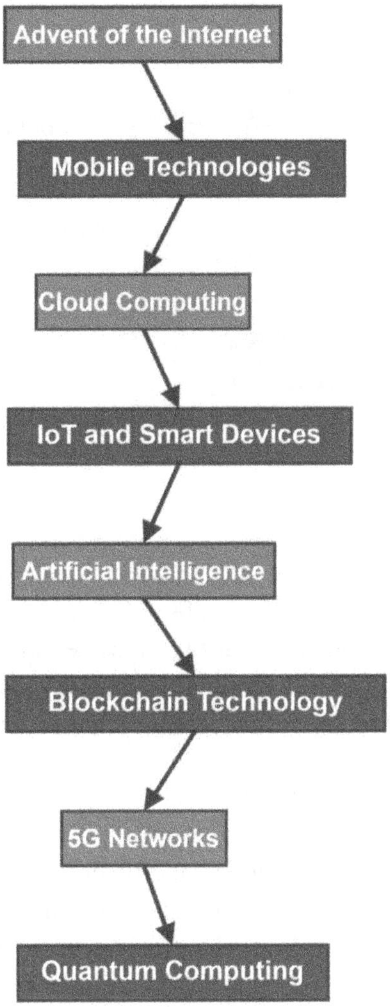

ROLE OF AI IN ENHANCING DIGITAL SERVICES

Artificial Intelligence (AI) is playing an increasingly crucial role in enhancing digital services across a wide range of industries, including Information and Communication Technology (ICT) and e-Services. By leveraging AI technologies, organizations can unlock new capabilities, improve efficiency, and deliver more personalized and intuitive experiences to their customers (Agrawal, Pitchai, et al., 2023; Koshariya et al., 2023; Samikannu et al., 2022).

Figure 2 illustrates the link between AI and enhanced digital services, where AI utilizes technologies to enhance efficiency, deliver personalized experiences, and unlock new capabilities, forming a feedback loop with enhanced digital services.

Figure 2. Role of AI in enhancing digital services

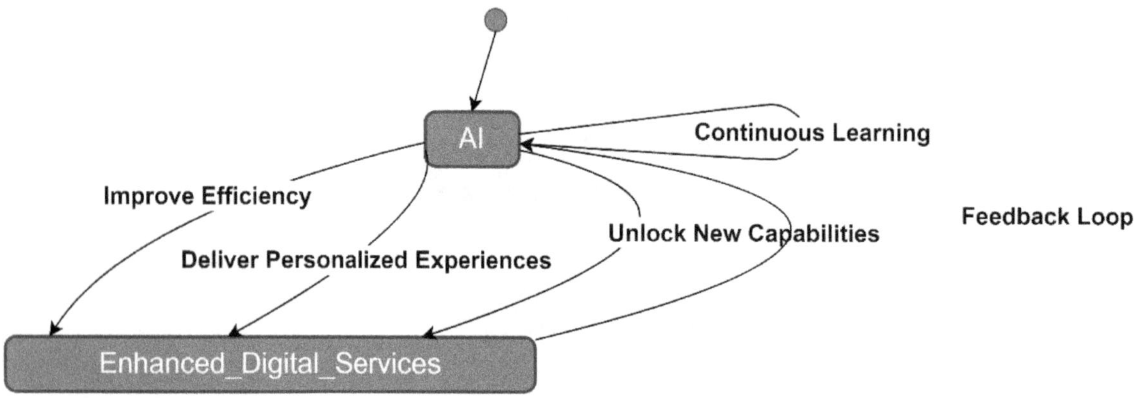

AI Technologies

AI is a range of technologies and techniques that enable machines to perform tasks that traditionally require human intelligence. Machine learning, a subset of AI, improves performance without explicit programming. Deep learning, a more advanced form, trains neural networks to recognize patterns and make predictions. Other AI technologies include natural language processing (NLP) and computer vision, which allow machines to interpret and analyze visual information (Das et al., 2024; Sharma et al., 2024).

Applications of AI in ICT and E-Services

AI is being utilized in ICT and e-Services to improve efficiency, automate processes, and provide personalized experiences. In ICT, AI-powered solutions optimize network traffic, detect security threats, and respond proactively. In e-Services, AI is revolutionizing customer interactions and service delivery through chatbots and virtual assistants. AI-driven recommendation engines analyze user behavior to deliver personalized content and product suggestions, enhancing the shopping experience and increasing sales conversion rates. Overall, AI is revolutionizing the way businesses operate and interact with their customers (Pachiappan et al., 2024).

Benefits of AI Integration

AI integration in digital services enhances efficiency and productivity by streamlining processes, reducing manual labor, and allocating resources more effectively. This allows employees to focus on strategic activities, driving innovation and growth. AI also allows organizations to deliver personalized experiences to customers by analyzing vast data, identifying patterns and insights, and tailoring content, recommendations, and interactions to individual preferences, enhancing customer satisfaction, engagement, and loyalty (Boopathi & Khang, 2023; Zekrifa et al., 2023).

AI is revolutionizing digital services in ICT and e-Services by providing insights and predictions based on data analysis. It can forecast customer demand, anticipate market trends, and optimize resource allocation, allowing organizations to stay ahead of competition and capitalize on opportunities. This leads to improved efficiency, personalized experiences, and better-informed decisions, driving innovation, growth, and a competitive advantage in the digital economy (Dhanya et al., 2023; Hussain et al., 2023).

ADVANCED ASSESSMENT METRICS FOR AI-DRIVEN SERVICES

Advanced assessment metrics for security, scalability, and performance enable organizations to evaluate AI-driven services' reliability, identify improvement areas, and mitigate risks. This proactive approach builds stakeholder trust, enhances user satisfaction, and drives success in the competitive AI-driven digital services market (Boopathi & Kumar, 2024; Pramila et al., 2023).

Figure 3 displays advanced assessment metrics for AI-driven services, including security, scalability, and performance metrics. These metrics evaluate the effectiveness and robustness of AI-driven services in various aspects, including data privacy, cybersecurity measures, adversarial robustness, ethical considerations, and throughput, latency, resource utilization, and fault tolerance.

Advanced Assessment Metrics for AI-Driven Services

This section explores the use of advanced evaluation metrics in evaluating the effectiveness and impact of AI-driven services, specifically focusing on user experience, security, scalability, and performance, which go beyond traditional measures (Naveeenkumar et al., 2024). Advanced assessment metrics are crucial for organizations to evaluate user experience in AI-driven services, providing valuable insights into their effectiveness and performance. This helps in continuous improvement, meeting user expectations, and enhancing satisfaction and engagement. Ensuring security, scalability, and performance is vital for delivering reliable solutions, making these metrics essential for evaluating AI-enabled systems.

Figure 3. Advanced assessment metrics for AI-driven services

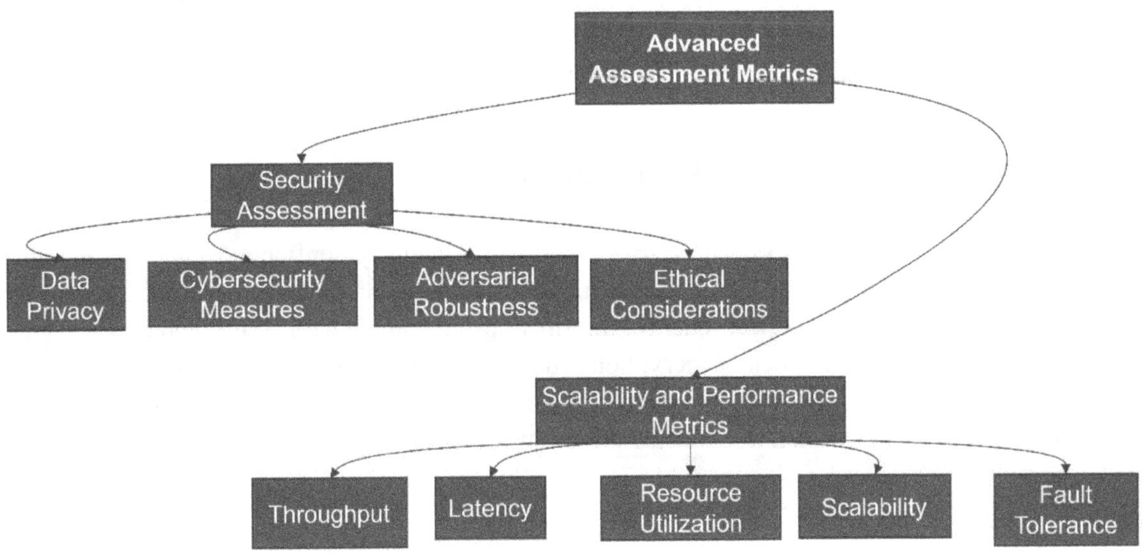

Metrics for Evaluating User Experience

- **User Engagement:** This metric measures the level of user interaction and engagement with AI-driven services. It includes metrics such as session duration, frequency of interactions, and depth of engagement. Higher user engagement indicates that the service is resonating with users and providing value.
- **User Satisfaction:** User satisfaction metrics assess users' subjective perception of the service's quality and usefulness. This can be measured through surveys, feedback forms, or sentiment analysis of user reviews. Positive sentiment and high satisfaction scores indicate that the service meets users' expectations and fulfills their needs effectively.
- **Ease of Use:** Ease of use metrics evaluate how intuitive and user-friendly the AI-driven service is. This includes factors such as navigation simplicity, clarity of instructions, and ease of completing tasks. A low learning curve and minimal user effort indicate that the service is well-designed and accessible to a wide range of users.
- **Personalization Effectiveness:** Personalization metrics assess the effectiveness of AI algorithms in delivering personalized experiences to users. This includes metrics such as recommendation accuracy, relevance of content suggestions, and alignment with user preferences. High personalization effectiveness indicates that the service effectively tailors content and recommendations to individual user profiles.
- **Response Time:** Response time metrics measure the speed at which the AI-driven service responds to user queries or commands. This includes metrics such as latency, processing time, and system responsiveness. Low response times are essential for providing a seamless and responsive user experience, especially in real-time interaction scenarios.
- **Error Rate:** Error rate metrics quantify the frequency and severity of errors or inaccuracies in the AI-driven service's outputs. This includes metrics such as error rate per interaction, error distribution across different tasks, and impact of errors on user experience. A low error rate indicates that the service reliably produces accurate results, enhancing user trust and confidence.
- **Adaptability and Flexibility:** These metrics assess the AI-driven service's ability to adapt to changing user needs, preferences, and contexts. This includes metrics such as adaptation speed, flexibility in handling diverse inputs, and responsiveness to user feedback. A highly adaptable and flexible service can accommodate varying user requirements and preferences, leading to a more satisfying user experience.

Security Assessment in AI-enabled Systems

AI-enabled systems' security assessment metrics evaluate data integrity, confidentiality, and availability. These metrics include data privacy, cybersecurity measures, adversarial robustness, and ethical considerations. Data privacy measures protect sensitive information and comply with GDPR and CCPA regulations. Cybersecurity measures, such as encryption and access controls, prevent unauthorized access and data breaches (Nanda et al., 2024; Rahamathunnisa et al., 2023). Adversarial robustness measures the system's resilience to attacks. Ethical considerations ensure fairness, transparency, and accountability in decision-making processes.

Scalability and Performance Metrics

AI-driven systems' scalability and performance metrics evaluate their capacity to handle increasing workloads, accommodate growing user bases, and maintain optimal performance under diverse conditions (Naveeenkumar et al., 2024).

- **Throughput**: Measuring the system's capacity to process a high volume of requests or transactions within a given time frame, ensuring responsiveness and efficiency.
- **Latency**: Evaluating the time taken for the system to respond to user requests or perform computations, minimizing delays and optimizing user experience.
- **Resource Utilization**: Monitoring resource consumption, such as CPU, memory, and storage, to ensure efficient allocation and utilization of computing resources.
- **Scalability**: Assessing the system's ability to scale horizontally or vertically to accommodate increased demand, whether through the addition of hardware resources or the deployment of distributed architectures.
- **Fault Tolerance**: Evaluating the system's resilience to failures and its ability to recover gracefully from errors or disruptions, minimizing downtime and ensuring continuous service availability.

AI IMPLEMENTATION IN REAL-WORLD SCENARIOS

Artificial Intelligence (AI) is not just a theoretical concept, but a real-world force driving innovation across industries like healthcare, finance, retail, and manufacturing. Organizations use AI to solve complex problems, streamline processes, and deliver value to customers and stakeholders (Rahamathunnisa et al., 2023; Ramudu et al., 2023).

Figure 4 showcases AI implementation in healthcare, finance, retail, and manufacturing industries, demonstrating its use to solve complex problems, streamline processes, and enhance customer and stakeholder value.

This introduction discusses the application of AI in various real-world scenarios, highlighting its practical applications and transformative impact. It highlights the challenges and benefits of AI implementation, revealing its potential to drive significant advancements in various industries. For instance,

Figure 4. AI implementation in real-world scenarios

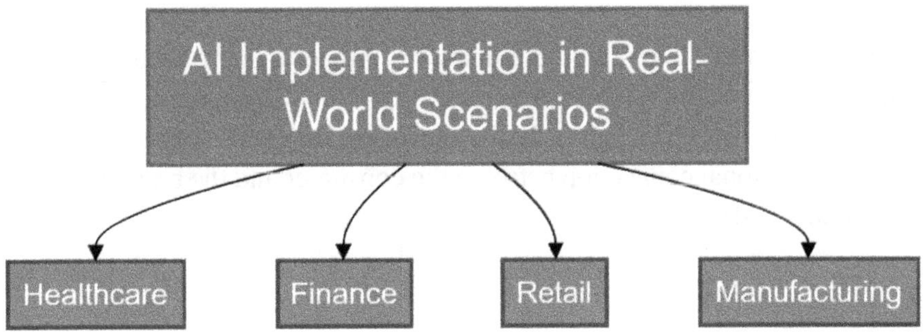

AI-powered diagnostic tools in healthcare are revolutionizing disease detection and treatment planning, while AI algorithms in finance are enabling fraud detection, risk assessment, and portfolio optimization, enabling informed decisions and risk mitigation. Overall, AI's potential to drive significant advancements in various domains is evident (Revathi et al., 2024).

AI is revolutionizing the retail industry by providing personalized recommendations, demand forecasting, and inventory management, enhancing customer experiences and operational efficiency. In manufacturing, AI-driven predictive maintenance systems optimize equipment performance, reduce downtime, and minimize maintenance costs by predicting failures before they occur. These real-world applications drive innovation, efficiency, and value creation, providing valuable insights into the practical applications of AI and its opportunities for organizations to achieve business objectives and stay competitive (Revathi et al., 2024). It explores AI implementations across various industries, highlighting challenges, success stories, and lessons learned. It aims to demonstrate the transformative potential of AI and inspire organizations to embrace it for innovation and strategic objectives.

AI-Driven Personalization in E-Commerce

In the competitive landscape of e-commerce, personalized experiences have emerged as a key differentiator for businesses seeking to engage customers and drive sales. Artificial Intelligence (AI) is revolutionizing e-commerce personalization by enabling retailers to tailor product recommendations, marketing messages, and user experiences to individual preferences and behavior patterns. This section explores how AI-driven personalization is transforming the e-commerce industry, enhancing customer satisfaction, and driving revenue growth (Singh & Adhikari, n.d.).

AI-driven personalization in e-commerce involves leveraging machine learning algorithms to analyze vast amounts of customer data and deliver targeted recommendations and experiences. By collecting and analyzing data on customer demographics, browsing history, purchase behavior, and preferences, AI algorithms can generate personalized product recommendations, suggest relevant content, and optimize the user journey to increase engagement and conversion rates.

Benefits of AI-Driven Personalization

The implementation of AI-driven personalization in e-commerce offers several benefits for both businesses and consumers. For businesses, personalized recommendations can lead to increased sales and revenue by driving impulse purchases, cross-selling, and upselling opportunities. By delivering relevant content and promotions tailored to individual preferences, businesses can enhance customer loyalty, increase repeat purchases, and improve customer lifetime value (Naveeenkumar et al., 2024).

For consumers, AI-driven personalization enhances the shopping experience by providing relevant product recommendations and streamlining the discovery process. By presenting users with products that align with their interests and preferences, AI-driven personalization reduces decision fatigue and enhances satisfaction. Moreover, personalized experiences create a sense of individuality and exclusivity, fostering a deeper emotional connection between the consumer and the brand (Naveeenkumar et al., 2024; Ravisankar et al., 2024).

Implementation Strategies and Best Practices

Successful implementation of AI-driven personalization in e-commerce requires a strategic approach and adherence to best practices (Rajeshwari et al., 2023).

- **Data Collection and Analysis**: Gathering and analyzing data on customer behavior, preferences, and interactions across multiple channels to generate actionable insights and recommendations.
- **Segmentation and Targeting**: Segmenting customers based on demographic, behavioral, and psychographic attributes to deliver targeted messaging and offers that resonate with specific audience segments.
- **Dynamic Content Personalization**: Dynamically adjusting website content, product recommendations, and promotional messages in real-time based on user interactions and preferences.
- **A/B Testing and Optimization**: Continuously testing and optimizing personalized experiences to identify the most effective strategies for driving engagement and conversion.
- **Privacy and Data Security**: Ensuring compliance with data protection regulations and maintaining transparency and trust with customers regarding data collection and usage practices.

AI-driven personalization is revolutionizing the e-commerce industry by providing tailored experiences that boost engagement, loyalty, and revenue. By analyzing customer data and providing personalized recommendations, retailers can create a seamless shopping experience, driving business growth and gaining a competitive advantage in the digital marketplace.

AI-powered Cybersecurity Solutions

Cybersecurity is a crucial priority for organizations in the digital world, as threats become more sophisticated and frequent. Traditional security measures are insufficient. Artificial Intelligence (AI) is revolutionizing cybersecurity by enabling rapid detection, prevention, and response to threats. This section explores the role of AI-powered cybersecurity solutions in safeguarding against evolving threats and improving overall security posture (Jaber & Fritsch, 2022).

The integration of AI-powered cybersecurity solutions into traditional security measures, such as firewalls and antivirus software, is demonstrated through machine learning algorithms, behavioral analytics, anomaly detection, threat intelligence, and automated response mechanisms (Figure 5).

AI-Powered Cybersecurity Solutions

AI-powered cybersecurity solutions use machine learning algorithms and advanced analytics to analyze vast data, identify potential security threats, detect anomalies in network traffic, identify malicious activities, and proactively defend against cyber attacks in real-time. By continuously learning from new data and evolving threat landscapes, these solutions respond with agility and precision (Sundaramoorthy et al., 2024).

Figure 5. Role of AI-powered cybersecurity solutions

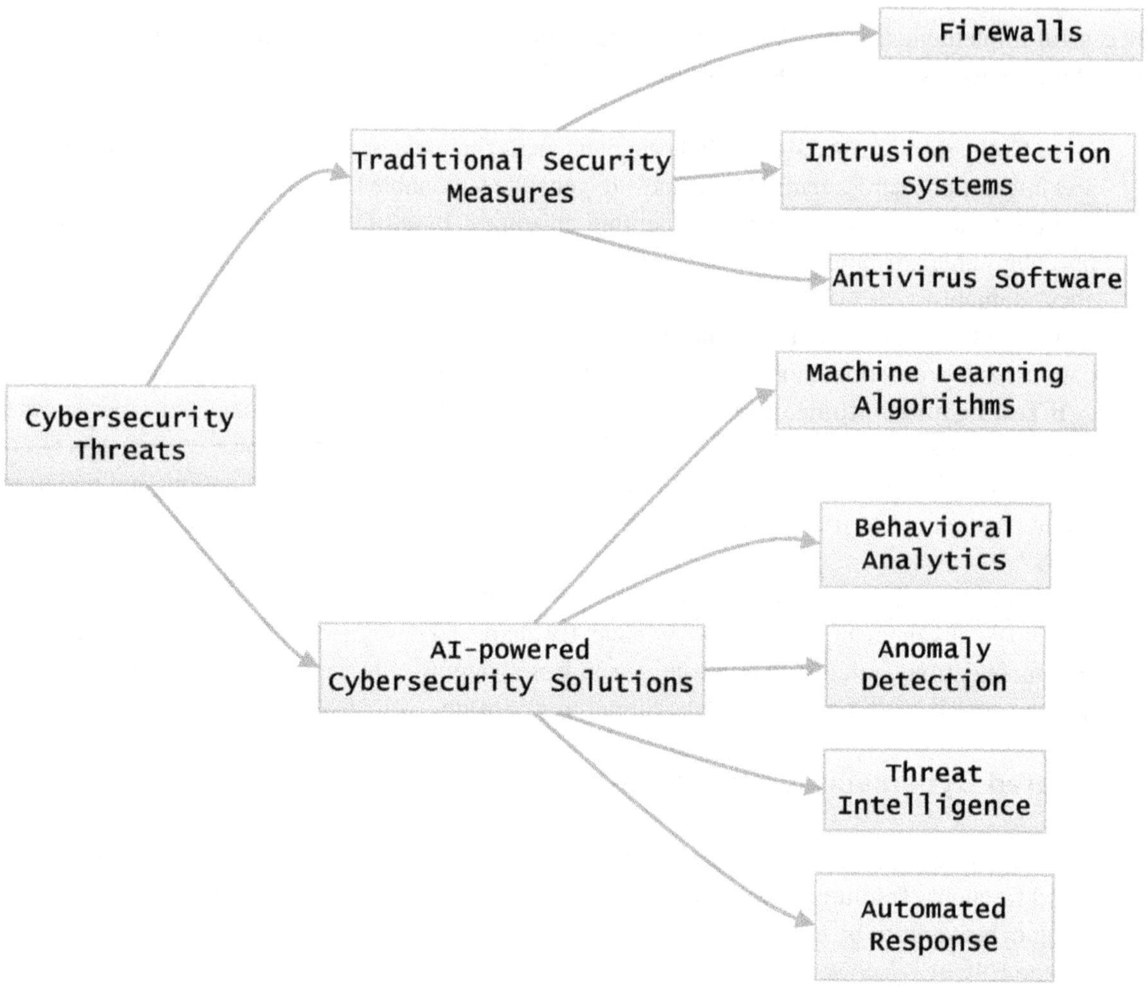

Benefits of AI-Powered Cybersecurity Solutions

The implementation of AI-powered cybersecurity solutions provides numerous significant advantages to organizations (Vegesna, 2023).

- **Advanced Threat Detection**: AI algorithms can detect and identify previously unseen cyber threats, including zero-day attacks and polymorphic malware, with greater accuracy than traditional signature-based methods.
- **Real-time Response**: AI-powered cybersecurity solutions can analyze and respond to cyber threats in real-time, enabling organizations to mitigate risks and minimize the impact of security incidents before they escalate.

- **Reduced False Positives**: By leveraging machine learning algorithms to analyze data and identify patterns, AI-powered cybersecurity solutions can reduce false positives and prioritize alerts based on the likelihood of a genuine security threat.
- **Enhanced Efficiency**: Automation capabilities inherent in AI-powered cybersecurity solutions enable organizations to streamline security operations, reduce manual effort, and allocate resources more effectively, improving overall efficiency and productivity.
- **Scalability**: AI-powered cybersecurity solutions can scale to accommodate the growing volume and complexity of cyber threats, ensuring organizations can effectively defend against evolving security risks as their digital footprint expands.

Implementation Strategies and Best Practices

The successful implementation of AI-powered cybersecurity solutions necessitates meticulous planning and adherence to best practices, including (Jaber & Fritsch, 2022; Vegesna, 2023). AI-powered cybersecurity solutions are revolutionizing organizations' protection against cyber threats by offering advanced threat detection, real-time response capabilities, and enhanced efficiency. By analyzing vast data and identifying potential security threats, these solutions strengthen security posture, mitigate risks, and protect sensitive data and systems from evolving attacks. As cyber threats evolve, AI-powered cybersecurity solutions will play a crucial role in safeguarding digital assets and ensuring business resilience.

- **Data Integration**: Integrating diverse sources of security data, including logs, network traffic, and endpoint telemetry, to provide comprehensive visibility into potential security threats.
- **Continuous Learning**: Training AI algorithms on large datasets of labeled and unlabeled data to continuously improve detection capabilities and adapt to evolving threat landscapes.
- **Human Oversight**: While AI can automate many aspects of cybersecurity, human oversight and intervention are essential to validate alerts, investigate security incidents, and make strategic decisions.
- **Collaboration and Threat Intelligence Sharing**: Sharing threat intelligence and collaborating with industry peers, government agencies, and cybersecurity experts to stay informed about emerging threats and best practices.
- **Compliance and Governance**: Ensuring compliance with relevant regulatory requirements and industry standards for data protection and cybersecurity, such as GDPR, HIPAA, and PCI DSS.

AI FOR PREDICTIVE MAINTENANCE IN ICT INFRASTRUCTURE

AI is revolutionizing predictive maintenance in ICT infrastructure, enhancing operational efficiency and reducing costs. This strategy enables organizations to identify potential issues before they cause downtime or service disruptions, thereby reducing the need for costly downtime or service disruptions (Hallaji et al., 2022).

AI-Driven Predictive Maintenance

AI-driven predictive maintenance uses machine learning algorithms to analyze data from sensors and monitoring devices to predict equipment failures or performance degradation. This helps organizations schedule maintenance more effectively, minimize unplanned downtime, and extend the lifespan of critical ICT infrastructure components (Agrawal, Pitchai, et al., 2023; Das et al., 2024; Durairaj et al., 2023).

Components of AI-Driven Predictive Maintenance

- **Data Collection**: AI-driven predictive maintenance relies on the collection of data from various sources, including sensors, IoT devices, and operational systems. This data can include information on equipment performance, environmental conditions, usage patterns, and maintenance history.
- **Data Analysis**: Machine learning algorithms are used to analyze the collected data and identify patterns indicative of potential equipment failures or performance degradation. These algorithms can detect anomalies, trends, and correlations that may not be apparent through traditional methods.
- **Predictive Modeling**: AI-driven predictive maintenance models are developed based on the analysis of historical data and the identification of patterns associated with specific failure modes or performance issues. These models can predict when equipment failures are likely to occur, allowing organizations to take proactive measures to prevent or mitigate them.
- **Alerting and Decision Support**: AI-driven predictive maintenance systems generate alerts and notifications when potential issues are detected, enabling organizations to prioritize maintenance activities and allocate resources more effectively. Decision support tools provide actionable insights and recommendations to help maintenance teams plan and execute maintenance tasks efficiently.

Benefits of AI-driven Predictive Maintenance

- **Reduced Downtime**: By identifying potential issues before they lead to equipment failures or service disruptions, AI-driven predictive maintenance helps organizations minimize unplanned downtime and maintain high levels of service availability.
- **Cost Savings**: Predictive maintenance allows organizations to optimize maintenance schedules, reduce unnecessary maintenance activities, and extend the lifespan of equipment, leading to significant cost savings over time.
- **Improved Operational Efficiency**: By automating the detection of potential issues and providing actionable insights, AI-driven predictive maintenance streamlines maintenance processes, reduces manual effort, and improves overall operational efficiency.
- **Enhanced Safety and Reliability**: Proactively addressing potential equipment failures helps ensure the safety and reliability of ICT infrastructure, protecting against costly accidents, data loss, and service interruptions.

Implementation Strategies and Best Practices

The successful implementation of AI-driven predictive maintenance in ICT infrastructure necessitates meticulous planning and execution, including (Keleko et al., 2022). AI-driven predictive maintenance is revolutionizing ICT infrastructure management, offering reduced downtime, cost savings, and improved operational efficiency. By utilizing machine learning algorithms, organizations can proactively address potential equipment failures, ensuring service availability and reliability. As AI technologies advance, adopting predictive maintenance becomes increasingly crucial for optimizing ICT infrastructure performance and reliability in the digital environment.

- **Data Integration and Quality**: Ensuring the availability of high-quality data from diverse sources and integrating it into a centralized data repository for analysis.
- **Model Development and Validation**: Developing and validating predictive maintenance models using historical data and domain expertise to ensure accuracy and reliability.
- **Integration with Maintenance Processes**: Integrating AI-driven predictive maintenance systems with existing maintenance processes and workflows to facilitate seamless execution of maintenance activities.
- **Continuous Monitoring and Improvement**: Continuously monitoring model performance and updating predictive maintenance algorithms as new data becomes available to ensure ongoing effectiveness and accuracy.
- **Collaboration and Knowledge Sharing**: Encouraging collaboration and knowledge sharing between maintenance teams, data scientists, and other stakeholders to leverage expertise and insights from diverse perspectives.

CHALLENGES AND OPPORTUNITIES IN IMPLEMENTING AI

Organizations must navigate technical hurdles, ethical considerations, and regulatory compliance to effectively utilize Artificial Intelligence (AI), which offers both opportunities and challenges, ensuring the full potential of this transformative technology (Ferreira et al., 2014; Hallaji et al., 2022; Vegesna, 2023).

Technical Challenges and Solutions

- **Data Quality and Availability**: Obtaining high-quality data in sufficient quantity is crucial for training AI models effectively. Organizations often face challenges related to data cleanliness, completeness, and accessibility. Solutions include data preprocessing techniques to clean and augment data, as well as data-sharing partnerships to access diverse datasets.
- **Algorithm Bias and Fairness**: AI algorithms may exhibit bias, leading to unfair outcomes, particularly in sensitive areas such as hiring or lending. Mitigating algorithmic bias involves using representative datasets, applying fairness-aware algorithms, and conducting regular audits to identify and address biases.
- **Model Interpretability and Explain-ability**: Black-box AI models can be challenging to interpret, leading to a lack of transparency and trust. Techniques such as model explain-ability

methods, model-agnostic interpretability techniques, and the use of transparent algorithms help improve the interpretability of AI models.

- **Scalability and Performance**: Scaling AI models to handle large datasets and high volumes of requests while maintaining performance is a technical challenge. Solutions include distributed computing architectures, optimization techniques, and the use of specialized hardware accelerators such as GPUs or TPUs.

Ethical Considerations in AI Adoption

- **Privacy and Data Protection**: AI systems often rely on large datasets containing sensitive information, raising concerns about privacy and data protection. Organizations must ensure compliance with data protection regulations such as GDPR and implement robust data anonymization and encryption techniques to safeguard personal information (Boopathi & Khang, 2023).
- **Bias and Fairness**: AI algorithms can perpetuate or amplify biases present in training data, leading to discriminatory outcomes. Addressing bias requires careful attention to dataset composition, algorithm design, and ongoing monitoring to detect and mitigate bias in AI systems.
- **Transparency and Accountability**: Transparency in AI systems is essential for ensuring trust and accountability. Organizations should strive to provide clear explanations of how AI decisions are made, enable auditing and accountability mechanisms, and establish processes for addressing errors or biases in AI systems.
- **Impact on Society and Employment**: The widespread adoption of AI has implications for society, including potential job displacement and socioeconomic inequality. Organizations should consider the broader societal impact of their AI initiatives and take proactive steps to mitigate negative consequences through measures such as reskilling and upskilling programs.

Regulatory Compliance and Data Privacy

- **Regulatory Compliance**: AI implementations must comply with relevant regulations and standards governing data privacy, security, and ethical use. Organizations should stay abreast of evolving regulatory requirements and ensure that their AI systems adhere to legal and ethical guidelines.
- **Data Privacy**: Protecting user data is paramount in AI implementations. Organizations must implement robust data privacy measures, including data encryption, access controls, and anonymization techniques, to safeguard sensitive information and maintain user trust.
- **Ethical Use of AI**: Ethical considerations extend beyond legal compliance to encompass broader ethical principles such as fairness, transparency, and accountability. Organizations should establish ethical guidelines for AI development and deployment and ensure that AI systems are used responsibly and ethically.

To effectively utilize AI, organizations must collaborate with technical experts, data scientists, ethicists, legal professionals, and policymakers to address technical challenges, ethical considerations, and regulatory compliance, thereby maximizing benefits for society.

FUTURE TRENDS AND INNOVATIONS

Emerging trends and innovations in ICT and e-Services are shaping the future, necessitating organizations to adapt to future-proof their digital services and remain competitive in the evolving landscape, as technology continues to evolve rapidly and incorporate AI-driven solutions (Hallaji et al., 2022).

Emerging Technologies Shaping the Future

- **5G Technology**: The rollout of 5G networks promises to revolutionize connectivity by delivering ultra-fast speeds, low latency, and massive connectivity. 5G technology will enable innovative applications such as Internet of Things (IoT) devices, augmented reality (AR), and virtual reality (VR), transforming how we interact with digital services (Agrawal, Shashibhushan, et al., 2023; Venkateswaran, Vidhya, Ayyannan, et al., 2023).
- **Edge Computing**: Edge computing brings processing power closer to the data source, enabling faster data processing and real-time insights. This trend is particularly relevant for applications requiring low latency, such as autonomous vehicles, smart cities, and industrial IoT (Boopathi, 2024b; Nanda et al., 2024).
- **Blockchain Technology**: Blockchain technology offers decentralized and secure transactions, making it suitable for applications such as cryptocurrency, supply chain management, and digital identity verification. As blockchain matures, it will enable new business models and enhance trust in digital transactions (Kumar et al., 2023; Sundaramoorthy et al., 2024).
- **Quantum Computing**: Quantum computing holds the potential to solve complex problems at speeds far beyond the capabilities of classical computers. While still in the early stages of development, quantum computing has the potential to revolutionize fields such as cryptography, drug discovery, and optimization (Sonia et al., 2024).

Predictions for AI in ICT and E-Services

- **AI-driven Personalization**: AI will continue to drive personalization in e-Services, delivering tailored experiences based on user preferences, behavior, and context. From personalized product recommendations to customized content delivery, AI will enable organizations to engage customers more effectively and drive conversion rates.
- **AI-powered Automation**: AI will increasingly automate routine tasks and processes across various industries, driving efficiency and productivity. In ICT, AI-powered automation will streamline network management, cybersecurity, and IT operations, enabling organizations to optimize resource allocation and improve service delivery.
- **AI-enabled Decision Support**: AI will play a crucial role in providing decision support across different domains, helping organizations make data-driven decisions and optimize business processes. From predictive analytics to prescriptive recommendations, AI-powered insights will empower organizations to stay ahead of the competition and seize new opportunities.

Strategies for Future-Proofing Digital Services

- **Invest in Emerging Technologies**: Organizations should stay abreast of emerging technologies such as 5G, edge computing, blockchain, and quantum computing, and explore how these technologies can enhance their digital services and create new value propositions.
- **Embrace AI-driven Innovation**: Organizations should embrace AI-driven innovation and explore opportunities to leverage AI technologies to automate processes, personalize experiences, and drive business growth. Investing in AI talent and infrastructure is essential for building AI capabilities and staying competitive in the digital age.
- **Adopt Agile and Adaptive Practices**: Agile and adaptive practices enable organizations to respond quickly to changing market dynamics and customer needs. By adopting agile methodologies and fostering a culture of innovation, organizations can iterate rapidly, experiment with new ideas, and stay ahead of emerging trends.
- **Focus on Customer Experience**: Customer experience will continue to be a key differentiator in the digital marketplace. Organizations should prioritize customer-centricity and focus on delivering seamless, personalized experiences across all touchpoints to drive customer satisfaction and loyalty.
- **Enhance Security and Trust**: As digital services become more pervasive, ensuring security and trust is paramount. Organizations should invest in robust cybersecurity measures, adhere to data privacy regulations, and prioritize transparency and accountability to build trust with customers and stakeholders.

Organizations can capitalize on the evolving landscape of ICT and e-Services by embracing emerging technologies, AI-driven innovation, and agile practices for future-proofing their digital services.

CONCLUSION AND RECOMMENDATIONS

The integration of Artificial Intelligence (AI) into Information and Communication Technology (ICT) and e-Services has led to a new era of innovation, efficiency, and personalization. Organizations are using AI technologies to enhance digital services, drive business growth, and stay competitive. This exploration examines the evolution of digital services, AI's role in ICT and e-Services, challenges and opportunities in AI implementation, and future trends in the industry. It emphasizes the importance of embracing emerging technologies and adopting agile practices. As organizations navigate the complexities of AI implementation, several recommendations emerge.

- **Invest in AI Talent and Infrastructure**: Organizations should prioritize building AI capabilities by investing in talent acquisition, training, and infrastructure. Developing in-house expertise in AI technologies will enable organizations to leverage AI effectively and drive innovation.
- **Embrace Ethical AI Practices**: Ethical considerations must guide AI development and deployment. Organizations should establish ethical guidelines for AI usage, prioritize transparency and accountability, and ensure fairness and equity in AI-driven decision-making processes.
- **Collaborate and Share Knowledge**: Collaboration and knowledge sharing are essential for driving AI innovation and addressing common challenges. Organizations should collaborate with industry peers, academic institutions, and research organizations to share best practices, insights, and lessons learned.

- **Prioritize Security and Data Privacy**: Security and data privacy must be central considerations in AI implementation. Organizations should implement robust cybersecurity measures, adhere to data protection regulations, and prioritize the security and privacy of user data to build trust and confidence among customers and stakeholders.
- **Stay Agile and Adaptive**: In a rapidly evolving digital landscape, agility and adaptability are critical. Organizations should embrace agile methodologies, iterate rapidly, and remain responsive to changing market dynamics, customer needs, and emerging technologies.

The recommendations suggest that organizations can harness the transformative potential of AI to unlock new opportunities, drive innovation, and deliver superior digital services that meet the evolving demands of customers and stakeholders in the digital age, thereby achieving sustainable growth, competitive advantage, and success in ICT and e-Services.

ABBREVIATIONS

- AI: Artificial Intelligence
- AR: Augmented Reality
- CCPA: California Consumer Privacy Act
- CPU: Central Processing Unit
- DSS: Decision Support System
- GDPR: General Data Protection Regulation
- GPU: Graphics Processing Unit
- HIPAA: Health Insurance Portability and Accountability Act
- ICT: Information and Communication Technology
- IN: Information Network
- IT: Information Technology
- NLP: Natural Language Processing
- PCI: Payment Card Industry
- TO: Technology Officer
- TPU: Tensor Processing Unit
- VR: Virtual Reality

REFERENCES

Afacan, G., & Arifoğlu, A. (2015). A new metric system for assessment of e-transformation. *International Journal of eBusiness and eGovernment Studies, 7*(1), 1–15.

Agarwal, R., & Thakur, V. (2019). Government eservice rating metrics. *Proceedings of the 12th International Conference on Theory and Practice of Electronic Governance*, 129–139. 10.1145/3326365.3326382

Agrawal, A. V., Pitchai, R., Senthamaraikannan, C., Balaji, N. A., Sajithra, S., & Boopathi, S. (2023). Digital Education System During the COVID-19 Pandemic. In Using Assistive Technology for Inclusive Learning in K-12 Classrooms (pp. 104–126). IGI Global. doi:10.4018/978-1-6684-6424-3.ch005

Agrawal, A. V., Shashibhushan, G., Pradeep, S., Padhi, S., Sugumar, D., & Boopathi, S. (2023). Synergizing Artificial Intelligence, 5G, and Cloud Computing for Efficient Energy Conversion Using Agricultural Waste. In Sustainable Science and Intelligent Technologies for Societal Development (pp. 475–497). IGI Global.

Boopathi, S. (2023). Deep Learning Techniques Applied for Automatic Sentence Generation. In Promoting Diversity, Equity, and Inclusion in Language Learning Environments (pp. 255–273). IGI Global. doi:10.4018/978-1-6684-3632-5.ch016

Boopathi, S. (2024). Balancing Innovation and Security in the Cloud: Navigating the Risks and Rewards of the Digital Age. In Improving Security, Privacy, and Trust in Cloud Computing (pp. 164–193). IGI Global.

Boopathi, S., & Khang, A. (2023). AI-Integrated Technology for a Secure and Ethical Healthcare Ecosystem. In *AI and IoT-Based Technologies for Precision Medicine* (pp. 36–59). IGI Global. doi:10.4018/979-8-3693-0876-9.ch003

Boopathi, S., & Kumar, P. (2024). Advanced bioprinting processes using additive manufacturing technologies: Revolutionizing tissue engineering. *3D Printing Technologies: Digital Manufacturing, Artificial Intelligence, Industry 4.0*, 95.

Das, S., Lekhya, G., Shreya, K., Shekinah, K. L., Babu, K. K., & Boopathi, S. (2024). Fostering Sustainability Education Through Cross-Disciplinary Collaborations and Research Partnerships: Interdisciplinary Synergy. In Facilitating Global Collaboration and Knowledge Sharing in Higher Education With Generative AI (pp. 60–88). IGI Global.

Dhanya, D., Kumar, S. S., Thilagavathy, A., Prasad, D., & Boopathi, S. (2023). Data Analytics and Artificial Intelligence in the Circular Economy: Case Studies. In Intelligent Engineering Applications and Applied Sciences for Sustainability (pp. 40–58). IGI Global.

Durairaj, M., Jayakumar, S., Karpagavalli, V., Maheswari, B. U., Boopathi, S., & ... (2023). Utilization of Digital Tools in the Indian Higher Education System During Health Crises. In *Multidisciplinary Approaches to Organizational Governance During Health Crises* (pp. 1–21). IGI Global. doi:10.4018/978-1-7998-9213-7.ch001

Ferreira, A., Leitão, P., & Vrba, P. (2014). Challenges of ICT and artificial intelligence in smart grids. *2014 IEEE International Workshop on Intelligent Energy Systems (IWIES)*, 6–11. 10.1109/IWIES.2014.6957039

Hallaji, S. M., Fang, Y., & Winfrey, B. K. (2022). Predictive maintenance of pumps in civil infrastructure: State-of-the-art, challenges and future directions. *Automation in Construction*, *134*, 104049. doi:10.1016/j.autcon.2021.104049

Hussain, Z., Babe, M., Saravanan, S., Srimathy, G., Roopa, H., & Boopathi, S. (2023). Optimizing Biomass-to-Biofuel Conversion: IoT and AI Integration for Enhanced Efficiency and Sustainability. In Circular Economy Implementation for Sustainability in the Built Environment (pp. 191–214). IGI Global.

Jaber, A., & Fritsch, L. (2022). Towards ai-powered cybersecurity attack modeling with simulation tools: Review of attack simulators. *International Conference on P2P, Parallel, Grid, Cloud and Internet Computing*, 249–257.

Keleko, A. T., Kamsu-Foguem, B., Ngouna, R. H., & Tongne, A. (2022). Artificial intelligence and real-time predictive maintenance in industry 4.0: A bibliometric analysis. *AI and Ethics*, *2*(4), 553–577. doi:10.1007/s43681-021-00132-6

Koshariya, A. K., Kalaiyarasi, D., Jovith, A. A., Sivakami, T., Hasan, D. S., & Boopathi, S. (2023). AI-Enabled IoT and WSN-Integrated Smart Agriculture System. In *Artificial Intelligence Tools and Technologies for Smart Farming and Agriculture Practices* (pp. 200–218). IGI Global. doi:10.4018/978-1-6684-8516-3.ch011

Kumar, P. R., Meenakshi, S., Shalini, S., Devi, S. R., & Boopathi, S. (2023). Soil Quality Prediction in Context Learning Approaches Using Deep Learning and Blockchain for Smart Agriculture. In Effective AI, Blockchain, and E-Governance Applications for Knowledge Discovery and Management (pp. 1–26). IGI Global. doi:10.4018/978-1-6684-9151-5.ch001

Mahmood, D., Latif, S., Anwar, A., Hussain, S. J., Jhanjhi, N., Sama, N. U., & Humayun, M. (2021). Utilization of ICT and AI techniques in harnessing residential energy consumption for an energy-aware smart city: A review. *International Journal of Advanced and Applied Sciences*, *8*(7), 50–66.

Montagnier, P., & Ek, I. (2021). AI measurement in ICT usage surveys. *RE:view*.

Nanda, A. K., Sharma, A., Augustine, P. J., Cyril, B. R., Kiran, V., & Sampath, B. (2024). Securing Cloud Infrastructure in IaaS and PaaS Environments. In Improving Security, Privacy, and Trust in Cloud Computing (pp. 1–33). IGI Global. doi:10.4018/979-8-3693-1431-9.ch001

Naveeenkumar, N., Rallapalli, S., Sasikala, K., Priya, P. V., Husain, J., & Boopathi, S. (2024). Enhancing Consumer Behavior and Experience Through AI-Driven Insights Optimization. In *AI Impacts in Digital Consumer Behavior* (pp. 1–35). IGI Global. doi:10.4018/979-8-3693-1918-5.ch001

Pachiappan, K., Anitha, K., Pitchai, R., Sangeetha, S., Satyanarayana, T., & Boopathi, S. (2024). Intelligent Machines, IoT, and AI in Revolutionizing Agriculture for Water Processing. In *Handbook of Research on AI and ML for Intelligent Machines and Systems* (pp. 374–399). IGI Global.

Pramila, P., Amudha, S., Saravanan, T., Sankar, S. R., Poongothai, E., & Boopathi, S. (2023). Design and Development of Robots for Medical Assistance: An Architectural Approach. In Contemporary Applications of Data Fusion for Advanced Healthcare Informatics (pp. 260–282). IGI Global.

Rahamathunnisa, U., Subhashini, P., Aancy, H. M., Meenakshi, S., Boopathi, S., & ... (2023). Solutions for Software Requirement Risks Using Artificial Intelligence Techniques. In *Handbook of Research on Data Science and Cybersecurity Innovations in Industry 4.0 Technologies* (pp. 45–64). IGI Global.

Rajeshwari, S., Praveenadevi, D., Revathy, S., & Sreekala, S. (2023). 15 Utilizing AI technologies to enhance e-commerce business operations. *Toward Artificial General Intelligence*, 309–330.

Ramudu, K., Mohan, V. M., Jyothirmai, D., Prasad, D., Agrawal, R., & Boopathi, S. (2023). Machine Learning and Artificial Intelligence in Disease Prediction: Applications, Challenges, Limitations, Case Studies, and Future Directions. In Contemporary Applications of Data Fusion for Advanced Healthcare Informatics (pp. 297–318). IGI Global.

Ravisankar, A., Shanthi, A., Lavanya, S., Ramaratnam, M., Krishnamoorthy, V., & Boopathi, S. (2024). Harnessing 6G for Consumer-Centric Business Strategies Across Electronic Industries. In AI Impacts in Digital Consumer Behavior (pp. 241–270). IGI Global.

Reggi, L., Arduini, D., Biagetti, M., & Zanfei, A. (2014). How advanced are Italian regions in terms of public e-services? The construction of a composite indicator to analyze patterns of innovation diffusion in the public sector. *Telecommunications Policy*, *38*(5–6), 514–529. doi:10.1016/j.telpol.2013.12.005

Revathi, S., Babu, M., Rajkumar, N., Meti, V. K. V., Kandavalli, S. R., & Boopathi, S. (2024). Unleashing the Future Potential of 4D Printing: Exploring Applications in Wearable Technology, Robotics, Energy, Transportation, and Fashion. In Human-Centered Approaches in Industry 5.0: Human-Machine Interaction, Virtual Reality Training, and Customer Sentiment Analysis (pp. 131–153). IGI Global.

Ronchi, A. M. (2019). *E-Services*. Springer. doi:10.1007/978-3-030-01842-9

Samikannu, R., Koshariya, A. K., Poornima, E., Ramesh, S., Kumar, A., & Boopathi, S. (2022). Sustainable Development in Modern Aquaponics Cultivation Systems Using IoT Technologies. In *Human Agro-Energy Optimization for Business and Industry* (pp. 105–127). IGI Global.

Seri, P., Bianchi, A., & Matteucci, N. (2014). Diffusion and usage of public e-services in Europe: An assessment of country level indicators and drivers. *Telecommunications Policy*, *38*(5–6), 496–513. doi:10.1016/j.telpol.2014.03.004

Sharma, D. M., Ramana, K. V., Jothilakshmi, R., Verma, R., Maheswari, B. U., & Boopathi, S. (2024). Integrating Generative AI Into K-12 Curriculums and Pedagogies in India: Opportunities and Challenges. *Facilitating Global Collaboration and Knowledge Sharing in Higher Education With Generative AI*, 133–161.

Singh, N., & Adhikari, D. (n.d.). *AI-Driven Personalization in eCommerce Advertising*. Academic Press.

Sonia, R., Gupta, N., Manikandan, K., Hemalatha, R., Kumar, M. J., & Boopathi, S. (2024). Strengthening Security, Privacy, and Trust in Artificial Intelligence Drones for Smart Cities. In *Analyzing and Mitigating Security Risks in Cloud Computing* (pp. 214–242). IGI Global. doi:10.4018/979-8-3693-3249-8.ch011

Stegaru, G., Danila, C., Sacala, I. S., Moisescu, M., & Stanescu, A. M. (2015). E-Services quality assessment framework for collaborative networks. *Enterprise Information Systems*, *9*(5–6), 583–606.

Sundaramoorthy, K., Singh, A., Sumathy, G., Maheshwari, A., Arunarani, A., & Boopathi, S. (2024). A Study on AI and Blockchain-Powered Smart Parking Models for Urban Mobility. In *Handbook of Research on AI and ML for Intelligent Machines and Systems* (pp. 223–250). IGI Global.

Vegesna, V. V. (2023). Privacy-Preserving Techniques in AI-Powered Cyber Security: Challenges and Opportunities. *International Journal of Machine Learning for Sustainable Development*, *5*(4), 1–8.

Venkateswaran, N., Kumar, S. S., Diwakar, G., Gnanasangeetha, D., & Boopathi, S. (2023). Synthetic Biology for Waste Water to Energy Conversion: IoT and AI Approaches. *Applications of Synthetic Biology in Health. Energy & Environment*, 360–384.

Venkateswaran, N., Vidhya, K., Ayyannan, M., Chavan, S. M., Sekar, K., & Boopathi, S. (2023). A Study on Smart Energy Management Framework Using Cloud Computing. In 5G, Artificial Intelligence, and Next Generation Internet of Things: Digital Innovation for Green and Sustainable Economies (pp. 189–212). IGI Global. doi:10.4018/978-1-6684-8634-4.ch009

Venkateswaran, N., Vidhya, R., Naik, D. A., Raj, T. M., Munjal, N., & Boopathi, S. (2023). Study on Sentence and Question Formation Using Deep Learning Techniques. In *Digital Natives as a Disruptive Force in Asian Businesses and Societies* (pp. 252–273). IGI Global. doi:10.4018/978-1-6684-6782-4.ch015

Zekrifa, D. M. S., Kulkarni, M., Bhagyalakshmi, A., Devireddy, N., Gupta, S., & Boopathi, S. (2023). Integrating Machine Learning and AI for Improved Hydrological Modeling and Water Resource Management. In *Artificial Intelligence Applications in Water Treatment and Water Resource Management* (pp. 46–70). IGI Global. doi:10.4018/978-1-6684-6791-6.ch003

Chapter 9
Industry 5.0:
Blue Wind Energy for Sustainable Urbanization and Intelligent Control of Energy

Shubhendu Shekher Shukla
https://orcid.org/0000-0002-6902-9608
SRM Business School, India

Manish Jain
Babu Banarasi Das University, India

Alka Jain
Babu Banarasi Das University, India

Saurabh Bajpai
https://orcid.org/0000-0002-1344-9996
Babu Banarasi Das University, India

Ashutosh Kumar Mishra
https://orcid.org/0000-0002-1094-0261
SRM Business School, India

Ankur Gupta
https://orcid.org/0000-0002-4651-5830
Vaish College of Engineering, India

Sabyasachi Pramanik
https://orcid.org/0000-0002-9431-8751
Haldia Institute of Technology, India

ABSTRACT

Blue wind energy combines offshore wind energy with cutting-edge technology, addressing sustainability in urbanization. This chapter investigates its application, focusing on integrating blue wind energy, AI, and IoT for smart energy management. Urgently needed due to urban energy demand and environmental concerns, conventional methods fall short. Blue wind energy, with AI and IoT, offers a sustainable alternative, but integration challenges exist. The amalgamation of blue wind energy, AI, and IoT presents a groundbreaking solution to urban energy needs. Urbanization necessitates sustainable energy solutions, with blue wind energy utilizing offshore wind resources effectively. Offshore wind farms near cities offer better energy production but require complex energy management systems for full potential realization.

DOI: 10.4018/979-8-3693-1343-5.ch009

INTRODUCTION

To address the increasing challenges posed by rapid urbanization, climate change, and increased energy consumption, the world must transition to sustainable urbanization. Given this, it is imperative to look into other energy sources, and blue wind energy stands out as a workable solution to these challenging issues. Because Blue Wind Energy makes use of airborne wind turbines that are linked to ground stations, it is a cutting-edge wind power technology. In this chapter, the potential of Blue Wind Energy as a fundamental component of Industry 5.0—a revolutionary industrial process combining green energy, artificial intelligence (AI), and the Internet of Things (IoT)—is examined (Kasinathan et al., 2022). The demand for clever and sustainable solutions increases as we approach Industry 5.0, which is characterized by the seamless fusion of digital and physical technologies. Urbanization, which increases energy consumption and drives a paradigm shift in favour of ecologically friendly alternatives, is a hallmark of modern civilization. This research investigates the revolutionary potential of Blue Wind Energy as a sustainable power source for urbanized environments, combined with the integration of Artificial Intelligence (AI) and the Internet of Things (IoT), in order to usher in a new era of intelligent energy management within the framework of Industry 5.0. The need for innovative and sustainable energy alternatives is made clear by the escalating issues with conventional energy sources, such as resource depletion and environmental degradation. Blue Wind Energy is a practical solution that generates power from wind energy with the least amount of negative environmental effect. This renewable energy source is particularly significant when taking urbanization into account since densely inhabited areas need efficient and environmentally friendly energy solutions. Industry 5.0 concepts are aligned with the potential effect of Blue Wind Energy systems via the integration of AI and IoT technology. Artificial Intelligence (AI) has the potential to enhance Blue Wind Energy system performance via its capacity to evaluate extensive datasets and make prompt judgments (Elrahmani et al., 2021). Simultaneously, the Internet of Things enables an intelligent and networked energy environment, facilitating smooth device control and communication for effective energy management. In the context of Industry 5.0, the combination of Blue Wind Energy, AI, and IoT offers a comprehensive and innovative way to handle the growing energy requirements of urbanized landscapes.

The Internet of Things and artificial intelligence are essential for optimizing all aspects of energy generation, distribution, and consumption. AI systems make predictive maintenance easier, which results in less downtime and more effective usage of wind turbines. IoT devices improve demand-side management and grid stability by providing real-time monitoring and control. The several uses and advantages of incorporating AI and IoT into the electricity system are highlighted in this study. Still, when this synergy is incorporated into urban environments, its real potential is unleashed. A dynamic, sustainable energy ecosystem is produced by the interplay of IoT-connected devices' responsiveness, AI-driven predictive analytics, and Blue Wind Energy's agility. Reduced energy waste, peak load cutting, and a markedly smaller carbon footprint are the outcomes. Relevance: This chapter shows how Blue Wind Energy may be successfully integrated with AI and IoT, demonstrating the enormous promise for more sustainable, green, and intelligent cities. The importance of sophisticated energy storage systems and smart grids as essential elements of the current energy environment are also emphasized in the report. The intelligent grid serves as the foundation for effective energy distribution, and AI and IoT are essential to its smooth operation. Rapid advancements in energy storage technology enable cities to successfully manage supply and demand while adjusting for wind energy's intermittent nature. The environmental effect of Blue Wind Energy, its economic viability, and a comparison with other energy sources are all included in this thorough evaluation of environmental and economic factors. In order to promote sustainable urbanization globally and encourage the deployment of blue wind energy in urban contexts, this study explores the necessary legislative and regulatory frameworks. In conclusion, this chapter tries to explain how Blue Wind Energy integrates with IoT and AI in the context of Industry 5.0, with a particular emphasis on how it might be used for sustainable urbanization. The goal of this chapter is to provide important insights into how energy systems that adhere to the ideas of the fourth industrial revolution will develop by examining the possible advantages, difficulties, and viability of this integrated approach. In the age of Industry 5.0, it hopes to clear the path for a more intelligent, sustainable, and green urban energy environment by using the combined potential of these technologies.

LITERATURE REVIEW

The 21st century is characterized by a dramatic acceleration of urbanization, which presents a number of issues, the most important of which is the growing need for energy in densely populated places. Traditional energy sources are becoming more and more unsustainable in terms of both ecology and economics as urban areas grow and change. Amidst these obstacles, the need of shifting towards sustainable and renewable energy options has emerged as a crucial area of focus for scholars, decision-makers, and business executives (Li et al., 2019).

A type of wind energy technology called "blue wind energy" seems to be a viable way to meet the expanding energy demands of metropolitan areas. By using wind currents over wide bodies of water, Blue Wind Energy, in contrast to traditional wind energy systems, takes use of the offshore wind's enormous energy potential. This novel method not only increases the efficiency of energy generation but also lessens some of the land use issues related to onshore wind farms. The inherent sustainability of Blue Wind Energy places it as a ray of hope for a more resilient and environmentally friendly energy future as the globe struggles with the effects of climate change (ElFar et al., 2021).

Blue Wind Energy systems' potential is multiplied by the incorporation of Artificial Intelligence (AI) and the Internet of Things (IoT), which is consistent with Industry 5.0 concepts. With its ability to do complex data analysis and machine learning, artificial intelligence (AI) has the potential to completely change how we optimize energy production and consumption. Blue Wind Energy systems can anticipate maintenance requirements, adjust to changing climatic conditions, and increase overall efficiency by using AI algorithms. Simultaneously, the Internet of Things enables a network of interconnected devices, enabling smooth communication among sensors, turbines, and energy grids. In the age of Industry 5.0, smart energy management—a critical component of sustainable urbanization—is made possible by this interconnection. With the advent of Industry 5.0, which is defined by the merging of digital and physical technologies, Blue Wind Energy's integration with AI and IoT is a critical step towards intelligent and sustainable urban energy systems. In order to fully understand the complex aspects of this integration, this study will examine its advantages, problems, and viability of using such a thorough strategy in the ever-changing context of Industry 5.0 (Singh, 2023). In doing so, we want to provide insightful information that will help shape the creation of intelligent, green, and resilient energy infrastructures for the future urbanized world (Bogdanov et al., 2021).

In light of the urgent issues surrounding urbanization, rising energy consumption, and the need of making the shift to sustainable practices in the age of Industry 5.0, this chapter is very important. According to (Khanh, P. T. et al. 2023), combining Blue Wind Energy with AI and the Internet of Things (IoT) is a novel way to address the energy requirements of quickly urbanizing areas. It is crucial to comprehend and use the potential of this integration for a number of strong reasons. First off, conventional energy sources become more insufficient as urban populations rise, and this has a noticeable negative effect on the environment. In addition to offering a clean, sustainable energy source, offshore wind energy solutions like Blue Wind Energy also help to reduce land use disputes that come with onshore alternatives. The technology under investigation is worth examining because it has the potential to change the way that sustainable urbanization is seen and provide a workable way to address the energy needs of growing cities. Second, the introduction of IoT and AI into Blue Wind Energy (Veeraiah, V. et al. 2023) systems is consistent with Industry 5.0's philosophy, which ushers in a new age of intelligent and networked technology. A revolutionary approach to smart energy management is presented by the integration of AI for predictive maintenance, performance optimization, and real-time decision-making with the capabilities of IoT for smooth communication and control. This creates a basis for robust and adaptable urban energy infrastructures in addition to improving the efficiency of energy generation and consumption. The chapter's importance stems from its addition to the larger conversation on sustainable practices in the context of Industry 5.0. By examining the complexities of Blue Wind Energy's interaction with AI and IoT, the study advances knowledge of how cutting-edge technologies might be used to build smarter, greener cities (Singh, 2024). Policymakers, industry stakeholders, and academics alike might benefit from the insights gained from this investigation, which could direct the creation of sustainable urban energy plans.

This chapter presents a comprehensive strategy for adopting renewable energy in urban settings, which adds to the current worldwide efforts to mitigate climate change. Combining Blue Wind Energy with AI and IoT is a step towards a more resilient and sustainable urban future—rather than just a technical integration. The significance of this paper lies in its potential to pave the way for a harmonious coexistence of urbanization, green energy, and intelligent technologies in the era of Industry 5.0, as we stand at the intersection of unprecedented technological advancements and environmental challenges. Fig 1 shows the chapter's significance.

Figure 1. Illustrates the chapter's significance

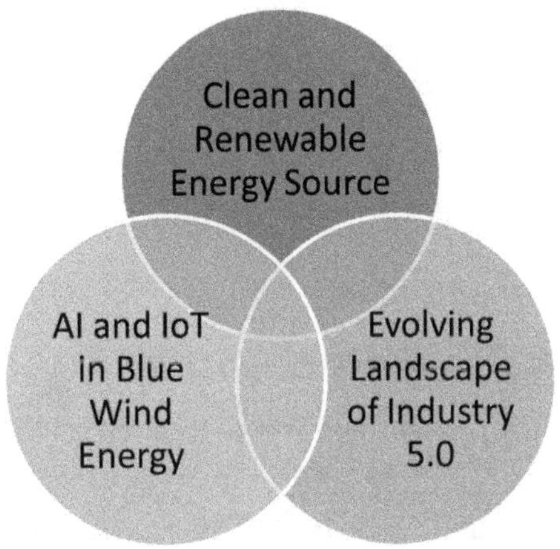

The Chapter's Objectives

In order to showcase blue wind energy as a practical green energy source and to guide future research and development in the subject of urban energy management in Industry 5.0, this study aims to provide incisive analysis that advances the discourse about sustainable energy solutions.

- investigate the potential applications of IoT and AI in intelligent energy management.
- assess the potential benefits and challenges of this integrated approach.

Overview, Definition, and Guiding Principles of Blue Wind Energy

Blue Wind Energy is a novel approach to wind power, focusing on the untapped potential of offshore wind resources. Blue Wind Energy is an extension of traditional wind energy technology that seeks to overcome some of the shortcomings of onshore wind farms by moving the turbines offshore. This intentional migration is a desirable alternative for generating sustainable energy in coastal locations since it has so many advantages. Blue Wind electricity generates electricity by harnessing the force of wind currents over large bodies of water, including seas or oceans. The term "blue" in "Blue Wind Energy" refers to the seascapes that are often home to these wind farms. By using offshore locations to mitigate land use restrictions and any aesthetic issues associated with onshore wind projects, Blue Wind Energy maximizes available space and minimizes visual impact on terrestrial environments. A key element of Blue Wind Energy is the physics of wind dynamics. Because of their regular and higher wind speeds than their onshore counterparts, offshore locations provide a more predictable and efficient source of

Figure 2. The chapter's goal

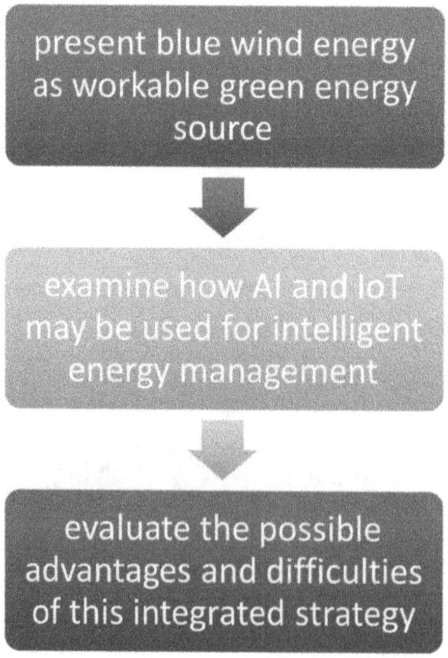

electricity. Wind is allowed to blow freely across large expanses of open water, increasing capacity factors and energy production. Furthermore, offshore wind farms' proximity to cities facilitates the transfer of produced energy to population centres by reducing transmission losses associated with long-distance power transportation. Blue wind energy systems typically consist of large turbines attached to towers fastened to the seafloor. These wind turbines convert wind energy from kinetic energy to electrical power via the spinning of blades connected to a generator. The generated energy is transported to the shore via submerged cables, where it might be integrated into the existing power system. Blue wind energy has major beneficial environmental impacts since it reduces greenhouse gas emissions, dependency on fossil fuels, and environmental damage caused by traditional energy sources. In an offshore environment, larger, more powerful turbines might be constructed to increase energy generating efficiency. In the context of renewable energy, Blue Wind Energy is a revolutionary approach. It does this by properly using offshore wind resources to provide sustainable, reliable, and environmentally beneficial electricity. The concepts of Blue Wind Energy serve as a beacon of innovation, providing a glimpse into the future of offshore wind technology and its potential role in forming a more sustainable energy ecosystem, as the world struggles with the imperative to shift towards greener energy alternatives. Fig 2 shows the chapter's goal.

Advantages and Difficulties of Wind Energy

Blue Wind Energy is a clean and renewable energy source with many advantages, but in order to reach its full potential and guarantee its place in a sustainable energy future, these issues must be resolved. In order to overcome these obstacles and increase the adoption and efficacy of Blue Wind Energy as a component of the global energy mix, it will be imperative that technological, legislative, and industrial developments continue.

Blue Wind Energy's Advantages

Rich Renewable Resource: Blue Wind Energy is a dependable and plentiful renewable energy source since it utilizes the extensive and steady offshore wind resources. Higher and more constant wind speeds are possible in an offshore setting, which increases the amount of energy produced. Decreased Land Use Conflicts: Blue Wind Energy systems do not compete for scarce land resources, in contrast to onshore wind farms. By locating turbines offshore, land use conflicts are lessened and the effects on terrestrial ecosystems are minimized, hence resolving issues with habitat destruction and aesthetics. Greater Capacity Factors: Blue Wind Energy systems have greater capacity factors since the offshore environment provides more consistent and powerful wind conditions. As a result, these systems are able to run at a larger proportion of their maximal capacity, producing more energy overall. Closeness to Population Centres: Since many cities are situated close to coastlines, Blue Wind Energy's offshore farm location enables the production of renewable energy to be positioned in close proximity to key population centres. Because of this close proximity, energy transmission losses and long-distance power transportation costs are decreased. Environmental Impact: By lowering greenhouse gas emissions and relying less on fossil fuels, Blue Wind Energy supports international efforts to mitigate climate change. When compared to onshore wind farms, the offshore position lessens the effect on nearby ecosystems and species.

Blue Wind Energy's Challenges

High Initial Costs: Installing and maintaining offshore wind farms requires a significant initial financial outlay. When compared to onshore wind projects, the cost of building and installing turbines in maritime locations, as well as the associated infrastructure, might be greater. Technological Difficulties: There are technological difficulties while operating in extreme offshore circumstances. Strong winds, wave pressure, and corrosive seawater must all be tolerated by turbines, necessitating sophisticated technical solutions to guarantee long-term dependability and endurance.

Logistics and Installation Challenges: Offshore wind turbine shipping and installation are difficult jobs requiring specialized equipment and boats. The constraints of placing turbines in deep water make the building and maintenance procedures more difficult. Grid Connection: Installing undersea cables, which may be costly and technically difficult, is necessary to connect offshore wind farms to the onshore electricity grid. Getting the most out of Blue Wind Energy requires a reliable and effective grid connection. Environmental Concerns: Although building and running offshore wind farms may have localized environmental effects, they are still a more ecologically benign alternative than many other energy sources. These include possible disruptions to shipping lanes, the visual landscape, and marine habitats.

Energy Demand and Sustainable Urbanization

An unparalleled age of city expansion and population concentration in urban areas has been brought about by the unstoppable trend of global urbanization. While this revolutionary process is a symbol of human progress, it has also resulted in a simultaneous increase in the need for energy. As a result, sustainable urbanization becomes vitally important and demands a paradigm change in the planning, construction, and energy systems of cities. The main obstacle posed by the urbanization trend is the growing requirement for energy to accommodate the demands of expanding populations. Cities are not just enormous consumers of energy but also real centres of innovation in technology, economic activity, and cultural vitality. A comprehensive approach to urban development is necessary to build resilient, dynamic communities that are also ecologically sustainable. This approach incorporates renewable energy sources, places a high priority on energy efficiency, and makes use of sophisticated technology. A future where urban centres are dynamic hubs of innovation, efficiency, and sustainability rather than just energy consumers is something that policymakers, city planners, industry stakeholders, and the general public are all working towards as we embark on the journey towards sustainable urbanization.

The Impact of Smart Cities on the World's Energy Use

Smart cities play a critical role in the world's energy usage since they are hubs of innovation, economic activity, and population density. Due to the concentrated demands of industry, transportation networks, and the varied needs of urban populations, cities now account for a significant portion of the global energy consumption. Urban energy consumption is enormous and complicated, which emphasizes how critical it is to address sustainability in cities in order to lessen its negative environmental effects. Strategies for boosting energy efficiency, deploying smart technology in cities, and embracing renewable energy sources become more and more important as urbanization picks up speed. As a result, cities are essential to the global effort to create a future in which energy is more resilient and sustainable, in addition to being large users of energy.

The Need to Switch to Green Energy Sources

Addressing urgent global issues like climate change, environmental degradation, and energy security is fundamentally dependent on the use of green energy sources. Green energy is a sustainable substitute for conventional fossil fuels. It is produced from renewable resources including solar, wind, hydro, and geothermal energy. Green energy uses the planet's natural processes instead of depleting limited resources or releasing damaging greenhouse gases, in contrast to fossil fuel reserves that are limited and cause pollution. According to (Sinha, M. et al. 2021), this shift is critical for lowering air pollution, promoting environmental sustainability, and lessening the negative consequences of climate change. By broadening the energy mix and lowering dependence on geopolitically vulnerable fossil fuel stocks, the shift to green energy improves energy security. Countries' geopolitical and economic stability is less reliant on the whims of oil price swings and the complex geopolitics of oil-producing areas. Green energy technologies can provide a route to energy independence by enabling countries to produce electricity on-site and lessen their reliance on swings in the world energy market. Making the switch to green energy promotes both economic expansion and scientific advancement. Research and development as well as the creation of jobs in emerging businesses are fuelled by investments in renewable energy technology. According to (Pramanik, S. et al. 2022), the green energy industry has the potential to stimulate economic growth by providing skilled job opportunities and elevating nations to the forefront of the global clean energy market. Making the switch to green energy is essential if we are to fight climate change, improve environmental sustainability, and ensure a diverse and robust energy supply in the future. This change represents a significant step towards a more sustainable and just global energy landscape as it not only lessens the environmental effect of conventional energy sources but also helps countries achieve economic prosperity and energy independence.

Urbanization's Effect on Energy Demand

Urbanization has a significant and varied effect on energy consumption. The concentration of economic activity, the expansion of infrastructure, and the density of population all contribute to an increase in the need for energy as more people move to urban areas. In addition to raising the need for transportation fuels, urbanization increases the requirement for energy to power homes, companies, and industries. Cities' energy consumption is further increased by the development of energy-intensive structures and the widespread use of electronic gadgets. Furthermore, higher living standards are often associated with urbanization, which raises demands for energy-intensive services.

Wind Energy Offshore

Unlike traditional onshore wind farms, offshore wind farms are situated near coastlines or at sea to benefit from higher and more consistent wind speeds. Offshore wind energy is a revolutionary advancement in the world of renewable energy as it harnesses the tremendous power of wind across vast bodies of water. Since it provides unique advantages and addresses some of the problems associated with onshore wind projects, this emerging business has attracted a lot of attention as a clean, renewable energy source. The much greater wind speeds that are typical over Open Ocean are the main advantages of offshore wind energy. Because the power produced by a wind turbine is proportional to the cube of the wind speed, these higher wind speeds lead to an increase in energy output. Because of this, offshore wind farms are able to attain greater capacity factors and run more reliably at or close to their full production. Because of its increased efficiency, offshore wind energy may contribute significantly to the total amount of renewable energy sources. Additionally, the restrictions related to land use that sometimes provide difficulties for onshore wind turbines are lessened by offshore wind projects. Large-scale wind farms may be installed in the ocean's huge expanses without taking up too much room or damaging nearby land. This feature is especially helpful in areas with high population density, where there may not be as many good onshore spots. Not to be overlooked is how offshore wind energy affects the ecosystem. Offshore wind energy is a clean and sustainable alternative to conventional fossil fuel-based energy sources since it generates power without releasing greenhouse gases or other dangerous pollutants into the atmosphere. Concerns about the aesthetics of onshore wind projects are mitigated by the submerged nature of offshore wind farms, which reduces visual and acoustic disruptions. Offshore wind energy development is not without difficulties, however. Due to the need for significant expenditures in specialized infrastructure, foundations, and turbines that can resist maritime conditions, offshore wind projects sometimes have greater initial capital costs than onshore installations. Offshore locations provide extra logistical challenges for grid connection, installation, and maintenance, requiring specialized boats and innovative technical solutions. Advancements in technology and governmental backing have accelerated the worldwide expansion of offshore wind farms in recent years. Leaders in offshore wind development are nations with long coasts, such China, Denmark, and the United Kingdom. The feasibility and efficiency of offshore wind energy are being improved by developments in turbine design, floating platforms, and grid integration; as a result, offshore wind energy is becoming a more crucial part of the shift to a low-carbon energy future.

Benefits of Wind Farms Offshore

The following benefits of offshore wind farms help explain why they are becoming more and more important in the field of renewable energy: Greater Wind Speeds: Compared to onshore places, offshore locations can have greater and more constant wind speeds. Offshore wind farms are more effective at converting wind energy into electricity because of this feature, which also leads to greater energy output and enhanced capacity factors.

Greater wind speeds over Open Water: Offshore wind farms may produce more power per turbine due to the greater wind speeds, which raises the total amount of energy produced. This is particularly crucial in heavily populated areas because there may not be many good onshore places. Mitigation of Visual and Noise Impact: Because offshore wind farms are underwater, they are less likely to cause visual or noise disruptions than onshore installations. Because of this feature, communities who are worried about the noise pollution and aesthetics of typical wind farms are more likely to approve offshore wind projects. Possibility of Larger Turbines: Larger turbines have the ability to catch more wind energy and provide greater power outputs, and this is made possible by offshore conditions. This feature helps to stabilize the grid and improves the dependability of offshore wind farms. Closeness to Population Centres: Since many cities are situated close to coastlines, offshore wind farms may be positioned strategically in close proximity to important population centres. This improves the effectiveness of energy distribution by lowering transmission losses and the expenses related to moving power across large distances. Environmental Benefits: Compared to conventional energy sources based on fossil fuels, offshore wind energy is a clean and ecologically beneficial option. It lessens the negative environmental effects of traditional energy production, such as air pollution and greenhouse gas emissions. Job Creation and Economic Growth: The planning, building, and upkeep of offshore wind farms provide employment opportunities

Figure 3. Offshore wind farm benefits

and promote economic expansion. This contributes to the development of a competent and long-lasting workforce by covering jobs in engineering, manufacture, installation, and continuing operations. Technological Developments: Design, material, and construction method breakthroughs are being driven by ongoing research and development in offshore wind technology. These developments support the ongoing enhancement of offshore wind farms' efficacy, affordability, and environmental impact.

The benefits provided by offshore wind farms place them in a critical position as the world turns its attention to renewable energy, positioning them as a key player in the shift to a more robust and sustainable energy future. Fig 3 shows the wind farm benefits.

Difficulties and Technological Progress: Difficulties With Offshore Wind Power

High Initial Costs: Compared to onshore projects, the capital costs of establishing offshore wind farms are much greater. Among the substantial up-front costs are the vessels, foundations, and specialized infrastructure that are required for installation.

Logistics and Installation Difficulties: Transporting and erecting wind turbines in an offshore setting may be logistically challenging, especially in deeper seas. Project complexity is increased by the need for specialized vessels and technical solutions for the deployment of foundations and grid connection. Maintenance and Repairs: Because of the severe maritime climate and the corrosive effects of seawater, accessing and maintaining turbines in offshore sites may be difficult. Creating economical and effective maintenance plans is essential to offshore wind farms' long-term survival.

Grid Connection: Installing undersea cables, an expensive and technically difficult procedure, is required to connect offshore wind farms to the onshore electricity grid. To fully profit from offshore wind energy, dependable and effective grid links are necessary. Environmental Concerns: There may be sporadic environmental effects from offshore wind farms, such as possible disruptions to animals, migratory paths, and marine ecosystems. One of the main challenges is balancing the environmental advantages of renewable energy with the protection of marine biodiversity. Technological Developments Handling Difficulties

Environmental Impact Assessments: The possible ecological implications of offshore wind farms are becoming more understood because to advancements in environmental impact assessment tools. With this information, projects may be designed with less negative effects on wildlife and marine ecosystems.

Unlocking the full potential of offshore wind energy requires persistent innovation and research to overcome these issues as technology advances. These developments help offshore wind become a more extensively used, ecologically friendly, and commercially feasible renewable energy source.

Notable Projects Using Offshore Wind Energy

A number of noteworthy offshore wind energy projects serve as trailblazing illustrations of the development and promise of the industry. One of the biggest offshore wind farms in the world right now is the Hornsea Wind Farm, which is situated off the coast of Yorkshire in the United Kingdom. With many stages, Hornsea will provide a significant amount of the UK's power requirements. The second noteworthy project is the Block Island Wind Farm, which is situated off the coast of Rhode Island and is the country's first offshore wind farm. Due to its success, offshore wind development in the United States has expanded.

Industry 5.0's Energy Management Uses AI and IoT

Through real-time issue detection and remediation, smart grids integrating Internet of Things (IoT) sensors improve the resilience and dependability of electricity distribution networks. Furthermore, demand-side management is facilitated by IoT-enabled industrial devices, which offer precise control over machinery and procedures to meet energy efficiency targets. The integration of AI and IoT in Industry 5.0's energy management goes beyond simple observation and control. Artificial intelligence (AI)-driven cognitive computing systems constantly optimizes energy use patterns by learning from and adapting to changing energy environments. When real-time data from IoT devices is incorporated into machine learning algorithms, these algorithms may make snap judgments to optimize energy consumption profiles, avoid equipment breakdowns, and balance loads. This degree of intelligent automation greatly helps achieve sustainability objectives and cost savings in addition to improving operational efficiency.

Predictive analytics (Gupta, A. et al. 2022) combined with AI and IoT in energy management encourages proactive maintenance. IoT-connected device performance data is analysed by AI algorithms to find trends that might point to equipment problems. Critical energy infrastructure has a longer lifetime thanks to this predictive maintenance technology, which also lowers maintenance costs and downtime. With its focus on integrating intelligent technologies, Industry 5.0 represents a shift away from reactive and manual energy management techniques and towards robust, self-optimizing systems. In the context of Industry 5.0, the integration of AI and IoT in energy management offers previously unheard-of advantages, but it also presents difficulties. It is necessary to address security issues pertaining to device interconnectivity and AI systems' possible susceptibility to cyber-attacks. Furthermore, significant expenditures in infrastructure, training, and technology adoption are needed for the implementation of these cutting-edge technologies. To guarantee smooth integration across various industrial ecosystems, standardization and interoperability also become essential factors to take into account.

AI's role in Industry 5.0's optimization of energy production and consumption the use of artificial intelligence by Industry 5.0 to optimize energy production and consumption is bringing about a fundamental shift in the way various sectors manage their energy resources. In the framework of the fourth industrial revolution, the convergence of digital and physical technologies is known as Industry 5.0, and artificial intelligence (AI) is a crucial element in enhancing the intelligence, sustainability, and efficiency of energy systems. AI's ability to analyse massive, complex information in real time makes it crucial for managing, predicting, and enhancing energy production. Machine learning algorithms examine weather patterns, historical data, and real-time energy consumption measurements to accurately forecast demand. By dynamically altering energy output, businesses may reduce waste and optimize resource utilization with the aid of these predictive skills. By ensuring that energy output closely matches demand patterns, artificial intelligence (AI)-powered energy production optimization helps to minimize overproduction. In Industry 5.0, the combination of artificial intelligence (AI) and the Internet of Things (IoT) enhances energy system optimization. Sensors and smart meters are among the Internet of Things devices that continually create real-time data on energy use and equipment performance. AI systems analyse this data and search for anomalies, inefficiencies, and potential growth opportunities. AI, for instance, may identify equipment problems, allowing for predictive maintenance to minimize energy use and avoid expensive downtime. AI-enabled cognitive computing systems are always learning and adapting to shifting energy environments. These systems have the ability to automatically decide how to use energy storage, respond to demand, and balance loads. AI's adaptable characteristics enable the development of self-optimizing energy systems that react quickly to changes in supply, demand, and environmental factors.

AI offers many advantages for Industry 5.0 (Dushyant, K. et al. 2022) energy production and consumption optimization. Cost savings, increased sustainability, and increased industry competitiveness are all a result of efficiency increases. Grid stability is further supported by AI-driven energy optimization, especially in situations where renewable energy sources with unpredictable outputs—like solar and wind—are widely used. AI supports a more robust and adaptable energy environment by intelligently controlling energy production and consumption, which is in line with Industry 5.0 objectives. But there are issues that need to be resolved, such data security, privacy issues, and the need for trained staff to deploy and oversee AI systems. Additionally necessary to guarantee the smooth integration of AI technology across various industrial contexts are standardization and interoperability. A new era of intelligent, sustainable, and effective industrial energy management is expected to be ushered in by the rising prominence of AI in optimizing energy systems as Industry 5.0 develops.

Internet of Things Uses for Control and Monitoring in Real-Time monitoring and control across several domains is one of the fundamental capabilities of the Internet of Things (IoT), which has emerged as a transformational technology with a wide range of applications. Numerous Internet of Things applications make use of real-time control and monitoring features. Smart Cities: By allowing real-time monitoring and management of several urban systems, IoT is essential to the development of smart cities. Smart traffic management systems optimize signal timings and reroute vehicles to ease congestion by using sensors and cameras to monitor traffic conditions in real time. IoT devices keep an eye on waste management, public safety, and air quality, enabling authorities to react quickly to changing circumstances. Industrial Internet of Things (IIoT) (Jayasingh, R. et al. 2022): IoT enables real-time production process monitoring and control in manufacturing and industry. Machinery sensors gather information on temperature, equipment operation, and other important parameters. Predictive maintenance is made possible by this real-time data, which also minimizes downtime and maximizes production efficiency. Smart Buildings: Internet of Things (IoT) applications in smart buildings includes real-time system monitoring and control for comfort and energy efficiency. Smart thermostats modify temperature and humidity according to outside factors and occupancy. IoT-enabled lighting systems dynamically alter brightness, while security systems provide real-time access management and monitoring. Agriculture: Precision agricultural methods brought out by IoT are revolutionizing the field. Field sensors monitor temperature, moisture content, and crop health in real time. Using this data as guidance, automated irrigation systems may optimize resource utilization by adjusting water distribution. The monitoring capabilities of drones with IoT devices are further enhanced.

Urbanization and Blue Wind Energy

Located offshore, Blue Wind Energy tackles the issues of land scarcity and aesthetic difficulties related to onshore wind projects. Blue Wind Energy maximizes space utilization and guarantees a more dependable and effective energy production process by using the strong and persistent winds across oceans and seas. The possibility of incorporating Blue Wind Energy into the energy mix of quickly expanding cities is further enhanced by the closeness of many metropolitan centres to coasts. The objectives of sustainable urbanization are in perfect harmony with the tenets of Blue Wind Energy. With their vast arrays of turbines fixed to the ocean below, offshore wind farms help lessen the environmental damage and greenhouse gas emissions that come with using traditional energy sources. By producing a sizable quantity of clean power, the technology helps to accelerate the shift to a low-carbon future and lessens the environmental effects of urban energy use. Furthermore, a decentralized energy infrastructure is essential to robust and sustainable urban growth and Blue Wind Energy makes this possible. Cities may increase energy security and diversify their energy sources by using offshore wind resources, which will lessen their reliance on centralized power plants. Blue Wind Energy's decentralized structure is also in line with the growing concept of smart cities, which emphasizes the need of distributed energy systems in fostering more responsive, flexible, and effective urban settings. There are obstacles to overcome when using Blue Wind Energy into urbanization initiatives, despite all of its benefits. Careful consideration is needed for factors such high initial capital costs, logistical challenges in offshore sites, and possible environmental issues. But continuing technical developments, legislative backing, and stakeholder cooperation are actively tackling these issues, opening the door for Blue Wind Energy to become a key component of the sustainable urbanization (Roy, A. et al. 2023) toolset. In the field of urban energy solutions, Blue Wind Energy is a shining example of innovation, providing a sustainable substitute for fossil fuels that power the world's growing cities. The addition of Blue Wind Energy to metropolitan energy portfolios marks a paradigm change towards greener, more ecologically friendly, and more efficient power production as urbanization picks up speed. Blue Wind Energy emerges as a revolutionary force in the goal of resilient and sustainable urban development, influencing how cities will use wind power to satisfy their energy demands in the future.

Smart Grids and Energy Storage: Smart Grids' Function in the Distribution of Urban Energy

In order to effectively handle the issues posed by increasing urbanization and the switch to renewable energy sources, smart grids and energy storage systems constitute a pivotal point in the modernization of urban energy distribution. Smart grids play a variety of roles in urban energy distribution because they increase grid stability and reliability by providing real-time insight into the whole energy network. Smart grids utilize advanced sensors, smart meters, and communication technologies to collect and analyse data on energy usage, grid performance, and any problems. To provide a consistent power supply for urban businesses and residents, real-time monitoring enables the early detection of issues, prompt response to blackouts, and optimization of grid performance.

Smart grids enable demand response systems that let consumers actively participate in energy management. Smart meters and Internet of Things (IoT) linked devices allow customers to access real-time information on their energy use, expenses, and environmental impact. With this information, customers may make educated choices, including shifting energy-intensive operations to off-peak hours when power prices are lower or when renewable energy generation is at its height. Demand-side flexibility plays a role in reducing peak demand, balancing the grid, and optimizing the pattern of total energy use. Energy storage devices may lessen the unpredictable and intermittent character of renewable energy sources when they are utilized in conjunction with smart grids. As urban areas include solar and wind power into their energy mix, the ability to store excess energy during high-generation times and release it during times of increased demand becomes more and more crucial. Energy may be effectively stored and released with the help of batteries and other energy storage devices, which act as a buffer to keep supply and demand in balance. This feature encourages the integration of a higher proportion of renewable energy into urban networks, reduces the need for additional fossil fuel-based backup supply, and contributes to grid stability.

With the help of smart grids and energy storage, urban transit will soon run on electricity. When smart grids are seamlessly integrated with electric vehicles (EVs), EVs may operate as mobile energy storage units. Through bidirectional charging, EVs may give extra energy back into the grid during peak demand or take energy when it is plentiful and affordable. This bidirectional flow promotes grid flexibility and helps the overall sustainability of urban transportation. In order to create an energy landscape that is contemporary, effective, and sustainable, smart grids play a critical role in urban energy distribution. Through the integration of cutting-edge technology, data analytics, and instantaneous communication with conventional power grids, smart grids maximize energy allocation, bolster dependability, and enable customers to take an active role in energy conservation. Smart grids facilitate the shift to a cleaner and more resilient urban energy infrastructure by addressing the difficulties associated with integrating renewable energy sources into urban networks when combined with energy storage technologies. Adoption of energy storage and smart grids is essential for creating a sustainable and future-proof urban energy ecosystem as cities continue to change.

How AI and IoT Help With Efficient Energy Distribution and Storage

The era of efficient energy storage and distribution is being ushered in by the synergistic integration of Artificial Intelligence (AI) (Andrushia, A. D. et al. 2023) and the Internet of Things (IoT). IoT sensors positioned across energy networks and storage systems serve as the nerve ends in this dynamic environment, continually gathering a multitude of real-time data on energy use, grid performance, and storage capacity. After processing this data, AI algorithms—the cognitive powerhouse—extracts useful information and makes defensible judgments. An intelligent energy ecosystem that adjusts and optimizes in response to changing circumstances is produced by the combination of real-time monitoring made possible by IoT and AI's predictive analytics capabilities. AI and IoT play a major role in predictive maintenance, wherein IoT sensors track the condition of energy infrastructure and AI algorithms anticipate any malfunctions or breakdowns. By using a proactive approach, downtime is decreased, dependability is improved, and the lifetime of crucial components is increased. Additionally, by using data from IoT-connected devices, the dynamic pair facilitates load control and demand response, enabling utilities to maximize peak demand reduction, balance loads, and optimizes energy distribution via AI-driven decision-making. An important area of research is energy storage efficiency, with AI algorithms optimizing cycles of charging and discharging depending on demand and grid circumstances in real time, and Internet of Things sensors keeping an eye on storage system performance. As a result, total efficiency is increased and stored energy is used wisely. Furthermore, IoT and AI work together to integrate renewable energy sources. IoT sensors on wind turbines and solar panels provide real-time data that AI algorithms use to estimate generating trends. This capacity helps to overcome the unpredictability of renewable energy sources and enable their smooth integration into the system. Artificial Intelligence (AI) plays a vital role in enhancing cybersecurity (Reepu, S. et al. 2023) in the digital age by monitoring network traffic for irregularities and instantly reacting to any attacks. By doing this, the energy infrastructure's networked equipment' integrity and security are guaranteed. A paradigm change towards a more intelligent, adaptable, and sustainable energy ecosystem is signalled by the use of AI and IoT in energy distribution and storage. This combination, which makes use of real-time data, predictive analytics, and adaptive decision-making, enables utilities and customers to effectively manage the complexity of contemporary energy needs and establishes the groundwork for a resilient and ecologically responsible energy future.

CONCLUSION

Together with the revolutionary potential of artificial intelligence (AI) and the internet of things (IoT), blue wind energy, smart grids, and energy storage represent a ground-breaking synergy that is set to completely reshape the field of sustainable urbanization and energy management in the industry 5.0 eras. Emerging as a shining example of innovation, Blue Wind Energy provides a cost-effective and environmentally friendly response to the growing energy needs of cities. By using the force of ocean winds, its offshore wind farms not only mitigate the problem of land scarcity but also make a substantial contribution towards the reduction of greenhouse gas emissions and the development of a robust energy infrastructure. The introduction of Smart Grids, strengthened by IoT and AI technologies, raises the bar for intelligence and efficiency in urban energy distribution. Cities' approaches to energy management and consumption have been revolutionized by the integration of renewable energy sources, demand response mechanisms, predictive maintenance, and real-time monitoring. Smart Grids' decentralized architecture empowers users, improves grid dependability, and establishes the foundation for flexible and responsive urban energy systems. With the support of AI and IoT, energy storage becomes more important in the pursuit of sustainable energy. These solutions lessen dependency on traditional backup sources, handle the intermittent nature of renewable energy sources, and enable the smooth integration of renewable energy into urban networks. They also improve storage operations in real time. The bidirectional flow of energy between storage devices and the grid, combined with breakthroughs in predictive analytics, highlights the transformational potential of AI and IoT in the field of energy storage. These interconnected technologies have a bright and wide future ahead of them. Sustained progress in artificial intelligence algorithms, machine learning frameworks, and Internet of Things sensor technologies will enhance the effectiveness, dependability, and flexibility of urban energy systems. The widespread use of these technologies will promote sustainability and resilience as Smart Cities (Mandal, A. et al. 2021), which are defined by intelligent and networked infrastructure, proliferate. These interconnected systems will mature as Industry 5.0 continues to develop, opening the door for ever more advanced energy management solutions. The establishment of cybersecurity protocols, standards, and interoperability will be crucial in guaranteeing the smooth integration of these technologies in various urban settings. Governments, businesses, and academic institutions working together will be essential to overcome obstacles and realizing the full promise of these revolutionary energy solutions. Cities will be powered by clean, intelligent, and adaptive energy systems in the future thanks to the synthesis of blue wind energy, smart grids, and energy storage with IoT and AI capabilities. As these technologies advance, they will together have a profound influence on energy management and sustainable urbanization, which will not only change how cities use and distribute energy but also greatly aid in the worldwide shift to a more robust and sustainable energy future. The integration of Artificial Intelligence (AI) and the Internet of Things (IoT) with Blue Wind Energy, Smart Grids, and Energy Storage presents a highly promising avenue for global adoption and scalability. This game-changing synergy positions itself as a paradigm for wider deployment by addressing important issues in sustainable development and urban energy management. With the help of AI and IoT, Blue Wind Energy, Smart Grids, and Energy Storage not only show promise for scalability but also provide a compelling case for widespread adoption. These integrated technologies provide a way forward for a genuinely global energy future that is robust, efficient, and sustainable as the globe navigates the problems of urbanization, climate change, and energy transition.

REFERENCES

Andrushia, A. D., Neebha, T. M., Patricia, A. T., Sagayam, K. M., & Pramanik, S. (2023). Capsule Network based Disease Classification for VitisVinifera Leaves. *Neural Computing & Applications, 2023.* Advance online publication. doi:10.1007/s00521-023-09058-y

Dushyant, K., Muskan, G., Gupta, A., & Pramanik, S. (2022). Utilizing Machine Learning and Deep Learning in Cyber security: An Innovative Approach. In M. M. Ghonge, S. Pramanik, R. Mangrulkar, & D. N. Le (Eds.), *Cyber security and Digital Forensics*. Wiley. doi:10.1002/9781119795667.ch12

ElFar, O. A., Chang, C. K., Leong, H. Y., Peter, A. P., Chew, K. W., & Show, P. L. (2021). Prospects of Industry 5.0 in algae: Customization of production and new advance technology for clean bioenergy generation. *Energy Conversion and Management: X, 10*, 100048.

Elrahmani, A., Hannun, J., Eljack, F., & Kazi, M. K. (2021). Status of renewable energy in the GCC region and future opportunities. *Current Opinion in Chemical Engineering*, *31*, 100664. doi:10.1016/j.coche.2020.100664

Gupta, A., Verma, A., & Pramanik, S. (2022). Security Aspects in Advanced Image Processing Techniques for COVID-19. In S. Pramanik, A. Sharma, S. Bhatia, & D. N. Le (Eds.), *An Interdisciplinary Approach to Modern Network Security*. CRC Press.

Jayasingh, R., & Kumar, J. (2022). Speckle noise removal by SORAMA segmentation in Digital Image processing to facilitate precise robotic surgery. *International Journal of Reliable and Quality E-Healthcare*, *11*(1), 1–19. Advance online publication. doi:10.4018/IJRQEH.295083

Kasinathan, P., Pugazhendhi, R., Elavarasan, R. M., Ramachandaramurthy, V. K., Ramanathan, V., Subramanian, S., & Alsharif, M. H. (2022). Realization of Sustainable Development Goals with Disruptive Technologies by Integrating Industry 5.0, Society 5.0, Smart Cities and Villages. *Sustainability (Basel)*, *14*(22), 15258. doi:10.3390/su142215258

Khanh, P. T., Ngọc, T. H., & Pramanik, S. (2023). Future of Smart Agriculture Techniques and Applications. In *Advanced Technologies and AI-Equipped IoT Applications in High Tech Agriculture*. doi:10.4018/978-1-6684-9231-4.ch021

Li, W., Lu, C., & Zhang, Y. W. (2019). Prospective exploration of future renewable portfolio standard schemes in China via a multi-sector CGE model. *Energy Policy*, *128*, 45–56. doi:10.1016/j.enpol.2018.12.054

Mandal, A., Dutta, S., & Pramanik, S. (2021). Machine Intelligence of Pi from Geometrical Figures with Variable Parameters using SCILab. In D. Samanta, R. R. Althar, S. Pramanik, & S. Dutta (Eds.), *Methodologies and Applications of Computational Statistics for Machine Learning* (pp. 38–63). IGI Global. doi:10.4018/978-1-7998-7701-1.ch003

Pramanik, S., Niranjanamurthy, M., & Panda, S. N. (2022). Using Green Energy Prediction in Data Centers for Scheduling Service Jobs. ICRITCSA 2022.

Reepu, S. (2023). Kumar, M. G. Chaudhary, K. G. Gupta, S. Pramanik and A. Gupta, Information Security and Privacy in IoT. In Handbook of Research in Advancements in AI and IoT Convergence Technologies. Academic Press.

Roy, A., & Pramanik, S. (2023). A Review of the Hydrogen Fuel Path to Emission Reduction in the Surface Transport Industry. *International Journal of Hydrogen Energy*. Advance online publication. doi:10.1016/j.ijhydene.2023.07.010

Singh, B. (2023). Tele-Health Monitoring Lensing Deep Neural Learning Structure: Ambient Patient Wellness via Wearable Devices for Real-Time Alerts and Interventions. *Indian Journal of Health and Medical Law*, *6*(2), 12–16.

Sinha, M., Chacko, E., Makhija, P., & Pramanik, S. (2021). Energy Efficient Smart Cities with Green IoT. In C. Chakrabarty (Ed.), *Green Technological Innovation for Sustainable Smart Societies: Post Pandemic Era*. Springer. doi:10.1007/978-3-030-73295-0_16

Veeraiah, V., Talukdar, V., Manikandan, K., Talukdar, S. B., Solavande, V. D., Pramanik, S., & Gupta, A. (2023). Machine Learning Frameworks in Carpooling. In Handbook of Research on AI and Machine Learning Applications in Customer Support and Analytics. IGI Global.

Chapter 10
Leveraging HR Metrics for an Effective Recruitment and Selection Process With Special Reference to the Manufacturing Sector in Coimbatore

Subhashini Durai
Bharathiar University, India

R. Krishnaveni
Terf's Academy College of Arts and Science, India

Geetha Manoharan
https://orcid.org/0000-0002-8644-8871
SR University, India

M. Nivedha
Robert Gordon University, UK

ABSTRACT

Any organization's growth and stability depend on its recruitment and selection process, which attracts top talent. HR metrics quantify and rate human resource processes. This study aims to integrate human resource metrics into the recruitment and selection process throughout. In this exploratory study, human resource managers discuss metrics and their use in evaluating recruitment and selection procedures. Manufacturing HR managers are being surveyed about the KPIs in question. Most HR managers (out of 15, at least 10 HR managers) have reported nine metrics as actively used in their firm, while a minority (out of 15, less than 10 HR managers) have reported 10 metrics as rarely used and six calculated metrics. This chapter will interest researchers and practitioners who identify, design, and deploy metrics to measure an organization's recruitment and selection process. The chapter identifies metrics to demonstrate how metrics encourage HR practitioners to adopt and measure skilled workforce in recruitment and selection. This contributes to the HR metrics debate.

DOI: 10.4018/979-8-3693-1343-5.ch010

INTRODUCTION

In India, the manufacturing sector is growing rapidly and is vital to economic growth and job creation. To compete, companies must hire and retain new and existing personnel to improve manufacturing potential. Recruitment and selection are crucial to hiring the appropriate individual at the right moment. Quantifiable findings are needed to assess a recruitment and selection process's correctness and reliability. HR metrics assess and evaluate organizational recruiting and selection processes (Durai D, S., Rudhramoorthy, K., & Sarkar, S., 2019). They also help make operational and strategic recruitment and selection decisions, making this study important.

Globally, HR departments are making evidence-based decisions to improve business activities. HR decisions are crucial to organizational decision-making. HR used to make qualitative decisions. The world is moving toward quantitative, evidence-based decisions. This research seeks to identify the key markers of organizational recruiting and selection effectiveness.

The most valuable asset in any firm is its people. When a company hires the right people, it improves results, retains employees, and achieves long-term goals. The recruitment and selection process ensures the right people are hired and promoted. In the recruiting process, recruitment is followed by selection and placement. Subhashini D, Krishnaveni R, & Geetha M (2022) state that an organization selects applicants with the highest qualifications to meet job requirements, taking into account environmental factors. The procedure separates acceptable applicants, who are more likely to succeed, from unsuitable ones. The selection procedure seeks candidates with the skills and credentials to perform the job.

The Progression of HR Metrics and Analytics

The 2004 Workforce Management (formerly Personnel Journal) article noted that Jac Fitz-enz proposed a new and non-conformist notion in 1978. Measure the impact of HR efforts on the company's finances. Responses included apathy, disagreement, and incredulity (Caudron, 2004). Over the past thirty years, Fitz-enz and a growing number of like-minded people have tirelessly improved HR measurement and educated HR professionals and top executives about its importance. HR KPIs including salary, staffing, hiring, and retention were defined precisely to start these activities. This led to the collection of data that can be compared across organizations. This enabled HR indicator comparisons to standards. Academics and professionals have expanded HR metric benchmarking to include employee training and development and other HR policies and practices. Profitable AI use recognizes business needs.

A major priority in the 1980s and 1990s was improving HR benchmarking. Although useful for HR professionals to compare their organization's HR indicators with similar or top-performing organizations, benchmarking offers limited insights on how to strategically exploit human resources for competitive advantage. HR professionals often had a harmful belief in simple, universal solutions. This thinking implies that we have achieved our HR duties if we can match our competitors'. In the recent decade, this has changed. Advanced software automating transactional personnel management and development has substantially expanded alternatives. Now that HR metrics data is more accessible, it may be integrated into other data sources. Integrating HR metrics with software creates new potential to collect commercial data on human resources. As their workloads are already full, many HR professionals doubt the value of taking this path. Next paragraphs will expand on this.

Previous inquiries that required manual computations can now be answered more easily and accurately. Example: identifying candidates most likely to accept a job offer, predicting employee turnover, and analyzing top-performing employees. Linkage analysis has become easier, but identifying human elements that drive corporate outcomes has not. By using human capital to compete, HR leaders boost business performance. Your organization's "people metrics." must be well-designed and interpreted to improve performance. HR analytics requires methodical data collection, analysis, and understanding to improve talent-related decisions and organisational performance. Analytics is transforming how HR professionals analyze the influence of personnel, the company's most precious resource, on its market success and goal.

Most organizations have mature HR processes. HR analytics supports the business case for the above procedures. If the business wants to maximise HR analytics' impact, two strategies stand out:

First, use HR analytics to link HR practices to business results: The areas of human resource management include integrating new hires, carefully selecting candidates, promoting a healthy work-life balance, surveying employees, 360-degree assessments, identifying and developing competencies, managing performance, and developing leadership skills. Each process must be examined to determine its ROI or NPV. If the viability of these procedures is communicated to management, it will be easy to encourage rapid action throughout the organization based on perceived impact. The process analytics approach revealed the organization's core HR elements, which HR analytics may help integrate into a strategic plan with a strong business focus. Succession planning uses varied firm operations' indicators. Use HR analytics with other interconnected business processes in the enterprise. Human resources analytics apply AI to identify well-positioned individuals, identify those who require support to upskill or reskill for future roles, and design talent management strategies to support their careers.

HR professionals should ask if corporate statistics are correct before making any judgments, like Caesars Entertainment Corporation CEO Garry Loveman. Or do we know?

Meaning of HR Metrics

"Without big data, you are blind and deaf in a freeway." Moore, Geoff

The field of Human Resources is HR. Strategically managing an organization's human capital is people resource management. An enterprise's human capital is often valued. A company's workforce's skills, expertise, and competencies are called human capital. Metrics help businesses track their operations and identify areas for improvement (M. Lourens, R. Raman, P. et al., 2022). Quantitative measurements are used to evaluate trends over time, usually annually (Manoharan G, Durai S & Gunaseelan A. R., 2022). HR metrics measure a company's human capital. These indicators measure HR efficiency and effectiveness. Individual indicators can help identify firm difficulties and manage financial success. The above metrics can describe a company's successes and failures. Human resources metrics measure effectiveness.

Any company's HR department is important to success. This strategy helps manage workers, who are responsible for many corporate operations. A firm may struggle to accept that its success depends on its employees' performance. Every organization must use separate human resources metrics and benchmarking procedures to achieve optimal employee performance in an era of constant change (Barinderjit S, Rachana J, Habibulla P et al., 2022). In addition, payroll, attendance monitoring, and timesheet management work smoothly. Sometimes called HR metrics, these outlines.

HR metrics gather and analyze data on numerous aspects of human resources management. HR evaluation includes employee performance and HR tasks. Due to their ability to assess and verify the firm's financial health, the above measurements are important (A. Bansal, J.K.S. Al-Safi, et al., 2023).

Performance management in human resources and employee satisfaction and productivity are further areas of study. HR metrics cover recruiting and retention, employee engagement, payroll administration, absenteeism, workforce numbers, leadership effectiveness, learning and development, and employee perks.

What Is the Scope of Measurement for HR Metrics?

Integrating HR data and workforce analytics requires collaboration. Workplaces evaluate many functions. This category includes task completion time, craftsmanship quality, employee satisfaction, welfare, and staff utilization efficiency. Well-defined human resources metrics can help firms meet the different needs and expectations of all stakeholders. HR analytics will use AI to automate and improve data accuracy.

What Is the Rationale for the Utilization of HR Metrics?

HR metrics include employee performance, retention, salary, engagement, cost-per-hire, and time-to-hire. This allows companies to closely monitor project performance and make appropriate modifications. Organizations evaluate a domain using HR metrics. These abilities can also help job seekers handle unexpected situations in inclusive, diverse, and well-being-focused companies. Workforce and human data analysis is essential to creating a culture of value. As its principles evolve, the company may lose employee confidence and loyalty if it doesn't handle this issue. Analytics can begin with HR metrics. The above activities are the first step in creating data-driven decisions that support the organization's goals.

What Are the Initial Steps for Implementing HR Metrics?

Utilize HR metrics to have a comprehensive understanding of the efficacy and inefficacy inside your organization. To initiate this process, commence by formulating a hypothesis or posing a research topic. Presented below are few such instances.

- Is the voluntary turnover rate higher than the desired level?
- What is the expense of that?
- Is the talent acquisition process progressing satisfactorily?
- Or, is your organization experiencing financial losses due to the recruitment of unsuitable candidates?

HR analytics can prove to be advantageous in the realm of forecasting forthcoming business requirements. The utilization of HR metrics can provide answers to these inquiries and facilitate the enhancement of long-term corporate decision-making.

What Is the Significance of Human Resources Metrics?

HR metrics help firms uncover patterns and trends by providing a measurable benchmark. These trends may indicate growth and success for the organization. Executives use these strategic planning measures. Employees are valuable resources and contribute to an organization's strategy. Executives and human resources specialists agree on the metrics the firm will track and their importance. These measurements help solve organizational issues and provide employee incentives. HR analytics help HR executives make better decisions and optimize HR management. They are vital to improving HR processes. Analytics isn't hard, but it takes time and effort. A basic procedure is: Find out about your employees. Consider the data in light of corporate strategy. Operations must be modified to improve efficiency. Assess the changes' efficacy. Adjust as needed.

What Are the Advantages of Adhering to Human Resources Metrics?

Human Resource analytics is crucial. Small enterprises without HR metrics analysis will perform poorly and lose competitiveness. Intense rivalry in the commercial world undermines scientific HR practices. Let us list some major benefits. Consider the components of each category while reading the following.

- Enhance the allocation of labor resources through the optimization of scheduling, bidding, hiring, and pay processes.
- Anticipate the outcomes of potential modifications using hypothetical scenarios, sometimes referred to as 'what if' analyses. These scenarios may involve changes in PTO policies, benefits, the introduction of extra shifts or locations, the implementation of hybrid schedules, or alterations to team composition.
- Enhance staff satisfaction and bolster employee retention
- Enhance human resources (HR) efficiency
- Mitigate compliance issues related to hiring rules, diversity regulations, overtime, minimum wage, exempt vs non-exempt categorization, Family and Medical Leave Act (FMLA), Payroll-Based Journal (PBJ), and Affordable Care Act (ACA)
- Optimize the return on investment (ROI) of HR programs, including employee engagement, wellness initiatives, financial planning, and performance management.
- Enhancing the efficiency of recruitment, onboarding, training, and compensation processes pertaining to the human capital of an organization.
- Assessing the potential impacts of changes made to various activities and processes, such as policies regarding personal time-off (B. Bijeta Nayak, G. Manoharan., et al., 2024), adjustments to employee benefits, team reorganization, and increased overtime hours.
- Maximizing the return on investment of human resources initiatives, encompassing employee engagement, wellness programs, financial planning support, and performance management.

There Are Several Significant Human Resources (HR) Metrics That Pertain to the Domain of Recruiting and Selection

The Variable of Interest in This Study Is the Time to Hire, Measured in Days

The 'time to hire' is crucial in recruitment. This metric measures the number of days between a candidate's employment application and acceptance. Measurement of time to hire gives useful information about recruiting process performance and candidate experience.

The rate at which the HR department evaluates, interviews, and accepts candidates is called recruitment efficiency. A lengthy hiring process may suggest operational inefficiencies. The hiring process length affects candidate experience. Candidates can withdraw from a lengthy recruitment procedure. Would you rather wait two weeks than two months to start a new job? High-demand applicants don't wait.

Avoid confusing "time to hire" with "time to fill." This statistic usually measures the time in days between a job request's approval and the candidate's acceptance. The above description matches SHRM and ISO 30414 views.

The Cost per Hire Is Calculated by Dividing the Overall Cost of Hiring by the Number of New Hires

The 'cost per hire (CPH)' measure, like time to hire, shows how much an organization spends on recruiting and onboarding new hires. Additionally, this indicates recruitment process efficacy. Determining rental cost might be difficult. Company methods for calculating this statistic varied until The Society of Human Resource Management and the American National Standards Institute reached a consensus and developed a standardized equation.

The sum of internal and external recruitment costs is divided by the total number of hires to calculate CPH. Hire fees and quantity will depend on a monthly or annual measurement period.

Early Turnover Rate

The early turnover rate, which refers to the percentage of recruits that depart within the initial year, is a significant metric to consider in assessing recruitment outcomes.

Arguably, this indicator holds significant importance in assessing the level of success in the hiring process inside an organization.

The early leaver statistic serves as an indicator of potential mismatches between individuals and either their employing organizations or their specific job roles. The occurrence of early turnover is also associated with significant financial costs. Typically, it requires a period of 6 to 12 months for people to acquire comprehensive familiarity with their roles and attain their 'Optimum Productivity Level'. Based on the findings of a survey conducted by Glassdoor in 2018, it was determined that the mean expense associated with employee turnover in the United Kingdom amounts to £11,000 per individual.

The variable of interest in this study is the duration, measured in months, since the most recent internal promotion received by employees.

This metric, which is relatively uncomplicated, serves as a valuable tool for elucidating the reasons for the departure of individuals with great potential.

Examples of HR metrics that are related to revenue can include metrics such as employee productivity, employee turnover rate, and employee engagement. These metrics provide insights into the impact of HR practices on the organization's financial performance, Dr BudhiSagar Mishra, Dr Lalit Mohan Pant, et al, (2022). Employee productivity measures the efficiency and effectiveness of employees in generating money for the organization.

The Metric of Revenue

The metric of revenue per employee is calculated by dividing the total revenue generated by a company by the total number of employees employed by the company.

This indicator quantifies the overall efficiency of the organization. The metric known as "revenue per employee" serves as a valuable indicator for assessing the caliber of individuals that an organization has recruited. Please refer to the Business Insider article to examine the performance of the leading 12 technology businesses globally in relation to this particular indicator.

The 9-Box Grid Box

The 9-box grid, also known as performance and potential, is a tool used to assess and evaluate individuals based on their performance and potential within an organization.

The utilization of a 9-box grid is observed in the assessment and visualization of an individual's performance and potential across three distinct levels. This methodology provides an assessment of personnel based on their performance levels, expertise, potential for growth, and exceptional abilities. This statistic is quite effective in distinguishing between desired and undesired turnover, as an illustrative example.

In a previous article, we discussed the methodologies employed to assess employee performance, encompassing both qualitative and quantitative approaches. Various metrics commonly used in organizations include the Net Promoter Score, management by objectives, number of errors, 360-degree feedback, and forced ranking, among others. The measure of billable hours per employee is a significant metric used in assessing the productivity and efficiency of an organization. It quantifies the number of hours that an employee spends on billable tasks, which directly contribute to generating revenue for the company.

Billable Hours of Employees

This performance statistic is important for legal firms and consulting firms. The association between this type of performance and worker engagement or other input indicators is intriguing. This measure can reveal insights when examined across departments and managers/partners. Employee utilization rate, which is the percentage of time employees spend on billable tasks during work hours, is also related to this number.

Engagement Rating

The degree of participation in an activity or event.

Active and engaged workers are more productive. Engagement as a key'soft' HR result is crucial. Even in a stressful work environment, those who are optimistic about their job and proud of their company are more engaged. Active workers perform better and see challenges more positively. Additionally, team involvement is a key indicator of team manager performance.

Additional examples of HR metrics include employee turnover rate, time to fill vacancies, training and development investment per employee, absenteeism rate, employee satisfaction score, and diversity and inclusion metrics. These metrics provide valuable insights into

The Cost of Human Resources (HR)

The cost of human resources (HR) per employee, for example, is $600.

This statistic quantifies the cost-effectiveness of human resources by measuring the monetary value.

The Ratio of Human Resources Experts

The ratio of human resources experts to employees, for example, is 1:60.

The HR-to-employee ratio is an additional metric that demonstrates the cost efficiency of the HR department. An organization that possesses well-established analytical capabilities should be capable of optimizing the productivity of its HR specialists, enabling them to do a greater volume of work with a reduced workforce.

The ratio of HR

The ratio of HR business partners to employees, denoted as 1:80, is the proportion of HR Business partners available to support and serve each employee within an organization.

An analogous measure to the one mentioned above. Once more, the implementation of advanced analytics skills will empower the Human Resources department to quantitatively assess and forecast the effects of HR policies. This measure has the potential to enhance the efficiency of the human resources department and decrease the number of business partners involved (Ramachandran et al., 2022).

The Turnover Rate

Employee attrition is often measured by the turnover rate, which is determined by dividing the number of departing employees by the total population.

This statistic measures an organization's annual staff turnover. In combination with a performance indicator, the 'turnover' statistic can track the difference in staff attrition rates between high and low performers.

Higher-performing employees should stay, while lower-performing employees should leave. This statistic also gives HR business partners a lot of information about the departments and positions where workers feel at home and where they don't want to work. Understanding turnover rates helps build recruitment strategies. Moreover, attrition may be a key indicator of management effectiveness.

To gain comprehensive insights into the methodology of calculating employee turnover, please refer to the provided hyperlink.

The Efficacy of Human Resources (HR) Software

This measure exhibits a higher level of complexity. The effectiveness of learning and development software may be assessed using several metrics, such as the number of active users, average time spent on the platform, session duration, total time spent on the platform per user per month, screen flow, and software retention. These metrics facilitate the assessment of employee preferences and effectiveness in order to inform HR decision-making.

Absenteeism

Absenteeism, also referred to as absence percentage, is a measure used to quantify the rate at which individuals are absent from their designated activities or responsibilities.

Similar to turnover, absenteeism is also a significant signal of employee unhappiness and can serve as a forecast of future turnover. The absenteeism rate might provide valuable insights for mitigating instances of leave, given that prolonged absences can incur significant expenses. The disparities seen among individual managers and departments serve as noteworthy indicators of possible issues and bottlenecks.

Optimal Approach for Measuring and Evaluating Human Resources (HR) Metrics

In order to optimize the utilization of data obtained through human resources (HR), we have sought insights from C-suite executives and other HR professionals regarding their most valuable recommendations. There are numerous strategies that may be employed to optimize the utilization of HR metrics, ranging from the timely collecting of data to maintaining a focus on the broader context.

Here are seven recommended methods to employ when doing an assessment of HR metrics:

- Ensure prompt data collection
- Align HR metrics with business objectives
- Emphasize the significance of employee engagement
- Generate relevant data tailored to specific audiences
- Extract insights from employee billable hours
- Prioritize year-over-year analysis over month-after-month comparisons
- Evaluate join ratio

What Is HR Analytics?

In order to comprehend the fundamental nature of HR analytics and elucidate its influence on business success, we sought the insights of Mick Collins, who holds the esteemed positions of Global Vice President, Workforce Analytics & Planning Solution Strategy, and Chief Expert at SAP Success Factors.

HR analytics is a systematic approach used to get valuable insights regarding the impact of investments in human capital assets on four key outcomes: revenue generation, expense reduction, risk mitigation, and strategic plan execution. According to Collins, the process involves the use of statistical techniques to integrated data from HR, talent management, financial (Rajesh, G. A., Ashtikar, S. P., et al., 2023), and operational sources. This statement was made during a private conversation with HR Technologist.

The primary focus of HR analytics lies inside the HR function and should not be misconstrued as being completely synonymous with people analytics or workforce analytics, contrary to popular belief.

The Key Features of HR Analytics

1. They handle C-suite business questions. A system that can answer each inquiry may require the purchase of numerous analytics tools to collect precise data for each query. One can also use a comprehensive method that evaluates multiple metrics to answer each business question.
2. The user-friendly interface makes these tools accessible to non-experts in data science. An easily comprehensible method is best for laypeople evaluating one or more metrics without disrupting the data scientist's workflow.

3. Software applications are hosted on cloud servers instead of local infrastructure. Cloud-based solutions enable accessibility without considerable IT engagement (Ponduri, S. B., Ahmad, S. S., et al., 2024). This allows Human Resources to use the solution as needed independently.
4. These systems feature statistical analysis and machine learning. Big data platforms need machine learning and natural language processing-powered data management systems (Ashiq, V. M., Fredrik, E. T., et al., 2023) to operate. This lets the device learn and reason autonomously, revealing information data scientists can evaluate.
5. These models use predictive analytics. Predictive analytics involves gathering insights from existing datasets to discover trends and forecast future occurrences. Collins claims analysts use statistics to anticipate the future. In particular, the question is whether the current termination rate will continue or increase as the labor market improves.
6. These devices have advanced visualization technologies. Visual representations of large amounts of data may help understand patterns and events. Complex data collected by an analytics engine cannot be adequately presented using standard charts and presentations. Advanced visualization software is needed.

Subscriptions make these services available. Software as a service (SaaS) platforms benefit from subscription models since they make the latest technology accessible. The large initial cost required to acquire an analytics system can be mitigated by these solutions, making analytics investment more economically viable.

COMMON DATA SOURCES HR ANALYTICS SOLUTIONS

I. Internal Data

Internal data refers to data that is expressly gathered from the human resources (HR) department of an organization. The fundamental human resources (HR) system has multiple data points that can be leveraged for the purpose of an HR analytics tool. An HRIS system encompasses various metrics within its framework, which may include:

The following information is typically included in an organization's personnel records:

1. Employee tenure: This refers to the length of time an employee has been employed by the organization.
2. Employee compensation: This encompasses the financial remuneration provided to employees, including salary, bonuses, and benefits.
3. Employee training records: These records document the training programs and courses that employees have completed to enhance their skills and knowledge.
4. Performance appraisal data: This data pertains to the evaluation of an employee's job performance, typically conducted through periodic assessments (Sudarshan E., R Indumathy., et al., 2022).
5. Reporting structure: This refers to the hierarchical arrangement of employees within the organization, outlining the lines of authority and reporting relationships.
6. Details on high-value, high-potential employees: This information pertains to employees who possess exceptional skills or potential for growth, often identified as key assets to the organization.

7. Details on any disciplinary action taken against an employee: This includes documentation of any formal actions or measures taken in response to an employee's violation of organizational policies or standards.

The primary obstacle in this context lies in the occasional disconnection of the data, which consequently undermines its reliability as a measure. The data scientist can contribute significantly in this context. The scattered data can be organized and grouped into meaningful data points, which can subsequently be utilized by the analytics tool.

II. External Data

External data is acquired through the establishment of collaborative partnerships with different departments within the firm. The inclusion of external data is crucial as it provides a broader and more comprehensive viewpoint that cannot be achieved solely via the utilization of internal organizational data.

1. Financial data:

The inclusion of organization-wide financial data is crucial in conducting HR analyses, as it enables the calculation of various metrics such as revenue per employee or cost of recruitment.

2. Organization-specific data:

The specific data requirements for HR analytics may vary depending on the nature of the firm and its primary offering, whether it be a product or a service.

According to Collins (, HR leaders at a global retail organization should utilize store sales, costs, and customer experience data to enhance their analytics engine. Conversely, HR professionals in a construction company should focus on operational data, namely health and safety information, as well as data about contingent labor costs.

3. Passive data from employees:

Employees consistently contribute data that is kept in the Human Resource Information System (HRIS) from the initial point of contact for employment. Furthermore, the utilization of data derived from individuals' social media posts, shares, and feedback surveys can serve as a valuable resource in informing the study of human resources data.

4. Historical data:

Various global economic, political, and environmental events exert influence on the patterns of employee behavior (I.A.K. Shaikh, C.N.S. Kumar, et al., 2023). The utilization of such data can provide valuable insights that are not attainable through internal data with inherent limitations.

The recession in 2008 constituted a worldwide phenomenon that brought about a shift in employees' perceptions of employment or labor. The emergence of the freelance, start-up, and gig economies gained momentum in response to the persistent job losses experienced by individuals. The utilization of data derived from a significant historical event of utmost importance might provide valuable insights into the potential reactions of the workforce in response to analogous transformations that may occur in subsequent periods. Subsequently, this tool can be employed to discern patterns within the existing labor force and forecast both voluntary and involuntary attrition.

10 Key Justifications for Google's Use of the People Analytics Method

The people analytics team has a direct reporting line to the Vice President, and there is a designated representative from the team in each significant HR function. The company manufactures a wide range of goods, such as non-anonymous staff surveys and dashboards. Furthermore, it strives to recognise meaningful connections and offer suggested courses of action. The objective is to replace subjective opinions with objective data and measurements.

Most individuals are now aware of Google's complimentary meals, 20% time policy, and diverse array of enjoyable pursuits. However, it is important to acknowledge that each of these initiatives was introduced and is sustained through the use of data. Google's people analytics approaches are remarkably innovative and impactful, leaving me in awe. Here are my Top 10 Google people management techniques, both past and present that showcase the company's data-driven approach:

1. Effective leader traits and manager duties A project. Oxygen studied substantial internal data and found that excellent managers are essential for optimal performance and employee retention. The study also identified eight leadership traits. Instead of technical expertise, regular individual coaching sessions that showed interest in the employee and provided frequent tailored feedback were found to be the key to leadership success. Managers are evaluated twice a year by employees in eight categories.

The PiLab No organization has a subset like Google's PiLab. It conducts empirical research within Google to determine the best human management and productivity tactics, including employee satisfaction prizes. The lab improved employee well-being by using evidence-based dish size changes to reduce calorie consumption at its eating facilities.

3. A retention algorithm Google created a mathematical system to predict which employees will become retention issues. This strategy lets management take proactive efforts before it's too late and customize retention solutions.
4. Mathematical forecasting Google values forward-thinking HR. They use predictive models and what-if research to improve their forecasts of people management difficulties and opportunities. It also uses analytics to improve personnel planning, which is vital for a growing organization.

Increasing diversity Google uses data to address diversity, unlike most companies. Thus, the people analytics team investigated the causes of the underrepresentation of diverse candidates, notably women in engineering, in recruiting, retention, and promotion. Its recruitment, retention, and career progression results were impressive and quantifiable.

6. Effective recruitment method Google, one of the few organizations that uses science in recruitment, created an algorithm to predict job success. The research also indicated that more than four

interviews did not significantly impact the hiring process, reducing hiring time. Google's strategic hiring process uses a collaborative decision-making method to avoid hiring managers making short-term choices based on their own requirements. Project Janus designed an algorithm for each major job category to analyze rejected resumes and locate promising candidates. Their miss rate was 1.5% after analysis. Thus, they hired several reevaluated candidates.

7. Valuing high achievers Google officials found a 300-fold performance gap between great and average engineers. Showing the value of great performers convinces management to invest in hiring, retaining, and developing them. Google's best-kept secret is that people operations professionals make the best business case in any industry. The key reason they have great executive support.

Workplace design promotes collaboration. Google prioritizes cross-functional collaboration. Exploration (learning), teamwork, and fun increase invention, according to research. Company workplaces are designed to promote learning, enjoyment, and collaboration. It even tracks employee café line time to improve teamwork. Fun management may seem unneeded, but research demonstrates that it attracts, retains, and fosters collaboration.

9. Enhancing knowledge exploration and acquisition Since most people learn by doing, experiential learning is prioritized over classroom instruction. Project rotations, failure lessons, and hosting Al Gore and Lady Gaga to speak to staff have improved exploration and education at Google. Google values self-directed learning and adaptability in employees.
10. It convinces with evidence, not force. The presentation of Google's people analytics team's final recommendations to executives and managers is what makes it successful. Instead than forcing its methods on managers, the organization acts as internal consultants, giving convincing facts and actionable recommendations to change. Due to its highly analytical audience of executives, this platform uses data to change preconceived views and influence. Empirical approaches must produce results. RBS's surveys helped management prioritize dignity after the financial crisis. Ameriprise's image of a limited-product store helped the HR department eliminate low-value services. IBM's efforts to build a robust talent pool increased consultant use. Khazanah's leadership audits convinced many companies to improve operations. Any analytics methodology must ensure that executives can use the data to make decisions.

REVIEW OF LITERATURE

Turner, D. W. (2010) states that an organization's success and performance depend on its human resource management, or deliberate allocation of workers to appropriate jobs and timeframes. As competition increases, companies must implement industry-specific recruitment and selection best practices. Most people agree that people are the most valuable resources in the global economy, according to Fitz-enz (1995). Other assets are commodities that can be bought at market prices. Human assets' ability to learn, gain skills, and contribute to economic growth makes them special. Fitz-enz states that assets other than human capital are commodities that may be bought at market prices.

Naveen, S., & Raju, D. N. M. (2014) examined manufacturing industry recruitment and selection efforts. They found that an effective recruitment and selection process should include job description and person specification, creation of a single recruitment specification, identification of suitable candidates, review and shortlisting of applicants, candidate selection, and employment contract negotiation. According to Mark Sullivan's 2009 article, the recruitment process includes planning, sourcing, screening, interviewing, hiring, and reporting. Quality of hire, applicant contentment, return on investment of applicant source, and time to fill are recruitment factors, according to the individual.

Human resources firm ICIMS (2015) analyzed ten critical recruiting metrics. These KPIs covered hiring origins, position filling times, and open requisition details. The metrics measured the number of applicants and interviewees, the number of offers extended and accepted, hiring manager and candidate satisfaction, the cost of each hire, regulatory compliance, hire quality, new hire turnover, and task completion. According to Garvey (2005), recruiting indications fall into two categories. 1) Incentives are measured by the number of hires, the time it takes to fill positions, the diversity of candidates and hires, the ratio of interviews to job offers extended, and the acceptance rate. 2) On the other hand, hiring manager and new hire satisfaction, efficiency measures, and offer-related indicators are not currently linked to incentive compensation.Study by Obeidat and Abdalla (2022). Environmental management is recognised as essential to the UN Sustainable Development agenda. Modern companies seek new ways to improve their environmental management. Common environmental management methods include Green HRM. Saritha Kumari Y., Aarthi D., et al., (2022) discuss how Green HRM might help circular economy (CR) business models. This research explains sustainable development's environmental element. Green HRM helps firms achieve sustainable and environmental goals, therefore this statement helps them use the potential synergy between Green HRM and Circular Economy. This study describes how HR analytics and HR matrices improve strategic decision-making for Green HRM, improving firms' environmental performance.

Shrivastava, S., & Dhaigude, A. S. (2022) discussed that American company Prime DataTechPvt. Ltd. (PDPL) was based in Bengaluru, India, provided database management systems, web development, cloud computing, and security. PDPL has won a Fortune 50 customer for their ERP system. Thus, PDPL is recruiting consultants and managers with the right qualifications and skills. According to PDPL CEO Jeffery Gladwell, potential employees may accept job offers but decline to work for the company. Using human resources analytics, he attempted to solve this problem. The person in issue ordered AishwaryaVerma to create a recruitment plan with Vaidya as CHRO. Verma was given one week to analyze HR recruitment records for insights. A prediction model that could reliably predict a candidate joining the company was the goal.

Samtani, D. D. (2022) identified that data transformation into organizational performance insights is a growing area of study for scholars and professionals. Thus, advanced analytics and management are gaining popularity. The growing usage of HR analytics by HR departments shows that this interest has expanded beyond HRM. Prescriptive analytics may assist Irish HR, according to this study. The article discusses how prescriptive analytics may help HR professionals evaluate recruitment and performance. To understand how HR services affect company culture, these topics are key. Prescriptive analytics may also solve major HR issues like recruitment and performance management.

Madhani, P. M. (2023) examined that managers can replace anecdotal experience, hierarchical systems, and risk aversion with data analysis, prediction, and experimental investigation using HR analytics. HR analytics emphasizes the value created by employees and the ability to capture and use it. A linear three-stage maturity model is used to explain the progression of HR analytics from conventional to modern. Firms must meet six requirements to implement human resources analytics, according to research. HR analytics optimises HRM activities like selection, appraisal, remuneration, rewards, and development to improve organisational performance. Research also shows many companies using HR analytics.

Bulsari, S. & Pandya, K. (2023) commented that HR analytics is evidence-based and supports decision-making to improve individual and organizational performance and financial gains, unlike intuition-driven alternatives. This chapter examines HR analytics theory and practice. Then, HR analytics is applied to recruiting, employee engagement, and retention. Two case studies for each of the three HR tasks are briefly discussed in this paper. HR analytics application statistics in organizations are briefly discussed in this discourse. This chapter also tackles top HR analytics implementation issues and moderating factors. Additionally, implementation issues are discussed. Discussion of HR analytics' future concludes the chapter. This chapter does not cover technical topics like regression models or machine learning methods due to the book's broad scope.

Susanto, P. C., Sawitri, N. N., Suroso, S., & Rony, Z. T. (2023) reports uses researcher replies to conduct a complete analysis of the factors. This study uses qualitative methods compatible with the literature. Literary studies apply scholarly methods to study and analyze literary texts. This study will theoretically analyze and examine variable relationships using Mendeley, Google Scholar, and other respected online media journals and sourcebooks (Shameem, A., Ramachandran, K. K., et al., 2023). Details of the research will be discussed. As coaching and leadership development have typically been studied separately, this study integrates components, which is rare. Researcher recommendations for variable exploration in this study are rare. Thus, future human resources research should use multiple methods and investigate different topics to improve the discipline (Joyce, P. R., Selvaraj, F. J., et al., 2024), especially in this study.

RESEARCH METHODOLOGY

This descriptive study seeks human resources metrics to quantify the recruiting and selection process and help manufacturing businesses make evidence-based decisions (Krishanveni & Subhashini, 2016). Industrial human resource managers were interviewed for the statistics. Cross-sectional data was used over longitudinal data because it showed HR managers' views on using HR metrics in recruiting and selection in respective industries.

Data was collected through interviews and questionnaires. Data from direct interviews with respondents was more relevant to the study. Entrepreneurs (B Nagarjuna, Y Srivastava, et al., 2022) delivered an initial summary of the project in person due to scheduling constraints. They received a questionnaire by mail to answer the questions at their convenience.

This study included industrial human resource managers with at least two years of experience. No age or gender restrictions applied. To gauge human resource managers' interest in the study, researchers met or called them. The researchers used purposive sampling. The study sampled 15 Coimbatore industrial HR managers. These managers had two years of experience.

Results

A detailed literature review was followed by an analysis to determine the best measures for recruiting and selection. The measurements are listed in tabular format with a statement or explanation explaining their function. Respondents were given 19 indicators and asked to rate their awareness and use in their workplace. HR managers were asked to list any other metrics they use in their recruitment processes beyond the 19 indicators.

Table 1. Recruiting metrics and its definitions

Sl.No.	Metrics	Description
1	Time to source	The time taken from bringing in the external candidates to the organization
2	Time to select	The time taken from the start of external recruitment of candidates till the end of selection test
3	Time to interview& assess	The time taken from external recruitment till final selection of candidates and extends up to selection interview
4	Time to offer	The time taken from the start of external recruitment till hiring decision of the recruiter
5	Time to accept	The time taken from the start external recruitment till job acceptance by the candidate
6	Time to hire	The time taken from the start of external recruitment till the on boarding of employee
7	Time to start	The time taken from the start of external recruitment till the employee takes over the actual job
8	Ratio: No of resumes/ candidates	The ratio of total no of resumes source to total no of candidates initially screened
9	Ratio: No of candidates/ interviews	The ratio of total no of candidates screened to total no of candidates selected for interview
10	Ratio: No of interviews/offers	The ratio of total no of candidates selected for interview to total no of candidates offered job
11	Ratio: No of offers/acceptance	The ratio total no of candidates offered job to total no of candidates accepted the offer
12	Hiring manager satisfaction	The percentage of satisfaction of hiring managers with the hiring process and the new hires
13	Candidate satisfaction	The percentage of new hires satisfied with the hiring process and job
14	Quality of hire	The value the newly hired employees bring into the organization which is a mix of performance, cultural fit and engagement
15	Source of hire	The segmentation and identification of the potential of each external recruitment source
16	Cost per hire	The total cost incurred to bring on board a new hire
17	New employee turnover rate	The rate of new hires leaving the organization within a given time period to the average no of number of workers
18	New employee retention rate	The rate of new hires retained in the organization after a given period of time to the average no of workers
19	Recruiting cost ratio	The ratio of total recruiting costs to the total compensation of new hires

Responses on the recruiting and selection metrics used more frequently in manufacturing sector:

Most of the respondents (out of fifteen respondents at least ten respondents) has stated that 'Hiring manager satisfaction' (15), 'Candidate Satisfaction' (15), 'Quality of hire' (15), Source of Hire' (15), Cost per hire' (15), 'New employee turnover rate' (15), 'Time to hire' (13), 'Ratio-No. of offers/acceptance' (13) and 'Ratio-No. of interviews/offers' (10) are most frequently used Recruiting and selection metrics in their organisation. The below figure1shows the most frequently used metrics on the basis of the responses given by the HR managers of manufacturing sector. Responses on the recruiting and selection metrics which are not used frequently in manufacturing sector:

Only few respondents (out of fifteen respondents below ten respondents) has stated that 'Time to Accept' (5), 'Time to offer' (5), 'Time to Select' (5), Recruiting cost Ratio' (6), 'No. of Candidates/ Interview' (6), 'Time to interview and assess' (6), 'New employee retention rate' (7), 'No. of resumes/ candidate' (7), 'Time to Source' (7) and 'Time to Start' (9) are used in their organisation. And these Recruiting and selection metrics are considered as not used frequently in manufacturing sectors which is shown in the below figure 1.

Figure 1. Recruitment and selection metrics used in manufacturing sectors in Coimbatore district

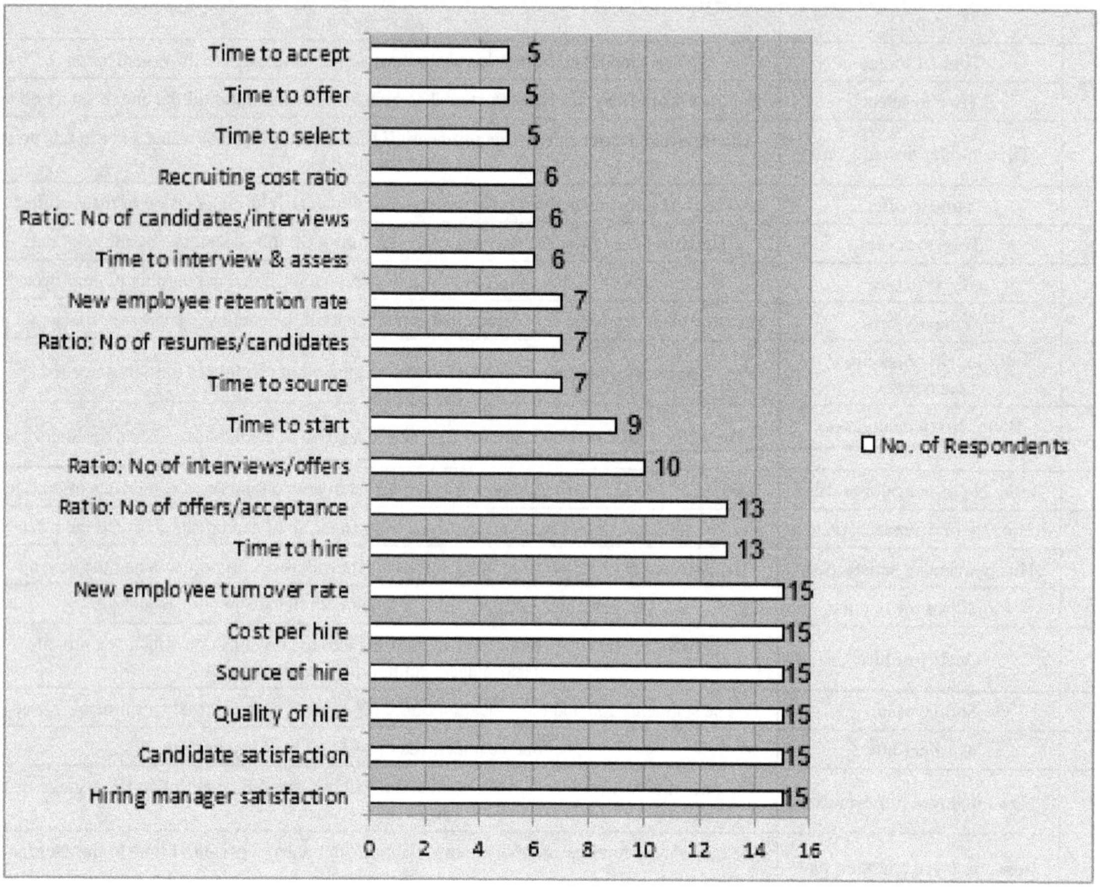

Other Metrics Suggested by the Respondents During Scheduling

During the interview the respondents were asked to specify any other metrics that are not mentioned in the questioner but are currently used in their organisation. Some of the respondents have suggested few metrics that they are currently using in their organisation for recruiting and selection process. These metrics are shown in the figure 2 below.

DISCUSSIONS

The case study extensively examines what business psychologist Xancam did in September 2008 to determine how organizations evaluate talent ROI (Yapp, 2009). Senior HR executives from British American Tobacco, Fujitsu, Premier Foods, Marks & Spencer, and PepsiCo participated in this study. The survey highlights the importance and challenges of assessing talent-related ROI. Also, it warns about risks without talent assessment.

The study asked participants about their organizations' quantitative measurements. Internal metrics like succession, retention, promotions, engagement, and diversity were preferred by most respondents.

Figure 2. Recruitment and selection metrics used in manufacturing sectors other than mentioned in the questioner in Coimbatore district

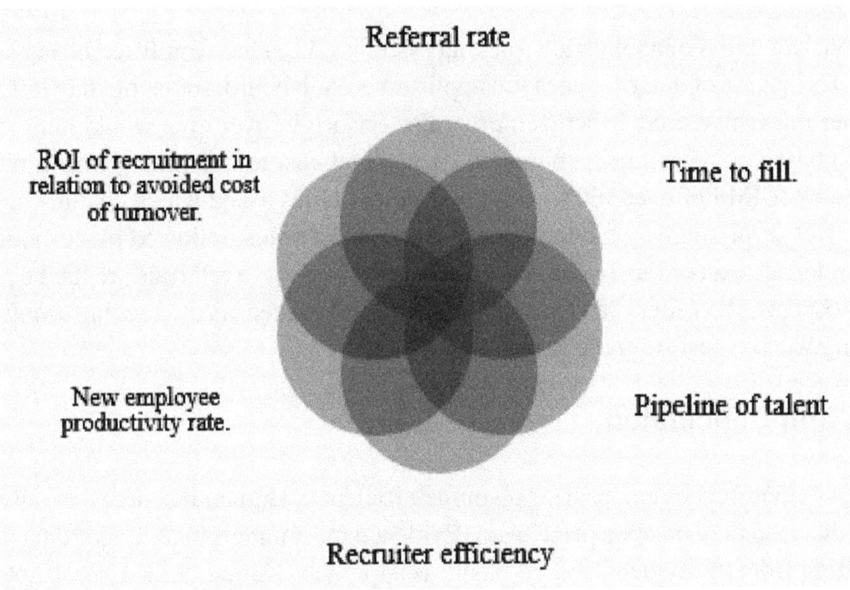

A few firms use metrics to evaluate talent-related initiatives for quantifiable results. The survey found that 58% of respondents measure talent management expenses using 'cost per individual'. Additionally, 53% of respondents measure the 'overall cost of talent management' and 43% measure the 'cost of talent management in relation to talent retention'. The 'cost of talent management in relation to productivity' is assessed by 40% of respondents, and the 'cost of individual talent management techniques' by 33%. Most organizations focus on top-line revenue and bottom-line profit, but few assess workplace productivity. Thus, manufacturing companies are assessing the ROI of efficient recruitment and selection.

The recruitment efficiency ratio and quality of hire are the best metrics for evaluating recruitment processes, according to Sullivan and Burnett (2009). Individual performance metrics, retention rates (both internal and external), manager satisfaction, applicant/employee satisfaction, and cost of hire are used to evaluate newly hired employees' on-the-job performance. Several metrics were examined by Shikari (2011) to determine the most significant hiring metrics that increased. Quality of fill, source of hiring, candidate satisfaction, pipeline development, recruiting cost ratio, recruitment efficiency ratio, and quality of hire are the factors. When individual recruiters affect the recruitment process, it's important to assess recruitment performance. Manufacturing companies are using this statistic to evaluate their efficiency.

Compared to traditional recruitment methods, Decker and Cornelius (2001) argue that recommendations, casual applications, and direct approaches offer significant advantages. According to Earle (2011), recruitment and selection maturity has five levels. Efficiency, effectiveness, marketing, retention, and planning are these levels (Manoharan, G., Durai, S, et al., 2024) Earle also provides key metrics for each level. Thus, manufacturing companies also use time to fill as a key recruitment metric. The measurement of newly hired employees' real on-the-job performance (Manoharan, G., Durai, S., et al., 2023) is the most important statistic. Though known as "quality of hire," it's a performance metric. This study seeks to prove that newly hired workers are more productive than average workers. New hire performance is also used to evaluate recruitment sources, recruiters' tools, and recruiters' performance.

Organizational adoption of application tracking systems (ATS) has simplified hiring source tracking and reporting. The source of entry for each job applicant is a job board, social media platform, employee referral, or other relevant source. Monitoring recruitment origin over time would help the team adjust work allocation based on recruitment source efficiency and cost to maximize recruiting expense ROI. A recent survey by ICIMS of over 360 recruitment professionals asked which channel attracts the most job applicants. Not surprisingly, job boards received the most votes, followed by corporate career sites and employee referrals. According to employee responses, employee referrals are the best way to attract high-quality prospects. Recruiters can learn about source effectiveness by tracking employment origin. They can distinguish the best from the worst sources.

Discussion and Conclusion

Today's business environment emphasizes resource efficiency. Human resources are an organization's most precious asset, so they must be prioritized. Evidence must underpin all major decisions. HR Analytics is benefiting from the evidence-based business approach (Kumar, S., Kumar, P., et al., 2024) HR Analytics enables data-driven HR decision-making and requires organizations to maintain sufficient quality data to prove HR investment ROI.

HR metrics are vital in modern HR organizations. HR leaders often call themselves business partners. They work with the business and use analytics and reporting to support important decisions (Manoharan, G., Durai, S., et al., 2024). Thus, HR indicators are crucial here. Many recognize the importance of HR measurements, especially when making data-driven decisions. All of these activities aim to improve employee and company welfare. Measurements depend on workforce size, money resources, timing restrictions, and resources. Manual data collection is unpleasant regardless of the need. Get a centralized HR metrics dashboard for strategic decision-making. Choosing the right HR metrics might be difficult, depending on your company. However, having a wide range of measurements that target different HR characteristics is beneficial (Deviprasad, S., Madhumithaa, N., et al., 2023).

HR executives should include these targets in manager and HR department goals. Additionally, they must be analyzed using meaningful reporting methods and presented in clear dashboards. These examples should demonstrate to the company the enormous impact and many benefits of a data-driven HR team. Subhashini D, Krishnaveni R, & Geetha M (2022) emphasize the importance of recruitment and selection processes in manufacturing and other industries. HR metrics quantify the performance of systems and people in an organization and suggest areas for development. Businesses can use the framework to improve recruiting and selection. New metrics users may start with the most common metrics and then improve them with the less common ones. To test the theoretical framework, empirical studies might be done. Frameworks for different sectors and industries can be developed with more research.

REFERENCES

Abdulwahid, A. H., Pattnaik, M., Palav, M. R., Babu, S. T., Manoharan, G., & Selvi, G. P. (2023, April). Library Management System Using Artificial Intelligence. In *2023 Eighth International Conference on Science Technology Engineering and Mathematics (ICONSTEM)* (pp. 1-7). IEEE.

Al-Safi, J. K. S., Bansal, A., Aarif, M., Almahairah, M. S. Z., Manoharan, G., & Alotoum, F. J. (2023). Assessment Based On IoT For Efficient Information Surveillance Regarding Harmful Strikes Upon Financial Collection. *2023 International Conference on Computer Communication and Informatics (ICCCI)*, 1-5. 10.1109/ICCCI56745.2023.10128500

Armstrong, M. (2006). A Handbook of Human Resource Management Practice (10th ed.). Cambridge University.

Ashiq, V. M., Fredrik, E. T., Kumar, N. K., Torres-Cruz, F., Colque, J. P. B., & Manoharan, G. (2023, September). A Deep Learning Approaches for Natural Language Processing and Sentiment Analysis in Social Media. In 2023 6th International Conference on Contemporary Computing and Informatics (IC3I) (Vol. 6, pp. 1746-1750). IEEE.

Bhavya, K. R., Dharmaraj, A., Pareek, P., Sathe, M. A., Tiwari, M., & Manoharan, G. (2023, September). Application of Soft Computing Techniques for Predictive Analytics in Financial Markets. In 2023 6th International Conference on Contemporary Computing and Informatics (IC3I) (Vol. 6, pp. 1756-1760). IEEE.

Bijeta Nayak, B., Manoharan, G., Sharma, V. K., Lourens, M., Kumar, A., & Hinge, P. (2024). Design and Empirical Analysis of a Artificial Intelligence-Based Human Resource Management Processing Systems for Detecting Personal Stress. 6th International Conference on Contemporary Computing and Informatics (IC3I), 2421-2426.

Bulsari, S., & Pandya, K. (2023). Future of HR Analytics: Applications to Recruitment, Employee Engagement, and Retention. In N. Sharma & K. Shalender (Eds.), *Managing Technology Integration for Human Resources in Industry 5.0* (pp. 140–162). IGI Global. doi:10.4018/978-1-6684-6745-9.ch009

Chotai, N. A., Tiwari, A., Aggarwal, S., Chandel, P. S., Dimari, A., & Manoharan, G. (2023, December). Importance of Employee Motivation and Satisfaction in the Workplace based on BiLSTM and ANN Approach. In 2023 2nd International Conference on Automation, Computing and Renewable Systems (ICACRS) (pp. 1141-1146). IEEE. 10.1109/ICACRS58579.2023.10404593

Deviprasad, S., Madhumithaa, N., Vikas, I. W., Yadav, A., & Manoharan, G. (2023). The Machine Learning-Based Task Automation Framework for Human Resource Management in MNC Companies. *Engineering Proceedings*, *59*(1), 63.

Durai, D. S., Rudhramoorthy, K., & Sarkar, S. (2019). HR metrics and workforce analytics: It is a journey, not a destination. *Human Resource Management International Digest*, *27*(1), 4–6. doi:10.1108/HRMID-08-2018-0167

Durai, S., Manoharan, G., Priya, T. S., Jayanthi, R., Razak, A., & Ashtikar, S. P. (2024). Quantifying the Impacts of Artificial Intelligence Implementations in Marketing. In Smart and Sustainable Interactive Marketing (pp. 120-144). IGI Global. doi:10.4018/979-8-3693-1339-8.ch008

Fitz-enz. (1995). How to measure human resource management (3rd ed.). Academic Press.

Garvey. (2005). The Next Generation of Hiring Metrics. Academic Press.

ICIMS. (2015). 10 Must-Track Metrics in Talent Acquisition. Academic Press.

Joyce, P. R., Selvaraj, F. J., Manoharan, G., Priya, C., Vijayalakshmi, R., Dwivedi, P. K., & Veerakumar, K. (2024). To Study The Role Of Marketing In Human Resource Management. *Migration Letters : An International Journal of Migration Studies*, *21*(S2), 1191–1196. doi:10.59670/ml.v21iS2.7072

Krishanveni, R., & Subhashini, D. (2016). Leveraging Metrics and Analytics for evidence based decisions in managing employee performance. International Journal of Contemporary management. *Theory into Practice*, *2*, 3.

Kumar, S., Kumar, P., Ahmad, S. S., Jayasaradadevi, P., Rajeyyagari, S., Manoharan, G., & Radhakrishnan, V. (2024). A Novel Approach for IoT-Based Cloud Computing Technology and its Impact on Business Entrepreneurship. *International Journal of Intelligent Systems and Applications in Engineering*, *12*(10s), 624–628.

Lourens, M., Raman, R., Vanitha, P., Singh, R., Manoharan, G., & Tiwari, M. (2022). Agile Technology and Artificial Intelligent Systems in Business Development. *2022 5th International Conference on Contemporary Computing and Informatics (IC3I)*, 1602-1607. 10.1109/IC3I56241.2022.10073410

Madhani, P. M. (2023). Human Resources Analytics: Leveraging Human Resources for Enhancing Business Performance. *Compensation and Benefits Review*, *55*(1), 31–45. doi:10.1177/08863687221131730

Manoharan, G., Durai, S., Ashtikar, S. P., & Kumari, N. (2024). Artificial Intelligence in Marketing Applications. In Artificial Intelligence for Business (pp. 40-70). Productivity Press.

Manoharan, G., Durai, S., & Rajesh, G. A. (2022). A case of designing performance metrics for sales associates in a retail store in Coimbatore, using the BEI technique. *AIP Conference Proceedings*, *2418*, 020015. doi:10.1063/5.0081824

Manoharan, G., Durai, S., Rajesh, G. A., & Ashtikar, S. P. (2023). Credit and Risk Analysis in the Financial and Banking Sectors: An Investigation. In Artificial Intelligence for Capital Markets (pp. 57-72). Chapman and Hall/CRC.

Manoharan, G., Durai, S., Rajesh, G. A., & Ashtikar, S. P. (2024). A Study on the Application of Expert Systems as a Support System for Business Decisions: A Literature Review. Artificial Intelligence and Knowledge Processing, 279-289.

Manoharan, G., Durai, S., Rajesh, G. A., Razak, A., Rao, C. B., & Ashtikar, S. P. (2023). An investigation into the effectiveness of smart city projects by identifying the framework for measuring performance. In *Artificial Intelligence and Machine Learning in Smart City Planning* (pp. 71–84). Elsevier. doi:10.1016/B978-0-323-99503-0.00004-1

Manoharan, G., Durai, S., Rajesh, G. A., Razak, A., Rao, C. B., & Ashtikar, S. P. (2023). A study of postgraduate students' perceptions of key components in ICCC to be used in artificial intelligence-based smart cities. In *Artificial Intelligence and Machine Learning in Smart City Planning* (pp. 117–133). Elsevier. doi:10.1016/B978-0-323-99503-0.00003-X

Naveen, S., & Raju, D. N. M. (2014). A study on recruitment & selection process with reference to three industries, cement industry, electronics industry, sugar industry in Krishna DtAp, India. IOSR Journal of Business and Management (IOSR-JBM), 15(5), 60-67.

Obeidat, S. M., & Abdalla, S. O. (2022). Achieving Sustainable Development Through Green HRM: The Role of HR Analytics. In J. Marx Gómez & L. O. Yesufu (Eds.), *Sustainable Development Through Data Analytics and Innovation. Progress in IS*. Springer. doi:10.1007/978-3-031-12527-0_10

Ofori, D., & Aryeetey, M. (2011). Recruitment and selection practices in small and medium enterprises. *International Journal of Business Administration*, *2*(3), 45–60. doi:10.5430/ijba.v2n3p45

Ponduri, S. B., Ahmad, S. S., Ravisankar, P., Thakur, D. J., Chawla, K., Chary, D. T., ... Sharma, S. (2024). A Study on Recent Trends of Technology and its Impact on Business and Hotel Industry. *Migration Letters : An International Journal of Migration Studies*, *21*(S1), 801–806.

Raghunadha Reddy, P., & Lakshmikeerthi, P. (2017). 'HR Analytics' - An Effective Evidence Based HRM Tool. *International Journal of Business and Management Invention*, *6*(7), 23–34.

Ramachandran, K. K., Mary, S. S. C., Painoli, A. K., Satyala, H., Singh, B., & Manoharan, G. (2022). Assessing the full impact of technological advances on business management techniques. The British Journal of Administrative Management. https://tbjam. org/vol58-special-issue-06

Samson, W. (2013).Recruitment of staff. International Journal of Selection, 14(6), 21-34.

Samtani, D. D. (2022). The Advantages of Using Prescriptive Analytics in Recruitment and Performance Management processes by HR professionals based in Ireland (Doctoral dissertation, Dublin, National College of Ireland).

Shaikh, I. A. K., Kumar, C. N. S., Rohini, P., Jafersadhiq, A., Manoharan, G., & Suryanarayana, V. (2023). AST-Graph Convolution Network and LSTM Based Employees Behavioral and Emotional Reactions to Corporate Social Irresponsibility. *2023 Second International Conference on Augmented Intelligence and Sustainable Systems (ICAISS)*, 966-971. 10.1109/ICAISS58487.2023.10250754

Shameem, A., Ramachandran, K. K., Sharma, A., Singh, R., Selvaraj, F. J., & Manoharan, G. (2023, May). The rising importance of AI in boosting the efficiency of online advertising in developing countries. In 2023 3rd International Conference on Advance Computing and Innovative Technologies in Engineering (ICACITE) (pp. 1762-1766). IEEE. 10.1109/ICACITE57410.2023.10182754

Shikari. (2011). Is hiring playing a great role? Academic Press.

Shrivastava, S., & Dhaigude, A. S. (2022). Prime Data Tech Pvt. Ltd: Resolving Employee Recruitment Dilemma using HR Analytics. Communications of the Association for Information Systems, 50. doi:10.17705/1CAIS.05027

Sinha, V., & Thaly, P. (2013). A review on changing trend of recruitment practice to enhance the quality of hiring in global organizations. *Management*, *18*(2), 141–156.

Subhashini Durai, K., & Manoharan, G. (2022). Leveraging HR metrics for effective recruitment & selection process in IT industries in Chennai and Coimbatore, Tamil Nadu. *AIP Conference Proceedings*, *2418*, 020011. doi:10.1063/5.0081942

Subhashini Durai, K., & Manoharan, G. (2022). Metric based performance management of employees – A case study of MSME unit in Coimbatore, Tamil Nadu. *AIP Conference Proceedings*, *2418*, 020013. doi:10.1063/5.0081943

Sullivan. (2009). Recruitment Process: Benchmark and Best Practice Study. Academic Press.

Susanto, P. C., Sawitri, N. N., Suroso, S., & Rony, Z. T. (2023). Human Resource Business Partners: Recruitment, Coaching, and Leadership Development. *International Journal of Integrative Sciences*, *2*(4), 457–470. doi:10.55927/ijis.v2i4.3680

Turner, D. W. (2010). Qualitative interview design: A practical guide for novice investigators. *The Qualitative Report*, *15*(3), 754–760. http://www.nova.edu/ssss/QR/QR15-3/qid.pdf

Wright, P. M., Gardner, T. M., Moynihan, L. M., & Allen, M. R. (2005). The relationship between HR Practices and firm performance: Examining causal order. *Personnel Psychology*, *58*(2), 409–447. doi:10.1111/j.1744-6570.2005.00487.x

Yapp, M. (2009). Measuring the ROI of talent management. *Strategic HR Review*, *8*(4), 5–10. doi:10.1108/14754390910963856

Zottoli, M. A., & Wanous, J. P. (2000). Recruitment source research: Current status and future directions. *Human Resource Management Review*, *10*(4), 353–382. doi:10.1016/S1053-4822(00)00032-2

Chapter 11
Moderation Effect of Training on Employee Job Performance in Retail Stores:
A Conceptual Framework for Industry 5.0 People Analytics

Amandeep Kaur
https://orcid.org/0009-0004-5716-7298
Lovely Professional University, India

Veer P. Gangwar
Lovely Professional University, India

Prabhjeet Kaur
Lovely Professional University, India

Lokesh Jasrai
Lovely Professional University, India

ABSTRACT

The current study tries to explore the relationship between training of employees and job performance in retail stores in Industry 5.0. It introduces a conceptual framework designed to interplay between training initiatives and employee job performance. On the other hand, chapters provide insights for practitioners and researchers in people analytics. Data analysis highlights the importance of employee performance in Punjab's diverse retail landscape and also emphasizes the need for effective training to meet customer demand and seasonal market changes, ensuring consistent customer satisfaction. The literature review provides insights into employee training's impact on job performance while focusing on the retail sector. Moderation analysis shows how training initiatives influence performance outcomes. In this chapter, the authors introduce a comprehensive conceptual framework that synthesizes literature and real-world illustrations and interplays between training and performance variables within the retail sector of Punjab. The analytical approach is used to establish a basis for future analysis and investigations, including of the approaches used for data collection. The data has been analyzed using 138 responses. The smart pls has been used to generate model analysis. The chapter provides practical implications for a conceptual framework for retail organizations and offers recommendations for optimizing employee performance through training programs and strategic decision-making in people analytics. In this chapter, the authors explain the role of attrition and attraction and analyze the moderating effects of training initiatives on the 'job performance' of employees in Punjab's retail stores, providing actionable strategies for organizations to optimize their workforce capabilities.

DOI: 10.4018/979-8-3693-1343-5.ch011

1. INTRODUCTION

Employee training helps in shaping 'job performance' and contributing to organizational success. Extensive literature demonstrates a positive approach between training programs and enhanced employee capabilities. These programs not only improve individual performance but also positively influence overall organizational outcomes. Various studies emphasize the transformative effect of training on employee skills, knowledge, and motivation, all of which are crucial components of job performance. Research shows that employee engagement and training have a strong and beneficial link in Pakistan's education sector, highlighting the wider effects of training on job performance (Anam Amin & Lodhi, 2013).

Additionally, a review study confirms that, as demonstrated by additional evidence in the field, '*training and development*' have a major impact on overall performance (Al Khawaldeh, 2023). A more recent study highlights training's moderately beneficial influence on worker performance, offering important new information about the complex connection that exists between training and employment results. According to a study conducted on faculty members at technical training institutes, the influence of training goes beyond improving individual skills to improve job satisfaction (Paposa & Kumar, 2019). The relationship between job performance and sustainable HRM practices is also explored, with training being recognized as a key mediator in this connection (Manzoor et al., 2019). This thorough analysis draws conclusions from a variety of research conducted in a range of industries in an effort to synthesize the body of evidence currently available regarding the effect of training on employee job performance. We want to offer a comprehensive view of the complex relationship between training programs and work performance by examining the pilot data and illuminating the elements that support their efficacy.

We are trying to understand the link between job success and employability training in retail stores in India. This chapter suggests a framework for seeing how training and results in retailing interact. It draws on existing information, real-world illustrations, and models. Training staff can boost job effectiveness and business results. Studies show that training can enhance employee's skills. This, in turn, ups both their individual success and the company's overall performance. Training plays a moderate but positive role in workers' job success. But that's not the only impact. It also creates job satisfaction and supports long-term HRM practices. The findings from literature also describes that faculty members of technical education institutes found that training is a crucial moderator in this relationship. The analysis shows that a variety of research has already been conducted in specific retail industries around the world. From the literature, studies have focused on industry 5.0 and saw the effect of training on employee job performance.

With relevance to Industrial 5.0 growth in India, significant efforts have been seen in recent years. This leads us to focus on employee job performance through dynamic training schedules. The study tries to develop an industry 5.0 focused conceptual framework that can focus on how job performance and training are related to the retail industry. The study tries to explore aspects of training, employee job performance, and the retail industry in Industry 5.0. The effectiveness of Industrial 5.0 in the retail industry provides a holistic understanding of people analytics. This understanding is crucial for researchers and practitioners in human resource management.

When industry 5.0 has globalization roots worldwide, its impact cannot be seen in the retail industry. With tough competition in the market, from smaller to bigger, every firm and organization is adopting an advanced technology approach. Here, people analytics plays its role. Assessment of employee performance through tools that assess employee performance on a monthly basis. The study focuses on basic questions related to training and development. To remain competitive, organizations must focus on employee's knowledge and skills, which are crucial for high performance and are integral to the human resource department. Training and development have become essential roles in organizations, as they significantly impact an organization's success by enhancing employee performance. Companies must navigate intense competition and evolving business climates, with employees being a company's most valuable asset. Training focuses on current employment, specific skills, and abilities to perform specific tasks, improving knowledge and abilities for specific professions. The study also considers the interests of both the organization and its personnel, and training is crucial for achieving organizational goals.

Industry 5.0 growth has pushed organizations to face global competition. This involves organizations that train employees at various stages of their careers. The enhanced training sessions will improve employee performance and improve competencies for adopting integrated technologies. In this advancement, human resource development plays an leading and supporting role in the management of staff resources. As stated by (Gowler & Legge, 1986, employees are the company's most valuable asset, as their growth impacts organizational growth and profitability. For better training in the age of Industry 5.0, companies need to focus on their retail effectiveness through training for their retail employees. This process impacts the interests of both the organization and its employees.

2. LITERATURE REVIEW

The role of industry 5.0 in the growth retail sector plays a major role. The retail sector was stagnant for some time during the 2009 financial crisis. The report also focused on the fact that only 5 to 10 were jobs that were not in existence when employees were deployed in 2022. It was also projected that there would be a radical change in skill sets in retail sector jobs. This assumption also reveals that 15 to 20 percent of employees feel a threat that they might lose their job in the retail industry if they didn't keep learning new skills (Bhat, 2020).. With the advancement of Industry 5.0 and the adoption of new technologies, skill sets should also need to upgrade.

Organizations always delves training programs which enables employees to get trained to enhance their knowledge and skills. This step involves the motivational approach like giving incentives to the employees who do well in the training. The purpose for initiating such training is to stimulate the employees to be more active in their training sessions. This encouragement leads employees to perform better. Organizations employers invest in employee training to improve employment conditions, increase productivity and reduce employee turnover. Proper training and development can increase organization standards among global partners. People analytics plays role in effective continuous auditing of employee performance to tailored training skills.

3. OBJECTIVES

- The chapter tries to evaluates the impact of '*training programs*' on '*employee job performance*' in Punjabi retail stores.
- To provide framework for enhancing workforce effectiveness by developing a model that integrates training outcomes and performance metrics.

Table 1. Relevant studies related to retail sector

Author	Gap in Literature	Findings	Constructs	Focus of Study
(Anam Amin & Lodhi, 2013)	Lack of focus on the retail sector in Punjab.	The study shows positive correlation between training and employee engagement.	'Employee training, Job performance'	Describes specific impact of employee engagement in training in retail.
(Al Khawaldeh, 2023)	Absence of recent studies on training in retail.	Moderate effect of overall training on improving worker performance.	'Overall training, Worker performance.'	Recent trends in training and their impact on worker performance.
(Kuruppu et al., 2021)	Emphasis on employee retention as a performance factor.	The study shows positive role of retention on employee performance.	'Employee retention, Employee performance.'	Exploration of the moderating role of retention on performance.

Table 2. Training as moderator in employee job performance in people analytics

Type of Study	Core Constructs	Gaps	Focus of Study	Future Questions	Reference
Review	People Analytics, Training, Ethical Considerations	Gaps in training and ethical issues not fully addressed.	Early stage of PA research, need for more exploration.	How can ethical considerations be integrated into People Analytics?	(Tursunbayeva et al., 2018)
Review	Performance Management, Performance Appraisal	Limited exploration of training's role in performance.	Focus on process-driven aspects, specifically performance appraisal.	How does training contribute to holistic performance management?	(Brown et al., 2019)
Analytical Study	People-Oriented Management, Job Performance	Effects of training on people-oriented management not detailed.	Combined effects of antecedents on job performance.	What specific aspects of training impact people-oriented management?	(López-Cabarcos et al., 2022)
Correlational Study	Work Engagement, Employee Satisfaction	Limited exploration of training's impact.	Individual-level correlations affecting employee satisfaction.	How can training interventions enhance work engagement?	(Sypniewska et al., 2023)
Analytical Study	Employee Psychological Well-being, Job Performance	Lack of specific details on training interventions.	Investigating the mediating role of affective well-being.	What training strategies contribute to improved psychological well-being?	(Kundi et al., 2020)
Analytical Study	Human Resources Analytics	Not explicitly focused on training as a moderator	Linking HR practices to organizational performance	How can HR analytics leverage training for improved organizational performance?	(Bahuguna et al., 2024)

4. FRAMEWORK

Mike West (2019) emphasizes the importance of activation, attrition, and activation in employee performance. Another study (Ahmad et al., 2020) examines the effects of performance appraisals on employee performance in Pakistan, while (Adekiya, 2024) use an employee performance rating survey to measure job time, quality, and quantity. Literature has contexted the term "people analytics", "work analytic", "talent analytic" and "HR analytic" in the same sense. Because the technological assessment of employee job performance are done through HR personnel to manage organization with competitive edge of industry 5.0.

Skill retention is a strategy enforced by employers to ensure critical skills remain valuable assets even during employee turnover (Masegare & Ngoepe, 2018; Rothman et al., 2013). It involves sharing knowledge with younger employees and varies over time. Municipalities conduct exit interviews to understand employee reasons for leaving. Employee rewards are a key cost for councils, representing about a quarter of all expenditure, and are used to reinforce partnership goals and display required behaviours and values (Pocock et al., 2001; Viglia et al., 2023).

Attitude and behavior of employees significantly impact an organization's productivity (Omisore & Adeleke, 2015). Training and education are crucial tools for transforming knowledge and competencies. Business organizations often link training programs to their objectives to ensure industry sustainability. Employee performance is directly related to organizational performance, as employees play a crucial role in sustaining operations (Hafeez & Akbar, 2015; Solomon et al., 2012). Therefore, improving employee involvement in decision-making through organized structures is essential for enhancing organizational performance. Attrition and attraction as main variable provide comprehensive approach in the model to check the relation in context employee job performance and training (Yahia et al., 2021).

5. CASE STUDIES EXAMPLES

The relevant case studies have been identified through secondary sources to signify the importance of regular training evaluation in many firms and organization to maintain the pace with changing dynamics of market. The technology enhancement also creates challenges among these retail sector to train their employees in accordance. Here are some case studies in view of retail sector signifying the importance of people analytics.

6. METHODOLOGY

This study has used quantitative approach with random sample to gather numerical data from 138 participants who are retailers in Punjab region. The purpose of the survey is to gather information about a particular question about the connection between 'employee job performance' and 'training programmes' (Lee et al., 2023). Survey technique and questionnaires as an instrument has been used to analyse data

Figure 1. Conceptual framework (authors own work)

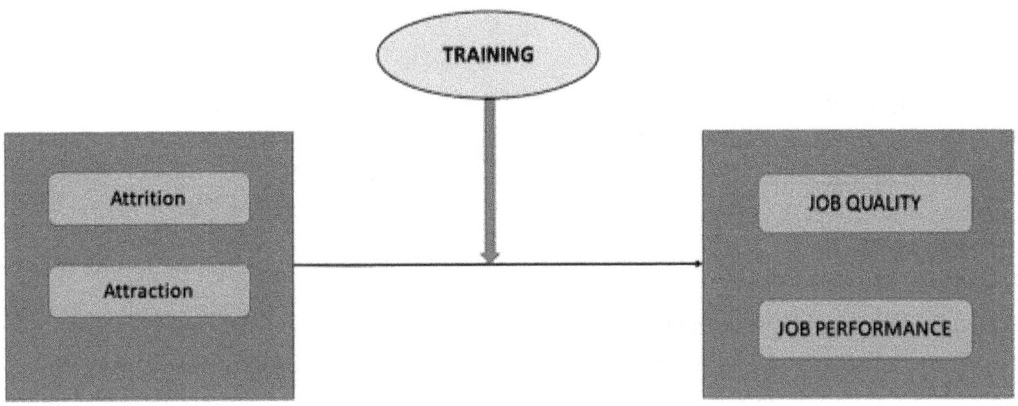

Table 3. Identification of core constructs for employee job performance people analytics

Author(s)	Type of Study	Findings	Constructs	Focus of Study
(Chalutz Ben-Gal, 2019)	Review	Provides an overview of ROI of HR analytics with a focus on practical implementation tools. Analyze basic HR parameters and discusses observations related to training and development.	HR parameters, Training and Development	Practical implementation tools in HR analytics.
(Fernandez & Gallardo-Gallardo, 2021)	Review	examines the main causes and obstacles to importance to adopt practices of HR analytics. explores the effects of training initiatives on employee performance and goes into great detail about HR measures and their applicability.	'HR analytics adoption, Training Programs, HR Metrics'	factors and obstacles influencing the use of HR analytics and the suitability of HR metrics.
(Husain et al., 2022)	Review	Discusses a broader perspective on human resource analytics, highlighting the evolution from traditional HR measurement and HRIS literature.	'HR Analytics, HR Measurement, HRIS Literature'	Evolution of HR analytics from traditional HR measurement.
(Chowdhury & Gkioulos, 2021)	Review	Conducts a literature review on cyber security training for critical infrastructure protection. Examines training delivery methods and conducts an analysis of metrics and key performance indicators.	'Cyber Security Training, Training Delivery Methods, Performance Metrics'	Cyber security training methods and metrics for critical infrastructure protection.
(Piwowar-Sulej, 2021)	Review	Conducts a hybrid literature review on core functions of Sustainable HR Management. Presents results of the analysis, including the implementation of green performance indicators and HR functions like training.	'Sustainable HR Management, Green Performance Indicators, HR Functions'	Core functions of Sustainable HR Management, including the implementation of green indicators.
(Santana & Díaz-Fernández, 2023)	Review	illustrates the skills needed for the era of artificial intelligence while outlining the main obstacles and a research plan. focuses on the fact that current HR analytics procedures will bring about revolutionary change.	'Competencies, Artificial Intelligence, Challenges, Research Agenda'	Visualization of competencies for the AI age and the potential transformation through HR analytics.
(Pino-Ortega et al., 2021)	Review	Conducts a systematic review on 'training design, performance analysis, and talent identification'. Identifies key variables through principal component analysis, aiming to target sport analysis performance.	'Training Design, Performance Analysis, Talent Identification, Team Sports Analysis'	Identification of key variables in training design and performance analysis for team sports.
(Garg et al., 2022)	Review	examines the applications of machine learning in the management of human resources. examines the ramifications, particularly if staff members are involved in the performance evaluation standards.	'Machine Learning, HR Management, Employee Contribution, Performance Measurement Criteria'	Applications of machine learning in HR management and employee involvement: implications.
(Giermindl et al., 2022)	Review	Identifies six perils related to people analytics and discusses their role for organizations. Proposes a matrix to aid managers in better decision-making.	'Perils of People Analytics'	Implications of perils for organizations and proposed decision-making matrix.

from retail employees in Punjab, India. The study has analysed the data statistically to brief out the results interpretation. The study also ensures ethical approaches through which information has been gathered from the participant consents.

Measurement Tool

In the study 7 Likert scale questionnaire has been used to do pilot survey in order get responses from the respondents in the area of Punjab (India). Items used for codes words like ATTR (Attrition), ARTN

Table 4. Case studies in relevance to retail sector

Focused	Authors
Numerous case studies illustrate how HR departments may successfully employ people analytics to solve HR and business difficulties have been produced as a result of the practitioner-focused approach.	(Harris et al., 2011; Kane, 2015; McIver et al., 2018)
The article offers case studies and HR analytical tools that show how people analytics are being used by multinational corporations to address business difficulties.	(Harris et al., 2011)
The report examines how firms are using cutting-edge technology for collecting employee data and offers a case study to demonstrate how successful this practice is.	(Kane, 2015)
The paper presents two case studies that show how companies are utilising people analytics to solve operational challenges.	(Rasmussen & Ulrich, 2015)
The study gives a general review of people analytics, covering definitions, applications, and disadvantages. provides a case study of how business difficulties are resolved using people analytics.	(Momin, 2015)
The case study looks at business intelligence's use in HR and shows how businesses may use people analytics to solve problems in the organization workspace.	(Pape, 2016)
The case study describes the beneficial role of people analytics in promoting diversity and inclusion in workplaces.	(Atewologun, 2014)
The case study highlights a retail company in Spain that effectively used people analytics to tackle its business obstacles.	(Simón & Ferreiro, 2018)

(attraction), JP (job performance), TRAN (training), and JQ (job quality) are stated in the table:6.3.1. and to do overall assessment of the model SMARTPLS software has been used.

7. RESULTS AND FINDINGS

Table 5 interpretation: The data's high KMO value and Bartlett's Test indicate its suitability for factor analysis due to its correlation and sufficient structure for identifying underlying factors.

Table 6 interpretation: The model's high R-squared value indicates its effective explanation of the dependent variable's variability, but caution advised due to the risk of overfitting. The regression model, with a value of 0.375, accounts for 37.5% of the total variation in *Job performance*, indicating that the independent variables arc significant. The adjusted R-squared, 0.357, accounts for 35.7% of *Job performance* variability, excluding unnecessary variables and penalizing the inclusion of unnecessary variables. The regression model, with an R-squared value of 0.252, accounts for 25.2% of the total variation in *job quality*, indicating its significant impact. The adjusted R-squared (0.229) adjusts the model's predictors, explaining 22.9% of *job quality* variability by the independent variable. R-squared values indicate the

Table 5. KMO and Bartlett's test

KMO and Bartlett's Testa		
Kaiser-Meyer-Olkin Measure of Sampling Adequacy.		.853
Bartlett's Test of Sphericity	Approx. Chi-Square	3804.380
	Df	351
	Sig.	.000

a. Based on correlations

Table 6. Adjusted R square

Constructs	R-square	R-Square Adjusted
JOB PERFORMANCE	0.437	0.416
JOB QUALITY	0.277	0.25

proportion of variability in *job performance and job quality* accounted for by independent variables in regression models. adjusted r-squared values provide a conservative estimate of model explanatory power. Higher R-squared values indicate better fit, but interpretation depends on analysis context.

Table 7 interpretation: Overall results of outer loading are above acceptable range of 0.7. only one item related to job performance that is JP1 is having value of 0.635. we have not excluded this item as it will affect the result effectiveness.

Table 7. Overall outer loading of the items

Relation	Outer Loadings
ATRN1 → "I believe that personalised branding and reputation of the firm do attract the talented individuals."	0.933
ATRN2 → "I agree that organizational onboarding recruitment does attract skilled individuals for the job."	0.896
ATRN3 → "I believe dynamic work culture of the organization also attract new employees."	0.930
ATRN4 → "I agree that perks and benefits also attractive towards potential hires."	0.926
ATTR1 → "I believe that turnover does impact negatively on overall performance."	0.899
ATTR2 → "I believe that effective training reduces employee attrition in the firm."	0.931
ATTR3→ "I believe that current organization do take measure to address employee attrition."	0.905
ATTR4 → "I believe that organization rewards employee and recognise their efforts."	0.950
JP1 → "I agree that organization rate my performance on the basis of productivity, efficiency and achieving goals."	0.635
JP4 → "I believe that training and opportunity provided by organization positively contribute to my job performance."	0.878
JP5 → "I agree that to some extent clear performance expectation and goals have been communicated by our superiors."	0.860
JP6 → "I am satisfied with feedback and recognition received from superiors."	0.836
JP7 → "I believe that tools and resources provided by organization supports our job performance."	0.814
JP8 → "I believe that culture and environment does impact overall ability to perform in the job."	0.864
JQ1 → "I am satisfied with current quality of job in the organization."	0.900
JQ2 → "I believe that my organization provides meaningful tasks which are goal oriented."	0.909
JQ3 → "I believe that organization recognises our contributions."	0.893
JQ4 → "I am satisfied with the opportunities for professional growth provided by organization to grow."	0.861
JQ5 → "I agree that workplace environment and culture positively contribute to the overall quality of my job. "	0.894
TRAN2 → "I believe that current training provided in the organization increase employee knowledge and skills."	0.848
TRAN3 → "I believe that current training content are relevant to our job responsibilities."	0.855
TRAN4 → "I believe that current training programs are designed to make employee ready for dynamic market challenges."	0.881
TRAN5 → "I believe the training does impact overall job quality and performance."	0.785
TRAINING x ATTRACTION -> TRAINING x ATTRACTION	1.000
TRAINING x ATTRITION -> TRAINING x ATTRITION	1.000

Table 8 interpretation: The validity and reliability evaluations of the *attraction, attrition, job performance, job quality, and training* measuring scales offer important information about the calibre of the information gathered. As evidenced by excellent Cronbach's Alpha, Composite dependability (rho_a and rho_c), and a decent Average Variance Extracted (AVE), *attraction* and *attrition* both exhibit outstanding dependability. These results imply that the metrics capture the intended structures consistently and that the constructions themselves account for a substantial amount of the observed variance, rather than the measurement error.

When it comes to job performance, the reliability metrics like Cronbach's alpha and composite reliability are good, but the average variance extracted (AVE) is a little bit lower than the other constructs, suggesting that there may be a little bit more measurement error. however, overall, the measurement items for job performance demonstrate satisfactory reliability. for job quality, the reliability statistics are excellent across all measures, implying high internal consistency and reliability of the measurement items. the AVE further suggests that the items reliably capture a substantial proportion of the variance in the job quality construct. finally, the measurement scale for training exhibit's good reliability, with high values for Cronbach's alpha and composite reliability. however, the AVE indicates a moderate level of measurement error compared to the other constructs. nonetheless, the overall reliability of the measurement items for training is deemed satisfactory.

Table 9 interpretation: These p values providing interrelation between variables. To provide effective model PLS-SEM bootstrapping has been used at the trail sample of 5000 as setting. In summary, the relation between these constructs shows that attraction -> *job performance, training -> job quality,*

Table 8. Construct reliability and validity

Constructs	Cronbach's Alpha	Composite Reliability (rho_a)	Composite Reliability (rho_c)	Average Variance Extracted (AVE)
ATTRACTION	0.941	0.948	0.957	0.848
ATTRITION	0.941	0.946	0.957	0.849
JOB PERFORMANCE	0.899	0.907	0.923	0.67
JOB QUALITY	0.935	0.937	0.951	0.795
TRAINING	0.864	0.878	0.907	0.71

Table 9. Assumed hypothesis from the network

Relation	Original Sample (O)	Sample Mean (M)	Standard Deviation (STDEV)	T statistics (|O/STDEV|)	P Values
Attraction -> job performance	0.229	0.203	0.122	1.871	0.061
Attraction -> job quality	0.393	0.385	0.106	3.720	0.000
Attrition -> job performance	0.304	0.304	0.110	2.762	0.006
Attrition -> job quality	0.198	0.199	0.096	2.068	0.039
Training -> job performance	0.312	0.349	0.132	2.369	0.018
Training -> job quality	0.075	0.089	0.094	0.799	0.424
Training X Attrition -> Job Quality	0.056	0.053	0.120	0.463	0.643
Training X Attraction -> Job Performance	0.191	0.153	0.130	1.466	0.143

training x attrition -> job quality, and training x attraction -> job performance cannot be accepted as the results of p values are below 0.05 significance level. The remaining results related to *attraction -> job quality, attrition -> job performance, and attrition -> job quality* can be accepted, indicating statistically significant relationships.

Table 10 interpretation: The table explains that from the data 47 percent respondents were male and 52 percent were males and 1 percent were others. From the age distribution 18 to25 and 26 to 35 having equally respondents. The majority of highest respondents were identified in age category of 36 to 45 with 36 percent Reponses. While from educational background we have respondents from bachelor's degree and master's degree with total of 49 percent and 33 percent responses as per data. The important details related to employment are that from all responses we have received full timers were maximum with 76 percentage and part timers with 22 percent whereas on contract basis only 2 percent response has been received. The last category provide base for the future gap that *why employee don't like to go for contact basis.*

The findings from the following results enables us to propose the model which is used to develop the association between these constructs to test out the questions drafted for the pilot study even though half of the hypothesis has been rejected but the pre study enable to testify the model that training does

Table 10. Details of demographics of data

Details	Responses	Percentage
Gender Distribution		
Male	72	52%
Female	65	47%
Others	1	1%
Total	138	100%
Age Distribution		
18-25	25	18%
26-35	25	18%
36-45	50	36%
46-above	38	28%
Total	138	100%
Educational Background		
High school	12	9%
Bachelor's Degree	68	49%
Master's Degree	46	33%
Doctorate	12	9%
Total	138	100%
Type of Employment		
Full Time	105	76%
Part time	30	22%
Contract	3	2%
Total	13	100

has positive significant impact on job performance in people analytics. Hence model has been run on basis of conceptual framework provided.

Following model has been generated using Smart PLS. the results of the collected data from 138 respondents were based on 7 Likert scale. At first 138 sample were run using bootstrapping at maximum of 5000 sample as adjusted setting. The second step involves the PLS-SEM algorithm using factor as option to run the model. The dotted line in the represented in the model from training construct associate the moderation effect on the attrition and attraction with job quality and job performance in people analytics. the analysis has been already interpreted with the results.

8. CONCLUSION AND FUTURE IMPLICATION

Studies about worker productivity highlight the significance of attrition and attraction. Performance reviews, skill retention measures, and employee awards are crucial to ensure critical talents remain relevant. Employee attitudes and behaviour have a substantial impact on efficiency, and training and education are critical tools for converting knowledge and competencies. Since workers are essential to maintaining operations, involving them in decision-making through formalized procedures is critical to improve their job performance. The study examines the fundamental metrics and adoption hurdles in the main areas of people analytics in industry 5.0 evolution. It investigates the evolution of HR assessment and HRIS literature and explain why security training and blended knowledge is needed for sustainable human resources administration are needed in industry 5.0. The study also covers abili-

Figure 2. PLS model of conceptual framework

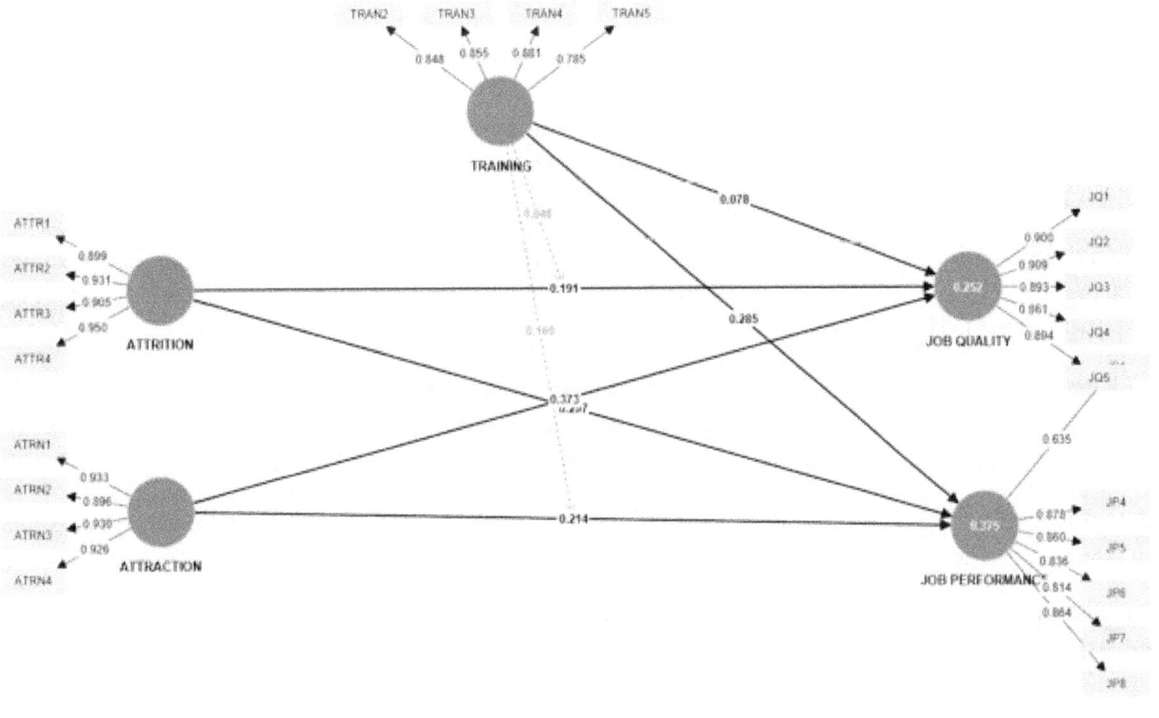

ties, training design, performance measurement, and talent discovery. Moreover, it examines machine learning applications in HR administration and lists six risks associated with people analytics. Higher ROI in theoretical and experimental studies is indicated by the review. The article presents case studies showcasing the successful use of people analytics in HR departments to solve HR and business issues. It examines how multinational corporations are using advanced technology to collect employee data, highlighting its benefits in promoting diversity and inclusion. The case study also highlights a retail company in Spain that effectively utilized people analytics to overcome its business challenges. Hence a conceptual framework has been provided to test the training moderation effect on job performance with other relevant variables. The reliability and validity assessments of the measurement scales for attraction, attrition, job performance, job quality, and training provide valuable insights into the quality of data collected. attraction and attrition demonstrate excellent reliability, with high Cronbach's alpha, composite reliability, and a good average variance extracted (AVE). job performance has good reliability metrics, but a lower average variance extracted (AVE) suggests potential measurement error. training has good reliability, but moderate measurement error. Hence, the following model can be utilised to test the future significance with more factors to test out employee job performance using people analytics in retail sector.

9. ACKNOWLEDGMENT

All the authors contribute equally to the study drafting. First and corresponding author Amandeep Kaur propose the conceptual idea regarding framework. Future studies with larger sample may produce effective results in the retail sector hence it is consented that this model can be utilised as base to conduct similar study.

REFERENCES

Adekiya, A. (2024). Perceived job insecurity and task performance: What aspect of performance is related to which facet of job insecurity. *Current Psychology (New Brunswick, N.J.)*, *43*(2), 1340–1358. doi:10.1007/s12144-023-04408-4 PMID:36852083

Ahmad, M., Raziq, M. M., Rehman, W. U., & Allen, M. M. (2020). High-performance work practices and organizational performance in Pakistan. *International Journal of Manpower*, *41*(3), 318–338. doi:10.1108/IJM-01-2019-0016

Al Khawaldeh, E. D. (2023). The Impact of Training on Improving Employee Performance: A Case Study on Employees in the Directorate of Education of Ma'an District. *International Journal of Professional Business Review*, *8*(10), e03520–e03520. doi:10.26668/businessreview/2023.v8i10.3520

Anam Amin, R. S., & Lodhi, M. R. N. (2013). The impact of employees training on the job performance in education sector of Pakistan. *Middle East Journal of Scientific Research*, *17*(9), 1273–1278.

Atewologun, D. (2014). Sites of intersectional identity salience. *Gender in Management*, *29*(5), 277–290. doi:10.1108/GM-12-2013-0140

Bahuguna, P. C., Srivastava, R., & Tiwari, S. (2024). Human resources analytics: Where do we go from here? *Benchmarking*, *31*(2), 640–668. doi:10.1108/BIJ-06-2022-0401

Bhat, T. (2020). India and Industry 4.0. Working paper, 218, Institute for studies in Industrial Development, New Delhi.

Brown, T. C., O'Kane, P., Mazumdar, B., & McCracken, M. (2019). Performance management: A scoping review of the literature and an agenda for future research. *Human Resource Development Review*, *18*(1), 47–82. doi:10.1177/1534484318798533

Chalutz Ben-Gal, H. (2019). An ROI-based review of HR analytics: Practical implementation tools. *Personnel Review*, *48*(6), 1429–1448. doi:10.1108/PR-11-2017-0362

Chowdhury, N., & Gkioulos, V. (2021). Cyber security training for critical infrastructure protection: A literature review. *Computer Science Review*, *40*, 100361. doi:10.1016/j.cosrev.2021.100361

Fernandez, V., & Gallardo-Gallardo, E. (2021). Tackling the HR digitalization challenge: Key factors and barriers to HR analytics adoption. *Competitiveness Review*, *31*(1), 162–187. doi:10.1108/CR-12-2019-0163

Garg, S., Sinha, S., Kar, A. K., & Mani, M. (2022). A review of machine learning applications in human resource management. *International Journal of Productivity and Performance Management*, *71*(5), 1590–1610. doi:10.1108/IJPPM-08-2020-0427

Giermindl, L. M., Strich, F., Christ, O., Leicht-Deobald, U., & Redzepi, A. (2022). The dark sides of people analytics: Reviewing the perils for organisations and employees. *European Journal of Information Systems*, *31*(3), 410–435. doi:10.1080/0960085X.2021.1927213

Hafeez, U., & Akbar, W. (2015). Impact of work-life balance on job satisfaction among school teachers of 21st century. *Australian Journal of Business and Management Research*, *4*(11), 25–37. doi:10.52283/NSWRCA.AJBMR.20150411A03

Harris, J. G., Craig, E., & Light, D. A. (2011). Talent and analytics: New approaches, higher ROI. *The Journal of Business Strategy*, *32*(6), 4–13. doi:10.1108/02756661111180087

Husain, R., Samad, T. A., & Qamar, Y. (2022). Past, present and future of luxury brands: A review and bibliometric analysis. *Journal of Fashion Marketing and Management*, *26*(4), 582–602. doi:10.1108/JFMM-02-2021-0046

Kane, G. C. (2015). People analytics through super-charged ID badges. *MIT Sloan Management Review*, *56*(4).

Kundi, Y. M., Aboramadan, M., Elhamalawi, E. M., & Shahid, S. (2020). Employee psychological well-being and job performance: Exploring mediating and moderating mechanisms. *The International Journal of Organizational Analysis*, *29*(3), 736–754. doi:10.1108/IJOA-05-2020-2204

Kuruppu, C., Kavirathne, C., & Karunarathna, N. (2021). The impact of training on employee performance in a selected apparel sector organization in Sri Lanka. *Global Journal of Management and Business Research. Administrative Management*, *21*(2), 5–12.

Lee, N. S. M. S., Hussain, S., Rashid, R. A., Raffar, M. A., & Aripin, N. (2023). The effect of training towards employee performance: An evidence from a public university in Malaysia. *International Journal of Information Management, 17*(3), 178–185.

López-Cabarcos, M. Á., Vázquez-Rodríguez, P., & Quiñoá-Piñeiro, L. M. (2022). An approach to employees' job performance through work environmental variables and leadership behaviours. *Journal of Business Research, 140*, 361–369. doi:10.1016/j.jbusres.2021.11.006

Manzoor, F., Wei, L., Bányai, T., Nurunnabi, M., & Subhan, Q. A. (2019). An Examination of Sustainable HRM Practices on Job Performance: An Application of Training as a Moderator. *Sustainability (Basel), 11*(8), 2263. doi:10.3390/su11082263

Masegare, P., & Ngoepe, M. (2018). A framework for incorporating implementation indicators of corporate governance for municipalities in South Africa. *Corporate Governance (Bradford), 18*(4), 581–593. doi:10.1108/CG-11-2016-0216

McIver, D., Lengnick-Hall, M. L., & Lengnick-Hall, C. A. (2018). A strategic approach to workforce analytics: Integrating science and agility. *Business Horizons, 61*(3), 397–407. doi:10.1016/j.bushor.2018.01.005

Momin, W. Y. M. (2015). HR analytics transforming human resource management. *International Journal of Applied Research, 1*(9), 688–692.

Omisore, B. O., & Adeleke, O. (2015). Work ethics, values, attitudes and performance in the Nigerian public service: Issues, challenges and the way forward. *Journal of Public Administration and Governance, 5*(1), 157–172. doi:10.5296/jpag.v5i1.7367

Pape, T. (2016). Prioritising data items for business analytics: Framework and application to human resources. *European Journal of Operational Research, 252*(2), 687–698. doi:10.1016/j.ejor.2016.01.052

Paposa, K. K., & Kumar, Y. M. (2019). Impact of training and development practices on job satisfaction: A study on faculty members of technical education institutes. *Management and Labour Studies, 44*(3), 248–262. doi:10.1177/0258042X19851649

Pino-Ortega, J., Rojas-Valverde, D., Gómez-Carmona, C. D., & Rico-González, M. (2021). Training design, performance analysis, and talent identification—A systematic review about the most relevant variables through the principal component analysis in Soccer, Basketball, and Rugby. *International Journal of Environmental Research and Public Health, 18*(5), 2642. doi:10.3390/ijerph18052642 PMID:33807971

Piwowar-Sulej, K. (2021). Core functions of Sustainable Human Resource Management. A hybrid literature review with the use of H-Classics methodology. *Sustainable Development (Bradford), 29*(4), 671–693. doi:10.1002/sd.2166

Pocock, B., Sexton, M., & Wilson, L. (2001). *Doing More, With Less: Tension and Change at Work in South Australian Local Government. Report of the Equity, Enterprise Bargaining and Employment Outcomes in South Australia Local Government Project.* Australian Services Union and the Australian Workers Union.

Rasmussen, T., & Ulrich, D. (2015). Learning from practice: How HR analytics avoids being a management fad. *Organizational Dynamics, 44*(3), 236–242. doi:10.1016/j.orgdyn.2015.05.008

Rothman, L. S., Gordon, I. E., Babikov, Y., Barbe, A., Benner, D. C., Bernath, P. F., Birk, M., Bizzocchi, L., Boudon, V., & Brown, L. R. (2013). The HITRAN2012 molecular spectroscopic database. *Journal of Quantitative Spectroscopy & Radiative Transfer*, *130*, 4–50. doi:10.1016/j.jqsrt.2013.07.002

Santana, M., & Díaz-Fernández, M. (2023). Competencies for the artificial intelligence age: Visualisation of the state of the art and future perspectives. *Review of Managerial Science*, *17*(6), 1971–2004. doi:10.1007/s11846-022-00613-w

Simón, C., & Ferreiro, E. (2018). Workforce analytics: A case study of scholar–practitioner collaboration. *Human Resource Management*, *57*(3), 781–793. doi:10.1002/hrm.21853

Solomon, M., Russell-Bennett, R., & Previte, J. (2012). *Consumer behaviour*. Pearson Higher Education AU.

Sypniewska, B., Baran, M., & Kłos, M. (2023). Work engagement and employee satisfaction in the practice of sustainable human resource management–based on the study of Polish employees. *The International Entrepreneurship and Management Journal*, *19*(3), 1069–1100. doi:10.1007/s11365-023-00834-9

Tursunbayeva, A., Di Lauro, S., & Pagliari, C. (2018). People analytics—A scoping review of conceptual boundaries and value propositions. *International Journal of Information Management*, *43*, 224–247. doi:10.1016/j.ijinfomgt.2018.08.002

Viglia, G., Pera, R., Dyussembayeva, S., Mifsud, M., & Hollebeek, L. D. (2023). Engagement and value cocreation within a multi-stakeholder service ecosystem. *Journal of Business Research*, *157*, 113584. doi:10.1016/j.jbusres.2022.113584

Yahia, N. B., Hlel, J., & Colomo-Palacios, R. (2021). From big data to deep data to support people analytics for employee attrition prediction. *IEEE Access : Practical Innovations, Open Solutions*, *9*, 60447–60458. doi:10.1109/ACCESS.2021.3074559

Chapter 12
Navigating HR Industry 5.0: Seizing Opportunities and Confronting Challenges

Rishi Shukla
https://orcid.org/0000-0003-0854-7302
Chitkara University, India

Sanjay Taneja
https://orcid.org/0000-0002-3632-4053
Graphic Era University, India

Shefali Saluja
https://orcid.org/0000-0002-8560-5150
Chitkara University, India

Ravi Kumar Jain
https://orcid.org/0000-0001-9912-8730
Sparsh Global, India

ABSTRACT

In HR Industry 5.0, the strategic HR value chain model aligns HR practices with organizational goals, emphasizing measurable outcomes, continuous improvement, and a people-centric approach. Leveraging strategic alignment and technological integration, organizations optimize talent acquisition, learning and development, performance management, and total rewards to drive sustainable growth. By prioritizing employee well-being, engagement, and development, organizations foster a positive workplace culture conducive to innovation and success in the digital age. The model offers a roadmap for navigating HR Industry 5.0, enabling organizations to seize opportunities and confront challenges in the dynamic landscape of modern business.

I. INTRODUCTION

In the ever-transforming landscape of human resources (HR), we stand at the precipice of HR Industry 5.0—a phase characterized by a convergence of cutting-edge technologies, globalization, and an unwavering focus on human-centric approaches. As we embark on this journey, it becomes imperative to comprehend the international projection of HR Industry 5.0, deciphering the plethora of opportunities and challenges it presents to organizations worldwide. This introduction serves as a gateway to our exploration, laying the groundwork for a comprehensive understanding of the intricacies and nuances inherent in this paradigm shift.

DOI: 10.4018/979-8-3693-1343-5.ch012

The Evolution of HR: A Brief Overview

Human resources, once perceived as a transactional function primarily concerned with administrative tasks and compliance, has undergone a remarkable evolution over the decades. From Personnel Management in the early 20th century to Human Resource Management (HRM) in the latter half, organizations have gradually recognized the strategic importance of their workforce. The advent of HR Industry 4.0 marked a pivotal moment, characterized by the integration of digital technologies such as Artificial Intelligence (AI), data analytics, and automation into HR practices. This digital transformation revolutionized talent acquisition, performance management, and employee engagement, paving the way for HR Industry 5.0.

HR Industry 5.0: The Nexus of Technology and Humanity

HR Industry 5.0 represents a fusion of advanced technologies with a renewed emphasis on human-centric approaches. At its core lies the recognition that technology should serve to augment—not replace—human capabilities, fostering a symbiotic relationship between man and machine. In this era, HR professionals harness the power of AI and predictive analytics to make data-driven decisions, optimize workforce productivity, and personalize employee experiences. Simultaneously, they prioritize empathy, emotional intelligence, and employee well-being, acknowledging that the human element remains indispensable in fostering innovation and driving organizational success.

The Importance of International Projection in HR

As organizations operate in an increasingly interconnected global economy, the significance of international projection in HR cannot be overstated. Multinational corporations navigate diverse cultural landscapes, regulatory frameworks, and talent pools, necessitating HR practices that transcend geographical boundaries. Whether expanding operations overseas, managing remote teams across continents, or fostering diversity and inclusion in multicultural workplaces (Iverson, 1996; Keir, 2016), HR professionals must adeptly navigate the complexities of global business environments. Moreover, in a world where talent knows no borders, organizations compete not only for market share but also for the best minds from around the globe.

II. INTERNATIONAL PROJECTION OF HR INDUSTRY 5.0

A. Globalization and Its Impact on HR Practices

The process of globalization has reshaped the business landscape, facilitating the expansion of organizations across borders and fostering unprecedented levels of interconnectedness. In this context, HR practices have had to adapt to the challenges and opportunities posed by operating in diverse cultural, regulatory, and economic environments. Globalization has not only increased the complexity of managing international workforces but has also necessitated a shift towards more standardized yet adaptable HR practices. As organizations expand their operations globally, they encounter a myriad of challenges ranging from differences in labor laws and cultural norms to variations in workforce demographics and talent expectations (Department of Personnel and Training, 2009; Hasan, Jawaad, & Butt, 2021; Soythong,

2023). For instance, a company based in the United States seeking to establish a presence in Asia must navigate cultural nuances in communication styles, hierarchical structures, and attitudes towards work-life balance. HR professionals play a critical role in facilitating this transition by designing policies and practices that accommodate local customs while aligning with overarching organizational goals.

Moreover, globalization has led to the emergence of virtual teams comprising members from diverse geographical locations. Managing such dispersed teams requires specialized HR strategies, including the implementation of virtual collaboration tools, cross-cultural training programs, and effective communication channels. HR Industry 5.0 emphasizes the importance of leveraging technology to overcome geographical barriers and foster collaboration, innovation, and knowledge sharing among remote teams.

B. Importance of Cultural Sensitivity in Multinational Corporations

Cultural sensitivity lies at the heart of successful HR management in multinational corporations (MNCs). Cultural differences impact various aspects of HR, including recruitment and selection, performance management, training and development, and employee relations. Failure to acknowledge and respect these differences can lead to misunderstandings, conflicts, and ultimately, decreased organizational effectiveness. MNCs must invest in cultural competency training for HR professionals and employees alike to navigate the complexities of working in diverse cultural contexts. This involves developing an understanding of cultural dimensions such as individualism vs. collectivism, power distance, uncertainty avoidance, and long-term vs. short-term orientation (Cartwright & Holmes, 2006; Reio & Ghosh, 2009). By fostering cultural intelligence, organizations can bridge cultural divides, promote inclusivity, and build cohesive multinational teams.

C. Adoption of HR Technologies on a Global Scale

The adoption of HR technologies has revolutionized the way organizations manage their global workforce. From cloud-based HRIS (Human Resource Information Systems) and talent management platforms to AI-driven recruitment tools and virtual reality-based training simulations, HR Industry 5.0 is characterized by a proliferation of innovative technologies aimed at enhancing HR efficiency, effectiveness, and employee experience (Bakker & Bakker, 2011; Brodie, Hollebeek, Jurić, & Ilić, 2011; H. M. MAHFUZUR RAHMAN et al., 2023; Hasan et al., 2021; Henson & Reardon, 2005; Lum, Kervin, Clark, Reid, & Sirola, 1998).

For multinational corporations, HR technologies offer several benefits, including centralized data management, real-time analytics, and automation of repetitive tasks (Madsen, Miller, & John, 2005). These technologies enable HR professionals to streamline processes, make data-driven decisions, and allocate resources more strategically across global operations. Furthermore, they facilitate seamless communication and collaboration among geographically dispersed teams, driving productivity and innovation.

However, the adoption of HR technologies also poses challenges, particularly concerning data privacy, security, and compliance with local regulations. MNCs must navigate these complexities by implementing robust data protection measures, ensuring transparency in data handling practices, and conducting regular audits to mitigate risks associated with data breaches and regulatory non-compliance.

In summary, the international projection of HR Industry 5.0 is characterized by the impact of globalization, the importance of cultural sensitivity, and the widespread adoption of HR technologies. In the following sections, we will delve deeper into these themes through a series of case studies that illustrate best practices and lessons learned in managing HR in a global context. Through these case studies, we aim to provide actionable insights that HR professionals can leverage to navigate the complexities of HR Industry 5.0 effectively.

III. CASE STUDIES

In this section, we will delve into case studies that exemplify best practices and challenges faced in navigating HR Industry 5.0 on an international scale. These case studies are hypothetical but serve as illustrative examples of organizations grappling with the complexities of global HR management, providing valuable insights into the strategies employed to seize opportunities and confront challenges.

1. Company A: Bridging Cultural Divide

Overview: Company A, a technology firm based in Silicon Valley, embarked on an ambitious expansion plan to establish a presence in China. Recognizing the importance of cultural integration in achieving success in the Chinese market, Company A devised comprehensive strategies to bridge the cultural divide between its American and Chinese employees.

Challenges: The expansion presented numerous challenges, including differences in communication styles, work ethics, and business practices between the two cultures. Company A faced resistance from Chinese employees who perceived American management styles as too hierarchical and individualistic. Additionally, navigating the intricacies of Chinese regulatory frameworks and business customs posed logistical challenges.

Strategies: Company A implemented cross-cultural training programs for employees from both regions, focusing on building cultural awareness, empathy, and effective communication skills. They also established mentorship programs pairing American and Chinese employees to facilitate knowledge exchange and mutual understanding. Furthermore, Company A adapted its business practices to align with Chinese cultural norms, emphasizing teamwork, harmony, and relationship-building in decision-making processes.

Outcomes: Through these initiatives, Company A successfully bridged the cultural divide and fostered a collaborative work environment conducive to innovation and growth. The cross-cultural training programs improved intercultural communication and reduced misunderstandings between American and Chinese employees. As a result, Company A achieved significant market penetration in China, establishing itself as a respected player in the local technology industry.

Key Takeaways: This case study highlights the importance of cultural sensitivity and adaptation in international HR management. By investing in cross-cultural training and fostering a culture of inclusivity, organizations can overcome cultural barriers and leverage diversity as a source of competitive advantage in global markets.

2. Company B: Leveraging Remote Work

Overview: Company B, a European financial institution, faced unprecedented challenges during the COVID-19 pandemic as lockdown measures forced employees to work remotely. In response, Company

B embraced remote work as a long-term strategy, leveraging HR technologies to facilitate virtual collaboration and maintain business continuity across its global operations.

Challenges: The sudden transition to remote work posed significant challenges, including adapting to new ways of working, maintaining team cohesion, and ensuring employee well-being in a virtual environment. Company B also faced technical challenges related to infrastructure readiness, cybersecurity, and data privacy concerns.

Strategies: Company B swiftly implemented remote work policies and provided employees with the necessary tools and resources to work effectively from home. They leveraged HR technologies such as video conferencing platforms, project management tools, and virtual collaboration software to facilitate seamless communication and collaboration among remote teams. Additionally, Company B prioritized employee well-being by offering virtual wellness programs, mental health resources, and flexible work arrangements to support employees during these challenging times.

Outcomes: The adoption of remote work practices enabled Company B to maintain business operations while safeguarding the health and safety of its employees. Employee productivity remained high, and collaboration among remote teams improved significantly. Moreover, the flexibility afforded by remote work arrangements allowed Company B to tap into a broader talent pool, enabling them to attract and retain top talent from around the world.

Key Takeaways: This case study underscores the importance of agility and adaptability in responding to crises and embracing new ways of working. By leveraging HR technologies and prioritizing employee well-being, organizations can successfully navigate challenges such as remote work and emerge stronger and more resilient in the face of adversity.

3. Company C: Enhancing Diversity and Inclusion

Overview: Company C, a multinational retail giant, recognized the strategic importance of diversity and inclusion (D&I) in driving innovation, fostering creativity, and enhancing organizational performance. They embarked on a journey to embed D&I principles into their HR practices across global subsidiaries.

Challenges: Despite espousing a commitment to diversity and inclusion, Company C faced challenges in translating these values into actionable initiatives across diverse cultural contexts. Differences in societal attitudes towards diversity, gender equality, and minority representation posed hurdles in achieving meaningful progress in D&I initiatives.

Strategies: Company C developed a comprehensive D&I strategy that encompassed recruitment and hiring practices, leadership development programs, and employee resource groups. They implemented unconscious bias training for hiring managers and established diversity quotas to ensure representation at all levels of the organization. Additionally, Company C fostered a culture of inclusivity by promoting open dialogue, celebrating diverse perspectives, and creating safe spaces for employees to voice their opinions and experiences.

Outcomes: Through these efforts, Company C significantly enhanced diversity and inclusion within its workforce, leading to improved employee engagement, retention, and performance. The implementation of diversity quotas resulted in a more representative leadership team, reflecting the diverse makeup of their customer base. Moreover, Company C's commitment to D&I positioned them as an employer of choice, attracting top talent from diverse backgrounds and driving innovation and creativity across the organization.

Key Takeaways: This case study underscores the strategic imperative of diversity and inclusion in fostering a culture of innovation and driving organizational success. By embedding D&I principles into HR practices, organizations can leverage diversity as a source of competitive advantage and create a more inclusive workplace where all employees feel valued, respected, and empowered to contribute their unique talents and perspectives.

4. Company D: Upskilling for the Future

Overview: Company D, a manufacturing conglomerate with operations in Asia and Europe, recognized the urgent need to upskill its workforce in response to rapid technological advancements and industry disruptions. They implemented proactive initiatives to equip employees with the digital skills needed to thrive in Industry 5.0.

Challenges: The traditional skill sets of Company D's workforce were becoming increasingly obsolete in the face of automation, robotics, and artificial intelligence. Moreover, resistance to change and a lack of awareness about the importance of upskilling posed challenges in gaining employee buy-in for the upskilling initiatives.

Strategies: Company D partnered with educational institutions, online learning platforms, and industry associations to develop customized training programs tailored to the needs of its workforce. They offered employees opportunities to acquire new skills through on-the-job training, workshops, and certification programs. Additionally, Company D provided financial incentives and career advancement opportunities to employees who demonstrated a commitment to continuous learning and professional development.

Outcomes: The upskilling initiatives led to a significant improvement in employee competencies, productivity, and job satisfaction. Employees embraced the opportunity to acquire new skills and adapt to evolving job roles, positioning themselves for career advancement and future-proofing their employability. Moreover, Company D's investment in upskilling enhanced its reputation as an employer that values employee development and fosters a culture of lifelong learning.

Key Takeaways: This case study highlights the importance of investing in employee development and upskilling to remain competitive in Industry 5.0. By empowering employees with the skills needed to thrive in a rapidly changing landscape, organizations can enhance their agility, innovation, and resilience, ensuring long-term success in the face of technological disruptions.

IV. THE IMPACT OF METAVERSE ON HR

The Metaverse, a virtual shared space where users interact with each other and digital objects in a computer-generated environment, is poised to revolutionize the future of work and HR practices. As technology continues to advance, the Metaverse presents both opportunities and challenges for HR professionals worldwide. In this section, we will explore the potential impact of the Metaverse on HR in the context of talent acquisition, employee engagement, and organizational culture.

A. Talent Acquisition in the Metaverse

The Metaverse offers HR professionals innovative ways to attract and recruit talent from around the globe. Virtual job fairs, career expos, and recruitment events hosted in the Metaverse provide organizations with a platform to showcase their employer brand and engage with potential candidates in immersive virtual environments. Job seekers can explore virtual job booths, interact with company representatives, and participate in virtual interviews—all from the comfort of their homes.

Moreover, the Metaverse enables organizations to assess candidates' skills and competencies through interactive simulations and virtual assessments. For example, companies can create virtual work environments where candidates can demonstrate their problem-solving abilities, teamwork skills, and creativity in real-time scenarios. By leveraging the Metaverse for talent acquisition, HR professionals can broaden their reach, reduce recruitment costs, and identify top talent more efficiently.

B. Employee Engagement in the Metaverse

In an era of remote work and distributed teams, the Metaverse offers HR professionals new opportunities to foster employee engagement and collaboration. Virtual offices and meeting spaces in the Metaverse provide employees with a digital environment where they can connect with colleagues, attend team meetings, and collaborate on projects in real-time. These virtual spaces can be customized to reflect the organization's culture and values, creating a sense of belonging and community among remote employees.

Furthermore, the Metaverse allows for immersive and interactive employee training and development programs. Instead of traditional classroom-style training sessions, employees can participate in virtual workshops, simulations, and role-playing exercises designed to enhance their skills and knowledge. By gamifying learning experiences and incorporating elements of virtual reality, HR professionals can create engaging and impactful training programs that resonate with employees.

C. Organizational Culture in the Metaverse

As organizations embrace the Metaverse, HR professionals must consider its implications for organizational culture and identity. Virtual work environments in the Metaverse may challenge traditional notions of workplace culture, requiring organizations to redefine their values, norms, and communication practices in a digital context. HR professionals play a crucial role in shaping and nurturing a positive and inclusive virtual culture that reflects the organization's core values and promotes collaboration and innovation.

Moreover, the Metaverse blurs the boundaries between work and leisure, raising questions about work-life balance and well-being. HR professionals must establish clear policies and guidelines to ensure that employees can disconnect and recharge outside of virtual work environments. Additionally, HR teams may need to provide support and resources to help employees navigate the challenges of virtual work, such as virtual fatigue and isolation.

In conclusion, the Metaverse holds immense potential to transform HR practices and the future of work. By embracing virtual recruitment methods, fostering employee engagement in virtual environments, and nurturing a positive virtual culture, HR professionals can harness the power of the Metaverse to drive organizational success in the digital age. However, they must also be mindful of the challenges and complexities inherent in virtual work and take proactive steps to address them. As the Metaverse continues to evolve, HR professionals must remain agile, innovative, and forward-thinking in their approach to HR management.

Strategic HR Value Chain Model

In the vibrant tapestry of modern business, it's the people who bring color, energy, and purpose to every organizational endeavor. Their talent, dedication, and creativity are the beating heart of success, propelling organizations forward in their quest for excellence. At the center of this human mosaic lies Human Resources (HR)—a vital force that cultivates, empowers, and celebrates the diverse talents and aspirations within an organization.

Enter the Strategic HR Value Chain Model—a compass guiding organizations on a journey of unlocking human potential, fostering growth, and nurturing a culture of fulfillment and achievement. This model is not just about processes and procedures; it's about the people—each one valued, supported, and encouraged to thrive.

Imagine a workplace where every employee feels not just a part of the team, but a cherished member of a close-knit family. Picture an environment where growth isn't just a corporate goal, but a shared journey of discovery and development. This is the promise of the Strategic HR Value Chain Model—a promise rooted in the belief that when people are at the forefront, success naturally follows.

1. Talent Acquisition and Deployment

Objective: Attract and deploy talent that aligns with organizational goals and values.

Measurable Metrics:

- Time-to-fill: Measure the time taken to fill open positions, indicating recruitment efficiency.
- Quality of hire: Assess the performance and fit of new hires against predefined criteria.
- Cost-per-hire: Calculate the cost incurred to recruit and onboard new employees.

2. Learning and Development

Objective: Develop employee skills and competencies to enhance performance and drive organizational growth.

Measurable Metrics:

- Training effectiveness: Evaluate the impact of training programs on employee performance and behavior.
- Skills proficiency: Assess employees' proficiency levels before and after training interventions.
- Return on investment (ROI) of training: Determine the financial impact of training initiatives on organizational outcomes.

3. Performance Management

Objective: Set clear performance expectations, provide regular feedback, and recognize and reward high performance.

Measurable Metrics:

- Key performance indicators (KPIs): Define and measure KPIs aligned with organizational goals and job roles.
- Performance ratings: Assess employee performance against predefined criteria and performance standards.
- Employee engagement scores: Measure employee engagement levels and correlation with performance ratings.

4. Total Rewards and Compensation

Objective: Design and implement competitive compensation and benefits packages to attract, retain, and motivate employees.

Measurable Metrics:

- Total compensation package: Calculate the total value of compensation and benefits provided to employees.
- Compensation competitiveness: Benchmark compensation levels against industry standards and competitors.
- Employee satisfaction with rewards: Measure employee satisfaction with compensation, benefits, and recognition programs.

5. Employee Engagement and Well-Being

Objective: Foster a positive work environment, promote employee engagement, and support employee well-being.

Measurable Metrics:

- Employee engagement survey results: Measure employee perceptions of job satisfaction, organizational commitment, and willingness to recommend the company as a great place to work.
- Employee turnover rate: Calculate the percentage of employees leaving the organization voluntarily.
- Health and wellness program participation: Track employee participation in health and wellness initiatives and programs.

6. HR Analytics and Insights

Objective: Utilize data analytics to gain insights into workforce trends, inform decision-making, and drive HR strategy.

Measurable Metrics:

- HR metrics dashboard: Monitor key HR metrics such as turnover rate, employee engagement scores, and recruitment metrics in real-time.
- Predictive analytics accuracy: Assess the accuracy of predictive models in forecasting workforce trends and future HR needs.
- Impact of HR initiatives: Measure the impact of HR interventions on organizational outcomes such as productivity, profitability, and customer satisfaction.

7. Strategic HR Alignment

Objective: Ensure alignment between HR practices and organizational goals to maximize organizational performance and effectiveness.

Measurable Metrics:

- HR alignment score: Assess the degree of alignment between HR strategies and organizational objectives based on key performance indicators.
- HR agility index: Measure HR's ability to respond quickly and effectively to changes in the business environment.
- Strategic HR contribution: Quantify the contribution of HR practices to achieving organizational goals and objectives.(See Table 1, Table 2, Table 3, Table 4, Table 5, Table 6)

The Strategic HR Value Chain Model provides a specialized and measurable framework for HR professionals to align HR practices with organizational objectives, measure outcomes at each stage of the HR value chain, and demonstrate the strategic impact of HR on organizational performance and effectiveness. By focusing on measurable metrics and outcomes, HR professionals can effectively evaluate the effectiveness of their HR practices and make data-driven decisions to drive organizational success. (See Table 1, Table 2, Table 3, Table 4, Table 5, Table 6).

Implementing the Strategic HR Value Chain Model requires a structured approach and collaboration across various functions within the organization. Here's a step-by-step guide on how an organization can implement this model effectively:

1. Assess Current State:
    - Conduct a comprehensive assessment of the organization's current HR practices, processes, and systems.
    - Identify strengths, weaknesses, opportunities, and threats (SWOT analysis) related to HR management.
    - Gather feedback from employees, managers, and key stakeholders to understand their perspectives on HR effectiveness and areas for improvement.
2. Define Organizational Objectives:
    - Align HR objectives with the organization's overall strategic goals and priorities.
    - Define key performance indicators (KPIs) and measurable outcomes that reflect the desired impact of HR practices on organizational success.
    - Ensure clarity and alignment of HR objectives with business objectives to drive strategic alignment and focus.
3. Design HR Value Chain:
    - Map out the HR value chain based on the Strategic HR Value Chain Model, identifying key stages and processes from talent acquisition to HR analytics.
    - Define the objectives, activities, and measurable metrics for each stage of the HR value chain.
    - Develop standardized processes, procedures, and guidelines to ensure consistency and effectiveness across HR functions.
4. Invest in Technology and Analytics:

- Invest in HR technologies and analytics tools that enable data-driven decision-making, monitoring, and evaluation of HR performance.
- Implement HRIS (Human Resource Information Systems), learning management systems, performance management tools, and analytics platforms to support HR processes and initiatives.
- Provide training and support to HR professionals on using technology and analytics tools effectively to drive HR performance and outcomes.

5. Develop Talent and Capability:
    - Invest in talent development and capability building for HR professionals to equip them with the skills, knowledge, and competencies required to implement the Strategic HR Value Chain Model.
    - Provide training, workshops, and certifications on HR best practices, strategic alignment, data analytics, and technology utilization.
    - Foster a culture of continuous learning, innovation, and collaboration within the HR team to drive excellence and effectiveness in HR management.
6. Implement Performance Management System:
    - Implement a robust performance management system that aligns individual and team goals with organizational objectives.
    - Define clear performance expectations, set SMART (Specific, Measurable, Achievable, Relevant, Time-bound) goals, and provide regular feedback and coaching to employees.
    - Evaluate employee performance based on predefined criteria and KPIs, recognizing and rewarding high performance and addressing performance gaps proactively.
7. Monitor, Evaluate, and Iterate:
    - Establish regular monitoring and evaluation mechanisms to track progress, measure outcomes, and identify areas for improvement.
    - Review HR metrics, analytics, and performance indicators regularly to assess the effectiveness of HR practices and initiatives.
    - Solicit feedback from employees, managers, and stakeholders to gather insights into HR performance and identify opportunities for enhancement.
    - Iterate and refine HR strategies, processes, and practices based on data-driven insights and feedback to drive continuous improvement and optimization.
8. Communicate and Engage:
    - Communicate HR objectives, initiatives, and outcomes transparently and effectively across the organization.
    - Engage employees, managers, and stakeholders in the HR transformation process, soliciting their input, participation, and support.
    - Foster open communication channels, feedback mechanisms, and forums for dialogue to ensure alignment, collaboration, and engagement in HR initiatives.

By following these steps and adopting a systematic approach, organizations can effectively implement the Strategic HR Value Chain Model, align HR practices with organizational objectives, and drive tangible results in terms of organizational performance, employee engagement, and HR effectiveness. Continuous monitoring, evaluation, and iteration are essential to ensure ongoing alignment and optimization of HR practices with evolving business needs and objectives.

CONCLUSION

In navigating the complexities of contemporary business landscapes, organizations are increasingly recognizing the pivotal role of Strategic Human Resource (HR) Management in driving sustainable growth and success. The implementation of the Strategic HR Value Chain Model underscores the transformative potential of aligning HR practices with organizational objectives, measuring outcomes at each stage of the HR value chain, and fostering a culture of continuous improvement and innovation. As we conclude this discourse on strategic HR management, it becomes evident that the strategic alignment of HR practices with organizational goals is not merely an aspiration but a fundamental imperative for organizations striving for excellence in the 21st-century global economy.

Strategic Alignment for Organizational Success

At the heart of the Strategic HR Value Chain Model lies the principle of strategic alignment, wherein HR practices are meticulously calibrated to support and advance organizational objectives. By defining clear performance expectations, setting measurable goals, and aligning HR initiatives with business priorities, organizations can enhance their agility, resilience, and competitiveness in dynamic and ever-evolving markets. The Strategic HR Value Chain serves as a blueprint for translating strategic intent into tangible HR actions, thereby maximizing organizational success.

Measurable Outcomes and Data-Driven Decision-Making

Central to the effectiveness of the Strategic HR Value Chain Model is the emphasis on measurable outcomes and data-driven decision-making. By adopting a systematic approach to HR management and leveraging HR analytics tools and techniques, organizations can gain actionable insights into workforce trends, performance metrics, and HR effectiveness. The implementation of HR metrics dashboards, predictive analytics models, and impact assessment methodologies enables HR professionals to monitor progress, identify areas for improvement, and make informed decisions to optimize HR strategies and practices.

Continuous Improvement and Innovation

In today's dynamic and competitive business environment, the pursuit of excellence is an ongoing journey rather than a destination. The Strategic HR Value Chain Model embodies a culture of continuous improvement and innovation, wherein HR practices are iteratively refined and enhanced to adapt to changing business needs and emerging trends. By fostering a culture of learning, experimentation, and collaboration, organizations can unleash the full potential of their HR function, drive innovation, and achieve sustained success in the long term.

Human-Centric Approach to HR Management

Amidst the rapid advancements in technology and automation, the Strategic HR Value Chain Model underscores the enduring importance of the human element in HR management. Beyond the metrics and analytics, HR professionals must uphold a human-centric approach that values empathy, inclusivity, and employee well-being. By prioritizing employee engagement, development, and satisfaction, organizations can cultivate a positive workplace culture that attracts top talent, fosters innovation, and nurtures high-performing teams.

Looking Ahead

As we reflect on the strategic imperatives outlined in the Strategic HR Value Chain Model, it becomes apparent that the future of HR management lies in its ability to evolve, adapt, and innovate in response to emerging challenges and opportunities. The strategic alignment of HR practices with organizational objectives, the emphasis on measurable outcomes and data-driven decision-making, the commitment to continuous improvement and innovation, and the human-centric approach to HR management will continue to guide organizations on their quest for excellence in the digital age.

In conclusion, the Strategic HR Value Chain Model serves as a guiding framework for organizations seeking to optimize their HR practices and maximize their impact on organizational success. By embracing strategic HR management principles, organizations can unlock the full potential of their workforce, drive innovation, and achieve sustainable growth and prosperity in an increasingly competitive and dynamic business environment.

REFERENCES

Bakker, A. B., & Bakker, A. B. (2011). An Evidence-Based Model of Work Engagement. *Current Directions in Psychological Science*, *20*(4), 265–269. Advance online publication. doi:10.1177/0963721411414534

Brodie, R. J., Hollebeek, L. D., Jurić, B., & Ilić, A. (2011). Customer engagement: Conceptual domain, fundamental propositions, and implications for research. *Journal of Service Research*, *14*(3), 252–271. doi:10.1177/1094670511411703

Cartwright, S., & Holmes, N. (2006). The meaning of work : The challenge of regaining employee engagement and reducing cynicism. doi:10.1016/j.hrmr.2006.03.012

Department of Personnel and Training. (2009). 6th Pay Commission, (11016), No.11016/2/2008-AIS-1I. Retrieved from https://ccis.nic.in/WriteReadData/CircularPortal/D2/D02ser/11016_2_2008-AIS-II.pdf

Hasan, T., Jawaad, M., & Butt, I. (2021). The influence of person–job fit, work–life balance, and work conditions on organizational commitment: Investigating the mediation of job satisfaction in the private sector of the emerging market. *Sustainability (Basel)*, *13*(12), 6622. Advance online publication. doi:10.3390/su13126622

Henson, S., & Reardon, T. (2005). Private agri-food standards: Implications for food policy and the agri-food system. *Food Policy*, *30*(3), 241–253. Advance online publication. doi:10.1016/j.foodpol.2005.05.002

Iverson, R. D. (1996). Employee acceptance of organizational change: The role of organizational commitment. *International Journal of Human Resource Management*, *7*(1), 122–149. Advance online publication. doi:10.1080/09585199600000121

Keir, M. Y. A. (2016). Staff Perceptions of how Human Resource Management Practices influence Organisational Performance: Mediating roles of Organisational Culture, Employees'. *Commitment and Employee Retention in Bahrain Private Universities*, (June), 1–241.

Lum, L., Kervin, J., Clark, K., Reid, F., & Sirola, W. (1998). Explaining nursing turnover intent: Job satisfaction, pay satisfaction, or organizational commitment? *Journal of Organizational Behavior*, *19*(3), 305–320. doi:10.1002/(SICI)1099-1379(199805)19:3<305::AID-JOB843>3.0.CO;2-N

Madsen, S. R., Miller, D., & John, C. R. (2005). Readiness for organizational change: Do organizational commitment and social relationships in the workplace make a difference? *Human Resource Development Quarterly*, *16*(2), 213–234. doi:10.1002/hrdq.1134

Reio, T., & Ghosh, R. (2009). Antecedents and Outcomes of Workplace Incivility. *Computational Complexity*, *2*(1), 1–9. doi:10.1002/hrdq

Soythong, K. (2023). The Effect of Quality of Work Life and Organizational Commitment to Employee Performance: A Case Study of Transportation Business in Nakhon Phanom Province of Thailand. Academic Press.

Chapter 13
Role of Industry 5.0 in Bancassurance: A Theoretical Perspective

Diksha Verma
Chandigarh Business School of Administration, Chandigarh Group of Colleges, India

Pooja Kansra
https://orcid.org/0000-0003-2229-0662
Lovely Professional University, India

Pawan Kumar
Lovely Professional University, India

ABSTRACT

The insurance companies cannot target every customer for selling insurance products as it is not possible for them to target customers at grand level, but banks can reach every customer even in rural or remote areas as well. Therefore, bancassurance as a mode of distribution is an approved and accepted method by all institutions nowadays along with Industry 5.0 concept which has relatively become new trend. Although various studies are available related to bancassurance, there is less discussion on bancassurance along with Industry 5.0. Because digital banking is quite a new concept and especially Industry 5.0 adopted by banks nowadays is an emerging concept therefore association of Industry 5.0 with bancassurance and their implications have been addressed in the present study. The present study will help to provide a comprehensive view of the role of Industry 5.0 in bancassurance and will be helpful to the bankers, government, policymakers, and researchers.

INTRODUCTION

The Indian insurance sector has come a long way in terms of growth and development since the time when insurance businesses were regulated by the public sector (Radhika, 2012; Mannar, 2015). Insurance

DOI: 10.4018/979-8-3693-1343-5.ch013

industry has relied on the public sector for a longer duration and has witnessed sluggish and uneven progress for those many years (Turkyilmaz et al., 2011; Pillai and Arumugan, 2023). A committee was made under the chairmanship of R.N. Malhotra in 1994 to examine the market conditions and implement the participation of private sector in insurance arena. It was found from the committee that only 22 percent were availing insurance and the rest were uninsured out of total strength of the country (Newar, 2013; Kumar, 2016; Agarwal, 2019). Various steps were initiated for improving insurance penetration among customers and also to accelerate the efficiency of insurers for overall growth of the industry (Mohamed et al., 2015). Thereafter, on the recommendations of IRDA in 1999 a bill was approved to reduce the restrictions and to allow the foreign players to enter Indian boundaries (Sinha, 2005; Kumaraswamy, 2012; Bhushan and Murtaza, 2014). More than 200 years old Indian insurance industry has witnessed several ups and downs (Shah and Chugan, 2018). The insurance industry has experienced considerable growth in terms of registered insurers, insurance premiums, number of policies and claims, etc. since its inception.

Insurance Sector in India

Insurance penetration and density are significant indicators of growth and development of insurance in the country (Rakshit, 2017; Shukla, 2018; Vimala and Alamelu, 2018). Nevertheless, rapid growth has been observed in the number of registered insurers and premiums underwritten (IRDA Annual Report, 2021-22) still, the penetration of insurance products amid the citizens of India is quite less. Irrespective of the extraordinary efforts for promotion of insurance in India like Jan-Dhan-AadharMobile policies, the nation has not performed well in this area. Various insurance schemes run by Indian Government including Atal Pension Scheme and other schemes by the name of Pradhan Mantri have been introduced by the government in recent years but the level of penetration is only 4.2 percent in comparison to a global penetration rate of 7.5 percent (Cafemutual, 2023). Insurance penetration in India was 4.2 percent in the year 2021-22 which was same as the previous year's penetration of 2020-21 which means no growth was reported in the year 2021-22 in penetration level. Globally if compared, as per 2021-22 survey, India was ranked at 27th position in terms of insurance penetration (IRDA Annual Report, 2021-22). Fortunately, the insurance density of India has shown consistent growth from 2001-02 to 2021-22 and globally India was ranked at 28th position in terms of density (IRDA Annual Report, 2021-22). Both of these metrics indorse that in both the terms discussed above Indian insurance sector is far behind other nations of the globe thus, even after so many years of its inception, future scope for development and growth is existing.

Bancassurance in India

The Indian banking system with major banking networks in the world has experienced a series of restructurings in the past years such as disinvestment by government in public sector banks, deregulation of interest rates, intense participation of private sector in banking industry (Kohli, 1999; Choudhury, 2007; Sawant, 2011; Anbalagan, 2017). There was a time when General Bank of India and the Bank of Hindustan were the only banks in country, however, both of them are now defunct (Nippatlapalli, 2013; Jadoun, 2015; Krishna, 2015). Later on, State Bank of India along with other banks came into presence which was earlier named as Bank of Bengal (Aravind and Nagamani, 2013; Maity and Sahu, 2017). In 1947, the RBI was authorized with comprehensive powers and authorities to regulate Indian commercial banks. Thereafter, it was observed that the quality of assets and capital competence provided by Indian banks became quite smooth and transparent in comparison to other countries (Lymberpoulos et al., 2004; Grover and Bhalla, 2013; Kaur and Kaur, 2022).

Currently, there are more than 1,20,000 bank branches in India. Banks with their persistent reach to metro and non-metro places make it possible for them to not only target the urban sector of nation but also consider all other sectors like rural sector or semi-urban sector. (Sinha, 2005; Karunagaran, 2006; Rajkumari, 2007) Still, penetrating the population through insurance has been an issue of concern in India (Nagaraja, 2015; Radhika and Satuluri, 2019; Routh et al., 2022). The decision of universalization of banking operations in India announced by the Narsimham Committee and the Khan Committee resulted in transforming both types of banks from traditional culture of earnings from accepting and depositing of funds to offering several products to their existing customers through its dispersed branches (Banerjee, 2009; Pal, 2013; Abey, 2016).

According to Economic Survey (2022) the rate of penetration of insurance in India is 4.2 percent which is low in comparison to the global average penetration of 7.5 percent. The share of contribution of bancassurance in health insurance was only 9 percent and share of individual agents was 35 percent which was very high if compared with contribution of bancassurance (IRDA Reports, 2021; Malti, 2022; Patnaik, 2022). Although the premium collection percentage was 4 percent but number of policies sold in the year has increased by more than 32 percent in the year 2021 in comparison to 2022 (Malti, 2022; IRDA Report 2021-22). If Indian Banks are considered, they are 1,20,000 in number constituting 65 percent of investments from households thus declaring it as the country of extreme opportunities for insurance companies to target customers (Muthumari & Pushpaveni, 2017).

After the entry of private as well as foreign banking companies with their innovative omni channels in banking sector, customers have become more demanding in terms of their services (Raghavan and Pai, 2021). Therefore, banks need to offer their goods and services in a way to approach customers more attractively (Wenninger, 2000; Temelkov, 2018). When several products are offered to the customers under one roof, it subsequently converts a branch into a wonderful destination for financial services for its customers (Karunagaran, 2006; Kumaraswamy, 2012). To compete in the market, banks are diversifying their services from earning interest income from lending and borrowing to inclusion of more dynamic and competitive offerings like underwriting of shares, equities, leasing, financing etc. (Karungaran, 2006; Hatt et al., 2018; Jing et al., 2021). Therefore, providing insurance is an additional service like various other services that is a natural consequence and is also acceptable by bankers as well as insurers (Saidenberg and Strahan, 1999; Block et al., 2008).

Industry 5.0 and Bancassurance

Banks mostly prefer selling their products through multiple channels rather than just focusing on selling through their branch (Tjioe, 2019). Due to innovations in technology and introduction of new alternatives, banks are also trying to focus on advancement in serving their same services that is what known as industry 5.0 (Komulainen and Makkonen, 2018). There is a complete shift from the previous banking system which was followed pre-nationalization (1969) to the system followed nowadays (Hamouda, 2019). The customer of a bank has now become a 'customer of the banking system'. Banks in the coming time will have to focus more on digital marketing, applications on mobile phones, social media platforms, etc. (Hamouda, Manel, 2019). Banking customers are much more exposed to digital experience by introduction of new and innovative financial products. Digitalization of channels of distribution of banking services has led to availability of different alternatives for the customers but on the other hand, it has led to challenges that are witnessed by the bankers. An information system is a way out of this which has helped in dealing with different multi and omnichannel scenarios (Pavlovski, 2013; Schmidt et al., 2016).

REVIEW OF LITERATURE

The transmuting pecuniary environment of the country has resulted in an impulsive change in the Indian Financial Industry (Sharma and Gupta, 2020). Financial organizations have started preferring strategic alliances and bancassurance is one such alliance across the gamut (Thalassinos, 2008). The major notion for combining banking and insurance services is to join the production and selling part for improved results (Ilona and Renata, 2009; Gujral, 2018). As per the report of Internet and Mobile Association of India, the contribution of bancassurance in India has augmented to 56 percent in 2019 from 27 percent in 2011 whereas the contribution of sales of insurance through the agency channel has declined to 24 percent from 42 percent in the same duration. Before COVID-19, Indian insurance companies started relying on bancassurance for increasing sales but later on slowed down due to the online pitching of customers for insurance by banks (Sengupta, 2021).

For increasing Indian insurance penetration, banking sector plays an important role (Kumaraswamy, 2012; Pani and Swain, 2013, Pallavi and Rai, 2018). There are 200 million middle-class people in the country. If this huge population is amalgamated with large banking networks in India, bancassurance can give fruitful results (Gupta 2006; Bala and Verma, 2012). Customers now are more agile towards their investment decisions considering various factors like tax reverts, easiness, accessibility, convenience etc. (Bawa and Bhagat, 2015). Before the introduction of IRDA Act, 1999 in India, the bancassurance term was quite unheard (Samal, 2019; Sadana and Kaur, 2023). However, after breaking the conservative norms of distribution of insurance and other financial services (Fan and Cheng, 2011; Bala and Verma, 2012 and Kumar, 2014) bankers, as well as insurers are preferring bancassurance in comparison to other channels of distribution for fetching customers and increasing the insurance penetration of the market (Popli and Rao, 2009; Grover and Bhalla, 2013).

A strong financial system with proper accessibility to financing products and services is required for the growth of a nation. Despite having more than 1.2 lakh branches of banks in Indian market, insurance penetration and density is quite low (Mishra, 2012; IRDA Annual Report, 2022; Jain, 2018). If average insurance density in India is compared with other developing countries, it stands at a low position. Although in recent years it has dramatically increased still it is far behind the ranking of developed nations (Pani & Swain, 2013). The penetration percentage of insurance in India is 3.7 percent of GDP in comparison to 6.31 percent of world's average level of insurance penetration (Sharma, 2021). However, other regions like China, Malaysia and Thailand have much higher penetration with 4.77 percent, 4.77 percent and 5.42 percent respectively (ASSOCHAM, 2021). The demand for insurance products is not a big concern as there is a huge market in India to conquer but making those customers buy insurance through banks is a big challenge (Dua et al., 2019).

Nowadays only insurance agent is not enough for selling insurance products and a strong method of distribution is required so that penetration level of insurance can be increased (Popli and Rao, 2009). The insurance companies cannot target every customer for selling insurance products as it is not possible for them at grand level but banks however can reach majority of customers in rural or remote areas. Therefore, bancassurance as a mode of distribution is an approved and accepted method by all 13 institutions nowadays (Pani and Swain, 2013). Due to large networks of banks with huge numbers of branches all over India, it becomes little convincing for bankers to reach their customers and motivating them to buy insurance through banks only and not by insurance agents. Banks have easy access to the database of their customers which makes it easy to advertise the products related to insurance in a very personalized and pertinent way (Bansal and Kanwal, 2018; Joshi, 2019). Due to the current dynamics of banking sector, high level of competition, etc. cost optimization for banks is required. The best method applicable in such a case may be adoption of digital channels and also to use proper administration for bancassurance. A large number of processes needed to be planned and automated when using 5.0 approach, both for banking companies as well as insurance companies also significant capital expenditure for expansion of software is required (Vasiliev, 2019; Ameen et al., 2021).

Bancassurance: It's Time to Go Digital

The world has transformed towards digitalization and there is no doubt in it. In this, era where existing as well as potential customers are interacting with digital platforms, insurance companies have the opportunities to use the widened data of endless customers. Dynamic life insurance products available with the companies are performing well in industry 5.0 where digital services are combined seamlessly with personal touch of human. The example is omni channel banking which is a business model where in which a customer can begin a service through one mode and end the same eservice through another mode. The most common example of this could be availing a loan service through bank using mobile application of particular bank and completing the required formalities in branch of the bank. The perfect omni channel banking provide synchronization in real-time between physical and digital services in which one person can start the service through one-point ad finish the same service through different point. The concept of bancassurance has been in world since last 40 years and successfully growing to reach new heights. Banks and insurance companies have adopted bancassurance effectively and trying to modify the services in better manner. Therefore, digitalization of bancassurance service is a new addition for improvement of services. Customers have started preferring digital services provided by banks and banking and insurance companies also have responded to the preferences of customers (Deshmukh, 2021). COVID-19 pandemic has been an amplifier for the banks to increase the sales of insurance that especially through digital mode. Almost all banks have adopted the concept of bancassurance through digital mode. The main requirements banks are fulfilling to adopt bancassurance in their companies involve

Moving Sales Towards Digital Platforms

Converting potential customers in to actual customers requires companies to totally overhaul the sales channel. The elimination of manual endorsing proves to be fruitful for the banks. Banks provide the forms to clients through digital platforms on which few of the information is prefilled that facilitate the customers and encourage them to fill the blanks quickly. Digital platforms are much convenient for the clients as well as bankers because both the parties become beneficiary of omnichannel approach.

Amplifying Personal Touch

Digital bancassurance channels have great scope for future. Banks have the ability to verify their client's tastes and preferences and also their money spending which allow banks to analyze the data of their customers and offer them personalized services. Banks use text messages, social media and other

Figure 1. Prerequisites of Industry 5.0 in bancassurance
Source: Author's Compilation

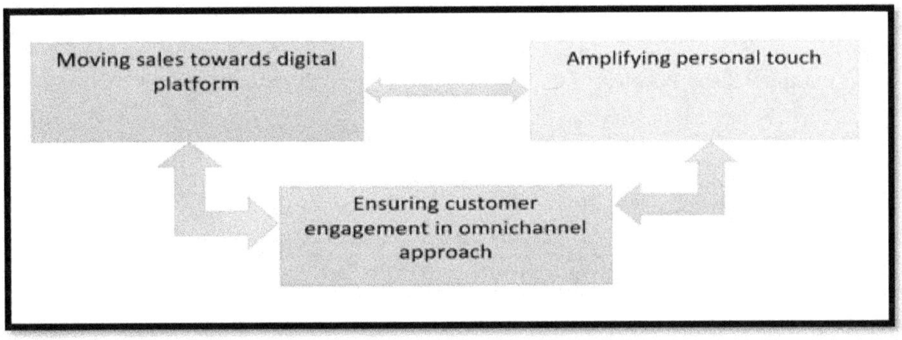

applications to personally target their customers for offering insurance services which make clients to take interest in that particular service. Ultimately it ca help the banks to sell more of their insurance services to their clients.

Ensuring Customer Engagement

For increasing sales of bancassurance, the most important that can be used by banks is industry 5.0 through omni channel approach. The foremost requirement is to enable sales with the help of mobile phones using applications, online websites which are safe and secure. While adopting omni channel for bancassurance, banks should keep in consideration that last point of completing any service should be at bank's branch. Client must visit the branch for availing insurance service that can be for any step whether initiating the service or finishing the same. Providing whole of the service through one mode will not fulfil the requirements of omni channel therefore, banks while providing bancassurance must take in to consideration all the channels applicable in omni channel to make the transaction successful.

Benefits of Industry 5.0 in Bancassurance

The concept of digital bancassurance is not that new in fact, it has already established its roots for providing the services to its customers with the help of block chain as well as omni channels. For other services like pension facility etc., also, digitalization of bancassurance is playing a vital role. Bancassurance on the other hand is witnessing growth year by year in both life as well as non-life insurance products with the help of digitalization and applicability of omni channels. However, there is some low percentage of banks which is not ready to adapt the change of digitalization for bancassurance. applicability of omni channel in bancassurance has definitely resulted in growth of sales of bancassurance over the years. A report by McKensy, 2019 stated that 118 banks in the whole world use digital bancassurance channels in which 19 percent share is for non-life insurance products and only 2 percent is for life insurance products. Globally banks have made bancassurance a recognizable product. The benefits of adopting omni channels in bancassurance have been discussed below to comprehend the theoretical perspective of concept.

Figure 2. Benefits of Industry 5.0 in bancassurance
Source: Author's Compilation

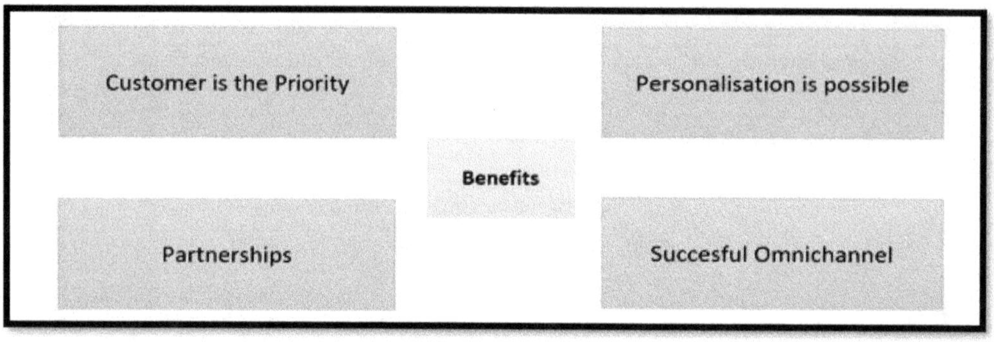

Customer Is the Priority

Customers are always the lifeline of banks and for providing any service to them bankers should always be on their toes. For providing bancassurance service to their customers, bankers always focus on customer-centric approach. Bancassurers always have offers and great services to serve their customers. Banks and insurance companies work together to provide customized products to their customers through physical as well as digital mode. Therefore, banks and insurance companies both are in position to grow with the help of digitalization.

Personalization Is Possible

Banks have the privilege of client's data in bulk because of providing other services to them. Thus, banks have the potential to personalize and customize their services to the customers because of their wide reach. Banks provide offers and services to their customers which are actually demanded by them according to their needs and preferences. Bankers personally approach the customers and provide relevant offers to them which are their requirements even if customers registered their preference through online channel, bankers have the opportunity to convert that potential preference into actual transaction at bank's branch through physical interaction.

Partnerships

As ecosystem transforms traditional practices of providing services, bancassurance was not that much old to adapt changes. It adopted the concept of omnichannel in bancassurance very smoothly that the partnership of bancassurance and omni channel is perceiving growth in the recent years. By proposing same service of bancassurance to the customers 24*7 through physical and digital mode have observed growth in the sales of bancassurance for both life as well as non-life insurance products. Partnership of bancassurance service with block chain technology and omni channel have seen growth in the recent years.

Successful Omnichannel in Industry 5.0

The concept of omni channel is quite different from the concept of multiple channels. Multichannel is an approach of providing same service to banks through different channels and omni channel is an approach of providing consistent interaction service between clients and service providers. As customer today is tech savvy, therefore prefer to take all the services through digital mode only and not wasting time in visiting the branches whether the service is availing insurance, taking loans or investing money in marketable securities. Customers prefer to make transaction through digital mode only. Providing customers with omni channels and advantage of giving same service through different channels or initiating the service through digital mode and winding up the same through offline mode has become a major reason for successful implementation of omnichannel in bancassurance.

Exhilarating Prospect

The collaboration of bancassurance with omnichannel is an exciting avenue for banks as well as insurance companies and to some extent it is beneficial for the customers as well. Banks are able to convert potential customers in to actual customers with the help of omnichannel approach and customers are able to access the bancassurance services of banks anywhere and anytime at single click. Undoubtedly bancassurance is growing fast but collaboration of omni channel with bancassurance has allowed banks to promote and develop the sales of bancassurance to high extent.

Challenges of Industry 5.0 in Bancassurance

The implementation of omni channel in banking strategies has been fruitful for the banks in recent years but it is a fact that banks have faced various challenges and difficulties in implementing omni channel with bancassurance. Proper maintenance of whole system requires huge cost, IT redesigning, change in culture etc. which have made collaboration of bancassurance with omni channel quite challenging for the banks. The figure below provides a comprehend view of few of the challenges faced by banks in collaborating bancassurance with omni channel.

Huge Cost Is Involved

Implementation of omni channel in any bank for any kind of service requires massive amount of investment by banks. For implementing omni channel in bancassurance also, huge cost is applied that becomes a big challenge for banks where there is shortage of funds.

IT Redesigning

For providing same service through digital as well as online mode, there is a need for complete IT redesigning. Banks need to maintain a system through which the same kind of services can be provided to the clients 24*7 without any problem or delay. Therefore, it becomes a challenge for the banks while implementing omni channel with bancassurance.

Figure 3. Challenges of Industry 5.0 in bancassurance
Source: Author's Compilation

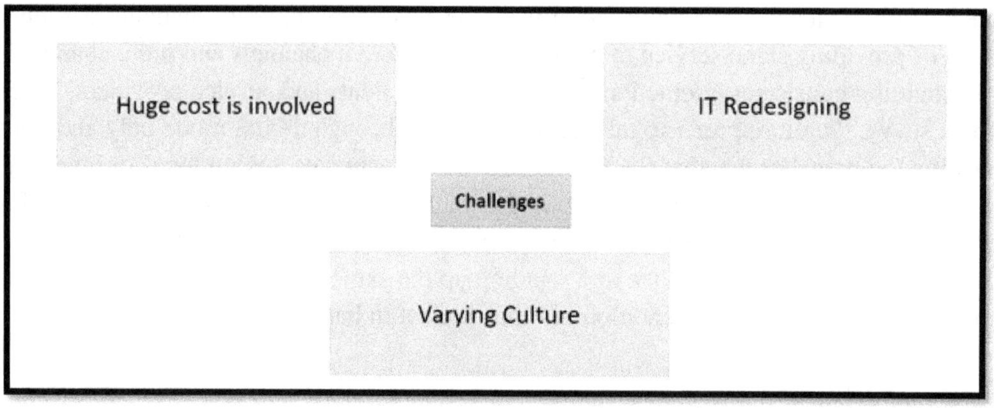

Varying Culture

Whenever any organization tries to change its native culture to the new one, challenges are being faced by them. Same thing applies on bank. When banks shift from traditional culture to digital one, challenge is being faced by banks.

The collaboration of omni channel with bancassurance is a new trend for providing services to the clients. There are numerous challenges in adjoining omni channel with bancassurance services but it is also a datum that bancassurance sales have witnessed growth in recent years. Providing same service to the customers physically and digitally is an important ingredient for growth of banks. Banks have proved that bancassurance services can be provided through various channels and that too effectively and efficiently.

Managerial Implications

A detailed discussion about digitalization of bancassurance services with the help of industry 5.0 above has shown that indeed implementation of industry 5.0 in providing bancassurance services has helped growing the sales of insurance products through banks. Banks have been trying hard to provide instantaneous services to their customers without the snag of time, labour and cost. Providing bancassurance products is one of the services that is provided by banks and has contributed in growth of banks in recent years. Although the concept of industry 5.0 is getting popular with every passing day, but on ground level customers are actually not that aware about omni channels provided by banks and that too in bancassurance. The digital bancassurance revolution aims to cater to these demands, enhancing value for customers, banks, and shareholders. Individualized insurance offerings delivered seamlessly meet consumer expectations for meaningful protection at equitable prices. To entice millennial customers, employing digital strategies is imperative. This demographic demands swift outcomes and substantial value. Banks and insurance companies must align their approaches to meet these expectations, including employing millennial staff for serving millennial clients while ensuring they possess comprehensive knowledge of insurance products. This particular group seeks quick results and significant value. Banks and insurance companies need to synchronize their strategies to meet these expectations. This involves hiring millennial employees to cater to millennial customers, ensuring they possess extensive expertise in insurance products. In this digital age, customer engagement is crucial. Therefore, well-trained bank employees are necessary, equipped not only to sell insurance but also to promptly address customer queries and ensure a seamless digital customer journey. Beyond digital means, organizing periodic "Customer Day" events can serve as an excellent platform for customer interaction and marketing bancassurance products. To enhance the effectiveness of the bancassurance channel, banks must prioritize ethical selling practices and invest in training their staff to provide tailored and trustworthy solutions to clients. Collaboration with insurance entities to improve underwriting efficiency and transparently communicate the claims process intricacies is essential. On the basis of discussion above, various managerial implications can be well-defined.

- Even if the world has entered in digital era, customers have misconception of losing their personal details if they transact digitally or online. Therefore, building trust among the bank customers ensuring them about safety of their credentials can be done.
- Making customers of the bank aware about concept of omni channels available in bancassurance can help in increasing sales of insurance services through banks. Therefore, customers must be made aware about omni channels and also difference between multi channels and omni channels.
- There is availability of strong financial system but the benefits of that system can be taken only when it is provided to all on same basis. Customers from remote areas are still not confident about taking insurance through banks. They still prefer to avail insurance from insurance agents. Therefore, buying insurance products from banks that too without visiting the banks is not risky needs to be shared with all. This can be done through banks only.
- Availability of same insurance services through physical mode and digital mode seems interesting for the customers but for bankers who are actually dealing with customers through offline and online mode become frustrating and curious sometimes. Therefore, bankers also need to be trained properly for selling insurance services to their actual as well as potential customers.
- Bancassurance services need premium payment, claim settlement kind of services. All the steps involved in completing an insurance purchase and further claim settlement require different formalities from the customer's side. Therefore, visit from customers in banks is essential for completing the process of insurance purchase. Thus, buying of insurance services through digital mode and paying premium online is not sufficient and customers must visit the banks for availing fruitful services.
- There is an immediate need to clarify and simplify the procedures involved in the bancassurance policies in order to bring clarity and transparency.

CONCLUSION

The banking sector is poised for significant transformation with the onset of Industrial Revolution 5.0, marked by the convergence of technological advancements across physical, digital, and biological domains. To navigate this evolving landscape, industrialists in banking must proactively embrace technological innovations and facilities. This entails harnessing artificial intelligence, machine learning, blockchain, and big data analytics to enhance operational efficiency and elevate customer experiences.

Moreover, investing in continuous skills development is imperative. Industrialists need to prioritize increasing awareness of industry-relevant technologies and enhancing proficiency in modern management methodologies. Additionally, preparing the workforce for technological shifts is crucial. This involves equipping employees with the necessary skills to collaborate effectively with automation technologies. While leveraging technology is essential, preserving a human-centric approach remains paramount, particularly in areas requiring human expertise such as customer service. Collaborating with the tech community and fostering organizational agility are also key strategies. By adopting these measures, industrialists can position their organizations to thrive amidst the opportunities and challenges presented by Industrial Revolution 5.0.

Utilizing digitally enabled interfaces can amalgamate the strengths of FinTech and Insurtech, simplifying data transfer. A digital repository for insurance documents can streamline policy administration, and integrating an agent firm's bancassurance platform with a bank's online services is another step forward for the coming future. Developing web platforms that consolidate all insurance policies in one location represents a notable advancement. Certain application interfaces have the capability to scan a customer's bank account for insurance contracts, provided banks grant permission to access customer data. However, this convenience must be balanced against potential intrusions into customers' privacy, necessitating careful handling of personal data. A needs-based selling approach is imperative for bancassurance's sustainable future. Without this, stricter regulatory norms may be required to safeguard customers from misinformation and unethical selling practices. Banks need to adopt a hybrid approach to engage customers effectively, leveraging social media alongside traditional marketing avenues. The emergence of online insurance purchases underscores the necessity for seamless integration between banking and insurance data in the digital realm. Banks are now appointing certified insurance facilitators, setting up specialized insurance counters, and incentivizing employees to offer insurance as part of comprehensive wealth management services. Today's customers seek comprehensive financial services from a single source, akin to a financial superstore. Ultimately, cultivating customer trust remains pivotal, necessitating a customer-centric approach and strategic outlook for the long-term success of bancassurance. In order to bolster the efficiency of the bancassurance channel, it is imperative for banks to place a premium on ethical sales practices. They should allocate resources towards training their personnel to deliver customized and reliable solutions to their clientele. Working in conjunction with insurance firms to enhance the efficiency of underwriting procedures and ensuring clear communication regarding the complexities of the claims process is paramount. Above all, fostering trust among customers is pivotal, demanding an approach centered around customers and a forward-thinking strategy that is indispensable for the sustained success of bancassurance.

REFERENCES

Abey, J. (2016). Mounting Role of Bancassurance in India. *International Journal of Business and Social Science*, *7*(4), 51–58.

Agarwal, M. K. (2019). Insurance Industry and The Government As A Facilitator of Change. *Deliberative Research*, *42*(1), 10–14.

Ameen, N., Tarhini, A., Shah, M., & Madichie, N. O. (2021). Going with the flow: Smart shopping malls and omnichannel retailing. *Journal of Services Marketing*, *35*(3), 325–348. doi:10.1108/JSM-02-2020-0066

Anbalagan, G. (2017). New technological changes in Indian Banking Sector. *International Journal of Scientific Research and Management*, *5*(9), 7015–7021. doi:10.18535/ijsrm/v5i9.11

Aravind, M., & Nagamani, P. (2013). Financial Analysis of State Bank of India during 2000- '12. *Asian Journal of Research in Business Economics and Management*, *3*(10), 170–184.

ASSOCHAM. (2021, June). *"Atmanirbhar Bharat" and insurance June 2021 Government's big leap towards making the insurance sector resilient*. https://www.assocham.org/uploads/files/1624941580.pdf

Bala, R., & Verma, A. (2012). Scope for the bancassurance in Indian life insurance sector: an analytical approach. *Asian-African Journal of Economics and Econometrics, 12*(1), 235-246.

Banerjee, A. (2009). Bancassurance: A Major Para-banking Activity. *Insurance Chronicle*, 35-38.

Bansal, J., & Kanwal, A. (2018). Qualitative research on issues and trends in the bancassurance model in India: An interview report. *International Journal of Banking. Risk and Insurance*, *6*(2), 67.

Bawa, S. K., & Chattha, S. (2016). Distribution Channels of Indian Life Insurance Industry: Understanding Customers' Awareness. *Business Analyst*, *37*(1), 63–80.

Bhushan, P., & Murtaza, M. A. (2014, December 22-24). *Bancassurance: The Indian Scenario* [Conference Presentation]. NIT-MTMI International Conference on Emerging Paradigms and Practices in Global Technology, Management & Business Issues, Department of Mechanical Engineering, National Institute of Technology Hamirpur (H.P) India.

Block, W., Snow, N., & Stringham, E. (2008). Banks, insurance companies, and discrimination. *Business and Society Review*, *113*(3), 403–419. doi:10.1111/j.1467-8594.2008.00326.x

Cafemutual. (2023, January 9). *Insurance penetration is just 4.2%, much less than the global average of 7%.* https://cafemutual.com/news/insurance/28335-insurance-penetration-is-just-42-much-less-than-the-global-average-of-7

Choudhury, K. (2007). Service quality dimensionality: A study of the Indian banking sector. *Journal of Asia-Pacific Business*, *8*(4), 21–38. doi:10.1300/J098v08n04_03

Deshmukh, A. (2021, June 7). *Reaping the benefits of digital bancassurance.* https://learnsure.ai/reaping-the-benefits-of-digital-bancassurance/

Dua, P., Sahay, N., & Deol, O. S. (2019). Bancassurance model and its impact on Financial Inclusion: Review and Analysis. *International Journal of Research and Analytical Reviews*, *6*(2), 661–669.

Fan, C. K., & Cheng, C. L. (2011). An examination of key factors influencing bancassurance success–Taiwan and mainland China evidence. *Service Industries Journal*, *31*(11), 1887–1902. doi:10.1080/02642069.2010.503888

Grover, N., & Bhalla, G. S. (2013). Level of awareness regarding bancassurance and choice of insurance product among bank customers in India. *Eurasian Journal of Business and Economics*, *6*(12), 63–77.

Gujral, T. M. (2018). Contemporary prominent development of bancassurance in India. *International Journal of Multidisciplinary Research Review*, *3*(10), 731–738.

Gupta, M. K. (2006, August 29). *Who/What drives Bancassurance in India?* [Conference Presentation]. 7th Asian Conference on Bancassurance and Alternative Channels, Mumbai.

Hamouda, M. (2019). Omni-channel banking integration quality and perceived value as drivers of consumers' satisfaction and loyalty. *Journal of Enterprise Information Management*, *32*(4), 608–625. doi:10.1108/JEIM-12-2018-0279

Hatt, S., Boeraeve, F., Artru, S., Dufrêne, M., & Francis, F. (2018). Spatial diversification of agroecosystems to enhance biological control and other regulating services: An agroecological perspective. *The Science of the Total Environment*, *621*(2), 600–611. doi:10.1016/j.scitotenv.2017.11.296 PMID:29195207

Ilona, T., & Renata, P. K. (2009). Tendencies for bancassurance development in the Polish market (Tendencje rozwoju bancassurance na rynku polskim). *Myśl Ekonomiczna i Prawna*, *4*, 174–182.

IRDA. (2022). *Annual Report*. Insurance Regulatory and Development Authority of India. https://irdai.gov.in/document-detail?documentId=1632108

Jadoun, A. S. (2015). The impact of E-Banking on customers in India. *International Research Journal of Management Sociology & Humanity*, *6*(3), 284–287.

Jain, M. (2018, January 15). Infographic: Little known facts about India's banking network. https://www.thehindubusinessline.com/economy/infographic-little-knownfacts about-indias-banking-network/article9381949.ece

Jing, H., Zou, K., & Cai, X. (2021). An Empirical Study on the Influence of Diversification on the Operating Cost of Commercial Banks. *Converter Magazine*, *2021*(5), 757–770.

Joshi, U. (2019). Perception among the Employees of Bank towards the Bancassurance in Nepal. *Nepalese Journal of Insurance and Social Security*, *2*(2), 71–80. doi:10.3126/njiss.v2i2.31830

Karunagaran, A. (2006). Bancassurance; A feasible Study for Banks in India. *Journal of Economics and Sustainable Development*, *4*(2), 24–34.

Kaur, N., & Kaur, R. (2022). Impact of bancassurance income on profitability of state bank of India. *An International Journal of Humanities and Management*, *8*(1), 48–54.

Kohli, R. (1999). Rural Bank Branches and financial reform. *Economic and Political Weekly*, *34*(3/4), 169–174.

Komulainen, H., & Makkonen, H. (2018). Customer experience in omni-channel banking services. *Journal of Financial Services Marketing*, *23*(3-4), 190–199. doi:10.1057/s41264-018-0057-6

Krishna, T. R. (2015). Banking Sector in India and Its Recent Developments. *International Journal of Multidisciplinary Educational Research*, *4*(1), 24–29.

Kumar, A. (2016). Impact of Liberlisation on Indian Insurance Industry. *International Journal of Management and Economics Review*, *1*(1), 1–10.

Kumaraswamy, D. S. (2012). Bancassurance: Tapping of Insurance into Banking Pursuit. *International Journal of Scientific and Research Publications*, *2*(7), 1–5.

Lymberpoulos, K., Chaniotakis, I. O., & Soureli, M. (2004). Opportunities for Banks to CrossSell Insurance Products in Greece. *Journal of Financial Services Marketing*, *9*(1), 34–48. doi:10.1057/palgrave.fsm.4770139

Maity, S., & Sahu, T. N. (2017). Pre-merger performance measures of state bank of India and its associate banks using data envelopment analysis. *Business Spectrum*, *7*(2), 16–26.

Malti, M. (2022, July 11). Total Number of Life Insurance Policies Sold in June 2022 Up 32%, Shows IRDAI Data. Outlook. https://www.outlookindia.com/business/total-number-of-life-insurance-policies-sold-in-june-2022-up-32-shows-irdai-data-news-208244

Mannar, B. R. (2015). The Indian market scenario of insurance sector. *Asia Pacific Journal of Research*, *1*(25), 88–98.

Mishra, N. (2012). Banc Assurance: Problems and Challenges in India. Integral Review. *Journal of Management*, *5*(1), 52–63.

Mohamed, O. E. B., Alhabshi, S. O., & Sharif, K. (2015). Factors influencing the penetration rate of Malaysian takaful industry from takaful managers' perspective. *The International Journal of Excellence in Islamic Banking and Finance*, *5*(1), 1–13. doi:10.12816/0024362

Muthumari, A., & Pushpaveni, K. (2017). A Study on Customer Service Loyalty Towards Bancassurance of Public and Private Sector Banks in Virudhunagar District, Tamilnadu. *Journal of Emerging Technologies and Innovative Research*, *4*(12), 385–392.

Nagaraja, B. (2015). Performance of insurance industry in India: A critical analysis. *International Journal of Multidisciplinary and Scientific Emerging Research*, *4*(1), 1045–1052.

Newar, L. R. (2013). Understanding Reforms in the Life Insurance Sector of India. *International Journal of Computer Applications in Engineering Sciences*, *3*(1), 18–23.

Nippatlapalli, A. R. (2013). A study on customer satisfaction of commercial banks: Case study on State Bank of India. *IOSR Journal of Business and Management*, *15*(1), 60–86. doi:10.9790/487X-1516086

Pal, R. (2013). Financial Sector Reforms: The Way to Socio-Economic Inclusion. *International Journal (Toronto, Ont.)*, *2*(1), 94–101.

Pallavi, D. R., & Rai, A. (2021). An Analysis of Customer Perception about Bancassurance: An Empirical Study. *Recent Trends in Management and Commerce, 2*(2), 79-86.

Pani, L. K., & Swain, S. (2013). Bancassurance and Indian banks. *International Journal of Research and Development-A Management Review*, *2*(1), 11–13.

Patnaik, A. (2022, July 30). Banking on bancassurance. Financial Express. https://www.financialexpress.com/opinion/banking-on-bancassurance/2611182/

Pavlovski, C. (2013). A Multi-Channel System Architecture for Banking. *International Journal of Computer Science. Engineering and Applications*, *3*(5), 1–12.

Pillai, R. H., & Arumugan, A. (2023). Comparative Analysis Between Banking and Insurance Sector on Perception of Transformational Leadership Styles. *International Journal of Professional Business Review: International Journal of Professional Business Review, 8*(5), 1–14. doi:10.26668/businessreview/2023.v8i5.1458

PopliG. S.RaoD. N. (2009). An Empirical Study of Bancassurance: Prospects and Challenges for selling Insurance Products through Banks in India. https://ssrn.com/abstract=1339471

Radhika, H. (2012). Role of IRDA in life insurance sector. *ZENITH International Journal of Business Economics & Management Research, 2*(9), 35–47.

Radhika, R., & Satuluri, R. K. (2019). A study on life insurance penetration in India. *International Journal of Human Resource Management and Research, 9*(1), 119–124. doi:10.24247/ijhrmrfeb201912

Raghavan, S., & Pai, R. (2021). Impact of Digital Banking and Artificial Intelligence on Retail Customer Engagement - A Case Study on HDFC Bank. *International Journal of Innovative Research in Science, Engineering and Technology, 10*(5), 4825–4834.

Rajkumari, M. (2007). A study on customer preference towards insurance services and bancassurance. *ICFAI Journal of Risk and Insurance, 4*(4), 49–60.

Rakshit, D. (2017). Analysis of growth of insurance density and insurance penetration in India after initiation of reforms in insurance sector. *International Journal of Research in Economics and Social Sciences, 7*(6), 164–171.

Routh, S., Joshi, L. K., & Dasgupta, S. (2022). Low Penetration: A Threat to Indian Life Insurance Sector. *International Research Journal of Modernization in Engineering Technology and Science, 4*(6), 5227–5233.

Sadana, D., & Kaur, K. (2023). A Study on Factors Contributing Growth of Bancassurance. *Journal of Corporate Finance Management and Banking System, 3*(02), 21–32. doi:10.55529/jcfmbs.32.21.32

Saidenberg, M. R., & Strahan, P. E. (1999). Are banks still important for financing large businesses? *Current Issues in Economics and Finance, 5*(12), 1–6.

Samal, A. (2019). Impact of Bancassurance on Financial Performance of Private Commercial Banks in India. *International Journal of Engineering and Advanced Technology, 8*(6S3), 2027-2034.

Sawant, B. S. (2011). Technological developments in Indian banking sector. *Indian Streams Research Journal, 1*(9), 1–4.

Schmidt, J., Drews, P., & Schirmer, I. (2016, August). *End-users' perspective on digitalization: A study on work order processing in the German banking industry* [Conference Presentation]. 22nd Americas Conference on Information Systems, San Diego.

Sengupta, R., Mishra, S. K., & Das, S. (2015). Emergence of Bancassurance in India-a Literature Review. *International Journal of Management and Social Sciences, 3*(8), 480–486.

Shah, D., & Chugan, P. K. (2018). The International BFSI Business from International Financial Services Centre (IFSC) in India: The Changing Scenario. In Sustainable Development: Future Trajectory (pp.19-28). Himalaya Publishing House.

Sharma, A. (2021, March 10). Economic Survey 2020-21: Insurance penetration 'extremely low' at 3.76%. Business Today. https://www.businesstoday.in/latest/economy-politics/story/economic-survey-2020-21-insurance-penetration-extremely-low-at-376-285890-2021-01-29

Sharma, G., & Gupta, S. (2020). Modelling the impact of corporate sustainability on economic performance with reference to Indian financial industry. *World Review of Entrepreneurship, Management and Sustainable Development, 16*(3), 317–328. doi:10.1504/WREMSD.2020.107272

Shukla, U. N. (2018). Enhancing life insurance penetration and density in India: Purchase intention modelling. *International Journal of Economics and Business Research, 15*(2), 141–154. doi:10.1504/IJEBR.2018.089683

SinhaT. (2005). Bancassurance in India: Who is tying the knot and why. *Available at* SSRN 715203 doi:10.2139/ssrn.715203

Temelkov, Z. (2018). Fintech firms opportunity or threat for banks? *International Journal of Information, Business and Management, 10*(1), 137–143.

Thalassinos, E. (2008). Trends and Developments in the European Financial Sector. *European Financial and Accounting Journal, 3*(3), 44–61. doi:10.18267/j.efaj.83

Tijoe, L. H. (2019). Bringing bancassurance into the digital era. *Linkedin.* https://www.linkedin.com/pulse/bringing-bancassurance-digital-era-lee-han-tjioe/

Turkyilmaz, A., Akman, G., Ozkan, C., & Pastuszak, Z. (2011). Empirical study of public sector employee loyalty and satisfaction. *Industrial Management & Data Systems, 111*(5), 675–696. doi:10.1108/02635571111137250

Vasiliev, S. A., & Serov, E. R. (2019). Omnichannel banking economy. *Risks, 7*(4), 1–11. doi:10.3390/risks7040115

Vimala, B., & Alamelu, K. (2018). Insurance penetration and insurance density in India–An analysis. *International Journal of Research and Analytical Reviews, 5*(4), 229–232.

Wenninger, J. (2000). The Emerging Role of Banks in E-Commerce. *Federal Reserve Bank of Newyork: Current Issues in Economics and Finance, 6*(3), 1–6.

Chapter 14
Role of Sociology in Adopting Digital HR for Sustainable Entrepreneurship:
Navigating Cultural Dynamics

K. Gunasekaran
Department of Mechanical Engineering, Metallizing Equipment Co. Pvt. Ltd., India

Boopathi S.
Department of Mechanical Engineering, Metallizing Equipment Co. Pvt. Ltd., India

ABSTRACT

This chapter delves into the connection between sociology and digital HR adoption, focusing on the cultural factors that influence this transition. It highlights how organizational culture, societal norms, and cultural values shape the implementation of digital HR strategies in entrepreneurial ventures. It emphasizes the role of digital HR in sustainable entrepreneurship, its efficiency, employee engagement, and strategic decision-making. It also highlights the importance of sensitivity to varying cultural norms and values in shaping attitudes towards digital HR adoption. It discusses the importance of bridging cultural gaps in digital HR implementation for sustainable growth and innovation. It emphasizes adaptability, openness to change, and cross-cultural communication. Digital HR tools can promote diversity, equity, and inclusion, contributing to sustainable entrepreneurship practices.

INTRODUCTION

The rise of digital technologies has significantly transformed the entrepreneurship landscape, transforming Human Resources (HR) functions from paper-based to sophisticated digital ecosystems. This introduction delves into the evolution of Digital HR within the entrepreneurial context, tracing its trajectory from traditional practices to innovative solutions shaping the future of workforce management. Digital HR is revolutionizing the way entrepreneurs manage their human capital, moving beyond administrative tasks

DOI: 10.4018/979-8-3693-1343-5.ch014

like payroll processing and compliance management to strategic workforce planning, talent acquisition, and performance management, as businesses embrace digital transformation and technology advancements (Ferreira & Ferreira, 2023).

Digital HR in entrepreneurship is evolving due to the growing recognition of human capital as a competitive advantage. Entrepreneurs recognize the importance of attracting, retaining, and developing top talent in a rapidly changing business landscape. Digital HR technologies help optimize workforce strategies, align talent management with business objectives, and drive innovation and growth. Digital HR solutions have democratized access to advanced HR capabilities, making them accessible to startups and small businesses. Cloud-based HR platforms, AI-powered analytics, and mobile applications are now accessible to entrepreneurs of all sizes, enabling them to compete more effectively in the talent marketplace and attract top talent (Rosário & Figueiredo, 2023).

Digital HR in entrepreneurship is evolving due to changing employee expectations. In a digital world, employees expect seamless HR services and personalized engagement. Digital HR technologies, such as self-service portals, mobile apps, and AI-driven chatbots, help entrepreneurs meet these expectations, enhancing employee satisfaction and productivity. The COVID-19 pandemic has accelerated the adoption of digital HR solutions by businesses transitioning to remote work environments. Entrepreneurs have been compelled to digitize HR processes to support distributed teams, facilitate remote collaboration, and ensure business continuity, making digital HR tools like virtual onboarding, remote performance management, and communication platforms indispensable (Rosário & Figueiredo, 2024).

Digital HR has evolved significantly in entrepreneurship, transforming workforce management and organizational development. Originating in administrative tasks, it now plays a crucial role in sustainable growth. This chapter explores the cultural factors influencing the adoption and implementation of digital HR strategies within entrepreneurial ventures, examining how sociological perspectives can enhance HR practices for sustainable entrepreneurship. The entrepreneurship landscape has undergone significant transformation due to technological advancements, with digital Human Resources (HR) practices revolutionizing workforce management. This introduction explores the evolution of digital HR within entrepreneurship, tracing its trajectory from traditional HR methodologies to its current role in shaping sustainable ventures (Reuther et al., 2023).

Historically, HR in entrepreneurial ventures was manual and inefficient. Digital technology has revolutionized HR operations by offering innovative solutions. Digital HR platforms, including software and cloud-based systems, have revolutionized talent acquisition, employee engagement, and performance evaluation, transforming the way entrepreneurs approach their operations. Digital HR has evolved to offer agility and scalability, allowing entrepreneurs to adapt to market conditions and scale operations efficiently. This flexibility allows for remote work arrangements and global talent sourcing, enabling entrepreneurs to build diverse teams. Digital HR technologies have democratized access to HR resources, leveling the playing field for startups and small businesses. With affordable and user-friendly HR software, entrepreneurs can leverage sophisticated tools to manage their human capital effectively, enabling them to navigate the complexities of today's competitive business landscape (Reuther et al., 2023).

The integration of data analytics and AI into digital HR platforms has provided valuable insights into workforce dynamics, enabling entrepreneurs to make informed decisions about talent management, succession planning, and organizational development. This analytical prowess helps identify and nurture top talent, mitigate retention risks, and foster a culture of continuous improvement. Digital HR platforms also enhance employee engagement and well-being, offering features like self-service portals, feedback mechanisms, and wellness programs. This holistic approach fosters a positive organizational culture conducive to innovation and growth (Sarma et al., 2024).

The evolution of digital HR in entrepreneurship has been a transformative journey, characterized by innovation, efficiency, and empowerment. From cost-saving measures to strategic enablers of sustainable ventures, digital HR has redefined how entrepreneurs manage their people. The study emphasizes the significant influence of technology on work and business, emphasizing the need to understand the cultural dynamics influencing the adoption of digital HR for sustainable entrepreneurship (Zaheer, 2022).

- Sociological theories provide frameworks for understanding how culture shapes organizational norms, values, and decision-making processes. By exploring cultural dynamics, entrepreneurs can identify potential barriers or facilitators to digital HR adoption within their specific cultural contexts.
- Sociological perspectives emphasize the importance of considering diverse stakeholder perspectives, including employees, management, and external stakeholders. By incorporating insights from various stakeholders, entrepreneurs can develop more inclusive and culturally sensitive digital HR strategies that resonate with different societal groups.
- Sociology sheds light on power dynamics within organizations and broader societal structures. By acknowledging power differentials, entrepreneurs can mitigate resistance to change, foster collaboration, and promote equitable access to digital HR resources, thereby advancing sustainability goals.
- Sociological perspectives underscore the value of diversity and inclusion in driving innovation and organizational resilience. By embracing diversity in digital HR practices, entrepreneurs can leverage the unique perspectives and talents of a diverse workforce, leading to more creative problem-solving and sustainable business outcomes.
- In an increasingly interconnected world, sociological perspectives help entrepreneurs navigate the cultural complexities of operating in global markets. By understanding cultural differences and adapting digital HR strategies accordingly, entrepreneurs can build culturally competent organizations capable of thriving in diverse international environments.

Sociological perspectives are crucial in promoting sustainable entrepreneurship by revealing cultural nuances that influence organizational behavior and technology adoption processes. By utilizing sociological insights, entrepreneurs can develop holistic, culturally responsive digital HR implementation strategies, prioritizing organizational success and societal well-being in sustainable ventures.

CULTURAL DYNAMICS

This section explores the role of sociology in understanding the complex interplay between technology, organizational culture, and societal norms in digital HR adoption for sustainable entrepreneurship, focusing on the influence of organizational culture, societal norms, and cultural values(Stuss, 2023).

Figure 1 provides a structured overview of the process involved in understanding and navigating the complexities of digital HR adoption within the context of organizational culture, societal norms, and cultural values, with the aim of fostering sustainable entrepreneurship.

Figure 1. Process and complexities of digital HR adoption

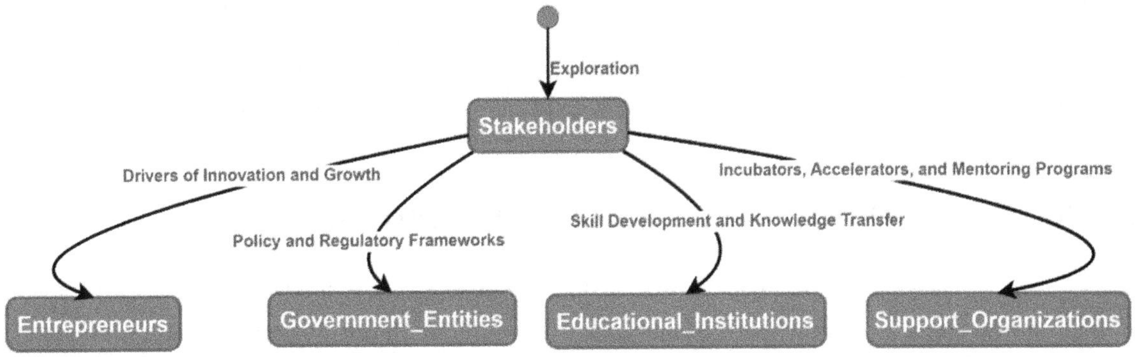

Conceptual Framework of Sociology in Digital HR Adoption

Sociology provides a comprehensive framework for understanding the adoption of digital HR practices in entrepreneurial ventures. It emphasizes the study of social structures, institutions, and interactions, providing insights into how individuals and groups are shaped by their social contexts. In the context of digital HR adoption, sociological perspectives highlight the cultural, social, and organizational factors that influence technology implementation processes (Rahamathunnisa et al., 2023). The notion of cultural embeddedness is central to the sociological framework, recognizing that technology adoption is deeply embedded within cultural and social contexts. Sociological theories like structuration theory and symbolic interactionism emphasize the reciprocal relationship between technology and society (Nave & Ferreira, 2022).

Influence of Organizational Culture

Organizational culture significantly influences attitudes towards technology adoption and innovation in entrepreneurial ventures. It is the shared values, beliefs, and norms that guide behavior within an organization. In the context of digital HR adoption, organizational culture can either facilitate or hinder the implementation of new technologies. Ventures with a culture of innovation, openness to change, and risk-taking are more likely to embrace digital HR initiatives. Conversely, organizations with entrenched bureaucratic structures, resistance to change, or lack of technological literacy may face barriers to digital HR adoption. Understanding these cultural norms is crucial for entrepreneurs to foster a culture that supports digital HR practices and sustainable entrepreneurship (Nave & Ferreira, 2022).

Societal Norms and Cultural Values

Societal norms and cultural values significantly influence attitudes towards technology adoption and utilization. Factors like collectivism vs. individualism, uncertainty avoidance, and power distance influence perceptions of technological innovation. Trust, transparency, and privacy also impact the acceptance of digital HR systems. Entrepreneurs must adapt their digital HR strategies to the cultural context, addressing cultural barriers through training and education. By respecting societal norms and cultural values, entrepreneurs can enhance the effectiveness of digital HR adoption initiatives and foster sustainable entrepreneurship in diverse cultural contexts (Thanasi-Boçe et al., 2023).

Understanding cultural dynamics is crucial for entrepreneurs implementing digital HR for sustainable entrepreneurship. Recognizing the impact of organizational culture, societal norms, and values helps navigate technology implementation complexities and fosters innovative, growth-oriented environments.

CULTURAL FACTORS SHAPING DIGITAL HR ADOPTION

This section explores the cultural factors influencing the adoption of digital HR practices in the rapidly evolving entrepreneurship landscape, focusing on the dynamics of cultural diversity within entrepreneurial environments (Purnomo et al., 2023).

Figure 2 illustrates the steps for navigating cultural factors affecting digital HR practices in entrepreneurship, emphasizing the need to align HR strategies with organizational culture and societal norms, while addressing cultural barriers for successful implementation.

Cultural Diversity in Entrepreneurial Ecosystems

Entrepreneurial ecosystems are characterized by cultural diversity, fostering innovation and collaboration among entrepreneurs, employees, and stakeholders. However, this diversity can also hinder digital HR adoption due to differences in norms, communication styles, and expectations. Entrepreneurs must navigate the complexities of managing diverse teams and accommodating varying cultural preferences in multicultural environments, ensuring the successful implementation of new technologies (Stuss, 2023).

Figure 2. Steps for navigating cultural factors affecting digital HR practices

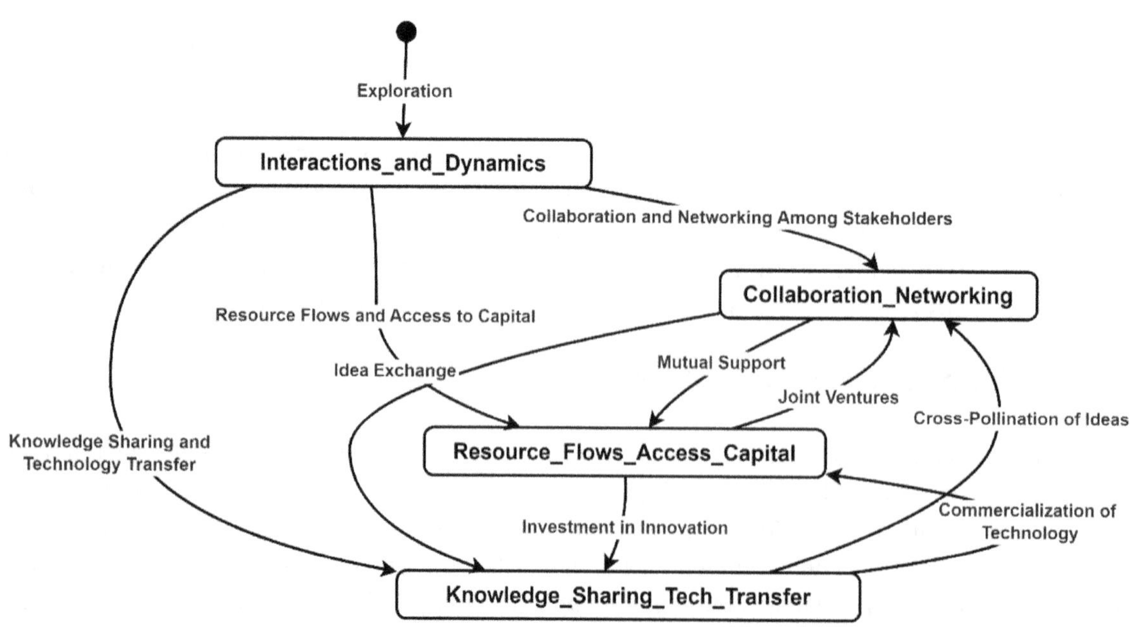

Cultural diversity in entrepreneurial ecosystems, including linguistic diversity, presents unique challenges for digital HR adoption. Language barriers can hinder communication and collaboration in multicultural workplaces, affecting the uptake of digital HR systems. Cultural diversity also encompasses values, beliefs, and social norms, necessitating entrepreneurs to adapt their digital HR strategies. Despite these challenges, cultural diversity offers opportunities for innovation and growth in digital HR adoption. By leveraging the collective wisdom and creativity of culturally diverse teams, entrepreneurs can leverage cultural diversity as a competitive advantage and organizational resilience.

Cultural diversity is a crucial element in entrepreneurial ecosystems, as it fosters inclusivity and sense of belonging. Digital HR practices that promote diversity, equity, and inclusion can enhance employee engagement, collaboration, and innovation within multicultural teams. Despite challenges, entrepreneurs can leverage cultural diversity as a source of strength and innovation to build sustainable ventures. By embracing cultural diversity and cultivating inclusive digital HR practices, entrepreneurs can harness the full potential of their diverse teams and drive success in the dynamic world of entrepreneurship (Reuther et al., 2023).

Cultural factors significantly influence attitudes towards technology and implementation success in sustainable entrepreneurship. The interplay between tradition and innovation can either facilitate or impede the adoption of digital HR practices within entrepreneurial ventures, highlighting the importance of cultural dynamics in this context.

Impact of Tradition

Tradition, a set of customs and beliefs passed down through generations, can act as a barrier to change, hindering the adoption of digital HR systems. This resistance may stem from fear of the unknown, reluctance to deviate from established practices, or a desire to preserve cultural heritage. Traditional HR management in entrepreneurial ventures may prioritize face-to-face interactions and hierarchical structures. Transitioning to digital HR systems requires overcoming cultural norms and convincing stakeholders of the benefits of technology-driven solutions. Entrepreneurs must address concerns, provide training, and foster a culture of experimentation. Cultural traditions vary across regions and industries, making it difficult to adopt digital HR practices in diverse contexts (Odeyemi et al., 2024).

Impact of Innovation

Innovation is a driving force in entrepreneurial ventures, promoting the adoption of new technologies and practices. Innovation-oriented cultures encourage experimentation, agility, and continuous improvement, fostering an environment conducive to digital HR adoption. Entrepreneurs who embrace innovation are more likely to use digital HR systems to enhance efficiency, foster collaboration, and gain a competitive edge. By utilizing AI, data analytics, and cloud-based platforms, they can revolutionize HR processes and unlock new growth opportunities (Rosário & Figueiredo, 2023, 2024).

Innovation-oriented cultures value creativity, flexibility, and adaptability, which are crucial for navigating digital HR adoption. Entrepreneurs who foster a culture of innovation empower employees to embrace change, experiment with new technologies, and drive digital transformation initiatives. The impact of tradition and innovation on digital HR adoption highlights the importance of cultural factors in shaping organizational behavior and technology adoption processes (Ravisankar et al., 2024; Venkateswaran et al., 2023). By understanding and navigating the interplay between tradition and innovation, entrepreneurs can foster sustainable entrepreneurship and harness the transformative power of digital HR for organizational success.

CHALLENGES AND OPPORTUNITIES

Digital HR practices in entrepreneurship present both challenges and opportunities, especially in bridging cultural gaps within organizations. Addressing these differences is crucial for successful implementation and fostering innovation, inclusivity, and sustainability (Dabić et al., 2023).

Figure 3 visually organizes the challenges and opportunities associated with digital HR practices in entrepreneurship, emphasizing the importance of effectively managing cultural differences to drive innovation, inclusivity, and sustainability within organizations.

Challenges

- **Cultural Resistance:** One of the primary challenges in bridging cultural gaps is overcoming resistance to change. Different cultural norms, values, and attitudes towards technology may hinder acceptance and adoption of digital HR systems within the organization.
- **Communication Barriers:** Cultural differences can lead to communication breakdowns, misunderstandings, and conflicts, particularly in multinational or multicultural teams. Language barri-

Figure 3. Challenges and opportunities associated with digital HR practices in entrepreneurship

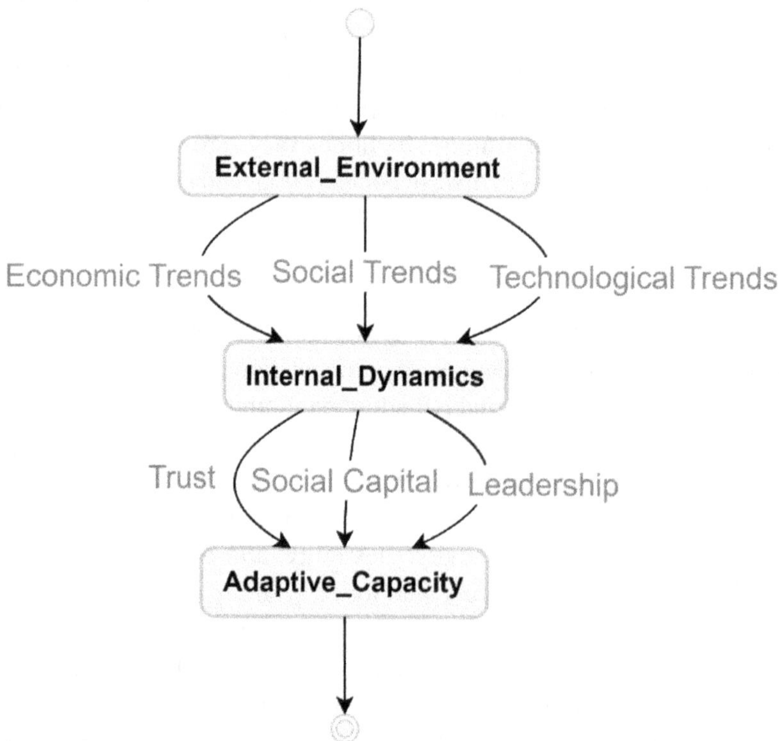

ers, non-verbal cues, and communication styles may impede effective collaboration and technology adoption.

- **Technological Literacy:** Disparities in technological literacy across different cultural groups may pose challenges to digital HR implementation. Employees with limited access to technology or digital skills may struggle to adapt to new systems, requiring comprehensive training and support programs.
- **Cultural Sensitivity:** Insensitivity to cultural norms and values can lead to alienation, resentment, and disengagement among employees. Ignoring cultural differences or imposing one-size-fits-all solutions may undermine trust and hinder digital HR adoption efforts.

Bridging cultural gaps in digital HR implementation presents both challenges and opportunities for entrepreneurship. By addressing cultural resistance, communication barriers, and technological literacy issues, entrepreneurs can harness the transformative potential of digital HR for sustainable organizational success. Diversity, including gender, ethnicity, culture, and cognitive diversity, can be harnessed as a strategic asset for driving innovation, enhancing performance, and fostering inclusive workplaces. This approach can help organizations navigate cultural complexities and achieve sustainable organizational success (Ren & Jackson, 2020).

Diversity in digital HR can be beneficial for sustainable entrepreneurship by addressing cultural barriers, bias, and communication issues. By leveraging diversity's benefits for innovation, talent acquisition, and employee engagement, entrepreneurs can create inclusive, resilient, and socially responsible ventures for long-term success (Sen, 2020).

Cultural diversity can enhance organizational perspectives, foster creativity, and drive innovation by leveraging the unique experiences of diverse cultural groups. It can also foster cross-cultural collaboration, facilitating knowledge sharing and collective problem-solving. Investing in cultural competency training can enhance awareness and understanding of diverse perspectives, promoting a culture of inclusion. A tailored approach to digital HR implementation, considering cultural preferences and priorities, can increase acceptance and adoption rates. Customizing HR systems, policies, and practices to align with cultural values can enhance user experience and effectiveness. Inclusive leadership, demonstrating cultural intelligence, empathy, and humility, can inspire trust and create an environment where diverse voices are valued and heard (Ravisankar et al., 2024; Venkateswaran et al., 2023). Overall, embracing cultural diversity can lead to more inclusive and effective digital HR strategies.

Challenges

- **Cultural Barriers:** Cultural differences can pose challenges to digital HR adoption, as diverse workforce populations may have varying levels of comfort and familiarity with technology. Entrepreneurs must address cultural barriers through targeted training, communication strategies, and cultural competence initiatives to ensure that digital HR systems are accessible and inclusive for all employees.
- **Bias and Discrimination:** Unconscious bias and discrimination can undermine diversity efforts and inhibit the effective utilization of digital HR technologies. Entrepreneurs must proactively address bias in recruitment, performance evaluation, and talent management processes to create equitable opportunities for all employees. Additionally, implementing bias-mitigation tools and fostering a culture of inclusion can help mitigate these challenges.

- **Communication and Language Barriers:** In multicultural workplaces, communication and language barriers may impede the adoption of digital HR systems and hinder effective collaboration. Entrepreneurs must prioritize clear and accessible communication channels, provide language support where necessary, and foster a culture of inclusivity to overcome these challenges and ensure that all employees can fully participate in digital HR initiatives.

Opportunities

- **Enhanced Creativity and Innovation:** Diversity of thought and perspective stimulates creativity and innovation, driving sustainable entrepreneurship forward. By leveraging digital HR platforms to facilitate collaboration and knowledge sharing among diverse teams, entrepreneurs can harness the collective intelligence of their workforce to generate novel ideas, solve complex problems, and seize new opportunities for growth.
- **Expanded Talent Pool:** Embracing diversity expands the talent pool, enabling organizations to attract and retain top talent from diverse backgrounds. Digital HR technologies, such as AI-driven recruitment platforms and remote work solutions, can help entrepreneurs access a broader talent pool, tap into diverse skill sets, and build high-performing teams capable of driving sustainable innovation and growth.
- **Improved Decision-Making:** Cognitive diversity, stemming from differences in perspectives, experiences, and cognitive styles, enhances decision-making processes within organizations. By leveraging digital HR analytics and data-driven insights, entrepreneurs can harness the diverse viewpoints of their workforce to make more informed decisions, mitigate risks, and capitalize on emerging opportunities in the dynamic business landscape.
- **Stronger Employee Engagement:** Inclusive workplaces foster a sense of belonging and engagement among employees, driving productivity, retention, and organizational performance. Digital HR tools, such as employee engagement surveys, feedback mechanisms, and recognition platforms, can help entrepreneurs cultivate a culture of inclusion, empower employees to contribute their unique talents, and foster a sense of collective purpose and commitment to sustainable entrepreneurship.

STRATEGIES FOR SUCCESSFUL ADOPTION

Cultivating an Adaptive Organizational Culture

This section emphasizes the importance of fostering an adaptive organizational culture for the successful adoption of digital HR practices in sustainable entrepreneurship, outlining strategies entrepreneurs can use to achieve this (Mukhuty et al., 2022).

Figure 4 visually illustrates the strategies for successful adoption of digital HR practices in sustainable entrepreneurship, highlighting the importance of both cultivating an adaptive organizational culture and promoting cross-cultural communication to achieve positive outcomes. An adaptive organizational culture is crucial for successful adoption of digital HR practices in sustainable entrepreneurship. This culture fosters open communication, empowers employees, promotes continuous learning, embraces

Figure 4. Strategies for successful adoption of digital HR practices

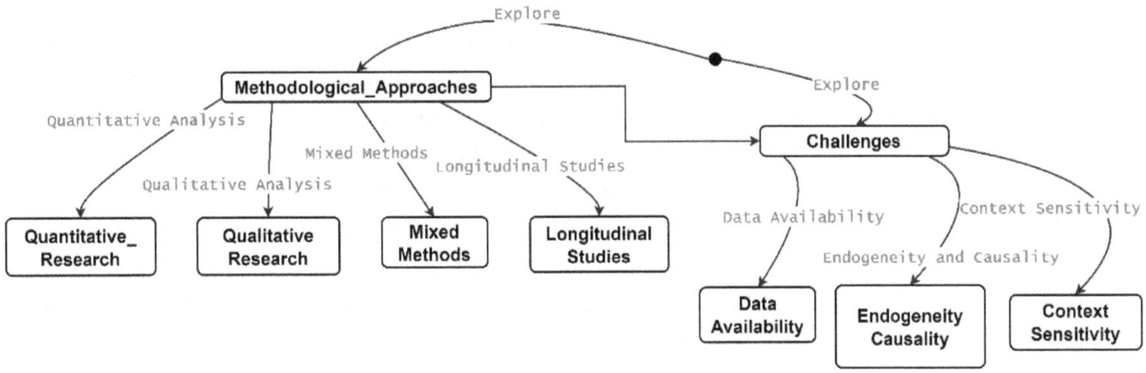

agility, and measures performance, driving organizational success and resilience in the digital age (Passaro et al., 2020).

- **Leadership Commitment and Vision:** Leadership plays a pivotal role in shaping organizational culture and driving digital HR adoption. Entrepreneurs must demonstrate a clear commitment to innovation and technology integration, articulating a compelling vision for the role of digital HR in achieving organizational objectives. By championing digital transformation initiatives and modeling behavior consistent with the desired cultural values, leaders can inspire confidence, build trust, and galvanize employees towards shared goals (Prabhuswamy et al., 2024).
- **Communication and Transparency:** Open and transparent communication is essential for building trust, fostering collaboration, and mitigating resistance to change. Entrepreneurs should communicate regularly with employees about the rationale for adopting digital HR practices, the expected benefits, and the support available for implementation. Providing opportunities for feedback, addressing concerns proactively, and soliciting input from employees can enhance engagement and ownership of the digital HR adoption process.
- **Empowerment and Inclusivity:** Empowering employees to participate in decision-making processes and contribute their ideas fosters a culture of ownership and accountability. Entrepreneurs should create opportunities for cross-functional collaboration, empower employees to experiment with new technologies, and recognize and reward innovative initiatives. Additionally, promoting diversity and inclusion ensures that all employees feel valued and included in the digital HR adoption journey, enhancing organizational resilience and fostering a sense of belonging.
- **Continuous Learning and Development:** Cultivating a culture of continuous learning and development is essential for building digital literacy and enabling employees to adapt to evolving technologies. Entrepreneurs should invest in training programs, workshops, and resources to enhance employees' digital skills and confidence in using digital HR platforms effectively. Encouraging a growth mindset, celebrating learning milestones, and providing opportunities for skill development and career advancement demonstrate a commitment to employee development and organizational agility.
- **Agility and Flexibility:** Embracing agility and flexibility enables organizations to adapt to changing market dynamics and seize emerging opportunities. Entrepreneurs should foster a culture that

embraces experimentation, iteration, and risk-taking, allowing for rapid prototyping and adjustment of digital HR strategies based on feedback and performance metrics. Encouraging flexibility in work arrangements, such as remote work options and flexible schedules, demonstrates responsiveness to employees' needs and preferences, fostering a culture of trust and autonomy.

- **Measurement and Evaluation:** The implementation of digital HR adoption strategies requires the establishment of metrics and key performance indicators (KPIs) to ensure continuous improvement and accountability. Entrepreneurs should define clear goals and objectives for digital HR initiatives, track progress against benchmarks, and solicit feedback from stakeholders to identify areas for refinement and optimization. Regular performance reviews and data-driven decision-making ensure that digital HR practices align with organizational priorities and contribute to sustainable entrepreneurship outcomes.

Promoting Cross-Cultural Communication

This section provides strategies for entrepreneurs to promote cross-cultural communication and facilitate the adoption of digital HR practices in diverse organizational settings, emphasizing the importance of effective communication in achieving successful outcomes (Djalic et al., 2021). Entrepreneurs can foster a culture of cross-cultural communication and collaboration by implementing strategies that promote cultural sensitivity, inclusivity, and openness to diversity. This fosters the successful adoption of digital HR practices, driving innovation, productivity, and sustainable entrepreneurship in a globalized business environment (Mahesh et al., n.d.).

- **Cultural Sensitivity Training:** Implementing cultural sensitivity training programs for employees can help raise awareness of cultural differences, reduce misunderstandings, and foster mutual respect and understanding. These programs should emphasize the importance of cultural diversity in the workplace, provide practical strategies for effective cross-cultural communication, and highlight the value of inclusive behaviors.
- **Multilingual Support:** Providing multilingual support for digital HR platforms and communication channels can enhance accessibility and inclusivity for employees from diverse linguistic backgrounds. By offering user interfaces, training materials, and support services in multiple languages, entrepreneurs can ensure that all employees can fully engage with digital HR tools and resources.
- **Cultural Liaisons or Ambassadors:** Designating cultural liaisons or ambassadors within the organization can facilitate communication and collaboration across cultural boundaries. These individuals, who possess cultural competence and language skills, can serve as bridges between different cultural groups, provide guidance on cultural norms and expectations, and help address cultural misunderstandings or conflicts that may arise during the digital HR adoption process.
- **Regular Feedback Mechanisms:** Establishing regular feedback mechanisms, such as surveys, focus groups, or open-door policies, can encourage employees to voice their opinions, concerns, and suggestions regarding digital HR initiatives. By soliciting feedback from diverse cultural perspectives, entrepreneurs can gain insights into the unique needs and preferences of different employee groups and tailor digital HR strategies accordingly.
- **Cross-Cultural Collaboration Platforms:** Leveraging digital collaboration platforms that support cross-cultural communication and teamwork can facilitate virtual collaboration among geo-

graphically dispersed teams. These platforms should incorporate features such as real-time messaging, video conferencing, document sharing, and project management tools to enable seamless communication and collaboration across cultural and geographical boundaries.

- **Inclusive Communication Practices:** Adopting inclusive communication practices, such as using plain language, avoiding jargon or culturally specific references, and providing visual aids or translations where necessary, can enhance understanding and engagement among diverse audiences. Entrepreneurs should strive to communicate clearly, respectfully, and inclusively, taking into account the cultural backgrounds and communication preferences of their employees.
- **Cultural Integration in HR Policies:** Integrating cultural considerations into HR policies and practices, such as recruitment, performance management, and employee development, can promote equity, fairness, and inclusion in the workplace. Entrepreneurs should ensure that HR policies are culturally sensitive, transparent, and adaptable to accommodate the diverse needs and preferences of employees from different cultural backgrounds (Saravanan et al., 2022).

DIGITAL HR AS A CATALYST FOR SUSTAINABLE ENTREPRENEURSHIP

Enhancing Efficiency and Innovation

Digital HR practices are transforming sustainable entrepreneurship by improving efficiency, fostering innovation, and driving long-term success. They optimize organizational processes, stimulate creativity, and enable adaptive responses to dynamic market conditions, making them a powerful catalyst for entrepreneurship (Mahesh et al., n.d.; Sipola et al., 2023).

Figure 5 demonstrates how digital HR practices enhance efficiency and innovation in sustainable entrepreneurship, promoting creativity, adaptive responses to market conditions, and long-term success by optimizing organizational processes.

Figure 5. Digital HR practices enhance efficiency and innovation in sustainable entrepreneurship

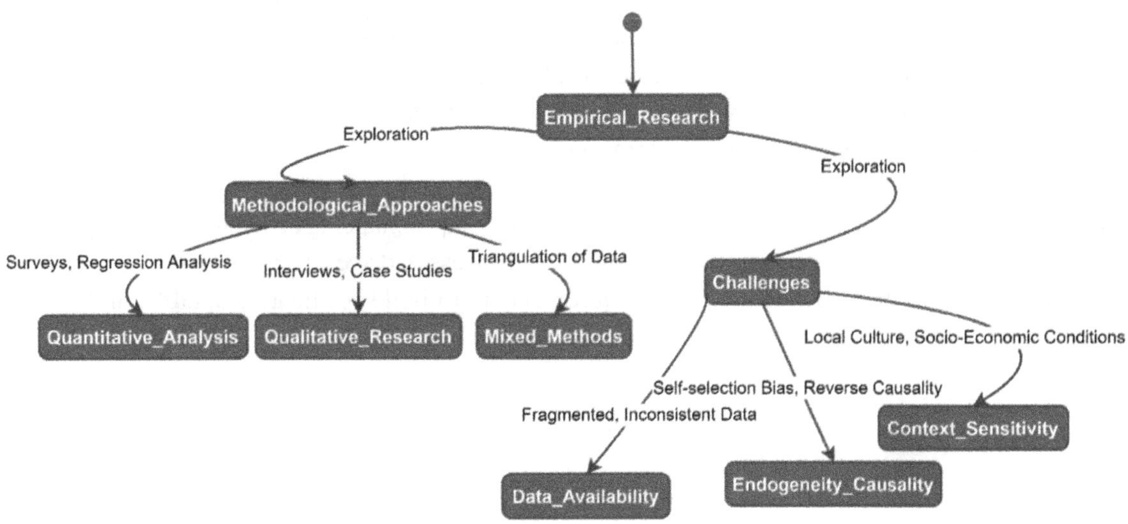

- **Streamlining Administrative Processes:** Digital HR platforms automate and streamline administrative HR processes, such as payroll management, time tracking, and leave management, reducing the burden of manual tasks and allowing employees to focus on more strategic activities. By eliminating inefficiencies and reducing administrative overhead, entrepreneurs can allocate resources more effectively, enhance productivity, and achieve cost savings that contribute to the sustainability of their ventures.
- **Facilitating Remote Work and Flexibility:** In today's increasingly digital and remote work environment, digital HR technologies play a crucial role in facilitating flexible work arrangements and supporting remote collaboration. Cloud-based HR systems enable employees to access HR services and information from anywhere, at any time, empowering them to work remotely without disruptions to productivity or communication. This flexibility enhances work-life balance, reduces commuting-related emissions, and contributes to environmental sustainability.
- **Driving Data-Driven Decision-Making:** Digital HR platforms leverage data analytics and insights to provide actionable intelligence on workforce trends, performance metrics, and talent management strategies. By harnessing data-driven insights, entrepreneurs can make informed decisions regarding recruitment, training, and succession planning, optimizing resource allocation and maximizing the potential of their human capital. Data-driven HR practices enable entrepreneurs to identify and address emerging challenges, capitalize on opportunities, and drive sustainable growth through evidence-based decision-making.
- **Fostering a Culture of Innovation:** Digital HR tools empower employees to contribute ideas, collaborate on projects, and share knowledge in real-time, fostering a culture of innovation and continuous improvement within entrepreneurial ventures. By providing platforms for idea generation, feedback, and collaboration, digital HR facilitates cross-functional collaboration, breaks down silos, and encourages creativity and experimentation. This culture of innovation enables entrepreneurs to adapt to changing market dynamics, anticipate future trends, and stay ahead of the competition in today's rapidly evolving business landscape.
- **Promoting Diversity and Inclusion:** Digital HR initiatives promote diversity and inclusion by providing equitable access to HR services, fostering a sense of belonging among employees, and eliminating bias in HR processes. By implementing diversity-focused recruitment strategies, unconscious bias training, and inclusive leadership practices, entrepreneurs can build diverse and inclusive teams that drive innovation, enhance problem-solving capabilities, and foster a culture of creativity and collaboration. A diverse workforce contributes to the sustainability of entrepreneurial ventures by bringing together a range of perspectives, experiences, and ideas that enrich organizational culture and drive long-term success.

Digital HR is a powerful tool for sustainable entrepreneurship, enhancing efficiency, fostering innovation, and promoting diversity and inclusion. It optimizes processes, drives data-driven decision-making, and fosters a culture of innovation, enabling entrepreneurs to build resilient, adaptable, and socially responsible ventures that contribute to society's betterment.

Fostering Diversity, Equity, and Inclusion

Digital HR can significantly promote diversity, equity, and inclusion (DEI) in organizations, thereby advancing DEI goals, fostering social responsibility, and driving sustainable business practices, thus fostering sustainable entrepreneurship (Sarma et al., 2024; Stuss, 2023).

- **Recruitment and Talent Acquisition:** Digital HR platforms enable entrepreneurs to reach a diverse talent pool and implement unbiased recruitment processes. By leveraging AI-driven recruitment tools that anonymize candidate information and eliminate unconscious bias, entrepreneurs can attract and hire candidates based on merit, skills, and qualifications, rather than demographic characteristics. This promotes diversity in the workforce and fosters a culture of inclusivity from the outset.
- **Training and Development:** Digital HR facilitates continuous learning and development opportunities for employees, regardless of their location or background. Virtual learning platforms, online courses, and e-learning modules can be customized to address the specific needs and preferences of diverse employee groups. By offering inclusive training programs that promote cultural competence, unconscious bias awareness, and inclusive leadership skills, entrepreneurs can cultivate a workforce that values diversity and embraces inclusion as a core organizational value.
- **Performance Management and Feedback:** Digital HR tools streamline performance management processes and provide objective performance metrics that promote transparency and fairness. By implementing 360-degree feedback mechanisms and regular performance reviews, entrepreneurs can ensure that all employees receive constructive feedback and recognition for their contributions, regardless of their cultural background or identity. This fosters a culture of equity and accountability and enables employees to thrive and grow within the organization.
- **Diversity Metrics and Analytics:** Digital HR analytics enable entrepreneurs to track diversity metrics and monitor progress towards DEI goals. By collecting data on workforce demographics, representation, and retention rates, entrepreneurs can identify areas for improvement, pinpoint systemic barriers to inclusion, and implement targeted interventions to promote diversity and equity within the organization. This data-driven approach enables entrepreneurs to make informed decisions and measure the impact of their DEI initiatives over time.
- **Employee Resource Groups (ERGs):** Digital HR platforms can facilitate the creation and management of employee resource groups (ERGs) that provide a forum for employees to connect, share experiences, and advocate for diversity and inclusion initiatives. By supporting ERGs focused on various dimensions of diversity, such as race, gender, sexual orientation, and disability, entrepreneurs can empower employees to drive meaningful change and foster a sense of belonging and community within the organization.
- **Inclusive Benefits and Policies:** Digital HR systems enable entrepreneurs to design and implement inclusive benefits packages and HR policies that address the diverse needs and preferences of their workforce. This may include flexible work arrangements, parental leave policies, healthcare benefits, and accommodations for employees with disabilities. By prioritizing inclusivity in benefits and policies, entrepreneurs can demonstrate their commitment to supporting the well-being and success of all employees, contributing to a more equitable and sustainable workplace culture.

Digital HR promotes sustainable entrepreneurship by promoting diversity, equity, and inclusion within organizations. It involves recruiting diverse talent, providing inclusive training, implementing unbiased performance management, tracking diversity metrics, supporting employee resource groups, and designing inclusive benefits and policies. This creates a workplace that values diversity, drives innovation, and contributes to long-term business success and societal well-being (Sen, 2020).

CONCLUSION

Digital HR practices offer a transformative opportunity for sustainable entrepreneurship, fostering diversity, equity, and inclusion (DEI) within organizational ecosystems. By leveraging digital HR, entrepreneurs can create inclusive workplaces, empower employees, drive innovation, and contribute to long-term business success and societal well-being. However, achieving full potential requires understanding cultural dynamics, addressing systemic barriers, and strategic implementation of DEI initiatives.

Future research in digital HR and sustainable entrepreneurship should concentrate on enhancing knowledge and practice in important areas.

- **Intersectionality and Multiple Identities:** Investigating the intersectionality of identities, such as race, gender, sexual orientation, and disability, in the context of digital HR adoption and DEI initiatives to understand how multiple dimensions of diversity intersect and influence employee experiences and outcomes.
- **Technology Accessibility and Inclusive Design:** Examining the accessibility of digital HR platforms and the effectiveness of inclusive design principles in promoting accessibility for employees with disabilities, ensuring that digital HR initiatives are accessible to all individuals, regardless of their abilities.
- **Long-Term Impact of DEI Initiatives:** Assessing the long-term impact of DEI initiatives on organizational performance, employee engagement, and sustainability outcomes to understand the effectiveness of digital HR in driving meaningful and lasting change within organizations.
- **Global Perspectives on DEI:** Exploring cultural variations in attitudes towards diversity, equity, and inclusion in different regions and industries to identify best practices for promoting DEI in diverse cultural contexts and globalized workplaces.
- **Ethical and Privacy Considerations:** Investigating ethical and privacy considerations associated with the use of digital HR technologies, including data privacy, algorithmic bias, and the ethical implications of AI-driven decision-making in HR processes.

The research suggests recommendations for entrepreneurs and organizational leaders to utilize digital HR for sustainable entrepreneurship, based on the findings.

- **Prioritize Diversity, Equity, and Inclusion:** Embed DEI principles into the core values and strategic objectives of the organization, fostering a culture of inclusivity, respect, and belonging that permeates all aspects of the business.
- **Invest in Cultural Competence:** Provide training and resources to employees and leaders to enhance cultural competence, promote cross-cultural communication, and address unconscious bias in HR practices and decision-making processes.

- **Collaborate Across Silos:** Break down silos within the organization and foster collaboration between HR, IT, and diversity and inclusion departments to ensure that digital HR initiatives are aligned with DEI goals and priorities.
- **Measure and Monitor Progress:** Implement metrics and analytics to track diversity, equity, and inclusion outcomes, monitor progress towards DEI goals, and identify areas for improvement, enabling data-driven decision-making and accountability.
- **Engage Stakeholders:** Involve employees, customers, and other stakeholders in the design and implementation of DEI initiatives, soliciting feedback, and fostering a sense of ownership and collective responsibility for driving change.

The implementation of these recommendations and the efficient use of digital HR can promote inclusive, resilient, and socially responsible business ventures for entrepreneurs in a diverse business environment.

ABBREVIATIONS

AI: Artificial Intelligence
COVID: Coronavirus Disease
DEI: Diversity, Equity, and Inclusion
ERG: Employee Resource Group
HR: Human Resources
IT: Information Technology
KPI: Key Performance Indicator

REFERENCES

Dabić, M., Maley, J. F., Švarc, J., & Poček, J. (2023). Future of digital work: Challenges for sustainable human resources management. *Journal of Innovation & Knowledge*, *8*(2), 100353. doi:10.1016/j.jik.2023.100353

Djalic, N., Nikolic, M., Bakator, M., & Erceg, Z. (2021). Modeling the influence of information systems on sustainable business performance and competitiveness. *Sustainability (Basel)*, *13*(17), 9619. doi:10.3390/su13179619

Ferreira, N. C., & Ferreira, J. J. (2023). Quo Vadis Sustainable Entrepreneurship? A Systematic Literature Review of Related Drivers and Inhibitors in SMEs. *IEEE Transactions on Engineering Management.*

Mahesh, K., Aithal, P., & Sharma, K. (n.d.). Green HRM and Teaching Sustainability in higher education Institutions: For Promoting Sustainable Education and Sustainable Development Goals. [IJCSBE]. *Education*, *8*(1), 261–271.

Mukhuty, S., Upadhyay, A., & Rothwell, H. (2022). Strategic sustainable development of Industry 4.0 through the lens of social responsibility: The role of human resource practices. *Business Strategy and the Environment*, *31*(5), 2068–2081. doi:10.1002/bse.3008

Nave, E., & Ferreira, J. J. (2022). A systematic international entrepreneurship review and future research agenda. *Cross Cultural & Strategic Management, 29*(3), 639–674. doi:10.1108/CCSM-11-2021-0204

Odeyemi, O., Usman, F. O., Mhlongo, N. Z., Elufioye, O. A., & Ike, C. U. (2024). *Sustainable entrepreneurship: A review of green business practices and environmental impact.* Academic Press.

Passaro, R., Quinto, I., Rippa, P., & Thomas, A. (2020). Evolution of collaborative networks supporting startup sustainability: Evidences from digital firms. *Sustainability (Basel), 12*(22), 9437. doi:10.3390/su12229437

Prabhuswamy, M., Tripathi, R., Vijayakumar, M., Thulasimani, T., Sundharesalingam, P., & Sampath, B. (2024). A Study on the Complex Nature of Higher Education Leadership: An Innovative Approach. In *Challenges of Globalization and Inclusivity in Academic Research* (pp. 202–223). IGI Global. doi:10.4018/979-8-3693-1371-8.ch013

Purnomo, A., Asitah, N., & Rosyidah, E. (2023). Understanding the Nexus between Green Entrepreneurship and Green Economy: A Review. *Journal of Economics and Business UBS, 12*(4), 2470–2484. doi:10.52644/joeb.v12i4.444

Rahamathunnisa, U., Sudhakar, K., Murugan, T. K., Thivaharan, S., Rajkumar, M., & Boopathi, S. (2023). Cloud Computing Principles for Optimizing Robot Task Offloading Processes. In *AI-Enabled Social Robotics in Human Care Services* (pp. 188–211). IGI Global. doi:10.4018/978-1-6684-8171-4.ch007

Ravisankar, A., Shanthi, A., Lavanya, S., Ramaratnam, M., Krishnamoorthy, V., & Boopathi, S. (2024). Harnessing 6G for Consumer-Centric Business Strategies Across Electronic Industries. In AI Impacts in Digital Consumer Behavior (pp. 241–270). IGI Global.

Ren, S., & Jackson, S. E. (2020). HRM institutional entrepreneurship for sustainable business organizations. *Human Resource Management Review, 30*(3), 100691. doi:10.1016/j.hrmr.2019.100691

Reuther, K., Dahle, Y., Schmidt, C., & Schösser, F. (2023). Motivational Facets of Sustainable Entrepreneurship: A Systematic Review and Future Research Agenda. *Sustainability (Basel), 15*(3), 2272. doi:10.3390/su15032272

Rosário, A. T., & Figueiredo, J. (2023). *Sustainable Entrepreneurship and Corporate Social Responsibility: Systematic Bibliometric Literature Review.*

Rosário, A. T., & Figueiredo, J. (2024). Sustainable entrepreneurship and corporate social responsibility: Analysing the state of research. *Sustainable Environment, 10*(1), 2324572. doi:10.1080/27658511.2024.2324572

Saravanan, A., Venkatasubramanian, R., Khare, R., Surakasi, R., Boopathi, S., Ray, S., & Sudhakar, M. (2022). Policy trends of renewable energy and non. *Renewable Energy.*

Sarma, S., Attaran, S., & Attaran, M. (2024). Sustainable entrepreneurship: Factors influencing opportunity recognition and exploitation. *International Journal of Entrepreneurship and Innovation, 25*(1), 56–69. doi:10.1177/14657503221093007

Sen, S. (2020). *Digital HR strategy: Achieving sustainable transformation in the digital age.* Kogan Page Publishers.

Sipola, J., Saunila, M., & Ukko, J. (2023). Adopting artificial intelligence in sustainable business. *Journal of Cleaner Production*, *426*, 139197. doi:10.1016/j.jclepro.2023.139197

Stuss, M. (2023). The concept of HR 4.0: A literature review. *International Entrepreneurship Review*, *9*(3).

Thanasi-Boçe, M., Kurtishi-Kastrati, S., Ramadani, V., & Zuferi, R. (2023). Sustainable Entrepreneurship in North Macedonia: Challenges and Perspectives. *Entrepreneurship Development in the Balkans: Perspective from Diverse Contexts*, 197–211.

Venkateswaran, N., Vidhya, R., Naik, D. A., Raj, T. M., Munjal, N., & Boopathi, S. (2023). Study on Sentence and Question Formation Using Deep Learning Techniques. In *Digital Natives as a Disruptive Force in Asian Businesses and Societies* (pp. 252–273). IGI Global. doi:10.4018/978-1-6684-6782-4.ch015

Zaheer, H. (2022). *Digital entrepreneurship: Review, trajectory and practice* [PhD Thesis]. Macquarie University.

Chapter 15
The Fusion of AI, IoT, and Agricultural Sensors for Self-Sustaining Agro-Technological Ecosystems:
Industry 5.0

S. Kalpana
Department of Artificial Intelligence and Data Science, Jai Shriram Engineering College, India

Kamunuri Ganapathi Babu
Department of Computer Science and Engineering, St. Martin's Engineering College, India

T. V. N. Padmavathi
Department of Food Safety and Quality Assurance, College of Food Science and Technology, India

Bhumika Sharma
https://orcid.org/0000-0002-3963-6036
Sharda School of Law, Sharda University, India

Hari B. S.
https://orcid.org/0000-0002-4778-3802
Department of Mechanical Engineering, Kongu Engineering College, India

M. Sudha
SSR Engineering College, India

ABSTRACT

This chapter explores the integration of artificial intelligence (AI), the internet of things (IoT), and agricultural sensors in creating self-sustaining ago-technological ecosystems. It delves into the historical foundations of agricultural technology, highlights the modern technologies' impact on farming practices, provides a detailed understanding of AI in agriculture, and highlights the role of agricultural sensors. The chapter discusses the integration of AI, IoT, and sensors in agriculture, focusing on the development of self-sustaining ecosystems. It discusses challenges in implementing these technologies and proposes solutions. Real-world case studies provide valuable insights. The chapter also explores the future trajectory of these advancements and their potential to revolutionize agriculture, offering a comprehensive guide for navigating technology-agriculture harmony for sustainable and efficient practices.

DOI: 10.4018/979-8-3693-1343-5.ch015

INTRODUCTION

Modern agriculture is a blend of technological innovation and sustainable practices, utilizing AI, IoT, and agricultural sensors to create self-sustaining ecosystems. This paradigm shift in farming practices has led to increased efficiency, productivity, and ecological responsibility, transforming the traditional agricultural foundations. The chapter explores the transformative impact of AI, IoT, and agricultural sensors on the agricultural landscape, highlighting their role in addressing challenges like a growing global population and climate change (Boopathi, 2024). It outlines how these technologies can synergize to create self-sustaining agricultural ecosystems, laying the groundwork for a comprehensive exploration of sustainable farming methods (Koshariya, Kalaiyarasi, et al., 2023a).

The second segment explores AI's potential in agriculture, highlighting its role in crop management, autonomous machinery, and resource optimization. It explores the integration of algorithms and machine learning in farming operations, highlighting its transformative impact on decision-making processes and reshaping the agricultural landscape. The third segment explores the integration of the Internet of Things (IoT) into agriculture, focusing on how IoT devices provide farmers with insights and control over their operations. The section aims to demystify the intricate web of interconnected devices that form the backbone of smart farming, enhancing efficiency and resource conservation (Koshariya, Khatoon, et al., 2023a).

This emphasizes the importance of agricultural sensors in modern farming practices, collecting data on soil health, weather patterns, and crop conditions. Understanding these sensors aids farmers in making informed decisions, optimizing inputs, and mitigating risks, enhancing the agro-technological ecosystem. The text envisions the convergence of AI, IoT, and agricultural sensors into self-sustaining ecosystems, promoting increased productivity and ecological sustainability. This exploration of the complex relationship between technology and agriculture aims for a harmonious future in the farming world (P. Kumar et al., 2023). The integration of Artificial Intelligence (AI), the Internet of Things (IoT), and agricultural sensors has transformed modern agriculture into a dynamic, interconnected ecosystem. This introduction highlights the importance of these technologies in contemporary farming practices, enhancing efficiency, promoting sustainability, and precision, and paving the way for a new era of farming(S. et al., 2022).

AI, IoT, and agricultural sensors have significantly transformed the agricultural sector, enabling informed decision-making and addressing challenges such as climate uncertainties and resource optimization. AI's ability to analyze vast datasets and make predictive insights drives agriculture away from traditional practices (Koshariya, Kalaiyarasi, et al., 2023b; Koshariya, Khatoon, et al., 2023b; P. Kumar et al., 2023). Its impact extends beyond traditional boundaries, with machine learning algorithms revolutionizing farming operations. From predictive analytics optimizing planting and harvesting schedules to autonomous machinery navigating fields with precision, AI has transformed farming methodologies, making them more efficient, responsive, and adaptable. This transformation is a testament to the transformative role of AI in modern agriculture (Agrawal et al., 2024).

The Internet of Things (IoT) is a crucial component in modern agriculture, connecting devices, machinery, and sensors to gather and transmit real-time data. It plays a vital role in precision agriculture, enabling smart irrigation systems, climate monitoring, and crop health sensors (Gnanaprakasam et al., 2023a; Jeevanantham et al., 2022; Sankar et al., 2023a). Agricultural sensors, acting as sensory organs, gather vital information from the fields, such as soil health, weather patterns, and crop conditions. Real-time data acquisition from these sensors provides farmers with actionable insights, enabling timely interventions, efficient resource allocation, and risk mitigation, thereby enhancing the resilience of the agricultural system (Sankar et al., 2023b).

The integration of AI, IoT, and agricultural sensors is seen as a roadmap for precision and sustainability in modern farming. The significance lies in their harmonious integration, paving the way for self-sustaining agro-technological ecosystems. This exploration aims to explore the intricate interplay between technology and agriculture, focusing on advancements that contribute to a more resilient, efficient, and sustainable future for farming. The concept of self-sustaining agro-technological ecosystems is a promising innovation in the rapidly changing agriculture landscape. It combines advanced technologies like AI, IoT, and agricultural sensors to create a dynamic and interconnected agricultural paradigm. This holistic approach optimizes productivity while nurturing the environment, making it a crucial solution for traditional farming methods in a rapidly changing world (Pachiappan et al., 2023).

The agricultural revolution requires a paradigm shift towards a more integrated and self-sufficient approach. Self-sustaining agro-technological ecosystems aim to redefine agriculture by combining nature and innovation. The integration of cutting-edge technologies is crucial for creating a dynamic and responsive agricultural ecosystem. AI, IoT, and agricultural sensors synergize to optimize operations and set the stage for a more sustainable and resilient farming future. This synergy transcends individual capabilities, enabling a harmonious coexistence between nature and innovation. The integration of AI, IoT, and agricultural sensors creates a technological symphony that optimizes agricultural operations (P. R. Kumar et al., 2023a).

The concept of self-sustaining agro-technological ecosystems emphasizes holistic resource management, integrating AI, IoT, and sensors to manage resources like water, fertilizers, and energy. This approach minimizes waste and environmental impact while maximizing yields. Beyond resource management, these ecosystems also promote environmental stewardship and biodiversity. By balancing productivity and environmental conservation through technology-driven monitoring, farmers can ensure the longevity of their operations and the health of their ecosystems. This approach goes beyond mere efficiency gains and promotes sustainable practices (Agrawal, Magulur, et al., 2023a).

The vision for farming in self-sustaining agro-technological ecosystems is a vision of innovation, resilience, and sustainability. Technology is not just a tool but an integral part of a balanced, regenerative agricultural system. This concept promotes a thriving coexistence between technology and agriculture. This chapter will explore the practical implementations and implications of self-sustaining agro-technological ecosystems in modern agriculture, highlighting the importance of technology in achieving this vision.

Scope: The chapter aims to explore the convergence of artificial intelligence (AI), the Internet of Things (IoT), and agricultural sensors within the context of modern agriculture. It begins by tracing the historical foundations of agricultural technology, providing a contextual understanding of how farming practices have evolved over time. The chapter then transitions to a discussion of contemporary technological advancements and their profound impact on agricultural operations.

Objectives

- To elucidate the historical evolution of agricultural technology, tracing its roots and pivotal developments that have shaped modern farming practices.
- To analyze the transformative effects of modern technologies such as AI, IoT, and agricultural sensors on traditional farming methods, highlighting their contributions to efficiency, productivity, and sustainability.

- To provide a comprehensive understanding of artificial intelligence applications within the agricultural sector, including machine learning algorithms, predictive analytics, and autonomous decision-making systems.
- To explore the significance of agricultural sensors in data collection, monitoring, and optimization of farming processes, emphasizing their role in enabling precision agriculture and resource management.
- To integrate AI, IoT, and sensors in agriculture to foster the development of self-sustaining agro-technological ecosystems, where farms operate efficiently with minimal human intervention, promoting sustainability and resilience.

FOUNDATIONS OF AGRICULTURAL TECHNOLOGY

Agriculture has a long history, with early technological interventions revolutionizing food production. Simple tools like plows and irrigation systems allowed early civilizations to cultivate larger areas and sustain growing populations (Agrawal, Magulur, et al., 2023b; Gnanaprakasam et al., 2023a; Sankar et al., 2023a). As societies progressed, innovations like the wheel and domesticated animals further transformed the agricultural landscape. Each technological leap in agriculture has been a pivotal chapter in human society advancement, laying the groundwork for the sophisticated technologies used in modern agro-technological ecosystems (Agrawal et al., 2024; S. et al., 2022).

Evolution of Farming Practices

The evolution of farming practices is closely linked to technological advancements, shaping human sustenance. Early farming relied on manual labor, but the Industrial Revolution introduced mechanization, increasing efficiency. The Green Revolution introduced high-yield crop varieties and chemical fertilizers, boosting productivity. This evolution reflects the need for sustainable and scalable food production, paving the way for the integration of AI, IoT, and agricultural sensors. The continuous dialogue between human ingenuity and technology continues to shape modern agriculture (Boopathi, Siva Kumar, et al., 2023).

The Role of Technology in Agriculture

At its core, the role of technology in agriculture has been a catalyst for progress and sustainability. The third segment elucidates how technology has become the linchpin of modern farming practices. From the advent of tractors and combine harvesters to precision agriculture utilizing GPS and satellite imaging, technology has continually redefined the efficiency and scope of farming operations. The integration of biotechnology, genetic engineering, and now AI, IoT, and agricultural sensors marks the pinnacle of this evolution. The role of technology is not merely about increasing yields; it's about fostering a balance between productivity and environmental responsibility. This historical evolution serves as a crucial backdrop, emphasizing that the integration of AI, IoT, and agricultural sensors is the latest chapter in a long narrative of human innovation in agriculture (Boopathi, Siva Kumar, et al., 2023).

AI IN AGRICULTURE

Artificial Intelligence (AI) is revolutionizing agriculture by reshaping traditional practices and promoting precision and efficiency. Machine learning algorithms and data analytics provide farmers with valuable insights, enabling smarter decision-making and sustainable resource management, thereby transforming the agricultural landscape (Agrawal et al., 2024). The use of Artificial Intelligence (AI) is significantly transforming the agricultural sector as shown in Figure 1.

- ***Crop Monitoring and Management:*** One of the pivotal applications of AI in agriculture lies in crop monitoring and management. AI algorithms process vast datasets derived from satellite imagery, drones, and ground-based sensors to assess crop health, detect diseases, and predict yield outcomes. This level of precision enables farmers to intervene proactively, optimizing irrigation, fertilization, and pest control strategies. AI-driven crop monitoring not only enhances productivity but also contributes to resource conservation and reduced environmental impact (Boopathi, 2024; P. R. Kumar et al., 2023b; Pachiappan et al., 2024).
- ***Precision Farming with AI:*** Precision farming, facilitated by AI, represents a paradigm shift from uniform agricultural practices to site-specific management. AI algorithms analyze diverse sets of data, including soil composition, weather patterns, and historical yield data, to prescribe precise actions for each part of a field. This targeted approach ensures optimal resource utilization, minimizing waste and environmental impact. AI-powered precision farming empowers farmers to tailor their interventions, enhancing productivity while simultaneously promoting sustainability (Agrawal, Magulur, et al., 2023a).
- ***Autonomous Machinery and Robotics:*** AI's influence extends to the realm of autonomous machinery and robotics, transforming the way tasks are executed on the farm. From autonomous tractors to robotic weeders, AI enables machines to navigate fields with precision, perform targeted actions, and adapt to changing conditions in real-time. This not only reduces the burden on labor but also enhances operational efficiency and cost-effectiveness. The integration of AI-driven robotics heralds a future where tasks are accomplished with unprecedented accuracy and speed (Maheswari et al., 2023).
- ***Predictive Analytics for Weather and Climate:*** AI's ability to analyze and predict weather patterns is a game-changer for agriculture. Predictive analytics, fueled by AI algorithms, offer farmers insights into upcoming weather events, allowing them to make informed decisions regarding planting, harvesting, and other critical activities. By anticipating climatic changes, farmers can mitigate risks associated with extreme weather conditions, contributing to improved crop resilience and

Figure 1. Artificial intelligence (AI) is revolutionizing agriculture

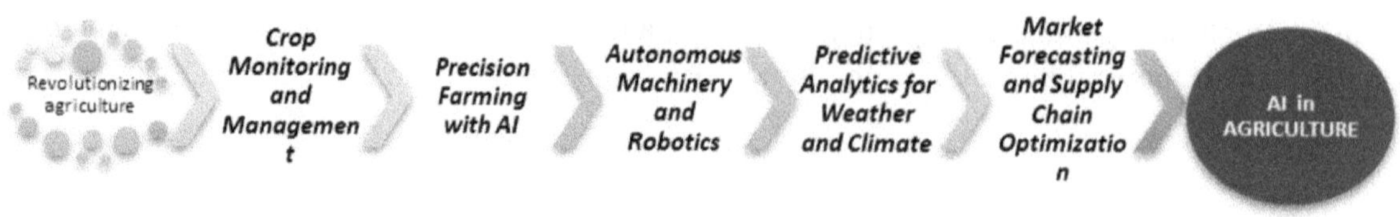

overall farm management (Agrawal, Shashibhushan, et al., 2023; Koshariya, Kalaiyarasi, et al., 2023b).

- ***Market Forecasting and Supply Chain Optimization:*** Beyond the field, AI contributes to market forecasting and supply chain optimization. Machine learning algorithms analyze market trends, commodity prices, and global demand to provide farmers with insights into potential market fluctuations (Mohanty, Venkateswaran, Ranjit, et al., 2023; Verma et al., 2024). This aids in strategic decision-making, such as crop selection and timing of sales, optimizing returns on investment. Additionally, AI facilitates supply chain efficiency, streamlining the distribution process and minimizing waste in the journey from farm to consumer (Dhanya et al., 2023).

AI's integration into agriculture is a technological revolution that enhances crop management and precision farming, offering sustainable, efficient, and resilient practices to tackle the challenges of a growing global population and changing environmental conditions.

AI Transforming in Farming Processes

The use of AI is revolutionizing farming processes, as depicted in Figure 2.

- ***Crop Monitoring and Disease Detection:*** AI-powered image recognition and machine learning algorithms analyze satellite imagery and drone data to monitor crop health. Early detection of diseases, nutrient deficiencies, or pest infestations allows farmers to take targeted actions, minimizing crop losses (Boopathi, Siva Kumar, et al., 2023).

Figure 2. AI transforming in farming processes

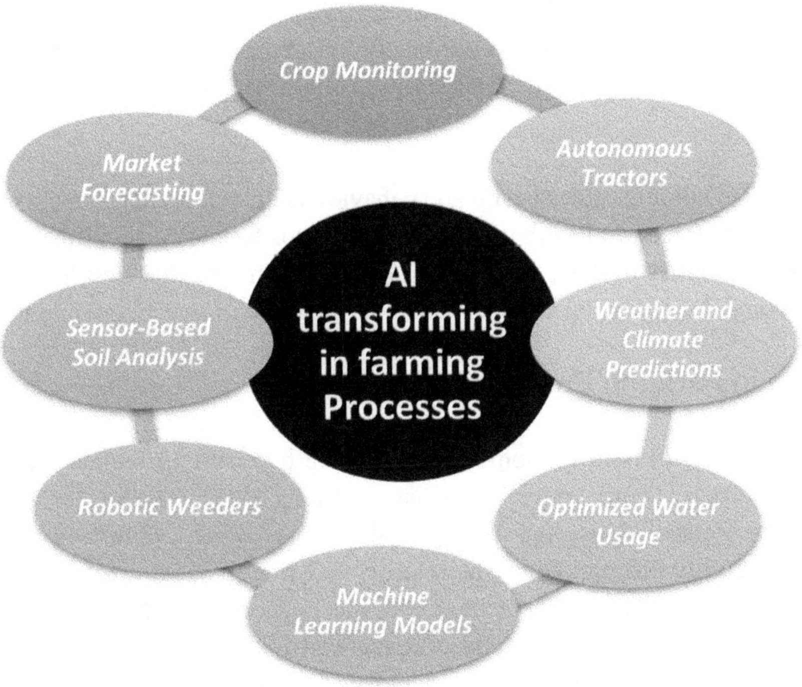

- ***Autonomous Tractors and Harvesters:*** AI enables the development of autonomous agricultural machinery. These machines use sensors and computer vision to navigate fields, plant seeds, apply fertilizers, and harvest crops with precision. This reduces the need for human labor, increases operational efficiency, and ensures consistent and accurate task execution.
- ***Weather and Climate Predictions:*** AI algorithms analyze historical weather data and satellite information to predict weather patterns. This helps farmers plan their activities based on upcoming weather conditions, reducing risks associated with adverse weather events and optimizing planting and harvesting schedules.
- ***Optimized Water Usage:*** AI-driven systems monitor soil moisture levels and weather forecasts to determine precise irrigation needs. By optimizing water usage, farmers can enhance crop yields, conserve water resources, and mitigate the environmental impact of excessive irrigation (Boopathi, Sureshkumar, et al., 2023; Hussain et al., 2023; Ingle et al., 2023).
- ***Machine Learning Models for Yield Estimation:*** AI models utilize data on weather conditions, soil quality, and historical yields to predict crop yields. This information assists farmers in making informed decisions regarding crop selection, resource allocation, and market planning (Syamala et al., 2023; Zekrifa et al., 2023).
- ***Robotic Weeders and AI-Powered Pest Control:*** AI technologies, such as computer vision and machine learning, are employed in robotic weeders that can identify and eliminate weeds without harming crops. AI also aids in the development of smart pest control systems, where drones or robots precisely apply pesticides based on real-time data analysis.
- ***Sensor-Based Soil Analysis:*** AI is used in conjunction with soil sensors to assess soil health and composition. These systems analyze data on nutrient levels, pH, and moisture content, providing farmers with actionable insights for soil management practices, including fertilization and crop rotation (Gnanaprakasam et al., 2023b).
- ***Market Forecasting and Logistics:*** AI analyzes market trends, demand patterns, and historical data to provide accurate market forecasts. This assists farmers in making strategic decisions about crop selection and timing of sales. Additionally, AI optimizes supply chain logistics, reducing waste and ensuring efficient delivery from farm to consumer (Mohanty, Venkateswaran, Ranjit P. S., et al., 2023).

AI-based systems monitor livestock health and behavior using sensors and cameras to collect data on movements, feeding patterns, and health indicators. This helps farmers detect illnesses early, optimize feeding, and improve animal welfare. AI-driven robotic systems identify and harvest ripe fruits and vegetables using computer vision, ensuring efficient and selective harvesting while minimizing waste.

IoT Integration in Farming Process

The Internet of Things (IoT) is revolutionizing agriculture by enabling seamless data exchange and analysis. Its integration has led to a new era of precision farming and smart practices. IoT's fundamentals include real-time data, connectivity, and intelligent decision-making, optimizing resource utilization and enhancing productivity in agriculture. The Internet of Things (IoT) is a network of interconnected devices with sensors, software, and other technologies that collect and exchange data. It can range from simple sensors to sophisticated machinery and equipment (Kavitha et al., 2023; Maguluri et al., 2023). In agriculture, IoT applications involve sensors deployed in fields, machinery, and livestock, creating a comprehensive network for data collection and sharing. The integration of IoT technology is being increasingly integrated into the farming process (Figure 3).

- ***IoT Components in Agriculture:*** The relevance of IoT in agriculture becomes evident when examining its important components. Sensors are the frontline soldiers of IoT in farming, measuring various parameters such as soil moisture, temperature, humidity, and crop health. Actuators enable automated responses based on the collected data, triggering actions like irrigation, fertilization, or pest control. Communication networks, often wireless, facilitate the transmission of data between devices and central systems. Cloud platforms serve as repositories for vast amounts of data, allowing for storage, analysis, and retrieval, while user interfaces provide farmers with intuitive ways to access and interpret this information (Reddy et al., 2023a).
- ***Precision Agriculture and Resource Optimization:*** One of the primary contributions of IoT to agriculture is the realization of precision farming. With sensors strategically placed throughout the agricultural landscape, farmers can monitor and manage their fields with unprecedented accuracy. Soil sensors, for example, measure moisture levels and nutrient content, allowing for precise irrigation and fertilization strategies. This not only optimizes resource usage but also mitigates environmental impact by reducing water and fertilizer runoff. Precision agriculture, enabled by IoT, empowers farmers to tailor their interventions based on real-time data, leading to more efficient and sustainable farming practices (Boopathi & Khang, 2023).
- ***Real-Time Monitoring and Decision Support:*** The real-time monitoring capabilities facilitated by IoT devices offer farmers a continuous stream of data on environmental conditions, crop health, and livestock status. This information is invaluable for timely decision-making. Farmers

Figure 3. IoT integration in farming process

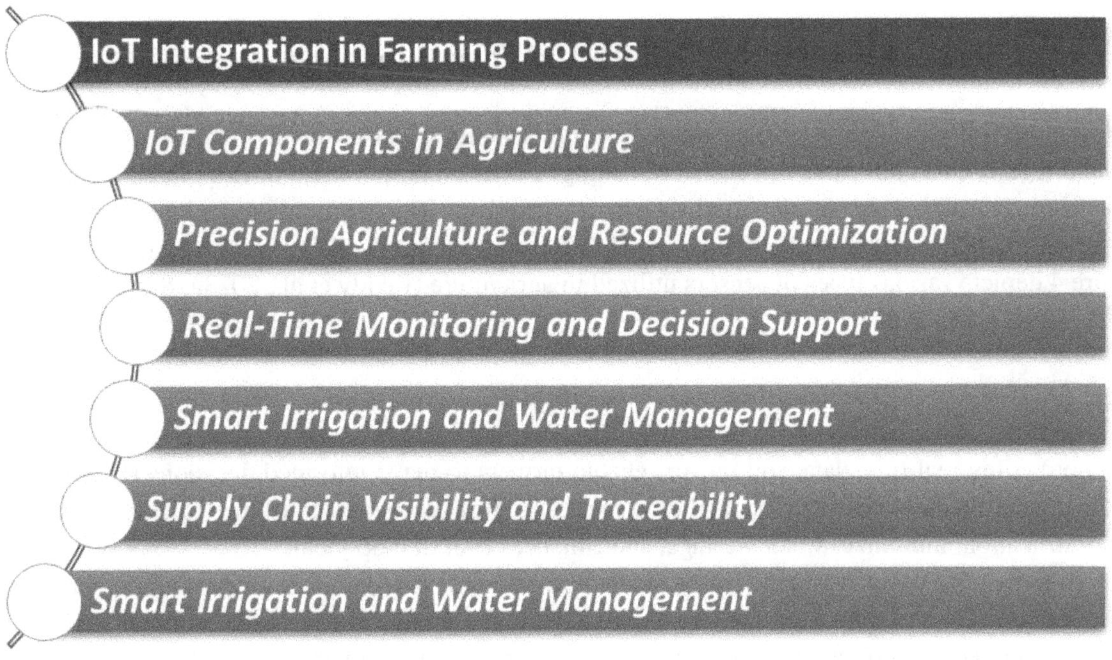

can receive alerts about potential issues, such as disease outbreaks or adverse weather conditions, enabling proactive interventions. This proactive approach enhances overall farm management, reduces the risk of crop losses, and contributes to increased yields (Kavitha et al., 2023; Maguluri et al., 2023).

- ***Smart Irrigation and Water Management:*** IoT plays a crucial role in addressing water scarcity challenges in agriculture through smart irrigation systems. Soil moisture sensors combined with weather data allow for precise irrigation scheduling. These systems ensure that crops receive the optimal amount of water, reducing waste and promoting water conservation. Smart irrigation, driven by IoT, not only enhances water use efficiency but also contributes to sustainable agricultural practices (Sankar et al., 2023b).
- ***Supply Chain Visibility and Traceability:*** Beyond the field, IoT enhances the entire agricultural supply chain. Sensors can track the condition of harvested crops during transportation and storage, ensuring quality and minimizing waste. IoT technologies contribute to supply chain visibility, providing stakeholders with real-time information on inventory levels, demand patterns, and logistics. This transparency not only streamlines operations but also facilitates traceability, allowing consumers to trace the journey of their food from farm to table.

The Internet of Things (IoT) is revolutionizing agriculture by providing real-time data, promoting precision farming, optimizing resource usage, and contributing to sustainable practices. However, challenges like data security, interoperability, and the digital divide need to be addressed. As technologies evolve, the future of IoT in agriculture holds promise, with innovations in edge computing, artificial intelligence, and 5G connectivity enhancing its capabilities. This synergy is crucial for global food security, environmental stewardship, and farming efficiency.

THE ROLE OF AGRICULTURAL SENSORS

Types of Sensors Used in Agriculture and Their Functions

Agriculture is undergoing a transformation driven by technological innovation, with sensors playing a crucial role in data collection and decision-making. These small, powerful devices facilitate precision agriculture, resource optimization, and sustainable practices. This exploration explores various types of sensors and their functions, highlighting their efficiency and productivity in farming operations. The figure 4 depicts various types of sensors utilized in agriculture (Reddy et al., 2023a; Samikannu et al., 2023; Satav et al., 2024).

- *Soil Sensors:* Soil sensors measure various parameters crucial for understanding soil health and fertility. These include moisture content, temperature, pH levels, and nutrient concentrations. By providing real-time data, soil sensors enable farmers to make informed decisions regarding irrigation schedules, fertilization, and crop selection. This precision contributes to efficient resource utilization, minimizes water wastage, and enhances overall crop yield.
- *Weather Sensors:* Weather sensors, including instruments like anemometers, barometers, and thermometers, monitor atmospheric conditions in and around the agricultural fields. These sensors collect data on temperature, humidity, wind speed, and precipitation. The information aids

Figure 4. Types of sensors used in agriculture

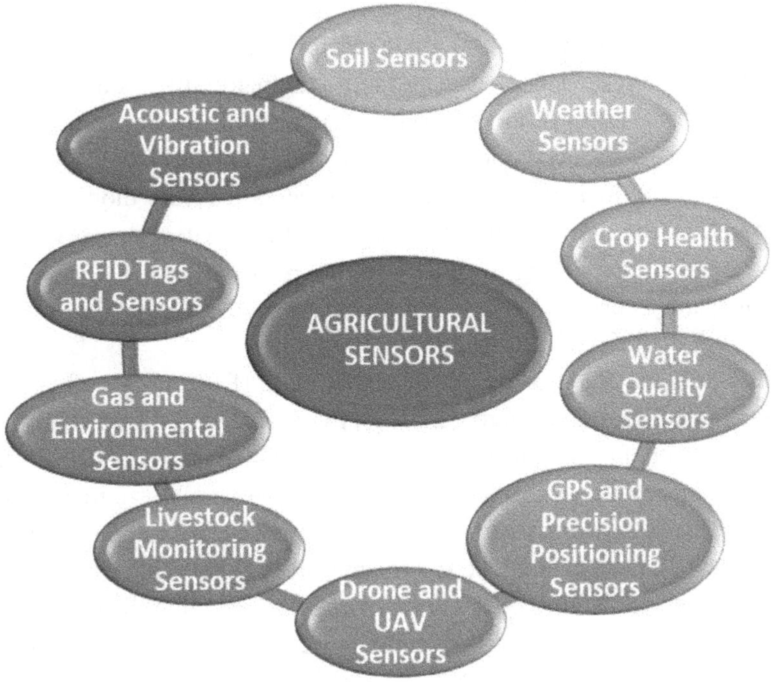

farmers in predicting weather patterns, optimizing planting and harvesting schedules, and mitigating risks associated with extreme weather events.

- *Crop Health Sensors:* Crop health sensors, often utilizing spectral imaging technology, assess the well-being of plants by analyzing their physiological characteristics. These sensors detect signs of stress, diseases, or nutrient deficiencies, allowing farmers to take targeted actions. Monitoring crop health in real-time facilitates early intervention, minimizing crop losses, and maximizing overall yield.
- *Water Quality Sensors:* Water quality sensors are crucial for monitoring the condition of irrigation water and water sources on the farm. These sensors measure parameters such as pH, dissolved oxygen, and nutrient levels. By ensuring that irrigation water meets quality standards, farmers can prevent soil salinity issues and optimize the efficiency of fertilization practices (Ali et al., 2024; P. R. Kumar et al., 2023b; Veeranjaneyulu et al., 2023).
- *GPS and Precision Positioning Sensors:* Global Positioning System (GPS) and precision positioning sensors provide accurate location information for agricultural machinery and equipment. These sensors enable precision agriculture practices by ensuring precise navigation for tractors, planters, and harvesters. This precision reduces overlap in operations, minimizes input wastage, and enhances the overall efficiency of field operations (Pachiappan et al., 2023; Rahamathunnisa, Sudhakar, et al., 2023).
- *Drone and UAV Sensors:* Drones and Unmanned Aerial Vehicles (UAVs) equipped with various sensors, including cameras and multispectral sensors, capture high-resolution images and data from above the fields. This aerial data is used for crop monitoring, disease detection, and yield

prediction. The information obtained through drone sensors aids in making data-driven decisions and optimizing farm management practices.

- *Livestock Monitoring Sensors:* Sensors designed for livestock monitoring track the health and behavior of animals. These sensors can measure parameters like body temperature, heart rate, and movement patterns. Livestock monitoring sensors enable early detection of illnesses, assist in optimizing feeding regimes, and contribute to overall animal welfare on the farm.
- *Gas and Environmental Sensors:* Gas and environmental sensors monitor air quality and environmental conditions in and around agricultural facilities. These sensors can detect gases like ammonia and methane, providing insights into the environmental impact of farming practices. Monitoring air quality ensures a safe environment for both crops and livestock (Arunprasad & Boopathi, 2019; Boopathi, 2022b, 2022a).
- *RFID Tags and Sensors:* Radio-Frequency Identification (RFID) tags, often combined with sensors, are used for tracking and managing inventory in agriculture. These sensors enable farmers to monitor the movement of assets, such as equipment, crops, or livestock. RFID technology contributes to supply chain visibility and traceability, enhancing overall farm management.
- *Acoustic and Vibration Sensors:* Acoustic and vibration sensors can be employed for pest detection in crops. These sensors pick up the sound patterns or vibrations associated with pest activity. Early detection allows for targeted pest control measures, reducing the need for widespread pesticide applications and minimizing environmental impact (Srinivas et al., 2023a).

The integration of various sensors in agriculture has significantly improved farmers' operations by providing real-time data, promoting precision, resource efficiency, and sustainable practices. As technology advances, the sophistication and capabilities of agricultural sensors are expected to grow, opening new opportunities for innovation in more efficient and environmentally conscious farming.

Impact of Sensors on Crop Monitoring and Management

The integration of sensors in agriculture has revolutionized crop monitoring and management practices, transforming the way farmers collect and utilize data. From soil and weather sensors to advanced imaging technologies, these sensors have revolutionized the agricultural landscape, offering important benefits and advancements that have reshaped the agricultural landscape (Kavitha et al., 2023; Maguluri et al., 2023).

- *Real-Time Data for Informed Decision-Making:* One of the most profound impacts of sensors on crop monitoring and management is the provision of real-time data. Soil sensors continuously measure crucial parameters such as moisture content, temperature, and nutrient levels. Weather sensors collect atmospheric data, while advanced imaging sensors monitor crop health. This influx of real-time information empowers farmers to make informed decisions promptly. Whether adjusting irrigation schedules, applying fertilizers, or identifying potential disease outbreaks, the immediacy of data ensures that interventions are timely and precisely tailored to the specific needs of the crops (Revathi et al., 2024).
- *Optimized Resource Utilization:* Sensors contribute to optimized resource utilization, a critical aspect of sustainable and efficient farming. Soil sensors, for instance, provide insights into the moisture levels in the soil. By integrating this information with weather data, farmers can implement precision irrigation, delivering the right amount of water at the right time. This not only conserves

water resources but also prevents over-irrigation, reducing the risk of soil salinity and minimizing environmental impact. Similarly, nutrient sensors assist in precisely managing fertilization, ensuring that crops receive the necessary nutrients without excess application (Boopathi & Sivakumar, 2013; Kalidas et al., 2012; Myilsamy & Sampath, 2017).

- *Enhanced Crop Health Monitoring:* The impact of sensors on crop health monitoring is monumental. Advanced imaging sensors, including multispectral and hyperspectral cameras mounted on drones or satellites, capture detailed information about crop conditions. These sensors can detect subtle variations in plant reflectance, indicating stress, diseases, or nutrient deficiencies. The early detection of such issues allows farmers to implement targeted interventions, preventing the spread of diseases and minimizing crop losses. Crop health sensors contribute to proactive management strategies, fostering resilient and healthier crops.
- *Precision Agriculture Practices:* The advent of sensors has facilitated the widespread adoption of precision agriculture practices. GPS and precision positioning sensors, when integrated with other sensors, enable precise navigation of agricultural machinery. This ensures that activities such as planting, fertilizing, and harvesting are executed with remarkable accuracy. Precision agriculture minimizes overlap, reduces input wastage, and enhances the overall efficiency of field operations. The impact is tangible, leading to increased yields, reduced costs, and more sustainable farming practices.
- *Data-Driven Decision Support Systems:* Sensors serve as the backbone for the development of data-driven decision support systems. These systems utilize the vast amount of data collected by sensors to provide farmers with actionable insights. Machine learning algorithms analyze historical and real-time data to generate predictions and recommendations. For instance, based on weather patterns and soil conditions, decision support systems can recommend optimal planting times or suggest specific crop varieties. This data-driven approach optimizes decision-making, enabling farmers to adapt to changing conditions and uncertainties in the agricultural environment.

CONVERGENCE OF AI, IOT, AND SENSORS

Synergistic Integration of AI, IoT, and Sensors for Sustainable Agriculture

The integration of Artificial Intelligence (AI), the Internet of Things (IoT), and sensors is revolutionizing agriculture by creating a harmonious ecosystem that promotes sustainable practices. This comprehensive study explores how these technologies work together, providing a comprehensive view of their integration for sustainable agriculture advancement (Rebecca et al., 2023).

- At the core of this synergy is the Internet of Things, acting as the nervous system of the agricultural ecosystem. IoT involves a network of interconnected devices equipped with sensors and actuators. These devices, deployed throughout the farm, collect and transmit data in real-time. Soil sensors monitor moisture levels, weather stations capture atmospheric conditions, and crop health sensors assess the vitality of plants. This vast array of IoT-enabled sensors forms the foundation upon which AI-driven intelligence is built.
- The synergy begins with the seamless acquisition of data from IoT-enabled sensors. Soil sensors provide insights into the composition and moisture levels of the soil, weather sensors capture

climatic conditions, and crop health sensors monitor the well-being of plants. The data collected is transmitted through interconnected networks, creating a web of information that is instantly accessible. This real-time data flow forms the basis for informed decision-making in agriculture.

- The data acquired by IoT devices serves as the raw material for Artificial Intelligence. AI, with its analytical prowess, processes and interprets this data. Machine learning algorithms, a subset of AI, analyze patterns, predict outcomes, and generate actionable insights. For example, AI can analyze historical weather patterns and current soil conditions to predict optimal planting times or recommend specific crops for cultivation. This analytical layer enhances the ability to extract meaningful information from the vast datasets generated by IoT sensors (Boopathi, 2023b; Jeevanantham et al., 2022; Reddy et al., 2023b; Samikannu et al., 2022).
- The marriage of AI and IoT gives rise to precision agriculture, a practice that optimizes resource utilization with surgical precision. AI algorithms, fueled by real-time data from IoT sensors, can prescribe precise actions for each part of a field. For instance, based on soil conditions, weather forecasts, and historical yield data, AI can recommend the exact amount of water, fertilizers, or pesticides needed for different areas of the farm. This targeted approach minimizes waste, reduces environmental impact, and enhances overall resource efficiency.
- The synergy of AI, IoT, and sensors facilitates autonomous decision-making in agriculture. AI algorithms, continuously learning from incoming data, can autonomously trigger actions through IoT-connected devices. For instance, if a crop health sensor detects signs of disease, the AI system can automatically initiate the release of targeted pesticides through automated spray systems. This swift response to emerging challenges enhances the resilience of the agricultural system, reducing the need for manual intervention (Boopathi, Kumar, et al., 2023; Gnanaprakasam et al., 2023a; P. R. Kumar et al., 2023b).
- The collaborative integration of AI, IoT, and sensors promotes sustainability and environmental stewardship. By continuously monitoring and optimizing resource usage, the system minimizes the ecological footprint of farming practices. Precision agriculture practices driven by AI and IoT contribute to soil health, water conservation, and biodiversity preservation. The collective intelligence of these technologies fosters a balanced approach that aligns agricultural productivity with long-term environmental sustainability (Pachiappan et al., 2024).
- The synergy extends to adaptive learning, wherein AI systems continuously evolve based on feedback from IoT sensors. This iterative process allows the system to adapt to changing environmental conditions, emerging challenges, and the unique dynamics of each farm. This adaptive learning loop ensures that the agricultural ecosystem becomes more resilient over time, optimizing its responses to a myriad of factors influencing crop growth and overall farm management.

BUILDING SELF-SUSTAINING ECOSYSTEMS

The Concept of Self-Sustaining Agricultural Ecosystems:

Self-sustaining agricultural ecosystems are a paradigm shift in farming, focusing on a holistic, regenerative approach that harmonizes with natural processes. These systems are productive, resilient, environmentally friendly, and maintain a balance between resource use and replenishment. Main principles and practices aim to create a sustainable relationship between agriculture and the environment, promoting a more balanced and sustainable farming system. The figure 5 depicts the process of creating self-sustaining ecosystems (Boopathi, Siva Kumar, et al., 2023; Domakonda et al., 2023; Kumar B et al., 2024).

- *Biodiversity and Crop Rotation:* At the core of self-sustaining agricultural ecosystems is the promotion of biodiversity. Instead of relying on monoculture, where a single crop is cultivated repeatedly, these ecosystems embrace diversity through crop rotation. Crop rotation involves alternating the types of crops planted in a given area over time. This practice not only helps break the cycles of pests and diseases but also fosters a healthier soil structure. Different crops have different nutrient requirements, and by diversifying, the ecosystem maintains a balanced nutrient profile while reducing the need for external inputs (Boopathi & Kumar, 2024; Venkateswaran, Kumar, et al., 2023).
- *Natural Pest Management:* Rather than relying solely on chemical interventions, self-sustaining agricultural ecosystems embrace natural pest management strategies. Beneficial insects, such as ladybugs and predatory beetles, are encouraged to thrive, providing a natural balance in controlling pest populations. Additionally, companion planting—cultivating different crops in proximity to benefit each other—helps repel pests and enhance overall resilience. This approach minimizes the need for synthetic pesticides, fostering a more ecologically balanced and sustainable agricultural system.
- *Water Conservation and Efficient Use:* Self-sustaining agricultural ecosystems prioritize water conservation and efficient use. Techniques such as rainwater harvesting, drip irrigation, and soil

Figure 5. Building self-sustaining ecosystems

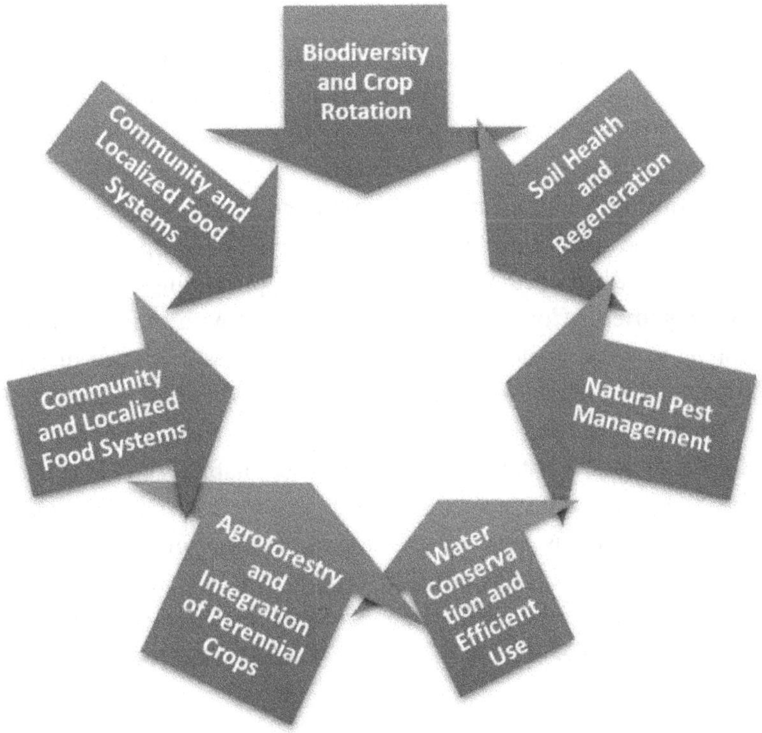

moisture monitoring are employed to optimize water resources. By understanding the water needs of different crops and landscapes, farmers can ensure that water is used judiciously, reducing waste and promoting sustainability. The emphasis on water efficiency contributes to the overall resilience of the agricultural ecosystem in the face of changing climate patterns (Kumar B et al., 2024; Rahamathunnisa, Sudhakar, et al., 2023).

- *Agroforestry and Integration of Perennial Crops:* Agroforestry, the integration of trees and shrubs into agricultural landscapes, is a significant component of self-sustaining ecosystems. Trees provide multiple benefits, including shade, windbreaks, and nutrient cycling. They also contribute to carbon sequestration, mitigating the impact of agriculture on climate change. Additionally, the integration of perennial crops, which have longer life cycles than annual crops, helps reduce the frequency of soil disturbance and contributes to the overall stability of the ecosystem.
- *Community and Localized Food Systems:* Self-sustaining agricultural ecosystems often emphasize community and localized food systems. By promoting local food production and consumption, these systems reduce the carbon footprint associated with long-distance transportation. Community-supported agriculture (CSA) models, farmers' markets, and direct-to-consumer sales create a direct connection between farmers and consumers, fostering a sense of shared responsibility for the health and sustainability of the agricultural ecosystem.

Strategies for Implementing and Maintaining Ecosystems

The successful establishment and maintenance of self-sustaining agricultural ecosystems necessitate a strategic approach that balances ecological principles, community involvement, and long-term sustainability (Boopathi, Siva Kumar, et al., 2023; Domakonda et al., 2023; Kumar B et al., 2024; Vijayakumar et al., 2023).

- **Farm Planning and Design:** The assessment of site conditions, including soil quality, topography, climate, and water availability, is crucial for understanding the land's natural features. Permaculture principles are implemented by dividing the farm into zones based on water needs, sunlight, and accessibility.
- **Biodiversity Promotion:** Implement crop rotation and companion planting to enhance biodiversity and disrupt pest and disease cycles. Incorporate perennial crops and agroforestry practices for long-term stability and diversification of plant species, promoting long-term stability.
- **Soil Health Management:** Cover cropping enriches soil with organic matter, nitrogen fixation, and soil erosion prevention, while minimum tillage practices minimize disturbance, preserve soil structure, and promote beneficial soil microorganism activity, enhancing soil structure and fertility (Boopathi, Kumar, et al., 2023; Gnanaprakasam et al., 2023a; P. R. Kumar et al., 2023b).
- **Natural Pest Management:** Establish beneficial insect habitats, such as flowering plants, to attract pollinators and predator insects, and cultivate disease-resistant crop varieties to reduce reliance on chemical interventions and promote natural pest control.
- **Water Conservation and Management:** Efficient drip irrigation systems and rainwater harvesting can minimize water wastage and reduce dependence on external water sources. Organic mulches can also help retain soil moisture, suppress weeds, and regulate soil temperature.

- **Agroforestry Integration:** Tree and shrub planting strategically provides shade, windbreaks, and wildlife habitat. Nitrogen-fixing trees enhance soil fertility. Alley cropping optimizes space by combining rows of trees or shrubs with crops.
- **Community Engagement:** Educational programs and workshops are conducted to raise awareness and understanding of self-sustaining agricultural practices among farmers and the local community, while establishing Community-Supported Agriculture (CSA) models fosters community involvement and support for sustainable agriculture.
- **Economic Viability:** Diversifying markets through marketing channels like farmers' markets and local grocery stores can boost economic resilience. Investing in value-added products like organic certification and agritourism can generate additional income and support farm financial sustainability.
- **Monitoring and Adaptive Management:** The text emphasizes the importance of data collection and adaptive management in managing soil health, crop performance, and ecosystem dynamics, utilizing sensors and analytics for informed decision-making and regularly assessing the effectiveness of implemented practices.
- **Government Support and Policies:** Advocate for sustainable agricultural policies and participate in government programs to support conservation, biodiversity, and financial support for regenerative farming practices.

CHALLENGES AND SOLUTIONS

Challenges in Implementing AI, IoT, and Sensor Technologies in Agriculture

The lack of reliable and affordable connectivity in rural areas hinders real-time data transmission, crucial for the effective functioning of advanced technologies. Additionally, there is a knowledge gap among farmers regarding the capabilities of these technologies (P. R. Kumar et al., 2023a; Pachiappan et al., 2023; Sankar et al., 2023b).

Proposed Solutions and Best Practices

- **Financial Support and Collaboration:** Governments and agricultural organizations can play a pivotal role in providing financial support and incentives for farmers to adopt AI, IoT, and sensor technologies. Collaborative efforts between private and public sectors can lead to the development of cost-effective solutions and shared infrastructure, making advanced technologies more accessible to a wider range of farmers.
- **Enhanced Connectivity:** Addressing the connectivity challenge requires investments in rural infrastructure. Governments and telecommunications companies can work together to expand and improve network coverage in agricultural areas. The promotion of low-power, wide-area (LPWA) networks and satellite-based communication systems can ensure reliable connectivity for IoT devices and sensors in remote locations.
- **Education and Training Programs:** Implementing comprehensive education and training programs is crucial. Agricultural extension services, technology providers, and NGOs can collaborate to conduct workshops, webinars, and on-farm training sessions. These initiatives should

focus on enhancing farmers' digital literacy, providing hands-on experience, and demonstrating the tangible benefits of AI, IoT, and sensors in agriculture (Das et al., 2024; Durairaj et al., 2023; Sharma et al., 2024).

- **Interoperability Standards:** The lack of interoperability among different systems and devices is a common challenge. Establishing industry-wide standards for data formats, communication protocols, and device interoperability is essential. This can be facilitated through the collaboration of industry stakeholders, standardization bodies, and technology developers to ensure seamless integration of diverse technologies.
- **Data Security and Privacy Concerns:** As AI, IoT, and sensors involve the collection and sharing of sensitive data, addressing concerns related to data security and privacy is imperative. Implementing robust encryption methods, secure authentication processes, and transparent data usage policies can build trust among farmers and stakeholders. Governments can also enact legislation to regulate data protection in agriculture (Rahamathunnisa, Subhashini, et al., 2023; Srinivas et al., 2023b).

CASE STUDIES

Case Study 1: FarmBot is a robotic farming system that uses AI, IoT, and agricultural sensors to optimize farming processes. It monitors soil moisture levels, nutrient concentrations, and crop growth stages, minimizing resource wastage and maximizing yield. The user-friendly interface allows farmers to remotely manage and customize farming operations, promoting efficiency and sustainability.

Case Study 2: Climate FieldView is a digital farming platform developed by The Climate Corporation, a subsidiary of Bayer, that uses AI and IoT to provide farmers with data-driven insights. It integrates with agricultural machinery and sensors, collecting and analyzing field data to generate recommendations for crop management, improving yield outcomes and profitability.

Case Study 3: Blue River Technology, acquired by John Deere, has developed See & Spray, an AI-powered agricultural spraying system that accurately identifies weeds in real-time and targets herbicide application, minimizing chemical usage and environmental impact, demonstrating how AI can enhance sustainability efforts in agriculture.

FUTURE DIRECTIONS

Future Directions in the Convergence of AI, IoT, and Agricultural Technology:

The future of agriculture holds exciting possibilities as the convergence of Artificial Intelligence (AI), the Internet of Things (IoT), and agricultural technology continues to evolve. One crucial trend is the increasing sophistication of AI algorithms for data analysis. As computing power grows and machine learning techniques advance, AI will become more adept at processing vast amounts of agricultural data. This will lead to more accurate predictions, personalized recommendations, and enhanced decision-making capabilities for farmers. AI will not only analyze historical data but also dynamically adapt to real-time changes, making agriculture more responsive and adaptive (Boopathi & Kanike, 2023; Pachiappan et al., 2023; Zekrifa et al., 2023).

Integration of Edge Computing: In the coming years, the integration of edge computing in agriculture is expected to gain prominence. Edge computing involves processing data closer to the source, reducing latency and enabling quicker responses. In the context of agriculture, this means that data from IoT sensors can be processed locally on the farm, allowing for rapid decision-making without relying heavily on cloud-based processing. This trend will enhance the efficiency and responsiveness of AI-driven systems in addressing the immediate needs of crops and livestock (Boopathi, 2023a; Venkateswaran, Vidhya, et al., 2023).

Blockchain Technology for Traceability: The evolution of self-sustaining agro-technological ecosystems will also involve the integration of blockchain technology. Blockchain can provide a secure and transparent ledger for recording and verifying transactions in the agricultural supply chain. This ensures traceability from farm to table, addressing concerns related to food safety and authenticity. Blockchain's decentralized and tamper-resistant nature will enhance transparency, trust, and accountability within the agricultural ecosystem (P. R. Kumar et al., 2023a; Sundaramoorthy et al., 2023).

Climate-Smart Agriculture: The future of agriculture will witness a growing emphasis on climate-smart practices facilitated by AI, IoT, and agricultural technology. Climate change poses challenges to traditional farming practices, and adaptive solutions are crucial. AI algorithms will analyze climate data, enabling farmers to make informed decisions on crop selection, irrigation scheduling, and pest management. IoT sensors will provide real-time insights into changing weather conditions, allowing for proactive adjustments to farming practices. The integration of climate-smart technologies will contribute to the resilience of agricultural ecosystems in the face of environmental uncertainties (Koshariya, Kalaiyarasi, et al., 2023a; P. R. Kumar et al., 2023a; Kumara et al., 2023).

Collaborative Ecosystems and Open Platforms: The future landscape of agricultural technology will see the emergence of collaborative ecosystems and open platforms. Interoperability will be a important focus, allowing different technologies and systems to seamlessly communicate and share data. Open platforms will encourage innovation and collaboration among diverse stakeholders, fostering the development of integrated solutions. This collaborative approach will not only accelerate technological advancements but also democratize access to cutting-edge agricultural technologies, benefitting farmers of all scales (Ingle et al., 2023; Janardhana et al., 2023).

Ethical and Social Implications

The integration of AI, IoT, and agricultural sensors in farming raises ethical and social concerns, including data privacy and ownership. It also raises concerns about job displacement and socioeconomic impact on rural communities. Automated farms may decrease manual labor demand, exacerbating disparities. To address these issues, reskilling and supporting affected workers is crucial, fostering inclusive growth and mitigating socioeconomic inequalities. AI, IoT, and agricultural sensors are revolutionizing farming practices, offering precision and resource optimization. However, they raise ethical concerns about overreliance, environmental degradation, and biodiversity loss. Balancing technological innovation with sustainable practices is crucial to minimize negative effects and preserve ecosystems. Accessibility and affordability of advanced technologies are also issues, especially for smallholder farmers in developing countries. Ensuring equitable access to technology and supporting capacity building and knowledge transfer is essential for inclusive agricultural development and global food security.

CONCLUSION

The chapter "Harmony in Harvest: The Fusion of AI, IoT, and Agricultural Sensors for Self-Sustaining Agro-Technological Ecosystems" explores the potential of AI, IoT, and agricultural sensors in revolutionizing traditional farming practices and developing self-sustaining agro-technological ecosystems, highlighting the transformative landscape of AI, IoT, and agricultural sensors.

The integration of AI, IoT, and sensors in agriculture is paving the way for a new era of precision, efficiency, and sustainability. AI algorithms enable farmers to make informed decisions, optimize resource utilization, and manage challenges like pest outbreaks. These technologies contribute to precision agriculture, reducing waste, enhancing productivity, and minimizing environmental impact. The future of agriculture is profound, with self-sustaining agro-technological ecosystems and advancements in edge computing, robotics, and blockchain. Climate-smart practices and collaborative ecosystems ensure agriculture becomes more resilient and aligns with global sustainability goals.

The integration of AI, IoT, and agricultural sensors is a promising solution to the challenges faced by the agricultural sector, such as feeding a growing population, mitigating climate change, and ensuring food security. This fusion of technologies can shape the future of food production, supply chains, and the overall agricultural ecosystem. It represents a transformative shift towards self-sustaining agro-technological ecosystems, where innovation meets stewardship, and technology becomes a catalyst for a greener, more abundant future in agriculture.

ABBREVIATIONS

IoT: Internet of Things
AI: Artificial Intelligence
ML: Machine Learning
GPS: Global Positioning System
UAVs: Unmanned Aerial Vehicles
RFID: Radio-Frequency Identification

REFERENCES

Agrawal, A. V., Magulur, L. P., Priya, S. G., Kaur, A., Singh, G., & Boopathi, S. (2023a). Smart Precision Agriculture Using IoT and WSN: In T. Murugan & N. E. (Eds.), Advances in Information Security, Privacy, and Ethics (pp. 524–541). IGI Global. doi:10.4018/978-1-6684-8145-5.ch026

Agrawal, A. V., Magulur, L. P., Priya, S. G., Kaur, A., Singh, G., & Boopathi, S. (2023b). Smart Precision Agriculture Using IoT and WSN. In *Handbook of Research on Data Science and Cybersecurity Innovations in Industry 4.0 Technologies* (pp. 524–541). IGI Global. doi:10.4018/978-1-6684-8145-5.ch026

Agrawal, A. V., Shashibhushan, G., Pradeep, S., Padhi, S., Sugumar, D., & Boopathi, S. (2023). Synergizing Artificial Intelligence, 5G, and Cloud Computing for Efficient Energy Conversion Using Agricultural Waste. In Sustainable Science and Intelligent Technologies for Societal Development (pp. 475–497). IGI Global.

Agrawal, A. V., Shashibhushan, G., Pradeep, S., Padhi, S. N., Sugumar, D., & Boopathi, S. (2024). Synergizing Artificial Intelligence, 5G, and Cloud Computing for Efficient Energy Conversion Using Agricultural Waste. In B. K. Mishra (Ed.), (pp. 475–497). Practice, Progress, and Proficiency in Sustainability. IGI Global. doi:10.4018/979-8-3693-1186-8.ch026

Ali, M. N., Senthil, T., Ilakkiya, T., Hasan, D. S., Ganapathy, N. B. S., & Boopathi, S. (2024). IoT's Role in Smart Manufacturing Transformation for Enhanced Household Product Quality. In *Advanced Applications in Osmotic Computing* (pp. 252–289). IGI Global. doi:10.4018/979-8-3693-1694-8.ch014

Arunprasad, R., & Boopathi, S. (2019). Chapter-4 Alternate Refrigerants for Minimization Environmental Impacts: A Review. In Advances in Engineering Technology (p. 75). AkiNik Publications New Delhi.

Boopathi, S. (2022a). An investigation on gas emission concentration and relative emission rate of the near-dry wire-cut electrical discharge machining process. *Environmental Science and Pollution Research International*, *29*(57), 86237–86246. doi:10.1007/s11356-021-17658-1 PMID:34837614

Boopathi, S. (2022b). Cryogenically treated and untreated stainless steel grade 317 in sustainable wire electrical discharge machining process: A comparative study. *Environmental Science and Pollution Research*, 1–10.

Boopathi, S. (2023a). Deep Learning Techniques Applied for Automatic Sentence Generation. In K. Becerra-Murillo & J. F. Gámez (Eds.), (pp. 255–273). Advances in Educational Technologies and Instructional Design. IGI Global. doi:10.4018/978-1-6684-3632-5.ch016

Boopathi, S. (2023b). Securing Healthcare Systems Integrated With IoT: Fundamentals, Applications, and Future Trends. In Dynamics of Swarm Intelligence Health Analysis for the Next Generation (pp. 186–209). IGI Global.

Boopathi, S. (2024). Sustainable Development Using IoT and AI Techniques for Water Utilization in Agriculture. In Sustainable Development in AI, Blockchain, and E-Governance Applications (pp. 204–228). IGI Global. doi:10.4018/979-8-3693-1722-8.ch012

Boopathi, S., & Kanike, U. K. (2023). Applications of Artificial Intelligent and Machine Learning Techniques in Image Processing. In B. K. Pandey, D. Pandey, R. Anand, D. S. Mane, & V. K. Nassa (Eds.), Advances in Computational Intelligence and Robotics. IGI Global. doi:10.4018/978-1-6684-8618-4.ch010

Boopathi, S., & Khang, A. (2023). AI-Integrated Technology for a Secure and Ethical Healthcare Ecosystem. In *AI and IoT-Based Technologies for Precision Medicine* (pp. 36–59). IGI Global. doi:10.4018/979-8-3693-0876-9.ch003

Boopathi, S., & Kumar, P. (2024). Advanced bioprinting processes using additive manufacturing technologies: Revolutionizing tissue engineering. *3D Printing Technologies: Digital Manufacturing, Artificial Intelligence, Industry 4.0*, 95.

Boopathi, S., Kumar, P. K. S., Meena, R. S., Sudhakar, M., & Associates. (2023). Sustainable Developments of Modern Soil-Less Agro-Cultivation Systems: Aquaponic Culture. In Human Agro-Energy Optimization for Business and Industry (pp. 69–87). IGI Global.

Boopathi, S., Siva Kumar, P. K., Meena, R. S. J., S. I., P., S. K., & Sudhakar, M. (2023). Sustainable Developments of Modern Soil-Less Agro-Cultivation Systems: Aquaponic Culture. In P. Vasant, R. Rodríguez-Aguilar, I. Litvinchev, & J. A. Marmolejo-Saucedo (Eds.), Advances in Environmental Engineering and Green Technologies (pp. 69–87). IGI Global. doi:10.4018/978-1-6684-4118-3.ch004

Boopathi, S., & Sivakumar, K. (2013). Experimental investigation and parameter optimization of near-dry wire-cut electrical discharge machining using multi-objective evolutionary algorithm. *International Journal of Advanced Manufacturing Technology*, *67*(9–12), 2639–2655. doi:10.1007/s00170-012-4680-4

Boopathi, S., Sureshkumar, M., & Sathiskumar, S. (2023). Parametric Optimization of LPG Refrigeration System Using Artificial Bee Colony Algorithm. In S. Tripathy, S. Samantaray, J. Ramkumar, & S. S. Mahapatra (Eds.), *Recent Advances in Mechanical Engineering* (pp. 97–105). Springer Nature Singapore. doi:10.1007/978-981-19-9493-7_10

Das, S., Lekhya, G., Shreya, K., Shekinah, K. L., Babu, K. K., & Boopathi, S. (2024). Fostering Sustainability Education Through Cross-Disciplinary Collaborations and Research Partnerships: Interdisciplinary Synergy. In Facilitating Global Collaboration and Knowledge Sharing in Higher Education With Generative AI (pp. 60–88). IGI Global.

Dhanya, D., Kumar, S. S., Thilagavathy, A., Prasad, D. V. S. S. S. V., & Boopathi, S. (2023). Data Analytics and Artificial Intelligence in the Circular Economy: Case Studies. In B. K. Mishra (Ed.), Advances in Civil and Industrial Engineering. IGI Global. doi:10.4018/979-8-3693-0044-2.ch003

Domakonda, V. K., Farooq, S., Chinthamreddy, S., Puviarasi, R., Sudhakar, M., & Boopathi, S. (2023). Sustainable Developments of Hybrid Floating Solar Power Plants: Photovoltaic System. In P. Vasant, R. Rodríguez-Aguilar, I. Litvinchev, & J. A. Marmolejo-Saucedo (Eds.), Advances in Environmental Engineering and Green Technologies. IGI Global. doi:10.4018/978-1-6684-4118-3.ch008

Durairaj, M., Jayakumar, S., Karpagavalli, V., Maheswari, B. U., Boopathi, S., & ... (2023). Utilization of Digital Tools in the Indian Higher Education System During Health Crises. In *Multidisciplinary Approaches to Organizational Governance During Health Crises* (pp. 1–21). IGI Global. doi:10.4018/978-1-7998-9213-7.ch001

Gnanaprakasam, C., Vankara, J., Sastry, A. S., Prajval, V., Gireesh, N., & Boopathi, S. (2023a). Long-Range and Low-Power Automated Soil Irrigation System Using Internet of Things: An Experimental Study. In Contemporary Developments in Agricultural Cyber-Physical Systems (pp. 87–104). IGI Global.

Gnanaprakasam, C., Vankara, J., Sastry, A. S., Prajval, V., Gireesh, N., & Boopathi, S. (2023b). Long-Range and Low-Power Automated Soil Irrigation System Using Internet of Things: An Experimental Study. In G. S. Karthick (Ed.), Advances in Environmental Engineering and Green Technologies. IGI Global. doi:10.4018/978-1-6684-7879-0.ch005

Hussain, Z., Babe, M., Saravanan, S., Srimathy, G., Roopa, H., & Boopathi, S. (2023). Optimizing Biomass-to-Biofuel Conversion: IoT and AI Integration for Enhanced Efficiency and Sustainability. In N. Cobîrzan, R. Muntean, & R.-A. Felseghi (Eds.), Advances in Finance, Accounting, and Economics. IGI Global. doi:10.4018/978-1-6684-8238-4.ch009

Ingle, R. B., Swathi, S., Mahendran, G., Senthil, T. S., Muralidharan, N., & Boopathi, S. (2023). Sustainability and Optimization of Green and Lean Manufacturing Processes Using Machine Learning Techniques. In N. Cobîrzan, R. Muntean, & R.-A. Felseghi (Eds.), Advances in Finance, Accounting, and Economics. IGI Global. doi:10.4018/978-1-6684-8238-4.ch012

Janardhana, K., Singh, V., Singh, S. N., Babu, T. S. R., Bano, S., & Boopathi, S. (2023). Utilization Process for Electronic Waste in Eco-Friendly Concrete: Experimental Study. In A. M. Rawani, M. K. Sahu, S. S. Chakarabarti, & A. K. Singh (Eds.), Practice, Progress, and Proficiency in Sustainability. IGI Global. doi:10.4018/978-1-6684-7573-7.ch011

Jeevanantham, Y. A., Saravanan, A., Vanitha, V., Boopathi, S., & Kumar, D. P. (2022). Implementation of Internet-of Things (IoT) in Soil Irrigation System. *IEEE Explore*, 1–5.

Kalidas, R., Boopathi, S., Sivakumar, K., & Mohankumar, P. (2012). Optimization of Machining Parameters of WEDM Process Based On the Taguchi Method. *IJEST, 6*(1).

Kavitha, C. R., Varalatchoumy, M., Mithuna, H. R., Bharathi, K., Geethalakshmi, N. M., & Boopathi, S. (2023). Energy Monitoring and Control in the Smart Grid: Integrated Intelligent IoT and ANFIS. In M. Arshad (Ed.), Advances in Bioinformatics and Biomedical Engineering. IGI Global. doi:10.4018/978-1-6684-6577-6.ch014

Koshariya, A. K., Kalaiyarasi, D., Jovith, A. A., Sivakami, T., Hasan, D. S., & Boopathi, S. (2023a). AI-Enabled IoT and WSN-Integrated Smart Agriculture System. In R. K. Gupta, A. Jain, J. Wang, S. K. Bharti, & S. Patel (Eds.), Practice, Progress, and Proficiency in Sustainability. IGI Global. doi:10.4018/978-1-6684-8516-3.ch011

Koshariya, A. K., Kalaiyarasi, D., Jovith, A. A., Sivakami, T., Hasan, D. S., & Boopathi, S. (2023b). AI-Enabled IoT and WSN-Integrated Smart Agriculture System. In *Artificial Intelligence Tools and Technologies for Smart Farming and Agriculture Practices* (pp. 200–218). IGI Global. doi:10.4018/978-1-6684-8516-3.ch011

Koshariya, A. K., Khatoon, S., Marathe, A. M., Suba, G. M., Baral, D., & Boopathi, S. (2023a). Agricultural Waste Management Systems Using Artificial Intelligence Techniques. In S. Kautish, N. K. Chaubey, S. B. Goyal, & P. Whig (Eds.), Advances in Computational Intelligence and Robotics. IGI Global. doi:10.4018/978-1-6684-8171-4.ch009

Koshariya, A. K., Khatoon, S., Marathe, A. M., Suba, G. M., Baral, D., & Boopathi, S. (2023b). Agricultural Waste Management Systems Using Artificial Intelligence Techniques. In *AI-Enabled Social Robotics in Human Care Services* (pp. 236–258). IGI Global. doi:10.4018/978-1-6684-8171-4.ch009

Kumar, B. M., Kumar, K. K., Sasikala, P., Sampath, B., Gopi, B., & Sundaram, S. (2024). Sustainable Green Energy Generation From Waste Water: IoT and ML Integration. In B. K. Mishra (Ed.), Practice, Progress, and Proficiency in Sustainability. IGI Global. doi:10.4018/979-8-3693-1186-8.ch024

Kumar, P., Sampath, B., Kumar, S., Babu, B. H., & Ahalya, N. (2023). Hydroponics, Aeroponics, and Aquaponics Technologies in Modern Agricultural Cultivation. In Trends, Paradigms, and Advances in Mechatronics Engineering (pp. 223–241). IGI Global.

Kumar, P. R., Meenakshi, S., Shalini, S., Devi, S. R., & Boopathi, S. (2023a). Soil Quality Prediction in Context Learning Approaches Using Deep Learning and Blockchain for Smart Agriculture. In R. Kumar, A. B. Abdul Hamid, & N. I. Binti Ya'akub (Eds.), Advances in Computational Intelligence and Robotics. IGI Global. doi:10.4018/978-1-6684-9151-5.ch001

Kumar, P. R., Meenakshi, S., Shalini, S., Devi, S. R., & Boopathi, S. (2023b). Soil Quality Prediction in Context Learning Approaches Using Deep Learning and Blockchain for Smart Agriculture. In Effective AI, Blockchain, and E-Governance Applications for Knowledge Discovery and Management (pp. 1–26). IGI Global. doi:10.4018/978-1-6684-9151-5.ch001

Kumara, V., Mohanaprakash, T. A., Fairooz, S., Jamal, K., Babu, T., & B., S. (2023). Experimental Study on a Reliable Smart Hydroponics System: In P. Vasant, R. Rodríguez-Aguilar, I. Litvinchev, & J. A. Marmolejo-Saucedo (Eds.), *Advances in Environmental Engineering and Green Technologies* (pp. 27–45). IGI Global. doi:10.4018/978-1-6684-4118-3.ch002

Maguluri, L. P., Ananth, J., Hariram, S., Geetha, C., Bhaskar, A., & Boopathi, S. (2023). Smart Vehicle-Emissions Monitoring System Using Internet of Things (IoT). In P. Srivastava, D. Ramteke, A. K. Bedyal, M. Gupta, & J. K. Sandhu (Eds.), Practice, Progress, and Proficiency in Sustainability. IGI Global. doi:10.4018/978-1-6684-8117-2.ch014

Maheswari, B. U., Imambi, S. S., Hasan, D., Meenakshi, S., Pratheep, V. G., & Boopathi, S. (2023). Internet of Things and Machine Learning-Integrated Smart Robotics. In M. K. Habib (Ed.), Advances in Computational Intelligence and Robotics. IGI Global. doi:10.4018/978-1-6684-7791-5.ch010

Mohanty, A., Venkateswaran, N., Ranjit, P., Tripathi, M. A., & Boopathi, S. (2023). Innovative Strategy for Profitable Automobile Industries: Working Capital Management. In Handbook of Research on Designing Sustainable Supply Chains to Achieve a Circular Economy (pp. 412–428). IGI Global.

Mohanty, A., Venkateswaran, N., Ranjit, P. S., Tripathi, M. A., & Boopathi, S. (2023). Innovative Strategy for Profitable Automobile Industries: Working Capital Management. In Y. Ramakrishna & S. N. Wahab (Eds.), Advances in Finance, Accounting, and Economics. IGI Global. doi:10.4018/978-1-6684-7664-2.ch020

Myilsamy, S., & Sampath, B. (2017). Grey Relational Optimization of Powder Mixed Near-Dry Wire Cut Electrical Discharge Machining of Inconel 718 Alloy. *Asian Journal of Research in Social Sciences and Humanities*, *7*(3), 18–25. doi:10.5958/2249-7315.2017.00157.5

Pachiappan, K., Anitha, K., Pitchai, R., Sangeetha, S., Satyanarayana, T., & Boopathi, S. (2024). Intelligent Machines, IoT, and AI in Revolutionizing Agriculture for Water Processing. In *Handbook of Research on AI and ML for Intelligent Machines and Systems* (pp. 374–399). IGI Global.

Pachiappan, K., Anitha, K., Pitchai, R., Sangeetha, S., Satyanarayana, T. V. V., & Boopathi, S. (2023). Intelligent Machines, IoT, and AI in Revolutionizing Agriculture for Water Processing. In B. B. Gupta & F. Colace (Eds.), Advances in Computational Intelligence and Robotics. IGI Global. doi:10.4018/978-1-6684-9999-3.ch015

Rahamathunnisa, U., Subhashini, P., Aancy, H. M., Meenakshi, S., Boopathi, S., & ... (2023). Solutions for Software Requirement Risks Using Artificial Intelligence Techniques. In *Handbook of Research on Data Science and Cybersecurity Innovations in Industry 4.0 Technologies* (pp. 45–64). IGI Global.

Rahamathunnisa, U., Sudhakar, K., Padhi, S. N., Bhattacharya, S., Shashibhushan, G., & Boopathi, S. (2023). Sustainable Energy Generation From Waste Water: IoT Integrated Technologies. In A. S. Etim (Ed.), Advances in Human and Social Aspects of Technology. IGI Global. doi:10.4018/978-1-6684-5347-6.ch010

Rebecca, B., Kumar, K. P. M., Padmini, S., Srivastava, B. K., Halder, S., & Boopathi, S. (2023). Convergence of Data Science-AI-Green Chemistry-Affordable Medicine: Transforming Drug Discovery. In B. B. Gupta & F. Colace (Eds.), Advances in Computational Intelligence and Robotics. IGI Global. doi:10.4018/978-1-6684-9999-3.ch014

Reddy, M. A., Reddy, B. M., Mukund, C., Venneti, K., Preethi, D., & Boopathi, S. (2023b). Social Health Protection During the COVID-Pandemic Using IoT. In *The COVID-19 Pandemic and the Digitalization of Diplomacy* (pp. 204–235). IGI Global. doi:10.4018/978-1-7998-8394-4.ch009

Reddy, M. A., Reddy, B. M., Mukund, C. S., Venneti, K., Preethi, D. M. D., & Boopathi, S. (2023a). Social Health Protection During the COVID-Pandemic Using IoT. In F. P. C. Endong (Ed.), Advances in Electronic Government, Digital Divide, and Regional Development. IGI Global. doi:10.4018/978-1-7998-8394-4.ch009

Revathi, S., Babu, M., Rajkumar, N., Meti, V. K. V., Kandavalli, S. R., & Boopathi, S. (2024). Unleashing the Future Potential of 4D Printing: Exploring Applications in Wearable Technology, Robotics, Energy, Transportation, and Fashion. In Human-Centered Approaches in Industry 5.0: Human-Machine Interaction, Virtual Reality Training, and Customer Sentiment Analysis (pp. 131–153). IGI Global.

S., P. K., Sampath, B., R., S. K., Babu, B. H., & N., A. (2022). Hydroponics, Aeroponics, and Aquaponics Technologies in Modern Agricultural Cultivation: In M. A. Mellal (Ed.), *Advances in Mechatronics and Mechanical Engineering* (pp. 223–241). IGI Global. doi:10.4018/978-1-6684-5887-7.ch012

Samikannu, R., Koshariya, A. K., Poornima, E., Ramesh, S., Kumar, A., & Boopathi, S. (2022). Sustainable Development in Modern Aquaponics Cultivation Systems Using IoT Technologies. In *Human Agro-Energy Optimization for Business and Industry* (pp. 105–127). IGI Global.

Samikannu, R., Koshariya, A. K., Poornima, E., Ramesh, S., Kumar, A., & Boopathi, S. (2023). Sustainable Development in Modern Aquaponics Cultivation Systems Using IoT Technologies. In P. Vasant, R. Rodríguez-Aguilar, I. Litvinchev, & J. A. Marmolejo-Saucedo (Eds.), Advances in Environmental Engineering and Green Technologies. IGI Global. doi:10.4018/978-1-6684-4118-3.ch006

Sankar, K. M., Booba, B., & Boopathi, S. (2023). Smart Agriculture Irrigation Monitoring System Using Internet of Things. In *Contemporary Developments in Agricultural Cyber-Physical Systems* (pp. 105–121). IGI Global. doi:10.4018/978-1-6684-7879-0.ch006

Satav, S. D., Hasan, D. S., Pitchai, R., Mohanaprakash, T. A., Sultanuddin, S. J., & Boopathi, S. (2024). Next Generation of Internet of Things (NGIoT) in Healthcare Systems. In B. K. Mishra (Ed.), Practice, Progress, and Proficiency in Sustainability. IGI Global. doi:10.4018/979-8-3693-1186-8.ch017

Sharma, D. M., Ramana, K. V., Jothilakshmi, R., Verma, R., Maheswari, B. U., & Boopathi, S. (2024). Integrating Generative AI Into K-12 Curriculums and Pedagogies in India: Opportunities and Challenges. *Facilitating Global Collaboration and Knowledge Sharing in Higher Education With Generative AI*, 133–161.

Srinivas, B., Maguluri, L. P., Naidu, K. V., Reddy, L. C. S., Deivakani, M., & Boopathi, S. (2023a). Architecture and Framework for Interfacing Cloud-Enabled Robots: In T. Murugan & N. E. (Eds.), Advances in Information Security, Privacy, and Ethics (pp. 542–560). IGI Global. doi:10.4018/978-1-6684-8145-5.ch027

Srinivas, B., Maguluri, L. P., Naidu, K. V., Reddy, L. C. S., Deivakani, M., & Boopathi, S. (2023b). Architecture and Framework for Interfacing Cloud-Enabled Robots. In *Handbook of Research on Data Science and Cybersecurity Innovations in Industry 4.0 Technologies* (pp. 542–560). IGI Global. doi:10.4018/978-1-6684-8145-5.ch027

Sundaramoorthy, K., Singh, A., Sumathy, G., Maheshwari, A., Arunarani, A. R., & Boopathi, S. (2023). A Study on AI and Blockchain-Powered Smart Parking Models for Urban Mobility. In B. B. Gupta & F. Colace (Eds.), Advances in Computational Intelligence and Robotics. IGI Global. doi:10.4018/978-1-6684-9999-3.ch010

Syamala, M. C. R., K., Pramila, P. V., Dash, S., Meenakshi, S., & Boopathi, S. (2023). Machine Learning-Integrated IoT-Based Smart Home Energy Management System: In P. Swarnalatha & S. Prabu (Eds.), Advances in Computational Intelligence and Robotics (pp. 219–235). IGI Global. doi:10.4018/978-1-6684-8098-4.ch013

Veeranjaneyulu, R., Boopathi, S., Kumari, R. K., Vidyarthi, A., Isaac, J. S., & Jaiganesh, V. (2023). Air Quality Improvement and Optimisation Using Machine Learning Technique. *IEEE- Explore*, 1–6.

Venkateswaran, N., Kumar, S. S., Diwakar, G., Gnanasangeetha, D., & Boopathi, S. (2023). Synthetic Biology for Waste Water to Energy Conversion: IoT and AI Approaches. *Applications of Synthetic Biology in Health. Energy & Environment*, 360–384.

Venkateswaran, N., Vidhya, R., Naik, D. A., Michael Raj, T. F., Munjal, N., & Boopathi, S. (2023). Study on Sentence and Question Formation Using Deep Learning Techniques. In O. Dastane, A. Aman, & N. S. Bin Mohd Satar (Eds.), Advances in Business Strategy and Competitive Advantage. IGI Global. doi:10.4018/978-1-6684-6782-4.ch015

Verma, R., Christiana, M. B. V., Maheswari, M., Srinivasan, V., Patro, P., Dari, S. S., & Boopathi, S. (2024). Intelligent Physarum Solver for Profit Maximization in Oligopolistic Supply Chain Networks. In *AI and Machine Learning Impacts in Intelligent Supply Chain* (pp. 156–179). IGI Global. doi:10.4018/979-8-3693-1347-3.ch011

Vijayakumar, G. N. S., Domakonda, V. K., Farooq, S., Kumar, B. S., Pradeep, N., & Boopathi, S. (2023). Sustainable Developments in Nano-Fluid Synthesis for Various Industrial Applications. In A. S. Etim (Ed.), Advances in Human and Social Aspects of Technology. IGI Global. doi:10.4018/978-1-6684-5347-6.ch003

Zekrifa, D. M. S., Kulkarni, M., Bhagyalakshmi, A., Devireddy, N., Gupta, S., & Boopathi, S. (2023). Integrating Machine Learning and AI for Improved Hydrological Modeling and Water Resource Management. In V. Shikuku (Ed.), Advances in Environmental Engineering and Green Technologies. IGI Global. doi:10.4018/978-1-6684-6791-6.ch003

Chapter 16
Unveiling and Mapping the Human Resource Technologies and Industry 5.0

Rajagopalan A.
School of Management, SASTRA University (Deemed), India

Vijayabanu C.
https://orcid.org/0000-0002-0125-4534
School of Management, SASTRA University (Deemed), India

ABSTRACT

Industries play a huge role in economic development. However, changes are due to the launch of modern technologies and the increasing complexity of new products, and it manufactures directly to the workers. Advanced technologies like artificial intelligence characterize the launch of Industry 5.0 which are useful in redesigning human resource technologies. The chapter helps to know about the technologies that improve HR processes and decision-making. The study consists of various technologies applied in human resource management to Industry 5.0 and its focus area. Then introduction to the concepts and technologies of this new 5.0 in HRM has evolved from different era. The convergence of this 5.0 is an increasing trend. There are many new and innovative methods to enhance the technologies. The chapter aims to understand the importance of applying technologies to various HR practices and it will be an eye-opener for students, research scholars, consultants, and practitioners based on various secondary sources and company practices.

INTRODUCTION

Over the years, Industries have played a major role in Economic Development. However, changes are due to the launch of modern technologies and the increasing complexity of new products and manufacture directly to the workers. Advanced technologies like Artificial intelligence characterize the Launch of Industry 5.0 and robotics are useful in redesigning Human resource technologies. This abstract helps in

DOI: 10.4018/979-8-3693-1343-5.ch016

exploring the implementation of Industry 5.0 in Human resource management. Industry 5.0 also called the fifth industrial revolution acts as a new and emerging phase of industrialisation where humans work along with advanced technologies and Artificial intelligence. Industry 5.0 and human resource technologies together refer to transformation cooperation between the human resource and modern technologies systems (Chin et al.,2021). Industry 5.0 refers to the latest shift in manufacturing, characterized by the integration of advanced technologies to optimize production processes and create smarter, more connected factories. With the help of professionals and powerful machines, the process gives business efficiency, sustainable, and secure production. Industry 5.0 is a new approach that has a positive impact on productivity and business (Aslam, 2020).This approach is not a passing trend. For quickly in change course when some particular strategy fails, digital HR use data analytics to track progress in each stage of employee life cycle, from assignation to learning and development to and off-boarding. It can improve HR processes by using analytics to determine what is and what is not in the constructed strategy (Cillo et al.,2022). The term digital HR refers to digital transformation which is a trend in the human resource industry as a whole, as well as in various technologies. Examples like Automation in recruitment, like posting goals, which helps HR professionals a better use of Processes. The current chapter helps to know about the technologies that improve HR processes and decision-making by leveraging digital platforms, automation, analytics, and artificial intelligence. Industry 4.0 is developing quickly, while the Period between the first three industrial revolutions took place over a century. To increase production and innovation in Industry 5.0, the industry revolution the most recent stage in the Industrial places a strong value on the integration of automation, artificial intelligence, and human collaboration. While Industry 4.0 focuses on technological advancements like Analytics in data, cyber systems, and the biggest exposure towards Artificial intelligence, machine learning, and other emerging technologies, Industry 5.0 is all about massive customization and personalization of these already standing tools (Echchakoui et al., 2020). The current human resource management must go through this process at the same time the rest of the others do. Industry 5.0 transformation has already become unchangeable. With the help of professionals and powerful AI tools, the process gives business efficiency, sustainability, and secure production (Leon, 2023). Industry 5.0 is a new approach that has a positive side on productivity and business. This approach is not a passing trend. It can improve HR Processes by using analytics to determine what is and what is not there in the constructed strategy. The term digital HR refers to digital transformation which is a trend in the human resource industry as a whole, as well as in various technologies. Examples like: Automation in recruitment, like posting goals, which helps HR professionals make better use of Processes. The current chapter helps to know about the technologies that improve HR processes and decision-making by leveraging digital platforms, automation, analytics, and artificial intelligence. Industry 4.0 is developing quickly, while the Period between the first three industrial revolutions took place over a century. Industry 5.0 shows how Industry 4.0 affects the society. Industries that adopted the change of Industry 5.0 earned mass and increased production of goods in the current study we are going to visualize the art of changing version 4.0 to version 5.0 in the Field of Social resource technologies (Howard, 2018). The convergence of human resource technologies and Industry 5.0 is a recent trend that stirs up businesses to manage their employees. Human resource technologies are some tools and systems that businesses use to control their employees, such as applicant tracking systems. Performance management software, training, and placements. The study starts with a quick and elaborative introduction to Industry 5.0 and its focus area. Then, there is an Introduction to several definitions and new concepts of era 5.0 from the viewpoint of different industry specialists and researchers. We will discuss some important features of Industry 5.0 compared to Industry 4.0. We will discuss some key technologies of Industry 5.0 and applications to be developed. The current study looks at some of the factors that influence HRM practices during this process the recent technology known as "Industry 5.0" aims to transform industries and human resource management into intelligent structures powered by artificial intelligence and the Internet. By sinking the Human resource AI tools and people, it looks forward to putting Artificial intelligence in service of people. The Chapter elaborately on the challenges faced by HR professionals about the adoption of this new industry 5.0. To make it happen, they should adopt digital technologies including artificial intelligence. Improving the skills of the employees to be updated about Industry 5.0.To obtain the resources efficiently and to provide more manufacturing solutions when compared to Industry 4.0, numerous technologies and applications are expected to assist Industry 5.0 in constructively increasing the production and innovativeness of products. The convergence of Industry 5.0 is an increasing trend, there are many new and innovative ways to enhance the technologies. When these technologies continue to advance, businesses will modify their HR practices if they want to make use of the options they offer. The chapter aims to understand the importance of applying technologies to various HR practices and it will be an eye-opener for students, research scholars, consultants and practitioners based on the methodology of secondary sources and company practices.

The chapter will help to understand the importance of applying technologies towards various HR practices and it will be an eye opener for students, research scholars, consultants and actioners. Sometimes, with the help of animals, they have been credible for the production and industry of various items such as motor vehicles, clothing, and houses. However, the landscape of industrial production endured a sincere transformation with Industry 1.0 in 1974. The expansion of industry revolutions starting from the first to the third revolution in 100 years takes simply 40 years to attain the fourth to third. In the year 1800, Industry1.0 emerged over the advancement of motorized invention structures for aquatic and steam-operated machinery. It results to enormous advances for the country as fabrication capability is higher. Version 2.0 occurred in the year 1870 with the thought of electrical control and production. This 2.0 focused on huge production and distribution of loads, which has raised the production of manufacturing companies.

Industry 3.0 raised in the year 1969 with notion of electric items, restricted automation, and Information technologies. The development of 4.0 was developed in 2011 with the idea of slight industrial works for the future. Industry 5.0 represents an evolving thought aimed at enlarging the conventional objective of producing goods and services individually for revenue maximization or remediation (Skobelev et al., 2017). It picturizes to make use of the distinctive creativity of human efforts in coordination with vast intellectual and detailed machinery. Various methodological prophets are confident that this new version of Industry 5.0 reintroduces a human touch to the industrial sector. This manifestation seeks to broaden the general goals of social and economic activities by absorbing the three fundamental elements: a human-centric approach, conservation and flexibility. With the elements, of human-centric approach factors in 5.0, the focus lies on classifying human needs and interests as their core objective.

Furthermore, it places considerable emphasis on meticulous assessment of the results of emerging technologies, with an idea of protecting basic human rights and values. The version 5.0 is hailed as the next big thing in the growth of the business, with an exciting objective (Tange., 2020).The big vision approach aims to achieve appropriate use of resources and other solutions that excel better than industry 4.0. The idea behind the emergence of the sector "5.0" is to increase the efficiency of the industrial revolution by combining human and machine cooperation. The future of industries is about the manufacturing of robots and industrial robots.

TECHNOLOGY REVOLUTION THROUGH INDUSTRY 5.0: AN OVERVIEW

The version number 5 pertains to the association amid people and robots, along with smart technologies. It revolves around how robotics enhances human productivity, particularly means of influencing the innovative machineries like Big Data analytics. What sets Industry 5.0 apart is its integration of people oriented, supportable, and spirited principles into the industrial landscape. Its global impact is intended to transform production processes by relieving humans of labour-intensive tasks. The term "Industry 5.0" denotes the start of a new industrial age driven by human creativity. It is based on the Recognise, Realise, Reduce, Reuse, and Recycle (6R) concept. Its main objectives are to improve people's quality of life, encourage innovation, and provide high-quality, customised goods (Adel, 2021).Industry 4.0 introduces revolutionary characteristics through automation, robotics, artificial intelligence, and machine learning, whereas the Fourth Revolt significantly improves this technology (Rada,2020).The next Industry 5.0 revolution is predicted to stress the precision and quality of products, changing manufacturing inside elite enterprises and supply networks. Sector 5.0 is revolutionizing the sector via increased automation and efficiency. Artificial intelligence can speed up predictive analysis to enable better decision-making, improve process efficiency, and automate repetitive processes.

Additionally, AI has the potential to quicken the creation of cutting-edge products and services like autonomous automobiles and customized customer care. In this context, industrial 5.0 is a forthcoming generation specifically for Industrial environments, represented by a concentration on human-centricity. Industry 5.0 represents a marvellous take-off from the Industry 4.0 (Letto et al., 2022).Different from antecedents, Industry 5.0 acts as solid spotlight on the Human-centric approach and hierarchize the systematic shifts regarding supportable industrial practises. The chapter holds significant importance as it establishes clear definitions and portrays the distinguishing features of industry 5.0.We will also talk about the structures of Industry 5.0 linked with Industrial evolutions and discuss the uses to progress in Diligence 5.0 by medical subjects, Recruitment, Payroll and others. The section drives through the various elements and suggests that all companies adapt to industry 5.0 (Y liu et al., 2020). The chapter will help to understand the significance and importance of application technologies in various HR practices and strategies.

REVIEW OF PAST LITERATURE-TECHNOLOGY IMPLICATIONS THROUGH 5.0 AND HRM

Industry 5.0 is envisioned as the supremacy of organisations, where humans and robots collaborate, facilitated by communication through the Social Networking System and various technologies (Masood et al, 2020).The industry is transitioning from past advancements, focusing on achieving unparalleled precision, reducing human resources time, and reinforcing processes through various technologies (Adadi and Beradda 2018).

Industry 5.0 enhances the established paradigm of Version 4.0 by emphasizing the essential role of exploration and revolution in guiding the transition toward sustainable, human-centric, and resilient changes across various industries globally (Braque, 2022).

Industry 5.0 is the upcoming industrial revolution that has the potential to transform entire diligence and also impact majority of HR practices. (Di Vaio et al, 2023). The various technologies of Version 5.0 are designed for various components which can integrate technology including cloud computing, big data analytics, smart materials, and human-machine interaction for various HR practices (Fazal and Muneta, 2023). Version 5.0 technology plays a crucial role in automating agreement processes among the HR organisation. However, smart contracts specifically manage aspects such as security and the automation of HR-related tasks (Long Liang, 2019).

Industry 5.0 focuses more on their effectiveness of human resources and their prevailing movement. Therefore, they rises the corporate efficacy at the process is accustomed created on some limits. (Peck Moore et al, 2018). Technology 5.0 represents the next stage of global governance and exemplifies symmetrical innovation. Thc primary objective is to establish secure pathways by segregating more human resource technology systems. (Poláková et al, 2023).

The term Industry 5.0 refers to the people working with the Digital era. It is about the robots who are helping humans to work faster by occupying the resources such as big data analytics (Javaid and Haleem, 2020). Industry 5.0 is defined by a radical partnership between people, organisations and systems employed together to explore advanced methods for improving and optimizing human productivity processes. (Panday and Kaur, 2023).

The 5.0 version is a valuable gift, tailored to seamlessly integrate with current resources and establish strong connections between humans and Technologies. Its adaptability aligns perfectly with modern business models, offering a flexible and efficient solution (Deepa, 2022).Industry 5.0 is about mass personalisation of these present technologies. While the whole world is going through these changes the current Human resource Management of the organisations also has to go through this transition. (Suchek Dey et al, 2022).

The fresh rebellion in which transformation is moving from Industry 4.0 While the industry 4.0 contains of scientific expansions in area of developments of data analytics, Cyber physical systems and more atmosphere in the atmosphere of Digitalisation. (Ganer kediya, 2022).Industry 5.0 revolves around the extensive customization of existing technologies for individualized experiences. As the global landscape undergoes these transformative shifts, the contemporary human resource management within organizations must also adapt to seamlessly navigate this transition. (Prem Singh, 2021).The revolution will be amplified among the humans and smart systems like develop especially in HR department. With this step, HR technologies like monotonous and repetitive tasks while peoples yield to creative side across the world. (Newman, 2018).

Industry 5.0 holds a high priority on protecting the encironment and welfare of its workforce in a way to inaugurate a workable source of wealth. It also highlight the human centric strategy that puts all workers in creative process used by the sector (Kalateh et al, 2022). Artifical intelligence and the human workers interaction, a collaboration and the potential of Human resource management strategies, where the people and robots will be working together, it is highlighting as a critical area on where HR managers should focus, where the humans will be received a special attention (Arsalan et al., 2021).

TECHNOLOGY EVOLUTION AND REVOLUTION FROM THE INDUSTRY 1.0 TO INDUSTRY 5.0

Industry is the process of converting resources and raw materials into high-quality products in order to provide commodities and services. The final products from industries progress through different stages, encompassing manufacturing, processing, assembly, packaging, and distribution (Aggarwal.,2019).

With time, the industrial sector has experienced multiple transformations as shown in above figure (1), collectively referred to as the "industrial revolution."

Industry 1.0: Manual Production to Automation

The primary goal of the evolution during Industry 1.0 was to transition from manual production methods to automation, playing a pivotal role in reshaping the global production landscape. Significant advancements in materials, manufacturing processes, transportation, and communication marked this revolution. The primary goal of the evolution during Industry 1.0 was to transition from manual production methods to automation, playing a pivotal role in reshaping the global production landscape. This revolution was marked by significant advancements in materials, manufacturing processes, transportation, and communication.

Industry 2.0: Mass Production With Integration of Human Resource

Industry 2.0 was started with Integration of Human resource technologies and the invention of other technologies such as assemblage line. The revolt helps to increase productivity, and emerging of new industries like automobiles industry, transforming some work practises comparing to the previous technological eras. This makes work classic than the previous technologies. They are characterized by the application of Visualization, the implementation of big data analysis, and the adoption of digital technologies. Industry 2.0 seeks to increase mass production by minimizing various non-productive efforts, aiming to enhance production through the deployment of automated workforce.

Industry 3.0: Automation and Use of Various Electronic Devices

This evolution begins with improvements in electronics and the creation and production of electronic devices like transistors, programmable memory controls, and computers. Processes were automated and human work was reduced. Examples are robots which performs multiple instruction tasks. The new concept like supply chain management was introduced. The rise of new technologies not only pay way for growth of system but also supported for a new origin like Bamboo HR, Big data and Cloud computing. The goal of Industry 3.0 is to seamlessly integrate digital tools and technologies into company operations, enabling the automation of various production-related processes. The advent of computers facilitated the introduction of new production and digital typesetters, all dependent on a combination of computer technology and human interaction.

Industry 4.0: Digitalisation/Automation

The objective is to enhance customization by integrating flexible Management systems and optimize Human resource management digitalisation through real-time data analysis. Organisation can make significant paces, such as predicting failures before they happen. Improvements in quality, reduced work pressure times, achieved through efficient manpower management practices (Aceto et al., 2019). The emergence in the Industry 4.0, signifying the fourth developed riot, configured the early century, installing a model shift characterized by high quality automation and seamless data exchange. Additionally, the fusion of these technology, particularly artificial intelligence and machine learning, allows for classier problem-solving and more agile decision-making, especially in organisation environment. The introduction of ground-breaking technologies like artificial intelligence and machine learning, which give industry improved decision-making and problem-solving capabilities, further fuels the human resource management. (Erro-Garcés et al., 2023).

Industry 5.0: Personalisation/Humans and Technology Collaboration

Last era is also referred to as Human technology partnership, which aims to combine the advantages of Industry 4.0 with a distinctly human touch. This manifestation underscores the significance of human creativity, innovation and problem-solving skills, which concurrently exploiting advanced technologies like AI and robotics. Industry 5.0 pave way for Human resource management in a collaborative work environment where the HR related technologies and humans collaborative with undertaking repetitive and hazardous tasks, permit humans to focus on sophisticated and creative endeavours (Mujumdar et al., 2021).This approach is relaxed to yield heightened efficiency, productivity and Work satisfaction. This progression represents a comprehensive and balanced approach to business, maximising the benefits of both people and technology in a future marked by creativity, effectiveness, and ethical business conduct. Industry 5.0 thrives to find the right balance between robotization and humans, blending the power of smart, precise, with human creativity and ingenuity.

- *Industry 1.0 pave way towards the rise of Manpower to automation, laying a foundation for beginning of digital tools in the area of Human resource management.*
- *Industry 2.0 revolves about the mass production with integration of Human resource management elements like Visualization, Big data analytics,*
- *Industry 3.0 initiated the automation in Human resource technologies incorporating advancement like machine learning, Artificial intelligence and Cloud computing technologies.*
- *Industry 4.0 established the foundation for emerging in Various HR technologies playing a vital role in Decision-making and Problem-solving issues.*
- *The present-generation Industry 5.0 is anticipated to progress further in the direction of advancements in cognitive computerization within the Human resource management.*

ROLE OF INDUSTRY REVOLUTION AND HRM

Human resource management, much like other well-designed areas, has gone through significant evolution over the centuries to adapt to the challenges posed by dynamic market conditions. The role of human resources as a crucial determinant of productivity, encompassing management strategy and capital, cannot be exaggerated. Furthermore, the intersection of evolving management philosophies and technological advancements has brought about disruptions in human resource functions. These changes have proven to be advantageous, contributing to the effective and efficient functioning of human resource management. To improve the proficiency and Innovation, the integration of updated automation and modish technologies into the industrial processes is decisive. Empower the growth of testable and editable processes to effectively meet the increasing the demands for products (CK Chang et al., 2020).Participate cyber and physical workings to create systems that can monitor and control physical developments with the help of computer-based processes. This industry 5.0 boost the real time data argument and adaptive manufacturing processes.

ROLE OF AI, DIGITALISATION, AND TECHNOLOGY IN HRM PRACTICES

In an effort to comprehend the nature of intelligence in living things, particularly humans, artificial intelligence emerged as a subject of study in the 1950s. The rise in information volume in catalogues, which is present in many real-world optimisation issues, has prompted researchers to look for other methods that can lead to effective solutions, such artificial intelligence and optimisation. Artificial intelligence tools and digital stages "intelligent status" has become more vital part for the business organisation and society

Application of AI into the Human resource practises can help a Company to issue a good outcome of the product along with effective workflow. Since these technologies can forecast, spot, and issue recommendations to Human resource team so that they can produce fare decisions after analysing any issues or data. Digitalisation in HRM is considered as elementary need in feature of the business organisation (Custers, 2012).Every business organisation has a long journey to go by assuming digitalisation. Employment and Talent obtaining are the first HR works, AI has been used to progress. From the job assigning to sending the job offers, these AI has significantly abridged the time spended on enrollment task. With the use of AI, these HR experts can bring out edited sequences of messages and communications for each candidate, guiding to improve concentration towards the work and response rates (Pillai and Sivathanu, 2020).AI can use to track and analyse conversion rates, allows recruiters and other managers to identify most successful strategies. HR and talent acquisition managers are ready to adopt this technology due to its cost-effectiveness and the advantages it brings to HR management. AI technology enhances efficiency by saving both time and costs for the talent acquisition department (Figure 1).

The digitization of Human Resource Management (HRM) has led to the gradual incorporation of AI into Human Resource Management Systems (HRMS) and HR systems. Digital HR technologies encompass a broad spectrum of tools and solutions designed to modernize and elevate various functions within human resources. These technologies like digital platforms, automation, and artificial intelligence to enhance HR processes and decision-making. The landscape of digital HR technologies is diverse, offering a wide array of tools and solution.

DIFFERENT TYPES OF HR TECHNOLOGIES AND ITS IMPLICATIONS

The different types of HR technologies and its application in organisation are shown in figure 2

Human Resource Information System (HRIS)

Software is called HRIS (Human Resources Information System). Solution designed to integrate and centralize employee information and HR-related data, encompassing elements such as labour force, benefits, performance reviews, and attendance. Its core functionalities are centered on efficient data management, Block chain web technologies and Visualization. HRIS stands as a prominent modern HR tool, gaining popularity in developed countries since the early 21st century. The adoption of HRIS by corporate organizations has emerged over the last five years, primarily within larger corporate enti-

Figure 1. Trends in human resource management

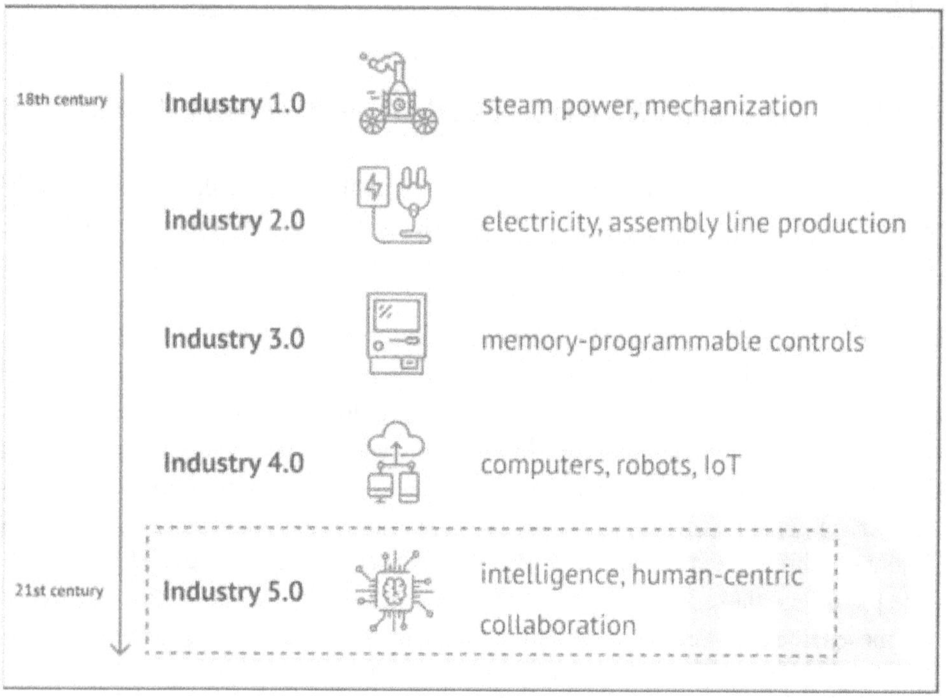

Figure 2. Different types of HR technologies and their Implications

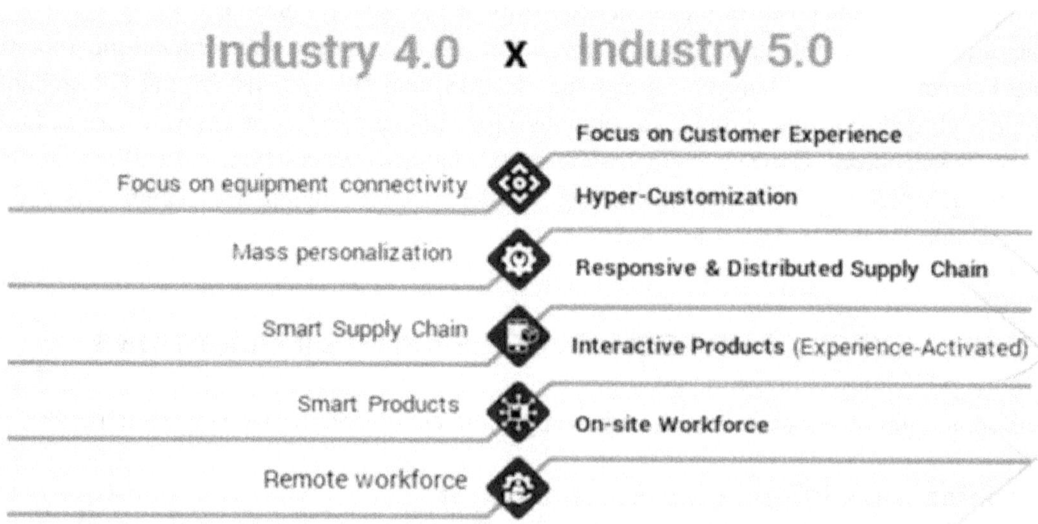

ties (Jahan and Sabrina, 2014).However, its implementation remains limited, with small businesses and public organizations lagging behind in recognizing the advantages of HRIS and showing minimal initiative to adopt the system. The primary obstacle to the success of HRIS is the lack of commitment from management. Although the high cost poses a significant limitation, the benefits of HRIS outweigh its drawbacks. Once implemented in an organization, both employees and management have acknowledged and experienced the positive outcomes

Case Example1: IBM (International business machine). IBM uses paperless online enrollment practices for all of its employees.

Applicant Tracking System (ATS)

ATS (Applicant Tracking System) software contributes to the modernization of the recruitment process by overseeing tasks such as managing job postings, applicant profiles, resume screening, interview scheduling, and fostering strong engagement with candidates. An Applicant Tracking System (ATS) is crafted to facilitate each step in the process of hiring the right candidate for a job. The Applicant Tracking System (ATS) offers wide-ranging Data analytics support for recruitment process by amalgamating completely recruiting tasks within a unified system. It facilitates the entire recruitment journey, starting from identifying a vacancy to on boarding the selected candidate. This system sets up a shared database for all the hiring steps, making it simple to manage recruitment without interruptions when using various tools. It should also assist in directly finding potential candidates in suitable databases or talent pools.

Case Example 2: Amazon uses this Applicant Tracking System (ATS) software that monitors resumes based on some unique keywords.

Learning Management System (LMS)

An Learning management system is used to distribute and manage training and development programs for the employee used in HR companies. It compromises the e-learning modules, Blockchain technologies, and assesses training outcomes. It is a learning management system eminent by its ability to integrate various media, support and many languages by integrating various resources and showcase the information in a proper manner. Its basic objective is to smoothen the construction of learning by interactive means. Moreover, it is critical to underscore that the usefulness of e-learning is not exclusively reliant on the Learning management system; a well-made course that combines innovative education organizations is equally vital. The mixture of a sincere learning management system and a solicitously planned course contributes to the overall quality of e-learning and boosts the possibility of widespread reception and assignment with this mode of education. Learning management system is notable by aptitude to participate in diverse media, powcr unusual workings, and present information in a structured manner.

Case Example 3: The organisation uses the Docebo learning tool, which allows employees to update their skills by e-learning through a unified Dashboard.

Performance Management Software

Performance Management software streamlines the task of goal-setting, orchestrates performance reviews, facilitates feedback, and assesses employee performance against predetermined benchmarks. Performance management is a wide-ranging process that discourses various aspects of performance within an entity. This process covers some sub-processes, including strategy definition (planning and goal setting), tactic implementation, Hr analytics, and performance measurement. Specifically, performance measurement is a distinct sub-process within the wide-ranging framework of performance management. Its principal attention is on categorizing, tracking, and collaborating performance results through the use of routine indicators. In spirit, performance measurement involves the assessment of results, providing a regular approach to assess how well objectives are being met. On the other hand, performance management covers outside measurement and involves taking action based on the evaluation results. This includes producing of informed decisions, executing improvements, and certifying that the targeted performance results are not only mediated but actively pursued and achieved.

Case Example 4: Adobe Software Company uses a performance management system for the feed-back process which is accurate and error free. The screening process done manually involves lots of time and energy

Employee Self-Service Portals

This system allows the employees to access and manage their personal HR-related information. It allows the employees to directly complete job- related tasks that were accepted by the HR teams. This supports and facilitates senior executive information and decision-making needs.

Case Example 5: Service now, an Software Company which offers employee service portals through a single unified portal for multi-department service distribution.

Payroll Software

Through task automation, the payroll system guarantees precision and efficiency in handling the intricate aspects of employee compensation. In essence, the payroll system stands as a pivotal component for HR organizations. The proposed payroll system seamlessly incorporates user authentication for employees, HR personnel, and administrators, ensuring secure access through designated usernames and passwords (Uppala, 2016).This user-friendly approach facilitates straightforward logins and contributes to an intuitive experience for all system users. The system adeptly tracks working hours, maintaining a comprehensive record of employee data.

Case Example 6: Deel Service Company has the Payroll system for remote teams which includes localized payments.

Time and Attendance Tracking

This system helps to manage their work hours, break time and attendance. This system, which is an Android mobile application, is a location-based smart time and attendance monitoring system built on the web services idea. On their Android smartphones, the staff member is required to install the corresponding APK files that were created for them. Various technologies include biometric devices, RFID cards and web-vase interfaces. The IP (internet protocol) address of the office internet must be saved by the employee. This location-based time and attendance monitoring system records your position and tracks your login and logout times (Sultana et al.,2015).The system establishes a connection to the office internet as soon as the employee walks into his workspace, sending the worker's ID and the current local time to the server. After that, the server obtains the local time and keeps the data in a database. Once more, the system alerts the office server when an employee departs the designated workspace.

Case Example 7: Zoho Company uses an Attendance tracking system for providing real-time insights into employee attendance and enhancing total HR processes.

Remote Work and Collaboration Tools

Though there is a rise in remote work, technologies such as video conferencing, Project management tools and other communication platforms permit remote groups to combine effectively. Remote collaboration is the practice of overcoming geographic distance as a hindrance to teamwork. It enables effective communication and productivity among a distributed team of employees, regardless of their location, with the aim of achieving a common goal. Tools for remote collaboration can play a key role in uniting even employees who are physically distant (Venkateswaran, 2012).Increase occupational cooperation by helping HR members connect to employees and information across geographical boundaries and rethinking of the workflows using fashionable combination able tools. Software like Slack, Project management, Trello, Zoom and Microsoft teams are used by HR teams to connect people from various places. All the while maintaining enterprise agreement and security. With the use of technologies like file sharing, unified workspace software, video conferencing, teleconferencing, and cross-channel messaging, remote workers may collaborate more effectively and be more productive in Organisations.

Case Example 8: Apple, Spotify and Salesforce, global companies are using software for connecting employees across globe without boundaries.

AI-Powered Recruitment Tools

AI Systems assist by analyzing the candidates' resumes, finding the best candidate for the job role, and conducting the preliminary candidate screenings through chatbots. This AI recruitment tool involves recruiting talented people by way of predictive analysis in the hiring process. Companies like ZOHO use advanced AI recruitment software which helps assist top talents and conduct behavioural improvement trials. Smart recruitment plays a crucial role in revolutionizing employment processes by incorporating advanced AI tools to simplify and automate the hiring process (Adadi and Berrada., 2018).For organizations aiming to enhance their recruitment procedures, AI-powered smart recruitment solutions can provide a competitive advantage in today's dynamic job market. Intelligence for the hiring process is software for the talent acquisition process, where machine learning can be used to filter those who are ideal candidates, as well as to mechanize some manual tasks in the recruitment process (Arslan et al., 2022).This technology is drafted to streamline or mechanize some parts of recruitment workflow, that to in case of repetitive and mass volume tasks.

Employee Engagement Applications:

These platforms quantify and improve the employee satisfaction, Well-being and engagement by way of Surveys and analytics. These platforms play a crucial role in quantifying and enhancing employee satisfaction, well-being, and engagement through the use of surveys and analytics. They are instrumental in instilling a people-first culture within organizations. Specifically designed to boost, track, measure, and understand workforce engagement, these tools come with a myriad of features that contribute to improving internal communications, gauging employee sentiments, shaping the employee experience, acknowledging achievements, and advocating for a healthy work-life balance. A key element of successful employee engagement strategies is personalization and leading platforms excel in providing flexibility to accommodate diverse user experiences.

Figure 3. AI application in HRMs

This adaptability ensures that the engagement tools can successfully meet the unique needs and preferences of every employee. By granting employees autonomy and flexibility in their work, these platforms promote enhanced internal cooperation and communication among staff members.

CHALLENGES OF HR ANALYTICS SOFTWARE

Skill Gap and Workforce Training

Companies may narrow the talent gap in three ways: by hiring more people, automating procedures, and focusing on employee retention. Businesses that feel that some employees are insufficient or lack the requisite knowledge may decide to use robotics, which is capable of doing tasks that people can (Compare et al.,2019).By taking advantage of the need to find a broad pool of people with the necessary skills, businesses may redefine themselves as learning organisations. A multitude of stakeholders are available to assist them with their upskilling and reskilling initiatives. One possible approach is to implement new professional skills certification models that are akin to those that are now in use and administered by various IT groups (Stone et al., 2015).By establishing objective and marketable credentials for a wide array of emerging job roles, such initiatives have the potential to enhance the efficacy of corporate training programs, boost labour market flexibility, and define clear skill sets..

Change Management and Adaptability

Collaborating Artificial intelligence with prevailing processes and schemes needs some experts to use it, but it is changed as a challenge in change management and adaptability for adapting it. The deployment of new technology, including AI, is a slow process, which further adds to the challenge of change management and adaptability. The distribution of new technology, including emerging technology (AI) is not a hurried process which adds a struggle of Change management and adaptability. The effective deployment of this AI should extend beyond urban and semi-urban regions, encompassing rural areas as well. The implementation must reach frontline workers, supervisors, and senior management, addressing their specific requirements for this transformative change (Serrror et al.,2020). Hence, senior experts perceive AI tools as revolutionary technology and are eager to embrace and integrate them into their foundational models.

Hiring and Retaining Talent

The impending era of Industry 5.0 will heavily rely on innovative technology like artificial intelligence (AI), robots, and data analytics. The industry's next iteration heavily relies on these cutting-edge technology. Consequently, in this quickly changing environment, finding and keeping tech-focused professionals becomes one of the biggest problems. For Industry 5.0 to flourish, workers must be motivated to learn new things and stay current. The establishment of a skill gap forces HR to negotiate a changing market and presents a significant barrier for organisations seeking to acquire talent. Because traditional HRM methods are becoming antiquated, business executives must assist staff members in reskilling or upskilling to meet changing work demands. The difficulty facing HRM is handling moral questions about using Automation and AI in the workplace. The HRM has difficulty addressing moral issues with automation and AI in the workplace. Ensuring proper technology implementation modifies the organization's perspective.

Data Privacy and Security

Privacy and security present substantial challenges for Industry 5.0, demanding a foundation of trust within ecosystems. In Industry 5.0, verification scales are utilized for communication with diverse devices, resilient against the potential impact of future quantum computing when deploying nodes for the Internet of Things (IoT). Digitalization technologies provide potential solutions to sustainability-related challenges faced by firms, emphasizing the necessity for modern businesses to comprehend these challenges and their consequences. This highlights the influence of external factors on a firm's activities or the industry at large. Examples include insufficient government support and policy, along with a dearth of broadband infrastructure. External barriers limit an organization's adaptability to changes and may hinder the transition for small manufacturing firms. Industry 5.0 can reap advantages from a blend of agile tools, engaging a diverse cross-section of individuals in product development, striking a harmonious balance between structure and flexibility.

Employee Well-Being and Work-LIFE BALANCE

Poor societal support, especially from supervisors, is consistently linked to burnout and can impact employees' well-being and work-life balance. The non-appearance of job resources, such as feedback and participation in decision-making, will be a gap in the organisational system. Job properties such as job control, the holding of feedback and learning opportunities are uniquely related to Well-being and work-life balance. Hence, HR must address the issues that are related to burnout and Stress. Furthermore, the advent of artificial intelligence has led to concerns that it may replace human labour, implying a scenario where people have no active role in work. However, this perspective is inherently flawed. Instead, these technologies are designed to enhance and streamline human tasks, making them more efficient and reducing the likelihood of burnout. In essence, rather than eliminating jobs, artificial intelligence serves to alleviate the burden on individuals, contributing to a healthier and more sustainable work environment.

Technology Usage With Ethics

Industry 5.0 raises moral concerns about the appropriate application of technology, namely in relation to data security, privacy, and the possibility of AI-powered system abuse. To guarantee the moral implementation of Industry 5.0 technologies and to handle any unsolved issues, certain rules and regulations are necessary. Mechanisation and AI technology integration may result in job losses in some industries, necessitating comprehensive training programmes to retrain and upskill employees and instill optimism in beneficial outcomes. Given the complexity and computerization of modern decision-making processes, it can be difficult to understand and articulate the reasoning behind some choices.

Future Implementations

Furthermore, when providing customers with increasingly sophisticated and analytical services, privacy-preserving statistical transactions, data accumulation privacy, and other ethical aspects need to be taken into account. Enterprises must embrace ethical strategies while integrating Industry 5.0 technology. Companies for example, set policies on data privacy and artificial intelligence (AI) and HR data will be used to spot patterns and forecast the size of the labour force in the future (Wollschlaeger et al., 2017). As a result, Industry 5.0 will have a significant impact and HRM will need to be flexible and sensitive to these developments. Industry 5.0 is projected to personalize service for employees, facilitated by cognitive-driven human resource challenges, where safety is considered as the foremost concern. Industries use digital computation by way of assessment and eliminate security weaknesses, especially while using extensive user and industrial data (Adel, 2021).

Additionally, when providing advanced and more analytical services to users, businesses must wisely consider factors like Privacy-preserving data transactions, ethical considerations related to data collections, and other privacy concerns. Ethical guidelines of Industry 5.0 technologies should be the top most priority for businesses. Therefore, the company must produce clear guidelines for ethical use of these Artificial intelligence technologies and other data privacy(Wollschlaeger et al., 2017).The role of Human resource management (HRM) is measured by automation, shifting from traditional HR activities like recruitment, Training and development, Policy Development, Record keeping to modern strategic HR functions like workforce planning and talent management; human resource data plays an important role in identifying trends and making calculations for future and future workforce needs. Therefore, impact of Industry 5.0 is significant, demanding Human resource management sectors to be more flexible and adaptive to the upcoming changes and upgradation in technologies.

CONCLUSION

The initial chapters of our work commenced by furnishing precise definitions of key Industry 5.0 concepts as perceived by HRM practitioners and industry communities. Subsequently, we delved into the evolutionary transformations of industries from the inaugural Industry 1.0 to the contemporary Industry 5.0, delineating their distinct phases and specialized nomenclatures. The discussion further progressed to illuminate each industrial era and its practical applications (Gupta,2019).The central focus of the chapter was on discerning the challenges associated with implementing HRM practices in the context of Industry 5.0.This chapter comprehensively encompasses various technologies, including the Human Resource Information System (HRIS), Applicant Tracking System (ATS), Learning Management System (LMS), Performance Management Software, Talent Management Software, Employee Self-Service Portals, Payroll Software, Time and Attendance Tracking, Remote Work and Collaboration Tools, AI Recruitment Tools, and Employee Engagement Tools (Lu., 2017).These platforms empower employees to operate autonomously and flexibly, fostering opportunities for heightened collaboration and communication within the organization. Advancing to Chapter 4, we elucidated the challenges confronted by HRM experts in Industry 5.0, encompassing ethical considerations in technology usage, skill gaps, and workforce training. Consequently, HRM emerges as a pivotal force in ensuring the success of organizations in Industry 5.0, harnessing the complete potential of both human and technological capabilities to propel innovation, productivity, and sustainable growth.

REFERENCES

Aceto, G., Persico, V., & Pescapé, A. (2019). A survey on information and communication technologies for industry 4.0: State-of-the-art, taxonomies, perspectives, and challenges. *IEEE Communications Surveys and Tutorials*, *21*(4), 3467–3501. doi:10.1109/COMST.2019.2938259

Adadi, A., & Berrada, M. (2018). Peeking inside the black-box: A survey on explainable artificial intelligence (XAI). *IEEE Access : Practical Innovations, Open Solutions*, *6*, 52138–52160. doi:10.1109/ACCESS.2018.2870052

Adel, A. (2022). Future of industry 5.0 in society: Human-centric solutions, challenges and prospective research areas. *Journal of Cloud Computing (Heidelberg, Germany)*, *11*(1), 40. doi:10.1186/s13677-022-00314-5 PMID:36101900

Aggarwal, M. (1784). History of the industrial revolution. Academic Press.

Arslan, A., Cooper, C., Khan, Z., Golgeci, I., & Ali, I. (2022). Artificial intelligence and human workers interaction at team level: A conceptual assessment of the challenges and potential HRM strategies. *International Journal of Manpower*, *43*(1), 75–88. doi:10.1108/IJM-01-2021-0052

Aslam, F., Aimin, W., Li, M., & Ur Rehman, K. (2020). Innovation in the era of IoT and industry 5.0: Absolute innovation management (AIM) framework. *Information (Basel)*, *11*(2), 124. doi:10.3390/info11020124

Cillo, V., Gregori, G. L., Daniele, L. M., Caputo, F., & Bitbol-Saba, N. (2022). Rethinking companies' culture through knowledge management lens during Industry 5.0 transition. *Journal of Knowledge Management*, *26*(10), 2485–2498. doi:10.1108/JKM-09-2021-0718

Compare, M., Baraldi, P., & Zio, E. (2019). Challenges to IoT-enabled predictive maintenance for industry 4.0. *IEEE Internet of Things Journal*, *7*(5), 4585–4597. doi:10.1109/JIOT.2019.2957029

Custers, M. (2012). Rethinking existing HR technologies for new gains in employee engagement and benefits. *Compensation and Benefits Review*, *44*(6), 332–335. doi:10.1177/0886368713476929

Di Vaio, A., Latif, B., Gunarathne, N., Gupta, M., & D'Adamo, I. (2023). Digitalization and artificial knowledge for accountability in SCM: a systematic literature review. *Journal of Enterprise Information Management.*

Echchakoui, S., & Barka, N. (2020). Industry 4.0 and its impact in plastics industry: A literature review. *Journal of Industrial Information Integration*, *20*, 100172. doi:10.1016/j.jii.2020.100172

ElFar, O. A., Chang, C. K., Leong, H. Y., Peter, A. P., Chew, K. W., & Show, P. L. (2021). Prospects of Industry 5.0 in algae: Customization of production and new advance technology for clean bioenergy generation. *Energy Conversion and Management: X*, *10*, 100048.

Erro-Garcés, A., & Aramendia-Muneta, M. E. (2023). The role of human resource management practices on the results of digitalisation. From Industry 4.0 to Industry 5.0. *Journal of Organizational Change Management*, *36*(4), 585–602. doi:10.1108/JOCM-11-2021-0354

Ganer, S. D., Kediya, S. O., Suchek, A. K., Dey, S. K., & Band, G. (2022, October). Analytical study of HRM practices in industry 5.0. *IOP Conference Series. Materials Science and Engineering*, *1259*(1), 012041. doi:10.1088/1757-899X/1259/1/012041

Gupta, S. (2023). An edge-computing based Industrial Gateway for Industry 4.0 using ARM TrustZone technology. *Journal of Industrial Information Integration*, *33*, 100441. doi:10.1016/j.jii.2023.100441

Howard, E. (2018). The evolution of the industrial ages: Industry 1.0 to 4.0. *Simio Forward Thinking, 5.*

Ietto, B., Ancillai, C., Sabatini, A., Carayannis, E. G., & Gregori, G. L. (2022). The role of external actors in SMEs' human-centered industry 4.0 adoption: An empirical perspective on Italian competence centers. *IEEE Transactions on Engineering Management.*

Jahan, S. (2014). Human resources information system (HRIS): A theoretical perspective. Academic Press.

Javaid, M., & Haleem, A. (2020). Critical components of Industry 5.0 towards a successful adoption in the field of manufacturing. *Journal of Industrial Integration and Management*, *5*(03), 327–348. doi:10.1142/S2424862220500141

Kalateh, S., Estrada-Jimenez, L. A., Pulikottil, T., Hojjati, S. N., & Barata, J. (2022, October). The human role in human-centric industry. In *IECON 2022–48th Annual Conference of the IEEE Industrial Electronics Society* (pp. 1-6). IEEE. 10.1109/IECON49645.2022.9968440

Leon, R. D. (2023). Employees' reskilling and upskilling for industry 5.0: Selecting the best professional development programmes. *Technology in Society*, *75*, 102393. doi:10.1016/j.techsoc.2023.102393

Liang, L., Feng, M., Cui, X., Zhou, S., Yin, X., Wang, X., Yang, M., Liu, C., Xie, R., Zhu, L., Yu, J., & Wei, X. (2019). The effect of exercise on cervical radiculopathy: A systematic review and meta-analysis. *Medicine*, *98*(45), e17733. doi:10.1097/MD.0000000000017733 PMID:31702624

Liu, Y., Ma, X., Shu, L., Hancke, G. P., & Abu-Mahfouz, A. M. (2020). From industry 4.0 to agriculture 4.0: Current status, enabling technologies, and research challenges. *IEEE Transactions on Industrial Informatics*, *17*(6), 4322–4334. doi:10.1109/TII.2020.3003910

Lu, Y. (2017). Industry 4.0: A survey on technologies, applications and open research issues. *Journal of Industrial Information Integration*, *6*, 1–10. doi:10.1016/j.jii.2017.04.005

Maddikunta, P. K. R., Pham, Q. V., Prabadevi, B., Deepa, N., Dev, K., Gadekallu, T. R., ... Liyanage, M. (2022). Industry 5.0: A survey on enabling technologies and potential applications. *Journal of Industrial Information Integration*, *26*, 100257. doi:10.1016/j.jii.2021.100257

Majumdar, A., Garg, H., & Jain, R. (2021). Managing the barriers of Industry 4.0 adoption and implementation in textile and clothing industry: Interpretive structural model and triple helix framework. *Computers in Industry*, *125*, 103372. doi:10.1016/j.compind.2020.103372

Masood, T., & Sonntag, P. (2020). Industry 4.0: Adoption challenges and benefits for SMEs. *Computers in Industry*, *121*, 103261. doi:10.1016/j.compind.2020.103261

Newman, N. (2018). *Journalism, media and technology trends and predictions 2018*. Reuters Institute for the Study of Journalism.

Panday, P., & Kaur, G. (2023). Talent management and employee outlook on industry 5.0. In Handbook of Research on Education Institutions, Skills, and Jobs in the Digital Era (pp. 299-306). IGI Global.

Peck, B. W., Van Abel, K. M., Moore, E. J., & Price, D. L. (2018). Rates and locations of regional metastases insinonasal malignancies: The Mayo Clinic experience. *Journal of Neurological Surgery. Part B, Skull Base*, *79*(03), 282–288. doi:10.1055/s-0037-1607288 PMID:29765826

Pillai, R., & Sivathanu, B. (2020). Adoption of artificial intelligence (AI) for talent acquisition in IT/ITeS organizations. *Benchmarking*, *27*(9), 2599–2629. doi:10.1108/BIJ-04-2020 0186

Poláková, M., Suleimanová, J. H., Madzík, P., Copuš, L., Molnárová, I., & Polednová, J. (2023). Soft skills and their importance in the labour market under the conditions of Industry 5.0. *Heliyon*, *9*(8), e18670. doi:10.1016/j.heliyon.2023.e18670 PMID:37593611

Rada, M. (2017). Industry 5.0 Definition. Academic Press.

Serror, M., Hack, S., Henze, M., Schuba, M., & Wehrle, K. (2020). Challenges and opportunities in securing the industrial internet of things. *IEEE Transactions on Industrial Informatics*, *17*(5), 2985–2996. doi:10.1109/TII.2020.3023507

Skobelev, P. O., & Borovik, S. Y. (2017). On the way from Industry 4.0 to Industry 5.0: From digital manufacturing to digital society. *Industry 4.0*, *2*(6), 307-311.

Stone, D. L., & Deadrick, D. L. (2015). Challenges and opportunities affecting the future of human resource management. *Human Resource Management Review*, *25*(2), 139–145. doi:10.1016/j.hrmr.2015.01.003

Sultana, S., Enayet, A., & Mouri, I. J. (2015). A smart, location based time and attendance tracking system using android application. *International Journal of Computer Science Engineering and Information Technology*, *5*(1), 1–5.

Tange, K., De Donno, M., Fafoutis, X., & Dragoni, N. (2020). A systematic survey of industrial Internet of Things security: Requirements and fog computing opportunities. *IEEE Communications Surveys and Tutorials*, *22*(4), 2489–2520. doi:10.1109/COMST.2020.3011208

Uppala, A. (2016). Creating Employee Self-Service Portal Concept. Academic Press.

Venkateswaran, N. (2012). Strategies for adopting talent management issues in software companies. *International Journal of Management, Economics and Social Sciences*, *1*(2), 33–41.

Wollschlaeger, M., Sauter, T., & Jasperneite, J. (2017). The future of industrial communication: Automation networks in the era of the internet of things and industry 4.0. *IEEE Industrial Electronics Magazine*, *11*(1), 17–27. doi:10.1109/MIE.2017.2649104

Compilation of References

Abdeldayem, M. M., & Aldulaimi, S. H. (2020). Trends and opportunities of artificial intelligence in human resource management: Aspirations for public sector in Bahrain. *International Journal of Scientific and Technology Research*, *9*(1), 3867–3871.

Abdulwahid, A. H., Pattnaik, M., Palav, M. R., Babu, S. T., Manoharan, G., & Selvi, G. P. (2023, April). Library Management System Using Artificial Intelligence. In *2023 Eighth International Conference on Science Technology Engineering and Mathematics (ICONSTEM)* (pp. 1-7). IEEE.

Abey, J. (2016). Mounting Role of Bancassurance in India. *International Journal of Business and Social Science*, *7*(4), 51–58.

Aceto, G., Persico, V., & Pescapé, A. (2019). A survey on information and communication technologies for industry 4.0: State-of-the-art, taxonomies, perspectives, and challenges. *IEEE Communications Surveys and Tutorials*, *21*(4), 3467–3501. doi:10.1109/COMST.2019.2938259

Adadi, A., & Berrada, M. (2018). Peeking inside the black-box: A survey on explainable artificial intelligence (XAI). *IEEE Access : Practical Innovations, Open Solutions*, *6*, 52138–52160. doi:10.1109/ACCESS.2018.2870052

Adekiya, A. (2024). Perceived job insecurity and task performance: What aspect of performance is related to which facet of job insecurity. *Current Psychology (New Brunswick, N.J.)*, *43*(2), 1340–1358. doi:10.1007/s12144-023-04408-4 PMID:36852083

Adel, A. (2022). Future of industry 5.0 in society: Human-centric solutions, challenges and prospective research areas. *Journal of Cloud Computing (Heidelberg, Germany)*, *11*(1), 40. doi:10.1186/s13677-022-00314-5 PMID:36101900

Afacan, G., & Arifoğlu, A. (2015). A new metric system for assessment of e-transformation. *International Journal of eBusiness and eGovernment Studies*, *7*(1), 1–15.

Agarwal, M. K. (2019). Insurance Industry and The Government As A Facilitator of Change. *Deliberative Research*, *42*(1), 10–14.

Agarwal, R., & Thakur, V. (2019). Government eservice rating metrics. *Proceedings of the 12th International Conference on Theory and Practice of Electronic Governance*, 129–139. 10.1145/3326365.3326382

Aggarwal, M. (1784). History of the industrial revolution. Academic Press.

Agrawal, A. V., Pitchai, R., Senthamaraikannan, C., Balaji, N. A., Sajithra, S., & Boopathi, S. (2023). Digital Education System During the COVID-19 Pandemic. In Using Assistive Technology for Inclusive Learning in K-12 Classrooms (pp. 104–126). IGI Global. doi:10.4018/978-1-6684-6424-3.ch005

Agrawal, A. V., Shashibhushan, G., Pradeep, S., Padhi, S., Sugumar, D., & Boopathi, S. (2023). Synergizing Artificial Intelligence, 5G, and Cloud Computing for Efficient Energy Conversion Using Agricultural Waste. In Sustainable Science and Intelligent Technologies for Societal Development (pp. 475–497). IGI Global.

Agrawal, A. V., Magulur, L. P., Priya, S. G., Kaur, A., Singh, G., & Boopathi, S. (2023). Smart Precision Agriculture Using IoT and WSN. In *Handbook of Research on Data Science and Cybersecurity Innovations in Industry 4.0 Technologies* (pp. 524–541). IGI Global. doi:10.4018/978-1-6684-8145-5.ch026

Agrawal, A. V., Shashibhushan, G., Pradeep, S., Padhi, S. N., Sugumar, D., & Boopathi, S. (2024). Synergizing Artificial Intelligence, 5G, and Cloud Computing for Efficient Energy Conversion Using Agricultural Waste. In B. K. Mishra (Ed.), (pp. 475–497). Practice, Progress, and Proficiency in Sustainability. IGI Global. doi:10.4018/979-8-3693-1186-8.ch026

Agyeman, C. M., & Ponniah, V. M. (2014). Employee demographic characteristics and their effects on turnover and retention in MSMEs. *International Journal of Recent Advances in Organizational Behaviour and Decision Sciences*, *1*(1), 12–29.

Ahmad, M., Raziq, M. M., Rehman, W. U., & Allen, M. M. (2020). High-performance work practices and organizational performance in Pakistan. *International Journal of Manpower*, *41*(3), 318–338. doi:10.1108/IJM-01-2019-0016

Akundi, A., Euresti, D., Luna, S., Ankobiah, W., Lopes, A., & Edinbarough, I. (2022). State of Industry 5.0—Analysis and Identification of Current Research Trends. *Applied System Innovation*, *5*(1), 1–14. doi:10.3390/asi5010027

Al Haziazi, M., Muthuraman, S., Al Yahyaei, N., & Al Balusi, A. (2021, March). Influence of HR Digital Transformation in the Cognitive Technology Era of the Sultanate of Oman. In *2021 7th International Conference on Information Management (ICIM)* (pp. 123-127). IEEE. 10.1109/ICIM52229.2021.9417155

Al Khawaldeh, E. D. (2023). The Impact of Training on Improving Employee Performance: A Case Study on Employees in the Directorate of Education of Ma'an District. *International Journal of Professional Business Review*, *8*(10), e03520–e03520. doi:10.26668/businessreview/2023.v8i10.3520

AlHamad, A., Alshurideh, M., Alomari, K., Kurdi, B., Alzoubi, H., Hamouche, S., & Al-Hawary, S. (2022). The effect of electronic human resources management on organizational health of telecommuni-cations companies in Jordan. *International Journal of Data and Network Science*, *6*(2), 429–438. doi:10.5267/j.ijdns.2021.12.011

Ali, M. N., Senthil, T., Ilakkiya, T., Hasan, D. S., Ganapathy, N. B. S., & Boopathi, S. (2024). IoT's Role in Smart Manufacturing Transformation for Enhanced Household Product Quality. In *Advanced Applications in Osmotic Computing* (pp. 252–289). IGI Global. doi:10.4018/979-8-3693-1694-8.ch014

Almalki, M. J., FitzGerald, G., & Clark, M. (2012). The relationship between quality of work life and turnover intention of primary health care nurses in Saudi Arabia. *BMC Health Services Research*, *12*(1), 1–11. doi:10.1186/1472-6963-12-314 PMID:22970764

Al-Safi, J. K. S., Bansal, A., Aarif, M., Almahairah, M. S. Z., Manoharan, G., & Alotoum, F. J. (2023). Assessment Based On IoT For Efficient Information Surveillance Regarding Harmful Strikes Upon Financial Collection. *2023 International Conference on Computer Communication and Informatics (ICCCI)*, 1-5. 10.1109/ICCCI56745.2023.10128500

Ambrosius, J. (2018). Strategic talent management in emerging markets and its impact on employee retention: Evidence from Brazilian MNCs. *Thunderbird International Business Review*, *60*(1), 53–68. doi:10.1002/tie.21799

Am, E. N., Affandi, A., Udobong, A., Sarwani, S., & Hernawan, H. (2020). „Implementation of human resource management in the adaptation period for new habits. *International Journal of Educational Administration, Management, and Leadership*, *1*(1), 19–26. doi:10.51629/ijeamal.v1i1.4

Ameen, N., Tarhini, A., Shah, M., & Madichie, N. O. (2021). Going with the flow: Smart shopping malls and omnichannel retailing. *Journal of Services Marketing*, *35*(3), 325–348. doi:10.1108/JSM-02-2020-0066

Anam Amin, R. S., & Lodhi, M. R. N. (2013). The impact of employees training on the job performance in education sector of Pakistan. *Middle East Journal of Scientific Research*, *17*(9), 1273–1278.

Anbalagan, G. (2017). New technological changes in Indian Banking Sector. *International Journal of Scientific Research and Management*, *5*(9), 7015–7021. doi:10.18535/ijsrm/v5i9.11

Ancarani, A., & Di Mauro, C. (2018). Successful digital transformations need a focus on the individual. In F. Schupp & H. Wöhner (Eds.), *Digitalisierung im Einkauf* (pp. 11–26). Springer Gabler. doi:10.1007/978-3-658-16909-1_2

Andrushia, A. D., Neebha, T. M., Patricia, A. T., Sagayam, K. M., & Pramanik, S. (2023). Capsule Network based Disease Classification for VitisVinifera Leaves. *Neural Computing & Applications*, *2023*. Advance online publication. doi:10.1007/s00521-023-09058-y

Aravind, M., & Nagamani, P. (2013). Financial Analysis of State Bank of India during 2000- '12. *Asian Journal of Research in Business Economics and Management*, *3*(10), 170–184.

Armstrong, M. (2006). A Handbook of Human Resource Management Practice (10th ed.). Cambridge University.

Arslan, A., Cooper, C., Khan, Z., Golgeci, I., & Ali, I. (2022). Artificial intelligence and human workers interaction at team level: A conceptual assessment of the challenges and potential HRM strategies. *International Journal of Manpower*, *43*(1), 75–88. doi:10.1108/IJM-01-2021-0052

Aruna, M., & Anitha, J. (2015). Employee retention enablers: Generation Y employees. *SCMS Journal of Indian Management*, *12*(3), 94.

Arunprasad, R., & Boopathi, S. (2019). Chapter-4 Alternate Refrigerants for Minimization Environmental Impacts: A Review. In Advances in Engineering Technology (p. 75). AkiNik Publications New Delhi.

Ashiq, V. M., Fredrik, E. T., Kumar, N. K., Torres-Cruz, F., Colque, J. P. B., & Manoharan, G. (2023, September). A Deep Learning Approaches for Natural Language Processing and Sentiment Analysis in Social Media. In 2023 6th International Conference on Contemporary Computing and Informatics (IC3I) (Vol. 6, pp. 1746-1750). IEEE.

Aslam, F., Aimin, W., Li, M., & Ur Rehman, K. (2020). Innovation in the era of IoT and industry 5.0: Absolute innovation management (AIM) framework. *Information (Basel)*, *11*(2), 124. doi:10.3390/info11020124

ASSOCHAM. (2021, June). *"Atmanirbhar Bharat" and insurance June 2021 Government's big leap towards making the insurance sector resilient*. https://www.assocham.org/uploads/files/1624941580.pdf

Atewologun, D. (2014). Sites of intersectional identity salience. *Gender in Management*, *29*(5), 277–290. doi:10.1108/GM-12-2013-0140

Aust, I., Matthews, B., & Muller-Camen, M. (2020). Common good HRM: A paradigm shift in sustainable HRM? *Human Resource Management Review*, *30*(3), 100705. doi:10.1016/j.hrmr.2019.100705

Azizi, M. R., Atlasi, R., Ziapour, A., Abbas, J., & Naemi, R. (2021). Innovative human resource management strategies during the COVID-19 pandemic: A systematic narrative review approach. *Heliyon*, *7*(6), e07233. doi:10.1016/j.heliyon.2021.e07233 PMID:34124399

Babu, B. S., Kamalakannan, J., Meenatchi, N., Karthik, S., & Boopathi, S. (2022). Economic impacts and reliability evaluation of battery by adopting Electric Vehicle. *IEEE Explore*, 1–6.

Bag, S., Srivastava, G., Cherrafi, A., Ali, A., & Singh, R. K. (2023). Data-driven insights for circular and sustainable food supply chains: An empirical exploration of big data and predictive analytics in enhancing social sustainability performance. *Business Strategy and the Environment.*

Bahuguna, P. C., Srivastava, R., & Tiwari, S. (2024). Human resources analytics: Where do we go from here? *Benchmarking, 31*(2), 640–668. doi:10.1108/BIJ-06-2022-0401

Bajer, J. (2017). „Digital transformation needs the human touch. *Strategic HR Review, 16*(2), 91–92. doi:10.1108/SHR-02-2017-0011

Bakker, A. B., & Bakker, A. B. (2011). An Evidence-Based Model of Work Engagement. *Current Directions in Psychological Science, 20*(4), 265–269. Advance online publication. doi:10.1177/0963721411414534

Bala, R., & Verma, A. (2012). Scope for the bancassurance in Indian life insurance sector: an analytical approach. *Asian-African Journal of Economics and Econometrics, 12*(1), 235-246.

Ballinger, G., Craig, E., Cross, R., & Gray, P. (2011). A stitch in time saves nine: Leveraging networks to reduce the costs of turnover. *California Management Review, 53*(4), 111–133. doi:10.1525/cmr.2011.53.4.111

Banerjee, A. (2009). Bancassurance: A Major Para-banking Activity. *Insurance Chronicle*, 35-38.

Bansal, J., & Kanwal, A. (2018). Qualitative research on issues and trends in the bancassurance model in India: An interview report. *International Journal of Banking. Risk and Insurance, 6*(2), 67.

Bawa, S. K., & Chattha, S. (2016). Distribution Channels of Indian Life Insurance Industry: Understanding Customers' Awareness. *Business Analyst, 37*(1), 63–80.

Berman, S., & Marshall, A. (2014). The next digital transformation: From an individual centered to an everyone-to-everyone economy. *Strategy and Leadership, 42*(5), 9–17. doi:10.1108/SL-07-2014-0048

Bharadwaj, A., El Sawy, O., Pavlou, P., & Venkatraman, N. (2013). Digital business strategy: Toward the next generation of insights. *Management Information Systems Quarterly, 37*(2), 471–482. doi:10.25300/MISQ/2013/37:2.3

Bhat, T. (2020). India and Industry 4.0. Working paper, 218, Institute for studies in Industrial Development, New Delhi.

Bhavya, K. R., Dharmaraj, A., Pareek, P., Sathe, M. A., Tiwari, M., & Manoharan, G. (2023, September). Application of Soft Computing Techniques for Predictive Analytics in Financial Markets. In 2023 6th International Conference on Contemporary Computing and Informatics (IC3I) (Vol. 6, pp. 1756-1760). IEEE.

Bhushan, P., & Murtaza, M. A. (2014, December 22-24). *Bancassurance: The Indian Scenario* [Conference Presentation]. NIT-MTMI International Conference on Emerging Paradigms and Practices in Global Technology, Management & Business Issues, Department of Mechanical Engineering, National Institute of Technology Hamirpur (H.P) India.

Bibi, P., Ahmad, A., & Majid, A. H. (2016). The moderating role of work environment on the relationship between compensation, job security, and employee's retention. *Journal of Economic & Management Perspectives, 10*(4), 726–738.

Bijeta Nayak, B., Manoharan, G., Sharma, V. K., Lourens, M., Kumar, A., & Hinge, P. (2024). Design and Empirical Analysis of a Artificial Intelligence-Based Human Resource Management Processing Systems for Detecting Personal Stress. 6th International Conference on Contemporary Computing and Informatics (IC3I), 2421-2426.

Billett, S. (2020). *Learning in the workplace: Strategies for effective practice.* Routledge. doi:10.4324/9781003116318

Block, W., Snow, N., & Stringham, E. (2008). Banks, insurance companies, and discrimination. *Business and Society Review, 113*(3), 403–419. doi:10.1111/j.1467-8594.2008.00326.x

Boopathi, S. (2021). Improving of Green Sand-Mould Quality using Taguchi Technique. *Journal of Engineering Research.*

Boopathi, S. (2022b). Cryogenically treated and untreated stainless steel grade 317 in sustainable wire electrical discharge machining process: A comparative study. *Environmental Science and Pollution Research*, 1–10.

Boopathi, S. (2023). Deep Learning Techniques Applied for Automatic Sentence Generation. In Promoting Diversity, Equity, and Inclusion in Language Learning Environments (pp. 255–273). IGI Global. doi:10.4018/978-1-6684-3632-5.ch016

Boopathi, S. (2023b). Securing Healthcare Systems Integrated With IoT: Fundamentals, Applications, and Future Trends. In Dynamics of Swarm Intelligence Health Analysis for the Next Generation (pp. 186–209). IGI Global.

Boopathi, S. (2024). Balancing Innovation and Security in the Cloud: Navigating the Risks and Rewards of the Digital Age. In Improving Security, Privacy, and Trust in Cloud Computing (pp. 164–193). IGI Global.

Boopathi, S. (2024). Implementation of Green Manufacturing Practices in Automobile Fields: A Review. *Sustainable Machining and Green Manufacturing*, 221–248.

Boopathi, S. (2024). Minimization of Manufacturing Industry Wastes Through the Green Lean Sigma Principle. *Sustainable Machining and Green Manufacturing*, 249–270.

Boopathi, S. (2024). Sustainable Development Using IoT and AI Techniques for Water Utilization in Agriculture. In Sustainable Development in AI, Blockchain, and E-Governance Applications (pp. 204–228). IGI Global. doi:10.4018/979-8-3693-1722-8.ch012

Boopathi, S. (2024b). Balancing Innovation and Security in the Cloud: Navigating the Risks and Rewards of the Digital Age. In Improving Security, Privacy, and Trust in Cloud Computing (pp. 164–193). IGI Global.

Boopathi, S. (2024c). Energy Cascade Conversion System and Energy-Efficient Infrastructure. In Sustainable Development in AI, Blockchain, and E-Governance Applications (pp. 47–71). IGI Global. doi:10.4018/979-8-3693-1722-8.ch004

Boopathi, S., & Kumar, P. (2024). Advanced bioprinting processes using additive manufacturing technologies: Revolutionizing tissue engineering. *3D Printing Technologies: Digital Manufacturing, Artificial Intelligence, Industry 4.0*, 95.

Boopathi, S., Khare, R., KG, J. C., Muni, T. V., & Khare, S. (2023). Additive Manufacturing Developments in the Medical Engineering Field. In Development, Properties, and Industrial Applications of 3D Printed Polymer Composites (pp. 86–106). IGI Global.

Boopathi, S., Kumar, P. K. S., Meena, R. S., Sudhakar, M., & Associates. (2023). Sustainable Developments of Modern Soil-Less Agro-Cultivation Systems: Aquaponic Culture. In Human Agro-Energy Optimization for Business and Industry (pp. 69–87). IGI Global.

Boopathi, S., Siva Kumar, P. K., Meena, R. S. J., S. I., P., S. K., & Sudhakar, M. (2023). Sustainable Developments of Modern Soil-Less Agro-Cultivation Systems: Aquaponic Culture. In P. Vasant, R. Rodríguez-Aguilar, I. Litvinchev, & J. A. Marmolejo-Saucedo (Eds.), Advances in Environmental Engineering and Green Technologies (pp. 69–87). IGI Global. doi:10.4018/978-1-6684-4118-3.ch004

Boopathi, S., Thillaivanan, A., Mohammed, A. A., Shanmugam, P., & VR, P. (2022). Experimental investigation on Abrasive Water Jet Machining of Neem Wood Plastic Composite. *IOP: Functional Composites and Structures, 4*, 025001.

Boopathi, S. (2022). Experimental investigation and multi-objective optimization of cryogenic Friction-stir-welding of AA2014 and AZ31B alloys using MOORA technique. *Materials Today. Communications, 33*, 104937. doi:10.1016/j.mtcomm.2022.104937

Boopathi, S. (2022a). An investigation on gas emission concentration and relative emission rate of the near-dry wire-cut electrical discharge machining process. *Environmental Science and Pollution Research International*, *29*(57), 86237–86246. doi:10.1007/s11356-021-17658-1 PMID:34837614

Boopathi, S. (2023). Internet of Things-Integrated Remote Patient Monitoring System: Healthcare Application. In *Dynamics of Swarm Intelligence Health Analysis for the Next Generation* (pp. 137–161). IGI Global. doi:10.4018/978-1-6684-6894-4.ch008

Boopathi, S. (2024a). Advancements in Machine Learning and AI for Intelligent Systems in Drone Applications for Smart City Developments. In *Futuristic e-Governance Security With Deep Learning Applications* (pp. 15–45). IGI Global. doi:10.4018/978-1-6684-9596-4.ch002

Boopathi, S., & Kanike, U. K. (2023). Applications of Artificial Intelligent and Machine Learning Techniques in Image Processing. In B. K. Pandey, D. Pandey, R. Anand, D. S. Mane, & V. K. Nassa (Eds.), Advances in Computational Intelligence and Robotics. IGI Global. doi:10.4018/978-1-6684-8618-4.ch010

Boopathi, S., & Khang, A. (2023). AI-Integrated Technology for a Secure and Ethical Healthcare Ecosystem. In *AI and IoT-Based Technologies for Precision Medicine* (pp. 36–59). IGI Global. doi:10.4018/979-8-3693-0876-9.ch003

Boopathi, S., & Myilsamy, S. (2021). Material removal rate and surface roughness study on Near-dry wire electrical discharge Machining process. *Materials Today: Proceedings*, *45*(9), 8149–8156. doi:10.1016/j.matpr.2021.02.267

Boopathi, S., & Sivakumar, K. (2013). Experimental investigation and parameter optimization of near-dry wire-cut electrical discharge machining using multi-objective evolutionary algorithm. *International Journal of Advanced Manufacturing Technology*, *67*(9–12), 2639–2655. doi:10.1007/s00170-012-4680-4

Boopathi, S., Sureshkumar, M., & Sathiskumar, S. (2023). Parametric Optimization of LPG Refrigeration System Using Artificial Bee Colony Algorithm. In S. Tripathy, S. Samantaray, J. Ramkumar, & S. S. Mahapatra (Eds.), *Recent Advances in Mechanical Engineering* (pp. 97–105). Springer Nature Singapore. doi:10.1007/978-981-19-9493-7_10

Branca, T. A., Fornai, B., Colla, V., Murri, M. M., Streppa, E., & Schröder, A. J. (2020). „The challenge of digitalization in the steel sector. *Metals*, *10*(2), 288–311. doi:10.3390/met10020288

Breque, M., De Nul, L., & Petridis, A. (2021). *Industry 5.0: Towards a sustainable, human-centric and resilient European industry*. Directorate-General for Research and Innovation. doi:10.2777/308407

Bresciani, S., Ferraris, A., Romano, M., & Santoro, G. (2021). Human resource management and digitalisation. In *Digital transformation management for agile organizations: A compass to sail the digital world* (pp. 117–138). Emerald Publishing Limited. doi:10.1108/978-1-80043-171-320211007

Brodie, R. J., Hollebeek, L. D., Jurić, B., & Ilić, A. (2011). Customer engagement: Conceptual domain, fundamental propositions, and implications for research. *Journal of Service Research*, *14*(3), 252–271. doi:10.1177/1094670511411703

Brown, T. C., O'Kane, P., Mazumdar, B., & McCracken, M. (2019). Performance management: A scoping review of the literature and an agenda for future research. *Human Resource Development Review*, *18*(1), 47–82. doi:10.1177/1534484318798533

Bryant, P. C., & Allen, D. (2013). Compensation, benefits and employee turnover: HR strategies for retaining top talent. *Compensation and Benefits Review*, *45*(3), 171–175. doi:10.1177/0886368713494342

Bulsari, S., & Pandya, K. (2023). Future of HR Analytics: Applications to Recruitment, Employee Engagement, and Retention. In N. Sharma & K. Shalender (Eds.), *Managing Technology Integration for Human Resources in Industry 5.0* (pp. 140–162). IGI Global. doi:10.4018/978-1-6684-6745-9.ch009

Burchardt, C., & Maisch, B. (2019). „Digitalization needs a cultural change–examples of applying Agility and Open Innovation to drive the digital transformation. *Procedia CIRP*, *84*, 112–117. doi:10.1016/j.procir.2019.05.009

Burnett, J. R., & Lisk, T. C. (2021). The future of employee engagement: Real-time monitoring and digital tools for engaging a workforce. In *International Perspectives on Employee Engagement* (pp. 117–128). Routledge. doi:10.4324/9781003142492-9

Cafemutual. (2023, January 9). *Insurance penetration is just 4.2%, much less than the global average of 7%.* https://cafemutual.com/news/insurance/28335-insurance-penetration-is-just-42-much-less-than-the-global-average-of-7

Cameron, K., & Sine, W. (1999). A framework for organizational quality culture. *The Quality Management Journal*, *6*(4), 7–25. doi:10.1080/10686967.1999.11919208

Cartwright, S., & Holmes, N. (2006). The meaning of work : The challenge of regaining employee engagement and reducing cynicism. doi:10.1016/j.hrmr.2006.03.012

Chalutz Ben-Gal, H. (2019). An ROI-based review of HR analytics: Practical implementation tools. *Personnel Review*, *48*(6), 1429–1448. doi:10.1108/PR-11-2017-0362

Charity, E. (2016). Human resource management practices and retention of core employees in the oil and gas industry in Nigeria. *Human Resource Management*, *6*(7).

Chatterjee, S., Nankervis, A., & Connell, J. (2014). Framing the emerging talent crisis in India and China: A human capital perspective. *SA Journal of Human Resource Management*, *1*(1), 25–43.

Chotai, N. A., Tiwari, A., Aggarwal, S., Chandel, P. S., Dimari, A., & Manoharan, G. (2023, December). Importance of Employee Motivation and Satisfaction in the Workplace based on BiLSTM and ANN Approach. In 2023 2nd International Conference on Automation, Computing and Renewable Systems (ICACRS) (pp. 1141-1146). IEEE. 10.1109/ICACRS58579.2023.10404593

Choudhury, K. (2007). Service quality dimensionality: A study of the Indian banking sector. *Journal of Asia-Pacific Business*, *8*(4), 21–38. doi:10.1300/J098v08n04_03

Chowdhury, N., & Gkioulos, V. (2021). Cyber security training for critical infrastructure protection: A literature review. *Computer Science Review*, *40*, 100361. doi:10.1016/j.cosrev.2021.100361

Cichosz, M. (2018). Digitalization and competitiveness in the logistics service industry. *Ementor*, *77*(5), 73–82. doi:10.15219/em77.1392

Cichosz, M., Wallenburg, C. M., & Knemeyer, A. M. (2020). „Digital transformation at logistics service providers: Barriers, success factors and leading practices. *International Journal of Logistics Management*, *31*(2), 209–238. doi:10.1108/IJLM-08-2019-0229

Ciliberto, C., Szopik-Depczyńska, K., Tarczyńska-Łuniewska, M., Ruggieri, A., & Ioppolo, G. (2021). Enabling the Circular Economy transition: A sustainable lean manufacturing recipe for Industry 4.0. *Business Strategy and the Environment*, *30*(7), 3255–3272. doi:10.1002/bse.2801

Cillo, V., Gregori, G. L., Daniele, L. M., Caputo, F., & Bitbol-Saba, N. (2022a). Rethinking companies' culture through knowledge management lens during Industry 5.0 transition. *Journal of Knowledge Management*, *26*(10), 2485–2498. doi:10.1108/JKM-09-2021-0718

Compare, M., Baraldi, P., & Zio, E. (2019). Challenges to IoT-enabled predictive maintenance for industry 4.0. *IEEE Internet of Things Journal*, *7*(5), 4585–4597. doi:10.1109/JIOT.2019.2957029

Cooke, F. L., Xiao, M., & Chen, Y. (2021). Still in search of strategic human resource management? A review and suggestions for future research with China as an example. *Human Resource Management*, *60*(1), 89–118. doi:10.1002/hrm.22029

Cortellazzo, L., Bruni, E., & Zampieri, R. (2019). The role of leadership in a digitalized world: A review. *Frontiers in Psychology*, *10*, 1–21. doi:10.3389/fpsyg.2019.01938 PMID:31507494

Costan, E., Gonzales, G., Gonzales, R., Enriquez, L., Costan, F., Suladay, D., Atibing, N. M., Aro, J. L., Evangelista, S. S., Maturan, F., Selerio, E. Jr, & Ocampo, L. (2021). Education 4.0 in developing economies: A systematic literature review of implementation barriers and future research agenda. *Sustainability (Basel)*, *13*(22), 12763. doi:10.3390/su132212763

Creswell, J. W., & Creswell, J. D. (2017). *Research design: Qualitative, quantitative, and mixed methods approaches.* Sage Publications.

Custers, M. (2012). Rethinking existing HR technologies for new gains in employee engagement and benefits. *Compensation and Benefits Review*, *44*(6), 332–335. doi:10.1177/0886368713476929

Dabić, M., Maley, J. F., Švarc, J., & Poček, J. (2023). Future of digital work: Challenges for sustainable human resources management. *Journal of Innovation & Knowledge*, *8*(2), 100353. doi:10.1016/j.jik.2023.100353

Das, S., Lekhya, G., Shreya, K., Shekinah, K. L., Babu, K. K., & Boopathi, S. (2024). Fostering Sustainability Education Through Cross-Disciplinary Collaborations and Research Partnerships: Interdisciplinary Synergy. In Facilitating Global Collaboration and Knowledge Sharing in Higher Education With Generative AI (pp. 60–88). IGI Global.

Das, P., Ramapraba, P., Seethalakshmi, K., Mary, M. A., Karthick, S., & Sampath, B. (2024). Sustainable Advanced Techniques for Enhancing the Image Process. In *Fostering Cross-Industry Sustainability With Intelligent Technologies* (pp. 350–374). IGI Global. doi:10.4018/979-8-3693-1638-2.ch022

De Klerk, J. J., Joubert, M., & Mosca, H. F. (2021). Is working from home the new workplace panacea? Lessons from the COVID-19 pandemic for the future world of work. *SA Journal of Industrial Psychology*, *47*(1), 1–14. doi:10.4102/sajip.v47i0.1883

Demartini, M., Pinna, C., Tonelli, F., Terzi, S., Sansone, C., & Testa, C. (2018). Food industry digitalization: From challenges and trends to opportunities and solutions. *IFAC-PapersOnLine*, *51*(11), 1371–1378. doi:10.1016/j.ifacol.2018.08.337

Demir, K. A., & Cicibaş, H. (2019). The next industrial revolution: Industry 5.0 and discussions on industry 4.0. *Industry 4.0 from the MIS Perspective*, (February), 247–260.

Demir, K. A., Döven, G., & Sezen, B. (2019). Industry 5.0 and human-robot co-working. *Procedia Computer Science*, *158*, 688–695. doi:10.1016/j.procs.2019.09.104

Denison, D. R., & Mishra, A. K. (1995). Toward a theory of organizational culture and effectiveness. *Organization Science*, *6*(2), 204–223. doi:10.1287/orsc.6.2.204

Department of Personnel and Training. (2009). 6th Pay Commission, (11016), No.11016/2/2008-AIS-1I. Retrieved from https://ccis.nic.in/WriteReadData/CircularPortal/D2/D02ser/11016_2_2008-AIS-II.pdf

Deshmukh, A. (2021, June 7). *Reaping the benefits of digital bancassurance.* https://learnsure.ai/reaping-the-benefits-of-digital-bancassurance/

Deviprasad, S., Madhumithaa, N., Vikas, I. W., Yadav, A., & Manoharan, G. (2023). The Machine Learning-Based Task Automation Framework for Human Resource Management in MNC Companies. *Engineering Proceedings*, *59*(1), 63.

Dhanya, D., Kumar, S. S., Thilagavathy, A., Prasad, D., & Boopathi, S. (2023). Data Analytics and Artificial Intelligence in the Circular Economy: Case Studies. In Intelligent Engineering Applications and Applied Sciences for Sustainability (pp. 40–58). IGI Global.

Dhanya, D., Kumar, S. S., Thilagavathy, A., Prasad, D. V. S. S. S. V., & Boopathi, S. (2023). Data Analytics and Artificial Intelligence in the Circular Economy: Case Studies. In B. K. Mishra (Ed.), Advances in Civil and Industrial Engineering. IGI Global. doi:10.4018/979-8-3693-0044-2.ch003

Di Vaio, A., Latif, B., Gunarathne, N., Gupta, M., & D'Adamo, I. (2023). Digitalization and artificial knowledge for accountability in SCM: a systematic literature review. *Journal of Enterprise Information Management.*

Divyashree, K. M., & Mithun, R. (2023). A study on digitalization in HRM practices. *Commerce and Management*, *II*, 95.

Djalic, N., Nikolic, M., Bakator, M., & Erceg, Z. (2021). Modeling the influence of information systems on sustainable business performance and competitiveness. *Sustainability (Basel)*, *13*(17), 9619. doi:10.3390/su13179619

Domakonda, V. K., Farooq, S., Chinthamreddy, S., Puviarasi, R., Sudhakar, M., & Boopathi, S. (2022). Sustainable Developments of Hybrid Floating Solar Power Plants: Photovoltaic System. In Human Agro-Energy Optimization for Business and Industry (pp. 148–167). IGI Global.

Domakonda, V. K., Farooq, S., Chinthamreddy, S., Puviarasi, R., Sudhakar, M., & Boopathi, S. (2023). Sustainable Developments of Hybrid Floating Solar Power Plants: Photovoltaic System. In P. Vasant, R. Rodríguez-Aguilar, I. Litvinchev, & J. A. Marmolejo-Saucedo (Eds.), Advances in Environmental Engineering and Green Technologies. IGI Global. doi:10.4018/978-1-6684-4118-3.ch008

Dua, P., Sahay, N., & Deol, O. S. (2019). Bancassurance model and its impact on Financial Inclusion: Review and Analysis. *International Journal of Research and Analytical Reviews*, *6*(2), 661–669.

Durai, S., Manoharan, G., Priya, T. S., Jayanthi, R., Razak, A., & Ashtikar, S. P. (2024). Quantifying the Impacts of Artificial Intelligence Implementations in Marketing. In Smart and Sustainable Interactive Marketing (pp. 120-144). IGI Global. doi:10.4018/979-8-3693-1339-8.ch008

Durai, D. S., Rudhramoorthy, K., & Sarkar, S. (2019). HR metrics and workforce analytics: It is a journey, not a destination. *Human Resource Management International Digest*, *27*(1), 4–6. doi:10.1108/HRMID-08-2018-0167

Durairaj, M., Jayakumar, S., Karpagavalli, V., Maheswari, B. U., Boopathi, S., & ... (2023). Utilization of Digital Tools in the Indian Higher Education System During Health Crises. In *Multidisciplinary Approaches to Organizational Governance During Health Crises* (pp. 1–21). IGI Global. doi:10.4018/978-1-7998-9213-7.ch001

Dushyant, K., Muskan, G., Gupta, A., & Pramanik, S. (2022). Utilizing Machine Learning and Deep Learning in Cyber security: An Innovative Approach. In M. M. Ghonge, S. Pramanik, R. Mangrulkar, & D. N. Le (Eds.), *Cyber security and Digital Forensics.* Wiley. doi:10.1002/9781119795667.ch12

Echchakoui, S., & Barka, N. (2020). Industry 4.0 and its impact in plastics industry: A literature review. *Journal of Industrial Information Integration*, *20*, 100172. doi:10.1016/j.jii.2020.100172

Edwin Cheng, T., Kamble, S. S., Belhadi, A., Ndubisi, N. O., Lai, K., & Kharat, M. G. (2022). Linkages between big data analytics, circular economy, sustainable supply chain flexibility, and sustainable performance in manufacturing firms. *International Journal of Production Research*, *60*(22), 6908–6922. doi:10.1080/00207543.2021.1906971

ElFar, O. A., Chang, C. K., Leong, H. Y., Peter, A. P., Chew, K. W., & Show, P. L. (2021). Prospects of Industry 5.0 in algae: Customization of production and new advance technology for clean bioenergy generation. *Energy Conversion and Management: X*, *10*, 100048.

Eliza, E. (2023). Human Resource Management Strategies to Improve Performance in the Digital Era. *Implikasi: Jurnal Manajemen Sumber Daya Manusia, 1*(2), 132–139.

Elrahmani, A., Hannun, J., Eljack, F., & Kazi, M. K. (2021). Status of renewable energy in the GCC region and future opportunities. *Current Opinion in Chemical Engineering, 31*, 100664. doi:10.1016/j.coche.2020.100664

Erro-Garcés, A., & Aramendia-Muneta, M. E. (2023). The role of human resource management practices on the results of digitalisation. From Industry 4.0 to Industry 5.0. *Journal of Organizational Change Management, 36*(4), 585–602. doi:10.1108/JOCM-11-2021-0354

Fahim, M. G. A. (2018). Strategic human resource management and public employee retention. *Review of Economics and Political Science, 3*(2), 20–39. doi:10.1108/REPS-07-2018-002

Fan, C. K., & Cheng, C. L. (2011). An examination of key factors influencing bancassurance success–Taiwan and mainland China evidence. *Service Industries Journal, 31*(11), 1887–1902. doi:10.1080/02642069.2010.503888

Fenech, R., Baguant, P., & Ivanov, D. (2019). „The changing role of human resource management in an era of digital transformation. *Journal of Management Information and Decision Sciences, 22*(2), 1–10.

Fernandez, V., & Gallardo-Gallardo, E. (2021). Tackling the HR digitalization challenge: Key factors and barriers to HR analytics adoption. *Competitiveness Review, 31*(1), 162–187. doi:10.1108/CR-12-2019-0163

Ferreira, A., Leitão, P., & Vrba, P. (2014). Challenges of ICT and artificial intelligence in smart grids. *2014 IEEE International Workshop on Intelligent Energy Systems (IWIES)*, 6–11. 10.1109/IWIES.2014.6957039

Ferreira, C., & Gonçalves, G. (2021). A systematic review on life extension strategies in industry: The case of remanufacturing and refurbishment. *Electronics (Basel), 10*(21), 2669. doi:10.3390/electronics10212669

Ferreira, N. C., & Ferreira, J. J. (2023). Quo Vadis Sustainable Entrepreneurship? A Systematic Literature Review of Related Drivers and Inhibitors in SMEs. *IEEE Transactions on Engineering Management.*

Fitz-enz. (1995). How to measure human resource management (3rd ed.). Academic Press.

Fitzgerald, M., Kruschwitz, N., Bonnet, D., & Welch, M. (2014). Embracing digital technology: A new strategic imperative. *MIT Sloan Management Review, 55*(2), 1–16.

Fletcher, L., Alfes, K., & Robinson, D. (2018). The relationship between perceived training and development and employee retention: The mediating role of work attitudes. *International Journal of Human Resource Management, 29*(18), 2701–2728. doi:10.1080/09585192.2016.1262888

Fukuda, K. (2020). Science, technology and innovation ecosystem transformation toward society 5.0. *International Journal of Production Economics, 220*(July), 107460. doi:10.1016/j.ijpe.2019.07.033

Gaines, B., Dugan, A., & Cherniack, M. (2018). The relationship between retirement expectations and job insecurity among the aging us workforce. *Innovation in Aging, 2*(Suppl 1).

Ganer, S. D., Kediya, S. O., Suchek, A. K., Dey, S. K., & Band, G. (2022, October). Analytical study of HRM practices in industry 5.0. *IOP Conference Series. Materials Science and Engineering, 1259*(1), 012041. doi:10.1088/1757-899X/1259/1/012041

Garg, S., Sinha, S., Kar, A. K., & Mani, M. (2022). A review of machine learning applications in human resource management. *International Journal of Productivity and Performance Management, 71*(5), 1590–1610. doi:10.1108/IJPPM-08-2020-0427

Garvey. (2005). The Next Generation of Hiring Metrics. Academic Press.

George, C. (2015). Retaining professional workers: What makes them stay? *Employee Relations*, *37*(1), 102–121. doi:10.1108/ER-10-2013-0151

Ghobakhloo, M., Iranmanesh, M., Mubarak, M. F., Mubarik, M., Rejeb, A., & Nilashi, M. (2022). Identifying industry 5.0 contributions to sustainable development: A strategy roadmap for delivering sustainability values. *Sustainable Production and Consumption*, *33*, 716–737. doi:10.1016/j.spc.2022.08.003

Giermindl, L. M., Strich, F., Christ, O., Leicht-Deobald, U., & Redzepi, A. (2022). The dark sides of people analytics: Reviewing the perils for organisations and employees. *European Journal of Information Systems*, *31*(3), 410–435. doi:10.1080/0960085X.2021.1927213

Gift, M. D. M., Senthil, T. S., Hasan, D. S., Alagarraja, K., Jayaseelan, P., & Boopathi, S. (2024). Additive Manufacturing and 3D Printing Innovations: Revolutionizing Industry 5.0. In Technological Advancements in Data Processing for Next Generation Intelligent Systems (pp. 255–287). IGI Global. doi:10.4018/979-8-3693-0968-1.ch010

Gilch, P. M., & Sieweke, J. (2021). Recruiting digital talent: The strategic role of recruitment in organisations' digital transformation. *German Journal of Human Resource Management*, *35*(1), 53–82. doi:10.1177/2397002220952734

Gnanaprakasam, C., Vankara, J., Sastry, A. S., Prajval, V., Gireesh, N., & Boopathi, S. (2023). Long-Range and Low-Power Automated Soil Irrigation System Using Internet of Things: An Experimental Study. In Contemporary Developments in Agricultural Cyber-Physical Systems (pp. 87–104). IGI Global.

Gnanaprakasam, C., Vankara, J., Sastry, A. S., Prajval, V., Gireesh, N., & Boopathi, S. (2023a). Long-Range and Low-Power Automated Soil Irrigation System Using Internet of Things: An Experimental Study. In Contemporary Developments in Agricultural Cyber-Physical Systems (pp. 87–104). IGI Global.

Gnanaprakasam, C., Vankara, J., Sastry, A. S., Prajval, V., Gireesh, N., & Boopathi, S. (2023b). Long-Range and Low-Power Automated Soil Irrigation System Using Internet of Things: An Experimental Study. In G. S. Karthick (Ed.), Advances in Environmental Engineering and Green Technologies. IGI Global. doi:10.4018/978-1-6684-7879-0.ch005

Gong, C., & Ribiere, V. (2021). Developing a unified definition of digital transformation. *Technovation*, *102*, 102217. doi:10.1016/j.technovation.2020.102217

Götz, M., & Jankowska, B. (2020). Adoption of Industry 4.0 Technologies and Company Competitiveness: Case Studies from a Post-Transition Economy. *National Research University Higher School of Economics*, *14*(4), 61–78. doi:10.17323/2500-2597.2020.4.61.78

Govindaraju, N. (2018). Demographic factors influence on employee retention. *International Journal of Engineering Studied and Technical Approach*, *7*, 10–20.

Grabowska, S., Saniuk, S., & Gajdzik, B. (2022). Industry 5.0: Improving humanization and sustainability of Industry 4.0. *Scientometrics*, *127*(6), 3117–3144. doi:10.1007/s11192-022-04370-1 PMID:35502439

Grover, N., & Bhalla, G. S. (2013). Level of awareness regarding bancassurance and choice of insurance product among bank customers in India. *Eurasian Journal of Business and Economics*, *6*(12), 63–77.

Gujral, T. M. (2018). Contemporary prominent development of bancassurance in India. *International Journal of Multidisciplinary Research Review*, *3*(10), 731–738.

Gupta, M. K. (2006, August 29). *Who/What drives Bancassurance in India?* [Conference Presentation]. 7th Asian Conference on Bancassurance and Alternative Channels, Mumbai.

Gupta, A., Verma, A., & Pramanik, S. (2022). Security Aspects in Advanced Image Processing Techniques for COVID-19. In S. Pramanik, A. Sharma, S. Bhatia, & D. N. Le (Eds.), *An Interdisciplinary Approach to Modern Network Security*. CRC Press.

Gupta, S. (2023). An edge-computing based Industrial Gateway for Industry 4.0 using ARM TrustZone technology. *Journal of Industrial Information Integration, 33*, 100441. doi:10.1016/j.jii.2023.100441

Hadi, R., Melumad, S., & Park, E. S. (2024). The Metaverse: A new digital frontier for consumer behavior. *Journal of Consumer Psychology, 34*(1), 142–166. doi:10.1002/jcpy.1356

Hafeez, U., & Akbar, W. (2015). Impact of work-life balance on job satisfaction among school teachers of 21st century. *Australian Journal of Business and Management Research, 4*(11), 25–37. doi:10.52283/NSWRCA.AJBMR.20150411A03

Haider, M., Rasli, A., Akhtar, C. S., Yusoff, R. B. M., Malik, O. M., Aamir, A., & Tariq, F. (2015). The impact of human resource practices on employee retention in the telecom sector. *International Journal of Economics and Financial Issues, 5*(1), 63–69.

Hair, J. F. Jr, Black, W. C., Babin, B. J., & Anderson, R. E. (2009). *Multivariate Data Analysis: A Global Perspective*. Pearson Education.

Hallaji, S. M., Fang, Y., & Winfrey, B. K. (2022). Predictive maintenance of pumps in civil infrastructure: State-of-the-art, challenges and future directions. *Automation in Construction, 134*, 104049. doi:10.1016/j.autcon.2021.104049

Hamouda, M. (2019). Omni-channel banking integration quality and perceived value as drivers of consumers' satisfaction and loyalty. *Journal of Enterprise Information Management, 32*(4), 608–625. doi:10.1108/JEIM-12-2018-0279

Hancock, J. I., Allen, D. G., Bosco, F. A., McDaniel, K. R., & Pierce, C. A. (2013). Meta-analytic review of employee turnover as a predictor of firm performance. *Journal of Management, 39*(3), 573–603. doi:10.1177/0149206311424943

Hanumanthakari, S., Gift, M. M., Kanimozhi, K., Bhavani, M. D., Bamane, K. D., & Boopathi, S. (2023). Biomining Method to Extract Metal Components Using Computer-Printed Circuit Board E-Waste. In *Handbook of Research on Safe Disposal Methods of Municipal Solid Wastes for a Sustainable Environment* (pp. 123–141). IGI Global. doi:10.4018/978-1-6684-8117-2.ch010

Harikaran, M., Boopathi, S., Gokulakannan, S., & Poonguzhali, M. (2023). Study on the Source of E-Waste Management and Disposal Methods. In *Sustainable Approaches and Strategies for E-Waste Management and Utilization* (pp. 39–60). IGI Global. doi:10.4018/978-1-6684-7573-7.ch003

Harris, J. G., Craig, E., & Light, D. A. (2011). Talent and analytics: New approaches, higher ROI. *The Journal of Business Strategy, 32*(6), 4–13. doi:10.1108/02756661111180087

Hasan, T., Jawaad, M., & Butt, I. (2021). The influence of person–job fit, work–life balance, and work conditions on organizational commitment: Investigating the mediation of job satisfaction in the private sector of the emerging market. *Sustainability (Basel), 13*(12), 6622. Advance online publication. doi:10.3390/su13126622

Hassan, W., Razi, A., Qamar, R., Jaffer, R., & Suhail, S. (2013). The effect of training on employee Retention. *Global Journal of Management and Business Research Administration and Management, 13*(6), 16–20.

Hatt, S., Boeraeve, F., Artru, S., Dufrêne, M., & Francis, F. (2018). Spatial diversification of agroecosystems to enhance biological control and other regulating services: An agroecological perspective. *The Science of the Total Environment, 621*(2), 600–611. doi:10.1016/j.scitotenv.2017.11.296 PMID:29195207

Hema, N., Krishnamoorthy, N., Chavan, S. M., Kumar, N., Sabarimuthu, M., & Boopathi, S. (2023). A Study on an Internet of Things (IoT)-Enabled Smart Solar Grid System. In *Handbook of Research on Deep Learning Techniques for Cloud-Based Industrial IoT* (pp. 290–308). IGI Global. doi:10.4018/978-1-6684-8098-4.ch017

Heneman, R. L., Greenberger, D. B., & Fox, J. A. (2002). Pay increase satisfaction: A reconceptualization of pay raise satisfaction based on changes in work and pay practices. *Human Resource Management Review, 12*(1), 63–74. doi:10.1016/S1053-4822(01)00041-9

Henson, S., & Reardon, T. (2005). Private agri-food standards: Implications for food policy and the agri-food system. *Food Policy, 30*(3), 241–253. Advance online publication. doi:10.1016/j.foodpol.2005.05.002

Hill, B., & Tande, C. (2006). *Total Rewards: The Employee Value Proposition.* Workspan.

Holtom, B. C., Mitchell, T. R., Lee, T. W., & Eberly, M. B. (2008). 5 turnover and retention research: A glance at the past, a closer review of the present, and a venture into the future. *The Academy of Management Annals, 2*(1), 231–274. doi:10.5465/19416520802211552

Horváth, D., & Szabó, R. Z. (2019). Driving forces and barriers of Industry 4.0: Do multinational and small and medium-sized companies have equal opportunities? *Technological Forecasting and Social Change, 146*, 119–132. doi:10.1016/j.techfore.2019.05.021

Howard, E. (2018). The evolution of the industrial ages: Industry 1.0 to 4.0. *Simio Forward Thinking, 5.*

Hugos, M. H. (2024). *Essentials of supply chain management.* John Wiley & Sons.

Humayun, M. (2021). Industrial Revolution 5.0 and the Role of Cutting Edge Technologies. *International Journal of Advanced Computer Science and Applications, 12*(12), 605–615. doi:10.14569/IJACSA.2021.0121276

Husain, R., Samad, T. A., & Qamar, Y. (2022). Past, present and future of luxury brands: A review and bibliometric analysis. *Journal of Fashion Marketing and Management, 26*(4), 582–602. doi:10.1108/JFMM-02-2021-0046

Hussain, Z., Babe, M., Saravanan, S., Srimathy, G., Roopa, H., & Boopathi, S. (2023). Optimizing Biomass-to-Biofuel Conversion: IoT and AI Integration for Enhanced Efficiency and Sustainability. In Circular Economy Implementation for Sustainability in the Built Environment (pp. 191–214). IGI Global.

Hussain, M., & Malik, M. (2020). Organizational enablers for circular economy in the context of sustainable supply chain management. *Journal of Cleaner Production, 256*, 120375. doi:10.1016/j.jclepro.2020.120375

Hussain, Z., Babe, M., Saravanan, S., Srimathy, G., Roopa, H., & Boopathi, S. (2023). Optimizing Biomass-to-Biofuel Conversion: IoT and AI Integration for Enhanced Efficiency and Sustainability. In N. Cobîrzan, R. Muntean, & R.-A. Felseghi (Eds.), Advances in Finance, Accounting, and Economics. IGI Global. doi:10.4018/978-1-6684-8238-4.ch009

ICIMS. (2015). 10 Must-Track Metrics in Talent Acquisition. Academic Press.

Ietto, B., Ancillai, C., Sabatini, A., Carayannis, E. G., & Gregori, G. L. (2022). The role of external actors in SMEs' human-centered industry 4.0 adoption: An empirical perspective on Italian competence centers. *IEEE Transactions on Engineering Management.*

Ilona, T., & Renata, P. K. (2009). Tendencies for bancassurance development in the Polish market (Tendencje rozwoju bancassurance na rynku polskim). *Myśl Ekonomiczna i Prawna, 4*, 174–182.

India Brand Equity Foundation (IBEF). (2022). Automobile industry in India. https://www.ibef.org/industry/india-automobiles

Ingle, R. B., Swathi, S., Mahendran, G., Senthil, T., Muralidharan, N., & Boopathi, S. (2023). Sustainability and Optimization of Green and Lean Manufacturing Processes Using Machine Learning Techniques. In *Circular Economy Implementation for Sustainability in the Built Environment* (pp. 261–285). IGI Global. doi:10.4018/978-1-6684-8238-4.ch012

Iqbal, S., & Hashmi, M. S. (2015). Impact of perceived organizational support on employee retention with mediating role of psychological empowerment. *Pakistan Journal of Commerce and Social Sciences*, *9*(1), 18–34.

IRDA. (2022). *Annual Report*. Insurance Regulatory and Development Authority of India. https://irdai.gov.in/document-detail?documentId=1632108

Iverson, R. D. (1996). Employee acceptance of organizational change: The role of organizational commitment. *International Journal of Human Resource Management*, *7*(1), 122–149. Advance online publication. doi:10.1080/09585199600000121

Jaber, A., & Fritsch, L. (2022). Towards ai-powered cybersecurity attack modeling with simulation tools: Review of attack simulators. *International Conference on P2P, Parallel, Grid, Cloud and Internet Computing*, 249–257.

Jadoun, A. S. (2015). The impact of E-Banking on customers in India. *International Research Journal of Management Sociology & Humanity*, *6*(3), 284–287.

Jaeger, B., & Upadhyay, A. (2020). Understanding barriers to circular economy: Cases from the manufacturing industry. *Journal of Enterprise Information Management*, *33*(4), 729–745. doi:10.1108/JEIM-02-2019-0047

Jahan, S. (2014). Human resources information system (HRIS): A theoretical perspective. Academic Press.

Jain, M. (2018, January 15). Infographic: Little known facts about India's banking network. https://www.thehindubusinessline.com/economy/infographic-little-knownfacts about-indias-banking-network/article9381949.ece

Janardhana, K., Singh, V., Singh, S. N., Babu, T. R., Bano, S., & Boopathi, S. (2023). Utilization Process for Electronic Waste in Eco-Friendly Concrete: Experimental Study. In Sustainable Approaches and Strategies for E-Waste Management and Utilization (pp. 204–223). IGI Global.

Janardhana, K., Singh, V., Singh, S. N., Babu, T. S. R., Bano, S., & Boopathi, S. (2023). Utilization Process for Electronic Waste in Eco-Friendly Concrete: Experimental Study. In A. M. Rawani, M. K. Sahu, S. S. Chakarabarti, & A. K. Singh (Eds.), Practice, Progress, and Proficiency in Sustainability. IGI Global. doi:10.4018/978-1-6684-7573-7.ch011

Javaid, M., & Haleem, A. (2020). Critical components of industry 5.0 towards a successful adoption in the field of manufacturing. *Journal of Industrial Integration and Management*, *5*(3), 327–348. doi:10.1142/S2424862220500141

Jayasingh, R., & Kumar, J. (2022). Speckle noise removal by SORAMA segmentation in Digital Image processing to facilitate precise robotic surgery. *International Journal of Reliable and Quality E-Healthcare*, *11*(1), 1–19. Advance online publication. doi:10.4018/IJRQEH.295083

Jeevanantham, Y. A., Saravanan, A., Vanitha, V., Boopathi, S., & Kumar, D. P. (2022). Implementation of Internet-of Things (IoT) in Soil Irrigation System. *IEEE Explore*, 1–5.

Jeya, R., Venkatakrishnan, G. R., Rengaraj, R., Rajalakshmi, M., Pradeep Mohan Kumar, K., & Boopathi, S. (2023). Water Resource Managements in Soil and Soilless Irrigation Systems Using AI Techniques. In Advances in Environmental Engineering and Green Technologies (pp. 245–266). IGI Global. doi:10.4018/979-8-3693-0338-2.ch014

Jing, H., Zou, K., & Cai, X. (2021). An Empirical Study on the Influence of Diversification on the Operating Cost of Commercial Banks. *Converter Magazine*, *2021*(5), 757–770.

Johnston, M. P. (2017). Secondary data analysis: A method of which the time has come. *Qualitative and Quantitative Methods in Libraries, 3*(3), 619-626.

Joshi, U. (2019). Perception among the Employees of Bank towards the Bancassurance in Nepal. *Nepalese Journal of Insurance and Social Security*, *2*(2), 71–80. doi:10.3126/njiss.v2i2.31830

Joyce, P. R., Selvaraj, F. J., Manoharan, G., Priya, C., Vijayalakshmi, R., Dwivedi, P. K., & Veerakumar, K. (2024). To Study The Role Of Marketing In Human Resource Management. *Migration Letters : An International Journal of Migration Studies*, *21*(S2), 1191–1196. doi:10.59670/ml.v21iS2.7072

Kagermann, H. (2015). Change through digitization - Value creation in the age of Industry 4.0. In *Management of permanent change* (pp. 23–45). Springer Gabler. doi:10.1007/978-3-658-05014-6_2

Kalateh, S., Estrada-Jimenez, L. A., Pulikottil, T., Hojjati, S. N., & Barata, J. (2022, October). The human role in human-centric industry. In *IECON 2022–48th Annual Conference of the IEEE Industrial Electronics Society* (pp. 1-6). IEEE. 10.1109/IECON49645.2022.9968440

Kalidas, R., Boopathi, S., Sivakumar, K., & Mohankumar, P. (2012). Optimization of Machining Parameters of WEDM Process Based On the Taguchi Method. *IJEST, 6*(1).

Kane, G. C. (2015). People analytics through super-charged ID badges. *MIT Sloan Management Review*, *56*(4).

Karmaker, C. L., Al Aziz, R., Ahmed, T., Misbauddin, S., & Moktadir, M. A. (2023). Impact of industry 4.0 technologies on sustainable supply chain performance: The mediating role of green supply chain management practices and circular economy. *Journal of Cleaner Production*, *419*, 138249. doi:10.1016/j.jclepro.2023.138249

Karmaker, C. L., Bari, A. M., Anam, M. Z., Ahmed, T., Ali, S. M., de Jesus Pacheco, D. A., & Moktadir, M. A. (2023). Industry 5.0 challenges for post-pandemic supply chain sustainability in an emerging economy. *International Journal of Production Economics*, *258*, 108806. doi:10.1016/j.ijpe.2023.108806

Karunagaran, A. (2006). Bancassurance; A feasible Study for Banks in India. *Journal of Economics and Sustainable Development*, *4*(2), 24–34.

Kasinathan, P., Pugazhendhi, R., Elavarasan, R. M., Ramachandaramurthy, V. K., Ramanathan, V., Subramanian, S., & Alsharif, M. H. (2022). Realization of Sustainable Development Goals with Disruptive Technologies by Integrating Industry 5.0, Society 5.0, Smart Cities and Villages. *Sustainability (Basel)*, *14*(22), 15258. doi:10.3390/su142215258

Kaur, A., & Dilawari, K. (2015). A study to identify the factors affecting employee retention. *International Journal of Scientific Research*, *6*(5), 1827–1831.

Kaur, N., & Kaur, R. (2022). Impact of bancassurance income on profitability of state bank of India. *An International Journal of Humanities and Management*, *8*(1), 48–54.

Kavitha, C. R., Varalatchoumy, M., Mithuna, H. R., Bharathi, K., Geethalakshmi, N. M., & Boopathi, S. (2023). Energy Monitoring and Control in the Smart Grid: Integrated Intelligent IoT and ANFIS. In M. Arshad (Ed.), Advances in Bioinformatics and Biomedical Engineering. IGI Global. doi:10.4018/978-1-6684-6577-6.ch014

Kazakova, E., & Lee, J. (2022). Sustainable manufacturing for a circular economy. *Sustainability (Basel)*, *14*(24), 17010. doi:10.3390/su142417010

Kazancoglu, I., Sagnak, M., Kumar Mangla, S., & Kazancoglu, Y. (2021). Circular economy and the policy: A framework for improving the corporate environmental management in supply chains. *Business Strategy and the Environment*, *30*(1), 590–608. doi:10.1002/bse.2641

Keir, M. Y. A. (2016). Staff Perceptions of how Human Resource Management Practices influence Organisational Performance: Mediating roles of Organisational Culture, Employees'. *Commitment and Employee Retention in Bahrain Private Universities*, (June), 1–241.

Keleko, A. T., Kamsu-Foguem, B., Ngouna, R. H., & Tongne, A. (2022). Artificial intelligence and real-time predictive maintenance in industry 4.0: A bibliometric analysis. *AI and Ethics*, *2*(4), 553–577. doi:10.1007/s43681-021-00132-6

Khalid, K., & Nawab, S. (2018). Employee participation and employee retention in view of compensation. *SAGE Open*, *8*(4). doi:10.1177/2158244018810067

Khalid, M. Y., Arif, Z. U., Ahmed, W., & Arshad, H. (2022). Recent trends in recycling and reusing techniques of different plastic polymers and their composite materials. *Sustainable Materials and Technologies*, *31*, e00382. doi:10.1016/j.susmat.2021.e00382

Khanh, P. T., Ngọc, T. H., & Pramanik, S. (2023). Future of Smart Agriculture Techniques and Applications. In *Advanced Technologies and AI-Equipped IoT Applications in High Tech Agriculture*. doi:10.4018/978-1-6684-9231-4.ch021

Kirilmaz, S. (2020). Digital Transformation and Human Resources Management: Digital HRApplication Examples of Businesses. *Pressacademia*, *11*(1), 224–225. doi:10.17261/Pressacademia.2020.1199

Kohli, R. (1999). Rural Bank Branches and financial reform. *Economic and Political Weekly*, *34*(3/4), 169–174.

Komulainen, H., & Makkonen, H. (2018). Customer experience in omni-channel banking services. *Journal of Financial Services Marketing*, *23*(3-4), 190–199. doi:10.1057/s41264-018-0057-6

Koshariya, A. K., Kalaiyarasi, D., Jovith, A. A., Sivakami, T., Hasan, D. S., & Boopathi, S. (2023). AI-Enabled IoT and WSN-Integrated Smart Agriculture System. In *Artificial Intelligence Tools and Technologies for Smart Farming and Agriculture Practices* (pp. 200–218). IGI Global. doi:10.4018/978-1-6684-8516-3.ch011

Koshariya, A. K., Khatoon, S., Marathe, A. M., Suba, G. M., Baral, D., & Boopathi, S. (2023). Agricultural Waste Management Systems Using Artificial Intelligence Techniques. In *AI-Enabled Social Robotics in Human Care Services* (pp. 236–258). IGI Global. doi:10.4018/978-1-6684-8171-4.ch009

Kraus, N., Kraus, K., Manzhura, O., Ishchenko, I., & Radzikhovska, Y. (2023). Digital Transformation of Business Processes of Enterprises on the Way to Becoming Industry 5.0 in the Gig Economy. *WSEAS Transactions on Business and Economics*, *93*(20), 1008–1029. doi:10.37394/23207.2023.20.93

Krishanveni, R., & Subhashini, D. (2016). Leveraging Metrics and Analytics for evidence based decisions in managing employee performance. International Journal of Contemporary management. *Theory into Practice*, *2*, 3.

Krishna, T. R. (2015). Banking Sector in India and Its Recent Developments. *International Journal of Multidisciplinary Educational Research*, *4*(1), 24–29.

Kshetri, N. (2021). Evolving uses of artificial intelligence in human resource management in emerging economies in the global South: Some preliminary evidence. *Management Research Review*, *44*(7), 970–990. doi:10.1108/MRR-03-2020-0168

Kumar, A., & Kaur, A. (2022, November). A Multivariate Analysis on Employee Competencies. *2022 5th International Conference on Multimedia, Signal Processing and Communication Technologies (IMPACT)*, 1-5. 10.1109/IMPACT55510.2022.10029153

Kumar, M., Kumar, K., Sasikala, P., Sampath, B., Gopi, B., & Sundaram, S. (2023). Sustainable Green Energy Generation From Waste Water: IoT and ML Integration. In Sustainable Science and Intelligent Technologies for Societal Development (pp. 440–463). IGI Global.

Kumar, P. R., Meenakshi, S., Shalini, S., Devi, S. R., & Boopathi, S. (2023). Soil Quality Prediction in Context Learning Approaches Using Deep Learning and Blockchain for Smart Agriculture. In Effective AI, Blockchain, and E-Governance Applications for Knowledge Discovery and Management (pp. 1–26). IGI Global. doi:10.4018/978-1-6684-9151-5.ch001

Kumar, P., Sampath, B., Kumar, S., Babu, B. H., & Ahalya, N. (2023). Hydroponics, Aeroponics, and Aquaponics Technologies in Modern Agricultural Cultivation. In Trends, Paradigms, and Advances in Mechatronics Engineering (pp. 223–241). IGI Global.

Kumara, V., Mohanaprakash, T. A., Fairooz, S., Jamal, K., Babu, T., & B., S. (2023). Experimental Study on a Reliable Smart Hydroponics System: In P. Vasant, R. Rodríguez-Aguilar, I. Litvinchev, & J. A. Marmolejo-Saucedo (Eds.), *Advances in Environmental Engineering and Green Technologies* (pp. 27–45). IGI Global. doi:10.4018/978-1-6684-4118-3.ch002

Kumar, A. (2016). Impact of Liberlisation on Indian Insurance Industry. *International Journal of Management and Economics Review*, *1*(1), 1–10.

Kumar, A., & Kaur, A. (2023). Predicting complaint voicing or exit amidst Indian consumers: A CHAID analysis. *Journal of Advances in Management Research*, *20*(1), 55–78. doi:10.1108/JAMR-03-2022-0054

Kumar, A., & Kaur, A. (2024). Indian consumers' tendency to exit amidst a complaint: A SEM approach. *International Journal of Management Practice*, *17*(1), 19–50. doi:10.1504/IJMP.2024.135189

Kumaraswamy, D. S. (2012). Bancassurance: Tapping of Insurance into Banking Pursuit. *International Journal of Scientific and Research Publications*, *2*(7), 1–5.

Kumar, B. M., Kumar, K. K., Sasikala, P., Sampath, B., Gopi, B., & Sundaram, S. (2024). Sustainable Green Energy Generation From Waste Water: IoT and ML Integration. In B. K. Mishra (Ed.), Practice, Progress, and Proficiency in Sustainability. IGI Global. doi:10.4018/979-8-3693-1186-8.ch024

Kumar, G. G., & Santhosh, C. (2014). Exploring the dimensions of employee retention in BPO industry in Kerala. *Asia Pacific Journal of Research*, *1*, 61–78.

Kumar, R., Gupta, P., Singh, S., & Jain, D. (2021). Human Empowerment by Industry 5.0 in Digital Era: Analysis of Enablers. *Lecture Notes in Mechanical Engineering*, (February), 401–410. doi:10.1007/978-981-33-4320-7_36

Kumar, S., Kumar, P., Ahmad, S. S., Jayasaradadevi, P., Rajeyyagari, S., Manoharan, G., & Radhakrishnan, V. (2024). A Novel Approach for IoT-Based Cloud Computing Technology and its Impact on Business Entrepreneurship. *International Journal of Intelligent Systems and Applications in Engineering*, *12*(10s), 624–628.

Kumar, V. M., & Babu, P. (2017). A review of the factors affecting employee retention in the workplace. *International Journal of Current Research*, *9*(11), 61791–61794.

Kundi, Y. M., Aboramadan, M., Elhamalawi, E. M., & Shahid, S. (2020). Employee psychological well-being and job performance: Exploring mediating and moderating mechanisms. *The International Journal of Organizational Analysis*, *29*(3), 736–754. doi:10.1108/IJOA-05-2020-2204

Kundu, S. C., & Lata, K. (2017). Effects of supportive work environment on employee retention: Mediating role of organizational engagement. *The International Journal of Organizational Analysis*, *25*(4), 703–722. doi:10.1108/IJOA-12-2016-1100

Kurek, D. (2021). Use of Modern IT Solutions in the HRM Activities: Process Automation and Digital Employer Branding. *European Research Studies*, *24*(1), 152–170. doi:10.35808/ersj/2035

Kuruppu, C., Kavirathne, C., & Karunarathna, N. (2021). The impact of training on employee performance in a selected apparel sector organization in Sri Lanka. *Global Journal of Management and Business Research. Administrative Management*, *21*(2), 5–12.

Laskowska, A., & Laskowski, J. F. (2022). "Silver" Generation at Work—Implications for Sustainable Human Capital Management in the Industry 5.0 Era. *Sustainability (Basel)*, *15*(1), 194. doi:10.3390/su15010194

Latha, K. L. (2013). A study on employee attrition and retention in manufacturing industries. *BVIMSR's. Journal of Management Research*, *5*(1), 1–23.

Lee, J., Bagheri, B., & Kao, H. A. (2015). A Cyber-Physical Systems architecture for Industry 4.0-based manufacturing systems. *Manufacturing Letters*, *3*(December), 18–23. doi:10.1016/j.mfglet.2014.12.001

Lee, N. S. M. S., Hussain, S., Rashid, R. A., Raffar, M. A., & Aripin, N. (2023). The effect of training towards employee performance: An evidence from a public university in Malaysia. *International Journal of Information Management*, *17*(3), 178–185.

Legner, C., Eymann, T., Hess, T., Matt, C., Böhmann, T., Drews, P., Mädche, A., Urbach, N., & Ahlemann, F. (2017). Digitalization: Opportunity and challenge for the business and information systems engineering community. *Business & Information Systems Engineering*, *59*(4), 301–308. doi:10.1007/s12599-017-0484-2

Leon, R. D. (2023). Employees' reskilling and upskilling for industry 5.0: Selecting the best professional development programmes. *Technology in Society*, *75*, 102393. doi:10.1016/j.techsoc.2023.102393

Liang, L., Feng, M., Cui, X., Zhou, S., Yin, X., Wang, X., Yang, M., Liu, C., Xie, R., Zhu, L., Yu, J., & Wei, X. (2019). The effect of exercise on cervical radiculopathy: A systematic review and meta-analysis. *Medicine*, *98*(45), e17733. doi:10.1097/MD.0000000000017733 PMID:31702624

Li, F. (2018). The digital transformation of business models in the creative industries: A holistic framework and emerging trends. *Technovation.*

Liu, Y., Ma, X., Shu, L., Hancke, G. P., & Abu-Mahfouz, A. M. (2020). From industry 4.0 to agriculture 4.0: Current status, enabling technologies, and research challenges. *IEEE Transactions on Industrial Informatics*, *17*(6), 4322–4334. doi:10.1109/TII.2020.3003910

Li, W., Lu, C., & Zhang, Y. W. (2019). Prospective exploration of future renewable portfolio standard schemes in China via a multi-sector CGE model. *Energy Policy*, *128*, 45–56. doi:10.1016/j.enpol.2018.12.054

López-Cabarcos, M. Á., Vázquez-Rodríguez, P., & Quiñoá-Piñeiro, L. M. (2022). An approach to employees' job performance through work environmental variables and leadership behaviours. *Journal of Business Research*, *140*, 361–369. doi:10.1016/j.jbusres.2021.11.006

Lourens, M., Raman, R., Vanitha, P., Singh, R., Manoharan, G., & Tiwari, M. (2022). Agile Technology and Artificial Intelligent Systems in Business Development. *2022 5th International Conference on Contemporary Computing and Informatics (IC3I)*, 1602-1607. 10.1109/IC3I56241.2022.10073410

Lu, H., Zhao, G., & Liu, S. (2024). Integrating circular economy and Industry 4.0 for sustainable supply chain management: A dynamic capability view. *Production Planning and Control*, *35*(2), 170–186. doi:10.1080/09537287.2022.2063198

Lumi, A. (2020). The impact of digitalisation on human resources development. *Prizren Social Science Journal*, *4*(3), 39–46. doi:10.32936/pssj.v4i3.178

Lum, L., Kervin, J., Clark, K., Reid, F., & Sirola, W. (1998). Explaining nursing turnover intent: Job satisfaction, pay satisfaction, or organizational commitment? *Journal of Organizational Behavior*, *19*(3), 305–320. doi:10.1002/(SICI)1099-1379(199805)19:3<305::AID-JOB843>3.0.CO;2-N

Lu, Y. (2017). Industry 4.0: A survey on technologies, applications and open research issues. *Journal of Industrial Information Integration*, *6*, 1–10. doi:10.1016/j.jii.2017.04.005

Lymberpoulos, K., Chaniotakis, I. O., & Soureli, M. (2004). Opportunities for Banks to CrossSell Insurance Products in Greece. *Journal of Financial Services Marketing*, *9*(1), 34–48. doi:10.1057/palgrave.fsm.4770139

Maddikunta, P. K. R., Pham, Q. V., B, P., Deepa, N., Dev, K., Gadekallu, T. R., Ruby, R., & Liyanage, M. (2022). Industry 5.0: A survey on enabling technologies and potential applications. *Journal of Industrial Information Integration*, *26*(July), 100257. Advance online publication. doi:10.1016/j.jii.2021.100257

Madhani, P. M. (2023). Human Resources Analytics: Leveraging Human Resources for Enhancing Business Performance. *Compensation and Benefits Review*, *55*(1), 31–45. doi:10.1177/08863687221131730

Madsen, S. R., Miller, D., & John, C. R. (2005). Readiness for organizational change: Do organizational commitment and social relationships in the workplace make a difference? *Human Resource Development Quarterly*, *16*(2), 213–234. doi:10.1002/hrdq.1134

Maguluri, L. P., Ananth, J., Hariram, S., Geetha, C., Bhaskar, A., & Boopathi, S. (2023). Smart Vehicle-Emissions Monitoring System Using Internet of Things (IoT). In P. Srivastava, D. Ramteke, A. K. Bedyal, M. Gupta, & J. K. Sandhu (Eds.), Practice, Progress, and Proficiency in Sustainability. IGI Global. doi:10.4018/978-1-6684-8117-2.ch014

Mahesh, K., Aithal, P., & Sharma, K. (n.d.). Green HRM and Teaching Sustainability in higher education Institutions: For Promoting Sustainable Education and Sustainable Development Goals. [IJCSBE]. *Education*, *8*(1), 261–271.

Maheswari, B. U., Imambi, S. S., Hasan, D., Meenakshi, S., Pratheep, V., & Boopathi, S. (2023). Internet of things and machine learning-integrated smart robotics. In Global Perspectives on Robotics and Autonomous Systems: Development and Applications (pp. 240–258). IGI Global. doi:10.4018/978-1-6684-7791-5.ch010

Mahmood, D., Latif, S., Anwar, A., Hussain, S. J., Jhanjhi, N., Sama, N. U., & Humayun, M. (2021). Utilization of ICT and AI techniques in harnessing residential energy consumption for an energy-aware smart city: A review. *International Journal of Advanced and Applied Sciences*, *8*(7), 50–66.

Maity, S., & Sahu, T. N. (2017). Pre-merger performance measures of state bank of India and its associate banks using data envelopment analysis. *Business Spectrum*, *7*(2), 16–26.

Majumdar, A., Garg, H., & Jain, R. (2021). Managing the barriers of Industry 4.0 adoption and implementation in textile and clothing industry: Interpretive structural model and triple helix framework. *Computers in Industry*, *125*, 103372. doi:10.1016/j.compind.2020.103372

Malathi, J., Kusha, K., Isaac, S., Ramesh, A., Rajendiran, M., & Boopathi, S. (2024). IoT-Enabled Remote Patient Monitoring for Chronic Disease Management and Cost Savings: Transforming Healthcare. In Advances in Explainable AI Applications for Smart Cities (pp. 371–388). IGI Global.

Malik, A., Srikanth, N. R., & Budhwar, P. (2020). Digitisation, artificial intelligence (AI) and HRM. *Human resource management: Strategic and international perspectives, 88.*

Malti, M. (2022, July 11). Total Number of Life Insurance Policies Sold in June 2022 Up 32%, Shows IRDAI Data. Outlook. https://www.outlookindia.com/business/total-number-of-life-insurance-policies-sold-in-june-2022-up-32-shows-irdai-data-news-208244

Mandal, A., Dutta, S., & Pramanik, S. (2021). Machine Intelligence of Pi from Geometrical Figures with Variable Parameters using SCILab. In D. Samanta, R. R. Althar, S. Pramanik, & S. Dutta (Eds.), *Methodologies and Applications of Computational Statistics for Machine Learning* (pp. 38–63). IGI Global. doi:10.4018/978-1-7998-7701-1.ch003

Mangal,, E., Lalwani, S., Dadhich, M., & Chauhan, D. (2021). A study of factors delivering competitive edge in employee retention. *Turkish Journal of Computer and Mathematics*, *12*(7), 2555–2571.

Manjula, P., & ... (2021). Human Resource Coping Strategies in „New Normal" and their Impact on Work Places: Systematic Review. *Journal of Contemporary Issues in Business and Government*, *27*(1), 1746–1759.

Mannar, B. R. (2015). The Indian market scenario of insurance sector. *Asia Pacific Journal of Research, 1*(25), 88–98.

Manoharan, G., Durai, S., Ashtikar, S. P., & Kumari, N. (2024). Artificial Intelligence in Marketing Applications. In Artificial Intelligence for Business (pp. 40-70). Productivity Press.

Manoharan, G., Durai, S., Rajesh, G. A., & Ashtikar, S. P. (2023). Credit and Risk Analysis in the Financial and Banking Sectors: An Investigation. In Artificial Intelligence for Capital Markets (pp. 57-72). Chapman and Hall/CRC.

Manoharan, G., Durai, S., Rajesh, G. A., & Ashtikar, S. P. (2024). A Study on the Application of Expert Systems as a Support System for Business Decisions: A Literature Review. Artificial Intelligence and Knowledge Processing, 279-289.

Manoharan, G., Durai, S., & Rajesh, G. A. (2022). A case of designing performance metrics for sales associates in a retail store in Coimbatore, using the BEI technique. *AIP Conference Proceedings, 2418*, 020015. doi:10.1063/5.0081824

Manoharan, G., Durai, S., Rajesh, G. A., Razak, A., Rao, C. B., & Ashtikar, S. P. (2023). A study of postgraduate students' perceptions of key components in ICCC to be used in artificial intelligence-based smart cities. In *Artificial Intelligence and Machine Learning in Smart City Planning* (pp. 117–133). Elsevier. doi:10.1016/B978-0-323-99503-0.00003-X

Manoharan, G., Durai, S., Rajesh, G. A., Razak, A., Rao, C. B., & Ashtikar, S. P. (2023). An investigation into the effectiveness of smart city projects by identifying the framework for measuring performance. In *Artificial Intelligence and Machine Learning in Smart City Planning* (pp. 71–84). Elsevier. doi:10.1016/B978-0-323-99503-0.00004-1

Manuti, A., & de Palma, P. D. (2018). How to Develop Digital HRM Practices in the Cognitive Technology Era: Evidences from a Case Study. In *Digital HR* (pp. 67–79). Palgrave Macmillan. doi:10.1007/978-3-319-60210-3_5

Manzoor, F., Wei, L., Bányai, T., Nurunnabi, M., & Subhan, Q. A. (2019). An Examination of Sustainable HRM Practices on Job Performance: An Application of Training as a Moderator. *Sustainability (Basel), 11*(8), 2263. doi:10.3390/su11082263

Maranesi, C., & De Giovanni, P. (2020). Modern circular economy: Corporate strategy, supply chain, and industrial symbiosis. *Sustainability (Basel), 12*(22), 9383. doi:10.3390/su12229383

Marler, J. H., & Parry, E. (2016). Human resource management, strategic involvement and e-HRM technology. *International Journal of Human Resource Management, 27*(19), 2233–2253. doi:10.1080/09585192.2015.1091980

Masegare, P., & Ngoepe, M. (2018). A framework for incorporating implementation indicators of corporate governance for municipalities in South Africa. *Corporate Governance (Bradford), 18*(4), 581–593. doi:10.1108/CG-11-2016-0216

Masood, T., & Sonntag, P. (2020). Industry 4.0: Adoption challenges and benefits for SMEs. *Computers in Industry, 121*, 103261. doi:10.1016/j.compind.2020.103261

McDonnell, A., Collings, D. G., & Burgess, J. (2012). Guest editors' note: Talent management in the Asia Pacific. *Asia Pacific Journal of Human Resources, 50*(4), 391–398. doi:10.1111/j.1744-7941.2012.00035.x

McIver, D., Lengnick-Hall, M. L., & Lengnick-Hall, C. A. (2018). A strategic approach to workforce analytics: Integrating science and agility. *Business Horizons, 61*(3), 397–407. doi:10.1016/j.bushor.2018.01.005

Mirković, V., Lukić, J., Lazarević, S., & Vojinović, Ž. (2019). Key characteristics of organizational structure that supports digital transformation. *International Scientific Conference Strategic Management and Decision Support Systems in Strategic Management*. 10.46541/978-86-7233-380-0_46

Mishra, N. (2012). Banc Assurance: Problems and Challenges in India. Integral Review. *Journal of Management, 5*(1), 52–63.

Mohamed, O. E. B., Alhabshi, S. O., & Sharif, K. (2015). Factors influencing the penetration rate of Malaysian takaful industry from takaful managers' perspective. *The International Journal of Excellence in Islamic Banking and Finance*, *5*(1), 1–13. doi:10.12816/0024362

Mohammed, A. (2015). The impact of talent management on employee engagement, retention and value addition in achieving organizational performance. *International Journal of Core Engineering & Management*, *1*(12), 142–152.

Mohanty, A., Venkateswaran, N., Ranjit, P., Tripathi, M. A., & Boopathi, S. (2023). Innovative Strategy for Profitable Automobile Industries: Working Capital Management. In Handbook of Research on Designing Sustainable Supply Chains to Achieve a Circular Economy (pp. 412–428). IGI Global.

Mohanty, A., Venkateswaran, N., Ranjit, P. S., Tripathi, M. A., & Boopathi, S. (2023). Innovative Strategy for Profitable Automobile Industries: Working Capital Management. In Y. Ramakrishna & S. N. Wahab (Eds.), Advances in Finance, Accounting, and Economics. IGI Global. doi:10.4018/978-1-6684-7664-2.ch020

Momin, W. Y. M. (2015). HR analytics transforming human resource management. *International Journal of Applied Research*, *1*(9), 688–692.

Montagnier, P., & Ek, I. (2021). AI measurement in ICT usage surveys. *RE:view*.

Montazeri, M. (2019). *Smart Additive Manufacturing: in-Process Sensing and Smart Additive Manufacturing: in-Process Sensing and Data Analytics for Online Defect Detection in Metal Data Analytics for Online Defect Detection in Metal Additive Manufacturing Processes Additive Man.* University of Nebraska - Lincoln. Retrieved from https://digitalcommons.unl.edu/mechengdisshttps://digitalcommons.unl.edu/mechengdiss/148

Mosca, M. (2020). *Digitalization of HRM: A study of success factors and consequences in the last decade* (Master's thesis, University of Twente).

Mourtzis, D., Angelopoulos, J., & Panopoulos, N. (2022). A Literature Review of the Challenges and Opportunities of the Transition from Industry 4.0 to Society 5.0. *Energies*, *15*(17), 6276. doi:10.3390/en15176276

Mukherjee, B., Chandra, B., & Singh, S. (2020). Talent retention in Indian public sector units (PSUs): An empirical investigation. *Kybernetes*, *49*(6), 1783–1810. doi:10.1108/K-03-2019-0165

Mukhuty, S., Upadhyay, A., & Rothwell, H. (2022). Strategic sustainable development of Industry 4.0 through the lens of social responsibility: The role of human resource practices. *Business Strategy and the Environment*, *31*(5), 2068–2081. doi:10.1002/bse.3008

Muo, I. K. (2013). Identifying and minimizing risks in the change management process: The case of Nigerian banking industry. *Issues in Business Management and Economics*, *1*(6), 148–162.

Murali, B., Padhi, S., Patil, C. K., Kumar, P. S., Santhanakrishnan, M., & Boopathi, S. (2023). Investigation on hardness and tensile strength of friction stir processing of Al6061/TiN surface composite. *Materials Today: Proceedings*.

Muthumari, A., & Pushpaveni, K. (2017). A Study on Customer Service Loyalty Towards Bancassurance of Public and Private Sector Banks in Virudhunagar District, Tamilnadu. *Journal of Emerging Technologies and Innovative Research*, *4*(12), 385–392.

Myilsamy Sureshkumar, Boopathi, & Sabareesh. (2018). The improving Wear Resistance Properties of Molybdenum Alloy Under Cryogenic Treatment. *International Journal of Mechanical and Production Engineering Research and Development*, *8*(7), 724–728.

Myilsamy, S., & Sampath, B. (2017). Grey Relational Optimization of Powder Mixed Near-Dry Wire Cut Electrical Discharge Machining of Inconel 718 Alloy. *Asian Journal of Research in Social Sciences and Humanities*, *7*(3), 18–25. doi:10.5958/2249-7315.2017.00157.5

Nagaraja, B. (2015). Performance of insurance industry in India: A critical analysis. *International Journal of Multidisciplinary and Scientific Emerging Research*, *4*(1), 1045–1052.

Nahavandi, S. (2019). Industry 5. 0—A Human-Centric Solution. *Sustainability*, *11*(4371), 43–71.

Nanda, A. K., Sharma, A., Augustine, P. J., Cyril, B. R., Kiran, V., & Sampath, B. (2024). Securing Cloud Infrastructure in IaaS and PaaS Environments. In Improving Security, Privacy, and Trust in Cloud Computing (pp. 1–33). IGI Global. doi:10.4018/979-8-3693-1431-9.ch001

Narayanan, A., Rajithakumar, S., & Menon, M. (2019). Talent management and employee retention: An integrative research framework. *Human Resource Development Review*, *18*(2), 228–247. doi:10.1177/1534484318812159

Nave, E., & Ferreira, J. J. (2022). A systematic international entrepreneurship review and future research agenda. *Cross Cultural & Strategic Management*, *29*(3), 639–674. doi:10.1108/CCSM-11-2021-0204

Naveeenkumar, N., Rallapalli, S., Sasikala, K., Priya, P. V., Husain, J., & Boopathi, S. (2024). Enhancing Consumer Behavior and Experience Through AI-Driven Insights Optimization. In *AI Impacts in Digital Consumer Behavior* (pp. 1–35). IGI Global. doi:10.4018/979-8-3693-1918-5.ch001

Naveen, S., & Raju, D. N. M. (2014). A study on recruitment & selection process with reference to three industries, cement industry, electronics industry, sugar industry in Krishna DtAp, India. IOSR Journal of Business and Management (IOSR-JBM), 15(5), 60-67.

Naz, S., Nisar, A., Khan, M., Ahmad, N., & Anwar, T. (2020). A study in the relationship between supportive work environment and employee retention: Role of organizational commitment and person-organization fit as mediator. *SAGE Open*, *4*(2), 1–20. doi:10.1177/2158244020924694

Newar, L. R. (2013). Understanding Reforms in the Life Insurance Sector of India. *International Journal of Computer Applications in Engineering Sciences*, *3*(1), 18–23.

Newman, N. (2018). *Journalism, media and technology trends and predictions 2018*. Reuters Institute for the Study of Journalism.

Nippatlapalli, A. R. (2013). A study on customer satisfaction of commercial banks: Case study on State Bank of India. *IOSR Journal of Business and Management*, *15*(1), 60–86. doi:10.9790/487X-1516086

Nishanth, J., Deshmukh, M. A., Kushwah, R., Kushwaha, K. K., Balaji, S., & Sampath, B. (2023). Particle Swarm Optimization of Hybrid Renewable Energy Systems. In *Intelligent Engineering Applications and Applied Sciences for Sustainability* (pp. 291–308). IGI Global. doi:10.4018/979-8-3693-0044-2.ch016

Nivlouei, F. B. (2014). Electronic Human Resource Management System: The Main Element in Capacitating Globalization Paradigm. *International Journal of Business and Social Science*, *5*(2), 147–159.

Obeidat, S. M., & Abdalla, S. O. (2022). Achieving Sustainable Development Through Green HRM: The Role of HR Analytics. In J. Marx Gómez & L. O. Yesufu (Eds.), *Sustainable Development Through Data Analytics and Innovation. Progress in IS*. Springer. doi:10.1007/978-3-031-12527-0_10

Odeyemi, O., Usman, F. O., Mhlongo, N. Z., Elufioye, O. A., & Ike, C. U. (2024). *Sustainable entrepreneurship: A review of green business practices and environmental impact*. Academic Press.

Ofori, D., & Aryeetey, M. (2011). Recruitment and selection practices in small and medium enterprises. *International Journal of Business Administration*, *2*(3), 45–60. doi:10.5430/ijba.v2n3p45

Oladapo, V. (2014). The impact of talent management on retention. *Journal of Business Studies Quarterly*, *5*(3).

Olaizola, I. G., Quartulli, M., Garcia, A., & Barandiaran, I. (2022). Artificial Intelligence from Industry 5.0 perspective: Is the Technology Ready to Meet the Challenge? *CEUR Workshop Proceedings*, 3214.

Omisore, B. O., & Adeleke, O. (2015). Work ethics, values, attitudes and performance in the Nigerian public service: Issues, challenges and the way forward. *Journal of Public Administration and Governance*, *5*(1), 157–172. doi:10.5296/jpag.v5i1.7367

Orlova, E. V. (2021). Design of personal trajectories for employees' professional development in the knowledge society under Industry 5.0. *Social Sciences (Basel, Switzerland)*, *10*(11), 427. doi:10.3390/socsci10110427

Özdemir, V., & Hekim, N. (2018). Birth of Industry 5.0: Making Sense of Big Data with Artificial Intelligence, "the Internet of Things" and Next-Generation Technology Policy. *OMICS: A Journal of Integrative Biology*, *22*(1), 65–76. doi:10.1089/omi.2017.0194 PMID:29293405

Pachiappan, K., Anitha, K., Pitchai, R., Sangeetha, S., Satyanarayana, T. V. V., & Boopathi, S. (2023). Intelligent Machines, IoT, and AI in Revolutionizing Agriculture for Water Processing. In B. B. Gupta & F. Colace (Eds.), Advances in Computational Intelligence and Robotics. IGI Global. doi:10.4018/978-1-6684-9999-3.ch015

Pachiappan, K., Anitha, K., Pitchai, R., Sangeetha, S., Satyanarayana, T., & Boopathi, S. (2024). Intelligent Machines, IoT, and AI in Revolutionizing Agriculture for Water Processing. In *Handbook of Research on AI and ML for Intelligent Machines and Systems* (pp. 374–399). IGI Global.

Palaniappan, M., Tirlangi, S., Mohamed, M. J. S., Moorthy, R. S., Valeti, S. V., & Boopathi, S. (2023). Fused Deposition Modelling of Polylactic Acid (PLA)-Based Polymer Composites: A Case Study. In Development, Properties, and Industrial Applications of 3D Printed Polymer Composites (pp. 66–85). IGI Global.

Pallavi, D. R., & Rai, A. (2021). An Analysis of Customer Perception about Bancassurance: An Empirical Study. *Recent Trends in Management and Commerce*, *2*(2), 79-86.

Pal, R. (2013). Financial Sector Reforms: The Way to Socio-Economic Inclusion. *International Journal (Toronto, Ont.)*, *2*(1), 94–101.

Panday, P., & Kaur, G. (2023). Talent management and employee outlook on industry 5.0. In Handbook of Research on Education Institutions, Skills, and Jobs in the Digital Era (pp. 299-306). IGI Global.

Pani, L. K., & Swain, S. (2013). Bancassurance and Indian banks. *International Journal of Research and Development-A Management Review*, *2*(1), 11–13.

Pape, T. (2016). Prioritising data items for business analytics: Framework and application to human resources. *European Journal of Operational Research*, *252*(2), 687–698. doi:10.1016/j.ejor.2016.01.052

Paposa, K. K., & Kumar, Y. M. (2019). Impact of training and development practices on job satisfaction: A study on faculty members of technical education institutes. *Management and Labour Studies*, *44*(3), 248–262. doi:10.1177/0258042X19851649

Parameswaran, H. (2021). Industry 5.0: Can it be a change management gizmo in Human resource development? *Parameswaran, Hima,(2021), Industry, 5.*

Paramita, D. (2020). *Digitalization in talent acquisition: A case study of AI in recruitment.*

Paramita, D. (2020). *Digitalization in talent acquisition: A case study of AI in recruitment*. Academic Press.

Parida, V., Sjödin, D., & Reim, W. (2019). Reviewing literature on digitalization, business model innovation, and sustainable industry: Past achievements and future promises. *Sustainability (Basel)*, *11*(2), 391–410. doi:10.3390/su11020391

Park, T. Y., & Shaw, J. D. (2013). Turnover rates and organizational performance: A meta-analysis. *The Journal of Applied Psychology*, *98*(2), 268–309. doi:10.1037/a0030723 PMID:23244224

Parviainen, P., Tihinen, M., Kääriäinen, J., & Teppola, S. (2017). Tackling the digitalization challenge: how to benefit from digitalization in practice. *International Journal of Information Systems and Project Management*, *5*(1), 63-77.

Paschek, D., Mocan, A., & Draghici, A. (2019). Industry 5. 0 – The Expected Impact of Next Industrial Revolution. *Managment Knowledge Learning International Conference*, 125–132. Retrieved from http://www.toknowpress.net/ISBN/978-961-6914-25-3/papers/ML19-017.pdf

Passaro, R., Quinto, I., Rippa, P., & Thomas, A. (2020). Evolution of collaborative networks supporting startup sustainability: Evidences from digital firms. *Sustainability (Basel)*, *12*(22), 9437. doi:10.3390/su12229437

Patnaik, A. (2022, July 30). Banking on bancassurance. Financial Express. https://www.financialexpress.com/opinion/banking-on-bancassurance/2611182/

Pavlovski, C. (2013). A Multi-Channel System Architecture for Banking. *International Journal of Computer Science. Engineering and Applications*, *3*(5), 1–12.

Peck, B. W., Van Abel, K. M., Moore, E. J., & Price, D. L. (2018). Rates and locations of regional metastases insinonasal malignancies: The Mayo Clinic experience. *Journal of Neurological Surgery. Part B, Skull Base*, *79*(03), 282–288. doi:10.1055/s-0037-1607288 PMID:29765826

Pillai, R. H., & Arumugan, A. (2023). Comparative Analysis Between Banking and Insurance Sector on Perception of Transformational Leadership Styles. *International Journal of Professional Business Review: International Journal of Professional Business Review*, *8*(5), 1–14. doi:10.26668/businessreview/2023.v8i5.1458

Pillai, R., & Sivathanu, B. (2020). Adoption of artificial intelligence (AI) for talent acquisition in IT/ITeS organizations. *Benchmarking*, *27*(9), 2599–2629. doi:10.1108/BIJ-04-2020-0186

Pino-Ortega, J., Rojas-Valverde, D., Gómez-Carmona, C. D., & Rico-González, M. (2021). Training design, performance analysis, and talent identification—A systematic review about the most relevant variables through the principal component analysis in Soccer, Basketball, and Rugby. *International Journal of Environmental Research and Public Health*, *18*(5), 2642. doi:10.3390/ijerph18052642 PMID:33807971

Piwowar-Sulej, K. (2021). Core functions of Sustainable Human Resource Management. A hybrid literature review with the use of H-Classics methodology. *Sustainable Development (Bradford)*, *29*(4), 671–693. doi:10.1002/sd.2166

Piwowar-Sulej, K. (2021). Human resources development as an element of sustainable HRM–with the focus on production engineers. *Journal of Cleaner Production*, *278*, 124008. doi:10.1016/j.jclepro.2020.124008 PMID:32901179

Pocock, B., Sexton, M., & Wilson, L. (2001). *Doing More, With Less: Tension and Change at Work in South Australian Local Government. Report of the Equity, Enterprise Bargaining and Employment Outcomes in South Australia Local Government Project*. Australian Services Union and the Australian Workers Union.

Poláková, M., Suleimanová, J. H., Madzík, P., Copuš, L., Molnárová, I., & Polednová, J. (2023). Soft skills and their importance in the labour market under the conditions of Industry 5.0. *Heliyon*, *9*(8), e18670. doi:10.1016/j.heliyon.2023.e18670 PMID:37593611

Ponduri, S. B., Ahmad, S. S., Ravisankar, P., Thakur, D. J., Chawla, K., Chary, D. T., ... Sharma, S. (2024). A Study on Recent Trends of Technology and its Impact on Business and Hotel Industry. *Migration Letters : An International Journal of Migration Studies*, *21*(S1), 801–806.

PopliG. S.RaoD. N. (2009). An Empirical Study of Bancassurance: Prospects and Challenges for selling Insurance Products through Banks in India. https://ssrn.com/abstract=1339471

Prabhuswamy, M., Tripathi, R., Vijayakumar, M., Thulasimani, T., Sundharesalingam, P., & Sampath, B. (2024). A Study on the Complex Nature of Higher Education Leadership: An Innovative Approach. In *Challenges of Globalization and Inclusivity in Academic Research* (pp. 202–223). IGI Global. doi:10.4018/979-8-3693-1371-8.ch013

Pramanik, S., Niranjanamurthy, M., & Panda, S. N. (2022). Using Green Energy Prediction in Data Centers for Scheduling Service Jobs. ICRITCSA 2022.

Pramila, P., Amudha, S., Saravanan, T., Sankar, S. R., Poongothai, E., & Boopathi, S. (2023). Design and Development of Robots for Medical Assistance: An Architectural Approach. In Contemporary Applications of Data Fusion for Advanced Healthcare Informatics (pp. 260–282). IGI Global.

Presbitero, A., Roxas, B., & Chadee, D. (2016). Looking beyond HRM practices in enhancing employee retention in BPOs: Focus on employee–organisation value fit. *International Journal of Human Resource Management*, *27*(6), 635–652. doi:10.1080/09585192.2015.1035306

Purnomo, A., Asitah, N., & Rosyidah, E. (2023). Understanding the Nexus between Green Entrepreneurship and Green Economy: A Review. *Journal of Economics and Business UBS*, *12*(4), 2470–2484. doi:10.52644/joeb.v12i4.444

Rachinger, M., Rauter, R., Müller, C., Vorraber, W., & Schirgi, E. (2019). Digitalization and its influence on business model innovation. *Journal of Manufacturing Technology Management*, *30*(8), 1143–1160. doi:10.1108/JMTM-01-2018-0020

Rada, M. (2017). Industry 5.0 Definition. Academic Press.

Radhika, H. (2012). Role of IRDA in life insurance sector. *ZENITH International Journal of Business Economics & Management Research*, *2*(9), 35–47.

Radhika, R., & Satuluri, R. K. (2019). A study on life insurance penetration in India. *International Journal of Human Resource Management and Research*, *9*(1), 119–124. doi:10.24247/ijhrmrfeb201912

Raghavan, S., & Pai, R. (2021). Impact of Digital Banking and Artificial Intelligence on Retail Customer Engagement - A Case Study on HDFC Bank. *International Journal of Innovative Research in Science, Engineering and Technology*, *10*(5), 4825–4834.

Raghunadha Reddy, P., & Lakshmikeerthi, P. (2017). 'HR Analytics' - An Effective Evidence Based HRM Tool. *International Journal of Business and Management Invention*, *6*(7), 23–34.

Rahamathunnisa, U., Sudhakar, K., Padhi, S., Bhattacharya, S., Shashibhushan, G., & Boopathi, S. (2024). Sustainable Energy Generation From Waste Water: IoT Integrated Technologies. In Adoption and Use of Technology Tools and Services by Economically Disadvantaged Communities: Implications for Growth and Sustainability (pp. 225–256). IGI Global.

Rahamathunnisa, U., Subhashini, P., Aancy, H. M., Meenakshi, S., Boopathi, S., & ... (2023). Solutions for Software Requirement Risks Using Artificial Intelligence Techniques. In *Handbook of Research on Data Science and Cybersecurity Innovations in Industry 4.0 Technologies* (pp. 45–64). IGI Global.

Rahamathunnisa, U., Sudhakar, K., Murugan, T. K., Thivaharan, S., Rajkumar, M., & Boopathi, S. (2023). Cloud Computing Principles for Optimizing Robot Task Offloading Processes. In *AI-Enabled Social Robotics in Human Care Services* (pp. 188–211). IGI Global. doi:10.4018/978-1-6684-8171-4.ch007

Rahamathunnisa, U., Sudhakar, K., Padhi, S. N., Bhattacharya, S., Shashibhushan, G., & Boopathi, S. (2023). Sustainable Energy Generation From Waste Water: IoT Integrated Technologies. In A. S. Etim (Ed.), Advances in Human and Social Aspects of Technology. IGI Global. doi:10.4018/978-1-6684-5347-6.ch010

Rahardja, U., Aini, Q., Budiarty, F., Yusup, M., & Alwiyah, A. (2021). Socio-economic impact of Blockchain utilization on Digital certificates. *Aptisi Transactions on Management*, *5*(2), 106–111. doi:10.33050/atm.v5i2.1508

Rajeshwari, S., Praveenadevi, D., Revathy, S., & Sreekala, S. (2023). 15 Utilizing AI technologies to enhance e-commerce business operations. *Toward Artificial General Intelligence,* 309–330.

Rajkumari, M. (2007). A study on customer preference towards insurance services and bancassurance. *ICFAI Journal of Risk and Insurance*, *4*(4), 49–60.

Rakhra, H. K. (2018). Study on factors influencing employee retention in companies. *International Journal of Public Sector Performance Management, 4*(1), 57-79.

Rakshit, D. (2017). Analysis of growth of insurance density and insurance penetration in India after initiation of reforms in insurance sector. *International Journal of Research in Economics and Social Sciences*, *7*(6), 164–171.

Ramachandran, K. K., Mary, S. S. C., Painoli, A. K., Satyala, H., Singh, B., & Manoharan, G. (2022). Assessing the full impact of technological advances on business management techniques. The British Journal of Administrative Management. https://tbjam. org/vol58-special-issue-06

Ramudu, K., Mohan, V. M., Jyothirmai, D., Prasad, D., Agrawal, R., & Boopathi, S. (2023). Machine Learning and Artificial Intelligence in Disease Prediction: Applications, Challenges, Limitations, Case Studies, and Future Directions. In Contemporary Applications of Data Fusion for Advanced Healthcare Informatics (pp. 297–318). IGI Global.

Rane, N. (2023). *Transformers in Industry 4.0, Industry 5.0, and Society 5.0: Roles and Challenges*. Academic Press.

Rani, N., & Samuel, A. (2016). A study on generational differences in work values and person-organization fit and its effect on turnover intention of Generation Y in India. *Management Research Review*, *39*(12), 1695–1719. doi:10.1108/MRR-10-2015-0249

Rashid, B. (2017). Digital Transformation And Innovation In Today's Business World. Available at https://www.forbes.com/sites/brianrashid/2017/06/13/digital-transformationandinnovation-in-todays-business-world

Rasmussen, T., & Ulrich, D. (2015). Learning from practice: How HR analytics avoids being a management fad. *Organizational Dynamics*, *44*(3), 236–242. doi:10.1016/j.orgdyn.2015.05.008

Ravisankar, A., Sampath, B., & Asif, M. M. (2023). Economic Studies on Automobile Management: Working Capital and Investment Analysis. In Multidisciplinary Approaches to Organizational Governance During Health Crises (pp. 169–198). IGI Global.

Ravisankar, A., Shanthi, A., Lavanya, S., Ramaratnam, M., Krishnamoorthy, V., & Boopathi, S. (2024). Harnessing 6G for Consumer-Centric Business Strategies Across Electronic Industries. In AI Impacts in Digital Consumer Behavior (pp. 241–270). IGI Global.

Rebecca, B., Kumar, K. P. M., Padmini, S., Srivastava, B. K., Halder, S., & Boopathi, S. (2023). Convergence of Data Science-AI-Green Chemistry-Affordable Medicine: Transforming Drug Discovery. In B. B. Gupta & F. Colace (Eds.), Advances in Computational Intelligence and Robotics. IGI Global. doi:10.4018/978-1-6684-9999-3.ch014

Rebecca, B., Kumar, K. P. M., Padmini, S., Srivastava, B. K., Halder, S., & Boopathi, S. (2024). Convergence of Data Science-AI-Green Chemistry-Affordable Medicine: Transforming Drug Discovery. In *Handbook of Research on AI and ML for Intelligent Machines and Systems* (pp. 348–373). IGI Global.

Reddy, M. A., Gaurav, A., Ushasukhanya, S., Rao, V. C. S., Bhattacharya, S., & Boopathi, S. (2023). Bio-Medical Wastes Handling Strategies During the COVID-19 Pandemic. In Multidisciplinary Approaches to Organizational Governance During Health Crises (pp. 90–111). IGI Global. doi:10.4018/978-1-7998-9213-7.ch006

Reddy, M. A., Reddy, B. M., Mukund, C., Venneti, K., Preethi, D., & Boopathi, S. (2023b). Social Health Protection During the COVID-Pandemic Using IoT. In *The COVID-19 Pandemic and the Digitalization of Diplomacy* (pp. 204–235). IGI Global. doi:10.4018/978-1-7998-8394-4.ch009

Reepu, S. (2023). Kumar, M. G. Chaudhary, K. G. Gupta, S. Pramanik and A. Gupta, Information Security and Privacy in IoT. In Handbook of Research in Advancements in AI and IoT Convergence Technologies. Academic Press.

Reggi, L., Arduini, D., Biagetti, M., & Zanfei, A. (2014). How advanced are Italian regions in terms of public e-services? The construction of a composite indicator to analyze patterns of innovation diffusion in the public sector. *Telecommunications Policy*, *38*(5–6), 514–529. doi:10.1016/j.telpol.2013.12.005

Reiche, B. S. (2008). The configuration of employee retention practices in multinational corporations' foreign subsidiaries. *International Business Review*, *17*(6), 676–687. doi:10.1016/j.ibusrev.2008.09.004

Reio, T., & Ghosh, R. (2009). Antecedents and Outcomes of Workplace Incivility. *Computational Complexity*, *2*(1), 1–9. doi:10.1002/hrdq

Renkema, M. (2021). AI, Digitalisation, and HRM: Foundations, Extensions, and New Directions on AI, Digitalisation, and HRM. In New Directions in the Future of Work (pp. 77-96). Emerald Publishing Limited.

Ren, S., & Jackson, S. E. (2020). HRM institutional entrepreneurship for sustainable business organizations. *Human Resource Management Review*, *30*(3), 100691. doi:10.1016/j.hrmr.2019.100691

Reuther, K., Dahle, Y., Schmidt, C., & Schösser, F. (2023). Motivational Facets of Sustainable Entrepreneurship: A Systematic Review and Future Research Agenda. *Sustainability (Basel)*, *15*(3), 2272. doi:10.3390/su15032272

Revathi, S., Babu, M., Rajkumar, N., Meti, V. K. V., Kandavalli, S. R., & Boopathi, S. (2024). Unleashing the Future Potential of 4D Printing: Exploring Applications in Wearable Technology, Robotics, Energy, Transportation, and Fashion. In Human-Centered Approaches in Industry 5.0: Human-Machine Interaction, Virtual Reality Training, and Customer Sentiment Analysis (pp. 131–153). IGI Global.

Rimon, G. (2017). Six surprising truths about how digital transformation will change HR. *Strategic HR Review*, *16*(2), 102–104. doi:10.1108/SHR-02-2017-0010

Ritter, T., & Pedersen, C. L. (2020). Digitization capability and the digitalization of business models in business-to-business firms: Past, present, and future. *Industrial Marketing Management*, *86*, 180–190. doi:10.1016/j.indmarman.2019.11.019

Ronchi, A. M. (2019). *E-Services*. Springer. doi:10.1007/978-3-030-01842-9

Rosário, A. T., & Figueiredo, J. (2023). *Sustainable Entrepreneurship and Corporate Social Responsibility: Systematic Bibliometric Literature Review*.

Rosário, A. T., & Figueiredo, J. (2024). Sustainable entrepreneurship and corporate social responsibility: Analysing the state of research. *Sustainable Environment*, *10*(1), 2324572. doi:10.1080/27658511.2024.2324572

Rothman, L. S., Gordon, I. E., Babikov, Y., Barbe, A., Benner, D. C., Bernath, P. F., Birk, M., Bizzocchi, L., Boudon, V., & Brown, L. R. (2013). The HITRAN2012 molecular spectroscopic database. *Journal of Quantitative Spectroscopy & Radiative Transfer*, *130*, 4–50. doi:10.1016/j.jqsrt.2013.07.002

Routh, S., Joshi, L. K., & Dasgupta, S. (2022). Low Penetration: A Threat to Indian Life Insurance Sector. *International Research Journal of Modernization in Engineering Technology and Science*, *4*(6), 5227–5233.

Roy, A., & Pramanik, S. (2023). A Review of the Hydrogen Fuel Path to Emission Reduction in the Surface Transport Industry. *International Journal of Hydrogen Energy*. Advance online publication. doi:10.1016/j.ijhydene.2023.07.010

S., P. K., Sampath, B., R., S. K., Babu, B. H., & N., A. (2022). Hydroponics, Aeroponics, and Aquaponics Technologies in Modern Agricultural Cultivation: In M. A. Mellal (Ed.), *Advances in Mechatronics and Mechanical Engineering* (pp. 223–241). IGI Global. doi:10.4018/978-1-6684-5887-7.ch012

Sadana, D., & Kaur, K. (2023). A Study on Factors Contributing Growth of Bancassurance. *Journal of Corporate Finance Management and Banking System*, *3*(02), 21–32. doi:10.55529/jcfmbs.32.21.32

Saidenberg, M. R., & Strahan, P. E. (1999). Are banks still important for financing large businesses? *Current Issues in Economics and Finance*, *5*(12), 1–6.

Sakellaridis, K., & Stiakakis, E. (2011). Business model change due to ICT integration: An application to the entertainment industry. *International Journal of Computer Information Systems and Industrial Management Applications*, *3*, 539–551.

Saks, A. M. (1995). Longitudinal field investigation of the moderating and mediating effects of self-efficacy on the relationship between training and newcomer adjustment. *The Journal of Applied Psychology*, *80*(2), 211–225. doi:10.1037/0021-9010.80.2.211 PMID:7737934

Samal, A. (2019). Impact of Bancassurance on Financial Performance of Private Commercial Banks in India. *International Journal of Engineering and Advanced Technology, 8*(6S3), 2027-2034.

Samikannu, R., Koshariya, A. K., Poornima, E., Ramesh, S., Kumar, A., & Boopathi, S. (2022). Sustainable Development in Modern Aquaponics Cultivation Systems Using IoT Technologies. In *Human Agro-Energy Optimization for Business and Industry* (pp. 105–127). IGI Global.

Samikannu, R., Koshariya, A. K., Poornima, E., Ramesh, S., Kumar, A., & Boopathi, S. (2023). Sustainable Development in Modern Aquaponics Cultivation Systems Using IoT Technologies. In P. Vasant, R. Rodríguez-Aguilar, I. Litvinchev, & J. A. Marmolejo-Saucedo (Eds.), Advances in Environmental Engineering and Green Technologies. IGI Global. doi:10.4018/978-1-6684-4118-3.ch006

Samoilovych, A., Popelo, O., Kychko, I., Samoilovych, O., & Olyfirenko, I. (2022). Management of Human Capital Development in The Era of the Digital Economy. *J. Intell. Manag. Decis*, *1*(1), 56–66. doi:10.56578/jimd010107

Samson, W. (2013).Recruitment of staff. International Journal of Selection, 14(6), 21-34.

Samtani, D. D. (2022). The Advantages of Using Prescriptive Analytics in Recruitment and Performance Management processes by HR professionals based in Ireland (Doctoral dissertation, Dublin, National College of Ireland).

Samuel, M. O., & Chipunza, C. (2009). Employee retention and turnover: Using motivational variables as a panacea. *African Journal of Business Management*, *3*(9).

Sánchez-Bayón, A., & Aznar, E. T. (2020). Business and labour culture changes in digital paradigm: Rise and fall of human resources and the emergence of talent development. *Cogito: Multidisciplinary Res. J.*, *12*, 225.

Sandhya, K., & Kumar, D. P. (2011). Employee retention by motivation. *Indian Journal of Science and Technology*, *4*(12), 1778–1782. doi:10.17485/ijst/2011/v4i12.34

Sankar, J. P., & Yogan, G. (2021). Human Resource Digital Transformation of IT Sector in India. *Webology*, *18*(1), 219–232. doi:10.14704/WEB/V18I1/WEB18085

Sankar, K. M., Booba, B., & Boopathi, S. (2023). Smart Agriculture Irrigation Monitoring System Using Internet of Things. In *Contemporary Developments in Agricultural Cyber-Physical Systems* (pp. 105–121). IGI Global. doi:10.4018/978-1-6684-7879-0.ch006

Santana, M., & Díaz-Fernández, M. (2023). Competencies for the artificial intelligence age: Visualisation of the state of the art and future perspectives. *Review of Managerial Science*, *17*(6), 1971–2004. doi:10.1007/s11846-022-00613-w

Saravanan, A., Venkatasubramanian, R., Khare, R., Surakasi, R., Boopathi, S., Ray, S., & Sudhakar, M. (2022). Policy trends of renewable energy and non. *Renewable Energy*.

Saravanan, M., Vasanth, M., Boopathi, S., Sureshkumar, M., & Haribalaji, V. (2022). Optimization of Quench Polish Quench (QPQ) Coating Process Using Taguchi Method. *Key Engineering Materials*, *935*, 83–91. doi:10.4028/p-z569vy

Sarma, S., Attaran, S., & Attaran, M. (2024). Sustainable entrepreneurship: Factors influencing opportunity recognition and exploitation. *International Journal of Entrepreneurship and Innovation*, *25*(1), 56–69. doi:10.1177/14657503221093007

Satav, S. D., Hasan, D. S., Pitchai, R., Mohanaprakash, T. A., Sultanuddin, S. J., & Boopathi, S. (2024). Next Generation of Internet of Things (NGIoT) in Healthcare Systems. In B. K. Mishra (Ed.), Practice, Progress, and Proficiency in Sustainability. IGI Global. doi:10.4018/979-8-3693-1186-8.ch017

Sawant, B. S. (2011). Technological developments in Indian banking sector. *Indian Streams Research Journal*, *1*(9), 1–4.

Schmidt, J., Drews, P., & Schirmer, I. (2016, August). *End-users' perspective on digitalization: A study on work order processing in the German banking industry* [Conference Presentation]. 22nd Americas Conference on Information Systems, San Diego.

Schwanholz, J., & Graham, T. (2018). Digital Transformation: New Opportunities and Challenges for Democracy? In J. Schwanholz, T. Graham, & P. T. Stoll (Eds.), *Managing Democracy in the Digital Age* (pp. 1–7). Springer. doi:10.1007/978-3-319-61708-4_1

Selmer, J., & Chiu, R. (2004). Required human resources competencies in the future: A framework for developing HR executives in Hong Kong. *Journal of World Business*, *39*(4), 324–336. doi:10.1016/j.jwb.2004.08.001

Sengeni, D., Padmapriya, G., Imambi, S. S., Suganthi, D., Suri, A., & Boopathi, S. (2023). Biomedical waste handling method using artificial intelligence techniques. In *Handbook of Research on Safe Disposal Methods of Municipal Solid Wastes for a Sustainable Environment* (pp. 306–323). IGI Global. doi:10.4018/978-1-6684-8117-2.ch022

Sengupta, R., Mishra, S. K., & Das, S. (2015). Emergence of Bancassurance in India-a Literature Review. *International Journal of Management and Social Sciences*, *3*(8), 480–486.

Sen, S. (2020). *Digital HR strategy: Achieving sustainable transformation in the digital age.* Kogan Page Publishers.

Senthil, T., Puviyarasan, M., Babu, S. R., Surakasi, R., Sampath, B., & Associates. (2023). Industrial Robot-Integrated Fused Deposition Modelling for the 3D Printing Process. In Development, Properties, and Industrial Applications of 3D Printed Polymer Composites (pp. 188–210). IGI Global.

Seri, P., Bianchi, A., & Matteucci, N. (2014). Diffusion and usage of public e-services in Europe: An assessment of country level indicators and drivers. *Telecommunications Policy*, *38*(5–6), 496–513. doi:10.1016/j.telpol.2014.03.004

Serror, M., Hack, S., Henze, M., Schuba, M., & Wehrle, K. (2020). Challenges and opportunities in securing the industrial internet of things. *IEEE Transactions on Industrial Informatics*, *17*(5), 2985–2996. doi:10.1109/TII.2020.3023507

Shaddiq, S., Irpan, M., & ... (2023). Governance of Human Resources Management in the Digital Era. *Journal of Business and Management Studies*, *5*(3), 80–96. doi:10.32996/jbms.2023.5.3.8

Shah, D., & Chugan, P. K. (2018). The International BFSI Business from International Financial Services Centre (IFSC) in India: The Changing Scenario. In Sustainable Development: Future Trajectory (pp.19-28). Himalaya Publishing House.

Shaikh, I. A. K., Kumar, C. N. S., Rohini, P., Jafersadhiq, A., Manoharan, G., & Suryanarayana, V. (2023). AST-Graph Convolution Network and LSTM Based Employees Behavioral and Emotional Reactions to Corporate Social Irresponsibility. *2023 Second International Conference on Augmented Intelligence and Sustainable Systems (ICAISS)*, 966-971. 10.1109/ICAISS58487.2023.10250754

Shameem, A., Ramachandran, K. K., Sharma, A., Singh, R., Selvaraj, F. J., & Manoharan, G. (2023, May). The rising importance of AI in boosting the efficiency of online advertising in developing countries. In 2023 3rd International Conference on Advance Computing and Innovative Technologies in Engineering (ICACITE) (pp. 1762-1766). IEEE. 10.1109/ICACITE57410.2023.10182754

Sharma, A. (2021, March 10). Economic Survey 2020-21: Insurance penetration 'extremely low' at 3.76%. Business Today. https://www.businesstoday.in/latest/economy-politics/story/economic-survey-2020-21-insurance-penetration-extremely-low-at-376-285890-2021-01-29

Sharma, D. M., Ramana, K. V., Jothilakshmi, R., Verma, R., Maheswari, B. U., & Boopathi, S. (2024). Integrating Generative AI Into K-12 Curriculums and Pedagogies in India: Opportunities and Challenges. *Facilitating Global Collaboration and Knowledge Sharing in Higher Education With Generative AI*, 133–161.

Sharma, A., Tyagi, R., Verma, A., & Paul, A. (2022). Review on Digitalisation and Artificial Intelligence in human Resource function of Energy sector. *Water and Energy International*, *65*(2), 38–46.

Sharma, G., & Gupta, S. (2020). Modelling the impact of corporate sustainability on economic performance with reference to Indian financial industry. *World Review of Entrepreneurship, Management and Sustainable Development*, *16*(3), 317–328. doi:10.1504/WREMSD.2020.107272

Shikari. (2011). Is hiring playing a great role? Academic Press.

Shrivastava, S., & Dhaigude, A. S. (2022). Prime Data Tech Pvt. Ltd: Resolving Employee Recruitment Dilemma using HR Analytics. Communications of the Association for Information Systems, 50. doi:10.17705/1CAIS.05027

Shukla, U. N. (2018). Enhancing life insurance penetration and density in India: Purchase intention modelling. *International Journal of Economics and Business Research*, *15*(2), 141–154. doi:10.1504/IJEBR.2018.089683

Sima, V., Gheorghe, I. G., Subić, J., & Nancu, D. (2020). Influences of the industry 4.0 revolution on the human capital development and consumer behavior: A systematic review. *Sustainability (Basel)*, *12*(10), 1–28. doi:10.3390/su12104035

Simón, C., & Ferreiro, E. (2018). Workforce analytics: A case study of scholar–practitioner collaboration. *Human Resource Management*, *57*(3), 781–793. doi:10.1002/hrm.21853

Singh, G., Tiwari, P., & Garg, V. (2023). HRM Digitalisation: Exploring Success and Outcomes. In The Adoption and Effect of Artificial Intelligence on Human Resources Management, Part B (pp. 199-219). Emerald Publishing Limited.

Singh, N., & Adhikari, D. (n.d.). *AI-Driven Personalization in eCommerce Advertising*. Academic Press.

Singh, B. (2023). Tele-Health Monitoring Lensing Deep Neural Learning Structure: Ambient Patient Wellness via Wearable Devices for Real-Time Alerts and Interventions. *Indian Journal of Health and Medical Law*, *6*(2), 12–16.

Sinha, M., Chacko, E., Makhija, P., & Pramanik, S. (2021). Energy Efficient Smart Cities with Green IoT. In C. Chakrabarty (Ed.), *Green Technological Innovation for Sustainable Smart Societies: Post Pandemic Era*. Springer. doi:10.1007/978-3-030-73295-0_16

SinhaT. (2005). Bancassurance in India: Who is tying the knot and why. *Available at* SSRN 715203 doi:10.2139/ssrn.715203

Sinha, V., & Thaly, P. (2013). A review on changing trend of recruitment practice to enhance the quality of hiring in global organizations. *Management*, *18*(2), 141–156.

Sinnott, G. C., Madison, G. H., & Pataki, G. E. (2002). *Employee Retention*. McGraw-Hill.

Sipola, J., Saunila, M., & Ukko, J. (2023). Adopting artificial intelligence in sustainable business. *Journal of Cleaner Production*, *426*, 139197. doi:10.1016/j.jclepro.2023.139197

Skobelev, P. O., & Borovik, S. Y. (2017). On the way from Industry 4.0 to Industry 5.0: From digital manufacturing to digital society. *Industry 4.0*, *2*(6), 307-311.

Skobelev, P., & Borovik, Y. (2017). On the Way From Industry 4. 0 To Industry 5.0. *International Scientific Journal "Industry 4.0,"* *2*(6), 307–311. Retrieved from https://stumejournals.com/journals/i4/2017/6/307/pdf

Solomon, M., Russell-Bennett, R., & Previte, J. (2012). *Consumer behaviour*. Pearson Higher Education AU.

Sonia, R., Gupta, N., Manikandan, K., Hemalatha, R., Kumar, M. J., & Boopathi, S. (2024). Strengthening Security, Privacy, and Trust in Artificial Intelligence Drones for Smart Cities. In *Analyzing and Mitigating Security Risks in Cloud Computing* (pp. 214–242). IGI Global. doi:10.4018/979-8-3693-3249-8.ch011

Soythong, K. (2023). The Effect of Quality of Work Life and Organizational Commitment to Employee Performance: A Case Study of Transportation Business in Nakhon Phanom Province of Thailand. Academic Press.

Srinivas, B., Maguluri, L. P., Naidu, K. V., Reddy, L. C. S., Deivakani, M., & Boopathi, S. (2023). Architecture and Framework for Interfacing Cloud-Enabled Robots. In *Handbook of Research on Data Science and Cybersecurity Innovations in Industry 4.0 Technologies* (pp. 542–560). IGI Global. doi:10.4018/978-1-6684-8145-5.ch027

Stegaru, G., Danila, C., Sacala, I. S., Moisescu, M., & Stanescu, A. M. (2015). E-Services quality assessment framework for collaborative networks. *Enterprise Information Systems*, *9*(5–6), 583–606.

Stone, D. L., & Deadrick, D. L. (2015). Challenges and opportunities affecting the future of human resource management. *Human Resource Management Review*, *25*(2), 139–145. doi:10.1016/j.hrmr.2015.01.003

Strohmeier, S. (2020). Digital human resource management: A conceptual clarification. *German Journal of Human Resource Management*, *34*(3), 345–365. doi:10.1177/2397002220921131

Stuss, M. (2023). The concept of HR 4.0: A literature review. *International Entrepreneurship Review*, *9*(3).

Subha, S., Inbamalar, T., Komala, C., Suresh, L. R., Boopathi, S., & Alaskar, K. (2023). A Remote Health Care Monitoring system using internet of medical things (IoMT). *IEEE Explore*, 1–6.

Subhashini Durai, K., & Manoharan, G. (2022). Leveraging HR metrics for effective recruitment & selection process in IT industries in Chennai and Coimbatore, Tamil Nadu. *AIP Conference Proceedings*, *2418*, 020011. doi:10.1063/5.0081942

Subhashini Durai, K., & Manoharan, G. (2022). Metric based performance management of employees – A case study of MSME unit in Coimbatore, Tamil Nadu. *AIP Conference Proceedings*, *2418*, 020013. doi:10.1063/5.0081943

Sulistyaningsih, E. (2023). Improving Human Resources Technology Innovation as a Business Growth Driver in the Society 5.0 Era. *ADI Journal on Recent Innovation*, *4*(2), 149–159.

Sullivan. (2009). Recruitment Process: Benchmark and Best Practice Study. Academic Press.

Sultana, S., Enayet, A., & Mouri, I. J. (2015). A smart, location based time and attendance tracking system using android application. *International Journal of Computer Science Engineering and Information Technology*, *5*(1), 1–5.

Sundaramoorthy, K., Singh, A., Sumathy, G., Maheshwari, A., Arunarani, A. R., & Boopathi, S. (2023). A Study on AI and Blockchain-Powered Smart Parking Models for Urban Mobility. In B. B. Gupta & F. Colace (Eds.), Advances in Computational Intelligence and Robotics. IGI Global. doi:10.4018/978-1-6684-9999-3.ch010

Sundaramoorthy, K., Singh, A., Sumathy, G., Maheshwari, A., Arunarani, A., & Boopathi, S. (2024). A Study on AI and Blockchain-Powered Smart Parking Models for Urban Mobility. In *Handbook of Research on AI and ML for Intelligent Machines and Systems* (pp. 223–250). IGI Global.

Susanto, P. C., Sawitri, N. N., Suroso, S., & Rony, Z. T. (2023). Human Resource Business Partners: Recruitment, Coaching, and Leadership Development. *International Journal of Integrative Sciences*, *2*(4), 457–470. doi:10.55927/ijis.v2i4.3680

Syamala, M., Komala, C., Pramila, P., Dash, S., Meenakshi, S., & Boopathi, S. (2023). Machine Learning-Integrated IoT-Based Smart Home Energy Management System. In *Handbook of Research on Deep Learning Techniques for Cloud-Based Industrial IoT* (pp. 219–235). IGI Global. doi:10.4018/978-1-6684-8098-4.ch013

Sypniewska, B., Baran, M., & Kłos, M. (2023). Work engagement and employee satisfaction in the practice of sustainable human resource management–based on the study of Polish employees. *The International Entrepreneurship and Management Journal*, *19*(3), 1069–1100. doi:10.1007/s11365-023-00834-9

Tange, K., De Donno, M., Fafoutis, X., & Dragoni, N. (2020). A systematic survey of industrial Internet of Things security: Requirements and fog computing opportunities. *IEEE Communications Surveys and Tutorials*, *22*(4), 2489–2520. doi:10.1109/COMST.2020.3011208

Tanwar, K., & Prasad, A. (2016). Exploring the relationship between employer branding and employee retention. *Global Business Review*, *17*(3), 186S–206S. doi:10.1177/0972150916631214

Tapiwa, G. G., Pedzisai, P., Bernard, N., & Mervis, C. (2022). Digitalisation of Human Resources Systems and Process Necessary for Public Sector Transformation in Zimbabwe. In *Transformational Human Resources Management in Zimbabwe: Solutions for the Public Sector in the 21st Century* (pp. 61–74). Springer Nature Singapore. doi:10.1007/978-981-19-4629-5_5

Technologies, A. I. Strategic HRM. In U. Hacioglu (Ed.), *Digital Business Strategies in Blockchain Ecosystems, Contributions to Management Science*. Springer.

Teclaw, R., Osatuke, K., Fishman, J., Moore, S. C., & Dyrenforth, S. (2014). Employee age and tenure within organizations: Relationship to workplace satisfaction and workplace climate perceptions. *The Health Care Manager*, *33*(1), 4–19. doi:10.1097/01.HCM.0000440616.31891.2d PMID:24463586

Temelkov, Z. (2018). Fintech firms opportunity or threat for banks? *International Journal of Information, Business and Management*, *10*(1), 137–143.

Tessema, M. T., Tesfom, G., Faircloth, M. A., Tesfagiorgis, M., & Teckle, P. (2022). The "great resignation": Causes, consequences, and creative HR management strategies. *Journal of Human Resource and Sustainability Studies*, *10*(1), 161–178. doi:10.4236/jhrss.2022.101011

Tett, R. P., & Meyer, J. P. (1993). Job satisfaction, organizational commitment, turnover intention, and turnover: Path analyses based on meta-analytic findings. *Personnel Psychology*, *46*(2), 259–293. doi:10.1111/j.1744-6570.1993.tb00874.x

Thalassinos, E. (2008). Trends and Developments in the European Financial Sector. *European Financial and Accounting Journal*, *3*(3), 44–61. doi:10.18267/j.efaj.83

Thanasi-Boçe, M., Kurtishi-Kastrati, S., Ramadani, V., & Zuferi, R. (2023). Sustainable Entrepreneurship in North Macedonia: Challenges and Perspectives. *Entrepreneurship Development in the Balkans: Perspective from Diverse Contexts*, 197–211.

Thite, M. (2022). Digital human resource development: Where are we? Where should we go and how do we go there? *Human Resource Development International*, *25*(1), 87–103. doi:10.1080/13678868.2020.1842982

Tijoe, L. H. (2019). Bringing bancassurance into the digital era. *Linkedin.* https://www.linkedin.com/pulse/bringing-bancassurance-digital-era-lee-han-tjioe/

Tiwari, M., & Mondal, S. R. (2022). Technological dynamism of workforce management for effective education service delivery during and after Covid-19. *HR Analytics and Digital HR Practices: Digitalization Post COVID*, *19*, 199–215. doi:10.1007/978-981-16-7099-2_8

Turkyilmaz, A., Akman, G., Ozkan, C., & Pastuszak, Z. (2011). Empirical study of public sector employee loyalty and satisfaction. *Industrial Management & Data Systems*, *111*(5), 675–696. doi:10.1108/02635571111137250

Turner, D. W. (2010). Qualitative interview design: A practical guide for novice investigators. *The Qualitative Report*, *15*(3), 754–760. http://www.nova.edu/ssss/QR/QR15-3/qid.pdf

Tursunbayeva, A., Di Lauro, S., & Pagliari, C. (2018). People analytics—A scoping review of conceptual boundaries and value propositions. *International Journal of Information Management*, *43*, 224–247. doi:10.1016/j.ijinfomgt.2018.08.002

Ulrich, D., Younger, J., Brockbank, W., & Ulrich, M. D. (2013). The state of the HR profession. *Human Resource Management*, *52*(3), 463–464. doi:10.1002/hrm.21536

Uppala, A. (2016). Creating Employee Self-Service Portal Concept. Academic Press.

Vasiliev, S. A., & Serov, E. R. (2019). Omnichannel banking economy. *Risks*, *7*(4), 1–11. doi:10.3390/risks7040115

Veeraiah, V., Talukdar, V., Manikandan, K., Talukdar, S. B., Solavande, V. D., Pramanik, S., & Gupta, A. (2023). Machine Learning Frameworks in Carpooling. In Handbook of Research on AI and Machine Learning Applications in Customer Support and Analytics. IGI Global.

Veeranjaneyulu, R., Boopathi, S., Kumari, R. K., Vidyarthi, A., Isaac, J. S., & Jaiganesh, V. (2023). Air Quality Improvement and Optimisation Using Machine Learning Technique. *IEEE- Explore*, 1–6.

Vegesna, V. V. (2023). Privacy-Preserving Techniques in AI-Powered Cyber Security: Challenges and Opportunities. *International Journal of Machine Learning for Sustainable Development*, *5*(4), 1–8.

Venkatasubramanian, V., Chitra, M., Sudha, R., Singh, V. P., Jefferson, K., & Boopathi, S. (2024). Examining the Impacts of Course Outcome Analysis in Indian Higher Education: Enhancing Educational Quality. In Challenges of Globalization and Inclusivity in Academic Research (pp. 124–145). IGI Global.

Venkateswaran, N., Vidhya, K., Ayyannan, M., Chavan, S. M., Sekar, K., & Boopathi, S. (2023). A Study on Smart Energy Management Framework Using Cloud Computing. In 5G, Artificial Intelligence, and Next Generation Internet of Things: Digital Innovation for Green and Sustainable Economies (pp. 189–212). IGI Global. doi:10.4018/978-1-6684-8634-4.ch009

Venkateswaran, N. (2012). Strategies for adopting talent management issues in software companies. *International Journal of Management, Economics and Social Sciences*, *1*(2), 33–41.

Venkateswaran, N., Kumar, S. S., Diwakar, G., Gnanasangeetha, D., & Boopathi, S. (2023). Synthetic Biology for Waste Water to Energy Conversion: IoT and AI Approaches. *Applications of Synthetic Biology in Health. Energy & Environment*, 360–384.

Venkateswaran, N., Vidhya, R., Naik, D. A., Raj, T. M., Munjal, N., & Boopathi, S. (2023). Study on Sentence and Question Formation Using Deep Learning Techniques. In *Digital Natives as a Disruptive Force in Asian Businesses and Societies* (pp. 252–273). IGI Global. doi:10.4018/978-1-6684-6782-4.ch015

Vennila, T., Karuna, M., Srivastava, B. K., Venugopal, J., Surakasi, R., & Sampath, B. (2022). New Strategies in Treatment and Enzymatic Processes: Ethanol Production From Sugarcane Bagasse. In Human Agro-Energy Optimization for Business and Industry (pp. 219–240). IGI Global.

Verma, D. S., & Chaurasia, R. (2016). A study to identify the factors affecting employee turnover in small scale industries. *International Journal of Engineering Sciences & Research Technology*, *5*(7), 638–652.

Verma, R., Christiana, M. B. V., Maheswari, M., Srinivasan, V., Patro, P., Dari, S. S., & Boopathi, S. (2024). Intelligent Physarum Solver for Profit Maximization in Oligopolistic Supply Chain Networks. In *AI and Machine Learning Impacts in Intelligent Supply Chain* (pp. 156–179). IGI Global. doi:10.4018/979-8-3693-1347-3.ch011

Viglia, G., Pera, R., Dyussembayeva, S., Mifsud, M., & Hollebeek, L. D. (2023). Engagement and value cocreation within a multi-stakeholder service ecosystem. *Journal of Business Research*, *157*, 113584. doi:10.1016/j.jbusres.2022.113584

Vignesh, S., Arulshri, K., SyedSajith, S., Kathiresan, S., Boopathi, S., & Dinesh Babu, P. (2018). Design and development of ornithopter and experimental analysis of flapping rate under various operating conditions. *Materials Today: Proceedings*, *5*(11), 25185–25194. doi:10.1016/j.matpr.2018.10.320

Vijayakumar, G. N. S., Domakonda, V. K., Farooq, S., Kumar, B. S., Pradeep, N., & Boopathi, S. (2024). Sustainable Developments in Nano-Fluid Synthesis for Various Industrial Applications. In Adoption and Use of Technology Tools and Services by Economically Disadvantaged Communities: Implications for Growth and Sustainability (pp. 48–81). IGI Global.

Vijayakumar, G. N. S., Domakonda, V. K., Farooq, S., Kumar, B. S., Pradeep, N., & Boopathi, S. (2023). Sustainable Developments in Nano-Fluid Synthesis for Various Industrial Applications. In A. S. Etim (Ed.), Advances in Human and Social Aspects of Technology. IGI Global. doi:10.4018/978-1-6684-5347-6.ch003

Vimala, B., & Alamelu, K. (2018). Insurance penetration and insurance density in India–An analysis. *International Journal of Research and Analytical Reviews*, *5*(4), 229–232.

Walangitan, N., Pangemanan, S., & Tumewu, F. (2014). The analysis of factors affecting employee retention at pt. hasjrat abadi manado. *Journal EMBA*, *2*(1), 490–498.

Wareth, H., & Amirah, N. (2020). A review of training and development towards employee retention in the banking sector. *The Journal of Management Theory and Practices*, *1*(2), 16–21.

Wargo, E., Carr Chellman, D., Budge, K., & Canfield Davis, K. (2021). On the digital frontier: Stakeholders in rural areas take on educational technology and schooling. *Journal of Research on Technology in Education*, *53*(2), 140–158. doi:10.1080/15391523.2020.1760753

Wenninger, J. (2000). The Emerging Role of Banks in E-Commerce. *Federal Reserve Bank of Newyork: Current Issues in Economics and Finance*, *6*(3), 1–6.

Wickramasurendra, J. M., Jagoda, D. J., & Rathnayake, R. M. L. (2021). Factors Influencing Social Media Addiction among G.C.E. Advanced Level Students in Sri Lanka: A Case Study in Colombo District, Sri Lanka. *Sri Lanka Journal of Social Sciences and Humanities*, *1*(2), 1–11. doi:10.4038/sljssh.v1i2.33

Wollschlaeger, M., Sauter, T., & Jasperneite, J. (2017). The future of industrial communication: Automation networks in the era of the internet of things and industry 4.0. *IEEE Industrial Electronics Magazine*, *11*(1), 17–27. doi:10.1109/MIE.2017.2649104

Wright, P. M., Gardner, T. M., Moynihan, L. M., & Allen, M. R. (2005). The relationship between HR Practices and firm performance: Examining causal order. *Personnel Psychology*, *58*(2), 409–447. doi:10.1111/j.1744-6570.2005.00487.x

Xiao, Z., Pramanik, A., Basak, A. K., Prakash, C., & Shankar, S. (2022). Material recovery and recycling of waste tyres-A review. *Cleaner Materials*, *5*, 100115. doi:10.1016/j.clema.2022.100115

Yahia, N. B., Hlel, J., & Colomo-Palacios, R. (2021). From big data to deep data to support people analytics for employee attrition prediction. *IEEE Access : Practical Innovations, Open Solutions*, *9*, 60447–60458. doi:10.1109/ACCESS.2021.3074559

Yapp, M. (2009). Measuring the ROI of talent management. *Strategic HR Review*, *8*(4), 5–10. doi:10.1108/14754390910963856

Yeves, J., Bargsted, M., Cortes, L., Merino, C., & Cavada, G. (2019). Age and perceived employability as moderators of job insecurity and job satisfaction: A moderated moderation model. *Frontiers in Psychology*, *10*, 10. doi:10.3389/fpsyg.2019.00799 PMID:31031675

Yupapin, P., Trabelsi, Y., Nattappan, A., & Boopathi, S. (2023). Performance improvement of wire-cut electrical discharge machining process using cryogenically treated super-conductive state of Monel-K500 alloy. *Iranian Journal of Science and Technology. Transaction of Mechanical Engineering*, *47*(1), 267–283. doi:10.1007/s40997-022-00513-0

Yusoff, R. M., Khan, F., Mubeen, A. & Azam, K. (2013). A study about factors influencing the university performance. *Sains Humanika, 64*(2).

Zacharaki, A., Vafeiadis, T., Kolokas, N., Vaxevani, A., Xu, Y., Peschl, M., Ioannidis, D., & Tzovaras, D. (2021). RECLAIM: Toward a new era of refurbishment and remanufacturing of industrial equipment. *Frontiers in Artificial Intelligence*, *3*, 570562. doi:10.3389/frai.2020.570562 PMID:33733214

Zahariev, A., Zaharieva, G., Mihaylova, M., & Ivanova, K. (2022). Digitalisation in human resource management: Evidence from the Bulgarian banking and insurance sectors. *Economic and Social Development: Book of Proceedings*, 261-269.

Zahariev, A., Ivanova, P., Zaharieva, G., Slaveva, K., Mihaylova, M., & Todorova, T. (2023). Interplay between CSR and the Digitalisation of Bulgarian Financial Enterprises: HRM Approach and Pandemic Evidence. *Journal of Risk and Financial Management, 16*(9), 385. doi:10.3390/jrfm16090385

Zaheer, H. (2022). *Digital entrepreneurship: Review, trajectory and practice* [PhD Thesis]. Macquarie University.

Zavyalova, E., Sokolov, D., Kucherov, D., & Lisovskaya, A. (2022). The digitalization of human resource management: Present and future. *Foresight and STI Governance*, *16*(2), 42–51. doi:10.17323/2500-2597.2022.2.42.51

Zehir, C., Karaboğa, T., & Başar, D. (2020). The transformation of human resource management and its impact on overall business performance: big data analytics and AI technologies in strategic HRM. *Digital Business Strategies in Blockchain Ecosystems: Transformational Design and Future of Global Business*, 265-279.

Zehir, C., Karaboğa, T., & Başar, D. (2020). The transformation of human resource management and its impact on overall business performance: Big data analytics and AI technologies in strategic HRM. *Digital Business Strategies in Blockchain Ecosystems: Transformational Design and Future of Global Business*, 265–279.

Zekrifa, D. M. S., Kulkarni, M., Bhagyalakshmi, A., Devireddy, N., Gupta, S., & Boopathi, S. (2023). Integrating Machine Learning and AI for Improved Hydrological Modeling and Water Resource Management. In *Artificial Intelligence Applications in Water Treatment and Water Resource Management* (pp. 46–70). IGI Global. doi:10.4018/978-1-6684-6791-6.ch003

Zhang, A., Venkatesh, V., Wang, J. X., Mani, V., Wan, M., & Qu, T. (2023). Drivers of industry 4.0-enabled smart waste management in supply chain operations: A circular economy perspective in china. *Production Planning and Control, 34*(10), 870–886. doi:10.1080/09537287.2021.1980909

Zhang, J., & Chen, Z. (2023). Exploring Human Resource Management Digital Transformation in the Digital Age. *Journal of the Knowledge Economy*, 1–17. doi:10.1007/s13132-023-01214-y

Zizic, M. C., Mladineo, M., Gjeldum, N., & Celent, L. (2022). From industry 4.0 towards industry 5.0: A review and analysis of paradigm shift for the people, organization and technology. *Energies, 15*(14), 5221. doi:10.3390/en15145221

Zottoli, M. A., & Wanous, J. P. (2000). Recruitment source research: Current status and future directions. *Human Resource Management Review, 10*(4), 353–382. doi:10.1016/S1053-4822(00)00032-2

About the Contributors

Pawan Kumar is working as full Professor in the Department of Marketing at Mittal School of Business, Lovely Professional University, Punjab, India. He has 15 years of experience in business academic research. His areas of interest in research include entrepreneurship, marketing, e-commerce, consumer behaviour, social media, technology innovation etc. He is an avid researcher. He is active in Ph.D research supervision and has good number of publications in Q1 and Q2 Journals to his credit in various research papers published Scopus indexed journals namely: The TQM Journal from Emerald, Visions: Journal of Business Perspectives from Sage, International Journal of Business and Globalization, International Journal of Business Information Systems from Inderscience and other national/international journals of repute.

Sunil Kumar, currently an Associate Professor at Faculty of Management Sciences, Shoolini University, possesses extensive academic and research experience. With a background in Business Administration, Sunil's research endeavors span multiple domains, including human resource management, e-training, and the application of artificial intelligence in business. His prolific contributions are evidenced by numerous research papers, book chapters, copyrights, and patents. Dr. Kumar has a knack for teaching with expertise in subjects like HR Analytics, Talent Management, Industrial Psychology, and more. He has also successfully guided PhD students and actively contributes to various academic administrative roles. Dr. Kumar's vast research landscape includes topics like AI-based chatbots in recruitment, e-training impact, and more. His papers have been published in esteemed journals like Journal of Workplace Learning and International Journal of Law and Management. Moreover, he has authored books and edited volumes touching upon themes related to the contemporary business environment. Dr. Sunil has been a dynamic participant in numerous workshops, ranging from data analysis to stress

Sumesh Singh Dadwal has 22 years of experience in research, teaching, e-Learning, quality management, and examination assessment in a wide range of business subjects. Currently, Sumesh is working as a Sr. Lecturer of Strategy and Course Director at LSBU Business School. Before joining LSBU, he worked as Sr. Lecturer, Dissertation Lead, and Programme Leader with Northumbria Universities London campus and also as an associate with London Graduate School and Regent College London (Bucks New University and the University of Bolton, UK). Dr Dawdal has also worked as an associate lecturer with Birkbeck College (UoL), University of West London, Plymouth University (GSM, London), Uni of Roehampton UK, and also worked as a Sr. lecturer and Programme Leader (MBA) at Glyndwr University London. Sumesh has hands-on experience in managing departments and in supporting the implementation of effective quality management systems. Previously, Dr Dawdal has also worked with QAA, UK, He has designed, developed, and supported for validation and review of the various programme. He has published in journals and books.

* * *

A. Rajagopalan is Doctoral (Ph.D.) Research Scholar in School of Management, SASTRA Deemed University, Thanjavur

Yashpal Azad is an Assistant Professor of Psychology at Eternal University, Sirmaur, India, with expertise in Cognitive Psychology and Organizational Behavior. His research interests span a broad spectrum, encompassing Interdisciplinary approaches to Psychology, Ethical Concerns in Research, Technological Advances in Educational Psychology, Neuro Psychology, Developmental Psychology, Consumer Behavior, Application of AI in Social Sciences and Research, Psychological well-being, and Social Psychology. Dr. Azad has demonstrated his scholarly acumen by authoring two edited volumes of research articles and actively serving as a reviewer for numerous reputable journals. Committed to academia and research, he consistently pushes the boundaries of knowledge in psychology and its interdisciplinary applications.

Hri B. S. is an Assistant Professor SrG in the Department of Mechanical Engineering at Kongu Engineering College, located in Perundurai, Erode, Tamil Nadu, India. Orchid Id: 0000-0002-4778-3802.

Smpath Boopathi is an accomplished individual with a strong academic background and extensive research experience. He completed his undergraduate studies in Mechanical Engineering and pursued his postgraduate studies in the field of Computer-Aided Design. Dr. Boopathi obtained his Ph.D. from Anna University, focusing his research on Manufacturing and optimization. Throughout his career, Dr. Boopathi has made significant contributions to the field of engineering. He has authored and published over 190 research articles in internationally peer-reviewed journals, highlighting his expertise and dedication to advancing knowledge in his area of specialization. His research output demonstrates his commitment to conducting rigorous and impactful research. In addition to his research publications, Dr. Boopathi has also been granted one patent and has three published patents to his name. This indicates his innovative thinking and ability to develop practical solutions to real-world engineering challenges. With 17 years of academic and research experience, Dr. Boopathi has enriched the engineering community through his teaching and mentorship roles. He has served in various engineering colleges in Tamilnadu, India, where he has imparted knowledge, guided students, and contributed to the overall academic development of the institutions. Dr. Sampath Boopathi's diverse background, ranging from mechanical engineering to computer-aided design, along with his specialization in manufacturing and optimization, positions him as a valuable asset in the field of engineering. His research contributions, patents, and extensive teaching experience exemplify his expertise and dedication to advancing engineering knowledge and fostering innovation.

Ait Dutt is a Professor and Associate Dean, in Lovely Professional University. As a tenured professor at Lovely Professional University, he has made indelible contributions to the academic landscape. His research spans a wide array of topics within operations management, His work has been published in prestigious journals. His research is characterized by its innovative thinking, rigorous empirical methodologies, and real-world applicability. Their publications have not only advanced theoretical frameworks but have also provided actionable insights for organizations seeking to enhance their operational efficiency and effectiveness.

Kamunuri Ganapathi Babu is an Assistant Professor in the Computer Science and Engineering department at St. Martin's Engineering College, situated in Secunderabad-Medchal, Telangana, India.

Akur Gupta has received the B.Tech and M.Tech in Computer Science and Engineering from Ganga Institute of Technology and Management, Kablana affiliated with Maharshi Dayanand University, Rohtak in 2015 and 2017. He is an Assistant Professor in the Department of Computer Science and Engineering at Vaish College of Engineering, Rohtak, and has been working there since January 2019. He has many publications in various reputed national/ international conferences, journals, and online book chapter contributions (Indexed by SCIE, Scopus, ESCI, ACM, DBLP, etc). He is doing research in the field of cloud computing, data security & machine learning. His research work in M.Tech was based on biometric security in cloud computing.

S Kalpana serves as an Assistant Professor in the Department of Artificial Intelligence and Data Science at Jai Shriram Engineering College, located on Dharapuram Road in Avinashipalayam, Tirupur, Tamil Nadu, India.

Pooja Kansra is currently working as professor in Mittal School of Business, Lovely Professional University. She has published various research papers in renowned journals indexed with Scopus, Web of Science, etc.

R Krishnaveni is working for Terf's Academy College of Arts and Science.

Amit Kumar is currently serving as an Assistant Professor at Akal College of Economics, Commerce and Management, Eternal University, Baru Sahib. He has received Bachelor's (B. Com) and Master's (MBA) from Himachal Pradesh University and Ph.D. (Consumer Complaining Behavior) from Jaypee University of Information Technology, Waknaghat, India. He has Qualified UGC-NET (Management) in 2013. He teaches post-graduate and undergraduate students and also guide master and Ph.D. students in the field of Marketing and HR. His research interests include consumer behavior, service marketing and customer relationship management. With 8+ years of teaching experience, his academic contribution includes publications including research papers, review papers (in various journals of national and international repute including SCOPUS and WOS) and one book. Morality, ethics, sincerity, hard work and being honest towards the job are the fundamentals of my life.

Pwan Kumar is working as professor in Mittal School of Business, Lovely Professional University, Jalandhar. He has published research papers in renowned journals indexed with Scopus, Web of Science, etc.

Getika Madaan is working as Assistant Professor, at the University centre for research and development Chandigarh University, Mohali, India.

Geetha Manoharan is currently working in Telangana as an assistant professor at SR University. She is the university-level PhD program coordinator and has also been given the additional responsibility of In Charge Director of Publications and Patents under the Research Division at SR University. Under her tutelage, students are inspired to reach their full potential in all areas of their education and beyond through experiential learning. It creates an atmosphere conducive to the growth of students into independent thinkers and avid readers. She has more than ten years of experience across the board in the business world, academia, and the academy. She has a keen interest in the study of organizational behavior and management. More than forty articles and books have been published in scholarly venues such as UGC-refereed, SCOPUS, Web of Science, and Springer. Over the past six-plus years, she has participated in varied research and student exchange programs at both the national and international levels. A total of five of her collaborative innovations in this area have already been published and patented. Emotional intelligence, self-efficacy, and work-life balance are among her specialties. She organizes programs for academic organizations. She belongs to several professional organizations, including the CMA and the CPC. The TIPSGLOBAL Institute of Coimbatore has recognized her twice (in 2017 and 2018) for her outstanding academic performance.

Ashutosh Mishra has extensive experience in academia and a solid foundation in finance and marketing. With Ph.D. in Management and a Post Graduate Diploma in Marketing and Finance (PGDM), Author is well-equipped to integrate extensive academic knowledge with a hands-on comprehension of management concepts. Author have spent the last 11 years molding the brains of the future generation because Author is passionate about education. Author have greatly benefited the academic community by encouraging a culture of critical thinking and intellectual curiosity. Author have made a substantial contribution to the area as a researcher by giving presentations at national and international conferences and publishing a large number of papers in prestigious publications. Author have received recognition for his innovative approach and contribution to the academic discourse for his Ph.D. thesis, "A Comprehensive Study of Consumer Behavior and Consumer Preference During the Shopping Hours in the Retail Sector with Reference to Lucknow Regions," which explores consumer purchasing behavior. Apart from his research pursuits, Author have been involved in several academic committees and have contributed significantly to curriculum creation, admissions, and examinations, guaranteeing that students have a comprehensive education that is in line with industry demands. Author is well-known for helping students navigate their academic and professional journeys outside of the classroom through mentoring and guidance. Author thinks that learning should be collaborative and inclusive, with an emphasis on pushing boundaries and encouraging students to reach their full potential. Every institution that Author work with benefits from his wealth of academic and real-world experience. His dedication to quality, together with his wealth of research experience and managerial skills, make him a strong contender to support the expansion and accomplishment of educational initiatives.

Sreshkumar Myilsamy completed his undergraduate in Mechanical Engineering and postgraduate in the field of Engineering Design. He completed his Ph.D. from Anna University, Chennai, Tamil Nādu, India.

T V. N. Padmavathi is an Assistant Professor specializing in Food Safety and Quality Assurance at the College of Food Science and Technology located in Rudrur, Nizamabad, Telangana, India.

Sbyasachi Pramanik is a professional IEEE member. He obtained a PhD in Computer Science and Engineering from Sri Satya Sai University of Technology and Medical Sciences, Bhopal, India. Presently, he is an Associate Professor, Department of Computer Science and Engineering, Haldia Institute of Technology, India. He has many publications in various reputed international conferences, journals, and book chapters (Indexed by SCIE, Scopus, ESCI, etc). He is doing research in the fields of Artificial Intelligence, Data Privacy, Cybersecurity, Network Security, and Machine Learning. He also serves on the editorial boards of several international journals. He is a reviewer of journal articles from IEEE, Springer, Elsevier, Inderscience, IET and IGI Global. He has reviewed many conference papers, has been a keynote speaker, session chair, and technical program committee member at many international conferences. He has authored a book on Wireless Sensor Network. He has edited 8 books from IGI Global, CRC Press, Springer and Wiley Publications.

Sefali Saluja is working as an Assistant Professor in Chitkara University holding Doctoral degree in Corporate Governance. She has conducted research on "Detection and Prevention of Corporate Frauds" in her PhD studies. She holds MBA degree in specialization of financial markets from Chitkara University and has graduated from Punjab University with Economics Honours. With total experience of 11 years. Out of which 4 years in Ernst & Young Pvt Ltd and 7 years in Chitkara University, Shefali has been an expert in the field of Ethics and Governance. During her experience in Ernst & Young Pvt Ltd -Risk Management, she has conducted internal auditing risk mitigations for various clients and received extra mile client service awards. She has successfully completed online course on "Forensic Accounting and Fraud Examination" from West Virginia University and delivered workshops on "Fraud Examination of Corporate Frauds" to various academicians and professionals in the field of Fraud Landscape. Her current job position includes various teaching and administrative related responsibilities in Chitkara university. She is managing NAAC Accreditation and AACSB Internal accreditation process for Chitkara Business School. Shefali has been continuously invited in many teaching opportunities for teaching a module on "Failing corporates" at Emden University, Germany. She was also invited by Telkom University, Indonesia and Providence University Taiwan to deliver online session on "Fraud Investigation". She has also delivered a module on "Business in Asia" to the students of Mondragon University, Spain. Recently, in 2023 she was invited by MSME association in Indonesia to train almost 100 MSMEs in Cirebon, Indonesia on "Business Opportunities' a community project. She is the member of Association of Certified Fraud Examiners (ACFE), USA and has been doing volunteer work for them since 2021. She is also visiting faculty with LINC Education, Australia. She is also handling Micro finance and Social Activities with United Nations. The activities are also live on YouTube. She is currently mentoring 2 professionals as PhD scholars under her supervision in the field of Corporate Fraud Detection and Prevention- Private and Public Sector. She has 14 copyrights and 4 granted patents as her intellectual contributions.

Bumika Sharma holds the position of Assistant Professor within the School of Law at Sharda School of Law, situated in Knowledge Park-III, Greater Noida, Gautam Budh Nagar, Uttar Pradesh, India. https://orcid.org/0000-0002-3963-6036.ed523cfb-e455-424b-906a-c509e3b8d9ca

Subhendu Shekher Shukla has completed his Ph.D (Management), M.Phil, MBA and MA (Sociology). Author is Member of Management Forum for American Association of International Researchers in American Research Institute for Policy Development, and Member of Editorial Board in several International peer reviewed Journals including Scopus Journals. He had worked with prominent IT Company (Wipro Technologies) as Project Manager for e-Governance that was a Central Government Project about e-District. Author holds more than 15 years of experience in academics, Research & Academic Administration. He is currently working as Assistant Professor in SRM Business School, Lucknow under the aegis of SR Group of Institutions, Lucknow in Department of Business Administration. During the academics author has publish 35 International Research Paper, 28 National Research Papers, attended 14 National Conferences and Seminars, 12 International Seminars. Author has already published 11 books on Marketing Analytics, Digital Marketing & E-Commerce, Rural Management, e-Governance and Computer Application in Management and Management Information System and Retail Management, Advertisement and Distribution Management, Rural Management. Author taught variety of subjects as Marketing, Sales and Distribution, Rural Marketing, Production and Operation management, Computer Application in Management.

R Sujatha is an academician with a profound passion for interdisciplinary research and teaching. Holding a Ph. D. in Network Security (Secured Authentication Protocol System) from Madurai Kamaraj University, she has dedicated her career to unraveling the complexities of the brain-mind relationship. With over two and a half decades of experience in academia, she has published more peer-reviewed articles in leading National and International journals, book chapters, and patents. Her innovative research has earned her recognition with the academic community awards and administration with Academic Leadership Award. Dr. R. Sujatha's commitment to education extends beyond research; she is deeply invested in mentoring the next generation of scholars. As a dedicated educator, she employs dynamic teaching methods to inspire her students and foster critical thinking skills. She is actively involved in collaborative projects that bridge the gap between academic and industry. She continues to push boundaries, driven by her curiosity and commitment to making meaningful contributions to both academia and society at large.

Sanjay Taneja is currently an Associate Professor in Research at Graphic Era University, Dehradun, India. His significant thrust areas are Banking Regulations, Banking and Finance (Fin Tech, Green Finance), Risks, Insurance Management, Green Economics and Management of Innovation in Insurance. He holds a double master's degree (MBA &M.Com.) in management with a specialization in Finance and Marketing. He received his PG degrees in Management (Gold Medalist) from Chaudhary Devi University, Sirsa, India in 2012. He earned his Doctor of Philosophy (Sponsored By ICSSR) in Banking and Finance entitled "An Appraisal of financial performance of Indian Banking Sector: A Comparative study of Public, Private and Foreign banks in 2016 from Chaudhary Devi University, Sirsa, India. He received his Post Doctoral Degree from faculty of Social Sciences, Department of Banking and Insurance, Usak University, Turkey entitled on "Impact of the European Green Deal on Carbon (CO2) Emission in Turkey" in 2023. He has published research papers in reputed SCOPUS/Web of Science/SCI/ABDC/UGC Care Journals. Prof. Taneja has more than fifty publications in total (Scopus/ABDC/Web of Science- 27).

C Vijayabanu is currently Professor at School of Management, SASTRA Deemed University in India She handles courses such as Human Resource Management, organizational behavior and specialization courses such Organisational Development & Change Management, Performance Management, etc. She brings to her classes enriched knowledge of 5 years of Research & 24 years of academic experience. She has produced 5 doctoral scholars successfully and currently Guiding 2 Ph.D. scholars. She has presented papers at international and national level conferences and seminars. She has published 100 plus research articles in referred Scopus and Web of Science Indexed journals. She has served on the editorial review boards of several academic journals, including Business theory and practice, Journal of Management Social Science and Humanities and Journal of Business Economics and Management.

Index

F

G

H

I

J

M

O

P

R

S

T

U

W

www.ingramcontent.com/pod-product-compliance
Lightning Source LLC
LaVergne TN
LVHW062120300926
849161LV00010B/2506
* 9 7 9 8 3 6 9 3 1 3 4 3 5 *